WOLFF TO KANT

A
HISTORY OF PHILOSOPHY

VOLUME VI
WOLFF TO KANT

BY
FREDERICK COPLESTON, S.J.

Professor Emeritus of Philosophy in the
University of London

SEARCH PRESS • LONDON

PAULIST PRESS • NEW JERSEY

Published in the United States by
Paulist Press
997 Macarthur Boulevard, Mahwah, N.J. 07430

Published in Great Britain by
Search Press Limited
Wellwood, North Farm Road
Tunbridge Wells, Kent TN2 3DR, England

First published 1960

ISBN (USA) 0-8091-0070-3
ISBN (UK) 0 85532 186 5

Printed and bound in the
United States of America

CONTENTS

v

PART IV

KANT

PREFACE

IT was my original intention to cover the philosophy of the seventeenth and eighteenth centuries in one volume, *Descartes to Kant*. But this did not prove to be possible. And I have divided the material between three volumes. Volume IV, *Descartes to Leibniz*, treats of the great rationalist systems on the Continent, while in Volume V, *Hobbes to Hume*, I have outlined the development of British philosophical thought up to and including the Scottish philosophy of common sense. In the present volume I consider the French and German Enlightenments, the rise of the philosophy of history, and the system of Kant.

However, though three volumes have been devoted to the philosophy of the seventeenth and eighteenth centuries, my original plan has been preserved to the extent that there is a common introductory chapter and a common Concluding Review. The former will be found, of course, at the beginning of the fourth volume. And the introductory remarks which relate to the subject-matter of the present volume will not be repeated here. As for the Concluding Review, it forms the final chapter of this book. In it I have attempted to discuss, not only from the historical but also from a more philosophical point of view, the nature, importance and value of the various styles of philosophizing in the seventeenth and eighteenth centuries. Thus the fourth, fifth and sixth volumes of this *History of Philosophy* form a trilogy.

PART I

THE FRENCH ENLIGHTENMENT

CHAPTER I

THE FRENCH ENLIGHTENMENT (1)

Introductory remarks—The scepticism of Bayle—Fontenelle—
Montesquieu and his study of law—Maupertuis—Voltaire and
deism—Vauvenargues—Condillac and the human mind—
Helvétius on Man.

1. THERE is perhaps a natural tendency in many minds to think
of the French Enlightenment primarily in terms of destructive
criticism and of an outspoken hostility towards Christianity, or at
any rate towards the Catholic Church. If we exclude Rousseau, the
best-known name among the French philosophers of the eighteenth
century is probably that of Voltaire. And this name conjures up in
the mind the picture of a brilliant and witty literary man who was
never tired of denouncing the Church as an enemy of reason and a
friend of intolerance. Further, if one knows anything about the
materialism of writers such as La Mettrie and d'Holbach, one may
be inclined to regard the Enlightenment in France as an anti-
religious movement which passed from the deism of Voltaire and
of Diderot in his earlier years to the atheism of d'Holbach and the
crudely materialistic outlook of a Cabanis. Given this interpretation of the Enlightenment, one's evaluation of it will depend very
largely upon one's religious convictions or lack of them. One man
will regard eighteenth-century French philosophy as a movement
which progressed ever further into impiety and which bore its
fruit in the profanation of the cathedral of Notre Dame at the
Revolution. Another man will regard it as a progressive liberation of mind from religious superstition and from ecclesiastical
tyranny.

Again, the impression is not uncommon that the French philosophers of the eighteenth century were all enemies of the existing
political system and that they prepared the way for the Revolution. Given this political interpretation, different evaluations of
the work of the philosophers are obviously possible. One may

regard them as irresponsible fomenters of revolution whose writings had practical effect in the Jacobin terror. Or one may regard them as representing a stage in an inevitable social-political development, as helping to initiate, that is to say, the stage of bourgeois democracy, which was fated in its turn to be replaced by the rule of the proletariat.

Both interpretations of the French Enlightenment, the interpretation in terms of an attitude towards religious institutions and towards religion itself and the interpretation in terms of an attitude towards political systems and towards political and social developments, have, of course, their foundations in fact. They are not perhaps equally well founded. On the one hand, though some philosophers certainly disliked the *ancien régime*, it would be a great mistake to regard all the typical philosophers of the Enlightenment as conscious fomenters of revolution. Voltaire, for example, though he desired certain reforms, was not really concerned with the promotion of democracy. He was concerned with freedom of expression for himself and his friends; but he could hardly be called a democrat. Benevolent despotism, especially if the benevolence was directed towards *les philosophes*, was more to his taste than popular rule. It was certainly not his intention to promote a revolution on the part of what he regarded as 'the rabble'. On the other hand, it is true that all the philosophers who are regarded as typical representatives of the French Enlightenment were opposed, in varying degrees, to the domination of the Church. Many of them were opposed to Christianity, and some at least were dogmatic atheists, strongly opposed to all religion, which they regarded as the product of ignorance and fear, as the enemy of intellectual progress and as prejudicial to true morality.

But though both the interpretation in terms of an attitude towards religion and also, though to a lesser extent, the interpretation in terms of political convictions have foundations in fact, it would give a thoroughly inadequate picture of eighteenth-century French philosophy, were one to describe it as a prolonged attack on throne and altar. Obviously, attacks on the Catholic Church, on revealed religion and, in certain cases, on religion in any form, were made in the name of reason. But the exercise of reason meant much more to the philosophers of the French Enlightenment than simply destructive criticism in the religious sphere. Destructive criticism was, so to speak, the negative side of the Enlightenment. The positive aspect consisted in the attempt to understand the world and especially man himself in his psychological, moral and social life.

By saying this I do not intend to minimize the philosophers' views on religious topics or to dismiss them as unimportant. To anyone, indeed, who shares the religious convictions of the present writer their attitude can hardly be a matter of indifference. But, quite apart from one's own beliefs, the attitude of *les philosophes* towards religion was clearly of cultural significance and importance. For it expresses a marked change from the outlook of the mediaeval culture, and it represents a different cultural stage. At the same time we have to remember that what we are witnessing is the growth and extension of the scientific outlook. The eighteenth-century French philosophers believed strongly in progress, that is, in the extension of the scientific outlook from physics to psychology, morality and man's social life. If they tended to reject revealed religion and sometimes all religion, this was partly due to their conviction that religion, either revealed religion in particular or religion in general, is an enemy of intellectual progress and of the unimpeded and clear use of reason. I certainly do not mean to imply that they were right in thinking this. There is no inherent incompatibility between religion and science. But my point is that if we dwell too exclusively on their destructive criticism in the religious sphere, we tend to lose sight of the philosopher's positive aims. And then we get only a one-sided view of the picture.

The French philosophers of the eighteenth century were considerably influenced by English thought, especially by Locke and Newton. Generally speaking, they were in agreement with the former's empiricism. The exercise of reason in philosophy did not mean for them the construction of great systems deduced from innate ideas or self-evident first principles. And in this sense they turned their backs on the speculative metaphysics of the preceding century. This is not to say that they had no concern at all with synthesis and were purely analytic thinkers in the sense of giving their attention to different particular problems and questions without any attempt to synthesize their various conclusions. But they were convinced that the right way of approach is to go to the phenomena themselves and by observation to learn their laws and causes. We can then go on to synthesize, forming universal principles and seeing particular facts in the light of universal truths. In other words, it came to be understood that it is a mistake to suppose that there is one ideal method, the deductive method of mathematics, which is applicable in all branches of study. Buffon, for example, saw this clearly; and his ideas had some influence on the mind of Diderot.

This empiricist approach to knowledge led in some cases, as in that of d'Alembert, to a position which can be described as positivistic. Metaphysics, if one means by this the study of trans-phenomenal reality, is the sphere of the unknowable. We cannot have certain knowledge in this field, and it is waste of time to look for it. The only sense in which we can have a rational metaphysics is by synthesizing the results of the empirical sciences. And in empirical science itself we are not concerned with 'essences' but with phenomena. In one sense, of course, we can talk about essences, but these are simply what Locke called 'nominal' essences. The word is not being used in a metaphysical sense.

It would, indeed, be a serious error were one to say that all the philosophers of the French Enlightenment were 'positivists'. Voltaire, for example, thought that we can prove the existence of God. So did Maupertuis. But we can discern an obvious approxi-mation to positivism in certain thinkers of the period. And so we can say that the philosophy of the eighteenth century helped to prepare the way for the positivism of the following century.

At the same time this interpretation of the French Enlighten-ment is one-sided: it is in a sense too philosophical. To illustrate what I mean, I take the example of Condillac. This philosopher was much influenced by Locke. And he set out to apply Locke's empiricism, as he understood it, to man's psychical faculties and operations, trying to show how they can all be explained in terms of 'transformed sensations'. Now, Condillac himself was not exactly what we would call a positivist. But it is doubtless possible to interpret his *Treatise on Sensations* as a move in the direction of positivism, as a stage in its development. It is also possible, however, to interpret it simply as a stage in the develop-ment of psychology. And psychology, considered in itself, is not necessarily connected with philosophical positivism.

Again, several philosophers of the French Enlightenment reflected on the connections between man's psychical life and its physiological conditions. And in certain cases, as in that of Cabanis, this resulted in the statement of a crude materialism. One may be tempted, therefore, to interpret the whole investiga-tion in terms of this result. At the same time it is possible to regard the dogmatic materialism of certain philosophers as a temporary aberration in the course of the development of a valuable line of study. In other words, if one looks on the psychological studies of the eighteenth-century philosophers as tentative experiments in the early stages of the development of this line of research, one may be inclined to attach less weight to exaggerations and crudities than if one restricts one's mental horizon simply to the French Enlightenment considered in itself. Of course, when one is concerned, as in these chapters, with the thought of a particular period and of a particular group of men, one has to draw attention to these exaggerations and crudities. But it is as well to keep at the back of one's mind an over-all picture and to remind oneself that these features belong to a certain stage in a line of development which stretches forward into the future and which is capable of supplying at a later date criticism and correction of earlier aberrations.

In general, therefore, we may look on the philosophy of the French Enlightenment as an attempt to develop what Hume called 'the science of man'. True, this description does not fit all the facts. We find, for example, cosmological theories. But it draws attention to the interest of eighteenth-century philosophers in doing for human psychical and social life what Newton had done for the physical universe. And in endeavouring to accomplish this aim they adopted an approach which was inspired by the empiricism of Locke rather than by the speculative systems of the preceding century.

It is worth noting also that the philosophers of the French Enlightenment, like a number of English moralists, endeavoured to separate ethics from metaphysics and theology. Their moral ideas certainly differed considerably, ranging, for instance, from the ethical idealism of Diderot to the low-grade utilitarianism of La Mettrie. But they were more or less at one in attempting to set morality on its own feet, so to speak. This is really the significance of Bayle's assertion that a State composed of atheists was quite possible and of La Mettrie's addition that it was not only possible but desirable. It would, however, be incorrect to say that all *les philosophes* agreed with this point of view. In Voltaire's opinion, for instance, if God did not exist, it would be necessary to invent Him, precisely for the moral welfare of society. But, generally speaking, the philosophy of the Enlightenment included a separation of ethics from metaphysical and theological considerations.

Whether this separation is tenable or not, is, of course, open to dispute.

Finally we may remind ourselves that eighteenth-century philosophy in France, as in England, was mainly the work of men who were not professors of philosophy in universities and who frequently had extra-philosophical interests. Hume in England was an historian as well as a philosopher. Voltaire in France wrote dramas. Maupertuis went on an expedition to the Arctic with a view to making a contribution towards determining the shape of the earth at its extremities by exact measurements of a degree of latitude. D'Alembert was an eminent mathematician. Montesquieu and Voltaire were of some importance in the development of historiography. La Mettrie was a doctor. In the eighteenth century we are still in the time when some knowledge of philosophical ideas was regarded as a cultural requirement and when philosophy had not yet become an academic preserve. Further, there is still a close connection between philosophy and the sciences, a connection which has, indeed, been a fairly general characteristic of French philosophical thought.

2. Among the French writers who prepared the way for the Enlightenment in France the most influential was probably Pierre Bayle (1647–1706), author of the famous *Dictionnaire historique et critique* (1695–7). Brought up as a Protestant, Bayle became a Catholic for a time, returning afterwards to Protestantism. In spite, however, of his adherence to the Reformed Church it was his conviction that the Catholics had no monopoly of intolerance. And during his residence at Rotterdam, where he lived from 1680 onwards, he advocated toleration and attacked the Calvinist theologian Jurieu for his intolerant attitude.

In Bayle's opinion, the current theological controversies were confused and pointless. Take, for example, the controversy about the relations between grace and free will. Thomists, Jansenists and Calvinists are all united in hostility towards Molinism. And there is really no fundamental difference between them. Yet the Thomists protest that they are not Jansenists, and the latter repudiate Calvinism, while the Calvinists denounce the others. As for the Molinists, they have recourse to sophistical arguments in their endeavour to show that the doctrine of St. Augustine was different from that of the Jansenists. In general, human beings are only too prone to believe that there are differences where there are no differences and that there are indissoluble connections between different positions when there are no such connections. So many controversies depend for their life and vigour on prejudice and lack of clear judgment.

More important, however, than Bayle's views about current controversy in dogmatic theology were his views about metaphysics and philosophical or natural theology. The human reason, he thought, is better adapted for the detection of errors than for the discovery of positive truth, and this is especially the case with regard to metaphysics. It is, indeed, commonly recognized that a philosopher has the right to criticize any particular proof of God's existence, provided that he does not deny that God's existence can be proved in some way. But in point of fact all the proofs which have ever been offered have been subjected to destructive criticism. Again, nobody has ever solved the problem of evil. Nor is this surprising. For it is not possible to achieve any rational reconciliation of the evil in the world with the affirmation of an infinite, omniscient and omnipotent God. The Manichaeans, with their dualistic philosophy, gave a much better explanation of evil than any explanation proposed by the orthodox. At the same time the metaphysical hypothesis of the Manichaeans was absurd. As for the immortality of the soul, no evident proof of it has been forthcoming.

Bayle did not say that the doctrines of God's existence and of immortality are false. Rather did he place faith outside the sphere of reason. This statement needs, however, a qualification. For Bayle did not simply say that religious truths are incapable of rational proof, though they do not contradict reason. His position was rather that these truths contain much that is repugnant to reason. There is therefore all the more merit, he suggested, whether sincerely or not, in accepting revelation. In any case, if the truths of religion pertain to the sphere of the non-rational, there is no point in indulging in theological argument and controversy. Toleration should take the place of controversy.

It is to be noted that Bayle separated not only religion and reason but also religion and morality. That is to say, he insisted that it is a great mistake to suppose that religious convictions and motives are necessary for leading a moral life. Non-religious motives can be just as efficacious, or even stronger, than religious motives. And it would be quite possible to have a moral society which consisted of people who did not believe in immortality, or, indeed, in God. After all, says Bayle in his article on the Sadducees in the *Dictionnaire*, the Sadducees, who did not believe in any resurrection, were better than the Pharisees, who did. Experience of life does not suggest that there is any indissoluble connection between belief and practice. We thus come to the concept of the autonomous moral human being who stands in no need of religious belief in order to lead a virtuous life.

Subsequent writers of the French Enlightenment, Diderot, for example, made ample use of Bayle's *Dictionnaire*. The work was also not without some influence on the German *Aufklärung*. In 1767 Frederick the Great wrote to Voltaire that Bayle had begun the battle, that a number of English philosophers had followed in his wake, and that Voltaire was destined to finish the fight.

3. Bernard le Bovier de Fontenelle (1657–1757) is perhaps best known as a popularizer of scientific ideas. He started his literary career with, among other productions, an unsuccessful play. But he soon perceived that contemporary society would welcome clear and intelligible accounts of the new physics. And his attempt to fulfil this need met with such success that he became secretary of the *Académie des Sciences*. In general he was a defender of the Cartesian physics; and in his *Entretiens sur la pluralité des mondes* (1686) he popularized Cartesian astronomical theories. He was not, indeed, blind to the importance of Newton, and in 1727 he published a *Eulogy of Newton*. But he defended Descartes' theory of vortices in his *Théorie des tourbillons cartésiens* (1752) and attacked Newton's principle of gravitation which seemed to him to involve postulating an occult entity. Manuscript notes which were found in his study after his death make it clear that in the latter part of his life his mind was moving definitely towards empiricism. All our ideas are reducible in the long run to the data of sense-experience.

Besides helping to spread the knowledge of scientific ideas in eighteenth-century France, Fontenelle also contributed, in a somewhat indirect way, to the growth of scepticism in regard to religious truths. He published, for instance, small works on *The Origin of Fables* and on *The History of Oracles*. In the first of these he rejected the view that myths or fables are due, not to the intelligence, but to the play of the imaginative faculty. Greek myths, for instance, originated in the desire to explain phenomena; they were the product of intelligence, even if the imagination played a part in elaborating them. The intellect of man in earlier epochs was not essentially different from the intellect of modern man. Both primitive and modern man try to explain phenomena, to reduce the unknown to the known. The difference between them is this. In earlier times positive knowledge was scanty, and the mind was forced to have recourse to mythological explanations. In the modern world, however, positive knowledge has grown to such an extent that scientific explanation is taking the place of mythological explanation. The implication of this view is obvious enough, though it is not explicitly stated by Fontenelle.

In his writing on oracles Fontenelle maintained that there was no cogent reason for saying either that the pagan oracles were due to the activity of demons or that the oracles were reduced to silence by the coming of Christ. The argument in favour of the power and divinity of Christ which consists in saying that the pagan oracles were silenced lacks, therefore, any historical foundation. The particular points at issue can hardly be said to possess great importance. But the implication seems to be that Christian apologists are accustomed to have recourse to worthless arguments.

Fontenelle was not, however, an atheist. His idea was that God manifests Himself in the law-governed system of Nature, not in history, where human passion and caprice reign. In other words, God for Fontenelle was not the God of any historic religion, revealing Himself in history and giving rise to dogmatic systems, but the God of Nature, revealed in the scientific conception of the world. There were, indeed, atheists among the eighteenth-century French philosophers; but deism, or, as Voltaire called it, theism, was rather more common, even though atheism was found more frequently among the French than among their English contemporaries.

4. It has already been remarked that the philosophers of the French Enlightenment endeavoured to understand man's social and political life. One of the most important works in this field was Montesquieu's treatise on law. Charles de Sécondat (1689–1755), Baron de la Brède et de Montesquieu, was an enthusiast for liberty and an enemy of despotism. In 1721 he published *Lettres persanes*, which were a satire on the political and ecclesiastical conditions in France. From 1728 to 1729 he was in England, where he conceived a great admiration for certain features of the English political system. In 1734 he published *Considérations sur les causes de la grandeur et de la décadence des Romains*. Finally in 1748 there appeared his work on law, *De l'esprit des lois*, which was the fruit of some seventeen years' labour.

In his work on law Montesquieu undertakes a comparative study of society, law and government. His factual knowledge was not, indeed, sufficiently accurate and extensive for an enterprise conceived on so vast a scale; but the enterprise itself, a comparative sociological survey, was of importance. True, Montesquieu had had certain predecessors. Aristotle in particular had initiated the compilation of studies of a great number of Greek constitutions. But Montesquieu's project must be seen in the light of contemporary philosophy. He was applying in the field of politics and law the inductive empirical approach which was applied by other philosophers in other fields.

It was not, however, Montesquieu's aim simply to describe social, political and legal phenomena, to register and describe a large number of particular facts. He wished to understand the facts, to use the comparative survey of phenomena as the basis for a systematic study of the principles of historical development. 'I first of all examined men, and I came to the belief that in this infinite diversity of laws and customs they were not guided solely by their whims. I formulated principles, and I saw particular cases fitting these principles as of themselves, the histories of all nations being only the consequences (of these principles) and every special law being bound to another law or depending on another more general law.'[1] Thus Montesquieu approached his subject, not simply in the spirit of a positivistic sociologist, but rather as a philosopher of history.

Looked at under one of its aspects, Montesquieu's theory of society, government and law consists of generalizations, often over-hasty generalizations, from historical data. The different systems of positive law in different political societies are relative to a variety of factors; to the character of the people, to the nature and principles of the forms of government, to climate and economic conditions, and so on. The totality of these relations forms 'the spirit of laws'. And it is this spirit which Montesquieu undertakes to examine.

Montesquieu speaks first of the relation of laws to government. He divides government into three kinds, 'republican, monarchical and despotic'.[2] A republic can be either a democracy, when the body of the people possess the supreme power, or an aristocracy, when only a part of the people possess supreme power. In a monarchy the prince governs in accordance with certain fundamental laws,

---

[1] *De l'esprit des lois*, Preface.　　　　[2] *Ibid.*, II, I.

and there are generally 'intermediate powers'. In a despotic State there are no such fundamental laws and no 'depositary' of law. 'Hence it is that religion has generally so much influence in these countries, because it forms a kind of permanent depositary, and if this cannot be said of religion, it may be said of the customs which are respected instead of laws.'[1] The principle of republican government is civic virtue; that of monarchical government is honour; and that of despotism is fear. Given these forms of government and their principles, certain types of legal systems will probably prevail. 'There is this difference between the nature and form of government; its nature is that by which it is constituted, and its principle that by which it is made to act. The one is its particular structure, and the other is the human passions which set it in motion. Now, laws ought to be no less relative to the principle than to the nature of each government.'[2]

Now, I have described Montesquieu's theory as though it were meant to be simply an empirical generalization. And one of the obvious objections against it, when so interpreted, is that his classification is traditional and artificial and that it is quite inadequate as a description of the historical data. But it is important to note that Montesquieu is speaking of ideal types of government. Behind, for example, all actual despotisms we can discern an ideal type of despotic government. But it by no means follows that any given despotism will faithfully embody this ideal or pure type, either in its structure or in its 'principle'. We cannot legitimately conclude from the theory of types that in any given republic the operative principle is civic virtue or that in any given despotism the operative principle of behaviour is fear. At the same time, in so far as a given form of government fails to embody its ideal type, it is spoken of as being imperfect. 'Such are the principles of the three governments: which does not mean that in a certain republic people are virtuous, but that they ought to be. This does not prove that in a certain monarchy people have a sense of honour, and that in a particular despotic State people have a sense of fear, but that they ought to have it. Without these qualities a government will be imperfect.'[3] Montesquieu can say, therefore, that under a given form of government a certain system of laws ought to be found rather than that it *is* found. The enlightened legislator will see to it that the laws correspond to the type of political society; but they do not do so necessarily.

[1] *De l'esprit des lois*, II, 4.   [2] *Ibid.*, III, 1.   [3] *Ibid.*, III, 11

Analogous statements can be made about the relation of laws to climatic and economic conditions. Climate, for instance, helps to form the character and passions of a people. The character of the English differs from that of the Sicilians. And laws 'should be adapted in such a manner to the people for whom they are framed as to render it very unlikely for those of one nation to be proper for another'.[1] Montesquieu does not say that climate and economic conditions determine systems of laws in such a way that no intelligent control is possible. They do, indeed, exercise a powerful influence on forms of government and on systems of law; but this influence is not equivalent to that of a determining fate. The wise legislator will adapt law to the climatic and economic conditions. But this may mean, for example, that in certain circumstances he will have to react consciously to the adverse effects of climate on character and behaviour. Man is not simply the plaything of infra-human conditions and factors.

We may perhaps distinguish two important ideas in Montesquieu's theory. There is first the idea of systems of law as the result of a complex of empirical factors. Here we have a generalization from historical data, a generalization which can be used as an hypothesis in a further interpretation of man's social and political life. Secondly, there is the idea of operative ideals in human societies. That is to say, Montesquieu's theory of types, though narrow enough as it stands, might perhaps be taken as meaning that each political society is the imperfect embodiment of an ideal which has been an implicit formative factor in its development and towards which it is tending or from which it is departing. The task of the wise legislator will be to discern the nature of this operative ideal and to adapt legislation to its progressive realization. If interpreted in this way, the theory of types appears as something more than a mere relic of Greek classifications of constitutions. One can say that Montesquieu is trying to express a genuine historical insight with the aid of somewhat antiquated categories.

If, however, we state Montesquieu's theory in this way, we imply that he is concerned simply with an understanding of historical data and that he is content with relativism. Systems of law are the results of different complexes of empirical factors. In each system we can see an operative ideal at work. But there is no absolute standard with reference to which the philosopher can compare and evaluate different political and legal systems.

[1] *De l'esprit des lois*, I, 3.

This interpretation, however, would be misleading on two counts. In the first place Montesquieu admitted immutable laws of justice. God, the creator and preserver of the world, has established laws or rules which govern the physical world.[1] And 'man, as a physical being, is, like other bodies, governed by invariable laws'.[2] As an intelligent or rational being, however, he is subject to laws which he is capable of transgressing. Some of these are of his own making; but others are not dependent on him. 'We must therefore acknowledge relations of justice antecedent to the positive law by which they are established.'[3] 'To say that there is nothing just or unjust but what is commanded or forbidden by positive laws is the same as saying that before the describing of a circle all the radii were not equal.'[4] Assuming the idea of a state of nature, Montesquieu remarks that prior to all positive laws there are 'those of nature, so called because they derive their force entirely from our frame and being'.[5] And in order to know these laws we must consider man as he was before the establishment of society. 'The laws received in such a state would be those of nature.'[6] Whether this idea fits in well with the other aspects of Montesquieu's theory may be disputable. But there is no doubt that he maintained the existence of a natural moral law which is antecedent to all positive laws established by political society. We can say, if we wish, that his treatise on law looks forward to a purely empirical and inductive treatment of political and legal institutions and that his theory of natural law was a hang-over from earlier philosophers of law. But this theory is none the less a real element in his thought.

In the second place Montesquieu was an enthusiast for liberty and not simply a detached observer of historical phenomena. Thus in the eleventh and twelfth books of *De l'esprit des lois* he sets out to analyse the conditions of political liberty; and as he disliked despotism, the implication is that a liberal constitution is the best. His analysis may take the form of giving a meaning to the word *liberty* as used in a political context and then examining the conditions under which it can be secured and maintained. And, theoretically speaking, this could be done by a political philosopher who had no liking for political liberty or who was indifferent towards it. But in his analysis Montesquieu had one eye on the English constitution, which he admired, and the other on the

---

[1] Laws in their most general sense are 'the necessary relations resulting from the nature of things' (*De l'esprit des lois*, 1, 1).
[2] *Ibid.*, 1, 1.   [3] *Ibid.*   [4] *Ibid.*   [5] *Ibid.*   [6] *Ibid.*

French political system, which he disliked. His discussion of political liberty is thus not simply an abstract analysis, at least so far as its spirit and motive are concerned. For he was inquiring how the French system could be so amended as to permit of and to retain liberty.

Political liberty, says Montesquieu, does not consist in unrestrained freedom but 'only in the power of doing what we ought to will and in not being constrained to do what we ought not to will'.[1] 'Liberty is a right of doing whatever the laws permit.'[2] In a free society no citizen is prevented from acting in a manner permitted by law, and no citizen is forced to act in one particular manner when the law allows him to follow his own inclination. This description of liberty is perhaps not very enlightening; but Montesquieu goes on to insist that political liberty involves the separation of powers. That is to say, the legislative, executive and judicial powers must not be vested in one man or one particular group of men. They must be separated or independent of one another in such a way that they can act as checks on one another and constitute a safeguard against despotism and the tyrannical abuse of power.

This statement of the condition of political liberty is arrived at, as Montesquieu explicitly says, by examination of the English constitution. In different States there have been and are different operative ideals. The ideal or end of Rome was increase of dominion, of the Jewish State the preservation and increase of religion, of China public tranquillity. But there is one nation, England, which has political liberty for the direct end of its constitution. Accordingly, 'to discover political liberty in a constitution no great labour is required. If we are capable of seeing where it exists, why should we go any further in search of it?'[3]

It has been said by some writers that Montesquieu saw the English constitution through the eyes of political theorists such as Harrington and Locke and that when he talked about the separation of powers as the signal mark of the English constitution he failed to understand that the Revolution of 1688 had finally settled the supremacy of Parliament. In other words, a man who relied simply on observation of the English constitution would not have fixed on the so-called separation of powers as its chief characteristic. But even if Montesquieu saw and interpreted the English constitution in the light of a theory about it, and even if

[1] *De l'esprit des lois*, XI, 3.   [2] *Ibid.*   [3] *Ibid.*, XI, 5.

the phrase 'separation of powers' was not an adequate description of the concrete situation, it seems clear that the phrase drew attention to real features of the situation. The judges did not, of course, constitute a 'power' in the sense that the legislative did; but at the same time they were not subject in the exercise of their functions to the capricious control of the monarch or his ministers. It may be said, with truth, that what Montesquieu admired in the English constitution was the result of a long process of development rather than of the application of an abstract theory about the 'separation of powers'. But he was not so hypnotized by a phrase that, having interpreted the English constitution as a separation of powers, he then demanded that it should be slavishly copied in his own country. 'How should I have such a design, I who think that the very excess of reason is not always desirable, and that men almost always accommodate themselves better to the mean than to extremes?'[1] Montesquieu desired a reform of the French political system, and observation of the English constitution suggested to him ways in which it might be reformed without a violent and drastic revolution.

Montesquieu's ideas about the balancing of powers exercised an influence both in America and in France, as in the case of the 1791 French Declaration of the Rights of Man and of Citizens. In later times, however, more emphasis has been laid on his pioneer work in the empirical and comparative study of political societies and of the connections between forms of government, legal systems and other conditioning factors.

5. In the section on Fontenelle attention was drawn to his defence of Cartesian physical theories. The displacement of Descartes by Newton can be illustrated by the activity of Pierre Louis Moreau de Maupertuis (1698–1759), who attacked the Cartesian theory of vortices and defended Newton's theory of gravitation. Indeed, his championship of Newton's theories contributed to his being elected a Fellow of the Royal Society. In 1736 he headed an expedition to Lapland which, as was mentioned in the first section of this chapter, he had undertaken, at the wish of King Louis XV, to make some exact measurements of a degree of latitude with a view to determining the shape of the earth. The results of these observations, published in 1738, confirmed Newton's theory that the surface of the earth is flattened towards the Poles.

In some respects Maupertuis's philosophical ideas were

---

[1] *De l'esprit des lois*, xi, 6.

empiricist, and even positivist. In 1750, when acting, on the invitation of Frederick the Great, as president of the Prussian Academy at Berlin, he published an *Essay on Cosmology*. In this work he speaks, for example, of the concept of force which originates in our experience of resistance in the physical overcoming of obstacles. 'The word *force* in its proper sense expresses a certain feeling which we experience when we wish to move a body which was at rest or to change or stop the movement of a body which was in motion. The perception which we then experience is so constantly accompanied by a change in the rest or movement of the body that we are unable to prevent ourselves from believing that it is the cause of this change. When, therefore, we see some change taking place in the rest or movement of a body, we do not fail to say that it is the effect of some force. And if we have no feeling of any effort made by us to contribute to this change, and if we only see some other bodies to which we can attribute this phenomenon, we place the *force* in them, as though it belonged to them.'[1] In its origin the idea of force is only 'a feeling of our soul',[2] and, as such, it cannot belong to the bodies to which we attribute it. There is, however, no harm in speaking about a moving force being present in bodies, provided that we remember that it is 'only a word invented to supply for our (lack of) knowledge, and that it signifies only a result of phenomena'.[3] In other words, we should not allow ourselves to be misled by our use of the word *force* into thinking that there is an occult entity corresponding to it. Force is measured 'only by its apparent effects'. In physical science we remain in the realm of phenomena. And the fundamental concepts of mechanics can be interpreted in terms of sensation. Indeed, Maupertuis believed that the impression of necessary connection in mathematical and mechanical principles can also be explained in empiricist terms, for instance by association and custom.

At the same time, however, Maupertuis proposed a teleological conception of natural laws. The fundamental principle in mechanics is the principle 'of the least quantity of action'.[4] This principle states that 'when some change takes place in Nature, the quantity of action employed for this change is always the least possible. It is from this principle that we deduce the laws of motion.'[5] In other words, Nature always employs the least possible amount of force or energy which is required to achieve her purpose. This law of the

---

[1] *Essai de cosmologie*, 2 *partie; Œuvres*, I, edit. 1756, pp. 29–30.
[2] *Ibid.*, p. 30. [3] *Ibid.*, p. 31. [4] *Ibid.*, p. 42. [5] *Ibid.*, pp. 42–3.

least possible quantity of action had already been employed by Fermat, the mathematician, in his study of optics; but Maupertuis gave it a universal application. Samuel König, a disciple of Leibniz, argued that the latter had anticipated Maupertuis in the statement of this law; and the French philosopher tried to refute the truth of this assertion. But the question of priority need not concern us here. The point is that Maupertuis felt himself entitled to argue that the teleological system of Nature shows it to be the work of an all-wise Creator. According to him, Descartes' principle of the conservation of energy seems to withdraw the world from the government of the Deity. 'But our principle, more conformable to the ideas which we ought to have of things, leaves the world in continual need of the power of the Creator, and it is a necessary consequence of the wisest employment of this power.'[1]

In the 1756 edition of his *Works* Maupertuis included a *Système de la Nature*, a Latin version of which had already been published under the pseudonym of Baumann with the date 1751. In this essay he denied the sharp Cartesian distinction between thought and extension. At bottom, says Maupertuis,[2] the reluctance which one feels to attribute intelligence to matter arises simply out of the fact that one always assumes that this intelligence must be like ours. In reality there is an infinity of degrees of intelligence, ranging from vague sensation to clear intellectual processes. And each entity possesses some degree of it. Maupertuis thus proposed a form of hylozoism, according to which even the lowest material things possess some degree of life and sensibility.

On the strength of this doctrine Maupertuis has sometimes been classed with the crude materialists of the French Enlightenment who will be mentioned later. But the philosopher objected to Diderot's interpretation of his theory as being equivalent to materialism and as doing away with the basis of any valid argument for the existence of God. In his *Reply to the Objections of M. Diderot* which he appended to the 1756 edition of the *Système de la Nature* Maupertuis observes that when Diderot wishes to substitute for the attribution to purely material things of elementary perceptions an attribution to them of sensation analogous to touch, he is simply playing with words. For sensation is a form of perception. And elementary perceptions are not the same as the clear and distinct perceptions which we enjoy. There is no real

---

[1] *Essai de cosmologie*, 2 *partie; Œuvres*, 1, edit. 1756, p. 44.
[2] *Système de la Nature*, LXII; *Œuvres*, 11, pp. 164–5.

difference between what 'Baumann' says and what Diderot wishes him to say. Obviously, these observations do not settle the question, whether Maupertuis is a materialist or not. But this is in any case a difficult question to answer. The philosopher appears to have maintained that higher degrees of 'perception' proceed from combinations of atoms or particles which enjoy elementary perception, but which are physical points rather than meta-physical points like Leibniz's monads. And it is certainly arguable that this is a materialist position. At the same time one must bear in mind the fact that for Maupertuis not only qualities but also extension are phenomena, psychic representations. And Brunet has even maintained[1] that in certain of its aspects his philosophy resembles Berkeley's immaterialist doctrine. The truth of the matter seems to be that though Maupertuis's writings contributed to the growth of materialism, his position is too equivocal to warrant our classing him without qualification with the materia-listic philosophers of the French Enlightenment. As for Diderot's interpretation, Maupertuis evidently suspected that he had his tongue in his cheek when he spoke of the 'terrible' consequences of Baumann's hypothesis, and that he merely wished to advertise these consequences while verbally rejecting them.

6. We have seen that both Fontenelle and Maupertuis believed that the cosmic system manifests the existence of God. Montes-quieu also believed in God. So did Voltaire. His name is associated with his violent and mocking attacks not only on the Catholic Church as an institution and on the shortcomings of ecclesiastics but also on Christian doctrines. But this does not alter the fact that he was no atheist.

François Marie Arouet (1694–1778), who later changed his name and styled himself M. de Voltaire, studied as a boy at the Jesuit college of Louis-le-Grand at Paris. After two visits to the Bastille he went to England in 1726 and remained there until 1729. It was during this sojourn in England that he made acquaintance with the writings of Locke and Newton and developed that admiration for the comparative freedom of English life which is evident in his *Philosophical Letters*.[2] Elsewhere Voltaire remarks that Newton, Locke and Clarke would have been persecuted in France,

---

[1] *Maupertuis*, Paris, 1929.
[2] Voltaire never met Hume, though he greatly admired him. On his part Hume was somewhat reserved in his attitude towards the French philosopher, though he was persuaded to write him an appreciative letter from Paris when Voltaire was at Ferney.

imprisoned at Rome, burned at Lisbon. This zeal for toleration did not, however, prevent him from expressing lively satisfaction when in 1761 he heard it reported that three priests had been burned at Lisbon by the anti-clerical government.

In 1734 Voltaire went to Cirey, and there he wrote his *Treatise on Metaphysics*, which he thought it more prudent not to publish. His *Philosophy of Newton* appeared in 1738. Voltaire took most of his philosophical ideas from thinkers such as Bayle, Locke and Newton; and he was undoubtedly successful in presenting these ideas in lucid and witty writings and in making them intelligible to French society. But he was not a profound philosopher. Though influenced by Locke, he was not in the same class as a philosopher. And though he wrote on Newton, he was not himself a mathematical physicist.

In 1750 Voltaire went to Berlin at the invitation of Frederick the Great, and in 1752 he composed his satire on Maupertuis, *Doctor Akakia*. This satire was displeasing to Frederick; and as the relations between the philosopher and his royal patron were becoming strained, Voltaire left Berlin in 1753 and went to reside near Geneva. His important *Essai sur les mœurs* appeared in 1756.

Voltaire acquired a property at Ferney in 1758. *Candide* appeared in 1759, the *Treatise on Tolerance* in 1763, the *Philosophical Dictionary* in 1764, *The Ignorant Philosopher* in 1766, a work on Bolingbroke in 1767, the *Profession of Faith of Theists* in 1768. In 1778 Voltaire went to Paris for the first performance of his play *Irène*. He received a tremendous ovation in the capital; but he died at Paris not long after the performance.

In the Beuchot edition of 1829–34 Voltaire's complete works comprise some seventy volumes. He was philosopher, dramatist, poet, historian and novelist. As a man, he certainly had some good points. He had a strong dose of common sense; and his call for a reform in the administration of justice, together with his efforts, even if inspired by very mixed motives, to bring certain miscarriages of justice to public attention, show a certain amount of humane feeling. But, in general, his character was not particularly admirable. He was vain, revengeful, cynical and intellectually unscrupulous. His attacks on Maupertuis, Rousseau and others do him little credit. But nothing, of course, that we may say about his defects of character can alter the fact that he sums up brilliantly in his writings the spirit of the French Enlightenment.

In his work on the elements of the Newtonian philosophy Voltaire maintains that Cartesianism leads straight to Spinozism. 'I have known many people whom Cartesianism has led to admit no other God than the immensity of things, and, on the contrary, I have seen no Newtonian who was not a theist in the strictest sense.'[1] 'The whole philosophy of Newton leads necessarily to the knowledge of a Supreme Being who has created everything and arranged everything freely.'[2] If there is a vacuum, matter must be finite. And if it is finite, it is contingent and dependent. Moreover, attraction and motion are not essential qualities of matter. Hence they must have been implanted by God.

In his *Treatise on Metaphysics* Voltaire offers two lines of argument for God's existence. The first is a proof from final causality. The world is compared to a watch; and Voltaire maintains that just as when one sees a watch, the hands of which mark the time, one concludes that it has been made by someone for the purpose of marking the time, so must one conclude from observation of Nature that it has been made by an intelligent Creator. The second argument is an argument from contingency on the lines laid down by Locke and Clarke. Later on, however, Voltaire left aside this second argument and confined himself to the first. At the end of the article on atheism in his *Philosophical Dictionary* he remarks that 'geometers who are not philosophers have rejected final causes, but true philosophers admit them. And, as a well-known author has said, a catechist announces God to infants whereas Newton demonstrates Him for the wise.' And in the article on Nature he argues that no mere assemblage could account for the universal harmony or system. 'They call me Nature, but I am all art.'

But though Voltaire maintained to the end his belief in the existence of God, there was a change in his view of the relation of the world to God. At first he shared more or less the cosmic optimism of Leibniz and Pope. Thus in his work on Newton he speaks of the atheist who denies God because of the evil in the world and then remarks that the terms *good* and *well-being* are equivocal. 'That which is bad in relation to you is good in the general system.'[3] Again, are we to abandon the conclusion about God's existence to which reason leads us because wolves devour sheep and because spiders catch flies? 'Do you not see, on the contrary, that these continual generations constantly devoured

---

[1] *Philosophie de Newton*, I, I.   [2] *Ibid.*   [3] *Ibid.*

and constantly reproduced, enter into the plan of the universe?'[1]

The problem of evil was, however, brought vividly to Voltaire's attention by the disastrous earthquake at Lisbon in 1755. And he expressed his reactions to this event in his poem on the disaster at Lisbon and in *Candide*. In the poem he appears to reaffirm the divine liberty; but in his later writings he makes creation necessary. God is the first or supreme cause, existing eternally. But the notion of a cause without an effect is absurd. Therefore the world must proceed eternally from God. It is not, indeed, a part of God, and it is contingent in the sense that it depends on Him for its existence. But creation is eternal and necessary. And as evil is inseparable from the world, it too is necessary. It depends, therefore, on God; but God did not choose to bring it about. We could hold God responsible for evil only if He created freely.

To turn to man. In the *Philosophie de Newton*[2] Voltaire remarks that several people who knew Locke had assured him that Newton once admitted to Locke that our knowledge of Nature is not great enough to allow us to state that it is impossible for God to add the gift of thinking to an extended thing. And it seems sufficiently clear that Voltaire considered the theory of the soul as an immaterial substantial being to be an unnecessary hypothesis. In the article on Soul in the *Philosophical Dictionary* he argues that terms such as 'spiritual soul' are simply words which cover our ignorance. The Greeks made a distinction between the sensitive and the intellectual soul. But the first certainly does not exist; 'it is nothing but the motion of your organs'. And reason can find no better proof for the existence of the higher soul than it can find for the existence of the lower soul. 'It is only by faith that thou canst know it.' Voltaire does not say here in so many words that there is no such thing as a spiritual and immortal soul. But his view is made sufficiently clear elsewhere.

As for human liberty in a psychological sense, Voltaire changed his mind. In the *Treatise on Metaphysics*[3] he defended the reality of liberty by an appeal to the immediate testimony of consciousness which resists all theoretical objections. In his *Philosophie de Newton*,[4] however, he makes a distinction. In certain trivial matters, when I have no motive inclining me to act in one way rather than in another, I may be said to have liberty of indifference. For example, if I have a choice of turning to the left or to the right,

---

[1] *Philosophie de Newton*, I, 1.   [2] I, 7.   [3] 7.   [4] I, 4.

and if I have no inclination to do the one and no aversion towards the other, the choice is the result of my own volition. Obviously, liberty of 'indifference' is here taken in a very literal sense. In all other cases when we are free we have the freedom which is called spontaneity; 'that is to say, when we have motives, our will is determined by them. And these motives are always the final result of the understanding or of instinct.'[1] Here liberty is admitted in name. But after having made this distinction Voltaire proceeds to say that 'everything has its cause; therefore your will has one. One cannot will, therefore, except as a consequence of the last idea that one has received. . . . This is why the wise Locke does not venture to pronounce the name *liberty*; a free will does not appear to him to be anything but a chimaera. He knows no other liberty than the power to do what one wills.'[2] In fine, 'we must admit that one can hardly reply to the objections against liberty except by a vague eloquence; a sad theme about which the wise man fears even to think. There is only one consoling reflection, namely that whatever system one embraces, by whatever fatalism one believes our actions to be determined, one will always act as though one were free.'[3] In the next chapter Voltaire proposes a series of objections against liberty of indifference.

In his article on Liberty in the *Philosophical Dictionary* Voltaire says roundly that liberty of indifference is 'a word without sense, invented by people who scarcely had any themselves'. What one wills is determined by motive; but one may be free to act or not to act, in the sense that it may or may not be in one's power to perform the action that one wills to perform. 'Your will is not free, but your actions are; you are free to act when you have the power to act.' In *The Ignorant Philosopher*[4] Voltaire maintains that the idea of a free will is absurd; for a free will would be a will without sufficient motive, and it would fall outside the course of Nature. It would be very odd if 'one little animal, five feet tall', were an exception to the universal reign of law. It would act by chance, and there is no chance. 'We have invented this word to express the known effect of any unknown cause.' As for the consciousness or feeling of freedom, this is quite compatible with determinism in our volition. It shows no more than that one can *do* as one pleases when one has the power to perform the action willed.

This assertion of determinism does not mean that Voltaire discarded the idea of the moral law. He expressed his agreement with

---

[1] *Philosophie de Newton*, I, 4. [2] *Ibid.* [3] *Ibid.* [4] 13.

Locke about the absence of any innate moral principles. But we are so fashioned by God that in the course of time we come to see the necessity of justice. True, Voltaire was accustomed to draw attention to the variability of moral convictions. Thus, in the *Treatise on Metaphysics*,[1] he remarks that what in one region is called virtue is called vice in another, and that moral rules are as variable as languages and fashions. At the same time 'there are natural laws with respect to which human beings in all parts of the world must agree'.[2] God has endowed man with certain inalienable feelings which are eternal bonds and give rise to the fundamental laws of human society. The content of the fundamental law seems to be very restricted and to consist mainly in not injuring others and in pursuing what is pleasurable to oneself provided that this does not involve wanton injury to one's neighbour. None the less, just as Voltaire always maintained a deistic (or, as he called it, a theistic) position, so he never surrendered completely to relativism in morals. Profound religious feeling of the type to be found in Pascal was certainly not a characteristic of Voltaire; nor was lofty moral idealism. But just as he rejected atheism, so did he reject extreme ethical relativism.

We have said that Voltaire came to adopt a determinist position in regard to human liberty in a psychological sense. At the same time he was a resolute defender of political liberty. Like Locke, he believed in a doctrine of human rights which should be respected by the State; and, like Montesquieu, he admired the conditions of freedom prevailing in England. But it is necessary to understand what he meant by political liberty. First and foremost he had liberty of thought and expression in mind. In other words, he was primarily concerned with liberty for *les philosophes*, at least when they agreed with Voltaire. He was not a democrat in the sense of wishing to promote popular rule. True, he advocated toleration, which he thought to be necessary for scientific and economic progress; and he disliked tyrannical despotism. But he mocked at Rousseau's ideas about equality, and his ideal was that of a benevolent monarchy, enlightened by the influence of the philosophers. He mistrusted dreamers and idealists; and his correspondence shows that in his opinion the rabble, as he pleasingly called the people, would always remain a rabble. Better conditions of freedom and toleration and better standards of judicial procedure could quite well be secured under the French monarchy,

[1] 9.   [2] *Ibid.*

provided that the power of the Church was broken and philosophical enlightenment substituted for Christian dogma and
superstition. Voltaire certainly never thought that salvation could
come from the people or from violent insurrection. Although,
therefore, his writings helped to prepare the ground for the
Revolution, it would be a great mistake to picture Voltaire as
looking forward to or as consciously intending to promote the
Revolution in the form which it was actually to take. His enemy
was not the monarchy, but rather the clergy. He was not interested
in liberalizing the constitution in the sense of advocating Montesquieu's 'separation of powers'. In fact one can even say that he
was interested in increasing the power of the monarchy, in the
sense that he wished it to be free of clerical influence.

These remarks are not to be taken as implying that Voltaire
was an enemy of progress. On the contrary, he was one of the most
influential disseminators of the idea of progress. But the term
meant for him the reign of reason, intellectual, scientific and
economic progress, rather than political progress, if one understands by this a transition to democracy or popular rule. For in his
opinion it was the enlightened monarchic ruler who was most likely
to promote progress in science, literature and toleration of ideas.

In spite of the fact that Montesquieu's theories have been
treated in this chapter, I propose to reserve Voltaire's opinions on
history for the chapter on the rise of the philosophy of history.

7. When one thinks of the period known as the Enlightenment
or Age of Reason, one naturally tends to think of an exaltation of
cool and critical intelligence. Yet it was Hume, one of the greatest
figures of the Enlightenment, who said that reason is and ought to
be the slave of the passions and who found the basis of moral life
in feeling. And in France Voltaire, whom one naturally pictures
as the very embodiment of critical, and somewhat superficial,
intelligence, declared that without the passions there would be no
human progress. For the passions are a motivating force in man;
they are the wheels which make the machines go.[1] Similarly, we
are told by Vauvenargues that 'our passions are not distinct from
ourselves; some of them are the whole foundation and the whole
substance of our soul'.[2] Man's true nature is to be found in the
passions rather than in the reason.

Luc de Clapiers, Marquis of Vauvenargues, was born in 1715.

---

[1] *Treatise on Metaphysics* 8.
[2] *Introduction to the Knowledge of the Human Mind*, II, 42.

From 1733 he was an army officer and took part in several campaigns until his health broke down. He spent the last two years of his life at Paris, where he was a friend of Voltaire and where he died in 1747. In the year preceding his death he published his *Introduction to the Knowledge of the Human Mind*, followed by *Critical Reflections on Some Poets*. Maxims and other pieces were added to subsequent (posthumous) editions.

The first book of Vauvenargues's work is devoted to the mind (*esprit*). 'The object of this first Book is to make known by definitions and reflections founded on experience, all those different qualities of men which are comprised under the name of mind. Those who seek for the physical causes of these same qualities might perhaps be able to speak of them with less uncertainty if in this work one succeeded in developing the effects of which they study the principles.'[1] Vauvenargues did not agree with those who tended to stress the equality of all minds. In his work he discusses briefly a number of qualities which are normally mutually exclusive and which give rise to different types of minds. He also stresses the concept of the genius, in whom we find a combination of normally independent qualities. 'I believe that there is no genius without activity. I believe that genius depends in great part on our passions. I believe that it arises from the meeting of many different qualities, and from the secret agreements of our inclinations with our (mental) lights. When one of these necessary conditions is wanting, there is no genius, or it is only imperfect. . . . It is the necessity of this meeting of mutually independent qualities which is apparently the cause of the fact that genius is always so rare.'[2]

In the second book Vauvenargues treats of the passions which, 'as Mr. Locke says',[3] are all founded on pleasure and pain. These last are to be referred respectively to perfection and imperfection. That is, man is naturally attached to his being, and if his being were in no way imperfect but developed itself always without hindrance or imperfection, he would feel nothing but pleasure. As it is, we experience both pleasure and pain; and 'it is from the experience of these two contraries that we derive the idea of good and evil'.[4] The passions (at least those which come 'by the organ of reflection' and are not merely immediate impressions of sense) are founded on 'the love of being or of the perfection of being, or

---

[1] *Introduction to the Knowledge of the Human Mind*, I, I.
[2] *Ibid.*, I, 15.   [3] *Ibid.*, II, 22.   [4] *Ibid.*

on the feeling of our imperfection'.[1] For example, there are people in whom the feeling of their imperfection is more vivid than the feeling of perfection, of capacity, of power. We then find passions such as anxiety, melancholy and so on. Great passions arise from the union of these two feelings, that of our power and that of our imperfection and weakness. For 'the feeling of our miseries impels us to go out of ourselves, and the feeling of our resources encourages us to do so and carries us thereto in hope'.[2]

In the third book Vauvenargues treats of moral good and evil. We have seen that the idea of good and evil are founded on experiences of pleasure and pain. But different people find pleasure and pain in different things. Their ideas of good and evil are therefore different. This, however, is not what is meant by moral good and evil. 'In order that something should be regarded as a good by the whole of society, it must tend to the advantage of the whole of society. And in order that something should be regarded as an evil, it must tend to the ruin of society. Here we have the great characteristic of moral good and evil.'[3] Men, being imperfect, are not self-sufficient; society is necessary for them. And social life involves fusing one's particular interest with the general interest. 'This is the foundation of all morality.'[4] But pursuit of the common good involves sacrifice, and it is not everyone who is spontaneously ready to make such sacrifices. Hence the necessity of law.

As for virtue and vice, 'preference for the general interest before one's personal interest is the only definition which is worthy of virtue and which fixes the idea of it. On the contrary, the mercenary sacrifice of the public happiness to one's own interest is the eternal mark of vice.'[5] Mandeville may hold that private vices are public benefits, and that commerce would not flourish without avarice and vanity. But though this is true in a sense, it must also be admitted that the good which is produced by vice is always mixed with great evils. And if these are held in check and subordinated to the public good, it is reason and virtue which do so.

Vauvenargues proposes, therefore, a utilitarian interpretation of morality. But just as in the first book he makes much of the concept of genius, so in the third he devotes a special discussion to greatness of soul. 'Greatness of soul is a sublime instinct which impels men to that which is great, of whatever nature it may be,

---

[1] *Introduction to the Knowledge of the Human Mind*, II, 22.
[2] *Ibid.*   [3] *Ibid.*, III, 43.   [4] *Ibid.*   [5] *Ibid.*

but which turns them towards good or evil according to their passions, their lights, their education, their fortune, etc.'[1] Greatness of soul is thus morally indifferent in itself. When united with vice, it is dangerous to society (Vauvenargues mentions Cataline); but it is still greatness of soul. 'Where there is greatness, we feel it in spite of ourselves. The glory of conquerors has always been attacked; the people have always suffered from it, and they have always respected it.[2] It is not surprising that Nietzsche, with his conception of the higher man standing 'beyond good and evil', felt sympathy with Vauvenargues. But the latter was not, of course, concerned to deny what he had already said about the social character of morality. He was drawing attention to the complexity of human nature and character. 'There are vices which do not exclude great qualities, and consequently there are great qualities which stand apart from virtue. I recognize this truth with sorrow. . . . (But) those who wish men to be altogether good or altogether evil do not know nature. In men all is mixed; everything there is limited; and even vice has its limits.'[3]

In Vauvenargues's *Maxims* we can find a number of sayings which obviously recall Pascal. 'Reason does not know the interests of the heart.'[4] 'Great thoughts come from the heart.'[5] We find too that insistence on the fundamental role of the passions to which attention has already been drawn. 'We owe perhaps to the passions the greatest advantages of the spirit.'[6] 'The passions have taught reason to man. In the infancy of all peoples, as in that of individuals, feeling has always preceded reflection and has been its first master.'[7] It is perhaps worth while mentioning this point as one may easily think of the Age of Reason as a period in which feeling and passion were habitually depreciated in favour of the coldly analytic reason.

It would not be quite correct to say that Vauvenargues was not a systematic writer on the ground that his writings consist more of aphorisms than of developed discussions. For in his work on the knowledge of the human mind there is a more or less systematic arrangement of his thoughts. But he acknowledged in his preliminary discourses that circumstances had not permitted him to fulfil his original plan. In any case Vauvenargues was more

---

[1] *Introduction to the Knowledge of the Human Mind*, III, 44.
[2] *Réflexions et maximes*, 222.
[3] *Introduction to the Knowledge of the Human Mind*, III, 44.
[4] *Réflexions et maximes*, 124.   [5] *Ibid.*, 127.
[6] *Ibid.*, 151.   [7] *Ibid.*, 154-5.

concerned with distinguishing and describing different qualities of mind and different passions than with investigating the causes, as he put it, of psychical phenomena. For a study of the way in which mental operations and functions are derived from a primitive foundation we have to turn to Condillac.

8. Étienne Bonnot de Condillac (1715–80) was first destined for the priesthood and entered the seminary of Saint-Sulpice. But he left the seminary in 1740 and took to philosophy. From 1758 to 1767 he was tutor to the son of the Duke of Parma.

Condillac's first publication was an *Essay on the Origin of Human Knowledge* (*Essai sur l'origine des connaissances humaines*, 1746), which bears the clear imprint of Locke's empiricism. This is not to say that Condillac simply reproduced the doctrine of the English philosopher. But he was in agreement with the latter's general principles that we must reduce complex to simple ideas and that we must assign to simple ideas an empirical or experiential origin.

In discussing the development of our mental life Condillac laid great stress on the part played by language. Ideas become fixed, as it were, only by being associated with a sign or word. When I look at the grass, for example, I have a sensation of green; a simple idea of green is transmitted to me by sense. But this isolated experience, which can, of course, be repeated indefinitely, becomes an object of reflection and can enter into combination with other ideas only by being linked with a sign or symbol, the word *green*. The fundamental material of knowledge is thus the association of an idea with a sign; and it is in virtue of this association that we are able to develop a complex intellectual life in accordance with our growing experience of the world and with our needs and purposes. True, language, that is to say ordinary language, is defective in the sense that we do not find in it that perfect correspondence between the sign and the signified which we find in mathematical language. None the less, we are intelligent beings, beings capable of reflection, because we possess the gift of language.

In his *Treatise on Systems* (*Traité des Systèmes*, 1749) Condillac subjects to adverse criticism the 'spirit of systems' as manifested in the philosophies of thinkers such as Descartes, Malebranche, Spinoza and Leibniz. The great rationalist philosophers tried to construct systems by proceeding from first principles and definitions. This is especially true of Spinoza. But the so-called geometrical system is useless for developing a real knowledge of the world. A philosopher may imagine that his definitions express an apprehension of essences; but in reality they are arbitrary. That is to say, they are arbitrary unless they are intended to state merely the senses in which certain words are used as a matter of fact. And if they are merely dictionary definitions, so to speak, they cannot do the job which they are supposed to do in the philosophical systems.

This does not mean, of course, that Condillac condemns all efforts to systematize knowledge. To subject to adverse criticism the spirit of systems, the attempt to develop a philosophy from reason alone in an *a priori* manner, is not to condemn synthesis. A system in the acceptable meaning of the word is an orderly disposition of the parts of a science so that the relations between them are clearly exhibited. There will certainly be principles. But principles will mean here known phenomena. Thus Newton constructed a system by using the known phenomena of gravitation as a principle and by then explaining phenomena such as the movements of the planets and the tides in the light of this principle.

We find similar ideas in Condillac's *Logic*, which appeared posthumously in 1780. The great metaphysicians of the seventeenth century followed a synthetic method, borrowed from geometry and proceeding by way of deduction from definitions. And this method, as we have seen, cannot give us real knowledge of Nature. The analytic method, however, remains always in the sphere of the given. We start from a confused given and analyse it into its distinct parts: we can recompose the whole in a systematic way. This is the natural method, the method which the mind naturally follows when we wish to develop our knowledge. How, for example, do we come to know a landscape or countryside? First we have a confused impression of it, and then we gradually arrive at a distinct knowledge of its various component features and come to see how these features together make up the whole. In developing a theory of method we are not called upon to elaborate an *a priori* notion of an ideal method; we should study how the mind actually works when it develops its knowledge. It will then be found that there is no one ideal and fixed method. The order in which we ought to study things depends on our need and purpose. And if we wish to study Nature, to acquire a real knowledge of things, we must remain within the sphere of the given, within the phenomenal order which is ultimately given to us in sense-experience.

Condillac is best known for his *Treatise on Sensations* (*Traité des sensations*, 1754). Locke had distinguished between ideas of sensation and ideas of reflection, admitting two founts of ideas, sensation and reflection or introspection. And in his early work on the origin of human knowledge Condillac had more or less assumed Locke's position. But in the *Treatise on Sensations* he made a clear break with Locke's theory of the dual origin of ideas. There is only one origin or fount, namely sensation.

In Condillac's opinion Locke gave only inadequate treatment to ideas of reflection, that is to say, to psychical phenomena. He analysed complex ideas, such as those of substance, into simple ideas; but he simply assumed the mental operations of comparing, judging, willing, and so on. There is room, therefore, for an advance on Locke. It has to be shown how these mental operations and functions are reducible in the long run to sensations. They cannot, of course, be all termed sensations; but they are 'transformed sensations'. That is to say, the whole edifice of the psychical life is built out of sensation. To show that this is the case is the task which Condillac sets himself in his *Treatise on Sensations*.

To make his point Condillac asks his readers to imagine a statue which is gradually endowed with the senses, beginning with the sense of smell. And he tries to show how the whole of man's mental life can be explained on the hypothesis that it arises out of sensations. The analogy of the statue is, indeed, somewhat artificial. But what Condillac wishes his readers to do is to imagine themselves bereft of all knowledge and to reconstruct with him their mental operations from the basis of elementary sensations. His approach to the problem of the origin of our ideas was stimulated by the data provided by the experiences of persons born blind who underwent successful operations for cataract at the hands of Cheselden, the London surgeon, and by Diderot's study of the psychology of the deaf and dumb. In the *Treatise on Sensations*,[1] he speaks at some length of the data provided by one of Cheselden's operations.

One of the chief features of this treatise is the way in which Condillac tries to show how each sense, taken separately, can generate all the faculties. Let us take, for example, a man (represented by the statue) whose range of knowledge is limited to the sense of smell. 'If we give the statue a rose to smell, to us it is a

---

[1] III, v.

statue smelling a rose, to itself it is smell of rose.'[1] That is to say, the man will have no idea of matter or of external things or of his own body. For his own consciousness he will be nothing but a sensation of smell. Now, suppose that the man only has this one sensation, the smell of a rose. This is 'attention'. And when the rose is taken away, an impression remains, stronger or weaker according as the attention was more or less lively or vivid. Here we have the dawn of memory. Attention to past sensation is memory, which is nothing but a mode of feeling. Then let us suppose that the man, after having repeatedly smelt the scents of roses and pinks, smells a rose. His passive attention is divided between the memories of the smells of roses and pinks. Then we have comparison, which consists in attending to two ideas at the same time. And 'when there is comparison there is judgment. . . . A judgment is only the perception of a relation between two ideas which are compared.'[2] Again, if the man, having a present disagreeable sensation of smell, recalls a past pleasant sensation, we have imagination. For memory and imagination do not differ in kind. Again, the man can form ideas, particular and abstract. Some smells are pleasant, others unpleasant. If the man contracts the habit of separating the ideas of satisfaction and dissatisfaction from their several particular modifications, he will possess abstract ideas. Similarly, he can form ideas of number when he recalls several distinct successive sensations.

Now, every sensation of smell is either agreeable or disagreeable. And if the man who now experiences a disagreeable sensation recalls a past agreeable sensation, he feels the need of re-attaining that happier state. This give rise to desire. For 'desire is nothing else than the action of these faculties when directed on the things of which we feel the need'.[3] And a desire which expels all others, or at least becomes dominant, is a passion. We thus arrive at the passions of love and hate. 'The statue loves a pleasant smell which it has or wishes to have. It hates an unpleasant smell which pains it.'[4] Further, if the statue remembers that the desire which it now experiences has been at other times followed by satisfaction, it thinks that it can fulfil its desire. It is then said to will. 'For by *will* we understand an absolute desire; that is, we think the thing desired is in our power.'[5]

Condillac thus endeavours to show that all mental operations

---

[1] *Treatise on Sensations*, 1, i, 2.   [2] *Ibid.*, 1, i, 15.
[3] *Ibid.*, 1, iii, 1.   [4] *Ibid.*, 1, iii, 5.   [5] *Ibid.*, 1, iii, 9.

can be derived from the sensation of smelling. Obviously, if we consider our faculties and operations simply as transformed sensations of smell, their range is extremely limited. And we can say the same of the consciousness of self in a man who is limited to the sense of smell. 'Its (the statue's) "I" is only the collection of the sensations which it experiences, and those which memory recalls to it.'[1] None the less, 'with one sense alone the understanding has as many faculties as with the five joined together'.[2] ('Understanding' is simply the name for all the cognitive faculties taken together.)

Hearing, taste and sight are then considered. But Condillac maintained that though the combination of smell, hearing, taste and sight multiplies the objects of a man's attention, desires and pleasures, it does not produce a judgment of externality. The statue will 'still see only itself. . . . It has no suspicion that it owes its modifications to outside causes. . . . It does not even know that it has a body.'[3] In other words, it is the sense of touch which is ultimately responsible for the judgment of externality. In his account of this matter Condillac's ideas varied somewhat. In the first edition of the *Treatise on Sensations* he made the knowledge of externality independent of movement. But in the second edition he admitted that the notion of externality does not arise independently of movement. In any case, however, it is touch which is primarily responsible for this notion. When a child moves its hand along parts of its body, 'it will feel itself in all parts of the body'.[4] 'But if it touches a foreign body, the "I" which feels itself modified in the hand does not feel itself modified in the foreign body. The "I" does not receive the response from the foreign body which it receives from the hand. The statue, therefore, judges these modes to be altogether outside it.'[5] And when touch is joined to other senses, the man gradually discovers his own several sense-organs and judges that sensations of smell, hearing, and so on are caused by external objects. For example, by touching a rose and making it approach or recede from the face, a man can come to form judgments about the organ of smell and about the external cause of his sensations of smell. Similarly, it is only by combination with touch that the eye learns how to see distance, size and movement. We have become so accustomed to judging size, shape, distance and situation by sight that we are naturally

---

[1] *Treatise on Sensations*, I, vi, 3.   [2] *Ibid.*, I, vii, I.   [3] *Ibid.*, I, xii, I–2.
[4] *Ibid.*, II, v, 4.   [5] *Ibid.*, II, v, 5.

inclined to think that these judgments are due simply to sight. But this is not the case.

It is perhaps worth while drawing attention in passing to a change of view on Condillac's part between the publication of his *Essay on the Origin of Human Knowledge* and his *Treatise on Sensations*. In the first work he seems to maintain that the link between idea and sign or symbol is necessary for intelligence. But in the second work this point of view is modified. When treating, for example, of the man who is limited to the sense of smell he admits that this man can have some idea of number. He can have the ideas of one and one and one. But, according to Condillac, 'memory does not distinctly grasp four units at once. Beyond three it presents only an indefinite multitude. . . . It is the art of ciphering which has taught us to enlarge our point of view.'[1] Thus in the *Treatise* Condillac maintains that intelligence and the use of ideas precedes language, though language is necessary for the development of our mental life beyond a rudimentary stage.

The upshot of the *Treatise* is that 'in the natural order all knowledge arises from sensations'.[2] All man's mental operations, even those which are generally reckoned his higher mental activities, can be explained as 'transformed sensations'. Thus Condillac was convinced that he had made a definite advance on the position of Locke. The latter had thought that the faculties of the soul are innate qualities; he had not suspected that they might have their origin in sensation itself. It might perhaps be objected that Condillac's statement is not quite accurate. For did not Locke suggest that it had not been shown to be impossible for God to confer on matter the faculty of thinking? But in point of fact Locke was concerned with analysing and tracing back to their empirical grounds the ideas about which our faculties are employed; he did not do the same thing for the faculties or psychical functions themselves.

Now, in his *Essay concerning Human Understanding*,[3] Locke had maintained that the will is determined by 'an uneasiness of the mind for want of some absent good'. It is uneasiness or disquiet which 'determines the will to the successive voluntary actions, whereof the greatest part of our lives is made up, and by which we are conducted through different courses to different ends'.[4] Condillac developed and extended the range of this idea. Thus in the *Extrait raisonné*, which he added to later editions of the

---

[1] *Treatise on Sensations* I, iv, 7.   [2] *Ibid.*, IV, ix, I.   [3] II, 21, 31 f.   [4] *Ibid.*, 33.

Treatise on Sensations, he maintains that 'uneasiness (*inquiétude*) is the first principle which gives us the habits of touching, seeing, hearing, feeling, tasting, comparing, judging, reflecting, desiring, loving, fearing, hoping, wishing, and that, in a word, it is through uneasiness that all habits of mind and body are born'. All psychical phenomena, therefore, depend on uneasiness, which is not so much anticipation of a good as uneasiness or disquietude under certain conditions. Thus one can say perhaps that Condillac gives a 'voluntaristic' foundation to the whole process by which man's mental life is developed. Attention must be explained with reference to felt need; and memory is directed by appetite and desire rather than by a mere mechanical association of ideas. In his *Traité des animaux*[1] he makes it clear that in his opinion the order of our ideas depends ultimately on need or interest. This is obviously a fruitful theory. It was to bear fruit later on in the voluntaristic interpretation of man's intellectual life which is found, for example, in Schopenhauer.

Condillac's theory of the mind, of mental operations as transformed sensations, appears at first sight to indicate a materialistic position. And this impression is increased by his habit of speaking of the 'faculties' of the soul as being derived from sensation, which may be taken to imply that the human soul itself is material. Moreover, does he not suggest that man is nothing but the sum of his acquirements? 'In giving it (the statue) successively new modes of being and new senses we saw it form desires, learn from experience to regulate and satisfy them, and pass from needs to needs, from cognitions to cognitions, from pleasures to pleasures. The statue is therefore nothing but the sum of all it has acquired. May not this be the same with men?'[2] Man may be the sum of his acquirements; and they are transformed sensations.

It can hardly be denied, I think, that Condillac's theory helped to promote a materialistic outlook, in that it exercised an influence on the materialists. But Condillac was not himself a materialist. In the first place he was not a materialist in the sense of one who holds that there are only bodies and their modifications. For not only did he affirm the existence of God as supreme cause but he also maintained the theory of an immaterial, spiritual soul. He did not intend to reduce the soul to a bundle of sensations. Rather did he presuppose the soul as a simple centre of unity and then attempt to reconstruct its activity on the basis of the

[1] II, 11.   [2] *Ibid.*, IV, ix, 3.

hypothesis that all psychical phenomena are ultimately derivable from sensations. Whether his reductive analysis and his acceptance of a spiritual soul in man fit well together is, of course, disputable. But in any case it is inaccurate to describe Condillac as a materialist.

In the second place Condillac left it an open question whether there are any extended things at all. As we have seen, he said at first that touch assures us of externality. But he soon realized that an account of the way in which the idea of externality arises is not the same thing as a proof that there are extended things. If we wish to say that sounds, tastes, odours and colours do not exist in objects we must also say that extension does not exist in them. Perhaps objects are extended, sonorous, tasty, odiferous and coloured; perhaps they are not. 'I maintain neither the one opinion nor the other, and I am waiting for someone to prove that they are what they appear to us to be, or that they are something else.'[1] It may be objected that if there is no extension, there are no objects. But this is untrue. 'All that we could reasonably infer would be that objects are existences which occasion sensations in us, and that they have properties about which we can have no certain knowledge.'[2] So far, therefore, from being a dogmatic materialist, Condillac leaves the door open for an immaterialist hypothesis, though he does not affirm this hypothesis.

It may be added that Condillac did not admit that his account of man's mental life involved sheer determinism. He appended to the *Treatise on Sensations* a dissertation on freedom, in which he discusses this point.

9. Condillac's attempt to show that all psychical phenomena are transformed sensations was continued by Claude Adrien Helvétius (1715–71) in his work *On the Mind* (*De l'esprit*, 1758). Helvétius came of a medical family whose original name, Schweizer, had been latinized. For a time he held the post of Farmer-General, but the opposition which his book on the mind aroused made it impossible for him to occupy posts in the royal service. So, apart from visits to England and to Berlin, he lived quietly on his estates. His book on man (*De l'homme, de ses facultés et de son éducation*) was published posthumously in 1772.

Helvétius reduces to sensation or sense-perception all the powers of the human understanding. It has been commonly held that man possesses faculties which transcend the level of sense.

---

[1] *Treatise on Sensations*, IV, v, *note*.   [2] *Ibid*.

But this is a false theory. Take judgment, for example. To judge is to perceive similarities and dissimilarities between individual ideas. If I judge that red is different from yellow, what I am doing is to perceive that the colour called 'red' affects my eyes differently from the way in which they are affected by the colour called 'yellow'. To judge, therefore, is simply to perceive.

This process of reductive analysis is applied also to man's ethical life. Self-love is the universal basis of human conduct, and self-love is directed to the acquisition of pleasure. 'Men love themselves: they all desire to be happy, and think their happiness would be complete if they were invested with a degree of power sufficient to procure them every sort of pleasure. The love of power, therefore, takes its rise from the love of pleasure.'[1] All phenomena such as the love of power are secondary; they are simply transformations of the fundamental love of pleasure. 'Corporeal sensibility is therefore the sole mover of man.'[2] Even virtues such as liberality and benevolence can be reduced to self-love, that is, to the love of pleasure. 'What is a benevolent man? One in whom a spectacle of misery produces a painful sensation.'[3] In the long run the benevolent man endeavours to relieve human unhappiness and misery simply because they cause in him painful sensations.

On the basis of this crude reductive psychology Helvétius erects a utilitarian theory of morality. In different societies men hold different moral opinions and attach different meanings to words such as *good* and *virtue*. And it is this fact, namely that different people attach different meanings to the same ethical terms, which causes so much confusion in discussion. Before we indulge in discussions about ethics, we ought, therefore, first to settle the meanings of words. And, 'the words once defined, a question is resolved almost as soon as proposed'.[4] But will not these definitions be arbitrary? Not, says Helvétius, if the work is performed by a free people. 'England is perhaps the only country in Europe from which the universe can expect and obtain this benefaction.'[5] If freedom of thought is presupposed, the common sense of mankind will find expression in agreement as to the proper meanings of ethical terms. 'True virtue is reputed such in all ages and all countries. The name of virtue should be given to such actions only as are useful to the public and conformable to the general

---

[1] *On Man*, 2, 7; translation by W. Hooper, 1777, I, 127.
[2] *Ibid.*, Hooper, I, p. 121.   [3] *Ibid.*, Hooper, I, p. 122.
[4] *Ibid.*, 2, 18; Hooper, I, p. 199.   [5] *Ibid.*, 2, 19; Hooper, I, p. 200.

interest.'[1] Although, therefore, self-interest is the fundamental and universal motive of conduct, public interest or utility is the norm of morality. And Helvétius tries to show how service of the common interest is psychologically possible. For example, if a child is taught to put itself in the place of the miserable and unfortunate, it will feel painful sensations, and self-love will stimulate a desire to relieve misery. In the course of time the force of association will set up a habit of benevolent impulses and conduct. Even if, therefore, self-love lies at the basis of all conduct, altruism is psychologically possible.

These considerations suggest that education is all-important in forming habits of conduct. Helvétius is one of the chief pioneers and promoters of utilitarian moral theory; but a special characteristic of his writings is his insistence on the power of education. 'Education can do all' and 'education makes us what we are'.[2] But the institution of a good system of education meets with serious obstacles. In the first place there is the clergy, and in the second place there is the fact that most governments are very imperfect or bad. We cannot have a good system of education until the power of the clergy has been broken and until a truly good system of government, with a corresponding good system of legislation, has been realized. The first and sole principle of morality is 'the public good is the supreme law'.[3] But few governments conduct themselves according to this law. Yet 'every important reformation in the moral part of education supposes one in the laws and form of government'.[4]

In the light of these ideas Helvétius inveighs against political despotism. Thus in the preface to his work *On Man* he speaks of the despotism to which France has been subjected, and adds that 'it is the characteristic of despotic power to extinguish both genius and virtue'.[5] Again, when speaking of the too unequal distribution of the national wealth, he remarks that 'for men to flatter themselves with this equal distribution among a people subject to arbitrary power is a folly'.[6] It is only in a free country that a gradual and more equitable redistribution of the national wealth can take place. We can say, therefore, that Helvétius was much more of a political reformer than was Voltaire; he was much more concerned than the latter with the overthrow of despotism and with the welfare of the people. This is one

---

[1] *On Man*, 2, 17; Hooper, I, p. 194.   [2] *Ibid.*, 10, 1; Hooper, II, pp. 392 and 395.
[3] *Ibid.*, 10, 10; Hooper, II, p. 436.   [4] *Ibid.*, Hooper, II, p. 433.
[5] Hooper, I, p. vi.   [6] *Ibid.*, 6, 9; Hooper, II, p. 105.

reason why he can be cited by left-wing writers as one of their predecessors.

Helvétius is tireless in attacking not only the clergy, particularly the Catholic priesthood, but also revealed or 'mysterious' religion, which he regardsas detrimental to the interests of society. True, when speaking of the accusation of impiety, he protests that he has not denied any Christian dogma. But it is quite evident from his writings that he does not seriously intend to accept anything but a form of natural religion or deism. And the content of this religion is interpreted in function of morality rather than in function of any theological beliefs. 'The will of God, just and good, is that the children of the earth should be happy and enjoy every pleasure compatible with the public welfare. Such is the true worship, that which philosophy should reveal to the world.'[1] Again, 'morality founded on true principles is the only true natural religion'.[2]

It can hardly be claimed that Helvétius was a profound philosopher. His reduction of all psychical functions to sensation is crude, and in ethics he gives no thorough analysis or defence of his basic ideas. These shortcomings were evident to some of the other thinkers of the French Enlightenment. Diderot, for example, objected to Helvétius's levelling-down tendency and to his explanation of all moral impulses in terms of veiled egotism. None the less, in his reductive analysis, in his insistence on intellectual enlightenment and on the power of education, and in his attacks on Church and State Helvétius represents some important aspects of eighteenth-century French philosophy, even if it is an exaggeration to speak of him as the typical thinker of the period.

[1] *On Man*, 1, 13; Hooper, 1, pp. 58–9.   [2] *Ibid.*, Hooper, 1, p. 60.

CHAPTER II

THE FRENCH ENLIGHTENMENT (2)

The Encyclopaedia; *Diderot and d'Alembert—Materialism; La Mettrie, d'Holbach and Cabanis—Natural history; Buffon, Robinet and Bonnet—The dynamism of Boscovich—The Physiocrats; Quesnay and Turgot—Final remarks.*

1. THE great literary repository of the ideas and ideals of the French Enlightenment was the *Encylopédie, ou Dictionnaire raisonné des arts et des métiers*. Suggested by a French translation of Chambers's *Cyclopaedia* or *Dictionary*, the *Encyclopaedia* was edited by Diderot and d'Alembert. The first volume was published in 1751, the second in the following year. The government then attempted to stop the work on the ground that it was prejudicial to the royal authority and to religion. However, by 1757 seven volumes had appeared. In 1758 d'Alembert retired from the editorship, and the French Government endeavoured to prevent the continuation of the project. But Diderot was eventually permitted to proceed with the printing, provided that no further volume was published until the whole work was complete. And in 1765 the final ten volumes (8–17) appeared, together with the fourth volume of plates, the first of which had been published in 1762. Subsequently other volumes of plates appeared, while a supplement in five volumes and indices in two volumes were printed at Amsterdam. The complete first edition of the *Encyclopaedia* (1751–80) consisted of thirty-five volumes. There were several foreign editions.

Quite apart from any controversy concerning the views expressed in the articles, the *Encyclopaedia*, as its editors freely acknowledged, left much to be desired. The articles varied greatly in standard and merit, and editorial supervision and co-ordination were lacking. In other words, we cannot expect to find in this work the conciseness, the concentration on clear and precise factual information, the systematic co-ordination and arrangement which are to be found in modern encyclopaedias. But in spite of all its defects the *Encyclopaedia* was a work of great importance. For its aim was not only to provide factual information for readers and to serve as a useful work of reference but also to guide and mould opinion. This is, of course, the reason why its publication aroused so much opposition. For it was the enemy both of the Church and of the existing political system. A certain amount of prudence was, indeed, observed in the writing of the articles; but the general attitude of the collaborators was perfectly clear. It was a large-scale manifesto by free-thinkers and rationalists; and its importance consists in its ideological aspect rather than in any permanent value as an encyclopaedia in the modern sense of the term.

Diderot and d'Alembert obtained collaborators who were of one mind when there was question, for example, of attacking the Church and revealed religion, but who differed considerably among themselves in other respects. Thus some articles were contributed by Voltaire, the deist, though when he thought that prudence rendered such conduct advisable, he did not hesitate to state, quite falsely, that he had had no connection with the *Encyclopaedia*. Another contributor, however, was the outspoken materialist d'Holbach, while the association of Helvétius with the work did nothing to commend it to the ecclesiastical authorities. The contributors included also Montesquieu and the economist Turgot.

D'Holbach will be considered in the section on materialism, while the ideas of Turgot will be discussed at the end of this chapter. In the present section I propose to confine myself to Diderot and d'Alembert.

(i) Denis Diderot (1713–84) was, like Voltaire, a pupil of the Jesuit College of Louis-le-Grand. Again like Voltaire, he came under the influence of English thought, and he translated several English works into French. Among them was the *Essai sur le mérite et la vertu* (1745), in which he added notes of his own to his translation of Shaftesbury's *Inquiry concerning Virtue and Merit*. And, as we have already seen, the idea of the *Encyclopaedia*, his life's work, was suggested to him by Chambers's *Cyclopaedia*. In 1746 he published *Pensées philosophiques* at the Hague and in 1749, at London, his *Lettre sur les aveugles à l'usage de ceux qui voient*. The views to which he gave expression earned him a few months' imprisonment at Vincennes, after which he devoted himself to the task of producing the *Encyclopaedia*. In 1754 there appeared at London his *Pensées sur l'interprétation de la nature*. A number of essays, such as the *Entretien entre d'Alembert et Diderot* and *Le rêve de d'Alembert* were not published during his lifetime. Diderot was by no means a rich man, and at one time he was in very difficult financial straits. But the Empress Catherine of Russia came to his assistance; and in 1773 he went to St. Petersburg, where he passed some months, partaking in frequent philosophical discussions with his benefactress. He was a noted conversationalist.

Diderot had no fixed system of philosophy. His thought was always on the move. We cannot say, for example, that he was a deist, an atheist or a pantheist; for his position changed. At the time when he wrote the *Pensées philosophiques* he was, indeed, a deist; and in the following year (1747) he wrote an essay on the sufficiency of natural religion, though it was not published until 1770. The historical religions, such as Judaism and Christianity, are mutually exclusive and intolerant. They are the creation of superstition. They began at certain periods in history, and they will all perish. But the historical religions all presuppose natural religion, which alone has always existed, which unites rather than separates men from one another, and which rests on the testimony which God has inscribed within us rather than on testimony provided by superstitious human beings. At a later stage of his development, however, Diderot abandoned deism for atheism and called on men to free themselves from the yoke of religion. Deism had cut off a dozen heads from the Hydra of religion; but from the one head which it had spared all the others would grow again.The only remedy is to make a clean sweep of all superstition. Yet Diderot later proposed a form of naturalistic pantheism. All parts of Nature ultimately form one individual, the Whole or All.

Similarly, the fluid character of his thought makes it impossible to state simply and unequivocally that Diderot was or was not a materialist. In his article on Locke in the *Encyclopaedia* he referred to the English philosopher's suggestion that it might not be impossible for God to confer on matter the capacity for thinking, and he evidently considered that thought developed out of sensibility. In the *Entretien entre d'Alembert et Diderot*, written in 1769, he gave clearer expression to a materialistic interpretation of man. Men and animals are really of the same nature, though their organizations differ. Differences in cognitive power and intelligence are simply the results of different physical organizations. And similar ideas appear in the *Rêve de d'Alembert* where it is implied that all psychological phenomena are reducible to physiological bases, and that the sense of freedom is illusory. Diderot was certainly influenced by Condillac's theory of the role of sensation in man's psychical life; but he came to criticize Condillac's sensationalism on the ground that the latter's analysis did not go far enough. We have to look beyond sensation to its physiological basis. And it is significant that Diderot assisted d'Holbach in the composition of his *Système de la nature* (1770), which was an outspoken exposition of materialism, even if the influence of d'Holbach on the development of his thought should not be exaggerated. At the same time we can find in Diderot a tendency to pan-psychism. He had a considerable admiration for Leibniz, whom he praised in the *Encyclopaedia*. And we find him later attributing perception to atoms, which correspond to Leibniz's monads. In certain combinations these atoms constitute animal organisms in which consciousness arises on the basis of the continuum formed by the atoms.

The fluid character of Diderot's interpretation of Nature and man is connected with his insistence on the experimental method in science and philosophy. In his work *On the Interpretation of Nature* he declared, wrongly of course, that mathematical science would soon come to a standstill, and that in less than a century there would not be three great geometers left in Europe. His conviction was that mathematics was limited by its own self-made concepts, and that it was incapable of giving us direct acquaintance with concrete reality. This acquaintance could be obtained only by the use of the experimental method, by the new scientific approach which constituted a successful rival not only to metaphysics but also to mathematics. And once we study Nature itself we find that it is changeable and elastic, rich in fresh possibilities, characterized by diversity and heterogeneity. Who knows all the species which have preceded ours? Who knows the species which will follow ours? Everything changes; no two atoms or molecules are perfectly alike; only the infinite whole is permanent. The order of Nature is not something static, but it is being perpetually born anew. We cannot, therefore, give any permanent interpretation of Nature in terms of our conceptual schemes and classifications. And one of the prime needs of thought is that it should keep itself open to new points of view and to new aspects of empirical reality.

Some historians have emphasized the discrepancy between the materialistic elements in Diderot's thought and his ethical idealism. On the one hand, his materialism does away with freedom and seems to make repentance and remorse pointless and useless. On the other hand, he reproached himself with having written his early erotic romance, *Bijoux indiscrets*; and he upheld the ideals of self-sacrifice, benevolence and humanity. He had no sympathy with those materialists who united the profession of materialism and atheism with low moral ideals; and he objected to Helvétius's attempt to explain all moral impulses and ideals in terms of veiled egotism. Indeed, he asserted the existence of immutable laws of natural morality. And, as an art critic, he extolled the free, creative activity of the artist.

However, even though we may agree with Rosenkranz, in his work on Diderot, that there is an inconsistency between the philosopher's materialism and his ethics, Diderot himself did not see any inconsistency. In his opinion there was no essential relation between ethical ideals and a belief in a spiritual soul in man. The derivation of thought from more rudimentary psychical activities does not entail the denial of high moral ideals. Thus in his article on Locke in the *Encyclopaedia*, to which we alluded above, he asks what difference it makes whether matter does or does not think. 'How can it possibly affect the idea of justice or injustice?' No evil moral consequences follow from the theory that thought emerges or evolves from sensibility. For man remains precisely what he is, and he is judged according to the good or evil purposes to which he devotes his powers, not according to whether thought is an original creation or an emergent from sensibility. In modern terms Diderot, who anticipated the evolutionary theory of Lamarck, is saying that the hypothesis of evolution does not affect the validity of man's moral ideals.

To some extent Diderot formed his ethical ideas under the influence of Shaftesbury's writings. But these ideas were not precisely fixed, except in the sense that he always upheld ideals of benevolence and humanity. He began at least by maintaining a 'rationalist' idea of immutable moral laws. But he found the basis of these laws in man's nature, that is to say, in the organic unity of man's impulses, passions and appetites, rather than in *a priori* commands of the reason. And he was hostile to the ascetic ideal as being contrary to nature. In other words, even if Diderot continued to uphold the idea of a natural law, he came to lay emphasis on its empirical basis and on its pragmatic effectiveness, when contrasted with a theological ethic, in promoting the common welfare.

(ii) Jean le Rond d'Alembert (1717–83) was born out of wedlock and was abandoned by his parents. He owed his name Jean le Rond or Lerond to the fact that he was found near the church of S. Jean le Rond at Paris. The surname was added later by himself. He was cared for by the wife of a glazier named Rousseau; but his real father, a certain Chevalier Destouches, settled an annuity on him, and he was thus enabled to study.

In 1738 d'Alembert was admitted as an advocate, but he did not practise as such. He then turned to medicine; but in a very short time he decided to give himself entirely to mathematics. He presented several papers, including his *Mémoire sur le calcul intégral* (1739) to the Academy of Sciences, and in 1741 he was made a member of this academy. His work in mathematics and science was of considerable importance. In 1741 he published his *Mémoire sur le réfraction des corps solides* and in 1743 his *Traité de dynamique*. In this treatise on dynamics he developed what is still known as 'd'Alembert's principle', and in 1744 he applied it in his *Traité de l'équilibre et du mouvement des fluides*. Subsequently he discovered the calculus of partial differences and applied it in his *Réflexion sur la cause générale des vents* (1747), which was crowned by the Prussian Academy. Among other writings we may mention his *Essai d'une nouvelle théorie sur la résistance des fluides* (1752) and his *Recherches sur différents points importants du système du monde* (1754–6).

As we have seen, d'Alembert was associated with Diderot in editing the *Encyclopaedia*, and he was the author of the *Discours préliminaire*. He also wrote a number of articles, chiefly, though not exclusively, on mathematical topics. But in 1758 he withdrew from collaboration in the work, wearied with opposition and the hazards of publication. In 1752 he had published *Mélanges de littérature, d'histoire et de philosophie*, and in 1759 there appeared his *Essai sur les éléments de philosophie*. In 1763 he visited Berlin, but he refused Frederick the Great's offer of the presidency of the Academy, just as in the previous year he had refused the invitation of Catherine of Russia to become tutor to her son on very generous terms. D'Alembert was a friend of David Hume, who held him in high esteem for his moral character and abilities and left him a legacy of £200 in his will. Being primarily a mathematician and scientist, d'Alembert was less exposed than other Encyclopaedists to suspicion and attack, and in 1755 he had been made a member of the Institute of Bologna on the recommendation of Pope Benedict XIV.

In his preliminary discourse in the *Encyclopaedia* d'Alembert declared that Locke was the creator of scientific philosophy, occupying a position which corresponded to that of Newton in physics. And in the *Elements of Philosophy* he asserted that the eighteenth century was the century of philosophy in a special sense. Natural philosophy had been revolutionized, and nearly all other fields of knowledge had made progress and assumed new forms. 'From the principles of the secular sciences to the foundations of religious revelation, from metaphysics to matters of taste, from music to morals, from the scholastic disputes of theologians to matters of trade, from the laws of princes to those of peoples, from natural law to the arbitrary laws of nations . . . everything has been discussed and analysed, or at least mentioned. The fruit or consequence of this general effervescence of minds has been to cast new light on some things and new shadows on others, just as the effect of the ebb and flow of the tides is to leave some things on the shore and to wash others away.'[1]

This does not mean that for d'Alembert intellectual progress consists simply, or even primarily, in the mere accumulation of new facts. In a manner reminiscent of Descartes he maintains that all the sciences put together are the unfolding of the human intelligence. And he stresses the function of unification. He assumes that the system of phenomena is homogeneous and uniform; and the aim of scientific knowledge is to show the unity and coherence of this system in the light of the principles which it exemplifies.

But this point has to be rightly understood. D'Alembert is not concerned with metaphysical principles. Nor is he concerned with ascertaining the essences of things in a metaphysical sense. Metaphysical theories and speculations lead us into antinomies and result in scepticism; they are not a source of knowledge. We cannot know the why and wherefore of things. We cannot even know that there is an external world. True, we inevitably act on the assumption that there is such a world; but this is a matter of instinct rather than of theoretical knowledge. And it is in no way required for the purpose of scientific philosophy that we should solve problems of this sort. It makes no difference to us, for example, whether we can penetrate to the essences of bodies, 'provided that, matter being supposed such as we conceive it, we can deduce from properties which we regard as primitive other

---

[1] *Eléments de Philosophie* in the 1759 edition of *Mélanges de littérature, d'histoir et de philosophie*, IV, pp. 3–6.

secondary properties which we perceive in matter, and that the general system of phenomena, always uniform and continuous, nowhere manifests to us a contradiction'.[1] To deduce phenomena from principles is not to deduce empirical data from metaphysical principles or from metaphysical essences; it is to deduce observed secondary properties from other observed properties which are regarded as more primitive. The business of scientific philosophy is to describe and correlate phenomena in a systematic way rather than to explain them in a metaphysical sense. Once we attempt to do the latter, we proceed beyond the bounds of what can properly be called knowledge.

We can say, therefore, that d'Alembert was a forerunner of positivism. Science has no need of occult qualities or substances or of metaphysical theories and explanations. And philosophy, like science, is concerned simply with phenomena, even if it considers a wider field of phenomena than is considered by the specialist in some particular limited branch of science. This does not mean, of course, that the natural philosopher is not concerned with explanation in any sense. On the basis of sense-experience he forms clear definitions, and he can deduce verifiable conclusions. But he cannot go beyond the range of phenomena or the empirically verifiable unless he wishes to enter a sphere where no sure knowledge is attainable. Metaphysics must either become a science of facts or remain the field of illusions. The study of the history of opinions shows us how men developed merely probable theories and how in some cases probability became, so to speak, truth, when it had been verified by patient investigation. So too the study of the history of the sciences suggests points of view for further investigation and theories which must be empirically tested.

In d'Alembert's moral theory we can see the same concern to separate ethics from theology and metaphysics which was commonly shared by the philosophers of the period. Morality is the consciousness of our duty towards our fellow-men. And the principles of morality all converge towards the same end, namely to showing us the intimate connection between our true interest and the performance of our social duty. The task of the moral philosopher is thus to make clear to man his place in society and his duty of employing his powers for the common welfare and happiness.

[1] *Eléments de Philosophie* in the 1759 edition of *Mélanges de littérature, d'histoire et de philosophie*, IV, p. 59.

We cannot legitimately call d'Alembert a materialist. For he abstained from pronouncements about the ultimate nature of things and mistrusted the dogmatic materialists and mechanists. Apart from his importance as a mathematician, the salient feature of his thought is probably his insistence on positivist methodology. Like Diderot, he thought that progress could pretty well be taken for granted, in the sense that intellectual enlightenment would bring with it social and moral progress. But in his conception of intellectual and scientific development he was profoundly influenced by Newton and the experimental method. His thought moved within the field traced out by contemporary scientific advance rather than in the framework of controversy about the ultimately spiritual or material nature of reality.

2. There were, however, some outspoken materialists belonging to the period of the French Enlightenment; and in this section something will be said about La Mettrie, d'Holbach and Cabanis.

(i) Julien Offray de La Mettrie (1709–51) was a doctor who was stimulated by observation in himself of the effects of fever on the mind and thought to inquire into the relations between physiological factors and psychical operations. His *Histoire naturelle de l'âme* appeared in 1745, and in the following year he was banished from France. In 1748 he published at Leyden *L'homme machine*, and in the same year he was banished from Holland and sought refuge with Frederick the Great. *L'homme plante* appeared at Potsdam in 1748.

In his *Natural History of the Soul* (later called *Treatise on the Soul*) La Mettrie argues that man's psychical life of thought and volition arises out of sensations and is developed by education. Where there are no senses, there are no ideas; the fewer the senses the fewer the ideas; and where there is little education or instruction, there is a paucity of ideas. The soul or mind depends essentially on bodily organization, and its natural history must be studied by exact observation of physiological processes. The senses, says La Mettrie, are his philosophers. The theory of a spiritual soul, intrinsically independent of the body, is an unnecessary hypothesis.

In *Man a Machine* La Mettrie refers to Descartes' description of the living body as a machine. But in his opinion Descartes had no warrant for asserting dualism, that is, for speaking of man as composed of a thinking substance, immaterial and free, and of an extended substance, the body. He should have applied his interpretation of the physical organism to the whole man. At the same time La Mettrie differs considerably from Descartes in his idea of matter. For this is not mere extension: it also possesses the power of movement and the capacity of sensation. At least, organized matter possesses a principle of motion which differentiates it from unorganized matter; and sensation arises from motion. We may not be able to explain or thoroughly understand this emergence; but we cannot thoroughly understand matter itself and its basic properties. It is sufficient that observation assures us that motion, the principle of organized matter, does emerge. And, given the principle of motion, not only sensation but all other forms of psychical life can arise. In fine, all forms of life depend ultimately on different forms of physical organization. Of course, the analogy of a machine is not adequate for describing man. We can also use the analogy of a plant. (Hence *L'homme plante*.) But this does not mean that there are radically different levels in Nature. We find differences of degree rather than of kind.

In matters of religion La Mettrie professed a complete agnosticism. But he was popularly regarded as an atheist. And, indeed, he tried to improve upon Bayle's assertion that a State composed of atheists is possible by adding that it is not only possible but also desirable. In other words, religion is not only quite independent of morality but also inimical to it. As for La Mettrie's ethical ideas, their nature is sufficiently indicated by the title of his work, *The Art of Enjoyment or the School of Pleasure*.[1] He did not possess the moral idealism of Diderot. Incidentally, this work was but one of a number of treatises published in the eighteenth century which represented the views of the circle of so-called 'libertines', though the views expressed ranged from the emphasis on sense pleasure, which was characteristic of La Mettrie, to more refined and intellectualized programmes for enjoyment.

(ii) La Mettrie's writings exercised a considerable influence; but the chief statement of a materialist position was the *Système de la nature ou des lois du monde physique et du monde morale* (1770) by the Baron Paul von Holbach (1723–89). Born in Germany, he resided at Paris and is generally known as d'Holbach. His house at Paris was a meeting-place for *les philosophes*, where they were entertained with lavish hospitality by the Baron and his wife who, incidentally, had no sympathy with her husband's philosophy. Hume, while at Paris, took part in these gatherings, though he did not care for d'Holbach's dogmatic atheism. He expressed his

---

[1] *L'art de jouir ou l'école de la volupté*, 1751.

attachment to the Baron, but among the members of the circle he preferred d'Alembert. Horace Walpole, however, who had no love for philosophers, remarks in his letters[1] that he had left off going to d'Holbach's dinners and that 'nonsense for nonsense, I like the Jesuits better than the philosophers'.

According to d'Holbach, Descartes was wrong in thinking that matter is inert of itself, so that motion has to be added from outside, as it were. Motion flows necessarily from the essence of matter, that is, from the nature of the atoms of which things are ultimately composed. Descartes was also wrong in thinking that matter is all of a piece, all of the same kind. Leibniz's principle of indiscernibles contains much more truth than the Cartesian notion of the homogeneity of matter. And there are different kinds of movement, each thing having its laws of motion which are inevitably obeyed.

Things as we know them empirically consist of different organizations of atoms, and their behaviours differ according to their several structures. Everywhere we find the phenomena of attraction and repulsion; but in the human sphere these take the form of love and hate. Further, each thing strives to preserve itself in being. And man too is impelled by self-love or self-interest. But this should not be taken as excluding a concern for the welfare of society. For man is a social being, and rational concern for one's own satisfaction and welfare goes hand in hand with concern for the general welfare. D'Holbach was a thorough-going materialist and determinist; but he did not intend to advocate a life of selfishness. As a man, he was known to have a humane and benevolent character. And among the anonymous works ascribed to him we find the *Système social ou principes naturels de la morale et de la politique* (London, 1773) and *La morale universelle* (Amsterdam, 1776).

The theory of a determined system of Nature, in which motion is not an extraneous element but an essential property of things, seemed to d'Holbach to rule out any need for postulating God or any supramundane being or beings. The order or system of the world is not the result of a divine plan, but of the nature of things and of their immanent laws. But d'Holbach was by no means content to profess agnosticism and to say that the religious hypothesis, as Hume called it, was unnecessary. In his opinion religion was the enemy of human happiness and progress. In a

[1] VI, 370.

well-known passage of the second book of the *System of Nature* he declares that ignorance and fear created the gods, that fancy, enthusiasm and deceit have adorned or disfigured the pictures formed of them, that weakness worships them, that credulity preserves them, and that tyranny supports belief in them for its own purposes. Belief in God, so far from making men happy, increases their anxiety and fear.

If, therefore, religion, a powerful instrument of political tyranny, could be overthrown, it would be easier to ensure the development of a rational social system in place of the system which is responsible for so much suffering and misery. In his writings d'Holbach was more outspoken in denunciation of the *ancien régime* than was usual among his colleagues. But he rejected revolution as a solution to political problems, and in his *Social System* he declared that revolution is worse than the disease which it is supposed to cure.

It is sometimes said that in his *System of Nature* d'Holbach combined and then carried to extremes the different tendencies of the writers of the French Enlightenment. And this is doubtless true to some extent. But his ideas were too extreme for many of his fellow-philosophers. Voltaire, for example, denounced the work for its atheism. And in Germany Frederick the Great drew attention to what he regarded as a flagrant contradiction. According to d'Holbach, human beings are as much subject to determinism as are other things. Yet he does not hesitate to denounce priests and governments in passionate terms and to demand a new social order, though this way of speaking makes no sense unless men are free and can reasonably be praised or blamed for their actions.

Finally, there is an often-quoted estimate of d'Holbach's work from a very different quarter. In *Wahrheit und Dichtung* (Book XI) Goethe speaks of his studies at Strasbourg and remarks that out of curiosity he and his friends had a look at the *System of Nature*. 'We could not conceive how such a book could be dangerous. It appeared to us so grey, so Cimmerian, so corpselike that we had difficulty in enduring its presence and shuddered before it as before a spectre.' To Goethe, d'Holbach's work seemed to deprive Nature and life of all that is precious.

(iii) Particularly crude expressions of materialism can be found in the writings of Pierre Jean Georges Cabanis (1757–1808), a physician and author of *Rapports du physique et du moral de l'homme.* He summed up his view of man in the words *Les nerfs—voilà tout l'homme* and declared that the brain secretes thought as the liver secretes bile. In this case, one would have thought, there are simply different sets of secretions, and it is somewhat difficult to decide which possesses the greater truth-value. It would, however, be misleading to suggest that the whole French Enlightenment should be evaluated in the light of the crude assertions made by materialists such as Cabanis. Indeed, we miss the significance of the materialist current of thought itself if we pay attention simply to these crudities. For its importance lies in its programmatic aspect rather than in the dogmatism against which d'Alembert and others protested. That is to say, its long-term importance lies in its aspect as a programme for studying the connections between physiological and psychological phenomena rather than in its dogmatic reduction of the latter to the former.

Cabanis protested that his concentration on the physiological bases of psychical life should not be taken to imply metaphysical materialism. As regards ultimate causes, he professed agnosticism. But in his view morality must be cut adrift from metaphysical and theological presuppositions and given a firm basis in the scientific study of man. One of his contributions to their study was his insistence on the unity of man's life. It is inappropriate, for example, to speak with Condillac of conferring this or that sense on a statue. The senses are not only interdependent but also intimately connected with other organic functions.

3. Diderot gave it as his opinion that under certain circumstances nothing is more wasteful than preoccupation with method. This is especially true, he said, of natural history in general and of botany in particular. He did not mean, of course, that any science can be profitably studied in a purely haphazard manner. What he meant was that we are simply wasting time if we are preoccupied with discovering some universal method which will be applicable to all the sciences. It is absurd, for example, to suppose that the method applicable in mathematics is applicable also in botany. The form of method and of systematization which is appropriate in the study of botany must be derived from the special character of the subject-matter of this science.

In forming this point of view Diderot was influenced to some extent by the earlier volumes of Buffon's *Histoire naturelle générale et particulière* (1749–88).

(i) In his introductory reflections in the work just mentioned Georges-Louis Leclerc de Buffon (1707–88) maintains that it is a great mistake to form one ideal of scientific method and then to attempt to force all branches of scientific research into the framework of this method. For example, in mathematics we fix clearly the meanings of our symbols, and we can proceed deductively, unfolding the implications of our starting-point; but we cannot do this when we are concerned, not, as in mathematics, with our concepts or with the meanings of symbols, as determined by ourselves, but with existent Nature. Truth is different in mathematics from what it is in the natural sciences. In the latter we must start with observation of phenomena, and only on the basis of observation can we form general conclusions with the aid of analogies. In the end we can see how particular facts are connected together and how universal truths are exemplified in these particular facts. But we cannot employ the deductive method of mathematics. Buffon was the keeper of the royal garden, and it is, indeed, clear that what he says applies with force in the field of botany.

Buffon's rejection of any rigid conception of one ideal and universally applicable scientific method was accompanied by a rejection of the notion that organisms fall into sharply defined classes or species which are separated from one another by rigid boundaries or limits. Even Linnaeus, in his botanical studies, went wrong in this respect. For he arbitrarily selected certain characteristics of plants as the key to classification, whereas we cannot understand Nature in this way. In Nature there is continuity; there are gradual transitions and not rigidly fixed types. In other words, Buffon substituted for the idea of a hierarchy of sharply delimited classes the idea of a series or chain of classes in each of which the members are grasped according to observed kinship. He did not reject the whole notion of classes or species. But the species is a group of members which are more alike to one another, in virtue of observed characteristics, than they are to other things. It is a mistake to suppose that our classifications express the apprehension of fixed essences. We can say, if we like, that Buffon understood classification in terms of what Locke called the 'nominal essence'. But his great point is that we must follow Nature as observed and keep our class-concepts elastic instead of constructing a fixed conceptual scheme and forcing Nature to fit it. If we were concerned merely with our ideas or definitions and their implications, the latter procedure would be apposite. But in botany, for example, we are concerned with knowing reality, not with an ideal system akin to that of mathematics.

It is probably true to say that Buffon's views helped in some way to prepare the way for the theory of evolution. All the same one is not entitled to conclude from his idea of the series or chain of species that he himself maintained this theory. He thought, indeed, of the several types of organisms being brought into existence in a continuous series as external conditions rendered survival possible. But he did not say that one species undergoes a process of transformation into another. He thought rather of a kind of ideal archetype of the living thing, representing the unity of the divine plan, which can take an indefinite number of possible concrete forms. And even though these concrete types are not fixed and rigid, the creation of each is a special act.

(ii) The idea of a series is represented also in the writings of Jean-Baptiste Robinet (1735–1820). For him Nature is faced with the problem of realizing in the most perfect manner possible the three vital functions of nutrition, growth and reproduction, functions which are found in some sense in all matter. Nature's solution to this problem is found in man, who is, therefore, the culmination of the series as far as the material world is concerned. But we can envisage a gradual liberation of activity, which is an essential note of a substance, from matter and from dependence on material organs. And this conception leads us to the idea of pure intelligence.

(iii) There are, however, considerable difficulties in the theory of a purely linear series. And we find Charles Bonnet (1720–93) suggesting that Nature may produce different main lines in the series, which themselves produce subordinate lines. With the German naturalist and traveller, Peter Simon Pallas (1741–1811), we find the analogy of a tree with different branches. For the matter of that, we find with Buffon himself the analogy of a network.

4. The Jesuit, Roger Joseph Boscovich (1711–87), obviously cannot be accounted one of the philosophers of the Enlightenment, if one means by the Enlightenment a movement of thought opposed to all supernatural religion. But the term should not be used simply in this restricted sense. True, we are dealing now with the French Enlightenment, and Boscovich, who was born at Ragusa, was not a Frenchman. But for ten years (1773–83) he acted as director of optics for the marine at Paris; and in any case

this is the most convenient place to make a few remarks about him.

In 1740 Boscovich was appointed professor of mathematics at the Roman College (now the Gregorian University), and while occupying this post he published essays on a variety of mathematical and astronomical topics. In 1758 he published at Vienna his *Philosophiae naturalis theoria, redacta ad unicam legem virium in natura existentium*. During a stay in England he was elected a Fellow of the Royal Society, and in 1769 he was invited by the Royal Society to undertake a journey to California to observe the transit of Venus, though acceptance was prevented by the fact that the Spanish Government had expelled the Jesuits from its territories. In 1785, after he had returned to Italy from Paris, he published *Opera pertinentia ad opticam et astronomiam* in five volumes. Among other works we may mention his *Elementa universae matheseos* (1754).

In Boscovich's opinion there is no such thing as actual contact between two bodies. The effect of Newton's theory of gravitation has been to show that action is action at a distance. We cannot, therefore, any longer suppose that motion or energy is communicated by immediate contact. Instead we must postulate atoms which attract and repel one another, but which never actually touch each other. Each atom has a position in space, and each possesses potential force, in the sense that any two atoms attract or repel one another. For all distances greater than a certain given distance this force is an attraction which varies as the inverse square of the distance. In the case of smaller distances the force is attraction in the case of one distance and repulsion in the case of the other. But here the laws governing attraction and repulsion have not yet been discovered, though, according to Boscovich, if we decrease the distance without limit, the force of repulsion increases without limit. Hence two atoms can never be in immediate contact. There are, of course, systems of atoms; but no system can occupy the same space as another. For when one system approaches another, there is a point at which the repulsion between the atoms of the two systems grows to such an extent that it cannot be overcome. Needless to say, Boscovich did not maintain that atoms are the only reality. He was speaking simply of bodies, and he went on to show how his theory of dynamic atomism could be applied in problems of mechanics and physics.

5. The Encyclopaedists were animated by the idea of progress as shown in the growth of the sciences and in a corresponding liberation from superstition. Intellectual enlightenment would be accompanied by a growth of toleration and by political and social reform. The idea of progress also finds a place in the theories of the group of eighteenth-century French economists who are known as the 'physiocrats'. This name was invented by Dupont de Nemours (1739–1817), who belonged to the group. The physiocrats originally called themselves economists, but their special name (compounded from the Greek words *phusis*, nature, and *kratein*, to rule) is an apt one because it draws attention to their fundamental tenet. This was that there are natural economic laws, and that economic progress depends on our allowing these laws to have unrestricted play.

It follows from this position that the government should interfere as little as possible in economic affairs. Society is founded on a contract whereby the individual submits to the limitation of his natural freedom in so far as its exercise is incompatible with the rights of other people. And government should limit itself to securing the fulfilment of the contract. If it tries to interfere in the field of economics, by restricting competition, for example, or by maintaining privileges and monopolies, it is trying to interfere with the operation of 'natural law'. And no good can come from such interference: Nature knows best.

This does not mean that the physiocrats were enthusiastic democrats, in the sense that they were zealous promoters of the idea of popular rule. On the contrary, they tended to look to enlightened autocracy as a means of implementing their policy. The doctrines of non-interference and *laissez-faire* lent themselves, indeed, to use in a revolutionary sense as part of a general demand for freedom; and they came in fact to be so used. But neither Quesnay nor Turgot, for instance, can be called an advocate of revolution or of the substitution of popular for monarchic rule.

(i) François Quesnay (1694–1774) studied medicine and surgery and became physician to Louis XV. But he devoted himself while at court to the study of economics, and it was round him and Jean de Gournay (1712–59) that the group of physiocrats centred. Quesnay wrote some articles on economic matters for the *Encyclopaedia*. He also published, among other writings, *Maximes générales de gouvernement économique d'un royaume agricole* (1758)

and, in the same year, a *Tableau économique avec son explication,
ou extrait des économies royales de Sully.*

According to Quesnay, national wealth is dependent on
agricultural productiveness. Those labours alone are truly productive which increase the quantity of raw materials. And
national wealth depends on the excess of these products over the
cost of producing them. Manufacture and commerce merely give
new forms to the wealth produced (raw materials include, for
instance, metals) and transfer wealth from one hand to another.
They are therefore 'sterile', not 'productive', though to say this is
not to say that they are not useful.

The interest of the landowner and of society are, therefore, one.
The greater the agricultural production, the greater the national
wealth. Or, as Quesnay put it, poor peasants, a poor kingdom; a
poor kingdom, a poor king. The increase of the 'net product',
therefore, should be the aim of the practical economist. Trade
distributes wealth; but the trading and manufacturing classes
make their gains at the expense of the nation, and the common
good requires that this expense should be reduced as much as
possible. The revenues of the State depend on the net product of
agricultural labour; and they should be derived from a land tax.

This peculiar emphasis on agricultural production at the
expense of industry and commerce was not shared by all the
physiocrats, but it was characteristic of some prominent members
of the group. Adam Smith, who made the acquaintance of
Quesnay during his visit to Paris in 1764–6, had a high opinion
of him; but though he was influenced to some extent by the
physiocrats, he did not agree with the description of industry and
commerce as 'sterile'.

(ii) Anne Robert Jacques Turgot, Baron de Laune (1727–81),
first studied for the priesthood but abandoned these studies before
ordination and subsequently occupied various parliamentary and
administrative posts. A friend of Voltaire, he also became
acquainted with Quesnay, Gournay, Dupont de Nemours and
other economists of the physiocratic school. Besides concerning
himself with practical economic reforms he wrote a number of
essays and articles, some for the *Encyclopaedia*. In 1770 he wrote
his *Lettres sur la liberté du commerce des grains*, and in 1776 he
published as a separate book his *Réflexions sur la formation et la
distribution des richesses*, which had first appeared in a journal in
1769–70. In 1774 he was appointed Minister of Marine and shortly

afterwards Comptroller-General. In the latter position, which was effectively that of minister of finance, he insisted on economy and succeeded in raising the national credit. At first he enjoyed the support of the king, but his plans for the abolition of privilege, the subjection of all classes to taxation and freedom of trade in corn won for him many enemies, while his schemes for an educational system and for poor-relief proved too much for the king. In the end he was forced to resign in 1776. For the rest of his life he gave himself to his studies.

As an economist Turgot shared Quesnay's ideas about land as the only source of wealth and about complete freedom in industry and commerce. But he was much more than an economist. For example, in his article on existence in the *Encyclopaedia* he developed a positivist interpretation. The given is a multiplicity of phenomena, the mutual relations of which are constantly changing. Yet in certain groups there are relatively persistent relations of co-ordination. One of these groups is what we call the self or ego, a particular group of perceptions related to perceptions or feelings of pleasure and pain. To affirm the existence of the external world is to affirm that other groups of phenomena, either immediately given or postulated, stand to the self in spatial or causal relations. Existence thus means for us existence as a subject or for a subject in the system of spatial and causal relations. The question what existence is in itself or what existent things are apart from the system of spatio-temporal and causal relations, is not a question which we are competent to answer. In other words we cannot solve metaphysical problems. Science is concerned with the description of phenomena, not with 'ultimate questions'.

Turgot is of importance in the development of a positivist interpretation of history. In human as distinct from animal history there is progress, in the sense that the intellectual achievements of one generation are taken over by, widened and surpassed by, the next. In each cultural period we can, indeed, find a certain recurring pattern. But by and large the intellectual advance of the human race passes through three main phases, the religious, the philosophical or metaphysical, and the scientific. In this third phase the mathematical and natural sciences triumph over speculative metaphysics and lay the foundation for further scientific advance and for new forms of social and economic life. Thus Turgot anticipated the interpretation of history which was to be expounded in the next century by Auguste Comte. And though from the point of view of economics he must be classed with Quesnay and the other physiocrats, from the wider philosophical point of view he can be classed with the editors of the *Encyclopaedia*, d'Alembert and Diderot.

6. The French Enlightenment is often associated, doubtless understandably, with the crude materialism and the anti-religious polemics of men such as Helvétius, La Mettrie and d'Holbach. And this is, of course, a real aspect of eighteenth-century French philosophy. But the spirit of the movement is probably better represented by men such as d'Alembert, Diderot and Turgot who tended to abstain from making dogmatic pronouncements about ultimate reality and who looked to scientific progress and the growth of toleration to bring about new and more rational forms of social and political life. Eighteenth-century French philosophy doubtless helped to prepare the way for the Revolution; but the philosophers themselves aimed, not at bloody revolution, but rather at the spread of knowledge and through the diffusion of knowledge at social reform. I do not mean to imply that the philosophical outlook of *les philosophes* was adequate or that I agree with their anti-metaphysical point of view. At the same time it is a mistake to regard them simply in the light of the dogmatic materialism of certain writers. As has been already indicated, to do this is to overlook the programmatic aspect of their work, the programme of extending the sphere of empirically verified knowledge as far as it will go. Crudities apart, they look forward, for instance, to the growth of empirical psychology and biology, to the development of sociological studies, and to the rise of political economy. In the next century the idealists felt the need for reconciling and synthesizing the religious, metaphysical and scientific outlooks. But this ideal presupposed, of course, the presence of the scientific and positivist outlook, and in helping to produce it the eighteenth-century philosophers were of considerable importance. As the idealists of the nineteenth century saw, the scientific outlook did not call for negation but rather for modification by incorporation in a wider synthesis. Whether they succeeded in providing this synthesis, is, of course, another question.

CHAPTER III

ROUSSEAU (1)

*Life and writings—The evils of civilization—The origin of in-
equality—The appearance of the theory of the general will—
Rousseau's philosophy of feeling.*

1. JEAN JACQUES ROUSSEAU was born at Geneva on June 28th,
1712, the son of a watchmaker. In 1725 he was apprenticed for
five years to an engraver; but after a while he ran away. The priest
of Confignon, a village near Geneva, introduced the boy to the
Baronne de Warens, who was to figure prominently in his life.
Under her influence Rousseau was converted to Catholicism, and
in 1728 he was received into the Church at Turin in a hospice for
catechumens, an institution of which he has given us a most
unfavourable picture in his *Confessions*. After a period of wandering and unsettled existence he rejoined Mme de Warens in 1731.
His life with her, first at Chambéry and afterwards at Les Char-
mettes, was later idealized by him as an idyllic episode. It was in
this period that he endeavoured by reading to make up for the
deficiencies of his earlier unsystematic education.

From 1738 to 1740 Rousseau acted as tutor to the children of a
M. de Mably, and while occupying this post he made the acquaintance of Condillac. In 1742 he went to Paris, only to proceed to
Venice in 1743 as secretary to the new French ambassador, the
Comte de Montaigu. The two men did not get on well together,
and in the following year Rousseau, dismissed for insolence,
returned to Paris. In 1745 he met Voltaire for the first time, and
in 1749 Diderot invited him to write the articles on music for the
Encyclopaedia. He was also introduced to d'Holbach's *salon*. In
the same year the Academy of Dijon offered a prize for the best
essay on the question whether the progress of the arts and
sciences had tended to the purification or to the corruption of
morality. Rousseau's *Discourse on the Arts and Sciences* was the
prize-winning essay, and it was published in 1750. Its author
became at once a famous man. But as he had indulged in an attack
on civilization and its corrupting effects on man, his views not
unnaturally met with strong opposition from *les philosophes*, and
a battle of words ensued. Rousseau was already well on his way to

a decisive break with the d'Holbach circle. However, undaunted by opposition, he decided to compete for another prize offered by the Dijon Academy, this time on the question, what is the origin of inequality among men and whether it is authorized by the natural law. His *Discourse on the Origin and Foundation of Inequality among Men* did not obtain the prize, but it was published in 1758. In it we are presented with a picture of natural man or man in the state of nature, that is to say, of man when the trappings and accretions of civilization have been stripped away. Man is naturally good, but civilization has brought with it inequality and a host of consequent evils. In the same year, 1755, Rousseau's article on political economy was printed in the *Encyclopaedia*. In 1758 it appeared separately as a *Discourse on Political Economy*. The idea of the general will makes its first appearance in this essay.

Rousseau had been for some time disgusted with life at Paris, a disgust which was reflected in his first two *Discourses*. And his mind turned towards his native city. Hence in 1754 he turned his back on the French capital and set out for Geneva. He was there received back into the Protestant Church. This change did not, indeed, signify any religious upheaval. For, as Rousseau observed, if his philosophical friends at Paris had done nothing else for him, they had at least undermined any belief he may have had in Catholic dogma. His main reason for formally returning to Protestantism was, as he admits, his wish to regain Genevan citizenship. But the philosopher did not remain long at Geneva. Returning to Paris in October 1754 he sent a copy of his *Discourse on Inequality*, when it appeared in the following year, to Voltaire who wrote to thank him for 'your new book against the human race'.

From 1756 until 1762 Rousseau lived in retirement at Montmorency. This was a period of great literary activity. In 1758 he wrote his *Lettre à d'Alembert sur les spectacles* relating to the article on Geneva in the *Encyclopaedia* in which d'Alembert had criticized the Genevan prohibition of theatrical performances. The year 1761 saw the publication of *La Nouvelle Héloïse*, Rousseau's novel. And in 1762 there appeared not only his most famous work, the *Social Contract* (*Du contrat social*) but also *Émile*, his book on education. By this time Rousseau had already quarrelled with Diderot. His decisive break with *les philosophes* found expression in his *Lettres morales*, though these were not published until 1861.

As a result of the publication of the *Social Contract* and *Emile* in 1762 Rousseau had to take refuge in Switzerland. But the reaction to his works at Geneva was also hostile, and in 1763 he formally renounced his Genevan citizenship. In 1765 he set out for Berlin, but on the way he decided to go to England; and in January 1766 he crossed the Channel with David Hume who had offered him sanctuary in England. It cannot be said that this visit was altogether successful. By this time Rousseau, always sensitive and suspicious, was suffering from persecution mania, and he became convinced that Hume was in league with his enemies. Hume, not understanding Rousseau's abnormal state of mind, was very angry, especially as he was engaged in procuring a royal pension for his friend; and, disregarding any advice to the contrary, he published in London and Paris his account of the affair. In May 1766 Rousseau returned to France, where he was received as a guest by the Prince de Conti. In 1770, after various wanderings, he returned to Paris, neglecting the fact that he was liable to arrest. But as a matter of fact he was left undisturbed by the police, though he was subjected to a campaign of literary vilification, especially by Grimm and Diderot. In May 1778 he left for Erménonville, as guest of the Marquis de Girardin, and it was there that he died on July 2nd. His *Confessions* and the *Rêveries du Promeneur Solitaire* were published posthumously (1782-9). The *Considerations on the Government of Poland* appeared in 1782.

The character and life of Rousseau provide ample material for the psychologist. True, some of the troubles were due to physical ill-health. He suffered for years from a bladder complaint, and he most probably died of uraemia. But from the beginning social adjustment was difficult for him; and though he was capable of deep affection and attachment, he was too sensitive, suspicious and intolerant to maintain constant friendships. A man much given to self-analysis, he often failed to understand either himself or others. A philosopher, he yet possessed a highly emotional temperament, and he drew attention to the tension between emotion and thought, heart and mind, which oppressed him. Romantic, emotional, possessing a genuine religious feeling yet self-centred and mentally unbalanced, it is in no way surprising that Rousseau broke with *les philosophes*. D'Holbach warned Hume that he was contemplating warming a viper in his bosom. And Hume later referred to Rousseau as 'the most singular of all human beings', though he afterwards acutely remarked that the

latter had only felt during the whole course of his life and that in
him sensibility had risen to an unexampled pitch. But all this, of
course, in no way affects Rousseau's importance in the history of
philosophy.[1]

2. 'It is a noble and beautiful spectacle to see man raising himself, so to speak, from nothing by his own exertions.'[2] These words
form the beginning of the first part of Rousseau's *Discourse on the
Arts and Sciences*. And we would naturally expect to find them
followed by a laudatory account of the blessings of civilization.
If they had been written by d'Alembert, for example, our expecta-
tions would doubtless have been fulfilled. But not so in the case of
Rousseau. We are soon told that 'the mind, as well as the body,
has its needs: those of the body are the basis of society, those of
the mind its ornaments'.[3] These words can, indeed, be taken in a
quite innocuous sense, even if they seem to imply that the fulfilment of all non-physical needs is no more than an unessential
ornament of society. But we straightway learn that the arts,
literature and the sciences fling garlands of flowers over the chains
which weigh men down and stifle in men's breasts the sense of
liberty for which they seem to have been born. These 'ornaments'
make men love their slavery. 'Necessity raised up thrones; the
arts and sciences have made them strong.'[4]

The way is thus prepared for a rhetorical attack on so-called
civilized society. Rousseau draws special attention to the artificiality of social life. In more rudimentary forms of society human
nature may not have been fundamentally better than it is now;
but men were sincere and open, letting themselves be seen as they
were. Now 'we no longer dare to seem what we really are, but lie
under a perpetual restraint'.[5] The herd of men all act exactly alike,
unless some very powerful motive intervenes; and sincere friendship and real confidence are banished. The veil of conventional
politeness covers all sorts of unworthy attitudes. Again, we may
not take the name of God in vain by vulgar oaths; but real
blasphemy does not disturb us. We do not indulge in extravagant
boasting; instead we subtly decry the merits of others and artfully
calumniate them. 'Our hatred of other nations diminishes, but

---

[1] In this and the next chapters the following abbreviations will be used: *D.A.*
for the *Discourse on the Arts and Sciences*; *D.I.* for the *Discourse on the Origin of
Inequality*; *D.P.* for the *Discourse on Political Economy*, *É.* for *Émile*; and *S.C.* for
the *Social Contract*. For the convenience of the reader page-references will be given
to the *Everyman's Library* editions of the *Social Contract* and *Discourses* and of
Émile, as these editions are easily available.
[2] *D.A.*, p. 130.   [3] *Ibid.*   [4] *Ibid.*, p. 131.   [5] *Ibid.*, p. 132.

patriotism dies with it. Ignorance is held in contempt; but a dangerous scepticism has succeeded it.'[1] Rousseau disliked and disapproved of the cosmopolitan spirit of the Enlightenment.

In his picture of civilized society Rousseau was obviously universalizing his experience at Paris, where he had hitherto appeared in fashionable society not on his own merits but in a humiliating position of dependence. However, some of what he says is doubtless true enough and provides material for the preacher. It is true, for instance, that in sophisticated society extravagant boasting is considered ludicrous but that the same end is sought for by the device of subtle depreciation of others. Rousseau, however, goes on to ascribe this state of affairs to the growth of the arts and sciences. 'Our minds have been corrupted in proportion as the arts and sciences have improved.'[2] And scientific advance is ascribed to 'vain curiosity'.[3] But it is one thing to draw attention to certain shadows in eighteenth-century society, and it is quite another thing to assign the advance of the arts and sciences as the cause of these defects.

To be sure, Rousseau endeavours to support his thesis by reference to history. Egypt, we are told, became the mother of philosophy (a very questionable proposition) and the fine arts, but soon she was conquered by Cambyses and subsequently by the Greeks, the Romans, the Arabs, and finally the Turks. In Greece, Rousseau tells us, the progress of the sciences soon produced dissolute manners and led to the imposition of the Macedonian yoke. 'Not all the eloquence of Demosthenes could breathe life into a body which luxury and the arts had once enervated.'[4] We can consider by contrast the virtues of the early Persians and of the Scythians, not to speak of the 'simplicity, innocence and virtue'[5] of the Germanic tribes who conquered the Romans. And we must not forget Sparta, 'eternal proof of the vanity of science'.[6]

In the second part of the *Discourse* we are roundly informed that 'astronomy was born of superstition, eloquence of ambition, hatred, falsehood and flattery; geometry of avarice; physics of an idle curiosity; and even moral philosophy of human pride. Thus the arts and sciences owe their birth to our vices.'[7] They arise out of evil, and they lead to evil consequences. They produce luxury and generate weakness. The military virtues of the Romans were extinguished in proportion as the latter cultivated the fine arts.

---

[1] *D.A.*, p. 133.   [2] *Ibid.*   [3] *Ibid.*, p. 134.   [4] *Ibid.*
[5] *Ibid.*, p. 135.   [6] *Ibid.*, p. 136.   [7] *Ibid.*, p. 140.

And 'if the cultivation of the sciences is prejudicial to military qualities, it is still more so to moral qualities'.[1] An expensive education is provided which teaches everything but moral probity and integrity. Literary, artistic and scientific proficiency are honoured, but moral virtue goes unrewarded. Towards the end of his *Discourse* Rousseau does, indeed, recall to mind the fact that he is addressing the Academy of Dijon and that he is competing for a literary prize. And he finds it advisable to say something in favour of men such as Francis Bacon, Descartes and Newton, 'those teachers of mankind'.[2] But he contrasts these geniuses, who were intended by Nature herself to be her disciples, with 'the herd of text-book authors',[3] who have indiscreetly broken open the doors of the sanctuary of the sciences and admitted an unworthy populace to information and ideas which it would be all the better for lacking. There can be little doubt whom Rousseau has in mind.

Rousseau's critics had no difficulty in showing the deficiencies in his historical knowledge and the weakness of his arguments in favour of the thesis that moral degeneration was caused by the growth of the arts and sciences. If he were alive today, he would doubtless point out how military needs have stimulated the development of scientific research in certain departments. And he would doubtless maintain that such advance has arisen from human vice and leads to evil consequences. But there is obviously another side to the pictures. Even if advance in atomic physics, for instance, has been stimulated in some sense by war, the fruits of research can be used for other than destructive purposes. Again, it is easy to criticize Rousseau's idealization of Sparta at the expense of Athens and his panegyric of the virtues of the Germanic tribes. However, Rousseau himself explicitly admitted the lack of logic and order in the work and its weakness in argument. In spite, however, of its obvious shortcomings the first *Discourse* possesses some importance as a counterblast to the Encyclopaedists' assumption that the advancement of the arts and sciences represents human progress in a general sense. True, it should not be taken as a complete and wholesale rejection of civilized society. It was the expression of feeling, of an attitude adopted in the light of an idea which came to Rousseau with the force of a sudden illumination. But later on, above all in the *Social Contract*, he undertakes to justify the transition from man's primitive state to

---

[1] *D.A.*, p. 147.   [2] *Ibid.*, p. 152.   [3] *Ibid.* p., 152.

that of organized society, and to inquire what form of social institution is most compatible with man's natural goodness and is least likely to corrupt and deprave him. Moreover, it appears that in 1750 or 1751 Rousseau began to plan a work on *Political Institutions* which he later abandoned after having extracted from his notes the substance of the *Social Contract*. And in this case he can hardly have held seriously, even at the time when he composed the first *Discourse*, that civilized society is so essentially evil that it must be totally rejected. At the same time it would be quite wrong to conclude that Rousseau was not sincere in what he said about the arts and sciences. The general idea that man has been corrupted by the growth of an artificial civilization and by rationalism remained with him, even if, to obtain an adequate picture of his philosophy, we have to balance it by his positive doctrine concerning the State and its function. In his later writings there is, indeed, a certain change of attitude, but it does not amount to a wholesale recantation of his earlier works.

3. If we assume that man has been corrupted by an artificial civilization, what is the natural state, the state of nature, from which he has been removed? That is to say, what positive meaning is to be attached to the term 'state of nature'? This question is discussed by Rousseau in his *Discourse on the Origin and Foundation of the Inequality of Mankind*.

We cannot, of course, observe the state of nature; for we are acquainted only with man in society. The really primitive condition of man eludes empirical investigation. Our interpretation, therefore, must take the form of a hypothetical account. 'Let us begin, then, by laying facts aside, as they do not affect the question. The investigations into which we may enter, in treating this subject, must not be considered as historical truths, but only as mere conditional and hypothetical reasonings, calculated to explain the nature of things rather than to ascertain their actual origin, just like the hypotheses which our physicists daily form about the formation of the world.'[1] In practice this means that we have to take man as we know him and then abstract from all supernatural gifts and from those faculties which he can acquire only in the course of a long process of social development. Indeed, we have to abstract from society itself.

When we act in this way, we find man 'satisfying his hunger at the first oak and slaking his thirst at the first brook; finding his

[1] *D.I.*, Introduction, pp. 175–6.

bed at the foot of the tree which afforded him a repast; and, with that, all his wants supplied'.[1] Such a man would be physically robust, unafraid of the animals which he surpasses in skill, if not in strength, subject to few causes of sickness and so standing in little need of medicines, and still less of doctors. His chief concern would be self-preservation. His senses of sight, hearing and smell would be refined, but not the senses of touch and taste, which are perfected by softness and sensuality.

How does savage man differ from the animal? 'It is not so much the understanding that constitutes the specific difference between the man and the brute, as the human quality of freedom . . . and it is particularly in his consciousness of this liberty that the spirituality of his soul is displayed. For physics may explain in some degree the mechanism of the senses and the formation of ideas; but in the power of willing or rather of choosing, and in the feeling of this power, nothing is to be found but acts which are purely spiritual and wholly inexplicable by the laws of mechanism.'[2] Rousseau thus rejects outright the adequacy of a purely materialistic and mechanistic interpretation of man.

A further quality which distinguishes man from the brute is the former's faculty of self-improvement, his perfectibility. But man was first governed by immediate wants and by instinct and feeling. 'To will and not to will, to desire and to fear, must be the first and almost the only operations of his soul until new circumstances occasion new development of his faculties.'[3] The desires of the savage never go beyond his physical wants. 'The only goods he recognizes in the universe are food, a female and sleep; the only evils he fears are pain and hunger.'[4]

Rousseau is imagining man 'wandering up and down the forests, without industry, without speech and without home, an equal stranger to war and to all ties, neither standing in need of his fellow-creatures nor having any desire to hurt them'.[5] Man is pictured, therefore, as devoid of social life and as not yet having reached the level of reflection. Can we say of such a man that he possesses moral qualities? In a strict sense, no; but it does not follow that man in a state of nature can be called vicious. We are not entitled to conclude that because man in his most primitive state had no idea of goodness, he was therefore bad. Again, where there are no 'mine' and 'thine', there are no clear concepts of

[1] *D.I.*, p. 177.   [2] *Ibid.*, p. 184.   [3] *Ibid.*, p. 185.
[4] *Ibid.*, p. 186.   [5] *Ibid.*, p. 203.

justice and injustice; but it does not follow that in the absence of these concepts men must behave in a violent and ruthless manner. Hobbes's picture of the state of nature as a state of war of all against all was unjustified. He was right in saying that self-love was the fundamental impulse; but self-love, in the sense of the impulse to self-preservation, does not of itself involve badness and violence. In the beginning the individual took little note of his fellows; and when he did so, the natural or innate feeling of compassion came into operation. It precedes all reflection, and even the brutes sometimes show it. To this theme of natural compassion and to its relation to self-love I shall return in the concluding section of this chapter. Meanwhile it is sufficient to note that for Rousseau man in the primitive state of nature is good. Even if he cannot be called good in a strictly moral sense, morality is simply a development of his natural feelings and impulses. Thus in his letter to Christophe de Beaumont, archbishop of Paris, which was printed in 1763, he could say roundly that the fundamental ethical principle is that man is naturally good and that there is no original perversity or sin in human nature.

It will have been noted that Rousseau pictures primitive man as without speech. And in the first part of the *Discourse on Inequality* he makes some reflections about the origins of language and about its importance in man's intellectual development. Language originated in 'the simple cry of nature';[1] but in the course of time conventional signs were established by common consent, a particular name being given to a particular thing. But Rousseau does not profess to be able to explain how the transition took place from this stage of linguistic development to the use of general terms expressing general ideas. 'General ideas cannot be introduced into the mind without the assistance of words, nor can the understanding seize them except by means of propositions.'[2] But the words seem to postulate ideas or thoughts. We are left, therefore, with a problem. There is also the problem of the relation of language to society. 'I leave to anyone who will undertake it the discussion of the difficult problem, which was most necessary, the existence of society for the invention of language, or the invention of language for the establishment of society.'[3] However, whatever the answers to such problems may be, the development of man's intellectual life would be unthinkable apart from the development of language.

[1] *D.I.*, p. 191.   [2] *Ibid.*, p. 192   [3] *Ibid.*, p. 194.

In the second part of the *Discourse on Inequality* Rousseau discusses the transition from the state of nature to organized society. He imagines how men gradually came to experience the advantage of common undertakings and how they thus came, on separate occasions at least, to develop a sense of social bonds. But the point on which Rousseau lays special emphasis is the establishment of private property. 'The first man who, having enclosed a piece of ground, bethought himself of saying *This is mine*, and found people simple enough to believe him, was the real founder of civil society.'[1] Property was introduced, equality disappeared, forests became smiling fields, slavery and misery arose with the crops. 'Metallurgy and agriculture were the two arts which produced this great revolution.'[2] Moral distinctions between justice and injustice also appeared. But this is not to say that men were better than they had been in the state of nature. 'Usurpations by the rich, robbery by the poor, and the unbridled passions of both, suppressed the cries of natural compassion and the still feeble voice of justice and filled men with avarice, ambition and vice. . . . The new-born state of society thus gave rise to a horrible state of war.'[3] In other words, private property was the result of man's departure from his state of primitive simplicity, and it brought untold evils in its train.

We have seen that Rousseau's primitive state of nature did not correspond to Hobbes's state of nature; it was not a condition of affairs of which it would be true to say, *Homo homini lupus*. But the form of society which has just been described was likened by Rousseau to a state of war, and in this respect it is similar to Hobbes's state of nature, though in some other important respects it is dissimilar. For example, moral distinctions arise for Rousseau in the state of civil society which, considered in abstraction, precedes the formation of political society,[4] whereas for Hobbes moral distinctions really follow the covenant whereby political society and government are established.

Given the insecurity and other evils which attend the establishment and development of the institution of private property, the establishment of political society, government and law was a foregone conclusion. 'All ran headlong to their chains in hope of securing their liberty; or they had just wit enough to perceive the advantage of political institutions, without sufficient experience

[1] *D.I.*, p. 207.   [2] *Ibid.*, p. 215.   [3] *Ibid.*, p. 219.
[4] Hegel in the next century made a distinction between civil society and the State.

to enable them to foresee the dangers.'[1] Government and law were thus established by common consent. But Rousseau is not the man to wax enthusiastic over this development. On the contrary, the institution of political society 'bound new fetters on the poor and gave new powers to the rich; irretrievably destroyed natural liberty, fixed eternally the law of property and inequality, converted clever usurpation into unalterable right, and, for the advantage of a few ambitious individuals, subjected all mankind to perpetual labour, slavery and wretchedness'.[2]

Rousseau declares, therefore, that he is content to adopt the common opinion and to regard the establishment of political society as 'a real contract between the people and the chiefs chosen by them; a contract by which both parties bind themselves to observe the laws therein expressed, which form the bonds of their union'.[3] But we can go on to ask, what was the course of development of political society? Did it begin with arbitrary power and despotism, or was despotism a later development? Rousseau's answer to this question is unequivocal. 'I regard it then as certain that government did not begin with arbitrary power, but that this is the depravation, the extreme term, of government and brings it back finally to just that law of the strongest which it was originally designed to remedy.'[4]

In the state of nature there was only natural or physical inequality, which consists in inequality of natural gifts and talents, whether physical or mental. And it is useless to ask, what is its source? For the very name shows that it is established by Nature. The subject of the *Discourse*, therefore, is what Rousseau calls 'moral or political inequality'.[5] This is due originally to the development of our faculties, and it is 'rendered permanent and legitimate by the establishment of property and laws'.[6] We can say, in addition, that whenever it is not proportionate to natural or physical inequality, it is at variance with natural right. It is wrong, for instance, that 'the privileged few should gorge themselves with superfluities while the starving multitude is in want of the bare necessities of life'.[7] And when we arrive at despotism, we have come, as it were, full circle. The subjects, being all reduced to slaves, return to their first equality. And as their master is unrestrained, all moral distinctions and principles of equity vanish. Men have then returned to a state of nature. Yet it differs

---

[1] *D.I.*, p. 221. [2] *Ibid.* [3] *Ibid.*, p. 228. [4] *Ibid.*
[5] *Ibid.*, p. 174. [6] *Ibid.*, p. 238. [7] *Ibid.*

from the original state of nature. For the latter was a state of innocence and simplicity, whereas the former is the result of corruption.

As we saw, Rousseau proposed to begin his *Discourse* by laying facts aside and by developing an hypothesis, that is, an hypothetical account of the origin of inequality. And according to his hypothesis moral or political inequality can be attributed not only to the improvement of the human faculties but also, and above all, to the establishment first of private property and then of political society, government and law. In the end we have a sharp antithesis between the natural goodness and simplicity of primitive man on the one hand and, on the other, the corruption of civilized man and the evils of organized society. At the same time perfectibility was assigned as one of the distinguishing marks of man as distinct from the brute. We can understand, therefore, the objection raised by Charles Bonnet (1720–93), writing under the pseudonym of Philopolis, that if perfectibility is a natural attribute of man, civilized society is natural. And this is obviously by no means the only objection which can be brought against the *Discourse on Inequality*.

But though Rousseau repeats in this *Discourse* the attack on the idea of progress which he had made in the first *Discourse*, he makes it clear at the end that he does not advocate the absurd idea of destroying society. 'What, then, is to be done? Must societies be totally abolished? Must *meum* and *tuum* be annihilated, and must we return to the forests to live among bears?'[1] Those who wish can return to the woods; but those who, like Rousseau, cannot subsist on acorns or live without laws or magistrates will, while maintaining a healthy contempt for the edifice of civilization, show concern for the reform of society. The way thus lies open for a more positive doctrine of political society. And in point of fact one of Rousseau's main ideas, that of the social or political contract, appears, as we have seen, in the *Discourse on Inequality*.

4. Another of Rousseau's leading ideas, that of the general will, makes its appearance in the *Discourse on Political Economy*. Having distinguished between the State and the family, Rousseau goes on to say that the former is 'a moral being possessed of a will'.[2] This general will, which always tends to the preservation and welfare of the whole and of every part, and which is the source of the laws, constitutes for all the members of the State,

[1] *D.I.*, p. 245.   [2] *D.P.*, p. 253.

in their relations to one another and to it, the rule of what is just or unjust'.[1] It is idle, for instance, to say that Spartan children were morally guilty of theft when they stole to supplement their meagre repasts. For they were acting in accordance with the general will of the Spartan State. And this was for them the measure of just and unjust, right and wrong.

When one remembers that the *Discourse on Political Economy* was written about the same time as the *Discourse on Inequality*, and possibly even just before the latter, one may well be astonished at the difference in tone between the two works. But, as was mentioned in the second section of this chapter, it appears that Rousseau had formed positive ideas about the State before he competed for the prizes offered by the Dijon Academy by writing rhetorical essays on set subjects. In the *Discourse on Inequality* the ideas of the state of nature and of the transition to organized society are discussed, and the theory of political society as resting on a contract makes its appearance; but neither of the first two *Discourses* was intended to be a systematic treatise on political theory. Then in the *Discourse on Political Economy* we find a sketch of the theory of the general will. This work gives, indeed, the impression of being closer in spirit to the *Social Contract* than to the first two *Discourses*; but the concept of the general will is not proposed as though it had just been thought of by Rousseau for the first time.

To return to the theory of the general will. If we take a particular society within the State, say a religious body, this society possesses a will which is general in relation to its members; that is to say, it possesses a common will directed to the attainment of the ends of the society. But this will is particular if it is considered in relation to the general will of the State. Now, moral goodness involves identification of one's particular will with the general will. It follows, therefore, that a man may be a good member of some religious body, for example, but a bad citizen. For though his will may be at one with the general will of the former, this general will may be at variance with the general will of the State which comprises the religious body within itself.

Rousseau assumes that the general will is directed towards the common good or interest, that 'the most general will is always the most just also, and that the voice of the people is in fact the voice of God'.[2] The general will of the State, being more general than the

---

[1] *D.P.*, p. 253.   [2] *Ibid.*, p. 254.

general will of any society within the State, must prevail; for it is
more just and directed to a more universal good. We can conclude,
therefore, that 'the first and most important rule of legitimate or
popular government, that is to say, of government whose object
is the good of the people, is . . . to follow in everything the general
will'.[1] Again, 'if you would have the general will accomplished,
bring all the particular wills into conformity with it; in other
words, as virtue is nothing more than this conformity of the
particular wills with the general will, establish the reign of virtue'.[2]
But if virtue is nothing more than conformity with the general
will, to establish the reign of virtue can be nothing more than to
conform all particular wills to the general will. Hence public
education, on the necessity of which Rousseau lays stress, must be
directed to facilitating and securing this conformity.

A distinction is drawn by Rousseau between sovereignty and
government. The sovereign is the power which possesses the right
of legislation; the government's function is executive and administrative, that is, to administer the law. 'The first duty of the
legislator is to make the laws conformable to the general will.'[3]
And 'the general will is always on the side which is most favourable to the public interest, that is to say, most equitable; so that
it is needful only to act justly to be certain of following the general
will'.[4]

What are we to understand by the general will? There is a natural
temptation to interpret Rousseau as identifying the infallible
general will with the voice of the people as expressed by vote in
assembly. But he does not make this identification. In a large
State such general assemblies of the whole people are impracticable; but even when a general assembly is practicable, 'it is by
no means certain that its decision would be the expression of the
general will'.[5] Of course, if one speaks at all about a quasi-mystical
general will of the State, which stands in need of articulate
expression, one will inevitably tend to identify it with the
expressed decision of the legislature or with the expressed will of
some supposed mouthpiece of the people. And this tendency is
certainly present in Rousseau. It could hardly be otherwise, given
his premises. But it is no more than a tendency; it is not a position
which he formally adopts. He explicitly allows, for instance, that
an actual decision of the sovereign legislature may fail to be a true

[1] *D.P.*, p. 255.   [2] *Ibid.*, p. 260.   [3] *Ibid.*, p. 258.
[4] *Ibid.*, p. 259.   [5] *Ibid.*

expression of the general will. It may be the expression of private interests which for some reason or other have wrongly prevailed. To say, for example, that the general will is the criterion of what is just and what is unjust is not, therefore, to say that no criticism of the laws of the State on the score of injustice is possible. That is why Rousseau can say that the legislator's first duty is to make the laws conform to the general will, and that it is needful only to act justly to be certain of following the general will. Such statements obviously suppose that law is not necessarily or inevitably the true expression of the general will, and that not even common decisions of a general assembly are immune from moral criticism.

As far as the *Discourse on Political Economy* is concerned, Rousseau evidently assumes that there is something higher than the State. We have seen that, according to him, the more general will is also the most just. We can say, therefore, that just as the wills of individuals and of particular societies within the State are particular wills in relation to the general will of the State, so is the will of an individual State a particular will if it is looked at in relation to 'the great city of the world . . . whose general will is always the will of nature, and of which the different States and peoples are individual members'.[1] In other words, there seems to be at the back of Rousseau's mind the traditional concept of a natural moral law, engraven on men's hearts, obedience to which necessarily conduces to human happiness and welfare. And the general will of a political society is a particular canalization, so to speak, of the universal orientation of the human will to the good. The legislator's task is to conform the laws to this general will; and the citizen's task is to bring his particular will into harmony with the general will.

If this general will represents, in a given political society, the universal orientation of the human will to the good of man, it represents what every member of the society 'really' wills. This enables Rousseau to answer the objection that membership of society and obedience to law involve restraint and curtailment of liberty. Men are free by nature. And they unite in societies to assure not only their property and life but also their liberty. In point of fact, however, they become subject to restraint when they form organized societies; they become subjects instead of masters. And is it not paradoxical in the extreme to suggest that men become free or preserve freedom by becoming subjects? Rousseau

[1] *D.P.*, p. 253.

answers by appealing to the idea of law. 'It is to law alone that men owe justice and liberty.'[1] But this answer can be effective only in so far as law expresses the general will and in so far as the latter represents the 'real' will of everyone and what everyone's reason 'really' dictates. In obeying the law a man is thus obeying his own reason and judgment and following his own real will. And to follow one's own judgment and will is to be free. Hence the obedient citizen is the truly free man; for he obeys a law which expresses his own real will. This notion was to be of considerable importance in later philosophy.

In the *Discourse on Political Economy*, therefore, which, as has been already remarked, differs strikingly in tone from the first two *Discourses*, we find an emphatic statement of the most significant theory of the *Social Contract*, namely that of the general will. The theory gives rise to considerable difficulties and problems; but further discussion is best postponed to the next chapter. The concluding section of this chapter, however, may help to throw a little more light on Rousseau's general outlook.

In the final pages of the *Discourse on Political Economy* Rousseau deals with the subject of taxation. In his opinion the most equitable system of taxation, and consequently the one best suited to a society of free men, would be a capitation tax in proportion to the amount of property which a man possesses over and above the necessities of life. Those who possess only the latter should pay nothing at all. As for the other citizens, the tax should be levied, not in simple ratio to the property of the taxed, but in compound ratio to the difference of their conditions and the superfluity of their possessions. It is perfectly just that the more wealthy a man is, the more he should pay in taxation. For one thing, the rich derive great advantages from the social contract. Society protects their possessions and opens to them easy access to lucrative positions of eminence and power. They enjoy many advantages which the poor fail to enjoy. Hence, as the richer a man is, the more he gets out of the State, so to speak, he should be taxed in proportion to his wealth. There should also be heavy taxes on all luxuries. For then either the rich will substitute socially useful for socially useless expenses or the State will receive high taxes. In either case the State will gain.

If we care to translate Rousseau's ideas into modern terms, we can say that he advocated a system of graduated income-tax,

[1] *D.P.*, p. 256.

according to which those with very low incomes would pay nothing at all while those possessing incomes above a certain level would pay a tax constantly increasing as we go up the scale. This is not, of course, exactly what he says. For he thinks in terms of property and of 'superfluities' rather than in terms of income. But it indicates the spirit of his proposals. And it is significant that he speaks of these proposals as tending insensibly 'to bring all fortunes nearer to that middle condition which constitutes the genuine strength of the State'.[1]

5. It was Rousseau's constant thesis that the fundamental impulse in man is self-love. Our wants give rise to our passions; and as primitive man's wants were purely physical, self-preservation was 'his chief and almost sole concern'.[2] In *Émile* we are told that 'our first duties are to ourselves; our first feelings are centred on self; all our instincts are at first directed to our own preservation and on our own welfare'.[3] Again, 'the origin of our passions, the root and spring of all the rest, the only one which is born with man, which never leaves him as long as he lives, is self-love; this passion is primitive, instinctive, it precedes all the rest, which are in a sense only modifications of it'.[4]

But this fundamental passion of self-love is not to be confused with egoism. For egoism is a feeling which arises only in society, and which leads a man always to prefer himself to others. 'In the true state of nature egoism did not exist.'[5] For primitive man did not make the comparisons which are required for egoism to be possible. Self-love, considered in itself, is 'always good, always in accordance with the order of nature'.[6] In his letter to the archbishop of Paris Rousseau says that self-love is 'a passion indifferent in itself to good and evil; it becomes good or evil only by accident and according to the circumstances in which it develops'.[7] But whether it is called good or indifferent, it is certainly not evil, and it is not to be identified with what is called egoism.

Primitive man is also depicted as moved by natural pity or compassion, which Rousseau describes as 'the pure emotion of nature, prior to all kinds of reflection'.[8] This feeling comes into operation, of course, only when a man has taken note in some sense of his fellows; but he does not reason to the desirability of compassion; he simply feels it. It is a natural impulse.

Rousseau may sometimes seem to imply that compassion is a

---

[1] *D.P.*, p. 286.   [2] *D.I.*, p. 183.   [3] *É.*, II, p. 61.
[4] *É.*, IV, p. 173.   [5] *D.I.*, p. 197, note 2.   [6] *É.*, IV, p. 174.
[7] *Œuvres*, 1865, III, p. 647.   [8] *D.I.*, p. 198.

feeling or passion different from and originally independent of self-love. Thus he speaks of compassion as 'a natural feeling which, by moderating the violence of love of self in each individual, contributes to the preservation of the whole species'.[1] And he goes on to add that in the hypothetical state of nature compassion supplies the place of laws, morals and virtues. But though we can distinguish between self-love and compassion, the latter is really a derivative of the former. We are told in *Émile* that 'the child's first sentiment is self-love (and that) his second, which is derived from it, is love of those about him'.[2] True, Rousseau is here speaking of something which goes beyond natural pity or compassion. But later he undertakes to tell us how pity, 'the first relative sentiment which touches the human heart according to the order of nature'[3] is born. We are informed that the individual sympathizes with or feels compassion for, not those who are happier than himself, but only those who are more unfortunate than he is and who are suffering from ills from which he does not believe himself to be immune. In other words, man originally feels pity because he identifies himself with the sufferer. And in this case it is not so much that the original impulse of self-love is accompanied and modified by an independent natural feeling of pity and compassion as that the latter is comprised in the former and grows out of it when man takes note of his fellows. In this sense it is the 'first relative sentiment'.

Now, all morality is founded on these natural feelings. In his letter to the archbishop of Paris, Rousseau remarks that love of self is not a simple passion. For man is a composite being, sensitive and intelligent. Sense-appetite tends to the good of the body, while the desire of the intelligent part of man, the desire or love of order, tends to the good of the soul. 'This last love, developed and rendered active, bears the name conscience';[4] but the operations of conscience, the love of order, postulate knowledge of order. It is, therefore, only when man has begun to take note of his fellows and to apprehend relations and make comparisons that he comes to have such ideas as justice and order, and that conscience can operate. Given the necessary reflection, moral concepts are formed and virtues and vices arise. But all these are founded on man's fundamental feelings. The concept of justice, for example, is founded on self-love. 'Thus the first notion of justice

[1] *D.I.*, p. 199.   [2] *É.*, IV, p. 174.
[3] *Ibid.*, p. 184.   [4] *Œuvres*, 1865, III, p. 64.

springs not from what we owe to others, but from what is due to us.'[1] Again, from the natural emotion of compassion 'flow all those social virtues of which he (Mandeville) denied man the possession. What is generosity, clemency or humanity but compassion applied to the weak, to the guilty, or to mankind in general?'[2] And conscience, as we have seen, is founded on love of self as present in man as an intelligent or rational being.

If our whole moral life depends on our fundamental impulses or passions, it is not surprising to find Rousseau attacking those who maintain that moral education consists in extirpating them. 'Our passions are the chief means of self-preservation; to try to destroy them is therefore as absurd as it is useless; this would be to overcome nature, to reshape God's handiwork.'[3] In point of fact moral development consists in the right direction and extension of the fundamental passion of self-love. 'Extend self-love to others and it is transformed into virtue, a virtue which has its root in the heart of every one of us.'[4] Self-love is capable of development into the love of all mankind and the promotion of the general happiness which are the concern of every truly virtuous man.

Morality is thus the unthwarted and unprevented development of man's natural passions and feelings. Vice is not natural to man; it constitutes a distortion of his nature. 'Our natural passions are few in number; they are the means to freedom, they tend to self-preservation. All those which enslave and destroy us have another source; nature does not bestow them on us; we seize on them in her despite.'[5] For instance, the rise of civilization has multiplied man's wants and needs, and this has given rise to selfishness and to the 'hateful and angry passions'. It is easy, therefore, to understand Rousseau's insistence that it is the simple, those who stand nearest to nature and whose feelings and passions have been least corrupted by an artificial civilization, who are most open to the voice of conscience. 'Virtue! Sublime science of simple minds, are such industry and preparation needed if we are to know you? Are not your principles graven on every heart? Need we do more, to learn your laws, than examine ourselves and listen to the voice of conscience, when the passions are silent? This is the true philosophy, with which we must learn to be content.'[6] And Rousseau makes the Savoyard priest assert that 'there is therefore at the bottom of our hearts an innate principle of justice and virtue by

---

[1] *É.*, II, p. 61.   [2] *D.I.*, p. 199.   [3] *É.*, IV, p. 173.
[4] *Ibid.*, p. 215.   [5] *Ibid.*, p. 173.   [6] *D.A.*, pp. 153-4.

which, in spite of our maxims, we judge our own actions or those
of others to be good or evil; and it is this principle which I call
conscience'.[1] 'To exist is to feel; our feeling is undoubtedly earlier
than our intelligence, and we had feelings before we had ideas. . . .
To know good is not to love it; this knowledge is not innate in
man. But as soon as his reason leads him to perceive it, his conscience impels him to love it. It is this feeling which is innate.'[2]
Hence, although Rousseau does not deny, but rather asserts, that
reason and reflection have a part to play in the development of
morality, he lays the emphasis on feeling. 'What I feel to be right
is right, what I feel to be wrong is wrong . . . it is only when we
haggle with conscience that we have recourse to the subtleties of
argument.'[3] These words are put into the mouth of the simple
Savoyard priest, it is true; but they represent a real element in
Rousseau's thought.

The word 'feeling', when used in the last quotation, signifies, of
course, immediate apprehension or intuition rather than feeling
in the sense in which the sentiment of pity is a feeling. And the
word has more or less the same meaning when the Savoyard priest
uses it in connection with recognition of God's existence. The
world is an ordered system of interrelated entities, and this fact
manifests the existence of divine intelligence. 'Let us listen to the
inner voice of feeling; what healthy mind can reject its evidence?'[4]
'I believe, therefore, that the world is governed by a wise and
powerful will; I see it or rather I feel it, and it is a great thing to
know this.'[5] 'I see God everywhere in his works; I feel him within
myself.'[6] Again, I know that I am a free, active being. 'In vain do
you argue this point with me; I feel it, and it is this feeling which
speaks to me more forcibly than the reason which disputes it.'[7]

We have seen that morality develops when man begins to
recognize his relations with his fellows. Rousseau can say, therefore, that 'society must be studied in the individual and the
individual in society; those who desire to treat politics and morals
apart from one another will never understand either'.[8] If one is
acquainted only with the *Social Contract*, one might perhaps be
inclined to interpret this statement as meaning that moral distinctions are settled simply by the general will expressed in positive
legislation. But we ought to bear in mind the first part of the
statement, namely that society must be studied in the individual.

[1] *É.*, IV, p. 252.   [2] *Ibid.*, p. 253.   [3] *Ibid.*, p. 249.   [4] *Ibid.*, p. 237.
[5] *Ibid.*, p. 239.   [6] *Ibid.*   [7] *Ibid.*, p. 242.   [8] *Ibid.*, p. 197.

What we have said hitherto shows that for Rousseau Nature her-self has directed our will to the good for man. But we possess no innate idea of this good. Hence we can form erroneous ideas of it. There is no guarantee, therefore, that what individual citizens, even when they are gathered together in assembly, think to be for the common good actually is for the common good. At the same time there is, underlying all distorted passions and erroneous ideas, a universal and natural direction of the will to the good. Hence it is the business of the legislator to interpret this will and to bring the laws into conformity with it. And this is why Rousseau can say in the *Social Contract* that 'the general will is always right and tends to the public advantage; but it does not follow that the deliberations of the people are always equally correct. Our will is always for our own good, but we do not always see what that is; the people is never corrupted, but it is often deceived, and on such occasions only does it seem to will what is bad.'[1]

I do not suggest that this aspect of Rousseau's theory of the general will, a theory which owes much to the traditional concep-tion of natural law, is the most significant aspect from the point of view of the historical development of political theory. And other aspects will be discussed in the next chapter. But if we bear in mind the relation between the concept of the infallible general will and Rousseau's moral theory as developed in other writings, it becomes easier to understand how he came to propose this concept in the first place.

Rousseau's exaltation of intuition and of inner feeling or sentiment (*sentiment intérieur*) gave expression to a revulsion against arid rationalism which was not uncommon in the second half of the eighteenth century. It also gave to this revolt a power-ful impetus. The cult of intuition and sensibility owed much to Rousseau. As for the profession of faith of the Savoyard priest, with its founding of belief in God and in immortality on feeling rather than on sheer reasoning, this exercised a considerable influence on Robespierre and his followers. But in the long run Rosseau's sentimental deism perhaps worked more in favour of the restoration of Catholicism than against it.

[1] *S.C.*, ii, 3, p. 25.

CHAPTER IV

ROUSSEAU (2)

*The social contract—Sovereignty, the general will and freedom—
Government—Concluding remarks.*

1. ROUSSEAU states the first problem to be considered in the
Social Contract in these terms: 'Man is born free; and everywhere
he is in chains. One thinks himself the master of others, and still
remains a greater slave than they. How did this change come
about? I do not know. What can make it legitimate? This question
I think I can answer.'[1] Having postulated an original state of
nature in which men were free, Rousseau is obliged either to condemn the social order in which man's primitive freedom no longer
exists and to say that men should shake off their bonds as soon as
possible or to justify it in some way. The first course is ruled out,
because 'the social order is a sacred right which is the basis of all
other rights'.[2] Hence Rousseau is compelled to show that the
social order is justified and legitimate.

In solving his problem Rousseau has recourse to the contractual theory which we have already met in different forms in
the philosophies of Hobbes and Locke. He is unwilling to found
the social order on force; for might does not confer right. 'Force is
a physical power, and I fail to see what moral effect it can have.
To yield to force is an act of necessity, not of will—at most it is an
act of prudence. In what sense can it be called a duty?'[3] If citizens
have a duty of obedience, it cannot be founded simply on the
possession of power by the person or persons to whom obedience
is rendered. At the same time there is no natural right to legislate
for society. For society and the state of nature are distinct. The
social order, therefore, to be legitimate and justified, must be
founded on agreement or convention.

Rousseau proposes the hypothesis that men have reached the
point at which the obstacles to their preservation in the state of
nature are greater than their resources for maintaining themselves
in this state. They must, therefore, unite together and form an
association. But the problem is not simply to find a form of
association which will protect the persons and goods of each

[1] *S.C.*, I, 3, p. 5.   [2] *Ibid.*   [3] *S.C.*, I, 3, p. 8.

member. It is also that of finding an association in which each member will still obey himself alone and remain as free as before. 'This is the fundamental problem of which the *Social Contract* provides the solution.'[1]

In essence the social compact or contract can be expressed as follows. 'Each of us puts his person and all his power in common under the supreme direction of the general will, and, in our corporate capacity, we receive each member as an indivisible part of the whole.'[2] This act of association immediately creates a moral and collective body, a public person, the republic or body politic. It is called the State when considered as passive, the Sovereign when considered as active, and a Power when compared with other similar bodies. Its members are called collectively the people, while, taken individually, they are called citizens, as sharing in the sovereign power, and subjects, as being under the laws of the State.

This theory of the social contract obviously differs from that of Hobbes. According to the latter's theory individuals agree to hand over their rights to a sovereign who stands outside the covenant, not being a party to it. Government is thus set up by the same agreement that creates an organized society: in fact, the existence of the body politic really depends on its relation to the sovereign who might, indeed, be an assembly and not an individual, but who is distinguishable from the contracting parties. In Rousseau's theory, however, the original contract creates a sovereign which is identical with the contracting parties taken collectively, and nothing at all is said about government. For Rousseau, the government is simply an executive power which is dependent for its power on the sovereign assembly or body politic. Hobbes's problem was one of social cohesion. Given his view of man and of the state of nature, he was faced with the task of finding an effective counterbalance to the centrifugal forces in human nature. Or, more concretely, he was faced with the problem of finding an effective remedy for the greatest evil of society, namely civil war. He found the solution in centralized government, in a theory of sovereignty which emphasized above all things the position of the government. And as he accepted the hypothesis of the state of nature, he had to incorporate this emphasis on government into his account of the covenant whereby the transition from the state of nature to that of organized society is effected. Rousseau's

[1] *S.C.*, 1, 6, p. 14.   [2] *Ibid.*, p. 15.

problem, however, was different. Given his insistence on liberty, and given his desire to show that the change from the state of nature to that of organized society was not a substitution of slavery for freedom for the sake of mere security, he felt himself compelled to show that in society a higher form of liberty is acquired than the one enjoyed in the state of nature. One would not, therefore, expect to find him emphasizing the idea of government in his account of the social contract or the idea of the contracting parties handing over their rights to a sovereign who stands outside the contract. Instead, we find him emphasizing a mutual agreement between the contracting parties which creates a new moral entity in which each member realizes himself more fully than he could do in the state of nature.

Obviously, this signifies a marked change of attitude and tone between the first two *Discourses* and the *Social Contract*. True, in the *Discourse on Inequality* we can see, as was remarked in the last chapter, some elements of Rousseau's mature political theory making their appearance. But the first *Discourse* inevitably gives the impression that for Rousseau political society is an evil, whereas in the *Social Contract* we find man's true nature being fulfilled, as it were, in the social order. He becomes, 'instead of a stupid and unimaginative animal . . . an intelligent being and a man'.[1] There is not, indeed, a pure contradiction between the first *Discourse* and the *Social Contract*. In the former Rousseau is speaking of the evils of civilized society as it actually existed, particularly in France, whereas in the *Social Contract* he is speaking rather of political society as it ought to be. And even in the latter work, while extolling the benefits which man acquires by the social contract, he remarks that 'the abuses of this new condition often degrade him below that which he left'.[2] At the same time it can hardly be denied that there is a remarkable change of tone and emphasis. And the same is true of the relation of the *Social Contract* to the *Discourse on Inequality*. The impression given by the latter is that man, naturally good, acquires moral ideas and moral qualities in the strict sense during a gradual process of development in which civil society, in the sense of loose social bonds, precedes the formation of organized political society. But in the *Social Contract* Rousseau speaks as though through the institution of political society man passes at once from a non-moral to a moral state. 'The passage from the state of nature to

[1] *S.C.*, I, 8, p. 19.   [2] *Ibid.*

the civil state produces a very remarkable change in man, by substituting justice for instinct in his conduct, and giving his actions the morality which they had formerly lacked.'[1] The State becomes the source of justice and the basis of rights. Here again there is perhaps no sheer contradiction. The social contract is after all nothing but a philosophical fiction, as Hume puts it; and we can, if we like, regard Rousseau as making a theoretical or logical, rather than an historical, distinction between man in society and man considered in abstraction from society. As a mere isolated individual, man, while not vicious or bad in himself, is not properly a moral being: it is only in society that his intellectual and moral life develops. And this is substantially what Rousseau had said in the *Discourse on Inequality*. At the same time there is a change of tone. True, this change of tone can be explained in large part by difference of purpose. In the *Discourse* Rousseau was concerned with the origins of inequality, and he ascribes to the institution of society the origin of what he calls 'moral or political inequality'. The emphasis is on inequality, as is indicated by the title of the *Discourse*. In the *Social Contract* Rousseau is concerned with the benefits which man acquires from the institution of society, such as the substitution of civil and moral for merely 'natural' liberty. But though the change in tone is explicable largely in terms of difference of purpose, it is there none the less. In the *Social Contract*, a new, and more important, aspect of Rousseau's political theory is displayed.

We can see, therefore, how misleading the opening words of the first chapter of the *Social Contract* can be, if they are taken as an adequate statement of Rousseau's position. 'Man is born free; and everywhere he is in chains.' These words formulate a problem, not a solution. The solution is to be found in the idea of the transformation of natural into civil and moral liberty. 'What a man loses by the social contract is his natural liberty and an unlimited right to everything which he tries to get and succeeds in getting; what he gains is civil liberty and the proprietorship of all he possesses.'[2] Natural liberty is limited only by the strength of the individual; civil liberty is limited by the general will, with which the real will of each member of society is one. Mere possession is the effect of force or of the right of first occupation; proprietorship is founded on a positive title, it is a right conferred by the State. 'Over and above all this, we might add to what man acquires in

---

[1] *S.C.*, I, 8, p. 18.   [2] *Ibid.*, p. 19.

the civil state moral liberty, which alone makes him truly master of himself. For the mere impulse of appetite is slavery while obedience to a law which we prescribe to ourselves is liberty.'[1] In some forms of society, in a tyrannical and capricious dictatorship for example, men are indeed reduced to slavery, and they may be worse off than in the state of nature. But this is accidental, in the sense that it does not follow from the essence of the State. If we consider the State in its essence, we must say that its institution is an incalculable benefit to man.

By accepting the contractual theory Rousseau is faced, of course, with the same difficulty with which Locke was faced. Are we to say that the original contracting parties bound not only themselves but also their descendants? And, if so, what is our justification for saying this? Rousseau does not appear to consider this problem explicitly, though he makes it clear that the citizens of a State can at any time agree to dissolve the contract. 'There neither is nor can be any kind of fundamental law binding on the body of the people—not even the social contract itself.'[2] Again, 'there is in the State no fundamental law that cannot be revoked, not excluding the social compact itself; for if all the citizens assembled of one accord to break the compact, it is impossible to doubt that it would be quite legitimately broken'.[3] As for individuals taken singly, Rousseau refers to Grotius's opinion that each man can renounce his membership of his own State and recover his natural liberty by leaving the country. He appears to endorse this opinion by adding that 'it would be indeed absurd if all the citizens in assembly could not do what each can do by himself'.[4] (Rousseau appends a note to say that flight from the country to escape one's obligations in the hour of need would be a criminal and punishable act.) Presumably he considered that as the social contract brings into existence a new moral being, this being continues to exist, in spite of the fact that some members die and new members are born, unless the members collectively dissolve the contract in one of their periodic assemblies. The membership in the State does not effect the latter's continual existence as a moral being.

2. We have seen that according to Rousseau the public person which is formed by the union of individuals through the social contract is called, when considered as active, the sovereign. This means in effect that the sovereign is the whole body of the people

[1] S.C., I, 8, p. 19.   [2] S.C., I, 7, p. 17.   [3] S.C., III, 18, p. 89.   [4] Ibid.

as legislating, as the source of law. Now, law is the expression of will. Rousseau can say, therefore, that sovereignty is 'nothing less than the exercise of the general will'.[1] Each citizen has a dual capacity. As a member of the moral being which is the source of law he is a member of the sovereign. Considered as standing under the law and bound to obey it, he is a subject. The individual possesses, of course, a particular will, and this may be at variance with the general will. It is his civic duty to conform his particular will to the general will of the sovereign, of which he is himself a member.

Sovereignty, Rousseau insists, is inalienable. For it consists in the exercise of the general will, and this will cannot be alienated or transferred. One may transfer power, but not will. This is why Rousseau later insists that the people cannot elect representatives in the full sense of the word; it can only elect deputies. 'Sovereignty, for the same reason as makes it inalienable, cannot be represented; it lies essentially in the general will, and will does not admit of representation. It is either the same or other; there is no intermediate possibility. The deputies of the people, therefore, are not and cannot be its representatives: they are merely its stewards, and can carry through no definitive acts. Every law the people has not ratified in person is null and void. . . .'[2] (Rousseau draws the conclusion that the people of England are free only during the election of members of parliament, and that then they relapse into slavery.)

For the same reason sovereignty is indivisible. For the will, the exercise of which is called sovereignty, is the general will, and this cannot be divided. Divide it, and you have only particular wills, and thus no sovereignty. We cannot divide sovereignty into various powers, such as legislative and executive powers. The executive power or government is neither the sovereign nor a part of it: it is concerned with the administration of law and is a mere instrument of the sovereign. For Rousseau, therefore, the sovereign is the legislative, and this is the people. In a given State the nominal sovereign may be a person or persons other than the people; but the true sovereign is always the people. Needless to say, by 'people' Rousseau does not mean one class in the State, as distinct from another class or from other classes; he means the whole body of citizens. We may also note that he uses the word 'legislator' in a technical sense of his own, to mean a person who

[1] *S.C.*, II, 1, p. 22.   [2] *S.C.*, III, 15, p. 83.

draws up laws, as Lycurgus is said to have drawn up laws for the Spartans. But a legislator in this sense does not, of course, possess sovereign power. His function is advisory or illuminative, in the sense that his task is to enlighten the sovereign people so that it may act with a clear idea of what the common interest really is here and now.

Sovereignty, therefore, is said to be the exercise of the general will: and the sovereign is the people, in whom this will resides. But what is meant by the general will?

The natural temptation, of course, is to understand the term 'general will' primarily in relation to the willing subject, the sovereign people, in its legislative function. We may then be easily led to think that the general will can be identified to all intents and purposes with the decision expressed in a majority vote of the assembly. And if we interpret Rousseau in this sense, we shall be likely to comment that his description of the general will as infallible and as always tending to the public advantage is both absurd and pernicious. Absurd, because there is no guarantee that a law enacted by a popular assembly really will be to the public advantage; pernicious, because it encourages tyranny and intolerance. But the interpretation on which these conclusions are based is incorrect; in any case it places the emphasis wrongly.

We must recall to mind first of all Rousseau's famous distinction between the general will (*volonté générale*) and the will of all (*volonté de tous*). 'There is often a great deal of difference between the will of all and the general will. The latter considers only the common interest, while the former takes private interest into account and is no more than a sum of particular wills.'[1] The general will is, indeed, general in the sense that it is the will of a universal subject, the sovereign people; but the emphasis is placed by Rousseau on universality of object, namely the common interest or good or advantage. And this general will cannot be identified without more ado with the sum of particular wills as manifested in a majority, or even in a unanimous, vote. For the result of voting may give expression to a mistaken idea of what the common good involves and demands; and a law which is enacted as the result of voting may conceivably be detrimental to the public advantage. 'Of itself the people always wills the good, but of itself it by no means always sees it. The general will is always in the right, but the judgment which guides it is not always

[1] *S.C.*, II, 3, p. 25.

enlightened . . . the public wills the good it does not see.'[1] It is this fact which 'makes a legislator necessary',[2] in the sense described above.

The 'will of all', therefore, is not infallible; it is only the 'general will' which is infallible and always right. And this means that it is always directed to the common good. It is clear, I think, that Rousseau has extended his concept of the natural goodness of man to the new moral being which arises through the social contract. The individual, impelled fundamentally by self-love (not, we may recall, to be identified with egoism in a morally depreciative sense), naturally seeks his own good, though it does not necessarily follow that he has a clear idea of its true nature.[3] The 'public person' which the social contract brings into existence also seeks inevitably its own good, the common good. But the people do not always understand where their true good lies. Hence they stand in need of enlightenment in order that the general will may be properly expressed.

Let us suppose for the sake of argument that it makes sense to speak of the State as a moral entity which is capable of willing. If we say that its will, the general will, is always right, and if we distinguish between this will and the will of all considered as the sum of particular wills, then the statement that the general will is infallible does not commit us to the statement that every law which is passed by the popular assembly is necessarily the law which is most conducive to the public advantage in the given circumstances. There is still room for possibly justified criticism. At the same time we run the risk of being reduced to the utterance of a tautology. For if we say that the general will is always right, and if we mean by this that the general will is always directed to the common good, the question arises whether we are saying anything more than that the will for the common good is the will for the common good; if, that is to say, we define the general will in terms of a universal object, namely the common good or interest. It might be maintained, therefore, that Rousseau can be saved from an uncritical worship of the legislative decisions of public assemblies only by reducing what he says to an innocuous tautology.

The comment might then be made that what is really required is a clear account of what it means to speak about the State as a

[1] *S.C.*, II, 6, p. 34.   [2] *Ibid.*
[3] We may compare the Scholastic doctrine that, whatever a man wills, he wills *sub specie boni*.

moral entity with a will. If this will is not identical with the will of all, what exactly is it? Is it something over and above all particular wills? Or is it rather particular wills taken collectively and considered according to their natural orientation towards the good rather than as directed by the particular concepts of the good in the minds of their owners? In the first case we are faced with an ontological problem. That is to say, we are faced with the problem of the ontological status of the subsistent general will. In the second case some reconsideration by Rousseau of his initial individualism would seem to be demanded. For the will of A is directed towards A's good, and the will of B is directed towards B's good. If, therefore, we wish to say that the wills of A, B, C, and so on, considered in their natural orientation towards the good, form collectively the general will (which is directed towards the common good), it seems that we ought to maintain that men are by nature and from the beginning social beings and that their wills are directed naturally not only towards their private good, but also to the common good, or to their private goods as comprised within the common good or as contributing to it. I think that something of this was, indeed, in the back of Rousseau's mind. But by first presenting us with an individualistic picture of man and by then advancing the idea of a new moral public person with a will of its own, he has left in obscurity the precise nature of the general will and its precise relation to particular wills. There is, indeed, little indication that Rousseau gave to these problems the prolonged reflection which they require. We can discern in his political philosophy various lines of thought which it is difficult to harmonize. The most significant line of thought is doubtless the idea of the State as an organic entity with a will of its own, which is in some rather undefined sense the 'true' will of each member of the State. To this notion I shall return presently.

I do not mean to imply that for Rousseau there is no connection between the general will and the legislative activity of the sovereign people. To say, as he does, that there is often a great deal of difference between the will of all and the general will, is not to say that they never coincide. And one of Rousseau's problems as a political theorist was to suggest means of ensuring, so far as this can be done, that the infallible general will attains concrete expression in law. One of the means which he suggests has already been noted, namely the employment of a wise 'legislator'. Another means is the prevention, so far as this is practicable, of partial societies within the State. The point is this. If each citizen votes entirely independently, the differences between them, according to Rousseau, will cancel out, 'and the general will remains as the sum of the differences'.[1] If, however, factions and parties are formed, each with its (relatively speaking) general will, the differences become less numerous, and the result is less general and less expressive of the general will. Worse still, when one association or party is so strong or numerous that its will inevitably prevails over those of the other citizens, the result is not expressive in any way of the general will of the State, but only of a particular will (particular, that is, in relation to the general will of the State, even if it is general in relation to the members of the association or party). Rousseau's conclusion is that 'it is therefore essential, if the general will is to be able to express itself, that there should be no partial society within the State, and that each citizen should think only his own thoughts'.[2]

This is, of course, one reason why Rousseau shows dislike of the Christian Church. 'Wherever the clergy is a corporate body, it is master and legislator in its own country. . . . Of all Christian writers, the philosopher Hobbes alone has seen the evil and how to remedy it, and has dared to propose the reunion of the two heads of the eagle, and the restoration throughout of political unity. . . . But he should have seen that the masterful spirit of Christianity is incompatible with his system, and that the priestly interest would always be stronger than that of the State.'[3] True, when Rousseau speaks against the Christian Church and in favour of a purely civil religion, he is not directly engaged in discussing the general will and its expression. But his remarks are none the less obviously relevant. For if the Church sets itself up as a quasi-sovereign, its influence will inevitably interfere with the expression of the general will of the true sovereign, namely the people.

It should be noted how Rousseau assumes that if the citizens are duly enlightened, and if partial societies within the State are suppressed (or, where this is not possible, rendered so numerous that their diverging interests and influences cancel out), the majority vote will inevitably express the general will. 'If, when the people, being furnished with adequate information, held its deliberations, the citizens had no communication one with another, the grand total of the small differences would always give the

---

[1] *S.C.*, II, 3, p. 25.   [2] *Ibid.*, p. 26.   [3] *S.C.*, IV, 8, p. 116.

general will, and the decision would always be good.'[1] Again, 'there is but one law which, from its nature, needs unanimous consent. This is the social compact. . . . Apart from this primitive contract, the vote of the majority always binds the rest. . . . The general will is found by counting votes.'[2] This does not exactly contradict what Rousseau says about the distinction between the general will and the will of all. For the distinction is meant to allow for the possibility of private interests, especially the interest of partial groups and associations determining the decision of the people in assembly. And when this abuse takes place, the result of voting does not represent the general will. But when such abuses are avoided, the result will certainly give expression to the general will.

Of course, in one sense this is obviously true; namely in the sense that the will of a majority is more general than the will of a minority. But this is a truism. And it is not all that Rousseau has in mind. For a law which is the expression of the general will is for him a law which tends to or secures or preserves the common good or interest. If, therefore, the influence of group interests is avoided, the expressed will of the assembly is infallibly conducive to the public good. Criticism of the assembly's expressed will would seem to be legitimate only on the ground of undue influence by private party and group interests. If we assume that each citizen is 'thinking his own thoughts' and is not exposed to illegitimate pressures, there does not seem to be any ground left, on Rousseau's premises, for criticizing the expressed will of the assembly, even if it is expressed only by a majority vote. It is true that he asserts that the majority should approach unanimity in proportion to the gravity of the matters to be decided; but this does not alter the fact that 'the general will is formed by counting votes (and that) all the qualities of the general will still reside in the majority'.[3]

Rousseau's discussion of the general will is closely connected with the problem of freedom. As we have seen, he wished to justify the transition from the hypothetical state of nature to that of organized political society. Believing that man is naturally free and that freedom is an inestimable value, he felt himself compelled to show that through the social contract, which gives rise to the State, man, instead of losing freedom, acquires a higher kind of it. For 'to renounce liberty is to renounce being a man'.[4]

[1] S.C., II, 3, pp. 25–6.   [2] S.C., IV, 2, p. 94.
[3] Ibid.   [4] S.C., I, 4, p. 10.

Rousseau maintained, therefore, that by the social contract natural liberty is exchanged for civil liberty. But it is obvious that in society men are compelled to obey the law. If they do not do so, they are punished. And, given this situation, is it possible to hold that by exchanging the state of nature, in which man was free to do whatever he had the physical capacity for doing, for the state of political society he became more, and not less, free than before, or at least that he acquired a truer and fuller freedom? Rousseau's treatment of this problem is celebrated.

In the first place the social contract must be understood as including the tacit undertaking to submit to the general will and that whoever refuses to do this shall be subjected to compulsion. 'The citizen gives his consent to all the laws, including those which are passed in spite of his opposition, and even those which punish him when he dares to break any of them.'[1]

In the second place, and this is the salient point, the general will is each man's real will. And the expression of the general will is the expression of each citizen's real will. Now, to follow one's own will is to act freely. Hence to be compelled to conform one's will to the general will is to be compelled to be free. It is to be brought into a state where one wills what one 'really' wills.

Here we have Rousseau's famous paradox. 'In order that the social compact may not be an empty formula, it tacitly includes the undertaking, which alone can give force to the rest, that whoever refuses to obey the general will shall be compelled to do so by the whole body. This means nothing less than that he will be forced to be free.'[2] Again, '. . . the general will is found by counting votes. When, therefore, the opinion which is contrary to my own prevails, this proves neither more nor less than that I was mistaken, and that what I thought to be the general will was not so. If my particular will had carried the day I should have achieved the opposite of what was my will; and I should not have been free.'[3]

It is difficult to see how the fact that an opinion different from my own prevails by a majority vote 'proves' that I was mistaken. Rousseau simply assumes that it does. However, passing over this point we can draw attention to the ambiguous use of the word *free*. Another man might be content to say that if freedom means freedom to do whatever one wishes to do and is physically capable of doing, it is, indeed, curtailed by membership of the State. But curtailment of one's freedom by law is essential to the well-being

[1] *S.C.*, IV, 2, p. 93.   [2] *S.C.*, I, 7, p. 18.   [3] *S.C.*, IV, 2, p. 94.

of society, and, in view of the fact that the advantages of society outweigh its disadvantages, such curtailment needs no other justification than its utility. The only relevant problem is that of restricting it to the minimum required by the common good. This purely empirical and utilitarian approach was not, however, to the taste of Rousseau. He wishes to show that apparent curtailment of liberty is not really a curtailment at all. Hence he is led into the paradoxical position of maintaining that one can be forced to be free. And the very fact that the position immediately strikes one as being paradoxical suggests that the word *free* is being given a sense which, whatever it may be, is different from the sense or senses which it normally bears. To apply this word to a man who is forced, for example, to obey a certain law does not conduce to clarity. It is to suggest, by applying a word outside its normal range of meaning, that force and compulsion are not really force and compulsion.

Linguistic criticism may appear tiresome and superficial to some minds. But it has in reality a considerable practical importance. For the transference of laudatory names or epithets to situations which lie outside their normal range of meaning is a stock device of political propagandists who wish to render these situations more acceptable. Thus the term *democracy*, perhaps with the prefix 'true' or 'real', is sometimes applied to a state of affairs in which the few tyrannize over the many with the aid of force and terror. And to call compulsion 'being forced to be free' is an instance of the same kind of thing. Later we find Robespierre saying that the will of the Jacobins was the general will and calling the revolutionary government the despotism of liberty. Linguistic criticism can throw some much-needed light on these troubled waters.

These remarks are not, of course, intended to suggest that Rousseau himself was in any way a friend of despotism or tyranny or terror. His paradox proceeded, not from a desire to make people believe that black is white, but from the difficulty of justifying a normal feature of social life, restriction of personal caprice by universal laws, in face of the picture which he had given of the state of nature. And though it is only proper to point out the dangers inherent in the use of such paradoxes, it is also true that to confine oneself to linguistic criticism of the type to which I have alluded would be to fail to note the historical importance of Rousseau's theory of the general will and the different ways in which it is capable of development. This is perhaps one reason why such criticism can appear tiresome and superficial. But further remarks on Rousseau's theory will be reserved for the final section of this chapter. Meanwhile I turn to the subject of government.

3. Every free action, says Rousseau, is produced by the concurrence of two causes. One is a moral cause, namely the will which determines the act, the other a physical cause, namely the physical power which executes the act. Both causes are required. A paralytic may will to run; but, lacking the physical power to do so, he stays where he is.

Applying this distinction to the body politic we must distinguish between the legislative power, namely the sovereign people, and the executive power or government. The former gives expression to the general will in universal laws and does not concern itself with particular actions or persons. The latter applies and enforces the law, and it is concerned, therefore, with particular actions and persons. 'I call *government*, or supreme administration, the legitimate exercise of the executive power, and prince or magistrate the man or the body entrusted with this administration.'[1]

The action by which a people puts itself under a prince is not a contract: 'it is simply and solely a commission'.[2] It follows that the sovereign can limit or modify or recover the executive power at its pleasure. Indeed, Rousseau envisages periodic assemblies of the sovereign people in which two questions should be voted on separately: 'does it please the sovereign to preserve the present form of government?' and 'does it please the people to leave its administration in the hands of those who are actually in charge of it?'[3] Obviously, Rousseau is here envisaging small States like Swiss cantons, where it is physically possible for the people to meet together periodically. However, the general principle, that the government is merely the instrument or minister of the sovereign people, holds good for all States. Of course, to say that the people can 'recover' the executive power does not mean that it can decide to exercise this power itself. Not even in a small Swiss canton could the people carry on day-by-day administration. And, on Rousseau's principles, the sovereign people is concerned in any case with legislation, not with administration, except in the sense that if it is dissatisfied with the existing government's administration, it is entitled to dismiss it and entrust the executive power to another government.

[1] *S.C.*, III, 1, p. 50.   [2] *Ibid.*   [3] *S.C.*, III, 18, p. 89.

The executive power, according to Rousseau, possesses 'a particular personality, a sensibility common to its members, and a force and will of its own making for its preservation'.[1] But this does not alter the fact that 'the State exists by itself and the government only through the sovereign'.[2] This dependence does not, indeed, prevent the government from acting with vigour and promptitude; but its dominant will ought to be the general will as expressed in law. If it comes to have a separate particular will which is more active and powerful than that of the sovereign, 'there would be, so to speak, two sovereigns, the one rightful and the other actual, the social union would evaporate instantly, and the body politic would be dissolved'.[3] Rousseau was no friend of capricious and tyrannical princes or governments.[4] They should be servants, and not masters, of the people.

Although Rousseau discusses types of government, it is unnecessary to say much about this subject. For he very sensibly refuses to assert that there is one ideal form of government, suitable for all peoples and circumstances. 'The question "What absolutely is the best government?" is unanswerable as well as indeterminate; or, rather, there are as many good answers as there are possible combinations in the absolute and relative situations of all nations.'[5] Again, 'there has been at all times much dispute concerning the best form of government, without consideration of the fact that each is in some cases the best, and in other cases the worst'.[6] We can say, however, that democratic governments suit small States, aristocratic governments those of middle size, and monarchical governments large States. But all forms of constitution are capable of abuse and degeneration. 'Were there a people of gods, their government would be democratic. So perfect a government is not for men.'[7] Rousseau is speaking here of democracy in the literal sense, which of all forms of constitution is the one most likely to give rise to factions and civil war. That monarchy is subject to abuse is obvious. The 'best and most natural arrangement' is that 'the wisest should govern the many, when it is assured that they will govern for its profit, and not for their own'.[8] But this is not, of course, assured. Aristocracy, like

---

[1] S.C., III, I, p. 53.   [2] Ibid.   [3] Ibid.
[4] The word tyrannical is here used in its ordinary sense. In Rousseau's technical language, however, a tyrant is one who usurps the royal authority, while a despot is one who usurps the sovereign power. 'Thus the tyrant cannot be a despot, but the despot is always a tyrant' (S.C., III, 10, p. 77).
[5] S.C., III, 9, p. 73.   [6] S.C., III, 3, p. 57.   [7] S.C., III, 4, p. 59.
[8] S.C., III, 5, pp. 60-1.

any other form of government, can degenerate. In fact, the tendency to degeneration is, in all forms of constitution, natural and inevitable. 'The body politic, as well as the human body, begins to die as soon as it is born, and it carries within itself the causes of its destruction.'[1] True, men have to endeavour to preserve the body politic in as healthy a condition as long as possible, just as they do with their own bodies. And this can best be done by separating clearly the executive from the legislative power and by various constitutional devices. But even the best constituted State will have an end, even if it survives longer than others, apart from unforeseen circumstances, just as a healthy and robust human body will eventually die, though of itself, and unforeseen accidents apart, it tends to outlive sickly and weak bodies.

4. A certain amount of what Rousseau says in the *Social Contract* is clearly related to his predilection for the small republic, like his own city of Geneva. It is only in a very small State that it would be possible, for example, for the citizens to meet together periodically and to exercise their legislative functions. The Greek city-State and the small Swiss republic furnished him with his ideal of the State in regard to size. Moreover, those extremes of wealth and poverty which disfigured contemporary France and which scandalized Rousseau were absent in the more simple life of the Swiss people. Again, the system of representation of which Rousseau disapproved is encouraged by the vastness of States, even if 'it comes to us from feudal government, from that iniquitous and absurd system which degrades humanity and dishonours the name of man'.[2] To be sure, Rousseau understood well enough that a very small State suffers from certain disadvantages, such as difficulty in defending itself; but he accepted the idea of federations of small States.

But Rousseau's predilection for small States constitutes a comparatively unimportant, though picturesque, aspect of his political theory. He was not so fanciful as to suppose that France, for instance, could in practice be reduced to a multiplicity of small States or to a confederation of such States. In any case his idea of the sovereignty of the people and his ideal of government for the people were of greater importance and influence than any of his ideas about the proper size for States. The idea of popular sovereignty was of some influence with Robespierre and the Jacobins. And we can say that when the slogans, Liberty and Equality,

---

[1] *S.C.*, III, 11, p. 77.   [2] *S.C.*, III, 15, p. 83.

spread through Europe, it was in part Rousseau's ideas which were spreading, though he was not himself an advocate of revolution. Rousseau was not a cosmopolitan: he disliked the cosmopolitanism of the Enlightenment and deprecated the lack of that patriotism and love of country which was characteristic of Sparta, the early Roman Republic and the Swiss people. We can say, therefore, at least that Rousseau's idea of national popular sovereignty had some affinity with the growth of national democracy as distinct from international socialism.

To estimate the practical influence of Rousseau's writings on political and social developments is, however, scarcely possible; we are forced to confine ourselves more or less to general indications. It is much easier, of course, to trace the influence of his theories on other philosophers. And the two thinkers who come immediately to mind are Kant and Hegel.

Rousseau's theory of the social contract is of little or no importance in this respect. He gave it prominence, indeed, as the title of his chief political work clearly shows; but it was merely an artificial device, taken over from other writers, to justify the transition from the hypothetical state of nature to that of political society. It was not a theory which had any future. Far more important was the doctrine of the general will. But this doctrine could be developed in at least two ways.

In the original draft of the *Social Contract* Rousseau speaks of the general will as being in each man a pure act of the understanding, which reasons on what a man may demand of his neighbour and on what his neighbour has a right to demand of him. The will is here depicted as rational. Let us add to this the doctrine expressed in the *Social Contract* that 'the mere impulse of appetite is slavery, while obedience to a law which we prescribe to ourselves is liberty'.[1] We then have an autonomous, rational will or practical reason whereby man in his higher nature, so to speak, legislates for himself and pronounces a moral law to which he, in his lower nature, is subject. And this law is universal, in the sense that reason prescribes what is right and, implicitly at least, what every man in the same circumstances ought to do. This notion of the autonomous will which legislates in the moral sphere is an obvious anticipation of the Kantian ethic. It may be objected that the Kantian will is purely rational, whereas Rousseau emphasizes the fact that reason would be ineffective as a guide to

[1] *S.C.*, 1, 8, p. 19.

action unless the law were graven on men's hearts in ineffaceable characters. The rational will needs a motive force which lies in man's fundamental impulses. This is true. It is true, that is to say, that Rousseau emphasizes the part played by *le sentiment intérieur* in man's moral life. But there is no intention of suggesting that Rousseau's theory of the general will and Kant's theory of the practical reason are one and the same thing. The point is simply that there are elements in the former's theory which are susceptible of development in a Kantian direction. And Kant was certainly influenced by Rousseau's writings.

The general will is not, however, universal simply in relation to its object. For Rousseau it is also universal in relation to its subject. That is to say, it is the will of the sovereign people, of the moral being or public person which is brought into existence by the social contract. And we have here the germs of the organic theory of the State which was developed by Hegel. The latter criticized and rejected the theory of the social contract; but he commended Rousseau for assigning will as the principle of the State.[1] Hegel did not, of course, take over Rousseau's theories of the State and of the general will; but he studied him and was influenced and stimulated by him in the development of his own political theory.

We have noted that Rousseau expressed a predilection for small States. In the sort of political society which he looked on as an ideal the general will would be manifested in what we may call a straightforward democratic manner, namely by the citizens voting in a popular assembly. But if we assume a large State, in which such assemblies are quite impracticable, the general will cannot find expression in direct legislation. It can find partial expression in periodic elections, but for legislative expression it needs interpretation by a man or by men other than the sovereign people. And it is no very far step to the conception of the infallible national will finding articulate expression through the lips of some leader. I do not mean that Rousseau would have approved such an interpretation of his theory. On the contrary, it would have aroused his abhorrence. And he could have pointed to sections of his writings which militate against it. At the same time the notion of a quasi-mystical will seeking articulate expression lends itself to exploitation of this kind.

There is, however, yet another way in which the theory of the

[1] Cf. *Philosophy of Right*, translated by T. M. Knox, Oxford, 1942, pp. 156–7.

general will could be developed. We can think of a nation as possessing some operative ideal which is partially expressed in its history and traditions and institutions, and which is plastic in the sense that it is not a fixed, articulate ideal but one which is gradually built up and which demands modification and reformulation in the light of the nation's development. And we can then perhaps speak of the task of legislators and of political theorists as being, in part at least, that of endeavouring to give concrete expression to this ideal and thus to show the nation what it 'really wants'. I do not suggest that this conception is immune from criticism. My point is that it is possible to put forward a theory of the general will without being forced to conceive the organ of interpretation as an infallible mouthpiece. The legislative and government may endeavour to see what is best for the nation in the light of its traditions, institutions and historical circumstances; but it does not follow that the interpretation of what is best either is or need be regarded as correct. It is possible to keep the idea of the nation wanting what is best for it and of the government and legislative as trying, or as under an obligation to try, to give expression to this will, without supposing that there is any infallible organ of interpretation and expression. In other words, it would be possible to adapt Rousseau's theory to the life of a democratic State as it is found in our western culture.

One main reason why diverse developments of Rousseau's theory are possible is, of course, the ambiguity which can be found in his statement of the theory. One important ambiguity is the following. When Rousseau says that the social order is the basis of all rights, his statement can be taken in an innocuous sense if we understand by 'right' legal right. The statement then becomes a truism. But when he says that legislation gives birth to morality,[1] this suggests that the State is the fount of moral distinctions. And if we couple this with his attack on partial societies and with his defence of a civil religion, as distinct from a revealed religion mediated by the Church, it is easy to understand how the view can be put forward that Rousseau's political theory points in the direction of totalitarianism. Yet he did not in fact think that morality depends simply on the State. After all, he insisted on the need of virtuous citizens if the State itself is to be good. He was thus faced with Plato's dilemma. There cannot be a good State without good citizens. But the citizens will not be good if the

[1] *S.C.*, IV, 7, p. III.

State, in its legislation and government, tends to deprave and corrupt them. This is one reason why Rousseau had recourse to the idea of an enlightened 'legislator' after the style of Solon or Lycurgus. But the mere fact that he was faced with this dilemma shows that he did not think that morality depends simply on the State; in the sense that whatever the State declares to be right is right. Moreover, he believed that a natural law is written in the hearts of men. And if he considered that, given certain conditions and precautions, this natural law would certainly find articulate expression in the declared will of the sovereign people, this optimism was due to his belief in man's natural goodness rather than to ethical positivism. It cannot, however, be denied that he made statements which smack of ethical positivism, in the sense that they seem to imply the derivation of morality from legislation and social opinion. In other words, his theory, taken as a whole, is ambiguous. Man always wills the good, but he can be mistaken as to its nature. Who is to interpret the moral law? The answer is ambiguous. Sometimes we are told that it is conscience, sometimes that it is the legislative. On the one hand, the voice of the legislative is not necessarily infallible; it may be influenced by selfish interests, and then it does not express the general will. Conscience presumably must be the deciding factor. On the other hand, a man must conform himself to the decision of the sovereign people: if necessary, he must be forced to be free. It can hardly be claimed that there is no ambiguity here. Hence, even though Rousseau himself laid stress on the law engraven in indelible characters on men's hearts and on the voice of conscience, we can understand the contention that there are incompatible elements in his theory, and that the new element is the tendency to eliminate the traditional conception of a natural moral law.

A final remark. We have considered Rousseau under the general heading of the French Enlightenment. And in view of the fact that he dissociated himself from the Encyclopaedists and the d'Holbach circle this may seem to be an inappropriate classification. Further, in the development of literature Rousseau exercised a powerful influence not only on French but also on German literature, particularly of the *Sturm und Drang* period. And this may appear to be an additional reason for separating him from the French Enlightenment. But Rousseau was not the originator of the literature of sensibility, even if he gave to it a powerful impetus; nor was he alone among eighteenth-century French philosophers and writers in stressing the importance of the passions and of feeling in human life. We have only to think of Vauvenargues, for example. The situation seems to be this. If we single out as the main features of the Enlightenment in France an arid rationalism, religious scepticism and a tendency to materialism, then we must say, of course, that Rousseau overcame the Enlightenment or passed beyond it. But we can equally well revise our conception of the period to include Rousseau: we can find in it something more than arid rationalism, materialism and religious scepticism. The fact of the matter is, however, that while he had his roots in the general movement of thought in eighteenth-century France, he is too outstanding a figure in the history of philosophy and literature for it to be profitable to give him a simple class-label and think that one has then satisfied all justice. He is and remains Jean-Jacques Rousseau, not a mere example of a type. Some of his theories, such as that of the social contract, are typical of the age and of little more than historical interest. In other aspects of his thought, political, educational and psychological, he looked forward to the future. And some of his problems, such as that of the relation between the individual and the State, are obviously as real now as when he wrote, even if we would give to his questions different formulations.

PART II

THE GERMAN ENLIGHTENMENT

CHAPTER V

THE GERMAN ENLIGHTENMENT (1)

Christian Thomasius—Christian Wolff—Followers and opponents of Wolff.

1. THE first phase of the Enlightenment (*Aufklärung*) in Germany is perhaps best represented by Christian Thomasius (1655–1728), son of the Jakob Thomasius who had been one of Leibniz's teachers. As a young man Christian Thomasius emphasized the superiority of the French to the Germans in the sphere of philosophy. The latter have an inclination to metaphysical abstractions which promote neither the common good nor individual happiness. Metaphysics does not yield real knowledge. Moreover, the 'learned' philosophy, taught in the universities, presupposes that the end of rational reflection is contemplation of abstract truth for its own sake. But this presupposition is a mistake. The value of philosophy lies in its utility, in its tendency to contribute to the social or common good and to the happiness or well-being of the individual. Philosophy, in other words, is an instrument of progress.

This hostility towards metaphysics and pure intellectualism was grounded to a certain extent in empiricism. The mind, according to Thomasius, must be purified of prejudices and preconceptions, especially of those characteristic of Aristotelianism and Scholasticism. But if he rejected Aristotelian and Scholastic metaphysics, he did not do so in order to substitute another metaphysics in their place. Thus Thomasius attacked, for example, the *Medicina mentis* of Tschirnhaus (1651–1708) who under the influence of Descartes and Spinoza advocated the application of the mathematical method in a philosophy of discovery and who extolled the attainment of truth as the noblest ideal of human life. For Thomasius it is clear that our natural knowledge depends on the senses. We possess no innate ideas, and we cannot discover truths about the world by a purely deductive method. Experience and observation are the only trustworthy sources of knowledge; and the bounds of this knowledge are determined by our senses. On the one hand, if there is anything so small that it makes no impression on the senses, we cannot know it. On the other hand, there are things so great that they exceed the capacity of our minds. We can know, for example, that the objects of the senses depend on a First Cause; but we cannot know, by philosophy at least, the nature of this cause. The dependence of our minds on sense-perception and the consequent limitation of our range of knowledge show the emptiness of metaphysical speculation. Nor should we allow ourselves to be led back into metaphysics by doubting the trustworthiness of the senses and by then attempting to give a philosophical proof of their trustworthiness. Doubt has, indeed, its proper place in our mental lives. For we ought to subject to doubt the opinions of the past which have proved of no utility to man. But sound common sense places a limit to doubt. We ought to avoid being entangled either in scepticism or in metaphysics. Rather should we devote ourselves to attaining knowledge of the world presented by the senses, not for the sake of knowledge, but for the sake of its utility.

But though Thomasius's idea of philosophy, as it appears in the *Einleitung zur Vernunftlehre* and in the *Ausübung der Vernunftlehre* (both 1691), is to a certain extent the expression of an empiricist outlook, those historians are probably right who connect it not only with social developments but also with the outlook of the Protestant Reformation. Of course, if we simply assert that the prominence given to the idea of the common good is an expression of the rise of the middle class, we lay ourselves open to the charge of exaggeration. For the idea of the common good was prominent in, for example, mediaeval philosophy. At the same time it is probably true that the utilitarian conception of philosophy, with its concentration on the idea of the enlightened reason using its capacities for the promotion of the common good, had some connection with the post-mediaeval structure of society, and that it is not unreasonable to speak of it as 'bourgeois' philosophy, provided that this word is not used as a term of abuse. As for the religious connection, there seems to be some truth in the view that this bourgeois philosophy was a secularized prolongation of the outlook of the Protestant Reformation. The true service of God is to be found in the ordinary forms of social life, not in the secluded contemplation of eternal verities or in turning away from the world in asceticism and mortification. This idea, when divorced from its strictly religious setting, easily leads to the conclusion that social progress and individual success in this world are marks of divine favour. And if philosophical reflection, as Luther thought, has little or no competence in the theological sphere, it seems to follow that it should be devoted to the promotion of the social good and of individual temporal happiness. Utility, not contemplation of the truth for its own sake, will be the chief motive of such reflection. That is to say, philosophy will be concerned with questions of ethics, social organization and law rather than with metaphysics and theology. It will centre round man; but its chief aim in considering man will be to promote his temporal good rather than to integrate a philosophical anthropology into a general metaphysics of Being. Man will be considered psychologically rather than metaphysically or from a theological point of view.

This does not mean, of course, that philosophy has to be anti-religious. As we have seen, the philosophy of the French Enlightenment was frequently hostile to Catholicism and, with certain thinkers, to religion in general, which was looked at as an enemy of social progress; but this point of view was certainly not characteristic either of the German Enlightenment in general or of Thomasius in particular. The latter was far from being an irreligious man. On the contrary, he was or came to be associated with pietism, a movement which arose in the Lutheran Church towards the end of the seventeenth century and which aimed at infusing a new devotional life into this religious body. But though one cannot legitimately say that pietism reduced religion simply to feeling, it had no sympathy with metaphysics or with Scholastic theology but laid emphasis on personal faith and interiority. Pietism, therefore, like empiricism, though for different reasons, contributed to the turning of philosophy away from metaphysics and natural theology.[1]

The conclusion of the *Vernunftlehre* or *Doctrine of Reason* is that metaphysics is useless and that reason should be employed to promote the good of man. Thomasius's ethical theory is set out in his *Einleitung zur Sittenlehre* (1692) and *Ausübung der Sittenlehre* (1696). But the theory undergoes a curious metamorphosis. We

---

[1] This statement is true as regards the direct influence of pietism on Thomasius and his followers; for it tended to remove religion and theology from the sphere of philosophical reflection. But the statement stands in need of qualification. For example, some knowledge of pietism is necessary, as will be seen in the next volume, for an understanding of the development of Hegel's thought.

are first told that the highest good of man is tranquillity of soul, the way to which is pointed out by the reason, the will being the faculty which leads man away from the good. This appears to be an individualistic ideal. But Thomasius goes on to argue that man is by nature a social being and that only as a member of society is he, properly speaking, a man. It follows that man cannot attain tranquillity of soul without the social bond, without love for his fellow-men; and the individual ought to sacrifice himself to the common good. Through mutual love there arises a common will which transcends the merely private and egoistic will. From this it seems to follow that the will cannot be characterized as bad. For 'rational love' is a manifestation of will; and from rational love the virtues arise. But Thomasius none the less wishes to hold that the human will is bad. The will is the slave of the fundamental impulses or drives such as the desires for wealth, honour and pleasure. Selflessness is unobtainable by our own efforts. Human choice and action can produce only sin: it is divine grace alone which is capable of rescuing man from his moral powerlessness. In other words, it is pietism which has the last word in Thomasius's ethical writings, and he explicitly reproaches himself for having thought that a man could develop a natural morality by his own power.

Thomasius is best known for his works in jurisprudence and international law. In 1688 he published *Institutionum jurisprudentiae divinae libri tres, in quibus fundamenta juris naturae secundum hypotheses ill. Pufendorfii perspicue demonstrantur*. In this work he wrote, as the title indicates, in dependence on the famous jurist, Samuel Pufendorf (1632–94). But he showed a greater degree of originality and independence in his later publication, *Fundamenta juris naturae et gentium ex sensu communi deducta* (1705). In it he begins with a consideration of man which is psychological, and not metaphysical, in character. He finds in man three fundamental drives: the desire to live as long and as happily as possible, the instinctive recoil from death and pain, and the desire for property and mastery. So long as reason does not control these impulses or drives, there exists the natural state of human society, which is a mixture of war and peace, tending always to degenerate into the former. This condition of affairs can be remedied only when rational reflection gains the upper hand and is directed towards securing for man the longest and happiest life possible. But what is a happy life? In the first place it is a just life; and the principle of justice is that we should not do to others what we do not wish them to do to us. On this principle is based natural law in the narrower sense, namely as directed to the preservation of external peaceful relations. In the second place a happy life is characterized by decency (*decorum*); and the principle of decency or of what is fitting is that we should do to others what we wish them to do to us. On this principle is based politics which is directed to the promotion of peace by benevolent action. In the third place a happy life demands virtue and self-respect (*honestum*); and the principle here is that we should do to ourselves what we wish others to do to themselves according to their capacities. On this principle is based ethics, which is directed to the attainment of inner peace.

We have here a rather different outlook from that suggested by Thomasius's remarks in his *Ausübung der Sittenlehre* about man's incapacity to develop a moral life by his own efforts. For in the *Fundamenta juris naturae et gentium ex sensu communi deducta* he clearly takes up the position that a natural law is derivable from the human reason, and that by the exercise of the latter man can overcome his egoistic impulses and promote the useful, namely the common good. Pufendorf had also derived the natural law from reason; but Thomasius separated natural law from metaphysics and theology more sharply than his predecessor had done. We find, therefore, a characteristic idea of the Enlightenment, that reason can heal the wounds of human life, and that exercise of· reason should be directed to the social good. The individual should find his own good in overcoming his egoistic desires and lusts and in subordinating himself to the good of society. This is not to say that Thomasius ever discarded belief in religion or in the supernatural. But he tended to separate religion, belonging to the sphere of faith, feeling and devotion, from the sphere of philosophical reflection. Calvinist emphasis on community appears in a secularized form; but it coexists for Thomasius with Lutheran pietism.

2. The chief representative of the second phase of the German Enlightenment is Christian Wolff (1679–1754). With Wolff, however, we find a very different outlook from that of Thomasius. The latter's hostility towards metaphysics, combined with pietism, is entirely absent. Instead we find a renewal of academic philosophy and School metaphysics, and a thorough-going rationalism. This must not be taken to imply that Wolff was a rationalist in the

sense of being anti-religious; he was nothing of the kind. But he developed a complete rational system of philosophy which included metaphysics and natural theology, and which exercised a powerful influence in the universities. True, he emphasized the practical end of philosophy and his aim was that of promoting the spread of understanding and virtue among men. But the characteristic note of his thought is its confidence in and insistence on the power of the human reason to attain certainty in the field of metaphysics, including metaphysical knowledge of God. This rationalism finds expression in the titles of his German writings which frequently begin with the words 'Rational Ideas of . . .' ('*Vernünftige Gedanken von* . . .'); for example, '*Rational Ideas of God, the World and the Soul of Man*' (1719). And his Latin works form together the 'Rational Philosophy' (*Philosophia rationalis*). The pietistic sundering of the sphere of faith from the sphere of reason and the elimination of metaphysics as uncertain and useless were quite foreign to Wolff's mind. In this sense he continued the great rationalist tradition of post-Renaissance continental philosophy. He wrote in considerable dependence on Leibniz, whose thought he expressed in a Scholastic and academic form. But though he lacked the originality of Leibniz and his other leading predecessors, he is a figure of importance in German philosophy. And when Kant discusses metaphysics and metaphysical proofs, it is often the Wolffian philosophy which he has in mind. For in his pre-critical period he had studied and assimilated the ideas of Wolff and his followers.

Wolff was born at Breslau, and at first he was destined for the study of theology, though he soon devoted himself to philosophy and lectured on the subject at Leipzig. Some notes on the *Medicina mentis* of Tschirnhaus brought him into contact with Leibniz, and it was on the latter's recommendation that Wolff was appointed professor of mathematics at Halle, where he lectured not only on mathematics but also on the various branches of philosophy. His views aroused, however, the opposition of his pietistic colleagues, who accused him of godlessness and prevailed upon Frederick William I to deprive him of his chair (1723). Indeed, Wolff was ordered, under pain of death, to leave Prussia within two days. He was received at Marburg, where he continued his activity as lecturer and writer, while his case aroused lively discussion throughout Germany. In 1740 he was recalled as professor to Halle by Frederick II, and subsequently he was awarded a title. Meanwhile the influence of his ideas was spreading through the German universities. He died at Halle in 1754.

In some respects Wolff was a thorough rationalist. Thus the ideal method was for him the deductive method. Its use outside formal logic and pure mathematics is rendered possible by the fact that the highest principle, that of non-contradiction, applies to all reality. From this principle we can derive the principle of sufficient reason which, like that of non-contradiction, is an ontological and not merely a logical principle. And the principle of sufficient reason is of great importance in philosophy. The world, for instance, must have its sufficient reason in a transcendent Being, namely in God.

Wolff was, of course, aware that the deductive method alone will not suffice for building up a system of philosophy, and still less for developing the empirical sciences. We cannot get along in the latter without experience and induction, and even in philosophy we require empirical elements. We must often be content, therefore, with probability. Some propositions are absolutely certain; for we cannot assert their opposites without contradiction. But there are many propositions which cannot be reduced to the principle of non-contradiction but which enjoy varying degrees of probability.

In other words, Wolff adopted Leibniz's distinction between truths of reason, the opposites of which cannot be asserted without contradiction and which are necessarily true, and truths of fact, which are not necessarily but contingently true. He applied the distinction in, for example, this way. The world is the system of interrelated finite things, and it is like a machine which works or moves necessarily in a certain way because it is what it is. But this necessity is hypothetical. If God had so willed, the world could have been other than what it is. It follows that there are many true statements about the world, the truth of which is not absolutely necessary. At the same time the world is ultimately composed of substances, each one of which exemplifies an essence that can, ideally at least, be conceived in a clear idea and defined. And if we possessed a knowledge of these essences, we could deduce a series of necessary truths. For when we conceive essences, we abstract from concrete existence and consider the order of possibility, irrespective of God's choice of this particular world. It is, indeed, arguable that Wolff's view that the world could be different from what it is does not fit in with his theory of essences.

For it might be maintained that, given the essences which compose the world, the world-order could only have been what it is. However, the point which I wish to make is that Wolff's rationalism, his emphasis on clear and distinct definable ideas and on deduction, leads him to describe philosophy as the science of the possible, of all possible things, a possible thing being anything which does not involve a contradiction.

Mention has been made of Leibniz, and there is no question, of course, that the latter's philosophy exercised a marked influence on Wolff's thought. We shall see examples of this influence shortly. But in reinstating the idea of essences Wolff makes explicit reference to the Scholastics; and though, given the widespread contempt for Scholasticism at the time, he is careful to maintain that he is improving on their ideas, he makes no secret of the fact that, following Leibniz, he has no sympathy with the wholesale condemnation of their opinions and work. And in point of fact it is quite clear that he was influenced by the Scholastics. But Wolff's concentration on being as essence puts one in mind of Scotus rather than of Aquinas. It was the later Scholasticism rather than the Thomist system which influenced his thought. Thus in his *Ontology* he refers with approval to Suárez, whose writings had enjoyed considerable success in the German universities, even in the Protestant ones.

The influence of Scholasticism can be seen in Wolff's division of philosophy. The fundamental division, which goes back, of course, to Aristotle, is into theoretical and practical philosophy. Theoretical philosophy or metaphysics is subdivided into ontology, dealing with being as such, rational psychology, concerned with the soul, cosmology, which treats of the cosmic system, and rational or natural theology which has as its subject-matter the existence and attributes of God. (Practical philosophy is divided, with Aristotle, into ethics, economics and politics.) The explicit separation of ontology or general metaphysics from natural theology does not go back to the Middle Ages; and it has sometimes been attributed to Wolff himself. But the separation had already been made by the Cartesian Clauberg (1622–65), who spoke of 'ontosophy' rather than of 'ontology', and the later term had been used by Jean-Baptiste Duhamel (1624–1706) a Scholastic, in his *Philosophia universalis*. Moreover, in his *Ontology* Wolff explicitly aimed at improving on the definitions given by the Scholastics and on their treatment of the science of being as being.

And although his division of philosophy differs from that, say, of St. Thomas Aquinas, his hierarchical arrangement of its branches was clearly developed under Scholastic influence.[1] This may not appear to be a matter of much importance; but it is at least interesting to observe that the Scholastic tradition found a continued life in the thought of one of the leading figures of the German Enlightenment, even if, from a strictly Thomist point of view, it was a rather debased form of Scholasticism which found a home in the Wolffian philosophy. This is certainly what is thought by those who, with Professor Gilson, contrast the 'existentialism' of Aquinas and his faithful followers with the 'essentialism' of later Scholastics.[2]

The Leibnizian influence can be clearly seen in Wolff's treatment of substance. Though he avoided the term 'monad', he postulated the existence of imperceptible simple substances which are without extension or figure, and no two of which are perfectly alike. The things which we perceive in the material world are aggregates of these substances or metaphysical atoms; and extension belongs, as with Leibniz, to the phenomenal order. The human body is, of course, also an aggregate of substances. But in man there is a soul which is a simple substance and the existence of which can be proved by reference to the fact of consciousness, self-consciousness and consciousness of the external world. Indeed, as far as the soul's existence is concerned, it is immediately evident to everyone in self-consciousness.

Wolff laid considerable emphasis on consciousness. The soul, as a simple substance, possesses active power; but this power consists in the soul's ability to represent to itself the world. And the different activities of the soul, of which the two fundamental forms are knowing and desiring, are simply different manifestations of this power of representation. As for the relation between soul and body, it must be described in terms of a pre-established harmony. As with Leibniz, there is no direct interaction between soul and body. God had so arranged things that the soul represents to itself the world according to the modifications which take place in the sense-organs of its body.

The principal proof of God's existence for Wolff is a cosmological argument. The world, the system of interrelated finite

---

[1] One must add that Wolff's division of philosophy had a considerable influence on subsequent Scholastic manuals and text-books.

[2] On this matter cf. Gilson's *Being and Some Philosophers* (second edition, corrected and enlarged, Toronto, 1952).

things, requires a sufficient reason for its existence and nature, and this sufficient reason is the divine will, though the divine choice has also its sufficient reason, namely in the attractive power of the best as conceived by God. This means, of course, that Wolff has to follow the main lines of the Leibnizian theodicy. Like Leibniz, he distinguishes between physical, moral and metaphysical evil. The latter, being the imperfection necessarily attendant on finitude, is inseparable from the world. As for physical and moral evil, the world requires at least their possibility. The question is really not whether God could have created the world without evil, but whether there is a sufficient reason for creating a world from which evil, or at least its possibility, cannot be absent. Wolff's answer is that God created the world with a view to being acknowledged, honoured and praised by man.

In all this we are obviously very far from Thomasius's view that the human mind is incapacitated for the attainment of truth in metaphysics and natural theology. Besides his cosmological proof of God's existence Wolff accepted the ontological argument, being persuaded that the development of this argument by Leibniz and himself had rendered it immune from the usual lines of criticism. The accusation of atheism which was brought against Wolff was absurd. But it is understandable that his enemies among pietists thought that he was putting reason in the place of faith and undermining their conception of religion.

Just as Wolff rejected the theory of man's intellectual incapacity in the sphere of metaphysics, so also did he reject the theory of man's moral incapacity, namely that man left to himself is incapable of doing anything but sin. His moral theory was based on the idea of perfection. The good is defined as that which makes us and our condition more perfect, while the bad is defined as that which makes us and our condition more imperfect. But Wolff admits that it was long ago recognized 'by the ancients' that we will only that which we regard as good, as in some way perfecting us, and that we will nothing which we regard as evil. In other words, he admits the Scholastic saying that man always chooses *sub specie boni*. Obviously, therefore, he has to find some criterion for distinguishing between good in the wide sense of the term, namely as including whatever is the object of the will's choice, and good in the moral sense, namely what we ought to strive for or choose. True, he emphasizes the idea of the perfection of our nature. But it is clear that this concept must be given some definite content which will enable us to discriminate between moral and immoral actions. In trying to do this Wolff gives prominence to the idea of the harmonization of the manifold elements of human nature under the rule of reason and of man's interior and exterior conditions. Some writers have maintained that by including external good in the *summum bonum* or end of human moral endeavour Wolff was giving expression to a 'Protestant ethic'. But, many centuries before, Aristotle had included a sufficiency of external goods in the good of man. In any case it must be noted that Wolff is anxious to avoid the individualism which may appear to be connected with an ethic of self-perfection. He therefore emphasizes the fact that man can perfect himself only if he strives to help his fellow-men and to rise above his purely egoistic impulses. Promotion of God's honour and of the common good belong to the idea of self-perfection. The 'natural law' ordains, therefore, that we should do that which makes ourselves and our condition and the condition of others more perfect, and that we should not do that which makes ourselves or others more imperfect.

Wolff asserts freedom as a condition of the moral life. But it is not at all easy for him to explain how freedom is possible, if it means that a man could have made another choice than the one that he has actually made. For, as we have seen, he regards Nature as analogous to a machine in which all movements are determined and (hypothetically) necessary. However, in spite of this difficulty Wolff continued to affirm that man is free. In justification of this position he appeals to the theory of the pre-established harmony between soul and body. There is no direct interaction between them. Hence, bodily conditions and sensual impulses, for example, cannot determine the soul's choices. Its choices spring from its own spontaneity, and they are therefore free.

But Wolff is also involved in difficulties about the relation of intellect to will in the moral life. According to him, a constant will to do only what corresponds with the natural moral law is the beginning and foundation of virtue. But can this constant direction of the will be produced by the intellect or reason, by knowledge of moral good and evil? Must not this production be an act of the will itself? As the constant direction of the will towards the objective moral good is not something which is given from the start, and as there is difficulty in showing how it can be produced by the intellect alone, Wolff stresses the need for and the important part played by education in the moral life. At the same time it is intellectual education, the formation of clear and distinct ideas, which he emphasizes. Hence, even if Wolff does not provide a completely satisfactory answer to the question how man by his own efforts can lead a truly moral life, it is clear that rationalism has for him the last word. The principal end of education is to produce those clear ideas of the moral vocation of man which can serve as motive-forces for the will. What is at the back of his mind seems clear enough. The will naturally seeks the good. But man can have mistaken ideas of the good. Hence the importance of developing true, clear and adequate ideas. The will can be rightly directed only by the intellect. Wolff may not succeed in explaining precisely how the intellect can govern the will and produce the right desires; but that it can do so in his opinion is beyond doubt.

Wolff sometimes speaks as though the aim of the education of the mind is to produce useful ideas. And if we bear in mind his insistence, when talking about our duties to ourselves and to our neighbour, that man ought to work and by this means maintain himself and promote the common good, we may perhaps be inclined to draw the conclusion that his moral ideal is simply that of the decent, hard-working citizen. We may conclude, in other words, that he has a thoroughly bourgeois conception of man's moral vocation, a conception which can be described as a secularized form of the Protestant notion of man's vocation in this world. But though this conception forms one element in his thought, it is not the only element. For he gives to the term 'useful' a wide range of meaning. Being useful to society does not mean simply faithful service as a manual labourer or as an official of some sort. The artist and the philosopher, for instance, develop their potentialities, perfect themselves, and are 'useful' to society. Education for life should not be taken in a narrow, Philistine sense. Wolff tries to combine a wide idea of education and self-perfection with an insistence on the duty of serving the common good, which he looks on as a characteristic note of his moral philosophy.

In view of Kant's idea that man has an obligation to seek moral perfection and that this perfection cannot be attained in a finite time, it is worth remarking that for Wolff before him moral perfection is not something which can be definitely attained here and now. Man cannot reach his objective and then rest on his oars, so to speak. The obligation to seek moral perfection involves an obligation to go on continually striving towards it, an obligation to strive endlessly after the complete harmonization of impulses and affects under the rule of reason. And this obligation falls both on the individual and on the human race in common.

On man's duties are based his rights. By nature all men are equal, and they have the same duties as men. They have, therefore, the same rights. For we have a natural right to all that enables us to fulfil our natural duties. There are also, of course, acquired rights; but as far as natural rights are concerned, all men are equal.

Wolff bases the State on a contract. But it has a natural justification in the fact that it is only in a large society that man can obtain for himself in sufficient measure the goods of life and defend them against aggression. The State exists, therefore, to promote the common good. As for government, this rests ultimately on the consent of the citizens, who may reserve to themselves the supreme power or transfer it to some form of government. Governmental power extends over only those activities of the citizens which are related to the attainment of the common good. However, Wolff conceded to the government wide powers of supervision with a view to the physical and spiritual well-being of the citizens. For he interpreted the common good in terms of human perfection, and not in purely economic terms.

Nations, says Wolff in his *Jus Gentium*,[1] are to be regarded as 'individual free persons living in a state of nature'. And just as there is a natural moral law which obliges individual men and gives rise to rights, so is there a natural law of nations or necessary law of nations, which is immutable and which gives rise to equal rights. This law is the natural moral law as applied to nations.

Further, all nations must be understood to have formed together, by presumed consent, a supreme State. For nature itself compels nations to form an international society for their common good. We must conclude, therefore, that the nations as a whole possess the right of compelling individual nations to fulfil their obligations towards the greater society. And just as in a democratic State the will of the majority must be considered to represent the will of the whole people, so in the supreme State the will of the majority of nations must be taken to represent the will of all nations. But how is this to be expressed, when nations cannot meet together in the way that is possible for groups of individuals? According to Wolff, we must take that to be the will of all nations

[1] *Prolegomena*, 2.

upon which they would agree if they followed right reason. And from this he concludes that what has been approved by the 'more civilized nations' is the law of nations.

The law derived from the concept of a society of nations is called by Wolff the 'voluntary law of nations'. And he places it under the general heading of 'the positive law of nations', together with stipulative law, resting on the express consent of nations, and customary law, resting on their tacit consent. But, quite apart from possible criticism of the idea of a supreme State with a fictitious ruler, it would seem more natural to place what Wolff calls the *jus gentium voluntarium* under the heading of the *jus gentium naturale* rather than under that of the *jus positivum*. For the latter classification would seem to demand the existence of an actual supreme or universal society rather than of a presumed society of nations. However, in asserting the existence of 'the voluntary law of nations' Wolff was influenced by Grotius, to whom he appeals, though he finds fault with the latter for not having distinguished properly between voluntary, stipulative and customary law. In any case the idea of a society of nations is of unquestionable value, whether we accept or reject Wolff's use of the idea.

If Wolff is compared with thinkers such as Descartes, Spinoza and Leibniz, he must doubtless be reckoned a minor figure in the history of philosophy. But if he is looked at in the context of the development of German thought, one's judgment will be different. Apart from Leibniz, Germany had produced little in the way of philosophy: the great period of German philosophy lay in the future. But meanwhile Wolff acted as a kind of philosophical educator of his nation. He is often accused, no doubt with justice, of aridity, dogmatism and formalism. But because of its comprehensiveness and its formal and orderly arrangement his system was able to provide a school-philosophy for the German universities. His influence spread throughout Germany and beyond, and his ideas may be said to have dominated in the German universities until the rise of the Kantian criticism. The system, which was no mean achievement in itself, thus stimulated the growth of philosophical reflection. He triumphed over his theological opponents, even if his philosophy was to be conquered by that of Kant and his successors. In other words, he occupies an important place in the history of German thought, and no accusations of lack of originality or of formalism can rob him of it.

3. The term 'Leibniz-Wolffian philosophy', which was rejected by Wolff himself, was coined by Georg Bernhard Bilfinger (1693–1750), who was for a time professor of philosophy at St. Petersburg and later (from 1731) professor of theology at Tübingen. *Dilucidationes philosophicae de Deo, anima humana, mundo et generalibus rerum affectionibus* (1725) helped to spread Wolff's system, though he did not follow the latter in everything. Among other disciples of Wolff we may name Ludwig Philipp Thümmig (1697–1728), who lost his chair at Halle at the same time as Wolff, and Johann Christoph Gottsched (1700–66), author of *Erste Gründe der gesamten Weltweisheit* (1733), who attempted to utilize the Wolffian philosophy in literary criticism. Mention must also be made of Martin Knutzen (1713–51), if for no other reason than that from 1734 he was professor of logic and metaphysics at Königsberg and numbered Kant among his hearers. He was a mathematician and astronomer as well as a philosopher, and he helped to arouse Kant's interest in Newtonian science. In the field of philosophy he was influenced by Leibniz and Wolff, but he was at the same time an independent thinker. Thus he abandoned the theory of the pre-established harmony in favour of a theory of efficient causality. Needless to say, Knutzen was not responsible for Kant's critical philosophy, but his lectures were one of the factors which contributed to form the latter's philosophical views in his pre-critical period. In religion Knutzen was inclined to pietism; but under the influence of Wolff he greatly modified the rejection of natural or philosophical theology which was one of the characteristics of the pietistic movement. Indeed, he published a *Philosophical Proof of the Truth of the Christian Religion* (1740). In other words, he tried to combine pietistic spirituality with Wolffian 'rationalism'.

A more important figure is Alexander Gottlieb Baumgarten (1714–62), professor at Frankfurt on the Oder, who produced a number of text-books in which he expounded and developed the Wolffian philosophy. His *Metaphysics*, for example, was used by Kant in his lectures, though not, of course, without criticism of its contents. But Baumgarten's importance does not lie primarily in his relationship to Kant, nor in his enrichment of the German philosophical vocabulary by his translations of Latin terms; it lies in the fact that he was the real founder of German aesthetic theory. In his *Meditationes philosophicae de nonnullis ad poema pertinentibus* (1735), which has been translated into English under the title *Reflections on Poetry*, he coined the word 'aesthetics' (*aesthetica*), and he developed his theories in the two volumes of his *Aesthetica* (1750–8).

Baumgarten's approach to aesthetics was determined to a great extent by Wolff's philosophy. The latter had deliberately omitted a treatment of art and of the beautiful; for the subject did not fit into the scheme of his philosophy. He was concerned with 'distinct' concepts, that is, with concepts which are communicable in words: he was not concerned with concepts which are 'clear' but not 'distinct', that is, with concepts which are clear but not communicable in words, such as the concept of a particular colour. And as he believed that the concepts concerned with the enjoyment of beauty are not distinct, he omitted a treatment of aesthetics. Further, when considering man's powers or faculties, he concentrated on the 'higher powers' (*vires superiores*), leaving aside to all intents and purposes the 'lower powers' (*vires inferiores*). And his belief that aesthetic enjoyment is a function of the lower powers, the faculties of sensation, was thus also a reason for omitting consideration of aesthetic theory. There was, therefore, a gap in the Wolffian philosophy, which Baumgarten set out to fill. And for a disciple of Wolff this involved a consideration of man's sensitive powers. The need for such a consideration had been rendered all the more acute by the increasing knowledge in Germany of British empiricism.

Baumgarten's idea of aesthetics was humanistic in character, in the sense that it was bound up with a view of man. At the beginning of the *Aesthetics* he remarks that 'the philosopher is a man among men; nor does he rightly think so great a part of human knowledge alien to himself'.[1] The philosopher must strive after a knowledge of sensibility, which plays such an important part in human life, and though he may not be able to create the beautiful as the artist does, he should seek for a systematic knowledge of the beautiful. Indeed, Baumgarten defines aesthetics as the science of the beautiful and of beautiful things. But beauty is perfection in the field of sensibility or sense knowledge. Hence aesthetics is the science of the perfection of sense knowledge. 'The goal of aesthetics is the perfection of sense knowledge as such. And this is beauty.'[2]

Aesthetics is also described by Baumgarten as the art of thinking beautifully (*ars pulchre cogitandi*). This unfortunate description or definition obviously lends itself to misunderstanding and misuse.

[1] Section 6.   [2] *Aesthetics*, section 14.

But Baumgarten was not saying that the science of aesthetics consists in knowing how to think 'beautiful thoughts'; he was referring to the art of using the so-called lower faculties properly with a view to their 'perfection'. And if we put his various definitions or descriptions together, we can say that he looked to aesthetics to provide a psychology of sensation, a logic of the senses, and a system for aesthetic criticism.

The idea of a logic of the senses is of importance. As a follower of Wolff, Baumgarten naturally arranged the philosophical sciences in a hierarchical order, and equally naturally he placed aesthetics in a subordinate position. For it is concerned with the inferior powers and with inferior knowledge. Aesthetics, if it is a science at all, must be the activity of thought; but as it does not treat of the province of distinct ideas, it must take an inferior place in the ladder, so to speak, of knowledge. At the same time Baumgarten saw that it will not do to treat aesthetic intuition as a form of purely logical thinking which has somehow failed to live up to the standards of logical thought. Yet it is not 'illogical'. Aesthetic intuition has its own inner law, its own logic. This is why he speaks of aesthetics as the art of the analogue of reason. 'Aesthetics (the theory of the liberal arts, inferior knowledge, the art of thinking beautifully, the analogue of reason) is the science of sensitive knowledge.'[1] Baumgarten may not always indicate very clearly whether he is speaking of aesthetic intuition itself or of our reflective and conceptual representation of it; but two things at least can be said. First, sensibility is not to be excluded from the sphere of knowledge on the ground that 'sense knowledge' is not purely logical or mathematical knowledge. Secondly, it is a peculiar kind of knowledge. For dealing with it we require a special epistemology, inferior knowledge or theory of knowledge (*gnoseologia inferior*). For the law which governs aesthetic intuition cannot be expressed in distinct and purely logical concepts; it is an 'analogue of reason'. Pure logic means abstraction, and abstraction means impoverishment, in the sense that the concrete and individual is sacrificed in favour of the abstract and universal. But aesthetic intuition bridges the gulf between the individual and the universal, the concrete and the abstract; its 'truth' is found within concrete qualities. And beauty is something which cannot be expressed in abstract concepts.

By including a variety of themes under the general heading of

[1] *Aesthetics*, section 1; cf. also *Prolegomena*, section 1.

aesthetics Baumgarten did not facilitate the making of clear generalizations. But the salient point of his aesthetic theory is his recognition of the fact that concepts such as beauty have their own peculiar use. He thus established aesthetics as an independent branch of philosophical inquiry. When speaking, for example, of the language of poetry, he makes it clear that we cannot force all uses of language into the same mould and interpret them in the same way. In poetry the words remain, as it were, saturated with immediate sensory content: 'the perfect language of sense is poetry'.[1] The language of poetry must be differentiated from the language of, say, physical science: the words do not function in the same way. But it does not follow that poetic statements are nonsense. They express and evoke vivid intuitions which are not irrational but possess their own analogue of reason. In Baumgarten's phrase they have the 'life of knowledge' (*vita cognitionis*).

We certainly ought not to exaggerate the importance of Baumgarten. In the first place he was not 'the father of aesthetics'. To go no further back in history, Shaftesbury and Hutcheson, for example, had already written on the subject in England. In the second place extravagant praise has sometimes been given to his achievements, and as an antidote we have only to consider the judgment of Benedetto Croce that 'save in its title and its first definitions Baumgarten's *Aesthetic* is covered with the mould of antiquity and commonplace'.[2] At the same time his importance in the development of aesthetic theory in Germany is undeniable. It is doubtless true, as Croce remarks, that he is of importance in the history of aesthetics as 'a science in formation . . . of aesthetics *condenda* not *condita*';[3] but he did at least recognize not only that there is such a thing as the philosophy of aesthetics but also that the language of aesthetics has its own peculiarities. He doubtless interpreted the subject in the light of the Wolffian philosophy; and he is open to the accusation of having spoken in too intellectualist terms, 'in terms of knowledge' and 'truth', for instance. But the point to remark is that he felt the inadequacy of a purely rationalist account of aesthetic intuition and enjoyment and that he paved the way for a further development of aesthetic theory. Whatever Baumgarten's shortcomings may have been he saw that there is a side of human life and activity which is a fit object of philosophical consideration but which cannot be understood by anyone who is

---

[1] *Meditations*, section 9.
[2] *Aesthetic*, translated by D. Ainslie, p. 218.
[3] *Ibid.*, p. 219.

determined to bring it into the sphere of abstract logical thinking on pain of exclusion from philosophy altogether.

Among the disciples of Baumgarten was Georg Friedrich Meier (1718–77) who expounded his master's doctrines at Halle and published *Principles of all the Beautiful Sciences* (*Anfangsgründe aller schönen Wissenschaften*) in three volumes (1748–50) and *Considerations on the First Principles of all Fine Arts and Sciences* (*Betrachtungen über den ersten Grundsätzen aller schönen Künste und Wissenchaften*) in 1757. As far as aesthetic theory is concerned, Moses Mendelssohn (1729–86), who will be mentioned again in the next chapter, was also influenced by Baumgarten. But there is no point in giving a list of names. It is sufficient to say that there was a plentiful crop of writings on aesthetics in the second half of the eighteenth century. Indeed in his *Sketch of the History and Literature of Aesthetics* (1799), J. Koller asserted that patriotic youth would be pleased to note that Germany had produced more literature on the subject than any other country.

Turning to Wolff's opponents and critics, we may mention first Joachim Lange (1670–1744) of Halle, who was one of the principal agents in obtaining Wolff's expulsion from the university in the name of orthodoxy and piety. A much more philosophically-minded thinker was Andrew Rüdiger (1673–1731), who lectured at Halle and Leipzig and attacked the notion that the mathematical method can be applied in philosophy. Mathematics is concerned with the sphere of the possible, whereas philosophy is concerned with the actual. The philosopher, therefore, should build on the foundation of experience, as given in sense-perception and self-consciousness; and he should derive his fundamental definitions and axioms from this source. Rüdiger also attacked, for example, the theory of a pre-established harmony between soul and body. The soul is extended, and there is physical interaction between soul and body.

Another opponent of Wolff was Christian August Crusius (1715–75), professor of philosophy and theology at Leipzig, who attacked the optimism and determinism of the Leibniz-Wolffian philosophy. As there are free beings in the world, namely men, we cannot interpret the world-system as a pre-established harmony. Further, Crusius criticized the use made by Leibniz and Wolff of the principle of sufficient reason, though this did not prevent him from substituting a fundamental principle of his own, namely the proposition that what cannot be thought is false and that what cannot be thought of as false is true.[1] From this illuminating proposition he derived three other principles; the principle of contradiction, that nothing can be and not be at the same time; the principle of inseparables, that those things which cannot be thought of separately cannot exist separately; and the principle of incompatibles, that those things which cannot be thought of as conjoined cannot exist in a state of conjunction. Obviously, Crusius was not really opposed to the spirit of Wolff's philosophy, even if he appeared to his contemporaries to be an opponent of Wolff because he rejected some of the latter's characteristic theses. Incidentally, Kant had a high opinion of Crusius, though he criticized his notion of metaphysics.

[1] The principle is applied by Crusius in this way, for example. The non-existence of the world is thinkable. Therefore it must have been created. Therefore there is a God.

CHAPTER VI

THE GERMAN ENLIGHTENMENT (2)

Introductory remarks; Frederick the Great; the 'popular philo-
sophers'—Deism: Reimarus; Mendelssohn—Lessing—Psycho-
logy—Educational theory.

1. (i) THE philosophy of Wolff and of his followers was in one
sense a high point of the German *Aufklärung*. It constituted a
programme, as it were, for bringing all provinces of human mental
activity before the bar of reason. This was, of course, the reason
why the pietistic Lutheran theologians opposed Wolff; for they
thought that his rationalism was the enemy of faith. The Wolffian
system also represented the rise of the educated middle class.
Reason should judge, for example, what is and what is not
acceptable in belief about God; the personal convictions of the
monarch or local sovereign should not be the deciding factor in
settling the religion of a people. Again, 'taste' and aesthetic judgment are not the prerogative of the aristocracy or of genius: the
philosophic reason can extend its sway to cover the aesthetic field.
Philosophy, it is true, is carried on by comparatively few people;
but reason is in itself universal. Belief, morals, forms of State and
government, aesthetics, all are subject to reason's impersonal
judgment.

These aspects of the Wolffian philosophy and its derivatives link
it with the general movement of the Enlightenment. At the same
time Wolff's system was, as we have seen, closely connected with
the thought of Leibniz, and so with the movement of rationalist
metaphysics in post-Renaissance philosophy on the European
continent. It thus stands somewhat apart from the spirit of the
Enlightenment as manifested in France and England. But in the
phase of the *Aufklärung* which will be briefly considered in this
chapter the influence of French and English thought becomes
more marked.

(ii) If one wishes to find a symbol of this influence, one can
hardly do better than consider Frederick the Great (1712–86).
Brought up by a French governess and tutor, he developed an
enthusiasm for French thought and literature, accompanied by a
certain contempt for German literature, which showed itself in his

preference for speaking and writing in the French language. True, he had at one time a strong sympathy with the philosophies of Leibniz and Wolff. And, as we saw in the last chapter, he reinstated the latter at Halle. Frederick had no sympathy with the Lutheran theologians who had secured Wolff's dismissal by Frederick William I. As far as religious beliefs were concerned, he was strongly in favour of toleration, not only of different dogmatic systems, but also of rationalism, agnosticism and even atheism. That a man of Wolff's eminence should be exiled from Prussia because he was not an adherent of pietism was something which the king could not countenance. In the course of time, however, his opinion of Wolff as a thinker changed, and he came under the predominating influence of French and English thought. In the chapters on the French Enlightenment we saw how Frederick invited philosophers such as Voltaire and Maupertuis to Potsdam, where he liked to converse with them on philosophical and literary matters. As for English thought, he had a high opinion of Locke and arranged for lectures to be given on his philosophy at Halle.

Though Frederick the Great believed in God, he had a strong inclination to scepticism; and Bayle was a writer whom he greatly appreciated. The king was very much of a freethinker. At the same time he developed a veneration for Marcus Aurelius, the Stoic emperor, and, like the Stoics, he laid great emphasis on the sense of duty and on virtue. Thus in his *Essay on Self-love considered as the Principle of Morals* (1770) he tried to show that self-love can be satisfied only through the attainment and practice of virtue which is the true good of man.

In view of Frederick's military exploits and of his successful determination to raise the political and military status of Prussia one may be tempted to regard the 'philosopher of Sans souci', as he called himself, with a cynical eye. But his praise of Marcus Aurelius was not merely idle talk. Nobody would wish to depict the Prussian monarch as a kind of uncanonized saint; but he undoubtedly possessed a strong sense of duty and of his reponsibilities, and his statement in *Antimachiavell* (1740) that the prince should regard himself as the first servant of his people was meant seriously. A despot he may have been; but he was an enlightened despot who concerned himself, for example, with enforcing the impartial administration of justice and with promoting the spread of education, from elementary education up to the reorganization and development of the Prussian Academy.[1] Through this concern with education Frederick was one of the leading figures of the German Enlightenment.

(iii) The spread of philosophical ideas in Germany was promoted by the so-called 'popular philosophers' who, without being creative thinkers, endeavoured to purvey philosophy to the educated public. Thus Christian Garve (1742-98) translated into German a number of works by English moralists, such as Ferguson, Paley and Adam Smith. Friedrich Justus Riedel (1742-85) helped to spread aesthetic ideas by his *Theory of the Fine Arts and Sciences* (1767), which has been called a mere compilation. Christian Friedrich Nicolai (1733-1811) exercised a considerable influence through his editorship, first of the *Bibliothek der schönen Wissenschaften* (1757-8), then of the *Briefe, die neueste Litteratur betreffend* (1759-65), and finally of the *Allgemeine deutsche Bibliothek* (1765-1805), literary journals which their editor succeeded in making pay for themselves. One may also mention, though he was scarcely a philosopher in the academic sense, Christoph Martin Wieland (1733-1813), first a pietist and then a literary figure and poet, who translated into German twenty-two plays of Shakespeare and, in his autobiographical novel, *Agathon* (1766), traced the history of the self-development of a young man, chiefly through the successive influences of different philosophies.

2. One effect of the influence of English and French thought on German thought was the rise of deism. In 1741 Tindal's *Christianity as old as the Creation* had appeared in German, and right at the beginning of the century John Toland had spent some time visiting the Courts of Hanover and Berlin.

(i) Prominent among the German deists was Hermann Samuel Reimarus (1694-1768), professor of Hebrew and Oriental languages at the Hamburg Gymnasium. His chief work was an *Apology for or Defence of the rational Worshippers of God* (*Apologie oder Schutzschrift für die vernünftigen Verehrer Gottes*). Reimarus did not publish the work, but in 1774-7 Lessing published some portions under the title of the *Wolffenbüttel Fragments*. Lessing did not give the name of the author, but pretended that he had found these fragments at Wolffenbüttel. Another portion was published at Berlin in 1786 under the pseudonym of C. A. E. Schmidt, and further excerpts appeared in 1850-2.

---

[1] It was his concern with education which made Frederick refuse to allow the publication in his territories of Pope Clement XIV's Bull suppressing the Society of Jesus. He did not wish the schools maintained by the Jesuits to be dissolved.

On the one hand Reimarus was opposed to purely materialistic mechanism. The world, as an intelligible system, is the self-revelation of God: the world-order is inexplicable without God. On the other hand he was a strong opponent of supernatural religion. The world is itself the divine revelation, and other so-called revelations are human inventions. Further, the idea of the world as a causally interconnected mechanical system is the great achievement of modern thought; and we can no longer accept the idea of miraculous and supernatural divine revelation. Miracles would be unworthy of God; for God achieves His purposes through a rationally intelligible system. In other words, Reimarus's natural theology follows the familiar deistic pattern.

(ii) The Jewish philosopher, Moses Mendelssohn (1729–86), who was a friend of Lessing and a correspondent of Kant, may be reckoned as one of the 'popular philosophers', in the sense that he helped to popularize the religious and philosophical ideas of the Enlightenment. But he is of some interest for his own sake.

In 1755 Lessing and Mendelssohn published an essay with the, at first sight at least, startling title, *Pope a Metaphysician!* (*Pope ein Metaphysiker!*). The Prussian Academy had announced an essay competition on the subject of Alexander Pope's alleged philosophical system, which Maupertuis considered to have been a digest of the Leibnizian philosophy. (The object was apparently to deliver an indirect blow at the reputation of Leibniz.) Lessing and Mendelssohn argued, however, that Pope was either a poet or a metaphysician, but not both; and that in point of fact he had no philosophical system. Philosophy and poetry are two quite different things. This differentiation between the conceptual and the aesthetic was expressed by Mendelssohn in more general terms in his *Letters on Sensations* (*Briefe über die Empfindungen*, 1755) and elsewhere. We must discriminate, he says in his fifth *Letter*, between the 'heavenly Venus', which consists in the perfect adequacy of concepts, and the 'earthly Venus' or beauty. Experience of the beautiful is not a matter of knowledge: we cannot grasp it by a process of analysis and definition. It is wrong to think that we should experience more perfect aesthetic enjoyment if we possessed more perfect cognitive powers. Nor is the beautiful an object of desire. In so far as something is desired, it ceases to be, if it ever has been, the object of aesthetic contemplation and enjoyment. Mendelssohn postulates, therefore, a distinct faculty which he calls the 'faculty of approval' (*Billigungsvermögen*). It is a special sign of beauty, he says in *Morgenstunden* (7), that it is contemplated with 'calm pleasure', whether we possess it or not. In thus insisting on the disinterested character of aesthetic contemplation Mendelssohn was writing to some extent under the influence of English aesthetic theory.

In the sphere of religion Mendelssohn maintained that the existence of God is capable of strict proof. His proofs, as given in *Morning Hours* (*Morgenstunden*, 1785), followed more or less the lines of the Wolffian system; and he accepted and defended the ontological argument. God is possible. But pure possibility is incompatible with the idea of a most perfect Being. Therefore God exists.

In his *Phaedo or on the Immortality of the Soul* (*Phädon oder über die Unsterblichkeit der Seele*, 1767) Mendelssohn tried to modernize Plato and argued that the soul is neither a mere harmony of the body nor a corruptible thing which can, as it were, waste away or disappear. Further, the soul has a natural and constant drive towards self-perfection; and it would be incompatible with the divine wisdom and goodness to create the human soul with this natural drive or impulse and then to render its fulfilment impossible by allowing the soul to relapse into nothingness.

The philosopher, therefore, can prove the existence of God and the immortality of the soul, the foundations of natural religion. In doing so he is simply giving a theoretical justification of truths which the human mind, left to itself, spontaneously recognizes, at least in a confused way. But this does not mean that the State is justified in trying to enforce uniform acceptance of specific religious beliefs. Nor is any religious body which demands of its members uniformity of belief entitled to invoke the aid of the State in attaining this end. The State is concerned with actions, not with beliefs. And though it should, of course, encourage, so far as this is compatible with freedom of thought, the formation of ideas which tend to issue in desirable activity, it should not extend its power of coercion from the sphere of action into that of thought. Toleration is the ideal, though, as Locke observed, we cannot tolerate those who seek to substitute intolerance for toleration.

Mendelssohn became involved in a famous dispute with Jacobi about Spinoza and pantheism. But something will be said about this in the section on Lessing, because the debate arose in connection with the latter's alleged Spinozism.

3. When Gotthold Ephraim Lessing (1729–81) entered the University of Leipzig he enrolled as a student of theology. But he soon abandoned theological studies for a literary career; and he is best known, of course, as a dramatist and as a literary and art critic. He must, however, be accorded a place in the history of philosophy. For though he was never a professional and systematic philosopher in the sense that Wolff was, he was deeply interested in philosophical questions, and his somewhat fragmentary ideas exercised considerable influence. More important, however, than any individual idea or thesis is the fact that his writings tended to form a unified literary expression of the spirit of the *Aufklärung*. This should not be taken to mean that his works simply reflected the ideas of others, as a kind of mirror. They did do this to some extent, of course. For example, *Nathan the Wise* (*Nathan der Weise*, 1779) expressed in dramatic form the ideal of religious toleration which was a prominent feature of the Enlightenment. But at the same time he developed the ideas which he took over from others. For instance, though he was somewhat influenced by the deism of Reimarus, he developed it partly under the inspiration of his understanding of Spinoza in a direction which put one in mind of later idealism rather than of what is usually understood by deism.

Lessing, as has already been mentioned, published some portions of Reimarus's chief work under the title of *Wolffenbüttel Fragments*. And this action led to his being attacked by some writers, especially, of course, by those who suspected that Lessing himself was the author and who at the same time disagreed with the views expressed in the *Fragments*. But as a matter of fact Lessing's view of religion was not that of Reimarus. The latter was convinced that the fundamental truths of natural religion can be strictly proved, whereas Lessing believed that no system of religious belief can be proved by universally valid arguments. Faith rests on inner experience, not on theoretical proofs.

Again, Lessing did not agree with Reimarus's attitude towards the positive, dogmatic religions. We cannot accept the radical distinction made by the rationalistic deists between the truths of natural religion, which can be proved by reason, and the dogmas of so-called revealed religion, which have to be rejected by the enlightened. I do not mean to suggest, of course, that Lessing accepted the idea of revelation in the orthodox sense. He rejected, for instance, the idea of the Bible as an unquestionable revelation, and he was himself a pioneer of the higher criticism which was to become so fashionable in the nineteenth century. But it was his conviction that the value of religious ideas and beliefs is to be judged by their effect on conduct or by their ability to affect conduct in a desirable way. The Christian way of life was already in existence not only before the canon of the New Testament was fixed but also before any of the Gospels were written. And criticism of the documents cannot affect the value of this way of life. Obviously, therefore, if all religious beliefs rest ultimately on experience, and if their value is to be estimated primarily by their tendency to promote moral perfection, the deistic distinction between the rationally provable truths of natural religion and the man-made dogmas of Christianity tends to fall away and disappear. Lessing's interpretation of the Christian dogmas was not the orthodox interpretation; but at the same time it allowed him to give a more positive valuation to Christianity than the rationalistic deists felt able to give it.

Lessing did not mean, of course, that in no case are better reasons available for accepting one religious or philosophical position rather than another. But for him it was a question of comparative degrees of truth and of an unending approximation to absolute truth rather than one of attaining at any given moment an absolute truth possessing final and universal validity. This point of view is symbolized by his famous remark that if God were to offer him with the right hand the complete truth and with the left the unending search for truth, he would choose the latter, even if it meant that he would always be in error. The possession of pure and final truth is for God alone.

This attitude has not unnaturally been criticized on various grounds. For example, the objection has often been made that, given his denial of man's possession of absolute and immutable truth, Lessing has no criterion for distinguishing degrees of truth. He can, indeed, maintain that degrees of truth are to be judged by their tendencies to promote different lines of conduct. But a problem obviously recurs in regard to distinguishing between more and less desirable types of conduct, between the moral and the immoral, and so on. But it is not possible to enter into discussion of these questions here. It is sufficient to point out in passing that such problems arise. The relevant point in a sketch of Lessing's ideas is rather the shift from the rationalist attitude of the deists to a 'dynamic', not to say fluid, idea of truth. The latter reappeared later on in contexts very different from that of Lessing's thought.

Lessing's idea of truth stands in close relation to his idea of history. In the *Education of the Human Race* (*Die Erziehung des Menschengeschlechts*, 1780) he asserts that 'what education is to the individual human being, that revelation is to the whole human race'.[1] Education is revelation made to the individual while revelation is the continual education of the human race. For Lessing, therefore, revelation means the divine education of the human race in history. It is a process which has been always going on, which is still taking place and which will continue in the future.

Further, revelation as the education of the human race in general is analogous to the education of the individual. The child is educated by means of sensible rewards and punishments. And in the childhood of the human race God could give 'no other religion, no other law, than one through the observance of or non-observance of which His people hoped or feared to be happy or unhappy here on earth'.[2] The childhood of the human race corresponds, therefore, more or less to the state of affairs depicted in the Old Testament. This is followed by the boyhood or youth of the human race, corresponding to the New Testament. Nobler motives for moral conduct than terrestrial punishments and rewards are brought to the fore; the immortality of the soul and eternal reward and punishment in the hereafter are preached. At the same time the conception of God as the God of Israel develops into the conception of the universal Father; and the ideal of inner purity of heart as a preparation for heaven takes the place of mere outward obedience to a law with a view to attaining temporal prosperity. To be sure, Christians have added theological speculations of their own to the teaching of Christ; but we should recognize in them a positive value. For they have stimulated the exercise of the reason and through them man has accustomed himself to think about spiritual things. Lessing mentions and rationalizes some particular dogmas; but the important point is not so much that he rationalizes them as that he sees in them a positive value. On this point he looks forward to Hegel rather than backwards to the deists. Finally, there is the manhood of the human race. 'It will certainly come, the time of a new, eternal Gospel, which has been promised to us in the elementary books of the New

---

[1] Section 1.   [2] *Education of the Human Race*, section 17.

Covenant.'[1] The term 'elementary books' is not a term of abuse,
For Lessing the books of the Old Testament are *Elementarbücher*
in comparison with the New Testament, while the books of the
latter are *Elementarbücher* in comparison with the further stage of
divine revelation. In this third stage of revelation man will do
good for the sake of the good and not for the sake of reward, either
terrestrial or celestial. Lessing lays the emphasis, therefore, on the
moral education of the human race. This is an unending process;
and Lessing even suggests a theory of palingenesis or reincarnation.
To say that he asserts the theory would be to say too much: he
suggests it in a series of questions. 'Why could not each individual
human being not have been present more than once in this world?
Is this hypothesis ridiculous because it is the oldest? . . . Why
should I not return as often as I have been to acquire new
knowledge, new capacities?'[2]

In 1783 Jacobi (whose ideas will be outlined in the next chapter)
wrote to Mendelssohn that when he had visited Lessing not long
before the latter's death, Lessing had openly admitted that he
was a Spinozist. To Jacobi this was a shocking admission; for he
held that pantheism was simply atheism under another name. As
for Mendelssohn, he was not a pantheist; but he was offended and
upset by Jacobi's correspondence, which he took as an attack not
only on Lessing but also, even if indirectly, on himself, as he was
planning an edition of Lessing's works. He therefore in his turn
attacked Jacobi in *Morning Hours*, whereupon the latter published
a reply, together with his correspondence with Mendelssohn
(1785). Both Herder and Goethe were drawn into the controversy,
and both disagreed with Jacobi's identification of Spinoza's
doctrine with atheism.

What Lessing said to Jacobi seems to have been that the
orthodox ideas of God were no longer of any use to him, that God
is one and all, and that if he had to call himself a disciple of any-
body, he could name nobody but Spinoza. And even if we allow
for the possibility of Lessing having taken a pleasure in shocking
Jacobi, there seems to be no doubt that he had been influenced by
Spinoza and that he recognized an affinity between his later ideas
of God and those of the great Jewish philosopher. Lessing believed,
for example, that human actions are determined. The world is one
system in which God is ultimately the universal cause. Further,
he clearly suggests that all things are comprised within the divine

---

[1] *Education of the Human Race*, section 86.   [2] *Ibid.*, sections 94–8.

Being. To see this we have only to look, for example, at the paragraphs entitled *On the Reality of Things outside God*, a short essay written for Mendelssohn. Referring to the theory that existent things are different from the divine ideas of these things, he asks: 'Why should not the ideas which God has of real things be these real things themselves?' It will be objected that in this case there are contingent things in the immutable essence of God. But 'has it never occurred to you, who are compelled to attribute to God ideas of contingent things, that ideas of contingent things are contingent ideas?' Lessing doubtless attached much more value to individuality than Spinoza did, and, as we have seen, he laid great stress on the movement of history towards a goal, that of moral perfection. His theories thus looked forward to some extent to later idealism with its emphasis on historical development rather than backward to Spinoza. But the question is not whether Lessing interpreted Spinoza correctly but whether there was some autobiographical truth in his remarks to Jacobi. And it seems to be clear that there was.

In one sense, of course, the so-called *Pantheismusstreit* (pantheism controversy) was not very profitable. The question whether pantheism is atheism under another name, is one which is best dealt with by defining terms. But the controversy had the effect of stimulating interest in Spinoza's philosophy, ideas about which were vague and inexact.

In the field of aesthetic theory Lessing set himself in his *Laokoon* (1766) to analyse the specific differentiating characteristics of poetry and of formative art, that is, painting and sculpture. The great critic Winckelmann (1717–68) had remarked that the artistic effect of the Laokoon in the Vatican is the same as that of Virgil's description of the Laocoon story in the *Aeneid*. Lessing used this remark as a point of departure. We have already seen how, in connection with Pope, he made a sharp distinction between philosophy and poetry. In the *Laokoon* he maintained that poetry is concerned with presenting human actions, and through them the life of the soul; and for this reason he condemned pictorially descriptive poetry. Sculpture, however, is concerned with the presentation of the body, particularly of ideal corporeal beauty. Further, Lessing tried to show how the materials employed by the different arts determine their characteristics.

If human action is the specific theme of poetry, this is particularly true of the drama, a subject to which Lessing gave his attention in the *Hamburgische Dramaturgie* (1767–9). In this work he insisted on the unity of the drama, a unity which consists essentially in unity of action. According to Lessing, the *Poetics* of Aristotle, the fruit of reflection on the great Greek tragedies, is 'as much an infallible work as the *Elements of Euclid*' (*Hamburgische Dramaturgie*, last chapter). At the same time he strongly attacked the French preoccupation with the 'three unities'. They misunderstood Aristotle when they insisted on unity of time and place as essential characteristics of drama. If they were right, Shakespeare would be no true dramatist. Lessing also made his own Aristotle's statement about the end of tragedy being 'the purging of pity and fear', interpreting pity as compassion, in a literal sense, and fear as self-regarding. Further, Aristotle was right in finding the essence of art in imitation. Drama imitates human actions; and tragedy imitates or presents a unity of human action in such a way as to ennoble man through its arousing of and 'purifying' of the passions of pity and fear. It has, therefore, a moral purpose.

These somewhat random, and in any case bald, observations give, it is true, a highly inadequate picture of Lessing as a writer on aesthetic theory and as a critic of the fine arts. He was not, indeed, an original thinker, in the sense of one who proposes new ideas in philosophy or in aesthetic theory. In the latter sphere he was much influenced by French, English and Swiss writers and, in regard to drama, by Aristotle. But though most of his ideas can be paralleled elsewhere, he had the gift of making these ideas live, and in this sense at least he was original and creative. In the preface to *Laokoon* he remarks that 'we Germans have no lack of systematic books'. His own work, he says, may not be as systematic and concise as that of Baumgarten, but he can flatter himself that whereas the latter admitted having taken many of the examples cited in his *Aesthetics* from Gesner's writings, 'my own example will taste more of the sources'. In other words, he endeavoured, as one would expect of a man who was himself a dramatist and poet, to base his aesthetic reflections on consideration of actual works of art and literature. It is thus doubtless true that Lessing's mind turned away from formalism and that, however dependent he may have been on other writers for his individual ideas, he presented them in a way which stimulated further, if different, reflections. The same can be said of his observations in the spheres of metaphysics and of the philosophy of history.

4. The period of the *Aufklärung* saw the beginnings of the study of psychology in Germany. An important figure in this field was Johann Nikolaus Tetens (1736–1807), who was professor of philosophy at Kiel for a time. In 1789 he accepted an invitation to take up a post at Copenhagen.

The general tendency of Tetens's thought was to mediate between the empiricist philosophy of England and the rationalist philosophy of the Continent. He was by no means an anti-metaphysician. Indeed, he published works on metaphysics and on the proofs of God's existence in which he affirmed the possibility and validity of metaphysics and of metaphysical proofs, while at the same time he endeavoured to ascertain why there are so few universally accepted metaphysical positions. But he insisted that in psychology we must start, not with metaphysical pre-suppositions, but with an analysis of psychical phenomena, though this analysis can form the basis for metaphysical reflections on the soul. Here we have an instance of the mediating tendency to which allusion has just been made.

Introspection must constitute the basis for scientific psychology, according to Tetens. But the soul is conscious of itself only in its activities, and of its activities only in so far as they are productive of psychical phenomena. The soul is not its own immediate object of intuition. In classifying the powers or faculties of the soul, therefore, and in attempting to determine the nature of the soul itself as ground of its activities we are necessarily dependent on hypotheses.

Together with the understanding, namely the activity of the soul as thinking and as productive of images, and willing, the activity whereby the soul produces changes (bodily movements, for instance) which are not themselves psychical representations, Tetens recognizes feeling as a distinguishable activity. We can distinguish, therefore, three powers of the soul, understanding, will and feeling, the latter being described as the receptivity or modifiability of the soul. He suggests, however, the hypothesis that these three powers are ultimately reducible to one fundamental power, the power of feeling and of self-activity, which is capable of progressive perfection. It is in the perfectibility of the soul's activity that man's difference from the animals is particularly conspicuous.

Tetens's *Philosophical Essays on Human Nature and Its Development* (2 vols., 1777) showed a predominantly analytic approach to psychology. A rather different approach was represented by the *Essay on the Soul* (1753) of Karl Kasimir von Creuz (1724–70). Like Tetens after him, von Creuz endeavoured to mediate between the English and continental (Leibnizian) philosophies of the soul. And, again like Tetens, he insisted on the empirical foundation of psychology. But he was concerned with reconciling Leibniz's view of the soul as a simple substance or monad with Hume's phenomenalistic analysis of the self. Von Creuz conceded to Hume that we cannot discover a point-like metaphysical ego which has no extension. At the same time he refused to allow that the self can be dissolved into discrete, separate phenomena. It has, indeed, parts, and in this sense it is extended; but the parts are not separable. And this inseparability of the parts of the soul distinguishes it from material things and constitutes a reason for affirming the soul's immortality, even if the ultimate grounds for this affirmation are to be found in divine revelation.

Of the two men Tetens was certainly of more importance for the development of psychology. He insisted, as we have seen, on a precise analytical approach. But at the same time he linked up analytical psychology with a general philosophy of human nature and its development, as the title of his chief work indicates. In his view we ought to study, not simply, for example, the origins of human ideas in experience, but the whole growth of the human intellectual life up to its expression in the different sciences. Again, his insistence on feeling as a distinct 'power' pointed towards a study of the expression of the life of feeling and sensibility in the world of art and literature.

5. The influence of Rousseau's *Émile* on educational theory in Germany during the *Aufklärung* was considerable. It was felt, for example, by Johann Bernhard Basedow (1723–90), author of, among other educational writings, a large tome named *Elementarwerk* (1774) which was designed as a kind of encyclopaedia for teachers and as a text for parents and children. But while Basedow was stimulated by Rousseau's idea of a 'natural' education, his pedagogical theory was not complicated by presuppositions about the deleterious effects of civilization on the human being. He was thus able to propose as the end and purpose of education preparation of children for a patriotic and happy life in the service of the common good. In his ideas about methods of teaching he was influenced by Comenius (1592–1671), author of *The Great Didactic*.

The stimulating effect of Rousseau was felt also by the famous

Swiss educationalist, Johann Heinrich Pestalozzi (1746–1827), who influenced the development of the German *Volksschulen* or elementary schools. But with Pestalozzi, as with Basedow, we find an emphasis on education for social life. He laid great stress on education in the family and in a rural community, and on education in general as the best instrument of social reform, provided, of course, that it fosters moral, and not merely intellectual, development.

Basedow was for a time a professor of moral philosophy; but Pestalozzi can scarcely be called a philosopher, and it would be out of place to discuss here his particular ideas in the field of pedagogy, however famous his name may be in the history of educational theory. It is sufficient to note that the Enlightenment in Germany, as elsewhere, produced its educational theorists. In England there was Locke, in France Rousseau, in Germany and Switzerland Basedow and Pestalozzi. And the idea of education for social life, represented by the two latter names, was in conformity with the general direction of thought in the *Aufklärung*.

CHAPTER VII

THE BREAK WITH THE ENLIGHTENMENT

Hamann—Herder—Jacobi—Concluding remarks.

1. AT the time of Wolff's death a very different type of man, Johann Georg Hamann (1730–88), was in his twenty-fourth year. Wolff was a great systematizer: Hamann had no use for philosophical systems. Wolff represented abstraction and the power of the discursive reason: Hamann hated what he regarded as one-sided abstraction and rejected the tyranny of the discursive reason. Wolff strove after clear and distinct ideas: Hamann dealt in oracular utterances which helped to earn for him the title of the Wizard (or Magus) of the North. In other words, Hamann set his face against the rationalism of the Enlightenment which represented for him the power of the devil rather than divine reason.

A native of Königsberg, Hamann was an unstable character who turned from one branch of study to another and from one occupation to another, ranging from posts as tutor in a family to minor posts in the commercial world. When reduced at one time to extreme poverty and an inner torment of spirit, he gave himself to the study of the Bible and developed the extreme pietism which was a characteristic of his writings. He numbered Herder and Jacobi among his friends, and he was also on friendly terms with Kant, though he vigorously criticized the latter's philosophy when Kant, awoken from his dogmatic slumbers, started to publish his *Critiques*.

It may seem that the Wizard of the North is out of place in a history of philosophy. But he gave expression, even if unsystematic and exaggerated expression, to ideas which were characteristic of the reaction against the Enlightenment, and he certainly exercised a considerable influence, even though his influence on Herder in particular has been exaggerated by some historians.

One of the main characteristics of Hamann's anti-rationalism was its religious setting. Let us take, for example, the controversy about language. Against the rationalistic view that man invented language, as though it was a kind of mechanical product, Herder maintained that language is coeval with mankind. Hamann was and always has been of the same opinion. But he was not content with saying that language is not an artificial invention of the human reason and then assigning some other empirical cause or causes. In his opinion language was in some mysterious way a communication of God, a divine revelation. Again, Hamann was convinced that poetry in particular is not the product of reason. On the contrary, poetry, as he says in 'Aesthetics in a Nutshell' (contained in *Crusades of a Philologist*, 1762), was the mother-tongue of mankind. The speech of primitive men was sensation and passion, and they understood nothing but images. It was in music, song and poetry that they expressed themselves. Moreover, great poetry is not the product of a superior reason: it is not to be attributed to a superior capacity of understanding and observing rules. Homer and Shakespeare created their works by genius, not by applying intellectually apprehended rules. But what is genius? The genius is a prophet whose inspiration is divine. Language and the arts are products of revelation.

Of course, such statements could be given a simple and common-sense interpretation. For example, as Goethe remarked, if it is true that God made man, and if language is natural to man as differentiated from the animals, it is true that God made language. Similarly, any theist (or pantheist for the matter of that) would be ready to attribute genius to the creative work of God. But Hamann expressed himself in an oracular style with a mystical colouring, which suggests that he meant something more, even if it is difficult to say what precisely he did mean.[1] In any case he was not content, for example, with insisting on the natural character of human speech and dissociating it from the idea of invention by reason: he insisted too on its divine origin.

Again, Hamann was not content with attacking the tyranny of the discursive reason and its pretended omnicompetence and with allowing a place in human life to faith in God and in divine revelation. His pietism led him to depreciate the reason and to find pleasure in the restriction of its power. It is significant that for him there is poetic, but not scientific, genius. We cannot speak of the great scientists as geniuses. For they work by reason, and this is not the organ of inspiration. And, in the religious sphere, it is not simply the case that the Wolffian natural theology is inadequate: it is thrown overboard in the name of faith. Again, while Hamann's view of history as a commentary on the word or

[1] What Hamann says is that at the beginning every phenomenon of Nature was for man a sign, a symbol, a guarantee of a divine communication, a living word. Language was a natural response to the perception of Nature as a divine word.

self-expression of God exercised a powerful influence on Herder's mind, the former was rather disconcerted by the latter's use of profane sources and by his attempt to apply a scientific method in his interpretation of history. In Hamann's eyes history, like the Scriptures, possesses an inner mystical or 'true' sense which is revealed by God rather than attained by the patient and untiring effort of the reason. In other words, Hamann tended to apply to the understanding of history the Protestant conception of the true sense of Scripture being revealed by the Holy Spirit to the silent and prayerful individual believer. The deeper exegesis, whether of the Bible or of history, is the work of God alone.

We cannot, however, dismiss Hamann as a mere pietist who, if he deserves any consideration at all by the philosopher, deserves it only in the sense that one may pay some attention to one's opponents. His view of history as a divine revelation, as a work of divine providence, which was shared by Herder, was to have considerable importance in the near future. For this view, transposed, it is true, into a system of speculative philosophy which would have seemed to Hamann an intolerable expression of rationalism, was to form an integral part of the Hegelian philosophy of history. Further, Hamann's anti-rationalism was bound up with a dislike of abstraction, which was not the product of mere prejudice. And a brief allusion must be made to this theme.

Goethe remarked[1] that Herder's utterances can be reduced to the principle that everything which man undertakes to perform, be it by word or by deed or in any other way, originates from the total, united powers of the personality. From the beginning man was poet, musician, thinker and worshipper in one. The rationalists of the Enlightenment, however, had, in Hamann's opinion, hypostatized the reason, speaking about 'the reason' and its performances as though it were something on its own and as though the ideal of human life consisted in reason's conquest of all spheres. Thus they tended to give man a false conception of himself and his activities. They abstracted one function of man's activity and turned it into the whole.

This hostility towards what he regards as false or one-sided abstractions is evident in Hamann's criticism of Kant's first *Critique*. In his *Metacritique on the Purism of Pure Reason*[2] Hamann

---

[1] *Dichtung und Wahrheit*, III, 12.
[2] This work, which was utilized by Herder in his own *Metacritique*, was not published during Hamann's lifetime. It was begun in 1781, the year in which the *Critique of Pure Reason* was published.

attacked the Kantian separations between reason, understanding and sense, and between form and matter in sensation and conceptualization. Kant deals in abstractions. There certainly is, for example, an activity called 'reasoning'; but there is no such thing as 'the reason' or 'the understanding'. There are simply different activities which are performed by one being, one organism, one person. Obviously, even if this line of criticism does not dispose of the *Critique of Pure Reason*, Hamann is making a good point. It is one which is not infrequently made in other contexts by philosophers whose general outlook is far removed from that of the Magus of the North.

2. Hamann was clearly opposed to the rationalism of the Enlightenment. When we turn to Herder, however, we find a man who started from the point of view of the *Aufklärung* (so far as one is justified in speaking of 'a' point of view) and who worked his way out of it. While, therefore, historians are perfectly entitled to speak of his break with the Enlightenment, it is also possible to speak of his development of certain lines of thought within the movement. What we choose to say about this matter depends to some extent, of course, on the way in which we define certain terms. If we mean by the Enlightenment the Wolffian rationalism and the individualism of a number of thinkers, it is obvious that Herder made a break with the *Aufklärung*. But if we give the term a wider range of meaning, including under it the first germs or seeds of positions to which Herder gave expression, the word 'break' may seem to be too sharp. It makes, however, for clarity if one follows the traditional practice and represents Herder as having reacted against and broken with the Enlightenment.

Johann Gottfried Herder (1744–1803) was born at Mohrungen in East Prussia, the son of a pietist schoolmaster. In 1762 he enrolled as a student of medicine at the University of Königsberg, though he presently changed to theology. He attended the lectures of Kant who was expounding the traditional Wolffian philosophy and giving courses on astronomy and geography; and Kant introduced him to the writings of Rousseau and Hume. At Königsberg Herder also formed a friendship with Hamann, though he can hardly have been at once deeply influenced by his anti-rationalist friend; for when he moved to Riga in 1764 he contributed essays and reviews to organs of the Enlightenment. In 1765 he was ordained a Protestant clergyman.

In 1766 there appeared anonymously at Leipzig the first two

parts of Herder's *Fragments concerning Recent German Literature* (*Ueber die neuere deutsche Literatur: Fragmente*). The work bore the date 1767, the year which saw its completion. In the course of this work Herder discussed problems concerning language, a subject which occupied a good deal of his thoughts. Like Mendelssohn and Lessing, he insisted on a distinction between poetic and scientific (in his terminology philosophical) language. But the distinction was given a genetic or historical setting. Herder distinguishes four stages of linguistic development, which are classified according to an analogy with human growth, an analogy suggested by Rousseau. First comes the childhood stage when language consists of signs of passions and feelings. Secondly there is the period of youth, the poetic age of language, when poetry and song are one. Thirdly there is the stage of manhood which, though it still possesses poetry, is marked by the development of prose. Fourthly and finally there is the old age of language, the philosophical age, when life and richness are sacrificed to pedantic accuracy.

The context in which this theory of language was placed was a discussion about the German language. We cannot enter here into the details of this discussion. It must suffice to say that Herder, because of his insistence on the difference between poetic and philosophical language, rejected the notion that what German poetry required was to develop logical clarity. This idea had been put forward by, for example, J. G. Sulzer (1720–79), for whom poets were mediators between speculative philosophy and the people. Herder also rejected the idea that the German language should be improved by imitation of foreign literature. German poetry can be great if it grows out of the spontaneous poetry of the people and is the fruit of national genius. Later on Herder was to do much to foster a revival of interest in folk-poetry. In this attitude he was opposed to those thinkers of the *Aufklärung* who despised the German language and thought that the only hope for German literature lay in 'imitation'.

All this may seem to have little to do with philosophy. But it is interesting to observe how Herder (and not Herder alone, of course) distinguished between different types of language. Further, Herder saw that the question of use is of great importance. If we investigate the origins of different types of language, we do so in order to examine their uses more carefully, he tells us. And the uses of language is a subject which is obviously much discussed in present-day English philosophy. Again, Herder's insistence on German and on the spontaneous poetry of the people as the basis for developed poetic literature can be regarded as an initial stage in the growth of his later philosophy of culture and history, which lays stress on the development of national cultures considered as totalities in which languages play an extremely important part.

In *Critical Forests* (*Kritische Wälder*, 1769) Herder took as his point of departure Lessing's *Laokoon*, though he had other critics in view besides Lessing, whom he recognized as an outstanding dramatist. In his work Herder touched on a variety of points, distinguishing sculpture and painting, for example, and arguing that though Homer was, indeed, the greatest of Greek poets, the creations of his poetic genius were historically conditioned and that his practice cannot be taken as a norm. This is obvious enough to us; but Herder's point of view is significant as representing an aspect of his sense of historical development and of his rejection of purely abstract and rationalistic criticism and theorizing.

In the fourth *Grove* of *Critical Forests*, which was not published in his lifetime, Herder subjected to trenchant criticism the ideas of Friedrich Justus Riedel (1742–86), author of a *Theory of the Fine Arts and Sciences* (1767). Riedel had asserted the existence of three fundamental faculties of the mind, common sense, conscience and taste, corresponding to three absolutes, the true, the good and the beautiful. Herder argued, for instance, that it is nonsense to suppose that there is a faculty called 'common sense' whereby man apprehends absolute truth immediately without a process of reasoning. Anti-Wolffian notions of this sort would make one return to the philosophy of Wolff if one thought it acceptable. Again, the theory of a faculty of taste, with its implication that whatever pleases is beautiful or at least what pleases the greater number of people is the more beautiful, is an absurdity. Baumgarten was much more on the right lines when he distinguished between logic and aesthetics but maintained at the same time that there can be and ought to be a science of aesthetics, a science of sensation, which would be an important part of the philosophy of man. For Herder, aesthetics would examine the logic of artistic symbolization. Like Baumgarten, he saw that aesthetics must be distinguished from abstract logic and from science; but his approach was more historical. What is required is an historical analysis of different cultures and of the development and nature of their respective aesthetic ideals. But, while rejecting Riedel's theory of the universal faculty of taste, corresponding to the absolutely beautiful, Herder wavers in his discussion of absolute beauty. It may seem that his idea of an historical approach, with its accompanying psychological and physiological investigations, should lead to a relativistic conception of beauty; and Herder does, indeed, make artistic beauty relative to different cultures and to different periods of those cultures. At the same time he seems to hold that through an historical approach it would be impossible to find a common denominator. For an historical approach does not mean merely registering different conceptions of artistic beauty: it involves also an examination of the factors, psychological, physiological and environmental, determining these conceptions. It is true that Riedel had himself defended a psychological approach to aesthetics, using the psychology of Johann Georg Darjes (1714–91), who had been influenced by the faculty psychology of Crusius. But Herder's point was that the psychological approach must be integrated into an historical approach. We cannot legitimately take a short cut by postulating a faculty which remains uniform in its operations in all cultures and which is correlative to an absolute, universal and unchanging ideal.

In 1769 Herder resigned his post as pastor at Riga and set out on a voyage to Nantes, going afterwards to Paris and then to Strasbourg, where he consorted with the young Goethe (1770–1). The literary fruit of his journey to Nantes was his *Travel Diary*. This work, though not intended for publication, is of considerable importance as manifesting a change of mind in its author. Looking backwards, he expresses his dissatisfaction with the lifeless technicalities of aesthetic criticism, describes his *Critical Forests* as useless, crude and miserable, and wishes that he had given himself to the study of French, of the natural sciences and of history; that is, to the acquisition of positive knowledge of the world and of men. If he had acted in this way, he says, he would not have become an inkpot and a repository of print. Looking forward, he envisages a new type of school and education in which the child will be led by gradual stages from acquaintance with its natural environment through a concrete presentation of geography, ethnography, physics and history to a systematic and more abstract study of such sciences. The method would thus be inductive, proceeding from the concrete to the abstract, so that abstract ideas would be grounded in experience. Religious and moral education would, of course, form an integral part of the general plan. And the result aimed at would be the development of a full and balanced human personality. In other words, Herder's mind in the *Travel Diary* is dominated by the ideas of positive knowledge and of education.

At Strasbourg Herder succeeded in conveying to Goethe some of his own interest in and appreciation for folk-poetry and the national cultural heritage. He also wrote his *Treatise on the Origin of Language (Abhandlung über den Ursprung der Sprache)*. Written at the end of 1770, it won a prize at the beginning of 1771 which had been offered by the Berlin Academy. Rejecting the extreme opposing views of the divine origin of language on the one hand and of its 'invention' on the other, Herder insists that the question of the origin of language, so far as it has any sense, is one which can be solved only on the basis of empirical evidence concerning the development and use, or uses, of language: it cannot be settled by dogmatic statements and *a priori* theorizing. In the course of his discussion he attacks the faculty psychology, maintains that primitive language and primitive poetry were one, and emphasizes the social function of poetry.

Herder did not like Strasbourg, and in 1771 he went to Bücke-burg as court preacher to the Count of Schaumburg-Lippe. Stimulated by James Macpherson's Ossianic forgeries, he contributed to a volume entitled *Of German Nature and Art (Von deutscher Art und Kunst*, 1773), an essay on Ossian and folk-songs, as well as another on Shakespeare. At this time Herder was revolting against the typical ideas of the Enlightenment, that it was the highest culmination of historical development and that the middle class was practically the unique source of enlightened reasonableness. He also asserted that the great rationalist systems of Descartes, Spinoza, Leibniz and others were poetic fictions, adding that the poetry of Berkeley was greater and better sustained. It is not surprising, therefore, that Herder completed his break with the *Enlightenment*, a break symbolized by *Another Philosophy of History (Auch eine Philosophie der Geschichte*, 1774).

In this work Herder gives an account of the successive ages of humanity, from the Golden Age of humanity's childhood onwards. But this scheme is not meant to be taken too seriously, as is clear from the fact that Herder states roundly that when one has depicted a whole age or a whole people, one is left with a general word. General characterizations are inherently weak. Indeed, there is a good deal of irony in Herder's account of historical ages. For Rome is said to represent the manhood of the human race. And the implication is that the eighteenth century, so lauded by the men of the Enlightenment, represents senility. And Herder does not hesitate to draw attention to the hollowness of some of the claims made on behalf of the eighteenth century. For instance, sublime ideas and principles are formed and expressed by the enlightened; but inclination and impulse to live with nobility and kindness are weakened. Again, enlightened Europe boasts its freedom, but the invisible slavery of class to class is passed over in silence, and the vices of Europe are exported to other continents.

More important, however, from a philosophical point of view than Herder's attack on the complacency of the men of the Enlightenment is his attack on their historiography. They approach history with a presupposition, namely that history represents an upward movement from religious mysticism and superstition to free and non-religious morality. But if we study history in the light of such presuppositions, we shall never succeed in understanding it in its concrete reality. We ought to study each culture and phase of culture on its own merits, seeking to enter into its complex life and to understand it, so far as possible, from within, without judgments about better and worse, happier and less happy. Each nation, says Herder, carries within itself its own happiness, and the same is true of each period of its development. We cannot say in general that youth is happier than childhood or that old age is more miserable than youth. Nor can we legitimately make analogous generalizations about nations in the course of their development.

Of course, there is a certain historicism in this attitude. But Herder is clearly insisting on an important truth, that if we wish really to understand the historical development of man, we must not force the historical data into the Procrustean bed of a preconceived scheme. This seems obvious enough to us now; but, given the general tendency of the Enlightenment to use history to prove a thesis, and a questionable thesis at that, Herder's point was by no means a truism at the time when he made it.

In 1776 Herder moved from Bückeburg to Weimar, where he was appointed General Superintendent or head of the Lutheran clergy. In 1778 he published an essay *Of the Cognition and Sensation of the Human Soul* (*Vom Erkennen und Empfinden der menschlichen*

Seele), in which he expressed his opinion that no psychology is possible which is not physiology at every step. This statement is markedly behaviouristic, though Herder postulated in physiology a vital force. He also wrote extensively on literary subjects, such as folk-songs and their cultural significance, on theological questions, on certain books of the Bible, and on the spirit of Hebrew poetry. But the outstanding work of this period was his *Ideas for the Philosophy of the History of Mankind (Ideen zur Philosophie der Geschichte der Menschheit)* which appeared in four parts from 1784 to 1791, the production of the work being interrupted by a journey to Italy (1788–9). A projected fifth part was never written. As I propose to discuss the *Ideas* in a later chapter, when dealing specifically with the rise of the philosophy of history, I shall say nothing about its contents here.

In the period from 1793 to 1797 there appeared Herder's *Letters for the Advancement of Humanity (Briefe zur Beförderung der Humanität)*, dealing with a heterogeneous collection of topics. One or two of the views which he expressed in the *Letters* will be mentioned later on in connection with the *Ideas*. The general theory of the work is that 'humanity', the ideal character of our race, is innate in us as a potentiality or predisposition and that it must be developed by formative education. The purpose of science, art and all other human institutions is to 'humanize' man, to develop the perfection of humanity. Herder raises the objection that this development would lead to the production of a Superman or of a being who was outside the human species; but he meets it by saying that perfect man would not be a Superman but simply the realization of 'humanity'. We may note that Herder's educational ideals were not confined simply to theory and writing; for he set himself to plan and carry into effect, so far as he could, a reform of education in the duchy of Weimar.

In his later years Herder published a number of theological writings, notably *Christian Writings* (1794–8), which are, in general, surprisingly rationalistic and much more what one would expect of a man of the Enlightenment than of a friend of Hamann. He also wrote in opposition to the critical philosophy of Kant of which he strongly disapproved. In 1799 he published a *Metacritique of the Critique of Pure Reason*, representing Kant's work as jugglery with words, as a linguistic monstrosity and as involving a wrong-headed perpetuation of the faculty psychology. This should not be taken to mean that Herder's criticism consisted of unintelligent abuse. On the contrary, it consisted of a reasoned examination of Kant's theories. For example, he maintained, as against the Kantian theory that mathematical propositions are synthetic, that they are 'identical', that is to say, that they are what Wittgenstein called 'tautologies'. Again, Herder rejected Kant's view of space and time. The geometer does not analyse the *a priori* form of space; for there is no such form. And even if Herder does not explain clearly what the geometer does analyse, it seems to be implied that he analyses the implications of his own axioms and fundamental postulates. But Herder's account of mathematics is only one particular instance of his criticism of Kant. His main line of thought is that Kant's whole enterprise is wrongly conceived. Even if there were a separate faculty called 'reason', it would be out of order to speak of 'criticizing' it. Rather should we start with language; for reasoning is not only expressed in language, it is also inseparable from it, though it is not coextensive with all the uses of language. Thinking, according to Herder, is inward speaking, while speaking in the ordinary sense is speaking aloud or thinking aloud, whichever you like. There is no 'reason' as an entity, there is only a process, an activity of man as a total personality, and language is an indispensable instrument of this process, merging with it. In fine, the *Critique of Pure Reason* is based, according to Herder, on an erroneous psychology.

In 1800 Herder published *Kalligone*, a criticism of Kant's *Critique of Judgment*. In his opinion Kant had no real understanding of aesthetics. Herder did not write a criticism of the second *Critique*; but this was not because he agreed with it. He intended to attack it but abandoned the idea, partly because he was advised not to do so and partly, probably more, because he was engaged on other work. Thus he undertook to edit a new literary periodical, *Adrastea* (1800–4), to which he was the main contributor, in the form of essays and poetic dramas.[1] The fifth volume of the periodical contained instalments of Herder's German translation of the *Romances of the Cid* (made from a French translation with consultation of a late Spanish version).

Herder died at Weimar on December 18th, 1803. From the foregoing account of his life and activity it should be clear that he was a man of many interests; and though he was not a great systematic philosopher, he was a fertile writer who exercised a great influence

[1] The fifth volume, dated 1803, appeared in 1804 after Herder's death. The sixth volume (1804) was also published posthumously.

on German life and thought. He has been called the teacher of the *Sturm und Drang* (Storm and Stress) movement in German litera- ture; but he certainly influenced also the succeeding romantic movement through his insistence on the significance of folk-songs, through his idea of the all-important role of language in culture and in the development of the aesthetic consciousness, through his idea of history as a divine revelation and through his defence of Spinoza in the pantheism controversy. A. W. Schlegel (1767–1845) and F. Schlegel (1772–1829) were both indebted to Herder. How- ever, as historians of German literature have remarked, it was the younger Herder, the rebel against the rationalism of the Enlighten- ment, who most influenced the romantic movement. In his later years Herder could not compete in the literary sphere with the influence of Goethe, which was inevitably felt even by those who disagreed with him.[1]

3. Mention has already been made of Jacobi in connection with the pantheism controversy. Friedrich Heinrich Jacobi (1743– 1819), who became president of the Academy of Sciences at Munich, was a philosopher of faith. He emphasized the fact that it was never his intention to construct an academic system of philosophy; on the contrary, his writings were the expression of his inner life and experience and were, so to speak, forced from him, as he put it, by a higher and irresistible power.

Jacobi had made a study of Spinoza, and in his opinion the latter's philosophy was the only logical system. For the human reason can pass, in its process of demonstrating truths, only from the conditioned to the conditioned: it cannot rise above the con- ditioned to a transcendent Deity. All metaphysical demonstrations of an ultimate ground of existence must lead, therefore, to monism, to the conception of a world-system, which, as Jacobi maintained in his correspondence with Mendelssohn, is equivalent to atheism. But this is not to say that Spinozism is to be accepted. On the contrary, it must be rejected in the name of faith, which is an affair of the heart (*Gemüt*) rather than of the speculative reason.

The result of this position is, of course, a complete separation between philosophy on the one hand and the sphere of faith on the other. To attempt to prove God's existence is equivalent to trying

---

[1] In his later years Herder became estranged from Goethe, who found the former afflicted by an 'ill-tempered spirit of contradiction'. As for Schiller, the other great representative of German classicism, he was never particularly enamoured of Herder and, as an admirer of Kant, he was offended by Herder's attack on the critical philosophy, which attack, indeed, was unfashionable and helped to isolate its author.

to reduce God to a conditioned being; and in the long run speculative metaphysics must result in atheism. It is better to recognize
Hume's services in exposing the pretensions of metaphysics, provided that we attribute full validity to faith. Just as we do not
prove the existence of the external world but enjoy an immediate
intuition in sense-perception of the existence of sense-objects, so
do we have (or can have) an immediate intuition of supersensible
reality, which we call 'faith'. In his later writings Jacobi spoke
of the higher reason (*Vernunft* as distinguished from *Verstand*)
whereby we apprehend immediately supersensible reality. If
somebody denies the existence of God, we cannot prove this
existence to him; but in his denial he shuts himself off from one
whole aspect of human experience. Or, rather, his denial is a result
of his blindness to all but our perception of the corporeal world and
our knowledge of the relations between finite things. Light comes
to us from the sphere of supersensible reality, but once we try to
grasp by the discursive reason this light and what it renders visible
to the higher or intuitive reason, the light fades and disappears.

To a certain extent Jacobi was in agreement with Kant. Thus
he believed that the field of knowledge, that is to say of scientific
or theoretical knowledge, is limited to the realm of possible
experience, where experience means sense-experience, and he was
in agreement with Kant about reason's incapacity to prove the
existence of supersensible realities. To this extent, therefore, he
welcomed the critical philosophy as making room for faith. But he
rejected the Kantian theory of the postulates of the practical
reason. Belief in God, for example, is not a practical postulate but
the result of faith, of an inner illumination of the higher reason.
Again, Jacobi rejected what he regarded as Kant's phenomenalism.
What we perceive are not phenomena linked together by subjective forms of intuition and categories of the understanding; they
are the real things themselves. Further, he insisted on the immediacy of moral intuition or sense as against what he looked on as
the empty formalism of the Kantian theory of the categorical
imperative. It may be argued that Jacobi misunderstood Kant;
but the point in mentioning his criticism of the critical philosophy
is to draw attention to the facts, first that he accepted it in so far
as it fell in with his idea of the incompetence of the discursive
reason to transcend the sphere of the sensible, and secondly that
he rejected it in so far as it seemed to rule out immediate apprehension of God and of moral values. It is also to be noted that in

Jacobi's view Kant's doctrine of the thing-in-itself was an anomaly, not in the sense that there are no metaphenomenal realities but in the sense that in the Kantian philosophy the affirmation of things-in-themselves can be justified only by use of the causal principle, though this is a subjectively grounded principle, according to Kant, and applicable only to phenomena.

4. We have seen that all three thinkers whom we have considered in this chapter not only opposed the rationalism of the Enlightenment but also subjected to criticism the new critical philosophy of Kant. It was from Kant, however, that the great movement of German speculative idealism in the first half of the nineteenth century took its rise. To be sure, some of the objections they brought against Kant were shared by the idealists. For instance, Jacobi's objection that the Kantian affirmation of the thing-in-itself, when taken together with his doctrine of the categories, placed Kant in an impossible position was raised also by Fichte. But the line of development taken by speculative idealism was not at all the line which either Hamann or Herder or Jacobi would have approved. (Jacobi charged Schelling with trying to conceal the Spinozistic consequences of his thought.) In this sense they were swimming against a current which was to prove too strong for them. At the same time Herder's idea of history as a progressive education of humanity and as a manifestation of providence, together with his insistence on organic totality, both in the cultural and in the psychological spheres, as against analytic splintering, were to be incorporated into the idealist movement, especially in the Hegelian system. It is true that Hamann also sponsored the idea of history as a kind of commentary on the divine *logos*. But his utterances were too oracular to have the effect of Herder's ideas. Historically speaking, therefore, the latter must be accounted the most important of the three.

It may be said that we ought to regard these three men, not simply in relation to subsequent philosophical development, but on their own merits, recognizing that they performed the useful function of drawing attention to and insisting on aspects of man's spiritual life which the rationalistic Enlightenment tended to ignore. This may well be true. At the same time one could hardly expect the human mind to rest content with the sort of dichotomy between faith and philosophy which was made by Hamann and Jacobi. If religion, as Herder maintained, is an integral part of human culture and not something man must grow out of, as some of the men of the Enlightenment had believed, man, in trying to understand his own cultural development, must try to understand religion. And this, of course, is one of the things which Hegel tried to do. In doing so he elevated the speculative reason above the immediacy of faith, and he thus adopted a position which was contrary to that of Hamann and Jacobi and which stimulated Kierkegaard to a reassertion of faith. We thus have the reaction of Hamann and Jacobi against the rationalism of the Enlightenment and, later, the reaction of Kierkegaard against the Hegelian form of rationalism. This suggests that Hamann and Jacobi in the late eighteenth century[1] and Kierkegaard in the nineteenth represent an important fact, the role of faith in human life. But it also suggests that a more satisfactory, that is, rationally satisfactory, synthesis of faith and philosophy is required than any which was offered by these protesters against an arid rationalism or an all-engulfing speculative intellect.

[1] Jacobi's activity continued into the early part of the nineteenth century.

PART III

THE RISE OF THE PHILOSOPHY OF HISTORY

CHAPTER VIII

BOSSUET AND VICO

Introductory remarks; the Greeks, St. Augustine—Bossuet—Vico—Montesquieu.

1. ACCORDING to Aristotle in the *Poetics*,[1] poetry is 'something more philosophical and of graver import than history, because its statements are of the nature rather of universals, whereas those of history are particular'.[2] Science and philosophy are concerned with the universal, whereas history is the sphere of the particular and of the contingent. Poetry, of course, is not philosophy or science; but it is 'more philosophical' than history. It is true that Aristotle makes general statements about historical development, which might possibly be classified under the heading of philosophy of history. For, like Plato before him, he speaks in the *Politics* of the various kinds of revolution which tend to occur under different institutions, of their causes and of the means of preventing them and of the tendencies in certain types of constitution to turn into other types. But such remarks are obviously general reflections on history of the kind which could perfectly well be made by the historian himself. If we mean by philosophy of history a total view of historical development purporting to show that this development, as made known by historical research, follows a rational pattern and fulfils some plan or exemplifies certain universal and necessary laws, we can hardly say that the Greeks elaborated a philosophy of history. They had, of course, their historians, such as Thucydides, but this is a different matter. True, the notion of a cyclic return in the history of the world was common enough, and this theory can, indeed, be called a philosophy of history. But it can scarcely be claimed that the Greeks elaborated the theory. And if we concentrate our attention on the tradition

---

[1] 1451b, 5–8.
[2] On the meaning of this statement, as far as poetry is concerned, see Vol. I, pp. 361–2.

which ultimately came to dominate Greek philosophy, namely the Platonic tradition, we find a marked tendency to belittle the importance of historical development, a tendency connected, of course, with the Platonic insistence on unchanging spiritual reality as the sphere of true being in contrast with the sphere of becoming. The most impressive expression of this tendency is probably that found in Plotinus,[1] when he depicts historical events as so many incidents in a play which must be set in sharp contrast with the interior life, the spiritual return of the soul to God. True, Plotinus does not subtract history from the rule of law and of 'providence'. And his view of human history must be accounted a philosophy of history, inasmuch as it is closely linked with his general philosophical outlook: it is part of his system, just as the Stoics' view of cosmic history as a series of cycles was part of their system. But the tendency of Plotinus is to belittle the events to which prominence is accorded by the historian. And in any case there is no idea of human history in general as a development towards a goal which is attained in and through history.

The idea of history not as a series of cycles but as a process of progressive development towards an ultimate goal is characteristic, not of Greek but of Jewish and Christian thought. But the intimate connection between this idea and the doctrines of the Messias in Judaism and of the Incarnation in Christianity, as well as with Jewish and Christian eschatological doctrines, leads to a theory of historical development which is theological in character, in the sense that it presupposes theological doctrines. The most notable example of a specifically Christian philosophy of history is, of course, the theory of St. Augustine as presented in his *De civitate Dei*, in which the history of the Jewish people and the foundation and growth of the Christian Church play important roles. I do not wish to repeat here what I have said in the second volume of this *History*[2] about St. Augustine's philosophy of history. It is sufficient to remark that he thought in terms of a total 'Christian wisdom' rather than in terms of a systematic distinction between theology and philosophy. The fact, therefore, that his view of history is largely a theological interpretation with reference to God's providential dealings with the Jews as manifested in the Old Testament and with reference to the Incarnation and its prolongation, so to speak, in the Church, Christ's mystical body, is in no way inconsistent with his general outlook. And it is,

[1] *Enneads*, III, 2.   [2] See Vol. II, pp. 85–9.

indeed, arguable, at least from a Christian point of view, both that
an interpretation of history as a process of development towards a
determinate goal cannot be anything else but a theological interpretation and that a non-theological interpretation of history, so
far as it is capable of validity, is reducible to the sort of statements
about history which historians themselves are competent to make.
In other words, it is arguable, from a Christian point of view, that
there can be no such thing as a philosophy of history, if this term
is understood to mean an interpretation of the whole of history as
an intelligible movement towards a determinate goal and if a
systematic distinction between philosophy and theology is presupposed. However, if it is claimed that there can be no such thing
as a philosophy of history in this sense, the claim must obviously
be understood with reference to a valid philosophy of history. For
it is clear enough that philosophies of history which do not presuppose theological doctrines have been and are presented. The
Marxist philosophy of history is a case in point. And though we
are not concerned with Marxism in this volume, we are concerned
with the transition from a theological to a non-theological interpretation of history.

2. Jacques Bénigne Bossuet (1627–1704), the great orator who
was bishop first of Condom and afterwards of Meaux, expounded
a theological interpretation of history in his *Discourse on Universal
History* (*Discours sur l'histoire universelle*, 1681). In his preface to
the work, dedicated to the Dauphin, he emphasizes two aspects of
universal history, the development of religion and that of empires.
For 'religion and political government are the two points on which
human affairs turn'.[1] Through a study of history princes can be
made aware of the abiding presence and importance of religion in
its successive forms and of the causes of political changes and of
the transition from one empire to another.

Obviously, these two themes could be treated by a non-religious
historian, without any theological presuppositions. But in his
Discourse on Universal History Bossuet has apologetic considerations in mind. In the first part he outlines twelve epochs:
Adam, or creation; Noe, or the Deluge; the vocation of Abraham;
Moses, or the written Law; the taking of Troy; Solomon, or the
building of the Temple; Romulus, or the foundation of Rome;
Cyrus, or the re-establishment of the Jews; Scipio, or the conquest
of Carthage; the birth of Jesus Christ; Constantine, or the peace of

---

[1] *Dessein général.*

the Church; and Charlemagne, or the establishment of the new empire. In other words, Bossuet is concerned with the providential dealings of God with the chosen people, with the spread of the Roman empire as a preparation for Christianity, with the Incarnation and with the establishment of the Church and of Christian society. Oriental empires enter upon the scene only in function of their relations with the Jewish people. India and China are omitted. The theological doctrines of creation, of divine providence, and of the Incarnation form the framework of the author's historical scheme. And the twelve epochs fall under seven 'ages of the world', the birth of Christ ushering in the seventh and last.

In the second part, devoted to the development of religion, apologetic considerations are again dominant. We pass from the creation through the time of the Patriarchs to the revelation of the Law to Moses; and from the kings and prophets to the Christian revelation. Bossuet discusses, indeed, some religions, such as those of Rome and Egypt, other than Judaism and Christianity; but his remarks are incidental to his main theme, that Christianity is the perfect development of religion. 'This Church, always attacked and never conquered, is a perpetual miracle and a striking testimony to the changelessness of the counsels of God.'[1]

The idea of divine providence is prominent also in the third part of the *Discourse*, which deals with the fortunes of empires. Thus we are told that 'these empires have for the most part a necessary connection with the history of the people of God'.[2] God used the Assyrians and Babylonians to punish the Jews, the Persians to re-establish them in their land, Alexander and his first successors to protect them, and the Romans to maintain their liberty against the kings of Syria. And when the Jews rejected Christ, God used these same Romans to chastise them, though the Romans did not understand the significance of the destruction of Jerusalem. Bossuet does not, of course, confine himself to such general familiar statements. He discusses the particular causes of the falls of a number of empires and States from Egypt to Rome, and he endeavours to draw lessons for the Dauphin from these discussions. His final conclusion is that no man can rule the course of history according to his own plans and wishes. A prince may intend to produce one effect by his actions and in actual fact produce another. 'There is no human power which does not serve,

[1] *Discourse*, Part II, 13.   [2] *Ibid.*, Part III, 1.

despite itself, other designs than its own: God alone knows how to reduce all to His will. That is why everything is surprising if we regard only particular causes; and yet everything proceeds according to an ordered development.'[1] In other words, historical changes have their particular causes, and the way in which these causes operate is by no means always foreseen or willed by men. But at the same time divine providence is fulfilled in and through the operations of these particular causes.

Perhaps we can say, therefore, that for Bossuet there are, as it were, two historical levels. There is the level of particular causes which are considered by the historian. The latter can determine, for instance, the particular causes which contributed to the fall of the Babylonian empire or of imperial Rome. But there is also the level of theological interpretation, according to which divine providence is fulfilled in and through historical events. But we are restricted in our knowledge of how divine providence is thus fulfilled in the cause of history. And this is obviously one reason why Bossuet dwells on the relations of Egypt, Assyria, Babylon and Persia to the Jewish people; for here he can have recourse to the teaching of the Old Testament.

Bossuet thus renewed in the seventeenth century St. Augustine's attempt to develop a philosophy of history. But, as has been remarked and as Bossuet was doubtless well aware, our ability to develop this sort of philosophy of history, namely in terms of the idea of divine providence, is very restricted. The chief significance of his *Discourse* is probably that it helped to draw attention to human history as the subject-matter of philosophical reflection.

3. A much more important figure in the rise of the philosophy of history is Giambattista Vico (1688-1744), one of the greatest of Italian philosophers. During Vico's lifetime a considerable amount of historical research was carried on. The Reformation and Counter-Reformation had both stimulated this work; and a further impetus, as historians have noted, was given by the rise of the national States and by dynastic interests. Thus Leibniz engaged in writing the history of the House of Brunswick, while in Italy Muratori, who was librarian to the Duke of Modena in the first half of the eighteenth century, was commissioned by his patron to prepare a history of the House of Este.[2] But historical research and accumulation of material for the writing of history is not the

---

[1] *Discourse*, Part III, 7.
[2] Muratori's great work was the *Rerum italicarum scriptores*.

same thing as historiography; and historiography or the writing of history is not the same thing as a theory or philosophy of history. For the latter we have to turn to Vico.

In 1699 Vico became professor of rhetoric in the university of Naples, a post which he held until 1741.[1] And in this capacity he delivered a number of inaugural lectures. The earlier ones show the influence of Cartesianism; but in that of 1708 he adopts a different attitude. The moderns, he says, have introduced great improvements in certain sciences, namely the physical sciences; but they have underestimated and depreciated the branches of study whose subject-matter depends on the human will and cannot be treated by the same method as, for instance, mathematics. These sciences include poetry, history, language, politics and jurisprudence. Further, the moderns have tried to extend the application of the demonstrative mathematical method of sciences where it can yield only apparent demonstration.

This point of view was developed more fully in his *Ancient Wisdom of the Italians* (*De antiquissima italorum sapientia*, 1710). In this work Vico attacks the philosophy of Descartes. In the first place, the *Cogito, ergo sum* cannot serve as an adequate refutation of scepticism or as a basis for scientific knowledge. For the certainty that one is thinking belongs to the level of unreflecting consciousness and not to the level of science. In the second place, clarity and distinctness of idea will not serve as a universal criterion of truth. It may appear to serve as a criterion of truth in mathematics. But it is applicable in geometry, for example, because geometry is a constructive science, in which the mind constructs or makes its own entities. Mathematical entities are not realities in the sense in which the objects of natural sciences are realities; they are fictions made by man. They are indeed clear and distinct; but they are so because the mind has itself constructed them. Construction of the object is therefore more fundamental than clarity and distinctness; and it provides us with the criterion of truth. 'The rule and criterion of truth is to have made it.'[2] But construction of the object does not mean precisely the same in physics, for instance, as in pure geometry. In the latter the objects are unreal entities, mental fictions; in the former they are not. Construction of the object in physics means using the experimental method. The things which we can prove in physics are

---

[1] In 1723 Vico competed for, but failed to obtain, the chair of civil law.
[2] *Opere*, I, 136; Bari, 1929.

those to which we can perform something similar. And the ideas of natural things which are clearest are those which we can support by experiments which imitate nature.

The statement of the principle *verum factum*, namely that the criterion of truth is to have made it, does not, therefore, lead to the conclusion that the geometrical method is of universal applicability in all sciences. Nor should it be taken to mean that the mind creates physical objects in the same sense in which it creates mathematical entities. We should not interpret Vico as maintaining that things are mental fictions or mere ideas. The making or constructing of the object should be understood in a cognitive rather than in an existential sense. When the mind reconstructs the structure of the object out of its elements, it attains certainty of truth in the very act of reconstruction. In this sense knowing and making are identified, *verum* and *factum* becoming one. God, creating all things, necessarily knows all things clearly. And a strict analogue to this truth is found only in human mathematical knowledge, where the objects or entities are mental fictions. We do not create Nature in the existential order. At the same time we have a scientific knowledge of Nature only in so far as we remake, as it were, the structure of the object in the cognitive order. And we cannot know that we are doing this correctly without the help of the experimental method. A deduction from purely abstract concepts created by ourselves cannot guarantee a knowledge of existent Nature, however clear and distinct these concepts may be.

The application of these ideas to history was not made in the *Ancient Wisdom of the Italians*; but it is easy to anticipate the general line which Vico's thought was to take. Human history is made by man; it is therefore understandable by man. The principles of historical science are to be found in the modifications of the human mind, in man's nature. Indeed, history lends itself to scientific investigation and reflection more easily than physical Nature. Nature was made by God alone, not man; hence God alone can have a full, adequate knowledge of Nature. But human society, human laws, language and literature, are all made by man. Hence man can truly understand them and the principles of their development. Here we have a reversal of the Cartesian position. The sciences which Descartes belittled in favour of physical science are given a position superior to the latter.

The principles of this new science were discussed by Vico in his great work, *Principles of a New Science concerning the Common*

Nature of the Nations (*Principi di una scienza nuova d'intorno alla comune natura delle nazioni*, 1725; 2nd edition, 1730; 3rd edition, 1744). In his autobiography Vico remarks that up to a certain date he admired two men above all, namely Plato and Tacitus. 'For with an incomparable metaphysical mind Tacitus contemplates man as he is, Plato as he should be.'[1] And we can connect with his admiration for these two men his aim in the *New Science* of determining the universal and eternal law of history and the ways in which this eternal law works itself out in the histories of individual peoples. The 'esoteric wisdom' of Plato is to be combined with the 'common wisdom' of Tacitus. But Vico adds the names of two other men to whom he recognizes a special debt. The first of these is Francis Bacon, from whose *De augmentis scientiarum* and *Novum organum* he derived a powerful inspiration in the development of his new science. (The title *New Science* may have been suggested by Bacon's *Novum organum*.) The second name is Grotius. Bacon saw that the sum of knowledge as existing in his time stood in need of being supplemented and amended, but, as far as law was concerned, he did not succeed in working out the laws governing human history. 'Grotius, however, embraces in a system of universal law the whole of philosophy and philology, including both parts of the latter, the history on the one hand of facts and events, both fabulous and real, and on the other of the three languages, Hebrew, Greek and Latin; that is to say, the three learned languages of antiquity that have been handed down to us by the Christian religion.'[2] Vico desired to carry further the work of Grotius. And we can connect with his reading of the philosophers of natural law, such as Grotius and Pufendorf (we may add Hobbes), his formulation of the problem of history as, in a large part, a problem concerning the origins of civilization. This is a theme to which he gives special attention in the *New Science*.

Vico was unwilling to start with Hobbes's 'licentious and violent men', Grotius's 'solitary, weak and needy simpletons' or Pufendorf's 'vagrants cast into the world without divine care or help', as he expresses the matter at the beginning of the first book of the first edition of the *New Science*. That is to say, he was unwilling to make an absolute start with men in these conditions. For Genesis does not suggest that Adam was originally in the state of nature described, for example, by Hobbes. So Vico allows a lapse of time

[1] *The Autobiography of Giambattista Vico*, translated by M. H. Fisch and T. G. Bergin, Cornell U.P., 1944, p. 138.
[2] *Autobiography*, p. 155.

for the process of man's bestialization to take place, among the Gentile races, that is to say. And then the problem arises how civilization developed.

Vico supposes that the first beginnings of civilization came with settled dwellings. The thunder and lightning of the sky god drove men, together with their women, into the shelter of caves. And these primitive habitations made possible the rise of the first stage of civilization, 'the age of the gods' or 'state of the families', when the father of the family was king, priest, moral arbiter and judge. This family-stage of civilization had three principles, namely, religion, marriage and burial of the dead.

In this primitive stage of civilization there were, however, ever-present tensions and inequalities. Among the vagrants, for instance, those who had not yet formed themselves into settled families which worshipped deities and tilled the soil in common, some were strong, others weak. And one can picture the weak taking refuge with settled families as dependents or serfs, to save themselves from their stronger and more violent fellows. We can then imagine the fathers of families uniting together against the serfs. That is to say, patrician and plebeian orders were gradually formed, and so there arose 'heroic states', in which the magistrates belonged to the patrician order. This was the second stage in the development of civilization; it was 'the age of the heroes'.

But this stage was inherently unstable. The patricians or nobles naturally wished to conserve the structure of society as it was; for they wished to preserve their position and privileges intact. But, equally naturally, the plebeians wished to change the structure of society. And in the course of time they succeeded in winning for themselves a share in one privilege after another, from a legal recognition of their marriages up to citizenship and eligibility for office. The age of the heroes thus gradually gave place to 'the age of men', characterized by democratic republics. It was the age of men, because the dignity of man as man, as a rational being, was at length recognized.

However, this third stage in the development of civilization held within itself the seeds of its own decay. Religion, which had been present from the start and which had been an all-important agent in man's rise to a civilized condition, tended, with the flowering of rationality, to give place to philosophy and barren intellectualism. Equality gave birth to a decline in public spirit and to the growth of licence. The laws certainly became more humane, and toleration

increased; but decadence accompanied this process of humaniza-
tion, until in the end society disintegrated from within or succumbed to external attack. This led, as at the close of the Roman
empire, to a reversion to barbarism.

After the completion of the cycle a new cycle begins. Thus in the
West the coming of Christianity heralded a new age of the gods.
The Middle Ages represented the age of the heroes in the new
cycle. And the seventeenth century, the century of the philosophies, was a phase of a renewed age of men. We find cycles in the
histories of individual peoples; and their particular cycles are the
working-out of a universal law. But this theory of cycles, which
Vico believed to be confirmed inductively, must not be misunderstood. Vico does not mean that historical events are determined or that precisely similar sets of particular events occur in
each cycle. Nor does he mean, for instance, that Christianity is a
temporary religious phenomenon which possesses a value relative
to one particular cycle, so that it must give place to another
religion in the future. What recurs is not the particular historical
facts or events but rather the general framework in which the
events occur. Or, better, it is the cycle of mentalities which recur.
Thus the primitive mentality, expressed in the language of sense,
imagination and passion is gradually succeeded by the emergence
of reflective rationality. This in turn becomes, as it were, cut off
from other layers of human nature and tends to develop into the
dissolvent criticism of the sceptical reason. And the dissolution of
society is not arrested until man recaptures the spontaneous
primitive mentality which brings with it a renewed contact with
God, a renewal of religion. Civilization 'in every case began with
religion and was completed by sciences, disciplines and arts'.[1]
There is a cycle of mentalities, of the forms of historical development, but not of the contents, the particular historical facts and
events. Vico's idea does, indeed, recall Greek theories of the cyclic
return; but he has no intention of affirming a fatalistic theory of
the necessary repetition of similar particular events. Nor does his
theory of cycles preclude all progress. For instance, Christianity
may correspond in a new cycle to what Vico calls the 'frightful
religions' of the first age of the gods; but it does not follow that
Christianity is not superior to them.

It is a great mistake to think that Vico offered nothing else in
his philosophy of history but a theory of cycles. There is much

[1] *Opere*, III, 5.

more to it than a tidy map of the development of each people or nation. For one thing we can find in his work a healthy counterblast to rationalism in the sense of an over-intellectualist interpretation of man and his history. The philosophers, says Vico, are incapable of forming for themselves a true idea of the origins of society; for they tend constantly to read back into the past their own ways of looking at things and to rationalize what was not the work of reason in the sense which they give to this word. Thus the philosophers of natural law depict for us men in the state of nature as making a contract or covenant which gives rise to society. But the real origins of society cannot have been of this kind. The factor which drove the vagrants or vagabonds into caves and suchlike primitive dwellings, there to establish more or less settled habitations, was fear; or, more generally, felt need.

This idea can be applied, not only to the philosophers of the seventeenth century, but also to those of the ancient world. The latter, subject to the same rationalizing tendency as their modern successors, attributed the laws of States to enlightened law-givers, such as Lycurgus at Sparta. But laws did not begin as the product of reflective reason, though in the course of time, as civilization developed, they have been subjected to revision by reason. The trouble is that philosophers, worshipping the reflective reason, find the essence of man in this reason. They think that it is reason alone which unites men and acts as a common bond, so that it must be the source of law, which is a unifying factor. The imagination, the senses and the passions separate men from one another. In reality, however, men in the first stages of development were ruled by imagination and feeling rather than by the reflective reason. True, reason was present; but it expressed itself in forms proper to imagination and feeling. Primitive religion was, psychologically, the spontaneous product of fear and of a sense of helplessness, not of reason in the philosophic sense; and primitive law was intimately associated with primitive religion. Both were the product, not of the philosophical reason, but of a logic of feeling and imagination. Law, in its origins, was custom as a natural growth, not the fruit of the planning intellect.

Vico laid great emphasis on poetry and mythology. Indeed, the third book of the *New Science* is entitled *On the Discovery of the True Homer*. If we wish to study the early stages of religion, morality, law, social organization and economics, we must refrain from mere abstract theorizing and study the data of philology, namely poetry and myth. And in interpreting, for instance, the Homeric poems we must avoid two erroneous ideas. First, we should not look on the myths as deliberate impostures, useful lies of the type commended by Plato in the *Republic*. Secondly, we should not rationalize them, as though their authors were giving allegorical expression to clearly conceived and rationally formulated ideas and theories. Rather are they the expression of the 'vulgar wisdom', the 'poetic wisdom', of a people; and they give us the key to the manner of thinking of peoples at the time when the myths were born. The Homeric poems, for instance, express in 'poetic characters' the religion, customs, social organization, economics and even scientific ideas of the Greeks in the heroic age. They are, as it were, the spontaneous literary expression or deposit of the mentality and life of a people at a given period of its development. Hence comes their great value for a reconstruction of history. Obviously, we are not called upon to accept everything as literal truth. Zeus, for instance, was not a real person, in the form in which he and his activities are described in the Homeric poems. At the same time he is not a mere literary device, symbolizing some abstract philosophical notion of deity. He is rather the imaginative expression of an early stage of contact with the divine. It is not that poetical descriptions of the divine covered, as it were, a philosophical theory of the divine, which was clearly formulated in reflective reason: the religious thinking of the period was poetical thinking. It had its own logic, but this was the logic of imagination and feeling rather than the abstract logic of the philosopher.

Another point to notice in Vico's philosophy of history is his insistence on the complex unity of each cultural period. Each 'age' or stage in a cycle has its own types of religion, law, social organization, and economics. Vico doubtless over-schematized; but he provided a programme, as it were, for a study of history which would not be confined to the narration of dynastic, political and military events but which would delve into the lives of peoples in successive phases of their histories and explore these lives in all their ramifications, exhibiting the connections between religion, morality, custom and law, social and political organization, economics, literature and art. At the same time he outlined programmes for the comparative study of the development both of human mentality in general and of particular sciences and arts.

History, therefore, reveals to us human nature. We cannot

attain a knowledge of human nature by simply considering man as he is, say, in the second period of the 'age of men' or by taking the philosopher as a standard. We have to turn to the gradual revelation of man's nature in history, in his poems, in his art, in his development of society and law, and so on. History is made by man; it is therefore understandable by man. And in studying history man attains a reflective awareness of his own nature, of what it has been and is and can be. It is silly to extol the achievements of the age of reason, the age of the philosophers, and despise the past and the primitive, for the whole course of history is the revelation of man. In the primitive age of the gods we see man as sense; in the age of heroes we see man as imagination; in the age of men we see man as reason.

The fact that history, whether we consider human actions or the monuments of art and literature or institutions, is made by man does not mean, however, that it is cut off from divine providence and that it is not in some sense the work of God. But for Vico divine providence operates primarily through the human mind and will; that is, through natural means and not primarily through miraculous intervention. Men have often intended one end and achieved another. For example, 'fathers meant to exercise without restraint their paternal power over their serfs, and they subjected them to the civil power from which cities arose. The ruling class of nobles meant to abuse their lordly freedom over the plebeians, and they had to submit to the laws which established popular freedom.'[1] Whatever individuals may have intended, through their actions civilization arose and developed. And in the second phase of the age of man, when free-thinkers, for instance, try to destroy religion, they contribute to the dissolution of society, to the end of a cultural cycle, and so to a rebirth of religion which is the chief factor in facilitating man's conquest of his egoistic passions and which leads to the growth of a new culture. Men act freely, but their free actions are the means by which the eternal purposes of divine providence are realized.

It is not quite accurate to say that Vico's *New Science* was entirely disregarded by his contemporaries. For certain particular theses became the subject of discussion. But the general significance of his ideas was certainly not appreciated; and Vico did not begin to come into his own until the nineteenth century. In 1787 Goethe visited Naples, and the *New Science* was brought to his

[1] *Opere*, IV, 2, 164.

attention. The great poet lent the work to Jacobi, and in 1811 Jacobi referred to what he considered to be Vico's anticipation of Kant. This passage was used by Coleridge in his *Theory of Life* (1816, published 1848), and in subsequent years he spoke with some enthusiasm of Vico. In France, Michelet published an abridged translation of Vico's main work (1827), and in 1835 he re-issued it, accompanied by a translation of the autobiography and of some other writings. In Italy, Rosmini and Gioberti interested themselves in Vico, and so did the idealists, such as Spaventa, who maintained that the entry of Hegelianism into Italy was, as it were, the homecoming of Vico to his native soil, on the ground that the latter was the precursor of German philosophy. But the modern spread of interest in Vico has been due above all to Benedetto Croce who represented him as the man who 'discovered the true nature of poetry and art and, so to speak, invented the science of aesthetic'.[1]

4. Montesquieu (1689–1755) does not refer in his published writings to Vico; but it seems probable that he made the acquaintance of the *New Science* when he was travelling in Italy in 1728, that is to say, before the publication of his famous works on the causes of the greatness and decadence of the Romans (1734) and on the spirit of laws (1748). The fact that he undertook a comparative study of society, law and government with a view to ascertaining the principles of historical development at once suggests that Vico exercised some influence on his mind, at least by way of stimulus, though it does not of itself prove that there was such an influence. However, Montesquieu's personal notes seem to show that Vico's theory of cycles and of the decay of civilization did exercise some influence on his mind, though its extent can hardly be ascertained.

As Montesquieu's ideas have been outlined already in the first chapter of this volume, no more will be said about them here. It is sufficient to point out that with both Vico and Montesquieu we find the idea of a comparative historical method, and that both men set out to use historical data as a basis for determining the laws governing the historical development of peoples. Of the two men Montesquieu, a thinker of the Enlightenment with a passion for liberty, had incomparably the greater success as far as his own time was concerned. Vico's star did not really begin to shine until the Enlightenment had run its course.

[1] B. Croce, *Aesthetic*, translated by D. Ainslie, London, 2nd edition, 1929, p. 220.

CHAPTER IX

VOLTAIRE TO HERDER

Introductory remarks—Voltaire—Condorcet—Lessing—Herder.

1. It has sometimes been maintained that the outlook of the eighteenth-century Enlightenment was unhistorical. If this were taken to mean that no history was written, the statement would be patently false. We have only to think of Montesquieu's *Histoire de la grandeur des Romains et de leur décadence* (1734), of Gibbon's *Decline and Fall of the Roman Empire* (1776–81), of Voltaire's *Histoire de Charles XII* (1731) and of his *Histoire du siècle de Louis XIV* (1751), and of Hume's historical works. Nor can it be said that the historiography of the eighteenth century was concerned simply with battles, diplomatic and political struggles and the doings of 'great men'. On the contrary, we see the rise of the idea of history as a history of human civilization. Charles Pinot Duclos, author of a *Histoire de Louis XI* (1745) and of *Considérations sur les mœurs de ce siècle* (1750), declared that he was concerned with the manners and customs of men rather than with wars or politics. In this attitude he was at one with Voltaire. The eighteenth century certainly saw a broadening of the idea of history.

When it is said that the outlook of the eighteenth-century Enlightenment was unhistorical, the statement may refer in part to the tendency shown by some writers to treat history as a form of *belles-lettres* and to make over-hasty judgments without real knowledge or understanding of the sources. More important, it refers to the tendency to treat the age of reason and enlightenment and its ideals as a kind of absolute standard of judgment and to despise the past except in so far as it could be interpreted as leading up to the age of *les philosophes*. This attitude of mind, with its accompanying tendency to use history to prove a thesis, namely the superiority of the eighteenth century in general and of the philosophers in particular, obviously did not conduce to an objective understanding of the past. It would be, indeed, an exaggeration to suggest that all the thinkers of the Enlightenment expounded a naïve theory of progress. A certain pessimism shows itself even in Voltaire. But, by and large, the philosophers were convinced that progress and the triumph of emancipated reason are synonymous; and their idea of reason made it difficult for them to understand either a primitive mentality or, for instance, the Middle Ages. When the philosophers wished to picture to themselves primitive man, they set before themselves modern man and stripped him of the qualities and habits which could be attributed to civilization, being careful to leave him the exercise of reason which would enable him to enter into the social contract. True, Vico saw the artificiality of this analytical method, and he looked to an examination of poetry, song, art, records of customs and of religious observance to afford a secure basis for an understanding of the mentality of earlier times. But Vico was a genius who stood somewhat apart from the Enlightenment, and who was consciously opposed to the exaggerated rationalism and intellectualism of so many of his contemporaries. His estimate of his own time was certainly not that of the average *philosophe*. As for the Middle Ages, the men of the Enlightenment were quite incapable of a sympathetic understanding of the mediaeval culture and outlook; the Middle Ages represented for them a darkness out of which the light of the reason had gradually emerged. Thus though they broadened the idea of historical study and made a valuable contribution to the future of historiography, they were too much inclined to use history to prove a thesis, to glorify the Enlightenment, and their prejudices made it difficult for them to penetrate with sympathetic understanding into cultures and outlooks which they felt to be very different from their own and which they were inclined to despise. It is in this sense that we should understand the accusation that the mentality of the Enlightenment was 'unhistorical'.

2. Voltaire, whose general philosophical position has been discussed in the first chapter of this volume, asserted that his *Essai sur les mœurs* (1740-9, published 1756) was intended as a continuation of the work of Bossuet. 'The illustrious Bossuet, who in his discourse on a part of the universal history grasped its true spirit, stopped at Charlemagne.'[1] Voltaire wishes to continue from where Bossuet left off, and the full title of his work is *An Essay on General History and on the Manners and Spirit of Nations from Charlemagne up to Our Days*. In point of fact, however, he goes back much further and begins with China, passing to India, Persia and Arabia, and then coming to the Church in West and East before Charlemagne.

[1] *Avant-propos.*

But though Voltaire announces his intention of continuing the work of Bossuet, it is obvious that his idea of history is very different from that of the bishop of Meaux. For Bossuet the important events in history are the creation, the dealings of God with the Jewish people, the Incarnation and the growth of the Church; and he envisages human history, from the creation to the last day, as a unity, as a manifestation of divine providence which is served even by human free choices. With Voltaire the theological outlook of St. Augustine and Bossuet is conspicuous by its absence. History is the field of the interplay of human wills and passions. Progress is possible in so far as man rises above the animal condition and in so far as reason dominates, particularly when it takes the form of that enlightened despotism which alone can bring true social reform. But the idea of history as the implementation of a divine plan and as moving towards a supernatural goal disappears. And with it there disappears any strong conviction about the unity and continuity of history.

In part, of course, Voltaire is simply putting forward the idea of an empirical study of history, without dogmatic presuppositions. He wrote a *Philosophie de l'histoire* (1765), which was prefixed to the 1769 edition of the *Essai sur les mœurs*; but there is little philosophy in it in any ordinary sense of the term. When he talks about the need for writing history in a philosophical spirit, he is referring to the need for excluding legends and fairy-stories. This is made clear, for instance, in his *Remarques sur l'histoire* where he asks whether a man of good sense, born in the eighteenth century, can be permitted to speak seriously about the oracles of Delphi. But Voltaire is ultimately demanding, of course, that supernatural explanations should be left out altogether. To write history in a philosophic spirit is to write in the spirit of a *philosophe*, a man of the Enlightenment. And 'the illustrious Bossuet' was not a *philosophe*.

The conviction that it is not the historian's business to entertain his reader with fabulous anecdotes and tall stories is one of the reasons why Voltaire advises people to study the history of modern, rather than of ancient, times. In his *Nouvelles considérations sur l'histoire* he remarks that to treat of ancient history is to mix a few truths with a thousand lies. But it is obvious that an historian of ancient times is not obliged to write in the chatty and gossipy manner of Herodotus or to accept as true all fable and legend. Quite apart from the fact that a study of such legends, and even of the oracles of Delphi can be, as Vico saw but Voltaire did not, of great use to the serious historian, the remedy for uncertain and fabulous history is patient research. But Voltaire had, of course, another reason for preferring the history of modern times, namely a conviction of the superiority of the modern world, and especially of the philosophers. In the brief *Remarques sur l'histoire* he expresses the wish that the young should begin a serious study of history 'at the time when it becomes really interesting for us; that is, it seems to me, towards the end of the fifteenth century'. It was then that Europe changed its aspect. In other words, the Middle Ages have no real interest for us.

This point of view comes out in a number of places in Voltaire's writings. We are told that past times are as if they had never been; that the world of the ancient Jews was so different from ours that one can hardly draw from it any rule of conduct applicable today; that study of ancient times satisfies curiosity, whereas study of modern times is a necessity; and so on. This attitude obviously constitutes a weak point in Voltaire as historian and philosopher of history.

But Voltaire has, of course, his strong points. In his little essay, *Nouvelles considérations sur l'histoire*, he remarks that after having read three or four thousand descriptions of battles and the contents of some hundreds of treaties he has scarcely found himself any wiser than before. 'I no more know the French and the Saracens by the battle of Charles Martel than I know the Tartars and the Turks by the victory which Tamerlane won over Bajazet.' Instead of a narration of battles and of the doings of kings and courts one should find in histories accounts of the dominant virtues and vices of nations, explanations of their power or feebleness, the story of the establishment and growth of arts and industries. In fine, for the man who wishes to read history 'as a citizen and philosopher' 'changes in manners and in the laws will be his great object of study'.[1] Similarly, at the beginning of the sixty-ninth chapter of the *Esprit des mœurs* Voltaire states: 'I should like to show what human society was at the time (the thirteenth and fourteenth centuries), how people lived in the intimacy of family life, which arts were cultivated, rather than to repeat so many disasters and combats, those deadly subjects of (ordinary) history, those well-worn examples of human malice.' The philosopher may have underestimated the importance of

[1] *Nouvelles considérations sur l'histoire.*

political and military history, but he certainly drew attention to aspects of human life which are now universally regarded as important parts of the subject-matter of the historian but which had been overlooked by chroniclers who were hypnotized by the deeds of generals and monarchs and heroes.

In his general ideas about history Voltaire was clearly not as profound as Montesquieu, whom he attacked, let alone Vico: but in his conception of social historiography we can see the expression of the development of the bourgeois consciousness. For him history should no longer be dynastic history, an instrument for the glorification or vilification, as the case might be, of potentates, but rather an account of the emergence of the life, arts, literature and science of the eighteenth century, or, more broadly, of the social life of man through the ages.

Finally, to balance what has been said about Voltaire's contempt for the pre-Renaissance world, it should be added that in the *Esprit des mœurs*, including the additions which he made to it, he paints on a vast canvas. He speaks not only of Europe but also of the Far East and of America, not only of the Christian world but also of the Mohammedan world and of the oriental religions. True, his knowledge is often very defective; but this does not alter the scope of his design. In one sense his history was less universal than that of Bossuet. For the latter's theological framework held together in an intelligible unity the whole history of the race. But in another, and more obvious, sense Voltaire's *Esprit des mœurs* was more universal than the bishop's *Discours sur l'histoire universelle*, namely in the sense that the former wrote about nations and cultures on which the latter did not touch.

3. In the section on the physiocrats in the second chapter of this volume attention was drawn to the theory of progress proposed by Turgot, who anticipated the view of history which was expounded in the nineteenth century by Auguste Comte. Turgot was, indeed, much more of a believer in progress than Voltaire had been. For in spite of his convictions about the superiority of the age of the Enlightenment the latter had no belief in laws governing human history. But I have no wish to repeat what has been already said about Turgot, and I turn instead to another leading exponent of the idea of progress in the later part of the eighteenth century, namely Condorcet.

Marie Jean Antoine Nicolas Caritat, Marquis de Condorcet (1743–94), was a mathematician as well as a philosopher. At the early age of twenty-two he composed a treatise on the integral calculus, which won for him the esteem of d'Alembert. For the latter, as well as for Voltaire and Turgot, whose lives he subsequently wrote (Turgot's in 1786 and Voltaire's in 1787), he had a great admiration. He took part in the preparation of the *Encyclopaedia*, and he was elected to the Academy of Sciences (1769) and to the French Academy (1782). In 1785 he published an essay on probability, a second edition of which, revised and enlarged, appeared in 1804 with the title *Éléments du calcul des probabilités et son application aux jeux de hasard, à la loterie et aux jugements des hommes.*

Condorcet also interested himself in economic matters, writing, under Turgot's influence, in defence of free trade in corn. In politics he was an enthusiastic democrat and republican. He welcomed the revolution and was elected a deputy in the Convention. But he possessed too independent a mind to survive for long in those tempestuous years. He criticized the constitution which had been adopted by the Convention in favour of the one which he had sponsored; he denounced the arrest of the Girondists; and, objecting on principle to the death penalty, he opposed the conduct of the Mountain, the left-wing group headed by Robespierre, Marat and Danton. His critical attitude resulted in his being declared an enemy of the Republic and an outlaw. For a time he lay in hiding in the house of a widow, Madame Vernet; but, becoming convinced that the house was watched and that he was endangering the life of his benefactress, he fled. In the end he was captured and died in a cell at Bourg-la-Reine. Whether he succumbed to a stroke, was poisoned or poisoned himself does not seem to be clear.

While in hiding from his enemies Condorcet wrote his work on progress, *Esquisse d'un tableau historique des progrès de l'esprit humain* (1794), which is his chief title to fame as a philosopher. His main general ideas are those of the perfectibility of man, of the history of the human race as a gradual progress from darkness to light, from barbarism to civilization, and of indefinite progress in the future. Thus, although he wrote the work in the shadow of the guillotine, it is pervaded by a spirit of optimism. The violence and evil of the times he explained principally in terms of the bad institutions and laws which had been created by rulers and priests. For he was an enemy, not only of the monarchy, but also of the priesthood, indeed of all religion. He looked to constitutional reform and to education as the chief means of promoting progress. In 1792 he was one of those who presented to the Assembly a plan for organizing State secularist education, which became the basis for the plan subsequently adopted by the Convention. According to his plan mathematics, natural, technical, moral and political science would form the chief subject-matters for instruction in more advanced education, the study of languages, living or dead, occupying a comparatively minor place in the syllabus. In other words, the emphasis would be put on the science of Nature and on the science of Man.

Condorcet's interpretation of past history is developed in the light of this idea of scientific culture. He distinguishes nine stages or epochs. In the first epoch men, emerging from a state of barbarism in which they differed only physically from the animals, united together into groups of hunters and fishers, recognizing family relationships and using language. In the second or pastoral stage of development inequality and slavery make their appearance, together with some rudimentary arts; and in the third period, the agricultural period, there is further progress. These three preliminary epochs are admittedly conjectural; but with the invention of the alphabetic script we pass from conjecture to historic fact. The culture of Greece represents for Condorcet the fourth epoch, and that of Rome the fifth. He then divides the mediaeval period into two epochs. The sixth closes with the Crusades, the seventh with the great invention of printing. The eighth epoch is more or less synonymous with the Renaissance, opening with the invention of printing and closing with the new turn given to philosophy by Descartes. The ninth epoch closes with the revolution of 1789. It embraces Newton's discovery of the true system of Nature, Locke's opening-up of the science of Man, that is, of human nature, and the discovery of the system of human society by Turgot, Rousseau and Price.

A future and tenth epoch is then envisaged by Condorcet. In it, he says, there will be progress towards equality between nations, towards equality between classes, and in the physical, moral and intellectual improvement of individuals. Equality for him does not mean mathematical equality, but rather freedom, accompanied by equality of rights.

Progress in the past is thus regarded as issuing in future progress. The justification for this optimistic belief is obviously the assumption that there is a kind of law of progress or of human development which permits inferences from the past to the future. But the factor on which Condorcet lays most stress as securing future progress is not some hypothetical law operating inevitably but education, that is, rational enlightenment, political reform and moral formation. In his view we can set no limits in advance to human progress and perfectibility. When treating of the tenth epoch he insists that indefinite progress is possible, not only in moral science (in, for instance, the reconciliation of self-interest with the common good), but also in physical science, technical science and even (as against Diderot's view) in mathematics.

Obviously, the interpretations of history given by Turgot and Condorcet prepared the way for the positivist system of Auguste Comte. Theology is regarded as disappearing as the light of the scientific reason grows in strength; and the same can be said of metaphysical philosophy, except in so far as this can be reduced to a synthesis of scientific laws. We can hardly say that Condorcet worshipped *les philosophes* and regarded them as the peak of historical advance. He admired Voltaire, it is true, and shared his violent anticlericalism. But he did not share his faith in enlightened despotism or his contempt for the people. He looked forward to a democratic and scientific civilization; and in spite of the defects of his *Essay*, both in its schematic framework and in many of its particular statements, he is in a sense much more modern than Voltaire. He does not so much canonize the eighteenth century as point to the future. Unfortunately he was blind to important aspects of reality and of man; but this blindness was shared, of course, by his nineteenth-century successors. And as for the dogma of progress, this has suffered a serious setback in the twentieth century.

4. The idea of progress was represented in Germany by Lessing. But, as we saw in the sixth chapter of this volume, his theory of progress in history had a theological setting. In *The Education of the Human Race* (1780) he declared that what education is to the individual human being, that revelation is to the whole human race. Progress is first and foremost the moral education of mankind by God. True, Lessing's conception of history differs very much from that of St. Augustine and Bossuet. For he did not, like them, regard Christianity as God's definitive revelation to man. Just as the Old Testament consisted of 'elementary books' in comparison with the New, so the New Testament consists of

'elementary books' with the further stage of divine revelation when men will be educated to the doing of good for its own sake and not for the sake of reward either in this life or the next. In this idea of passing beyond Christian morality, with its doctrine of sanctions, Lessing was in tune with the general current of moral theory characteristic of the Enlightenment. At the same time his conception of history as a progressive divine revelation permits at least some analogy between it and the philosophies of history of St. Augustine and Bossuet. It certainly bears the stamp of the eighteenth century; but it obviously differs very much from the theory of Condorcet, for whom historical progress is not the work of God but rather a liberation from religion.[1]

5. When we turn to Herder's philosophy of history, we find important differences from the characteristic theories of the Enlightenment. As we saw in the seventh chapter of this volume,[2] Herder attacked the self-complacency of the Enlightenment, the tendency of eighteenth-century philosophers to think that history led up to their own times by a process of progressive development. But, as we also saw, he did not base this attack simply on a disagreement with their interpretation of the Enlightenment: he attacked their general approach to history. For in his view they approached history with presuppositions, and they used it to prove a preconceived thesis. Their thesis certainly differed from that of Bossuet, but it was none the less a preconceived theory, namely that history represents an upward movement from religious mysticism and the slavery of superstition towards a free and non-religious morality. To be sure, the philosophers of the Enlightenment might reply that their interpretation was based on induction rather than on presuppositions. But Herder could retort that their selection of facts on which to base a general interpretation was itself guided by presuppositions. And his great point was that their approach to history prevented them from studying and understanding each culture on its own merits, according to its own spirit and complex unity. In his *Another Philosophy of History* (1774) Herder himself divided up history into ages or periods; but he also drew attention to the danger of such a proceeding. When we delimit an 'age' and describe it in a few generalizations, we tend to be left with mere words: the reality, the rich life of a people escapes us. It is only patient and thorough study of the data

[1] For further information about Lessing, the reader is referred back to Chapter VI, pp. 126–31.
[2] Pp. 138–46, to which the reader is referred for a further account of Herder.

which will enable us to understand the development of a people. And he himself laid emphasis, as we saw, on the poetry and early folk-songs of peoples as an important source for understanding the development of the human spirit. We can, indeed, hardly say that an emphasis on the understanding of the development of language and literature was in contradiction with the ideas of the Enlightenment. But Herder drew attention to the importance of the comparatively primitive in interpreting man and his history. We shall fail to appreciate the significance of earlier cultural phases if we persist in judging them simply with reference to a standard based on the rationalist ideals and presuppositions of eighteenth-century philosophers.

Herder's great work, *Ideas for the Philosophy of the History of Mankind* (*Ideen zur Philosophie der Geschichte der Menschheit*, 1784–91) was conceived on a gigantic scale. For, in the first two parts of the work, each of which contains five books, he treats of man's physical environment and organization, with anthropology and, to speak paradoxically, with the prehistorical period of man's development. It is only in the third part, comprising books XI–XV, that he comes to recorded history, carrying his account up to the fall of the Roman empire. This account is continued in the fourth part (books XVI–XX) up to about A.D. 1500. The fifth part was not written. However, ambitious as the scheme of his work certainly was, Herder did not make extravagant claims on its behalf. The very title, *Ideas for the Philosophy of the History of Mankind*, is significant in its modesty. And the author explicitly states that the work consists of 'stones for a building which only centuries can finish'.[1] He was not so foolish as to suppose that he could complete the edifice.

After treating of man's physical environment, that is, of the forces of the physical cosmos and of the position and history of the earth, Herder comes to the subject of organic life and of man himself. He does not expound evolution in the sense of maintaining that man has evolved from some species of animal; but he regards genera and species as forming a kind of pyramid, at the apex of which is man. Throughout all organic life we find, according to Herder, the manifestation of a vital force (obviously corresponding to Aristotle's *entelechy*), which, as we ascend the scale of genera and species, expresses itself in ever-increasing

---

[1] Preface, XIII, p. 6. References to the *Ideas* are, by volume and page, to the edition of Herder's works by A. Suphan, Berlin, 1877–1913.

differentiation of function. Herder's conception of this hierarchy is frankly teleological in character. The lower species in their ascending order prepare the way for the appearance of man as being capable of conceptual thinking, a rational and free being. Man in his appearance fulfils the purpose of Nature, that is, of God. But Herder notes that whereas on the level of pure instinct the fundamental drives of the organism function in an unerring manner, the possibility of error increases with the growth of the will. 'The weaker instinct becomes, the more does it fall under the command of arbitrary will (or caprice) and therefore also of error.'[1]

For Herder history is the natural history of human powers, actions and propensities, as modified by time and place. Though not expounding, at least not in any explicit fashion, the theory of transformistic evolution, he emphasizes man's continuity, so to speak, with his physical environment and with lower forms of life. He also emphasizes man's organization. Man is 'organized for' reason and freedom. He has come into the world to learn reason and acquire freedom. He can speak, therefore, of humanity (*Humanität*) being latent in man, as something which has to be developed. At first sight it may appear to constitute a contradiction in terms if one speaks of humanity being latent in man. But Herder uses the term in two senses. It may mean the ideal which man is capable of attaining; or it may mean the potentiality for attaining this ideal. The ideal is thus latent in man, and Herder can speak of man as being organized for humanity. As a physical entity, of course, man is already there. But he has a potentiality for the perfection of man, for 'humanity'.

Man is also said to be organized for religion. Indeed, religion and humanity are intimately connected, so that the former is described as the highest humanity. As for the origin of religion, this is due, according to Herder, to man's spontaneous inference from visible phenomena to their invisible cause. To say that religion is due to fear (to fear, for instance, of hostile, dangerous or threatening meteorological phenomena) is to assign a totally inadequate cause. 'It is saying nothing to say that fear invented the gods of most peoples. For fear, considered as such, does not invent anything; it simply awakens the understanding.'[2] Even false religions bear witness to man's power of recognizing God. He may infer the existence of beings which do not exist as he conceives them; but

---

[1] XIII, p. 102.   [2] *Ibid.*, p. 162.

he is justified in his inference from the visible to the invisible, from the phenomena to a hidden cause.

When treating of Herder in Chapter VII, we mentioned his statement in *Of the Cognition and Sensation of the Human Soul* (1778) that no psychology is possible which is not physiology at every step. It is worth mentioning, therefore, that in the fifth book of the first part of his *Ideas* Herder explicitly affirms the spirituality and immortality of the human soul. He describes the mind as a unity. The phenomena of association of ideas cannot be used as a proof of the contrary. Associated ideas belong to a being which 'calls up memories from its own energy . . . and connects ideas according to an internal attraction or repulsion, not according to some external mechanics'.[1] There are purely psychological laws according to which the soul carries out its activities and combines its concepts. This certainly takes place in conjunction with organic changes; but this does not alter the nature of the soul or mind. 'If the tool is worthless, the artist can do nothing.'[2] In other words, Herder has clarified his position as against materialism.

The second part of Herder's *Ideas* can be regarded as a sustained polemic against the tendency of the thinkers of the Enlightenment to despise the primitive. Certainly, there has been development from the more to the less primitive, a development in which reaction to physical environment (as with Montesquieu) was an important factor. And Herder gives a conjectural account of the development of the family into the clan, of the clan into a tribe with an elected leader, and of the tribe into a society with an hereditary monarch. But it is nonsense to suggest that primitive peoples were without any culture; and it is still greater nonsense to suggest that they were unhappy and miserable because they did not share the supposed privileges of the eighteenth century.

Further, Herder attacks the idea that history should be interpreted as a movement of progress towards the modern State. He implies at least that the development of a modern State had little to do with reason, and that it was due rather to purely historical factors. The members of a tribe may very well have been happier than many inhabitants of a great modern State, in which 'hundreds must go hungry so that one can strut and wallow in luxury'.[3] And Herder's dislike for authoritarian government is plain enough. When he published the second part he had to omit the statements that the best ruler is the one who contributes the most

[1] XIII, p. 183.   [2] *Ibid.*, p. 182.   [3] *Ibid.*, p. 340.

to making rulers unnecessary, and that governments are like bad doctors who treat their patients in such a way that the latter are in constant need of them. But what he did say was clear enough. In his view, 'the man who needs a lord is an animal; as soon as he becomes a human being he no longer needs a lord'.[1] So much for the ideal of enlightened despotism.

In all this Herder was partly engaged in an indirect attack on Kant. The latter had published a hostile review of the first part of *Ideas*; and in the second part Herder took the opportunity of attacking, indirectly, Kant's *Idea for a General History from a Cosmopolitan Point of View* (*Idee zu einer allgemeinen Geschichte in weltbürgerlicher Absicht*, 1784). Kant was prepared to neglect all stages of social organization except in so far as they could be seen as contributing to the development of the rational State. And a rational State must have a 'lord'; for man is so defective that he cannot live in society without one. Kant may very well have been right on this point; but Herder preferred to believe in man's natural goodness and perfectibility. In any case he was intent on rejecting the notion that history can profitably be interpreted as a progress towards the modern State, in the light of which all other forms of social organization must be judged.

In the third part of his *Ideas* Herder comes to recorded history. His general principle for the historian is that the latter's mind should be free from hypotheses, and that he ought not to take any particular nation or people as his favourite, despising or belittling other peoples. The historian of mankind must judge impartially and dispassionately, 'like the Creator of our race'.[2] Generally speaking, Herder makes a point of endeavouring to live up to this principle, though an animus against Rome manifests itself, with an accompanying indulgence towards the civilization of the Phoenicians.

Herder does not confine himself to Europe, but considers also the cultures of, for example, China, India, Egypt and the Jews, though his knowledge of China and India was, not unnaturally, deficient. Coming to Greece,[3] he finds a complete cultural cycle, the rise and decline of one people, and uses it to draw general conclusions. Every culture has its centre of gravity, and the deeper this centre of gravity lies in a balance of the culture's living active forces, the more solid and lasting is the culture. We can say

[1] XIII, p. 383.   [2] XIV, p. 85.
[3] Goethe consulted Herder as an authority on Greek culture.

therefore, that the peak of a culture is found when its active forces are most in equilibrium. But this peak is, of course, a point; that is to say, the centre of gravity inevitably moves, and the equilibrium is disturbed. The active forces may be so deployed that equilibrium is temporarily restored; but it cannot last for ever. Decline comes without fail sooner or later. Herder speaks as though the life of a culture were determined by natural laws: it is analogous to the life of a biological organism. The fate of Rome was predetermined not by divine intervention but by natural factors. Environment forced the Romans to become a military people, and this development shaped their history, their rise to greatness and their eventual decline. The empire became unbalanced, and it could not sustain itself.

In the fourth part of his *Ideas* Herder continues his account of European history from the fall of the Roman empire. In it he lays stress on the part played by Christianity in the development of European culture. It is true that we find an awareness of the importance of economic factors. Herder's account of the Crusades is a case in point. And he is by no means blind to the importance of technical inventions and of new scientific knowledge. But he is very far removed from the mentality of the Enlightenment, which regarded the desirable development of civilization as a movement away from religion. Herder may have been a liberal Christian, but he was profoundly convinced of the indispensable role of religion in human culture.

Inasmuch as Herder emphasizes ethnic groups, nations and cultures, and inasmuch as he emphasizes the part played by the Germanic peoples in the rise of Christian culture, a few misguided people, Nazis for instance, have tried to depict him as a nationalist and even as an adherent of a race-theory. But this interpretation is quite beside the mark. He nowhere suggests that the Germans should rule other nations. Indeed, he condemns, for instance, the behaviour of the Teutonic knights towards Germany's eastern neighbours; and in his writings he frequently attacks militarism and imperialism. His ideal was that of a harmonious unfolding of national cultures. Just as individuals are, or should be, free and yet united in society, so different nations should form a family, each making its own contribution to the development of 'humanity'. As for the race-theory, Herder believed that ethnic groupings form the most natural bases for States. And in his view one of the factors which contributed to the instability of Rome was precisely the way in which conquest of other peoples destroyed its ethnic unity. But this idea, whether valid or not, has nothing to do with the race-theory, if this is taken to mean the notion that one race is inherently superior to other races and has a right to rule them. As for the Jews, Herder was far from being an anti-Semite. But it would be waste of time to dwell more on this topic. No sensible, objective historian supposes that Herder's theory of history as a development of national cultures involves nationalism in the pejorative sense, militarism and imperialism, or the theory of the inherent superiority of a given race. Of course, in some sense he was a nationalist, but not in the sense that he claimed on behalf of his own nation rights which he was unwilling to concede to other nations.

Herder's philosophy of history is somewhat complex. In the first place we have his insistence on the need for an objective and dispassionate examination, free from preconceived theories, of each culture on its own merits. This is obviously an excellent rule for an historian. In the second place we have his theory of the life of a culture, on an analogy with the life of the organism; and this theory may appear to lend itself to interpretation in a manner reminiscent of Vico's theory of cycles. In the third place, however, we have his idea of 'humanity', which fits in better with a theory of progress than with a theory of cycles. But a harmonization is doubtless possible. Each culture has its cycle; but the general movement is towards the realization of man's immanent potentiality for 'humanity'.

Whether the progressive approximation to the ideal of humanity is inevitable or not for Herder, does not seem to be altogether clear. In his *Ideas* he remarks that 'the philosophy of final purposes has brought no advantage to natural history'.[1] It is absurd to suggest, for example, that the bad actions of Rome were necessary and required in order that Roman culture might develop and attain its peak. At the same time, although we cannot legitimately justify all actions in history on the ground that they were required for the fulfilment of some specific providential plan, Herder certainly appears to say that the gradual development of 'humanity' is inevitable. Thus he informs his readers that anything which can happen within the limits of given national, temporal and spatial circumstances, does happen.[2] And this appears to imply that if progressive approximation to the ideal of

[1] XIV, p. 202.   [2] *Ibid.*, p. 144.

humanity is possible, it will inevitably take place. Indeed, we are told that all destructive forces must ultimately yield to conserving forces and work for the development of the whole.[1]

A similar ambiguity appears in the series of *Letters for the Advancement of Humanity* (*Briefe zur Beförderung der Humanität*, 1793–7). In these *Letters*, in which Herder shows a greater readiness than before to recognize the capacity of political changes to contribute to the advance of mankind,[2] his general point of view seems to be that there is, and will be, by and large, a progressive movement towards the realization of the ideal of humanity. At the same time he insists on the necessity for education to develop man's innate potentialities. Without this unceasing formative education man would sink back into bestiality.[3] And such statements do not seem to imply the inevitability of progress. According to Herder, we can distinguish three phases in the development of the European spirit. First, there was that mixture of Roman and Germanic culture which produced the organization, religious and political, of Europe. Secondly, there were the Renaissance and Reformation. And, thirdly, there is the present phase, the result of which we are unable to predict.[4] Here again there seems to be some doubt about the future, though this doubt could, of course, be reconciled with a general belief in the forward march of humanity towards the ultimate development of its highest potentialities.

The situation can perhaps be expressed in this way. As an historian, hostile to the tendency to judge all cultures in the light of the civilization of his time, Herder was strongly inclined to historicism and relativism, which hardly fitted in with a dogma of progress. But as a philosopher, believing not only in man's natural goodness and perfectibility but also in the working of divine providence in and through men's actions, he was naturally inclined to the conclusion that man's highest potentialities will be eventually actualized in spite of all setbacks on the way.

[1] XIV, p. 213.
[2] He is more appreciative, for example, of Frederick the Great's measures of reform. And he at first intended to write optimistically of the French Revolution, though the appearance of the Terror led him to omit these sections.
[3] XVII, p. 138.
[4] In connection with this phase Herder speaks of the world-spirit (*Weltgeist*), a term which recurs with Hegel.

PART IV

KANT

CHAPTER X

KANT (1): LIFE AND WRITINGS

Kant's life and character—Earlier writings and the Newtonian physics—Philosophical writings of the pre-critical period—The dissertation of 1770 and its context—The conception of the critical philosophy.

1. IF we prescind from the history of his intellectual development and from the results of this development, we do not need to spend much time in recounting the facts of Kant's life. For it was singularly uneventful and devoid of dramatic incident. True, any philosopher's life is devoted primarily to reflection, not to external activity on the stage of public life. He is not a commander in the field or an Arctic explorer. And unless he is forced to drink poison like Socrates or is burned at the stake like Giordano Bruno, his life naturally tends to be undramatic. But Kant was not even a travelled man of the world like Leibniz. For he spent all his life in East Prussia. Nor did he occupy the position of a philosophical dictator in the university of a capital city, as Hegel later did at Berlin. He was simply an excellent professor in the not very distinguished university of a provincial town. Nor was his character such as to provide a happy hunting-ground for psychological analysts, as with Kierkegaard and Nietzsche. In his later years he was noted for his methodical regularity of life and for his punctuality; but it would hardly occur to anyone to think of him as an abnormal personality. But perhaps one can say that the contrast between his quiet and comparatively uneventful life and the greatness of his influence has itself a dramatic quality.

Immanuel Kant was born at Königsberg on April 22nd, 1724, the son of a saddler. Both as a child at home and at the Collegium Fridericianum, where he studied from 1732 until 1740, he was brought up in the spirit of the pietist movement. He continued throughout his life to appreciate the good qualities of sincere pietists; but it is evident that he reacted rather sharply against the religious observances to which he had to conform at the college. As for his formal schooling, he acquired a good knowledge of Latin.

In 1740 Kant entered upon his university studies in his home town and attended lectures in a wide variety of subjects. The main influence upon his mind, however, was that of Martin Knutzen, professor of logic and metaphysics. Knutzen was a disciple of Wolff; but he had a particular interest in natural science, lecturing in physics, astronomy and mathematics, as well as in philosophy. And Kant, who enjoyed the use of the professor's library, was stimulated by him to acquire a knowledge of Newtonian science. Indeed, Kant's first writings were mostly of a scientific nature, and he always retained a deep interest in the subject.

At the conclusion of his university studies Kant was driven by financial reasons to take posts as a family tutor in East Prussia; and this period of his life lasted some seven or eight years, finishing in 1755 when he took what we would call the doctorate and received permission to set up as a *Privatdozent* or lecturer. In 1756 he tried to obtain Knutzen's chair, rendered vacant by the latter's death. But Knutzen had been an 'extraordinary' professor, and the government, influenced by financial considerations, left the post unfilled. In 1764 Kant was offered the chair of poetry, but he declined it, no doubt wisely. In 1769 he refused a similar offer from Jena. Finally in March 1770 he was appointed 'ordinary' professor of logic and metaphysics at Königsberg. His period as a *Privatdozent* lasted, therefore, from 1755 until 1770, though for the last four years of this period a post as assistant librarian afforded him some additional financial support. (In 1772 he resigned this post as incompatible with his professorship.)

During these fifteen years, which belong to what is generally called Kant's pre-critical period, the philosopher gave an enormous number of lectures on a wide variety of topics. Thus at various times he lectured not only on logic, metaphysics and moral philosophy but also on physics, mathematics, geography, anthropology, pedagogy and mineralogy. From all accounts he was an excellent lecturer. It was the rule for professors and lecturers to expound text-books, and Kant had, of course, to conform to this rule. Thus he made use of Baumgarten's *Metaphysics*. But he did not hesitate to depart from his text or to criticize it, and his lectures were salted with humour, and even with stories. In his philosophical courses his main aim was to stimulate his hearers to think for themselves, to stand on their own feet, as he put it.

It must not be thought that Kant was a recluse. Later on he found himself compelled to economize with his time, but at the period of which we are writing he went a good deal into local society. Indeed, throughout his life he enjoyed social intercourse. Moreover, though he was far from being a travelled man, he took pleasure in meeting people who had experience of other countries, and he sometimes astonished them by his own knowledge, though this had been gained, of course, by reading. His interests were fairly wide. Thus the influence of Rousseau's writings stimulated a lively interest in educational reform, besides helping to develop his political views in a radical direction.

It is hardly to be expected, of course, that one should be able to designate the exact moment at which the pre-critical period of Kant's thought ended and the critical period began. That is to say, it would be unreasonable to expect that one should be able to state exactly when Kant rejected the Leibniz-Wolffian system of philosophy and began to work out his own system. However, for general purposes one can take his appointment as professor in 1770 as a convenient date. But the *Critique of Pure Reason* did not appear until 1781. During the intervening eleven years Kant was thinking out his philosophy. At the same time (or, rather, until 1796 inclusive) he was also engaged in lecturing. He continued to use Wolffian text-books in philosophy, and he also continued to give courses of lectures on non-philosophical subjects, those on anthropology and physical geography being particularly popular. It was his conviction that students needed factual knowledge of this kind, in order that they might understand the part played by experience in our knowledge. Philosophical theorizing in the void was by no means a Kantian ideal, even though a cursory glance at the first *Critique* might suggest that it was.

Once the first edition of the *Critique of Pure Reason* had appeared in 1781, Kant's other famous writings followed in quick succession. In 1783 he published *Prolegomena to any Future Metaphysics*, in 1785 the *Fundamental Principles of the Metaphysics of Morals*, in 1786 the *Metaphysical First Principles of Natural Science*, in 1787 the second edition of the *Critique of Pure Reason*, in 1788 the *Critique of Practical Reason*, in 1790 the *Critique of Judgment*, in 1793 *Religion within the Bounds of Reason Alone*, in 1795 a little treatise *On Perpetual Peace*, and in 1797 the

Metaphysics of Morals. It is understandable, therefore, that with this heavy programme Kant had to husband his time. And his order of the day, to which he faithfully adhered during his years as a professor, has become famous. Rising shortly before five in the morning, he spent the hour from five to six drinking tea, smoking a pipe, and thinking over his day's work. From six to seven he prepared his lecture, which began at seven or eight, according to the time of year, and lasted until nine or ten. He then devoted himself to writing until the midday meal, at which he always had company and which was prolonged for several hours, as Kant enjoyed conversation. Afterwards he took a daily walk of an hour or so, and the evening was given to reading and reflection. He retired to bed at ten o'clock.

Only once did Kant come into collision with political authority. This was in connection with his *Religion within the Bounds of Reason Alone.* In 1792 the first part of this work, entitled 'On the Radical Evil in Human Nature', had been passed by the censor on the ground that, like Kant's other writings, it was not intended for the general reader. But the second part, 'On the Conflict of the Good Principle with the Evil', failed to satisfy the censorship, on the ground that it attacked biblical theology. However, the whole work, consisting of four parts, was approved by the theological faculty of Königsberg and the philosophical faculty of Jena, and was published in 1793. Then trouble arose. In 1794 Frederick William II, successor to Frederick the Great on the throne of Prussia, expressed his displeasure at the book and accused Kant of misrepresenting and depreciating many fundamental principles of the Scriptures and of Christianity. The king threatened Kant with penalties if he should venture to repeat the offence. The philosopher declined to retract his opinions, but he promised to refrain from making any further public pronouncements, whether in lectures or in writing, on religion either natural or revealed. On the king's death, however, Kant considered that he was released from his promise, and in 1798 he published *The Conflict of the Faculties*, in which he discussed the relation between theology, in the sense of biblical belief, and philosophy or the critical reason.

Kant died on February 12th, 1804. He was already fifty-seven years old when he published his first famous work, the *Critique of Pure Reason*, and his literary production between 1781 and the time of his death constitutes an astonishing performance. In his last years he was working at a restatement of his philosophy, and the notes which were designed as material for a revised version of his system were published in a critical edition by Erich Adickes in 1920 under the title *Kants opus postumum*.

The salient trait in Kant's character was probably his moral earnestness and his devotion to the idea of duty, a devotion which found theoretical expression in his ethical writings. He was, as we have seen, a sociable man; he was also a kindly and benevolent one. Never rich, he was systematically careful in money matters; but he regularly assisted a number of poor persons. His thrift was certainly not accompanied by selfishness or hard-heartedness. Though scarcely a sentimental man, he was a sincere and loyal friend, and his conduct was marked by courtesy and respect for others. As regards religion, Kant was not given to the ordinary observances, and nobody could claim that he was inclined to mysticism. Nor was he precisely an orthodox Christian. But he certainly possessed a real belief in God. Though he maintained that morality is autonomous, in the sense that its principles are underived from theology, natural or revealed, he was also convinced that it implies or ultimately involves belief in God, in a sense which will be explained later. It would be an exaggeration to say that he had no idea of religious experience. And if one did say this, one would unfailingly arouse indignant references to Kant's reverence for the starry heavens above and the moral law within. At the same time he showed no real appreciation of the activities of adoration and prayer and of what Baron von Hügel called the mystical element in religion. But this does not mean, of course, that he had no reverence for God, even if his approach to religion was practically exclusively through the consciousness of moral obligation. The fact of the matter seems to be that just as Kant wrote on aesthetics and aesthetic experience without apparently possessing any personal and lively taste for, say, music, so he wrote on religion without possessing any deep understanding either of Christian piety or, for instance, of oriental mysticism. He was characterized by moral earnestness rather than by religious devotion, provided that this statement is not understood to mean that he was an irreligious man or that his assertion of belief in God was insincere. It was only on formal occasions which required his presence that he attended church services, and his remark to a friend that advance in moral goodness is accompanied by disuse of prayer reveals something of his character.

In politics Kant was inclined to republicanism, if this term is taken to include limited, constitutional monarchy. He sympathized with the Americans in the War of Independence, and later with the ideals at least of the French Revolution. Militarism and chauvinism were quite alien to his mind: the author of the *Treatise On Perpetual Peace* was not the kind of thinker of whom the Nazis were able to make plausible use. His political ideas were, of course, intimately associated with his conception of the value of the free, moral personality.

2. As we have seen, Kant's interest in scientific matters was stimulated by Martin Knutzen at the university of Königsberg. It is also evident that during the period which he spent as a family tutor in East Prussia he read extensively in scientific literature. For the doctorate dissertation which he submitted to the university in 1755 was on *Fire* (*De igne*): and in the same year he published a *General Natural History and Theory of the Heavens* (*Allgemeine Naturgeschichte und Theorie des Himmels*). This work had grown out of two previous essays (1754), one on the earth's motion round its axis, the other on the physical question whether the earth is growing old. In it he proposed an original anticipation of the nebular hypothesis advanced later by Laplace.

Instead, therefore, of the customary twofold division of Kant's intellectual life into the pre-critical period, when he was under the influence of the Leibniz-Wolffian system, and the critical period, when he was thinking out and expressing his own philosophy, some historians prefer a threefold division. That is to say, they think that we should recognize the existence of an initial period in which Kant was primarily concerned with problems of a scientific nature. This period would have lasted until 1755 or 1756, and the pre-critical philosophical period would fall more or less in the sixties.

There is, of course, something to be said in favour of this three-fold division. For it serves to draw attention to the predominantly scientific character of Kant's earlier writing. But for general purposes the traditional twofold division seems to me to be quite sufficient. After all, Kant did not abandon Newtonian physics for any other kind of physics. But he did abandon the Wolffian philosophical tradition in favour of an original philosophy. And this remains the important fact in his mental development. Further, the threefold division can be misleading. On the one hand Kant's earlier writings, though predominantly scientific, were not exclusively so. For instance, in 1755 his *De igne* was followed by another Latin dissertation entitled *A New Explanation of the First Principles of Metaphysical Knowledge* (*Principiorum primorum cognitionis metaphysicae nova dilucidatio*), which was composed in connection with receiving permission to lecture in the university as *Privatdozent*. On the other hand Kant published some scientific papers even during the critical period. Thus in 1785 he published an essay *On Volcanoes in the Moon* (*Ueber die Vulkane in Monde*).

It would, however, be a waste of time to pursue this question any further. The important point is that Kant, though never, so to speak, a practising physicist or astronomer, acquired a knowledge of Newtonian science, and that the validity of the scientific conception of the world remained for him a firm fact. The nature of scientific knowledge was, of course, open to discussion; and the range of applicability of scientific categories and concepts constituted a problem. But Kant never doubted the general validity of Newtonian physics within its own field; and his later problems arose on the basis of this conviction. How, for example, can we reconcile with the scientific conception of the world as a law-governed system, in which each event has its determinate and determining course, the world of moral experience which implies freedom? Again, what theoretical justification can we find for the universality of scientific statements and for the validity of scientific prediction in face of the empiricism of David Hume, which appears to deprive the scientific conception of the world of any rational, theoretical justification? I do not mean to imply that such problems were present from the beginning in Kant's mind; nor do I wish to anticipate at this point a discussion of the questions which gave rise at a later stage to his critical philosophy. But for an appreciation of his characteristic problematic it is essential to understand from the start that he accepted and continued to accept the validity of Newtonian science. Given this acceptance and given the empiricism of Hume, Kant found himself compelled in the course of time to raise questions about the nature of scientific knowledge. Again, given his acceptance of the scientific conception of the world and given at the same time his acceptance of the validity of moral experience, Kant found himself compelled in the course of time to discuss the reconciliation of the world of necessity with the world of freedom. Finally, given the facts of scientific advance and of the common acceptance of the classical physics, he found himself driven to ask whether the lack of comparable advance in metaphysics and of a common acceptance of any one metaphysical system did not demand a radical revision of our ideas of the nature and function of metaphysics. Kant's treatment of these problems lay in the future; but it presupposed that acceptance of Newtonian science which is manifested in his earlier writings.

3. When we speak of the pre-critical period in Kant's intellectual development, the reference is, of course, to the period which precedes the conception and working-out of his own original philosophy. In other words, the term must be taken in a technical sense and not in the sense of 'uncritical'. In this period he adhered more or less to the standpoint of the Wolffian philosophy; but he never accepted this philosophy in a slavish and uncritical manner. Already in 1755 he had criticized some doctrines of Leibniz and Wolff, such as the use made by them of the principle of sufficient reason, in his Latin work, *A New Explanation of the First Principles of Metaphysical Knowledge*. At this time his knowledge of the philosophy of Leibniz, as distinct from the scholasticized version of it elaborated by Wolff and his followers, was restricted and inadequate; but in the writings during the sixties we can see an increasingly critical attitude towards the Leibniz-Wolffian system, though it was not until the end of the decade that the critical point of view, in a technical sense of the term, made its appearance.

In 1762 Kant published *The False Subtlety of the Four Syllogistic Figures (Die falsche Spitzfindigkeit der vier syllogistischen Figuren)*, in which he maintained that the logical division of the syllogism into four figures is over-subtle and unnecessary. And at the end of the same year he published *The Only Possible Ground for a Demonstration of God's Existence (Der einzig mögliche Beweisgrund zu einer Demonstration des Daseins Gottes)*. As this work is of some interest a few brief remarks can be made about it here.

At the end of the essay Kant remarks that though 'it is thoroughly necessary to be convinced of God's existence, it is not quite so necessary that one should demonstrate it'.[1] For Providence has not willed that the only way of coming to a knowledge of God should be by way of metaphysical subtleties. Indeed, if this were the case, we should be in a sorry plight. For no really cogent demonstration, affording a certainty analogous to that of

[1] 3, 5; *W.*, II, p. 163. References to volume and page, preceded by the letter *W.*, are always to the edition of Kant's Works by the Prussian Academy of Sciences. See Bibliography.

mathematics, has yet been provided. However, it is natural that the professional philosopher should inquire whether a strict demonstration of God's existence is possible. And Kant's intention is to make a contribution to this inquiry.

All proofs of the existence of God must rest either on the concept of the possible or on the empirical idea of the existent. Further, each class can be divided into two sub-classes. In the first place we may attempt to argue either from possibility as a ground to the existence of God as a consequence or from possibility as a consequence to God's existence as the ground of this possibility. In the second place, that is, if we start with existing things, two courses are open to us. Either we can try to prove the existence of a first and independent cause of these things, and then show that such a cause must possess certain attributes, which make it proper to speak of it as God. Or we can try to prove at the same time both the existence and the attributes of God. Any proof of the existence of God must, according to Kant,[1] take one of these four forms.

The first line of argument mentioned, namely that from possibility as a ground to the existence of God as consequence, corresponds to the so-called ontological argument, from the idea of God to the divine existence, which was proposed in different forms by St. Anselm and Descartes and which was restated and accepted by Leibniz. It is rejected by Kant in *The Only Possible Ground* because, as he maintains, it presupposes that existence is a predicate, which is a false presupposition. The third line of argument, which corresponds to what Kant later calls the cosmological argument and which, he remarks, is much used by philosophers of the Wolffian School, is ruled out on the ground that we cannot demonstrate that a first cause must be what we call God. For the fourth line of argument, which corresponds to a teleological proof or proof from design, Kant shows, as he will continue to show in future, considerable respect, provided that emphasis is placed on the immanent teleology of the organism. None the less it does not, and cannot, amount to a demonstration of God's existence. For it brings us at best to a divine mind or intelligence which produces system and order and teleology in the world, not to a creator. In other words, it leaves us with a dualism, with superterrestrial mind on the one hand and with the material to be shaped on the other. As far as this argument alone is concerned, we are left in doubt whether this material is independent of or dependent on God.

[1] 3, 1; *W.*, II, pp. 154-5.

There remains, therefore, the second line of argument, that from possibility as consequence to the existence of God as its ground. And it is this line of argument which Kant proposes as the only possible basis for a demonstration of God's existence. There is, he tells us, no intrinsic logical contradiction in denying all existence whatsoever. But what we cannot legitimately do is to affirm possibility and at the same time to deny that there is an existent ground of possibility. And we must admit possibility. For we cannot deny it without thinking, and to think is to affirm implicitly the realm of possibility. And Kant proceeds to argue that this being must be one, simple, immutable, eternal, spiritual and whatever else is included in the meaning of the term 'God' as used in metaphysics.

As far as mediaeval philosophy is concerned, this line of argument reminds one much more of Duns Scotus, who tried to argue from possibility to the existence and attributes of God, than of St. Thomas Aquinas. True, in his Third Way Aquinas bases his argument on the concept of 'possible' beings; but his concept of possibility is derived from the empirical fact that some things come into being and pass away and are therefore 'possible' (what Scholastics generally call 'contingent'). And Kant is arguing that the existence of God is implied by all thinking rather than that the existence of contingent things manifests the existence of God. Perhaps we can say that what Kant is demanding is that the Leibnizian argument from eternal truths should be turned into a strict demonstration. In any case it is interesting to observe that his line of thought, though different from that of the ontological argument, is of an *a priori* character in comparison with, say, the argument from design, and that it presupposes a Leibnizian view of metaphysics as a non-empirical science. But this does not mean that he did not see any intrinsic difference between mathematics and metaphysics. A difference is clearly affirmed in a work to which reference will now be made.

In *The Only Possible Ground*[1] Kant spoke of metaphysics as 'a bottomless abyss' and as 'a dark ocean without shore and without lighthouses'. We hear something more explicit about the nature of metaphysics in his *Enquiry into the Distinctness of the Principles of Natural Theology and Morals (Untersuchung über die Deutlichkeit der Grundsätze der natürlichen Theologie und der Moral,* 1764). In the preceding year the Berlin Academy had offered a prize for

---

[1] Preface; *W.*, II, p. 66.

an essay on the question whether metaphysical truths in general and, in particular, the first principles of natural theology and morals are capable of the same degree of demonstrative certainty as the truths of geometry. If not, what are the peculiar nature and degree of the certainty which they enjoy? And is this degree sufficient to justify full conviction? Kant's essay did not win the prize, which went to a contribution by Mendelssohn; but it is naturally of considerable interest.

Kant insists that there are fundamental differences between mathematics and metaphysics.[1] Thus mathematics is a constructive science in the sense that it proceeds 'synthetically' constructing its definitions arbitrarily. The definition of a geometrical figure is not the result of analysing a previously possessed concept or idea: the concept arises through the definition. In philosophy (which Kant calls 'world-wisdom', *Weltweisheit*), however, definitions are obtained, when they are obtained, by analysis. That is to say, we have first of all an idea of something, though this idea is confused or inadequate; and we then endeavour to clarify it by comparing instances of its application and by performing a work of abstraction. In this sense philosophy proceeds analytically, and not synthetically. To illustrate the difference, Kant takes the example of time. We already have some idea and knowledge of time before we undertake a philosophical investigation of it. And this investigation takes the form of comparing and analysing diverse instances of the experience of time with a view to forming an adequate, abstract concept. 'But if I wished to try to arrive synthetically at a definition of time, what a happy chance I should have to meet with, for this concept to be precisely the one which completely expressed the previously given idea.'[2] That is to say, if I constructed a definition of time arbitrarily, as the geometer constructs his definitions, it would be a matter of mere chance if it happened to give explicit, abstract expression to the concrete idea of time which I, like anyone else, already possess.

It may be said that philosophers do as a matter of fact construct definitions 'synthetically'. For instance, Leibniz conceived for himself a simple substance possessing only obscure or confused representations and called it a slumbering monad. This is perfectly

---

[1] In an essay on the concept of negative quantity (1763) Kant had already explicitly rejected the notion that the mathematical method should be used in philosophy, though he also insisted that mathematical truths can be philosophically relevant and fertile (*W.*, II, pp. 167–8).

[2] *Enquiry*, I, I; *W.*, II, p. 277.

true. But the point is that when philosophers construct definitions arbitrarily, these definitions are not properly speaking *philosophical* definitions. 'Such determinations of the meaning of a word are never philosophical definitions; but if they are to be called clarifications at all, they are only grammatical clarifications.'[1] I can explain, if I wish, in what sense I intend to use the term 'slumbering monad'; but then I am acting as a grammarian rather than as a philosopher. Leibniz 'had not explained this monad, but imagined it; for the idea of it was not something given to him but something which he had himself created'.[2] Analogously, the mathematician often enough deals with concepts which are capable of philosophical analysis and which are not mere arbitrary constructions. The concept of space is a case in point. But such concepts are received by the mathematician; they are not, technically speaking, mathematical concepts in the same sense as the concept of, say, a polygon.

We can say, then, that while in mathematics I have no concept at all of my object until the definition provides one, in metaphysics[3] I have a concept which is already given to me, although it is confused, and I should try to make it clear, explicit and definite.[4] As St. Augustine says, I know very well what time is as long as nobody asks me for a definition. And in metaphysics I can very well know some truths about an object of thought and draw valid conclusions from these truths without being able to define the object. Kant gives the example of desire. There is much that I can say with truth about the nature of desire without being able to define it. In short, while in mathematics one begins with definitions, in metaphysics it is rather the other way about. And Kant concludes that the principle rule to be observed if certainty is to be obtained in metaphysics is to ascertain what it is that one knows immediately and with certainty of the subject-matter in question, and to determine the judgments to which this knowledge gives rise.

Metaphysics is thus different from mathematics. At the same time we must admit that philosophical theories have been for the most part like meteors, the brightness of which is no guarantee of their longevity. 'Metaphysics is without a doubt the most difficult of all human studies; only no metaphysics has yet been

[1] *Enquiry*, I, I; *W.*, II, p. 277.   [2] *Ibid.*
[3] Metaphysics is described by Kant as 'nothing else but philosophy about the ultimate principles of our knowledge' (*Enquiry*, 2; *W.*, II, p. 283).
[4] *Enquiry*, 2; *W.*, II, p. 283.

written.'[1] What is required is a change of method. 'The genuine method of metaphysics is fundamentally of the same kind as that which Newton introduced into natural science and which was there so fruitful.'[2] The metaphysician should start with some phenomena of 'inner experience', describe them accurately and ascertain the immediate judgments to which they give rise and of which we are certain. He can later inquire whether the diverse phenomena can be brought together under a single concept or definition, analogous to, say, the general law of gravitation. Kant, as we have seen, used Wolffian text-books in philosophy, and in metaphysics he made use of Baumgarten. Now, Baumgarten's method was that of starting with very general definitions and then proceeding to the more particular. And it is precisely this method which Kant rejects. The metaphysician is not concerned primarily with the relation of ground to consequent in a purely logical and formal sense. He is concerned with 'real grounds'; and he must start with the given.

As regards the particular questions proposed by the Berlin Academy concerning natural theology and morals, Kant still maintains in the *Enquiry* that the principles of natural theology are, or can be, certain. And he refers briefly to his demonstration of the existence of God as the actual ground of possibility. But in morals the situation is somewhat different. For one thing we must recognize the part played by feeling in the moral life. Kant refers to 'Hutcheson and others', and he remarks that 'it is first of all in our days that people have begun to see that while the power of representing truth is *knowledge*, that of perceiving the good is *feeling*, and that these two must not be confused with one another'.[3] (The influence of British moralists and writers on aesthetics is apparent also in Kant's *Observations on the Feeling of the Beautiful and Sublime* (*Beobachtungen über das Gefühl des Schönen und Erhabenen*, 1764).) But, quite apart from the part played by feeling in the moral life, the first principles of morality have not yet been made sufficiently clear. We find some anticipation of Kant's later ethical theory in the distinction which he makes between 'problematical necessity' (to attain end X, you must take means Y) and 'legal necessity' (you are obliged to do this, not as a means to something else, but as an end). At the same time he tells us that after much thought he has come to the

[1] *Enquiry*, 1, 4; *W.*, II, p. 283.
[2] *Enquiry*, 2; *W.*, II, p. 286.
[3] *Enquiry*, 4, 2; *W.*, II, pp. 299–300.

conclusion that the first formal principle of obligation is 'Do the most perfect thing which is possible for you'.[1] But we cannot deduce from this principle particular obligations, unless 'material' first principles are also given. All these themes need to be carefully examined and thought through before we can give to the first principles of morals the highest degree of philosophical certainty.

Kant's remarks in the *Enquiry* about clarifying our idea of time may perhaps suggest to the contemporary English reader that he is engaged in reducing philosophy to 'linguistic analysis', to an analysis of the use of terms. But he does not intend to deny the existential import of metaphysics. This is made clear, for instance, by what he has to say on natural theology. His point in this work is that a metaphysics which really employs the mathematical method will be confined to exhibiting relations of formal implication. If the metaphysician is to increase our knowledge of reality, he must cease trying to ape the mathematician and turn rather to a method analogous to that which was employed so successfully by Newton in natural science. He should, indeed, begin by clarifying the confused concepts of experience and giving them adequate and abstract expression; but he may then be able to proceed to inference and to the building-up of a metaphysics. It does not follow, however, that Kant possesses any great faith in the capacity of metaphysics for extending our theoretical knowledge beyond the sphere of the sciences. And when we are already aware of the later development of his thought, certain remarks in the *Enquiry* naturally suggest to our minds a tentative anticipation of his later point of view. Such a remark is the statement that metaphysics is concerned with the first principles of our knowledge. We should not, however, be justified in trying to father upon Kant at this stage the critical point of view. What we can say is that his recommendation to metaphysicians to substitute the Newtonian for the mathematical method should not blind us to his growing scepticism about the pretensions of speculative metaphysics. Indeed, the recommendation is partly an expression of this scepticism, or at least doubt. For it is linked with the conviction that whereas natural science has made good its claim to increase our knowledge of the world, metaphysics has not yet done so. And a suggestion as to how it might do so does not mean that Kant commits himself to the claims of speculative metaphysics. Indeed, he very soon makes it clear that this is far from being the case.

[1] *Enquiry*, 4, 2; *W*., II, p. 299.

In 1766 Kant published anonymously (though the author's identity was never a secret) a partly serious, partly humorous work entitled *Dreams of a Ghost-seer explained by Dreams of Metaphysics* (*Träume eines Geistersehers, erläutert durch Träume der Metaphysik*). For some time he had been curious about the visionary experiences of Immanuel Swedenborg; and he studied the latter's *Arcana coelestia*, the result of his reflections being *Dreams of a Ghost-seer*. As regards visionary experiences, Kant does not definitely either accept or reject their possible origin in the influence exerted by a world of spirits. On the one hand he gives us what he calls 'a fragment of esoteric philosophy',[1] in which, given the (unproved) assumption of a world of spirits, he suggests a way in which the influence of spirits on men's souls might be projected in imaginative visions. On the other hand he follows this up with 'a fragment of vulgar philosophy',[2] in which he suggests an explanation of experiences such as those of Swedenborg which would make their subjects fit candidates for medical attention and treatment. The reader is left to adopt which explanation he chooses. But the main point is not Kant's discussion of visionary experiences but rather his question whether the theories of speculative metaphysics, so far as they pretend to transcend experience, are in any stronger position than Swedenborg's visions. And he makes it clear that they are, in his opinion, in a weaker position. It may be that Swedenborg's visions were caused by contact with a world of spirits, even if this cannot be proved. But metaphysical theories are supposed to be rationally demonstrated; and this is what metaphysical theories about spiritual beings cannot be. We cannot even have positive conceptions of spirits. True, we can try to describe them by the aid of negations. But the possibility of this procedure rests, according to Kant, neither on experience nor on rational inference: it rests on our ignorance, on the limitations of our knowledge. The conclusion is that the doctrine of spirits must be excluded from metaphysics which, if it is to be scientific at all, must consist in determining 'the limits of knowledge which have been set by the nature of the human reason'.[3]

In adopting this attitude towards metaphysics Kant was influenced by the criticism of Hume. This seems to be made abundantly clear by what is said in *Dreams of a Ghost-seer* about

[1] *Dreams*, 1, 2; *W*., II, p. 329.
[2] *Dreams*, 1, 3; *W*., II, p. 342.
[3] *Dreams*, 2, 3; *W*., II, p. 369.

the causal relation. This must not be confused with the relation of logical implication. No logical contradiction is ever involved in affirming the cause and denying the effect. Causes and effects can be known only through experience. We cannot, therefore, employ the idea of causality to transcend experience (that is, sense-experience) and to attain knowledge of supersensible reality. Kant does not deny that there is supersensible reality: what he denies is that metaphysics can open the door to it in the way that meta-physicians of the past have thought that it could.

It is no good saying, Kant remarks, that traditional meta-physics is necessary for morality, in the sense that moral principles are dependent on metaphysical truths, such as the immortality of the soul and divine reward and punishment in the next life. Moral principles are not conclusions drawn from speculative meta-physics. At the same time moral faith (*der moralische Glaube*) may well point beyond the empirical world. 'It seems to be more in accordance with human nature and the purity of morals to ground the expectation of the future world on the experience of a virtuous soul than, conversely, to base its moral attitude on the hope of another world.'[1]

In the *Dreams of a Ghost-seer*, therefore, we find anticipations of Kant's later views. Speculative metaphysics of the traditional type is not, and cannot be, a source of scientific, demonstrated knowledge. Morality is autonomous and not dependent on meta-physics or on theology. That is to say, moral principles are not conclusions drawn from metaphysical or theological premises. At the same time morality may point beyond itself, in the sense that moral experience produces a (reasonable) moral faith in certain truths which cannot be demonstrated by the metaphysicians. But beyond the suggestion that metaphysics should take the form of a science of the limits of human knowledge Kant has not yet arrived at his characteristic conception of philosophy. The negative side of his thought is still prominent, namely the sceptical criticism of speculative metaphysics.

That Kant has not yet arrived at the critical standpoint is clear, for example, from the essay on space which he published in 1768. In this essay he developed some ideas of Leonard Euler (1707–83), for whom he had a great admiration, and maintained that 'absolute space possesses a reality of its own independently of the existence of all matter. . . .'[2] At the same time he shows himself

---

[1] *Dreams*, 2, 3; *W.*, II, p. 373.   [2] *W.*, II, p. 378.

conscious of the difficulties attending the theory that space is an independent, objective reality. And he remarks that absolute space is not an object of external perception but a fundamental concept which makes external perception possible.[1] This point of view was to be developed in his inaugural dissertation.

4. Kant's statement in the introduction to the *Prolegomena to Any Future Metaphysics* that it was David Hume who first interrupted his dogmatic slumbers is so often quoted or referred to that one may be inclined to overlook or underestimate the influence of Leibniz. In 1765 the latter's *New Essays concerning the Human Understanding* were at last published, and in 1768 there appeared Duten's edition of Leibniz's writings, containing the Leibniz-Clarke correspondence. Before these publications Kant had seen the thought of his great predecessor largely through the medium of the Wolffian philosophy; and it is clear that the fresh light shed on Leibniz had a profound effect on his mind. The first results of his reflections found expression in his inaugural dissertation as professor *On the Form and Principles of the Sensible and Intelligible World* (*De mundi sensibilis atque intelligibilis forma et principiis*, 1770).

To start with a particular point. As regards the Leibniz-Clarke correspondence, Kant was convinced that the former was right in maintaining against Newton and Clarke that space and time cannot be absolute realities or properties of things-in-themselves. If we try to retain Clarke's position, we shall find ourselves hopelessly involved in antinomies. Kant accepted, therefore, the view of Leibniz that space and time are phenomenal, and that they are not properties of things-in-themselves. At the same time he was not prepared to accept Leibniz's notion that they are confused ideas or representations. For in this case geometry, for instance, would not be the exact and certain science which it is. Kant speaks, therefore, of space and time as 'pure intuitions'.

In order to understand this position, we must go further back. In his inaugural dissertation Kant divides human knowledge into sensitive knowledge and intellectual knowledge. This distinction must not be understood as being between confused and distinct knowledge. For sensitive knowledge can be perfectly distinct, as it is, indeed, in the case of geometry, the prototype of such knowledge. And intellectual knowledge can be confused, as it not infrequently is in the case of metaphysics. The distinction must

[1] *W*., II, p. 383.

be understood rather in terms of objects, the objects of sensitive knowledge being sensible things, *sensibilia*, capable of affecting the sensibility (*sensualitas*) of the subject, which is the latter's receptivity or capacity for being affected by the presence of an object so as to produce a representation of it.

Leaving aside intellectual knowledge for the moment and attending to sensitive knowledge, we must distinguish therein between the matter and the form. The matter is what is given, namely sensations, that which is produced by the presence of sensible objects. The form is that which co-ordinates the matter; it is contributed, as it were, by the knowing subject and is the condition of sensitive knowledge. There are two such conditions, namely space and time. In the inaugural dissertation Kant speaks of them as 'concepts'. But he is careful to observe that they are not universal concepts *under* which sensible things are grouped but singular concepts *in* which *sensibilia* become the object of knowledge. These 'singular concepts' are described as 'pure intuitions'. The divine intuition is the archetype and active principle of things; but this is not the case with our intuitions which are said to be passive. Their function is simply to co-ordinate the sensations which are received and thus to make sensitive knowledge possible. '*Time is not something objective and real;* it is neither an accident, nor a substance, nor a relation; it is the subjective condition, necessary because of the nature of the human mind, of co-ordinating all *sensibilia* by a certain law, and it is a *pure intuition.* For we co-ordinate substances and accidents alike, as well according to simultaneity as to succession, only through the concept of time. . . .'[1] Again, '*space is not anything objective* and real; it is neither a substance nor an accident nor a relation; but it is *subjective* and ideal and proceeding from the nature of the mind by a stable law, as the scheme (*schema*) of co-ordinating all external *sensa*'.[2] The pure intuition of time is thus the necessary condition for all sensitive knowledge whatsoever. I cannot, for instance, be aware of my internal desires except in time. The pure intuition of space is the necessary condition for all knowledge of external *sensa*.

In order, therefore, to avoid the difficulties and antinomies which are involved if we hold either that space and time are independent, absolute realities or that they are real and objective

[1] *On the Form and Principles*, 3, 14, 5; *W.*, II, p. 400.
[2] *On the Form and Principles*, 3, 15, D; *W.*, II, p. 403.

properties of things, Kant suggests that they are subjective pure (that is, of themselves empty of all empirical content) intuitions which, together with sensations, the matter of sensitive knowledge, form what he calls in the dissertation 'appearances' (*apparentiae*). But this should obviously not be taken to mean that the human being consciously and deliberately applies these pure intuitions to sensations. The union of form and matter precedes all reflection. That is to say, because the human subject is what it is it necessarily perceives sensible objects in space and time. The act of distinguishing between form and matter is the work of philosophical reflection. But as far as our first awareness is concerned the union is something given, even though in subsequent reflection we can distinguish between what is due to the presence of sensible objects and what is contributed by the subject.

One can interpret Kant's point of view in this way. Let us assume with Hume that in sense-knowledge the given consists ultimately of impressions or sensations. The world of experience obviously does not consist simply of impressions or sensations or sense-data. The question arises, therefore, how the ultimately given is synthesized to form the world of experience. In Kant's terminology in the inaugural dissertation what are the form and principles of the sensible world? First of all (that is, first of all from the point of view of logical priority) the given elements are perceived in the pure intuitions or 'concepts' of space and time. There is spatial and temporal co-ordination. We then have 'appearances'. The mind then, through what Kant calls the logical use of the intellect, organizes the data of sense intuition, while leaving their fundamentally sensuous character intact. We then have the phenomenal world of 'experience'. 'From appearance to experience there is no way except by reflection according to the logical use of the intellect.'[1] In its logical use or function the mind simply organizes the data of sense intuition; and we then have the empirical concepts of experience. The empirical sciences are thus rendered possible by the logical use of the intellect. They belong to the sphere of sensitive knowledge, not in the sense that the intellect or understanding is not employed in these sciences (which would be an absurd notion), but in the sense that it does not provide new concepts out of its own resources, so to speak, but simply organizes logically the materials drawn from a sensuous source. The logical use of the intellect is not, indeed, confined to

[1] *On the Form and Principles*, 2, 5; *W.*, II, p. 394.

the organization of material derived from a sensuous source; but, when it is used in this way, its use does not turn sensitive knowledge into intellectual knowledge, in the sense in which Kant uses these terms in the dissertation.

What, then, does Kant mean by intellectual knowledge and by the intelligible world? Intellectual or rational knowledge is knowledge of objects which do not affect the senses: that is to say, it is knowledge, not of *sensibilia*, but of *intelligibilia*. And the latter together form the intelligible world. Sensitive knowledge is knowledge of objects as they *appear*, that is, as subjected to what Kant calls 'the laws of sensibility', namely the *a priori* conditions of space and time, whereas intellectual knowledge is knowledge of things *as they are* (*sicuti sunt*).[1] The empirical sciences come under the heading of sensitive knowledge, while metaphysics is the prime example of intellectual knowledge.

Now, this obviously suggests that in metaphysics the mind apprehends objects which transcend the senses; above all, God. But do we enjoy intuition of spiritual realities? Kant explicitly denies this. 'An *intuition* of intelligible objects is not given to man, but only a *symbolic knowledge*.'[2] That is to say, we conceive supersensible objects by means of universal concepts, not by direct intuition. What, then, is the justification for thinking that our conceptual representations of supersensible realities are valid?

The difficulty can be put in this way. Kant spoke, as we have seen, of the logical use of the understanding or intellect, the latter's function, that is, of comparing and organizing material derived from either a sensuous or a supersensuous source. In the case of material derived from a sensuous source the understanding has something to work on, namely the data derived from sense intuition, from the marriage, as it were, between sensations and the pure intuitions of space and time. But if we enjoy no intuition of supersensible reality, the understanding appears to have nothing to work on. For in its logical use it does not supply materials but logically organizes them.

The problem can be developed thus. Kant distinguished between the logical use of understanding or intellect and its 'real use'. According to its real use the intellect produces concepts from itself; that is, it forms concepts which are non-empirical in character. In the *New Essays* Leibniz had criticized Locke's

---

[1] *On the Form and Principles*, 2, 4; *W.*, II, p. 392.
[2] *On the Form and Principles*, 2, 10; *W.*, II, p. 396.

empiricism. We do not, as the latter had maintained, derive all our concepts empirically. On this matter Kant sided with Leibniz, though he did not follow the latter in speaking of innate ideas. 'Since, then, in metaphysics we do not find empirical principles, the concepts encountered therein must be sought, not in the senses, but in the very nature of the pure intellect, not as *innate (connati)* concepts, but as abstracted from the intrinsic laws of the mind (attending to its actions on the occasion of experience), and so as *acquired*. Of this kind are possibility, existence, necessity, substance, cause, etc., together with their opposites or correlates. . . .'[1] Thus the concepts of substance and cause, for instance, are derived, not from sense-experience, but from the mind itself on the occasion of experience. The question arises, however, whether in the absence of intuitive material as far as the intelligible world is concerned, these concepts can be used to grasp supersensible realities in such a way that we can make positive and certainly true statements about them. In other words, can there be a dogmatic metaphysics which has any valid claim to embodying knowledge of *intelligibilia*?

We have seen that Kant divides not only knowledge into sensitive and intellectual knowledge but also the world into the sensible and intelligible worlds. And this naturally suggests that intellectual knowledge is knowledge of *intelligibilia*, just as sensitive knowledge is knowledge of *sensibilia*. And inasmuch as supersensible realities belong to the class of *intelligibilia*, we would naturally expect Kant to maintain that dogmatic metaphysics, considered as a system of known truths, is possible. And in point of fact this twofold scheme of knowledge and of objects of knowledge, proposed under the influence of Leibniz, makes it difficult for him to throw dogmatic metaphysics overboard. At the same time he says enough in the dissertation to weaken very considerably the position of dogmatic metaphysics and to cast doubt upon its claims, even if he does not reject it outright and in so many words. And it is worth while dwelling briefly on this point which is of importance in the development of Kant's thought.

In the first place Kant asserts, as we have seen, that the 'real use' of the intellect in the sphere of *intelligibilia* gives us only symbolic knowledge. And this might suggest to someone trained in the Thomist tradition that Kant is saying that we can have valid knowledge of supersensible realities, though this knowledge

[1] *On the Form and Principles*, 2, 8; *W.*, II, p. 395.

is analogical in character. But what he seems to mean is that in the absence of intuitive material the extension of the 'real use' of the intellect (as producing from itself its concepts and axioms on the occasion of experience) into its dogmatic use provides us only with symbolic indications of supersensible realities, so that the description, for example, of God as first cause would be an instance of symbolism. And from this position to Kant's later position the distance is not very great. That is to say, it is easy to take the further step of maintaining that the primary function of concepts such as cause and substance is to synthesize further the data of sense intuition, and though it is, of course, psychologically possible to apply such concepts to supersensible realities the application does not yield scientific knowledge of these realities.

In the second place Kant discusses the following important point. In the natural sciences and in mathematics, where sense intuition supplies the data or material and where the intellect is employed only according to its logical use (that is, logically comparing and organizing the data but not supplying concepts and axioms from its own inner nature), 'use provides the method'.[1] That is to say, it is only after these sciences have already acquired a certain degree of development that we reflect on and analyse the method employed, considering how the method can be improved in detail. The situation is analogous to that obtaining in the case of language. Man did not first elaborate grammatical rules and then begin to employ language. The development of grammar followed, not preceded, the use of language. 'But in pure philosophy, such as is metaphysics, in which *the use of the intellect* concerning the principles is *real*, that is, where primitive concepts of things and relations and the very axioms are originally provided by the pure intellect itself, and where, since there are no intuitions, we are not immune from error, *method precedes all science*; and whatever is undertaken before the precepts of this method have been duly worked out and firmly established, seems to be rashly conceived and fit to be rejected as a vain and ridiculous activity of the mind.'[2] In dealing with material things, which affect the senses, we can come to know much about them without having first worked out a scientific method. But when we are dealing with supersensible realities, such as God, or with things in themselves as distinct from the way in which they appear to us in sense intuition, it is essential to ascertain first *how* we can come to know

---

[1] *On the Form and Principles*, 5, 23; *W*., II, p. 410.   [2] *Ibid.*, p. 411.

them. For in the absence of intuition the problem of method becomes all-important.

The chief rule of method, Kant tells us, must be to see that the principles of sensitive knowledge are not extended from sensible to supersensible realities. As we have seen, he made a sharp distinction between the sensuous and intellectual levels in human knowledge. And he insists that we must be on our guard against applying to supersensible realities concepts which are applicable only in the sphere of sensitive knowledge and against turning into universal principles the principles of sensitive knowledge. He gives as an example the axiom that whatever exists, exists somewhere and at some time. We are not entitled to state this universally, thus drawing down God, for example, into the spatio-temporal sphere. And the intellect in what Kant calls its 'critical use' (*usus elencticus*) has the office of exposing the unjustifiable character of such universal statements. The intellect in its critical use can thus keep the sphere of supersensible reality free, as it were, from contamination by the application of concepts and principles peculiar to sensitive knowledge.

But the critical use of the intellect must be distinguished from its dogmatic use. The fact that we can say, for instance, that God is not in space or time does not necessarily mean that we can attain positive and certain knowledge about God by the pure intellect. And, as has been already remarked, Kant has only to go on to say that the cognitive function of the primitive concepts of the pure intellect is that of further synthesizing the data of sense intuition for dogmatic metaphysics to be ruled out, if we mean by dogmatic metaphysics a system of certain truths about supersensible realities such as God and the immortal soul of man. Strictly speaking, the concept of cause, for instance, would then be inapplicable to God. Psychologically speaking, we could, of course, so apply it; but its use would give us only a symbolic indication of God, not scientific knowledge.

Kant does not maintain, and indeed never maintained, that there are no supersensible realities. And it may be objected that, given the doubt cast upon dogmatic metaphysics, he has no warrant for asserting that there are any such realities. But in the dissertation he does not reject dogmatic metaphysics in so many words, in explicit and clear terms. When he later comes to do so he also develops his theory of the postulates of the moral law, a theme which must be left aside for the present.

In the dissertation Kant speaks of the dogmatic use of the intellect as an extension of the general principles of the pure intellect to conceive a perfect *noumenon* or purely intelligible reality as the measure of all other realities. In the theoretical sphere (that is, in the sphere of being, of what is) this measure or exemplar is God, the supreme being. In the practical sphere (in the sphere of what ought to be effected through free action) it is moral perfection. Moral philosophy, therefore, as far as its fundamental principles are concerned, is said to belong to pure philosophy. Kant is saying that these principles depend on the reason itself, and not on sense-perception. He agreed with Hume that we cannot found moral principles on sense-perception. At the same time he was not prepared to make them the expression of feeling and to abandon the attempt to give them a purely rational foundation. Epicurus, accordingly, is worthy of severe reproof; and so are those, 'such as Shaftesbury and his followers',[1] who follow him to a certain extent. But Kant does not develop the subject. The elaboration of his moral philosophy lies in the future.

5. At the beginning of September 1770 Kant wrote to J. H. Lambert that he proposed during the winter to pursue his inquiries into pure moral philosophy, 'in which there are no empirical principles'.[2] He also mentioned his intention of revising and extending certain sections of his inaugural dissertation. In particular he wished to develop the idea of a particular, though negative, science which must precede metaphysics. This science, described as 'general phenomenology',[3] makes clear the range of validity of the principles of sensitive knowledge and thus prevents the unwarranted application of these principles in metaphysics. We have already seen that Kant spoke about this science in his dissertation, where, as afterwards in the letter, it is referred to as a 'propaedeutic' in relation to metaphysics.[4]

His reflections during the winter of 1770–1, however, led Kant to abandon the idea of extending the inaugural dissertation and to project instead a new work. Thus in June 1771 he wrote to Marcus Herz,[5] who had been one of his pupils, that he was engaged on a book which would bear the title *The Bounds of Sensibility and Reason* (*Die Grenzen der Sinnlichkeit und der Vernunft*). In this work he proposed to deal with the relations of the fundamental principles and laws, taken to be determined before experience of

---

[1] *On the Form and Principles*, 2, 9; *W.*, II, p. 396.   [2] *W.*, X, p. 97.
[3] *Ibid.*, p. 98.   [4] *W.*, II, p. 395, and X, p. 98.   [5] See *W.*, X, p. 123.

the sensible world, to the subjects involved in the theory of taste, in metaphysics and in morals. We have seen that in the inaugural dissertation of 1770 Kant expounded the theory that space and time are subjective 'laws' of the co-ordination of sensations, and that in the same dissertation he embraced the theory that the pure intellect derives from itself on the occasion of experience the fundamental concepts of metaphysics, and also the theory that the fundamental principles of morals are derived from the reason alone. He now proposes to undertake an investigation into the fundamental concepts and laws which originate in the nature of the subject and which are applied to the experiential data of aesthetics, metaphysics and morals. In other words, he proposes to cover in one volume the subjects which proved in the end to need three, namely the three *Critiques*. In this letter he speaks of the subjective principles 'not only of sensibility but also of the understanding' (*des Verstandes*).[1] He is thus well on his way to conceiving his great enterprise of isolating the *a priori* elements in human knowledge. The distinction between form and matter in knowledge must be investigated not merely in relation to sensibility, where the subjective elements are the pure intuitions of space and time, but also in relation to the understanding and to the part which it plays in synthesizing the given. And the range of inquiry is to cover not only theoretical knowledge but also moral and aesthetic experience.

In another letter to Herz, written in February 1772, Kant refers again to his projected book on *The Bounds of Sensibility and Reason*. According to his original plan the book would have consisted of two parts, one theoretical, the other practical. The first part would have been subdivided into two sections, treating respectively of general phenomenology and of metaphysics considered according to its nature and method. The second part would also have consisted of two sections, dealing respectively with the general principles of the feeling of taste and with the ultimate grounds of morality. But while thinking out the first part Kant noticed, he tells Herz, that something essential was wanting, namely a thorough treatment of the relation of mental presentations (*Vorstellungen*) to the objects of knowledge. And something must be said here about Kant's remarks on this theme; for they show him at grips with his critical problem.

Our sensuous representations do not create a problem, provided

---

[1] See *W.*, **x**, p. 122.

that they are the result of the subject's being affected by the object. True, sensible objects appear to us in a certain way because we are what we are, that is, because of the *a priori* intuitions of space and time. But in sensitive knowledge the form is applied to a matter which is passively received; our sensibility is affected by things external to us. Hence there is no great problem about the objective reference of our sensuous representations. But the situation is different when we turn to intellectual presentations. Abstractly speaking, the objective conformity of concept with object would be guaranteed if the intellect produced its objects through its concepts; that is, if it created the objects by conceiving or thinking them. But it is only the divine intellect which is an archetypal intellect in this sense. We cannot suppose that the human intellect creates its objects by thinking them. Kant never accepted pure idealism in this sense. At the same time the pure concepts of the understanding are not, according to Kant, abstracted from sense-experience. The pure concepts of the understanding must 'have their origins in the nature of the soul, yet so that they neither are caused by the object nor bring the object into being'.[1] But in this case the question immediately arises how these concepts refer to objects and how objects conform to the concepts. Kant remarks that in his inaugural dissertation he had contented himself with a negative account of the matter. That is to say, he had contented himself with saying that 'intellectual presentations . . . are not modifications of the soul by the object',[2] passing over in silence the question how these intellectual presentations or pure concepts of the understanding refer to objects when they are not affected by the latter.

Given Kant's assumption, namely that the pure concepts of the understanding and the axioms of the pure reason[3] are not empirically derived, this question is obviously a pertinent one. And the only way of answering it in the end, if the assumption is to be maintained, will be to abandon the statement of the dissertation that sensuous presentations present us with objects as they appear while intellectual presentations give us objects as they are, and to say instead that the pure concepts of the understanding have as their cognitive function the further synthesizing of the

[1] *W.*, x, p. 130.　　　[2] *Ibid.*
[3] Kant's terminology is still fluid. He speaks of 'the pure concepts of the understanding' (*die reinen Verstandesbegriffe*), of 'intellectual presentations' (*intellectuale* [*sic*] *Vorstellungen*), and of 'the axioms of the pure reason' (*die axiomata der reinen Vernunft*).

data of sense intuition. That is to say, Kant will have to maintain that pure concepts of the understanding are, as it were, subjective forms by which we necessarily conceive (because the mind is what it is) the data of sense intuition. Objects will then conform to our concepts, and our concepts will refer to objects, because these concepts are *a priori* conditions of the possibility of objects of knowledge, performing a function analogous to that of the pure intuitions of space and time, though at a higher, namely an intellectual, level. In other words, Kant will be able to maintain his sharp distinction between sense and intellect; but he will have to abandon the notion that while sense presentations give us things as they appear, intellectual presentations give us things as they are in themselves. Instead there will be an ascending process of synthesis whereby empirical reality is constituted. The sensuous and intellectual forms of the human subject remaining constant, and things being knowable only in so far as subjected to these forms, there will always be conformity between objects and our concepts.

To return to the letter to Herz. Plato, says Kant, postulated an intuition of the divinity in a previous existence as the source of the pure concepts and fundamental principles of the understanding. Malebranche postulated a present and continuing intuition of divine ideas. Crusius assumed that God implanted in the soul certain rules of judgment and certain concepts such that they will agree with objects according to a pre-established harmony. But all such theories have recourse to a *Deus ex machina* and they raise more problems than they solve. Some other explanations of the conformity between concepts and objects must therefore be sought. And Kant informs Herz that his inquiry into 'transcendental philosophy' (namely his attempt to reduce the concepts of the pure reason to a certain number of categories) is now sufficiently advanced for him to offer a *Critique of the Pure Reason* (*eine Kritik der reinen Vernunft*),[1] which will deal with the nature both of theoretical and of practical (moral) knowledge. The first part should be published within three months; and it will treat of the sources, method and limits of metaphysics. In the second part, to be published later, he will deal with the basic principles of morality.

The work did not, however, progress as rapidly as Kant at first imagined that it would. As he struggled with his problems, he

[1] *W.*, x, p. 132.

became more and more conscious of their complexity. After a time he saw that he would have to divide up the matter which he hoped to treat in one *Critique*. In the end he became worried about the delay and put together the *Critique of Pure Reason* (*Kritik der reinen Vernunft*) in four or five months. It appeared in 1781. In this famous work Kant treats of mathematical and scientific knowledge and endeavours to justify the objectivity of this knowledge in the face of the empiricism of David Hume. He does this by proposing his 'Copernican revolution', that is, the theory that objects conform to the mind rather than the other way round. Because the structure of human sensibility and of the human mind is constant, objects will always appear to us in certain ways. We are thus enabled to make universal scientific judgments which hold good not only for actual but also for possible experience. The Newtonian science is thus theoretically justified despite the dissolvent tendencies of empiricism. From this position it follows, however, that the pure concepts of the understanding do not enable us to apprehend things in themselves, apart from the way in which they appear to us, or supersensible realities. And in the first *Critique* Kant tries to explain how speculative metaphysics of the traditional type arose and why it is foredoomed to failure. The problems which lie at the basis of the *Critique of Pure Reason* will be discussed in the next chapter.

Kant found that the *Critique of Pure Reason* was misunderstood, and that there were complaints about its obscurity. He therefore published *Prolegomena to Any Future Metaphysics* (*Prolegomena zu einer jeden künftigen Metaphysik*, 1783), a shorter work which was designed, not to supplement the *Critique*, but to act as a kind of introduction or explanation. In 1787 he published a second edition of the *Critique*. In references the first edition is referred to as *A*, the second as *B*.

Meanwhile Kant had turned his attention to the fundamental principles of morals. And in 1785 he published his *Fundamental Principles* (or *Groundwork*) *of the Metaphysics of Morals* (*Grundlegung zur Metaphysik der Sitten*). And this was followed in 1788 by the *Critique of Practical Reason* (*Kritik der praktischen Vernunft*), though in between he had published, not only the second edition of the *Critique of Pure Reason*, but also *Metaphysical First Principles of Natural Science* (*Metaphysische Anfangsgründe der Naturwissenschaft*, 1786). Kant's moral theory will be dealt with in a later chapter. It is sufficient to say here that, just as in the first *Critique* he endeavoured to isolate and give a systematic account of the *a priori* elements in scientific knowledge, so in his moral writings he tried to isolate and give a systematic account of the *a priori* or formal elements in morality. Thus he endeavoured to ground obligation and the universality of the moral law not on feeling but on the practical reason, that is, on reason as legislating for human conduct. This does not mean that he tried to deduce from reason alone all the concrete duties which Smith or Brown encounters in his life. Nor did he think that we could work out a set of concrete moral laws, binding on man as such, without any reference to empirically given material. But he believed that in the moral judgment there is, as it were, a 'form' which can be derived from the practical reason and which is applied to empirically given material. The situation in morals is thus analogous to some extent with that in science. Both in science and in man's moral life, that is, both in theoretical and in practical knowledge, there is the given, the 'matter', and there is the 'formal' and *a priori* element. And it is with the latter that Kant is chiefly concerned in his ethical writings. In this sense he is concerned with the 'metaphysics' of morals.

But Kant is also concerned in his ethical writings with metaphysics in another sense. For he tries to establish as postulates of the moral law the great truths of freedom, immortality and God. Thus the principal truths which, according to the first *Critique*, are incapable of scientific demonstration, are later re-introduced as postulates of moral or practical faith. This theory is not a mere appendix to the Kantian philosophy, still less a superfluous excrescence. For it is an essential part of Kant's attempt to harmonize the world of Newtonian science with the world of moral experience and of religious faith. The notion that pure concepts of the understanding can give us theoretical knowledge of things in themselves and of a supersensible world has been ruled out in the first *Critique*. At the same time room has been made for 'faith'. And in the ethical writings the truths of human freedom, immortality and the existence of God are brought in, not as scientifically demonstrable, but as implications of the moral law, in the sense that recognition of the fact of moral obligation is seen to demand or postulate a practical faith in these truths. Thus Kant still maintains that there is a supersensible sphere; but he finds the key to it, not in dogmatic metaphysics, but in moral experience.

It will be recalled that in his projected work on *The Bounds of*

Sensibility and Reason Kant had intended to deal not only with metaphysics and morals but also with the fundamental principles of the theory of taste (*die Geschmackslehre*). The aesthetic judgment or judgment of taste was at length treated in the third *Critique*, the *Critique of Judgment* (*Kritik der Urteilskraft*), which appeared in 1790. This work consists of two main parts, the first dealing with the aesthetic judgment, the second with the teleological judgment or judgment of purposiveness in Nature; and it is of considerable importance. For in it Kant tries, as far as our consciousness is concerned at least, to bridge the gulf between the mechanistic world of Nature as presented in physical science and the world of morality, freedom and faith. That is to say, he tries to show how the mind passes from the one to the other; and he attempts the rather difficult task of showing how the transition is reasonable without at the same time going back on what he has already said about the vanity of dogmatic metaphysics and about the position of moral or practical faith as our only means of access to the supersensible world. The contents of the work will be discussed later. But it is worth while noting how deeply Kant was concerned with the reconciliation of the scientific outlook with that of the moral and religious man.

In 1791 Kant published an article 'On the failure of all Philosophical Attempts at a Theodicy' (*Ueber das Miszlingen aller philosophischen Versuche in der Theologie*), in which he maintained that in theodicy or philosophical theology we are concerned with matters of faith rather than with scientifically demonstrable truth. And this was followed in 1793 by *Religion within the Bounds of Reason Alone* (*Die Religion innerhalb der Grenzen der blossen Vernunft*). Mention has been made in an earlier section of this chapter of the trouble to which publication of this book gave rise. Reference has also been made to the small treatise *On Perpetual Peace* (*Zum ewigen Frieden*, 1795) in which perpetual peace, grounded on a moral basis, is depicted as a practical ideal of historical and political development.[1] Finally, in 1797, there appeared the two works which form the two parts of the *Metaphysics of Morals* (*Metaphysik der Sitten*), namely the *Metaphysical Elements of the Theory of Right* (*Metaphysische Anfangsgründe der Rechtslehre*) and the *Metaphysical Elements of the Theory of Virtue* (*Metaphysische Anfangsgründe der Tugendlehre*).

[1] On history Kant had published in 1784 his *Idea for a General History from a Cosmopolitan Point of View* (*Idee zu einer allgemeinen Geschichte in weltbürgerlicher Absicht*).

We have seen that the human mind does not, on Kant's view, constitute or create the object in its totality. That is to say, although things as perceived and known are relative to us in the sense that we perceive and know them only through the *a priori* forms embedded in the structure of the human subject, there are things-in-themselves, even if we cannot know them as they are in themselves. To put the matter crudely, we no more create things according to their ontological existence than the man who wears red-tinted spectacles creates the things which he sees. If we assume that the spectacles can never be detached, the man will never see things except as red, and their appearance will be due to a factor in the perceiving subject. But it does not follow that things do not exist independently of the perceiving subject. Hence Kant refused to allow that Fichte's suppression of the thing-in-itself represented a legitimate development of his own philosophy. At the same time it can hardly be denied that some of the notes which form part of the *Opus Postumum* indicate that towards the end of his life Kant was developing his thought in such a way that it is reasonable to see in it an anticipation of German speculative idealism. However, it is illegitimate to found one's interpretation of the direction of Kant's thought in his later years on one set of notes to the exclusion of other notes which express a somewhat different point of view. And if we take the *Opus Postumum* as a whole it seems that we must conclude that Kant never abandoned altogether the realistic elements in his thought. But something more will be said about the *Opus Postumum* at a later stage of the discussion of Kant's philosophy.

CHAPTER XI

KANT (2): THE PROBLEMS OF THE FIRST *CRITIQUE*

The general problem of metaphysics—The problem of a priori knowledge—The divisions of this problem—Kant's Copernican revolution—Sensibility, understanding, reason, and the structure of the first Critique*—The significance of the first* Critique *in the context of the general problem of Kant's philosophy.*

1. IF we look at the prefaces to the first and second editions of the *Critique of Pure Reason* and at the foreword to and first sections of the *Prolegomena to Any Future Metaphysics*,[1] we find the author placing an obvious emphasis on the problem of metaphysics. Is metaphysics possible or not? Obviously, the question is not whether it is possible to write metaphysical treatises or to indulge in metaphysical speculation. The question is whether metaphysics is capable of extending our knowledge of reality. For Kant, the chief problems of metaphysics are God, freedom and immortality. We can therefore express the question in this way. Is metaphysics capable of giving us sure knowledge of the existence and nature of God, of human freedom, and of the existence in man of a spiritual, immortal soul?

A question of this sort clearly presupposes a doubt. And there is, in Kant's opinion, abundant reason for such initial doubt, that is, for raising the problem of metaphysics. Time was when metaphysics 'was called the queen of all the sciences; and if one takes the will for the deed, she certainly deserved this title of honour on account of the outstanding importance of her subject-matter'.[2]

---

[1] References to Kant's writings in Chapters XI–XIII are to be interpreted as follows. *A* denotes the first edition and *B* the second edition of the *Critique of Pure Reason*. These will be found respectively in Volumes IV and III of the critical edition of Kant's works edited by the Prussian Academy of Sciences (see Bibliography). The numbers placed after *A* and *B* refer to sections as given in this edition (the sections corresponding to pagination in the original German editions). For the translation of passages I am responsible. But as the great majority of passages quoted in translation are taken from *B*, the references are generally valid for Professor N. Kemp Smith's translation of *B* (see Bibliography), as this translation embodies the division into sections referred to above. (Professor Kemp Smith's translation also contains the preface to *A*, as well as the Deduction of the Categories as given in *A*.)

Prol. denotes *Prolegomena to Any Future Metaphysics*, which is contained in Volume IV of the critical German edition. Numbers following *Prol.* refer to sections in the German edition. This division into sections is reproduced in, for example, the translation by J. P. Mahaffy and J. H. Bernard (see Bibliography).

[2] *A*, VIII.

Kant never denied the importance of the main themes of which metaphysics treats. But now, he observes, metaphysics has fallen into disrepute. And this is easily understandable. Mathematics and the natural sciences have advanced, and there is in these fields a great area of generally accepted knowledge. Nobody seriously questions this fact. But metaphysics appears to be an arena for endless disputes. 'One can point to no single book, as one can point to a Euclid, and say: This is metaphysics, here you will find the noblest object of this science, the knowledge of a supreme Being and of a future world, provided by the principles of pure reason.'[1] The fact of the matter is that metaphysics, unlike physics, has not found any sure scientific method the application of which will enable it to solve its problems. And this leads us to ask, 'why is it that here no sure path of science has yet been found? Is it perhaps impossible to find one?'[2]

The inconclusiveness of metaphysics, its inability hitherto to find a reliable method which will lead to certain conclusions, its constant tendency to retrace its steps and to start all over again; such characteristics have helped to produce a widespread indifference towards metaphysics and its claims. True, in one sense this indifference is unjustified; for it is 'vain to profess indifference in regard to such inquiries, the objects of which cannot be a matter of indifference to human nature'.[3] Moreover, those who profess to be indifferentists are prone to make metaphysical pronouncements of their own, even if they are unaware of the fact. At the same time this indifference is not, in Kant's view, the fruit of mere levity of mind: rather is it the expression of a contemporary maturity of judgment which refuses to be satisfied with illusory knowledge or pseudo-science. It should serve, therefore, as a stimulus to undertake a critical investigation of metaphysics, summoning the latter before the tribunal of reason.

What form must this critical investigation take? To be in a position to answer this question we must recall what metaphysics means for Kant. As we saw in the last chapter, he disagreed with Locke's theory that all our concepts are ultimately derived from experience. He did not, indeed, accept the opposite theory of innate ideas. But at the same time he believed that there are concepts and principles which the reason derives from within itself on the occasion of experience. A child is not born with, for example, an idea of causality. But on the occasion of experience its reason

[1] *Prol.*, 4.   [2] *B*, xv.   [3] *A*, x.

derives the concept from within itself. It is an *a priori* concept in the sense that it is not derived from experience but is applied to and in a sense governs experience. There are, therefore, *a priori* concepts and principles which are grounded in the mind's own structure. These concepts are 'pure', in the sense that they are, of themselves, empty of all empirical content or material. Now, the metaphysicians have assumed that reason can apply these concepts and principles so as to apprehend supersensible realities and things-in-themselves, that is, not merely as they appear to us. There have thus arisen the various systems of dogmatic metaphysics. But the assumption was over-hasty. We cannot take it for granted that the *a priori* concepts and principles of the reason can be used to transcend experience; that is, to know realities which are not given in experience. First of all we must undertake a critical investigation into the powers of the pure reason itself. This is the task which the dogmatic philosophers neglected, dogmatism being described as the assumption that it is possible to make progress in knowledge simply on the basis of pure philosophical concepts by employing principles which reason has long been in the habit of employing, 'without having inquired in what way and with what right reason has arrived at these principles. Dogmatism is thus the dogmatic procedure of the pure reason without previous criticism of its own powers.'[1] It is this criticism which Kant proposes to undertake.

The tribunal before which metaphysics is to be brought is, therefore, 'nothing else than the critical investigation (*Kritik*) of pure reason itself', which means 'a critical inquiry into the faculty of reason with reference to all the cognitions to which it may strive to attain independently of all experience'.[2] The question is, then, 'what and how much can understanding and reason[3] know, apart from all experience'.[4] Let us assume with Kant that speculative metaphysics is a non-empirical science (or alleged science) which claims to transcend experience, attaining to a knowledge of purely intelligible (non-sensible) realities by means of *a priori* concepts and principles. Given this view of metaphysics, the validity of its claim will obviously be determined by the answer to the question, what and how much can the mind know apart from experience.

To answer this question a critical inquiry into the faculty of

[1] *B*, xxxv.   [2] *A*, xii.
[3] The distinction between understanding and reason can be passed over for the moment. It will be explained later.   [4] *A*, xvii.

reason, as Kant puts it, is required. What this means will, I hope, become clearer during the course of this chapter. But it may be as well to point out at once that Kant is not referring to a psychological inquiry into the nature of reason considered as a psychical entity; that is, with reason as an object among objects. He is concerned with reason in regard to the *a priori* cognition which it makes possible. That is to say, he is concerned with the pure conditions in the human subject as such for knowing objects. Such an inquiry is termed 'transcendental'.

One of the main tasks of the *Critique of Pure Reason* is to show in a systematic manner what these conditions are. And it is important to understand what sort of conditions Kant is talking about. There are obviously empirical conditions for perceiving things and for learning truths. For instance, I cannot see things in complete darkness; light is required for vision. And there are many scientific truths which cannot be discovered without the aid of instruments. Further, there are empirical conditions which are subjective, in the sense that they are conditions on the part of the knowing subject himself. I cannot see things if I am suffering from certain diseases of the eye in an advanced state. And there are obviously people who cannot, practically speaking, understand subjects which others understand with comparative ease. But Kant is not concerned with empirical conditions: he is concerned with the non-empirical or 'pure' conditions of human knowledge as such. In other words, he is concerned with the formal elements of pure consciousness. Tom, Dick and Harry, namely particular people with their particular limitations, do not enter into the matter at all. Or, rather, they enter into it only as exemplifying the human subject as such. That is to say, conditions of knowledge which hold for the human subject as such will obviously hold for Tom, Dick and Harry. But it is with the necessary conditions for knowing objects that Kant is concerned, not with variable empirical conditions. And if the conditions turn out to be such that realities transcending sense-experience cannot be objects of knowledge, the claims of speculative metaphysics will have been shown to be hollow and vain.

Now, Kant mentions Wolff with respect as 'the greatest of all dogmatic philosophers'.[1] And it is clear that when he speaks about dogmatic metaphysics, he has in mind principally, though not exclusively, the Leibniz-Wolffian system. We may be inclined to

[1] *B*, xxxvi.

object, therefore, that his inquiry into the possibility or impossibility of metaphysics is really an inquiry into the capacity of a certain type of metaphysics to extend our knowledge of reality, and that it is thus too restricted in scope. For there are other ideas of metaphysics besides that of Wolff. But though it is quite true that Kant pays insufficient attention to other conceptions of metaphysics, it is possible to exaggerate the importance of this line of objection. For instance, concepts such as those of cause and substance are employed in other metaphysical systems besides that of Wolff. Yet if the status and function of these concepts were what Kant, in the course of the first *Critique*, declares them to be, they could not be used to attain knowledge of supersensible realities. The Kantian critique of the powers of reason would thus, if valid, affect many other metaphysical systems besides that of Wolff. In other words, Kant's field of inquiry may be too narrow in its starting-point, in the sense that metaphysics means for him a particular type of metaphysics; but the inquiry is developed in such a way that the conclusions arrived at have a very wide range of application.

It may be as well to note that Kant does not always use the term 'metaphysics' in precisely the same sense. The inquiry into the powers of reason in regard to pure *a priori* cognition is called critical philosophy, while the systematic presentation of the whole body of philosophical knowledge attained or attainable by the power of pure reason (that is, *a priori*) is called metaphysics. When the latter term is used in this sense, critical philosophy is a preparation for or propaedeutic to metaphysics, and thus falls outside metaphysics. But the term 'metaphysics' may also be given to the whole of pure (non-empirical) philosophy, including so-called critical philosophy; and in this case critical philosophy counts as the first part of metaphysics. Again, if we take the term 'metaphysics' as meaning the systematic presentation of the whole body of philosophical knowledge attained by the power of pure reason, we may mean by 'knowledge', knowledge in a strict sense, or we may include the pretended or illusory knowledge which many philosophers have thought to be attainable by pure reason. If we understand the word 'knowledge' in the first of these two senses, Kant obviously does not reject metaphysics. On the contrary, he thought that it could, at least in principle, be systematically and completely developed. And his own *Metaphysical First Elements of Natural Science* is a contribution. But if the term 'metaphysics' is used to mean pretended or illusory knowledge of supersensible realities, one of the tasks of the critical philosophy is to expose the hollowness of the claims made on behalf of this pseudo-science. Finally, we must distinguish between metaphysics as a natural disposition and metaphysics considered as a science. The mind has a natural tendency to raise such problems as those of God and immortality; and though we should try to understand why this is the case, Kant neither wishes to eradicate the tendency nor believes that it is possible to do so, even if it were desirable. Metaphysics as a natural disposition is actual, and therefore it is obviously possible. But metaphysics as a science, if we mean by this a scientific knowledge of super-sensible beings, has never, according to Kant, been a reality. For all the alleged demonstrations hitherto produced can be shown to be invalid, that is, pseudo-demonstrations. Hence we can very properly ask whether metaphysics, considered as a science, is possible.

All this may sound very complicated and confusing. But it is not so confusing in practice as it sounds when briefly summarized. In the first place Kant himself refers to the different uses of the term 'metaphysics'.[1] In the second place the context makes it clear in what sense Kant is using the term in a particular passage. But the fact that the term bears more than one meaning in his writings is of some importance. For if one is ignorant of it, one may rashly conclude that he contradicts himself, admitting metaphysics in one place, rejecting it in another, when there is perhaps really no contradiction at all.

2. But though the possibility of metaphysics as a science (that is, as a science with objects of its own, transcending sense-experience) is for Kant an important problem, it is only part of the general problem considered in the *Critique of Pure Reason*. This general problem may be said to be that of the possibility of *a priori* knowledge.

Now, by *a priori* knowledge Kant does not mean knowledge which is relatively *a priori*; that is, in relation to this or that experience or to this or that kind of experience. If someone puts a garment too near the fire so that it is singed or burned, we may say that he might have known *a priori* that this would happen. That is to say, on the basis of past experience the man might have known antecedently to his action what its effect would be. He

---

[1] See, for example, *B* 869–70.

need not have waited to see what would happen. But this antecedent knowledge would be *a priori* only in relation to a particular experience. And it is not of such relatively *a priori* knowledge that Kant is thinking. He is thinking of knowledge which is *a priori* in relation to all experience.

But here we have to be careful not to draw the conclusion that Kant is thinking about innate ideas, supposed to be present in the human mind before experience in a temporal sense of the word 'before'. Pure *a priori* knowledge does not mean knowledge which is explicitly present in the mind before it has begun to experience anything at all: it means knowledge which is underived from experience, even if it makes its appearance as what we would ordinarily call 'knowledge' only on the occasion of experience. Consider the following famous and often-quoted statements. 'That all our knowledge begins with experience there can be no doubt. . . . But though all our knowledge begins *with* experience, it does not follow that it all arises *out of* experience.'[1] Kant agrees with the empiricists, such as Locke, to the extent of saying that 'all our knowledge begins with experience'. Our knowledge, he thinks, must begin with experience because the cognitive faculty, as he puts it, requires to be brought into exercise by our senses being affected by objects. Given sensations, the raw material of experience, the mind can set to work. At the same time, however, even if no knowledge is temporally antecedent to experience, it is possible that the cognitive faculty supplies *a priori* elements from within itself on the occasion of sense-impressions. In this sense the *a priori* elements would be underived from experience.

Now, why should Kant think that it is possible for there to be any *a priori* knowledge at all? The answer is that he was convinced that there evidently is such knowledge. He agreed with David Hume that we cannot derive necessity and strict universality[2] from experience. It follows, therefore, that 'necessity and strict universality are sure marks of *a priori* knowledge and are inseparably connected with one another'.[3] And it is easy to show that we possess knowledge which finds expression in necessary and universal judgments. 'If one desires an example from the

---

[1] *B*, 1.

[2] Universality which is based on induction is not, for Kant, strict but 'assumed and comparative' and admits of exceptions. If, on the basis of my personal experience, I say that human beings do not live more than a hundred years, the universality of the judgment is 'assumed'. Strict universality admits of no possible exception.

[3] *B*, 4.

sciences, one needs only to look at any proposition in mathematics. If one desires an example from the commonest operations of the understanding, the proposition that every change must have a cause can serve one's purposes.'[1] This last proposition is, in Kant's terminology, 'impure' in the sense that the concept of change is derived from experience. But the proposition is none the less *a priori*, even if it is not an example of pure *a priori* knowledge. For it is a necessary and strictly universal judgment.

There is, therefore, a considerable area of *a priori* knowledge. Kant acknowledged his debt to Hume. 'I freely confess that it was the thought of David Hume which many years ago first interrupted my dogmatic slumbers and gave an entirely new direction to my inquiries in the field of speculative philosophy.'[2] But though Kant had been convinced by Hume's discussion of the principle of causality that the element of necessity in the judgment cannot be justified on purely empiricist lines, he refused to accept Hume's psychological account of its origin in terms of the association of ideas. If I say that every event must have a cause, my judgment expresses *a priori* knowledge: it is not simply the expression of an habitual expectation mechanically produced by the association of ideas. The necessity, Kant insists, is not 'purely subjective';[3] the dependence of any event or happening or change on a cause is known, and it is known *a priori*. That is to say, my judgment is not simply a generalization from my experience of particular cases; nor does it stand in need of experiential confirmation before its truth can be known. Though, therefore, Hume was right in saying that a necessary relation between event and cause is not given in experience, his psychological explanation of the origin of the idea of necessity was inadequate. We have here an instance of *a priori* knowledge. But it is by no means the only instance. Hume may have devoted his attention principally to the causal relation; but Kant 'soon found that the concept of connection between cause and effect is by no means the only one through which the understanding thinks connections between things *a priori*'.[4] There is, therefore, a considerable area of *a priori* knowledge.

But if there certainly is *a priori* knowledge, why should Kant ask how it is possible? For if it is actual, it is obviously possible. The answer is, of course, that in the case of those fields (pure mathematics and pure physics) where, Kant is convinced, there

[1] *B*, 4-5.   [2] *Prol.*, Foreword.   [3] *B*, 5.   [4] *Prol.*, Foreword.

evidently is *a priori* knowledge, the question is not how this knowledge is *possible* (better, *whether* it is possible) but *how* it is possible. Granted its possibility (for it is actual), how is it that it is possible? How is it that we can have the *a priori* knowledge which we have, for example, in mathematics?

In the case of speculative metaphysics, however, the claim to possess *a priori* knowledge is suspect. Here, therefore, we ask whether it is possible rather than how it is possible. If metaphysics provides us with knowledge of God or of immortality, for instance, such knowledge must, on Kant's view of metaphysics, be *a priori*. It must be independent of experience, in the sense that it does not logically depend on purely empirical judgments. But does speculative metaphysics provide us with such knowledge? Is it even capable in principle of doing so?

3. We must now try to make these problems more precise. And to do so we must refer to Kant's distinction between different types of judgment.

In the first place we must distinguish between analytic and synthetic judgments. Analytic judgments are those in which the predicate is contained, at least implicitly, in the concept of the subject. They are said to be 'explicative judgments' (*Erläuterungs-urteile*)[1] because the predicate does not add to the concept of the subject anything which is not already contained in it, explicitly or implicitly. And their truth depends on the law of contradiction. We cannot deny the proposition without involving ourselves in logical contradiction. Kant cites as an example 'all bodies are extended'. For the idea of extension is contained in the idea of body. Synthetic judgments, however, affirm or deny of a subject a predicate which is not contained in the concept of the subject. They are called, therefore, 'ampliative' or 'augmentative judgments' (*Erweiterungsurteile*),[2] because they add something to the concept of the subject. According to Kant, 'all bodies are heavy' is an example of a synthetic judgment; for the idea of weight or heaviness is not contained in the concept of body as such.

We must now make a further distinction within the general class of synthetic judgments. In all synthetic judgments, as we have seen, something is added to the concept of the subject. A connection is affirmed (to restrict our attention to the affirmative judgment) between predicate and subject, but the predicate cannot be got out of the subject, so to speak, by mere analysis.

B, 11; *A*, 7.   [2] *Ibid.*

Now, this connection may be purely factual and contingent: it is then given only in and through experience. And when this is the case, the judgment is synthetic *a posteriori*. Take the proposition, 'All members of tribe X are short', and let us suppose that this is a true proposition. It is synthetic: for we cannot elicit the idea of shortness by mere analysis from the concept of membership of tribe X.[1] But the connection between shortness and membership of the tribe is given only in and through experience; and the judgment is simply the result of a series of observations. Its universality is not strict but assumed and comparative. Even if there does not happen to be at the moment any member of the tribe who is not short, there may be one or more tall members in the future. We cannot know *a priori* that all members are short: it is simply a matter of contingent fact.

But, according to Kant, there is another class of synthetic propositions, in which the connection between predicate and subject, though not knowable by mere analysis of the concept of the subject, is none the less necessary and strictly universal. These are called synthetic *a priori* propositions. Kant gives us an example. 'Everything which happens has its cause.'[2] The proposition is synthetic because the predicate, having a cause, is not contained in the concept of what happens, that is, of an event. It is an ampliative, not an explicative judgment. But it is at the same time *a priori*. For it is characterized by necessity and strict universality, the marks of *a priori* judgments. The proposition, 'everything which happens has its cause', does not mean that, so far as our experience goes, all events have had causes and that it is reasonable to expect, until experience shows otherwise, that future events also will have causes. It means that every event, without any possible exception, will have a cause. The proposition is, of course, dependent on experience in one sense, namely that it is by experience that we become acquainted with things happening, with events. But the connection between predicate and subject is given *a priori*. It is not a mere generalization from experience, reached by induction; nor does it stand in need of experiential confirmation. We know *a priori* or in advance that every event must have a cause; and the observation of such a connection in

[1] The judgment could, of course, be turned into an analytic judgment by so defining membership of the tribe that it includes the idea of shortness. But then we should be moving in the realm of verbal definitions and their implications; we should not be dealing with empirical reality, with the tribe as it actually exists.
[2] *B*, 13; *A*, 9.

the case of events falling within the field of an experience adds nothing to the certainty of the judgment.

It would be out of place, I think, to interrupt the course of Kant's problematic by discussing the highly controversial question of synthetic *a priori* propositions. But for the benefit of any reader who may not already be well aware of the fact, it is only fitting to note that the existence of synthetic *a priori* propositions is widely challenged by modern logicians, especially, of course, by empiricists and positivists. Their approach to the matter is rather different from that of Kant, but I do not wish to dwell upon this theme. The main point is that while the general distinction between analytic and synthetic propositions causes no difficulty, many philosophers refuse to admit that there are any synthetic propositions which are *a priori*. If a proposition is necessary, it is analytic. If a proposition is not analytic, it is synthetic *a posteriori*, to use Kant's language. In other words, the empiricist contention is that if a proposition does more than analyse the meanings of terms or illustrate the meanings of symbols, if, that is to say, it gives us information about non-linguistic reality, the connection between predicate and subject is not, and cannot be, necessary. In fine, all synthetic propositions are, in Kant's terminology, *a posteriori*. A proposition whose truth rests simply on the principle of contradiction is, as Kant said, analytic. A proposition whose truth does not rest on the principle of contradiction cannot be necessarily true. There is no room for a third class of propositions besides analytic propositions on the one hand and empirical propositions (corresponding to Kant's synthetic *a posteriori* judgments) on the other.

Kant, however, was convinced that there are synthetic *a priori* propositions; that is, propositions which are not merely 'explicative' but which extend our knowledge of reality and which are at the same time *a priori* (that is, necessary and strictly universal). The general problem, therefore, how is *a priori* cognition possible, can be expressed thus. How are synthetic *a priori* propositions possible? How is it that we can know anything at all about reality *a priori*? But this general question can be split up into several more particular questions by considering where synthetic *a priori* propositions are to be found.

They are to be found, in the first place, in mathematics. 'First of all it must be noted that mathematical propositions proper are always judgments *a priori* and not empirical, because they include the concept of necessity, which cannot be derived from experience.'[1] The proposition $7+5=12$ is not an empirical generalization admitting of possible exceptions. It is a necessary proposition. At the same time, however, this proposition, according to Kant, is not analytic in the sense described above: it is synthetic. The concept of twelve is not obtained, and cannot be obtained, by mere analysis of the idea of the union between seven and five. For this idea does not of itself imply the concept of twelve as the particular number resulting from the union. We cannot arrive at the notion of *12* except with the aid of intuition. 'The arithmetical proposition is therefore always synthetic.'[2] That is to say, it is synthetic *a priori*; for, as we have seen, it is a necessary proposition and so cannot be synthetic *a posteriori*.

Similarly, the propositions of pure geometry are also synthetic *a priori* propositions. For instance, 'that a straight line between two points is the shortest, is a synthetic proposition. For my concept of *straight* contains no notion of quantity, but only of quality. The concept of *the shortest* is thus wholly an addition, and it cannot be derived by any analysis from the concept of a straight line. Intuition must therefore lend its aid here, by means of which alone is this synthesis possible.'[3] But besides being synthetic the proposition is necessary, and so *a priori*. It is not an empirical generalization.

Geometers, Kant remarks, can make use of some analytical propositions; but he insists that all the propositions of pure mathematics proper are synthetic *a priori* propositions. Pure mathematics is not for him, as it was for Leibniz, a simply analytic science, depending on the principle of contradiction: it is constructional in character. Something more will be said in the next chapter about Kant's conception of mathematics, when we treat of his theory of space and time. Meanwhile it is sufficient to note the question which arises from his doctrine that mathematical propositions are synthetic *a priori* propositions; namely how is pure mathematical science possible? We certainly do know mathematical truths *a priori*. But how is it possible to do so?

In the second place, synthetic *a priori* propositions are also found in physics. Take, for instance, the proposition, 'in all changes of the corporeal (material) world the quantity of matter remains unchanged'. This proposition, according to Kant, is necessary and therefore *a priori*. But it is also synthetic. For in the

[1] *B*, 14.   [2] *B*, 16.   [3] *Ibid.*

concept of matter we do not think its permanence, but merely its presence in space, which it fills. Physics in general, of course, does not consist simply of synthetic *a priori* propositions. But 'natural science (physics) contains within itself synthetic *a priori* judgments as principles'.[1] And if we call the complex of these principles pure natural science or pure physics, the question arises, 'How is pure natural science or physics possible?' We possess *a priori* knowledge in this sphere. But how is it possible for us to possess it?

Kant believed that there are also *synthetic a priori* propositions in morals. But this subject can be left to the chapter on his ethical theory, as we are treating here of the problems raised and discussed in the *Critique of Pure Reason*. We come, therefore, to the subject of metaphysics. And if we consider metaphysics, we find that it does not aim simply at analysing concepts. It contains, indeed, analytic propositions; but they are not, properly speaking, metaphysical propositions. Metaphysics aims at extending our knowledge of reality. Its propositions must, therefore, be synthetic. At the same time, if it is not (and it is not) an empirical science, its propositions must be *a priori*. It follows, therefore, that if metaphysics is possible, it must consist of synthetic *a priori* propositions. 'And so metaphysics, according to its aim at least, consists simply of synthetic *a priori* propositions.'[2] As an example Kant cites the proposition, 'the world must have a first beginning'.[3]

But, as we have seen, the claim of metaphysics to be a science is in doubt. The question, therefore, is not so much *how* metaphysics as a science is possible as *whether* it is possible. At this point, however, we must refer to a distinction which we have already made, the distinction between metaphysics as a natural disposition and metaphysics as a science. As Kant believes that the human reason is naturally impelled to raise problems which cannot be answered empirically, he can quite properly ask how metaphysics, considered as a natural disposition, is possible. But inasmuch as he doubts whether the claim of metaphysics to constitute a science, capable of answering its own problems, is justified, the question here is really whether metaphysics considered as a science is possible.

We are faced, therefore, with four questions. First, how is pure mathematical science possible? Secondly, how is pure natural science or pure physics possible? Thirdly, how is metaphysics, considered as a natural disposition, possible? Fourthly, is meta-physics, considered as a science, possible? Kant treats of these questions in the *Critique of Pure Reason*.

4. If we consider the general question, how is *a priori* know-ledge possible or how are synthetic *a priori* judgments possible, and if at the same time we bear in mind Kant's agreement with Hume concerning the impossibility of deriving necessity and strict universality from empirical data, we can see how difficult it would be for him to maintain that knowledge consists simply in the con-formity of the mind to its objects. The reason for this is obvious. If, to know objects, the mind must conform itself to them, and if at the same time it cannot find in these objects, considered as empirically given, necessary connections, it becomes impossible to explain how we can make necessary and strictly universal judgments which are as a matter of fact verified and which, as we know in advance or *a priori*, must always be verified. It is not merely that we find, for instance, that experienced events have causes: we also know in advance that every event must have a cause. But if we reduce experience to the merely given, we cannot discover there a necessary causal relation. It is thus impossible to explain our knowledge that every event must have a cause on the hypothesis that knowledge consists simply in the mind's conforming itself to objects.

Kant therefore suggested another hypothesis. 'Hitherto it has been assumed that all our knowledge must conform to objects. But all attempts to ascertain anything about them *a priori* by concepts, and thus to extend our knowledge, came to nothing on this assumption. Let us try, then, whether we may not make better progress in the tasks of metaphysics if we assume that objects must conform to our knowledge. This at all events accords better with the possibility which we are seeking, namely of a knowledge of objects *a priori*, which would determine something about them before they are given to us.'[1]

This hypothesis, Kant observes, is analogous to that proposed by Copernicus. The latter saw that though the sun appears to move across the earth from east to west, we cannot justifiably conclude from this that the earth is fixed and that the sun moves round a fixed earth, for the very good reason that the observed movement of the sun would be precisely the same (that is to say, the pheno-mena would be precisely what they are) if it were the earth which

[1] *B*, xvi.

was moving round the sun, and the human observer with it. The immediate phenomena would be the same on either hypothesis. The question is whether there are not astronomical phenomena which can only be explained on the heliocentric hypothesis, or which at any rate are explained better and more economically on the heliocentric than on the geocentric hypothesis. And subsequent astronomical investigation showed that this is indeed the case. In an analogous manner, Kant suggests, empirical reality would remain what it is even on the hypothesis that for objects to be known (that is, for them to *be* objects, if we mean by 'object' an object of knowledge) they must conform to the mind rather than the other way about. And if *a priori* knowledge can be explained on the new but not on the old hypothesis, this is obviously an argument in favour of the former.

Kant's 'Copernican revolution' does not imply the view that reality can be reduced to the human mind and its ideas. He is not suggesting that the human mind creates things, as far as their existence is concerned, by thinking them. What he is suggesting is that we cannot know things, that they cannot be objects of knowledge for us, except in so far as they are subjected to certain *a priori* conditions of knowledge on the part of the subject. If we assume that the human mind is purely passive in knowledge, we cannot explain the *a priori* knowledge which we undoubtedly possess. Let us assume, therefore, that the mind is active. This activity does not mean creation of beings out of nothing. It means rather that the mind imposes, as it were, on the ultimate material of experience its own forms of cognition, determined by the structure of human sensibility and understanding, and that things cannot be known except through the medium of these forms. But if we speak of the mind imposing its own cognitive forms on the raw material, so to speak, of knowledge, this must not be taken to mean that the human subject does this deliberately, consciously and of set purpose. The object as given to conscious experience, the object *about* which we think (a tree, for instance), is already subjected to those cognitive forms which the human subject imposes by a natural necessity, because it is what it is; that is, because of its natural structure as a knowing subject. The cognitive forms thus determine the possibility of objects, if 'object' is taken to refer to object of knowledge precisely as such. If the word were taken to refer to things in themselves, that is, to things as they exist apart from any relation to the knowing subject, we could not, of course, say that they are determined by the human mind.

Perhaps the matter can be made a little clearer by reverting to the admittedly crude illustration of a man with red-tinted spectacles. On the one hand it is obvious that the man who sees the world as red because he is wearing red-tinted spectacles does not create the things which he sees in the sense in which God is Creator. Unless there existed things which affected him, that is, which stimulated his power of vision, he would not see anything at all. On the other hand nothing could be seen by him, that is, nothing could be for him an object of vision unless it were seen as red. At the same time, to make the analogy at all applicable, we must add the following important point. A man who puts on red-tinted spectacles does so deliberately: it is by his own choice that he sees things as red. We have to imagine, therefore, a man who is born with his power of vision so constituted that he sees all things as red. The world presented to him in experience is then a red world. This is really the point of departure for his reflection. Two hypotheses are then possible. It may be that everything *is* red. Or it may be that things have different colours,[1] but that they appear as red because of some subjective factor (as is, indeed, the case in the analogy). Spontaneously, the man would naturally embrace the first hypothesis. But it may be that in the course of time he finds a difficulty in explaining certain facts on this hypothesis. Thus he may be led to envisage and consider the alternative hypothesis. And if he finds that certain facts can be explained on this second hypothesis which cannot be explained on the hypothesis that all things are really red, he will embrace the second. He will never, indeed, be able to see the 'real' colours of things: appearances will be the same for him after his change of hypothesis as before, just as the apparent movement of the sun is precisely the same for the man who accepts the heliocentric hypothesis as it is for the man who accepts the geocentric hypothesis. But he will know why things appear as they do. The man who accepts the heliocentric hypothesis will know that the apparent movement of the sun round the earth is due to the earth's movement and to his own with it. The man who sees all things as red will have reason to suppose that this appearance of things is due to a condition in himself. Analogously, the man who accepts

[1] For purposes of this analogy I must be allowed to use ordinary everyday language. It is obviously an analogy or illustration, not a considered statement about the ontological status of colours.

Kant's 'Copernican revolution' will have reason to believe, let it be assumed, that certain ways in which things appear to him (as spatially co-ordinated, for instance, and as connected with one another by necessary causal relations) are due to subjective *a priori* conditions of knowledge in himself. He will not, indeed, be able to know things apart from their subjection to these *a priori* conditions or forms; but he will know why the empirical world is what it is for his consciousness.

We have already noted Kant's reference in his foreword to the *Prolegomena* to Hume's influence on his thought. In the preface to the second edition of the *Critique of Pure Reason* he draws attention to the influence of mathematics and physics in suggesting to him the idea of his 'Copernican revolution'. In mathematics a revolution must have occurred at a very early stage. Whoever the Greek may have been who first demonstrated the properties of the isosceles triangle, a new light must have flashed upon his mind. For he saw that it was not sufficient to contemplate either the visible diagram of the triangle or the idea of it in his mind. He had to demonstrate the properties of the triangle by a process of active construction. And, in general, mathematics became a science only when it became constructional in accordance with *a priori* concepts. As for physics, the revolution in this sphere came at a much later date. With the experiments of Galileo, Torricelli and others a new light broke upon physicists. They understood at last that though the scientist must, indeed, approach Nature to learn from her, he must not do so simply in the spirit of a pupil. Rather must he approach Nature as a judge, compelling her to answer the questions which he proposes, as a judge insists on witnesses answering the questions proposed to them according to a plan. He must come to Nature with principles in one hand and experiment in the other and make her answer questions proposed according to his design or purpose. He must not allow himself simply to follow her about like a child in leading-strings. It was only when physicists saw that Nature must be made to conform, as it were, to their preconceived designs[1] that real progress in the science became possible. And these revolutions in mathematics and physics suggest that we may possibly get along better in metaphysics if we assume that objects mnst conform to

[1] Obviously, Kant does not envisage the physicist as simply reading preconceived theories into Nature. He is thinking of the process of hypothesis, deduction and controlled experiment, in which the physicist is clearly no mere passive recipient of impressions from Nature.

the mind rather than the other way round. As Hume showed, *a priori* cognition cannot be explained on the second supposition. Let us see, therefore, if it can be explained on the first.

How can the 'Copernican revolution' help to explain *a priori* cognition? An example may help to give a preliminary idea. We know that every event must have a cause. But, as Hume showed, no amount of observation of particular events will serve to produce this knowledge. From this Hume concluded that we cannot be said to *know* that every event has a cause. All we can do is to try to find a psychological explanation of our belief or persuasion.[1] For Kant, however, we certainly do know that every event must have a cause. And this is an instance of *a priori* cognition. On what condition is it possible? It is possible only on condition that objects, to be objects (that is, to be known), must be subjected to the *a priori* concepts or categories of the human understanding, of which causality is one. For in this case nothing will ever enter the field of our experience except as exemplifying the causal relation, just as, to revert to our former illustration, nothing can ever enter the field of vision of the man whose power of vision is so constituted that he sees all things as red, except as red. If objects of experience are of necessity partially determined or constituted as such by the imposition of mental categories, and if causality is one of these, we can know in advance or *a priori* that nothing will ever happen, within the whole field of human experience, without a cause. And by extending this idea beyond the single example of causality we can explain the possibility of the whole range of *a priori* cognition.

Now, I have spoken of Kant's 'hypothesis'. And as regards its initial conception it was, of course, an hypothesis. 'Let us see whether we can get on better by assuming that . . .' represents the sort of way in which Kant introduces his idea. But he notes that, though the idea was suggested by the revolution in natural philosophy or physics, we cannot, in the critical philosophy, experiment with objects in a manner analogous to that in which the physicist can make experiments. We are concerned with the relation between objects and consciousness in general, and we cannot remove objects out of their relation to the knowing subject in order to see whether this does or does not make a difference to them. Such a procedure is impossible in principle. At the same

---

[1] In the Foreword to the *Prolegomena* Kant rightly notes that Hume never questioned the fact that the concept of cause is indispensable for life.

time, however, if on the new hypothesis we can explain what cannot be explained in any other way, and if at the same time we succeed in demonstrating the laws which lie *a priori* at the basis of Nature (considered as the sum of possible objects of experience), we shall have succeeded in proving the validity of the point of view which was at first assumed as an hypothesis.

5. Now, 'there are two sources of human knowledge, which perhaps spring from a common but to us unknown root, namely sensibility and understanding. Through the former objects are *given* to us; through the latter they are *thought*.'[1] Kant here distinguishes between sense or sensibility (*Sinnlichkeit*) and understanding (*Verstand*), telling us that objects are *given* through sense and *thought* through the understanding. But this statement, if taken alone and without reference to the context, might easily give rise to a misconception of his meaning, and a few words of comment are necessary.

We have seen that Kant does not agree with the empiricists that all human knowledge is derived from experience. For there is *a priori* knowledge, which cannot be explained on purely empiricist principles. At the same time he agrees with the empiricists on this point, that objects are given to us in sense-experience. But the word 'given' can be misleading. To put the matter rather crudely, thought can get to work on objects only when they are given to sense; but it does not follow that what is 'given' is not already a synthesis of matter and form, the form being imposed by human sensibility. And it was Kant's conviction that the given is in fact such a synthesis. The word 'given' must therefore be taken as meaning given to consciousness, without the implication that the senses apprehend things-in-themselves, things as they exist independently of the synthesizing activity of the human subject. Sense-experience itself involves such an activity, namely synthesis in the *a priori* sense intuitions of space and time. Things-in-themselves are never given to us as objects: that which the understanding finds before it, so to speak, as the given is already a synthesis of form and matter. The understanding then further synthesizes the data of sense intuition under its own pure (non-empirical) concepts or categories.

Sensibility and understanding, therefore, co-operate in constituting experience and in determining objects as objects, though their contributions are distinguishable. Now, this means that the

---

[1] *B*, 29; *A*, 19.

function of the pure concepts or categories of the understanding (*Verstand*) is to synthesize the data of sense intuition. They are therefore inapplicable to realities which are not, and cannot be, given in sense-experience. And it follows that no metaphysics which consists in using the pure concepts or categories of the understanding (such as the concepts of cause and substance) to transcend experience, as Kant puts it, and to describe supersensible reality can legitimately claim to be a science. Indeed, one of the philosopher's tasks is to expose the hollowness of any such claim.

The function of the pure concepts or categories of the understanding is thus to synthesize the manifold of sense: their use lies in their application to the data of sense intuition. But there are also certain ideas which, while not being mere abstractions from experience, are at the same time not applicable to the data of sense intuition. They transcend experience in the sense that no objects are given, or can be given, within experience which correspond to them. Such, for instance, are the ideas of the soul as a spiritual principle and of God. How are such ideas produced? The human mind has a natural tendency to seek unconditioned principles of unity. Thus it seeks the unconditioned[1] principle of unity of all categorical thinking in the idea of the soul as a thinking subject or ego. And it seeks the unconditioned principles of unity of all objects of experience in the idea of God, the supremely perfect Being.

These 'transcendental Ideas', as Kant calls them, are ascribed by him to the reason (*Vernunft*). We must note, therefore, that Kant uses this word with varying degrees of strictness. When he calls the first *Critique* the *Critique of Pure Reason* (*Kritik der reinen Vernunft*), the word 'reason', as covering the general contents of the work, includes sensibility, understanding and reason in the narrower sense. In this narrower sense reason (*Vernunft*) is distinguished from understanding (*Verstand*), and still more from sensibility (*Sinnlichkeit*). It refers to the human intellect as seeking to unify a manifold referring it to an unconditioned principle, such as God.

Now, this natural tendency of the reason, considered in itself, is in no way belittled by Kant. On the contrary, he considers that the transcendental Ideas exercise an important regulative

---

[1] 'Unconditioned' as transcending the subjective conditions of sensibility and understanding.

function. For example, the Idea of the world as a totality, the total system of causally related phenomena, constantly spurs us on to develop ever wider scientific explanatory hypotheses, ever wider conceptual syntheses of phenomena. It serves, in other words, as a kind of ideal goal, the notion of which stimulates the mind to renewed effort.

The question arises, however, whether these Ideas possess more than a regulative function. Can they be the source of a theoretical knowledge of corresponding realities? It is Kant's conviction that they cannot. In his view any attempt to use these Ideas as the basis for metaphysics as a science is foredoomed to failure. If we do so, we shall find ourselves involved in logical fallacies and antinomies. Given our possession of these Ideas, it is easy to understand the temptation to use them in a 'transcendent' manner; that is, to extend our theoretical knowledge beyond the field of experience. But it is a temptation to be resisted.

Bearing in mind the considerations outlined in this section, we can easily understand the general structure of the *Critique of Pure Reason*. The work is divided into two broad divisions, the first of which is entitled *Transcendental Doctrine of Elements* (*Transzendentale Elementarlehre*). This deals, as the word 'transcendental'[1] indicates, with the *a priori* elements (forms or conditions) of knowledge. It is subdivided into two main parts, *The Transcendental Aesthetic* (*Die transzendentale Aesthetik*) and *The Transcendental Logic* (*Die transzendentale Logik*). In the first of these Kant deals with the *a priori* forms of sensibility and shows how the synthetic *a priori* propositions of mathematics are possible. The *Transcendental Logic* is subdivided into *The Transcendental Analytic* (*Die transzendentale Analytik*) and *The Transcendental Dialectic* (*Die transzendentale Dialektik*). In the *Analytic* Kant treats of the pure concepts or categories of the understanding and shows how the synthetic *a priori* propositions of natural science are possible. In the *Dialectic* he considers two main themes, first the natural disposition to metaphysics, and secondly the question whether metaphysics (that is, speculative metaphysics of the traditional type) can be a science. As has already been remarked, he affirms the value of metaphysics considered as a natural disposition but denies its claim to constitute a true science which give us theoretical knowledge of purely intelligible reality.

[1] 'I call all knowledge *transcendental* which is occupied not so much with objects as with our mode of cognition of objects, so far as this is possible *a priori*' (*B*, 25; *A*, 11–12).

The second of the two broad divisions of the *Critique of Pure Reason* is entitled *Transcendental Doctrine of Method* (*Transzendentale Methodenlehre*). In the place of speculative or 'transcendent' metaphysics, claiming to be a science of realities which transcend experience, Kant envisages a 'transcendental' metaphysics, which would comprise the complete system of *a priori* cognition, including the metaphysical foundations of natural science. He does not profess to provide this transcendental system in the *Critique of Pure Reason*. If we regard the complete system of *a priori* cognition as an edifice, we can say that the *Transcendental Doctrine of Elements*, the first broad division of the *Critique*, examines the materials and their functions, while the *Transcendental Doctrine of Method* considers the plan of the edifice and is 'the determination of the formal conditions for a complete system of pure Reason'.[1] Kant can say, therefore, that the *Critique of Pure Reason* sketches the plan of the edifice architectonically, and that it is 'the complete idea of transcendental philosophy, but not this science itself'.[2] Strictly speaking, the *Critique of Pure Reason* is only a propaedeutic to the system of transcendental philosophy or metaphysics. But if we use the latter term in a wider sense, we can, of course, say that the contents of the *Critique*, the doctrine of elements and the doctrine of method, constitute the first part of transcendental philosophy or metaphysics.

6. In the last chapter mention was made of the fact that in *Dreams of a Ghost-seer* Kant declared that metaphysics is the science of the boundaries or limits of human reason. In the *Critique of Pure Reason* he endeavours to fulfil this programme. But reason must be understood to mean the theoretical or speculative reason; better, reason in its theoretical function. We cannot have theoretical knowledge of realities which are not given in sense-experience or which are incapable of being so given. There is, of course, reason's critical reflection on itself; but the result of such reflection is primarily to reveal the conditions of scientific knowledge, the conditions of the possibility of objects. It does not open to us a world of supersensible reality as an object of theoretical knowledge.

At the same time this delimitation of the boundaries of theoretical or scientific knowledge does not show that God, for example, is unthinkable or that the term is meaningless. What it does is to put freedom, immortality and God beyond the range of

---

[1] *B*, 735–6.   [2] *B*, 28; *A*, 13.

either proof or disproof. The criticism of metaphysics, therefore, which is to be found in the *Transcendental Dialectic* opens the way for practical or moral faith, resting on the moral consciousness. Thus Kant can say[1] that he has to do away with knowledge to make room for faith, and that his destructive criticism of metaphysics' claim to be a science strikes a blow at the root of materialism, fatalism and atheism. For the truths that there is a spiritual soul, that man is free and that God exists no longer rest on fallacious arguments which afford a ground for those who deny these truths; they are moved to the sphere of the practical or moral reason and become objects of faith rather than of knowledge (this term being taken in a sense analogous to that in which it is used with reference to mathematics and natural science).

It is a great mistake to look on this theory as a mere sop to the orthodox and devout or as a mere act of prudence on Kant's part. For it is part of his solution to the great problem of reconciling the world of science on the one hand with, on the other, the world of the moral and religious consciousness. Science (that is, classical physics) involves a conception of causal laws which do not admit of freedom. And man, considered as a member of the cosmic system studied by the scientist, is no exception. But scientific knowledge has its limits, and its limits are determined by the *a priori* forms of human sensibility and understanding. There is thus no valid reason whatsoever for saying that the limits of our scientific or theoretical knowledge are identical with the limits of reality. And the moral consciousness, when its practical implications are developed, takes us beyond the sensible sphere. As a phenomenal being, man must be considered as subject to causal laws and as determined; but the moral consciousness, itself a reality, involves the idea of freedom. Though, therefore, we cannot demonstrate scientifically that man is free, belief in freedom is demanded by the moral consciousness.

This point of view is certainly beset with difficulties. Not only do we have the division between sensible, phenomenal reality and noumenal, purely intelligible reality, but we are also faced in particular with the difficult conception of man as phenomenally determined but noumenally free, as determined and free at the same time, though under different aspects. But it would be out of place to discuss the difficulties here. My point in mentioning Kant's point of view was twofold. First, I wished to draw attention once

---

[1] *B*, xxx.

again to the general problem of the reconciliation of the world of Newtonian physics with the world of reality and religion. For if we bear this general problem in mind, we are less likely to lose sight of the wood for the trees. Secondly, I wished to indicate that the *Critique of Pure Reason* does not stand by itself in lonely isolation from Kant's other writings but that it forms a part of a total philosophy which is gradually revealed in successive works. True, the first *Critique* has its own problems, and to this extent it stands by itself. But, quite apart from the fact that inquiry into *a priori* cognition has yet to be pursued in the field of the practical reason, the conclusions of the first *Critique* form only a part of the solution to a general problem which underlies all Kant's thinking. And it is important to understand this fact from the start.

CHAPTER XII

KANT (3): SCIENTIFIC KNOWLEDGE

*Space and time—Mathematics—The pure concepts or categories
of the understanding—The justification of the application of the
categories—The schematism of the categories—Synthetic* a priori
*principles—The possibility of the pure science of Nature—
Phenomena and noumena—The refutation of idealism—Concluding remarks.*

I. THE only way, says Kant at the beginning of the *Transcendental Aesthetic*, in which our knowledge can relate immediately to
objects is by means of an intuition.[1] And an intuition can take
place only in so far as an object is given to us. The divine intellect
is said to be both intuitive and archetypal. That is to say, the
divine intuition creates its objects. But this is not the case with
human intuition, which presupposes an object. And this means
that the human subject must be affected by the object in some
way. Now, the capacity for receiving representations (*Vorstellungen*) of objects by being affected by them is named 'sensibility'
(*Sinnlichkeit*). 'By means of sensibility, therefore, objects are
given to us, and it alone provides us with intuitions.'[2]

If these remarks are taken purely by themselves, the term
'sensibility' has a wide meaning, being simply cognitive receptivity or the capacity for receiving representations of objects by
being affected by them. But we must remember that Kant looks
on the divine intuition, considered precisely in contrast with
human intuition, as being not only archetypal but intellectual. It
follows, therefore, that human intuition is sense intuition. And
sensibility thus means the capacity for receiving representations
of objects by being sensibly affected by them. 'The effect of an
object upon the faculty of representation, so far as we are affected
by the object, is sensation' (*Empfindung*).[3] Kant agrees, therefore,
with the empiricists to the extent of saying that human cognition
of objects requires sensation. The mind requires to be put in contact, as it were, with things through an affection of the senses.

---

[1] The word 'intuition' (*Anschauung*) can refer either to the act of intuiting or
to what is intuited. In the present context the word is used in the first sense. But
Kant frequently uses it in the second sense.
[2] *B*, 33; *A*, 19.   [3] *B*, 34; *A*, 19.

Kant takes it for granted that the senses are acted upon by external things; and the effect of this action upon the faculty of representation is called 'sensation'. The latter is thus a subjective representation; but this does not mean that it is caused by the subject.

Sense intuition cannot, however, be reduced simply to the *a posteriori* affections of our senses by things. The object of an empirical sensuous intuition is called by Kant 'appearance' (*Erscheinung*). And in the appearance we can distinguish two elements. First there is its matter. This is described as 'that which corresponds to sensation'.[1] Secondly, there is the form of appearance. And this is described as 'that which enables the manifold of appearance to be arranged in certain relations'.[2] Now, the form, as distinct from the matter, cannot be itself sensation, if the matter is described as that which corresponds to sensation. Hence, while the matter is given is *a posteriori*, the form must lie on the side of the subject: that is to say, it must be *a priori*, an *a priori* form of sensibility, pertaining to the very structure of sensibility and constituting a necessary condition of all sense intuition. According to Kant, there are two pure forms of sensibility, space and time. Space is not, indeed, a necessary condition of *all* empirical intuitions; but this point can be passed over for the moment. It is sufficient to note that Kant parts company with the pure empiricists by finding an *a priori* element in all sense-experience.

Perhaps at this point some remarks should be made about Kant's terminology, even at the cost of interrupting the exposition of his theory of space and time. First, the term 'representation' (*Vorstellung*) is used in a very wide sense to cover a variety of cognitive states. Hence the term 'faculty of representation' is pretty well equivalent to 'mind' (*Gemüt*), a term which is also used in an extremely wide sense. Secondly, the term object (*Gegenstand*) is not used consistently in one sense. Thus in the definition of sensation quoted above 'object' must refer to what Kant later calls thing-in-itself, and which is unknown. But 'object' generally means object of knowledge. Thirdly, in the first edition of the *Critique of Pure Reason* Kant distinguishes between 'appearance' and 'phenomenon'. 'Appearances, so far as they are thought as objects according to the unity of the categories, are

---

[1] *B*, 34; *A*, 20.
[2] *B*, 34. In *A*, 20 the wording is somewhat different.

called *phenomena*.'[1] Hence 'appearance' should mean the content of a sense intuition when this content is considered as 'undetermined' or uncategorized, while 'phenomenon' should mean categorized objects. In point of fact, however, Kant often uses the term 'appearance' (*Erscheinung*) in both senses.

A further remark. We have seen that the matter of appearances is described as that which 'corresponds to' sensation. Elsewhere, however, we are told that sensation itself can be called 'the matter of sense-knowledge'.[2] And perhaps these two ways of speaking can be regarded as expressions of two different tendencies in Kant's thought. The external thing which affects the subject is itself unknown; but by affecting the senses it produces a representation. Now, Kant sometimes tends to speak as though all appearances were subjective representations. And, when this point of view is dominant, it is natural for him to describe sensation itself as the matter of appearance. For sensation is described, as we have seen, as the effect of an object upon the faculty of representation. But Kant also speaks as though phenomena were objects which are not simply subjective representations; and this represents, indeed, his dominant outlook. If, then, we think away the contribution of the categories of the understanding to phenomena and come down to appearances (in the narrower sense of the word), it is natural to speak of the matter of an appearance as being that which 'corresponds to' sensation.

The last three paragraphs can be described, not as a digression, but as a series of footnotes in the text, if one may be permitted a contradiction in terms. However, a brief development of the idea suggested in the final sentence of the last paragraph may serve to clarify Kant's position and carry forward our account of it. The approach is proposed by Kant himself.[3]

The world of common experience obviously consists of things with various qualities, things which stand in various relations to one another. That is to say, we ordinarily talk about perceiving things, each of which can be described in terms of qualities, and each of which stands in various relations to other things. And perception in this sense is clearly the work of understanding and sense in co-operation. But from the total process we can try to abstract all that is contributed by the understanding, in order to arrive at empirical intuition, or perception in a narrow sense. We then come by logical analysis to appearances, to what we may

[1] *A*, 248.   [2] *A*, 50; *B*, 74; *Prol.*, 11.   [3] Cf. *A*, 20–2; *B*, 35–6.

call perhaps sense-contents or sense-data. But we can carry the analysis further. For within the content of sense-experience we can distinguish between the material element, that which corresponds to indeterminate sensation, and the formal element, the spatio-temporal relations of the manifold of appearance.[1] And the purpose of the *Transcendental Aesthetic* is to isolate and study the formal elements, considered as a necessary condition of experience.

The matter can be expressed in this way. The very lowest level conceivable of anything which could be called a knowledge of or acquaintance with objects involves at least an adverting to the representations produced by the action of things upon our senses. But we cannot advert to sensations without relating them in space and time. For instance, to advert to two sensations, that is, to be conscious of them, involves relating the one to the other within time, within an order of temporal succession. One sensation comes before or after or at the same time as another. Space and time constitute the framework, as it were, in which the manifold of sensation is ordered or arranged. They thus at the same time diversify and unify (in spatio-temporal relations) the indeterminate matter of appearance.

This does not mean, of course, that we are at first aware of unordered sensations, and that we then subject them to the *a priori* forms of space and time. For we are never faced, as it were, with unordered sensations. Nor could we be. Indeed, Kant's main point is that space and time are *a priori* necessary conditions of sense-experience. What is given, therefore, in empirical intuition, namely that of which we are aware, is, so to speak, already ordered. The ordering is a condition of awareness or consciousness, not a consequence of it. True, within the appearance we can distinguish, by a process of logical abstraction or analysis, between matter and form. But as soon as we abstract in thought the subjectively contributed form of appearance, the object of which we are aware disappears. In fine, the objects of sensuous or empirical intuition are, as given to consciousness, already subject to the *a priori* forms of sensibility. The ordering or relating takes place within sensuous intuition, not after it.

Attention can now be drawn to the distinction which Kant makes between outer or external sense, by means of which we

---

[1] Strictly speaking, the form of appearance is, as we have seen, that which enables the manifold of appearances (sensations or that which corresponds to sensations) to be ordered in certain relations. But we can speak of the relations as the formal element in appearance.

perceive objects external to us (or, as he puts it, represent to ourselves objects as external to us), and inner or internal sense, by
means of which we perceive our interior states.[1] Space is said to
be 'the form of all appearances of the external senses, that is,
the subjective condition of sensibility, under which alone external
intuition is possible for us'.[2] All objects external to us are, and must
be, represented as being in space. Time is said to be 'the form of
the internal sense, that is, of the intuition of ourselves[3] and of
our internal state'.[4] Our psychical states are perceived in time, as
following one another or as simultaneous, but not as in space.[5]

Inasmuch as Kant immediately proceeds to say that time is the
a priori formal condition of all appearances whatsoever, whereas
space is the *a priori* formal condition of external appearances only,
it may appear that he is contradicting himself. But his meaning is
this. All representations (*Vorstellungen*), whether they have or
have not external things as their objects, are determinations of
the mind.[6] And, as such, they belong to our internal state. Hence
they must all be subject to the formal condition of inner sense or
intuition, namely time. But time is thus only the mediate condition of external appearances, whereas it is the immediate
condition of all internal appearances.

Now, we have been speaking of space and time as pure forms of
sensibility and as forms of intuition. But we have already drawn
attention[7] to the different ways in which Kant uses the term
'intuition'. And in what he calls the 'metaphysical exposition' of
the ideas of space and time he refers to them as being themselves
a priori intuitions. They are not empirically derived concepts. I
cannot derive the representation of space *a posteriori*, from the
experienced relations between external appearances; for I cannot
represent external appearances as having spatial relations except
within space. Nor could I represent appearances as existing simultaneously or successively unless the representation of time were
already present. For I represent them as existing simultaneously

---

[1] Kant would agree with Hume that in introspection we perceive psychical
states but not a permanent ego or soul. More will be said on this subject later.
[2] *B*, 42; *A*, 26.
[3] Kant is referring to the empirical ego, not to the spiritual soul.
[4] *B*, 49; *A*, 33.
[5] We may recall that Hume remarked that we cannot properly speak of one
internal state as being to the left or right of another.
[6] *Das Gemüt* is customarily translated 'mind'. The word is used by Kant in a
very wide sense, and it must not, of course, be taken as equivalent to 'understanding' (*Verstand*).
[7] See p. 235, note 1.

or successively within time. I can think away all external appearances, and the representation of space still remains, as a condition of their possibility. Similarly, I can think away all internal states, but the representation of time still remains. Space and time, therefore, cannot be empirically derived concepts. Further, they cannot be concepts at all, if we mean by concepts general ideas. Our ideas of spaces are formed by introducing limitations within a unitary space, which is presupposed as their necessary foundation; and our ideas of different times or stretches of time are formed in an analogous manner. But we cannot, according to Kant, split up general concepts in this way. Space and time are particulars rather than general concepts. And they are found on the perceptual level; they are presupposed by the concepts of the understanding, not the other way round. We must conclude, therefore, that they are *a priori* intuitions on the level of sense, though we must not, of course, take this as meaning that in the representations of unitary space and time we intuit non-mental existent realities. The representations of space and time are necessary conditions for perception; but they are conditions on the side of the subject.

Are space and time, therefore, unreal for Kant? The answer to this question depends on the meanings which we attach to the words 'real' and 'unreal'. Appearances, objects given in empirical intuition, are, so to speak, already temporalized and, in the case of appearances represented as external to ourselves, spatialized. Empirical reality is, therefore, spatio-temporal, and it follows that space and time must be said to possess empirical reality. If the question whether space and time are real is equivalent to the question whether empirical reality is characterized by spatio-temporal relations, the answer must be affirmative. We experience only appearances, and appearances are what they are, possible objects of experience, only through the union of form and matter; that is, through the ordering of the indeterminate and formless matter of sensation by the application of the pure forms of sensibility. There can never be an object of outer sense which is not in space; and there can never be any object, whether of outer or inner sense, which is not in time.[1] Hence empirical reality must necessarily be characterized by spatial and temporal relations. It is not proper to say that appearances *seem* to be in space; they *are* in space and time. It may be objected that, according to Kant,

---

[1] 'Object' must here be taken, of course, in the sense of object of human knowledge or object for us.

space and time are subjective forms of sensibility, and that they therefore should be called ideal rather than real. But the point is that, for Kant, there can be no empirical reality apart from the imposition of these forms. They enter into the constitution as it were of empirical reality; and they are thus themselves empirically real.

At the same time, however, inasmuch as space and time are *a priori* forms of human sensibility, the range of their application is extended only to things as appearing to us. There is no reason to suppose that they apply to things-in-themselves, apart from their appearance to us. Indeed, they cannot do so. For they are essentially conditions for the possibility of appearances. While, therefore, it is correct to say, for instance, that all appearances are in time, it is quite incorrect to say that all things or all realities are in time. If there are realities which cannot affect our senses and which cannot belong to empirical reality, they cannot be in space and time. That is to say, they cannot have spatio-temporal relations. By transcending empirical reality they transcend the whole spatio-temporal order. Moreover, those realities which do affect our senses, when taken as they are in themselves and apart from being objects of experience, are not in space and time. There may be some ground in things in virtue of which a thing possesses, as a phenomenon, certain spatial relations and not others; but this ground is unknown and it necessarily remains unknown. It is not itself a spatial relation. For space and time have no application to non-phenomenal reality.

Kant's formula is, therefore, this. Space and time are empirically real but transcendentally ideal. They are empirically real in the sense that what is given in experience is in space (if it is an object of the external senses) and in time. Space and time are not, Kant insists, illusions. We can distinguish between reality and illusion as well on his theory as on the opposite theory. But space and time are transcendentally ideal in the sense that the sphere of phenomena is the only sphere of their validity, and that they do not apply to things-in-themselves, considered apart from their appearance to us.[1] This transcendental ideality, however, leaves the empirical reality of the spatio-temporal order entirely unimpaired. Kant would not admit, therefore, that his view could properly be assimilated to the Berkeleian idealism, according to which to exist is to perceive or to be perceived. For he affirmed the

---

[1] We must remember that to appear means being subjected to the *a priori* forms of sensibility.

existence of things-in-themselves, which are not perceived.[1] His Copernican revolution, he insists, no more impairs the empirical reality of the world of experience than the heliocentric hypothesis alters or denies the phenomena. It is a question of explaining phenomena, not of denying them. And his view of space and time is capable of explaining the *a priori* knowledge founded on these intuitions, which no other view is capable of explaining. To this *a priori* knowledge we must now turn.

2. Kant gives what he calls a 'transcendental exposition' of both space and time. 'By a transcendental exposition I understand the explanation of a conception as a principle from which the possibility of other synthetic *a priori* cognitions can be discerned. For this purpose it is required, first that such cognitions do really flow from the given conception, and secondly that these cognitions are possible only on the presupposition of a given way of explaining this conception.'[2] In his transcendental exposition of time Kant does not tell us very much beyond the facts, first that the concept of change, and with it the concept of motion (considered as change of place), is possible only in and through the representation of time, and secondly that we cannot explain the synthetic *a priori* cognition exhibited in the general doctrine of motion except on the presupposition that time is an *a priori* intuition. When treating of space, however, he speaks at some length[3] of mathematics, in particular of geometry. And his general thesis is that the possibility of mathematical knowledge, which is synthetic *a priori* in character, can be explained only on the theory that space and time are pure *a priori* intuitions.

Let us take the proposition, 'It is possible to construct a figure with three straight lines'. We cannot deduce this proposition by mere analysis of the concepts of a straight line and of the number three. We have to construct the object (a triangle) or, as Kant puts it, to give ourselves an object in intuition. This cannot be an empirical intuition. For then it could not give rise to a necessary proposition. It must be, therefore, an *a priori* intuition. And from this it follows that the object (the triangle) cannot be either a thing-in-itself or a mental image, as it were, of a thing-in-itself. It

---

[1] Whether or not he could do so consistently is a question which need not concern us for the moment.

[2] *B*, 40.

[3] That is, if we take the section entitled 'transcendental exposition of the conception of space' together with the relevant parts of the 'general remarks on the Transcendental Aesthetic'.

cannot be a thing-in-itself, for things-in-themselves, by definition, do not appear to us. And even if we grant the possibility of intuiting a thing-in-itself, this intuition could not be *a priori*. The thing would have to be presented to me in an *a posteriori* intellectual intuition, if such were possible to us. Nor can we suppose that the object (the triangle) is a mental image or representation of a thing-in-itself. For the necessary propositions which we are enabled to make by constructing a triangle are made about the triangle itself. For instance, we can demonstrate the properties of *the* isosceles triangle, so to speak. And we have no warrant for supposing that what is necessarily true of a representation is true of a thing-in-itself. How, then, can we construct in intuition objects which enable us to enunciate synthetic *a priori* propositions? We can do so only on condition that there is in us a faculty (*Vermögen*) of *a priori* intuition, which is the universal, necessary condition for the possibility of objects of external intuition. Mathematics is not a purely analytic science which gives us information only about the contents of concepts or meanings of terms. It gives us information *a priori* about objects of external intuition. But this is not possible unless the intuitions required for the construction of mathematics are all grounded in *a priori* intuitions which are the necessary conditions for the very possibility of objects of external intuition. Thus 'geometry is a science which determines the properties of space synthetically, and yet *a priori*'.[1] But we could not determine the properties of space in this way unless space were a pure form of human sensibility, a pure *a priori* intuition which is the necessary condition for all objects of external intuition.

The matter can perhaps be made somewhat clearer by referring to Kant's discussion in the *Prolegomena* of the objectivity of mathematics, that is, of its applicability to objects. Geometry, to take one particular branch of mathematics, is constructed *a priori*. Nevertheless we know very well that its propositions are necessary, in the sense that empirical reality must always conform to them. The geometer determines *a priori* the properties of space, and his propositions will always be true of the empirical spatial order. But how can he make necessarily true *a priori* statements which have objective validity in reference to the external, empirical world? It is possible for him to do this only if the space, whose properties he determines, is a pure form of human sensibility, by which form alone objects are given to us and which applies only to phenomena, not to things-in-themselves. Once we accept this explanation, 'it is quite easy to understand and at the same time to prove indisputably that all external objects of our sensible world must necessarily accord in all strictness with the propositions of geometry'.[1]

Kant thus uses the *a priori* character of mathematics to prove his theory of space and time. And it is of interest to note the relation of his position to that of Plato. The latter also was convinced of the *a priori* character of mathematics. But he explained it by postulating an intuition of 'mathematical objects', intelligible particulars which are not phenomena and which subsist in some sense in their own right. This line of explanation is ruled out on Kant's principles; and he accuses Plato of abandoning the world of sense and taking flight into an empty ideal realm where the mind can find no sure support. However, he shares Plato's conviction of the *a priori* character of mathematical knowledge, though his explanation of it is different.

Some references to Leibniz may help to throw some further light on Kant's view of mathematics. For Leibniz all mathematical propositions, including axioms, can be demonstrated with the aid of definitions and the principle of contradiction. For Kant fundamental axioms cannot be demonstrated by recourse to the principle of contradiction. Geometry is thus axiomatic in character. But Kant maintains that the fundamental axioms of geometry express insights into the essential nature of space represented in a subjective *a priori* intuition. And it is obvious that it is possible to hold both that the axioms are indemonstrable and that they do not express insights into the essential nature of space. For they might be held to be free postulates, as, for instance, by the mathematician, D. Hilbert.

Again, in developing mathematical science the mind, according to Leibniz, proceeds analytically. We only require definitions and the principle of contradiction, and we can then proceed by analysis. For Kant, as we have seen, mathematics is not a purely analytic science: it is synthetic, requiring intuition and proceeding constructionally. And this is as true of arithmetic as it is of geometry. Now, if we accept the view, represented above all by Bertrand Russell, that mathematics is ultimately reducible to logic, in the sense that pure mathematics could in principle be

---

[1] *Prol.*, 13, remark 1.

deduced from certain primitive logical concepts and indemonstrable propositions, we shall naturally reject Kant's theory. We shall regard this theory as refuted by the *Principles of Mathematics* and *Principia Mathematica*. But Russell's view of mathematics as purely analytic is not, of course, by any means universally accepted. And if we think, with L. E. J. Brouwer for example, that mathematics does in fact involve intuition, we shall naturally attach more value to Kant's theory, even if we do not accept his account of space and time. However, as I am not myself a mathematician, I cannot profitably attempt to decide how much truth there is in the theory. I can only draw attention to the fact that modern philosophers of mathematics are by no means all agreed that mathematics is what Kant said it was not, namely a purely analytic science.

Attention must, however, also be drawn to a feature of Kant's theory of geometry which has led critics to maintain that the theory has been discredited by subsequent mathematical developments. By space Kant meant Euclidean space, and by geometry he meant Euclidean geometry.[1] It follows, therefore, that if the geometer reads off, so to speak, the properties of space, the geometry of Euclid is the only geometry. Euclidean geometry will necessarily apply to empirical reality, but no other geometrical system will apply. Since Kant's time, however, non-Euclidean geometries have been developed, and it has been shown that Euclidean space is but one of the conceivable spaces. Moreover, Euclidean geometry is not the only one which will fit reality, as it were; which geometry is to be used depends on the mathematician's purpose and the problems with which he has to deal. It would, indeed, be absurd to blame Kant for having a prejudice in favour of Euclidean geometry. At the same time the development of other geometries has rendered his position untenable.

To be accurate, it is rash to say without qualification that Kant excluded the possibility of any non-Euclidean geometry. For we find him saying, for instance, that 'there is no contradiction in the concept of a figure which is enclosed within two straight lines. For the concepts of two straight lines and of their intersection contain no negation of a figure. The impossibility is found, not in the concept in itself, but in the construction of the concept in space; that is, in the conditions and determinations of space. But these have their own objective reality; that is, they apply to possible

---

[1] Leibniz had also understood by space Euclidean space.

things, because they contain in themselves *a priori* the form of experience in general.'[1] But even if we take this passage as saying by implication that a non-Euclidean geometry is a bare logical possibility, Kant clearly states that such a geometry cannot be constructed in intuition. And this is really, for Kant, the same thing as to say that there cannot be a non-Euclidean geometrical system. Non-Euclidean geometry may be thinkable in the sense that it is not ruled out simply by application of the principle of contradiction. But, as we have seen, mathematics for Kant does not rest simply on the principle of contradiction; it is not an analytic but a synthetic science. Hence constructibility is essential for a geometrical system. And to say that only Euclidean geometry can be constructed is really to say that there cannot be non-Euclidean systems.

If, therefore, we assume the constructional character of geometry, and if non-Euclidean geometries can be constructed, it follows at any rate that Kant's theory of geometry cannot be accepted as it stands. And if non-Euclidean systems can be applied, this tells against Kant's theory that the intuition of Euclidean space is a universal and necessary condition for the possibility of objects. But whether or not it would be possible to revise the Kantian theory of the subjectivity of space in such a way as to allow for subsequent mathematical developments is not a matter on which I feel disposed to offer any opinion. From the purely mathematical point of view it is not a question of any importance. From the philosophical point of view it has, indeed, importance; but then there may be other reasons for denying Kant's theory of the transcendental ideality of space and time.[2]

However, if we assume that Kant has proved the truth of his theory of space and time, he may be said to have answered his first question, namely how is mathematical science possible. How can we explain the possibility of the synthetic *a priori* cognition which we undoubtedly possess in mathematics? It is explicable if, and only if, space and time are empirically real but transcendentally ideal in the sense described above.

A final remark. It may have occurred to the reader that it is very odd of Kant to treat mathematics on the level of sensibility. But the latter did not imagine, of course, that arithmetic and

---

[1] *B*, 268; *A*, 220–1.

[2] In a sense Leibniz also maintained the transcendental ideality of space and time, but with reference to God's thinking, not, as with Kant, to ours. And for Kant the difference is all-important.

geometry are developed by the senses without the use of the understanding. The question was what is the necessary foundation for the work of the mind in developing systems of mathematical propositions. And for Kant the *a priori* forms of sensibility, the pure intuitions of space and time, constitute this necessary foundation. In his view all human intuition is sensuous, and if intuition is required in mathematics, it must be sensuous in character. He may well have been wrong in thinking that all human intuition is necessarily sensuous. But at any rate he was not guilty of the absurdity of supposing that the senses construct mathematical systems without the co-operation of the understanding.

3. We can begin our treatment of the *Transcendental Analytic* by developing a little this important point of the co-operation of sense and understanding in human knowledge.

Human knowledge arises from two chief sources in the mind (*Gemüt*). The first is the faculty or power of receiving impressions; and through this an object is given to us. Sense intuition provides us with data, and we cannot obtain objects as data in any other way. The second main source of human knowledge is the power of thinking the data by means of concepts. The receptivity of the mind for impressions is called sensibility (*Sinnlichkeit*). The faculty of spontaneously producing representations is called understanding (*Verstand*). And the co-operation of both faculties is required for knowledge of objects. 'Without sensibility no object would be given to us, and without the understanding no object would be thought. Thoughts without content are empty; intuitions without concepts are blind. . . . These two powers or faculties cannot exchange their functions. The understanding is incapable of intuiting, and the senses are incapable of thinking. It is only from the united co-operation of the two that knowledge can arise.'[1]

But though the co-operation of both powers is required for knowledge, we ought not to overlook the differences between them. And we can distinguish between sensibility and its laws on the one hand and understanding and its laws on the other. The science of the laws of sensibility has already been considered. We must therefore now turn our attention to the science of the laws of the understanding, namely logic.

The logic with which we are here concerned is not, however,

[1] *B*, 75; *A*, 51.

formal logic, which regards only the forms of thinking and abstracts from its content and from differences in the kinds of objects about which we can think.[1] We are concerned with what Kant calls 'transcendental logic'. It is not offered as a substitute for traditional formal logic, which Kant simply accepts. It is offered as an additional, and new, science. Like pure formal logic, it is concerned with the *a priori* principles of thought, but, unlike the former science, it does not abstract from all the content of knowledge, that is, from the relation of knowledge to its object. For it is concerned with the *a priori* concepts and principles of the understanding and with their application to objects; not, indeed, with their application to this or that particular kind of object, but with their application to objects in general. In other words, transcendental logic is concerned with the *a priori* knowledge of objects so far as this is the work of the understanding. Transcendental aesthetic, which we have already considered, studies the pure forms of sensibility as the *a priori* conditions necessary for objects being given to us in *sense intuition*. Transcendental logic studies the *a priori* concepts and principles of the understanding as necessary conditions for objects (that is, the data of sense intuition) being *thought*.

The matter can be put this way. It was Kant's conviction that there are in the understanding *a priori* concepts by which the manifold of phenomena is synthesized. Causality is one of them. There is room, therefore, for a systematic study of these concepts and of the principles grounded in them. In pursuing this study we shall discover the ways in which human understanding necessarily synthesizes phenomena and makes knowledge possible.

The second part of the *Transcendental Logic*, namely the *Transcendental Dialectic*, is concerned with the misuse of these *a priori* concepts and principles and with their illegitimate extension from the objects given in sense intuition to things in general, including those which cannot be given to us as objects in the proper sense. But consideration of this second part must be left for the next chapter. We are concerned at present with the first part, namely the *Transcendental Analytic*. And our first task is to ascertain the *a priori* concepts of the understanding (*Analytic of Concepts*).

But how are we to set about this task? Obviously, we are not

---

[1] For example, in systematically mapping out, so to speak, the forms of deductive thinking we are concerned simply with these forms themselves. And the whole matter can be expressed symbolically, without reference to objects.

called upon to make a complete inventory of all possible concepts and then to separate the *a priori* concepts from those which are *a posteriori* or empirical, abstracted from sense-experience. Even if this were practically possible, we should have to possess a criterion or method for distinguishing between *a priori* and empirical concepts. And if we were in possession of a method for ascertaining which concepts are purely *a priori*, it might be that the use of the method would enable us to achieve our purpose without making any such general inventory. The question is, therefore, whether there is in fact a way of ascertaining the *a priori* concepts of the understanding in a direct and systematic manner. We need a principle or, as Kant puts it, a 'transcendental clue' (*Leitfaden*) for discovering these concepts.

Kant finds this clue in the faculty of judgment, which for him is the same as the power of thought. 'We can reduce all operations of the understanding to judgments, so that the understanding can be represented as the power of judging. For it is, according to what has been said above, a power of thinking.'[1] Now, what is a judgment? To judge, which is the same as to think, is to unify different representations to form one cognition by means of concepts.[2] In judgment, therefore, representations are synthesized by means of concepts. Now, we can obviously set no limit to the number of possible judgments, if we are talking about particular judgments. But we can determine the number of possible ways of judging, that is, the number of logical types of judgment, considered according to their form. And, in Kant's opinion, logicians have already done so. But they have not carried the matter further and inquired into the reason why these, and only these, forms of judgment are possible. It is, however, precisely here that we can find our 'transcendental clue'. For each form of judgment is determined by an *a priori* concept. And in order, therefore, to discover the list of the pure *a priori* concepts of the understanding, we have only to examine the table of possible logical types of judgment.

We can put the matter in this way. The understanding does not intuit; it judges. And to judge is to synthesize. Now, there are certain fundamental ways of synthesizing (functions of unity in

[1] *B*, 94; *A*, 69.
[2] According to Kant, judgment is *mediate* knowledge of an object, a representation of a representation of an object. No representation, except an intuition, relates immediately to an object. A concept relates immediately only to some other representation, either to an intuition or to another concept.

judgment, as Kant puts it), exhibited in the possible logical types or forms of judgment. And these exhibit the *a priori* structure of the understanding, considered as a unifying or synthesizing power. We can thus discover the fundamental synthesizing functions of the understanding. 'The functions of the understanding can thus all be found, if one can completely exhibit the functions of unity in judgments. And the following section will show that this can be done quite easily.'[1]

Hitherto we have generally spoken of the pure or *a priori* *concepts* of the understanding. But Kant also calls them *categories*. And this is probably a better word. The understanding, which is the unifying or synthesizing or judging power, possesses an *a priori* categorial structure. That is to say, because it is what it is, it necessarily synthesizes representations in certain fundamental ways, according to certain basic categories. Without this synthesizing knowledge of objects is not possible. Hence the categories of the understanding are *a priori* conditions for knowledge. That is, they are *a priori* conditions for the possibility of objects being thought. And without being thought the objects cannot really be said to be known. For, as we have seen, sensibility and understanding co-operate in the production of knowledge, though their functions differ and can be considered separately.

Kant's table of types of judgment or of logical functions of judgment can now be given. For the sake of convenience I give at the same time his table of categories. The total scheme shows which category corresponds, or is supposed to correspond, to which logical function. The tables are to be found in the first chapter of the *Analytic of Concepts*.[2]

Judgments	*Categories*
1. Quantity.	1. Quantity.
(i) Universal.	(i) Unity.
(ii) Particular.	(ii) Plurality.
(iii) Singular.	(iii) Totality.
2. Quality.	2. Quality.
(iv) Affirmative.	(iv) Reality.
(v) Negative.	(v) Negation.
(vi) Infinite.	(vi) Limitation.

[1] *B*, 94; *A*, 69.   [2] *B*, 95 and 106; *A*, 70 and 80.

Judgments	*Categories*
3. Relation.	3. Relation.
(vii) Categorical.	(vii) Inherence and subsistence (substance and accident).
(viii) Hypothetical.	(viii) Causality and dependence (cause and effect).
(ix) Disjunctive.	(ix) Community (reciprocity between agent and patient).
4. Modality.	4. Modality.
(x) Problematic	(x) Possibility—impossibility.
(xi) Assertoric.	(xi) Existence—non-existence.
(xii) Apodictic.	(xii) Necessity—contingency.

Kant remarks about the list of categories that it has not been made in a haphazard fashion, like Aristotle's list of categories, but by the systematic application of a principle. It thus contains all the original pure concepts or categories of the understanding. There are, indeed, other pure concepts of the understanding but these are derived (*a priori*) and subsidiary. Kant proposes to call them *predicables*, to distinguish them from the categories (*praedicamenta*); but he does not undertake to give a list of them; that is, to work out the complete system of original and derived pure concepts of the understanding. It is enough for his purpose to have given the list of the original concepts or categories.

Kant was, however, over-optimistic in thinking that he had given a complete list of categories. For it is clear that his principle for determining what they were was dependent on the acceptance of certain views about judgment, which were taken from the logic of his time. And so it was open to his successors to revise his list, even when they accepted the general idea of *a priori* categories.

It is worth remarking, perhaps, that according to Kant the third category in each triad arises out of the combination of the second with the first. Thus totality is plurality regarded as unity; limitation is reality combined with negation; community is the causality of a substance reciprocally determining and determined by another substance; and necessity is existence given through the possibility of existence.[1] This interpretation of the triadic scheme may seem to be somewhat far-fetched; but in view of the central

---

[1] Thus the concept of a necessary being would be the concept of a being whose possibility involves existence, that is, which cannot be merely possible. But *this* concept is not, for Kant, objectively applicable.

position occupied later in the Hegelian philosophy by the idea of triadic development through thesis, antithesis and synthesis it is worth while drawing attention here to Kant's remarks.

4. According to Kant, therefore, there are twelve *a priori* categories of the understanding. But what is the justification for their employment in synthesizing phenomena? What is the justification for their application to objects? Such a problem does not arise in connection with the employment of the *a priori* forms of sensibility. For, as we have seen, no objects can be given to us at all except through the subjection of the indeterminate matter of sensation to the forms of space and time. Hence it would be foolish to ask how we are justified in applying the forms of sensibility to objects. For these forms are a necessary condition of there being objects at all. But the situation in regard to the categories of the understanding is different. Objects are already there, so to speak, given in sense intuition. Might not these objects, namely appearances, be such that the application to them of the categories of the understanding distorts or misrepresents them? We need to show that the application is justified.

The giving of such a justification is called by Kant the transcendental deduction of the categories. The word 'deduction' can easily be misunderstood. For it suggests a systematic discovery of what the categories are. And this has already been done. In the present context, therefore, deduction means justification, as Kant indeed explains. As for the word 'transcendental', its meaning is best understood by contrasting it with the word 'empirical'. Kant is not concerned to justify the application of the categories by showing that their employment is empirically fruitful, in this or that science, for example. He is concerned to justify their application by showing that they are *a priori* conditions of all experience. He can say, therefore, that the whole aim of the transcendental deduction is to show that the *a priori* concepts or categories of the understanding are *a priori* conditions of the possibility of experience.

The problem can be defined more closely. Space and time are also *a priori* conditions of experience. But they are conditions which are necessarily required in order that objects should be given to us. The task of the transcendental deduction, therefore, is to show that the categories are conditions which are necessarily required for objects to be *thought*. In other words, a justification of the application of the categories to objects must take the form of showing that objects cannot be thought except through the synthesizing categories of the understanding. And as the thinking of objects is required for knowledge of them, to show that objects cannot be thought save through the categories is to show that they cannot be known except through the categories. And to show this is to show that the employment of the categories is justified; that is, that they have objective validity.

This line of thought is clearly involved in Kant's Copernican revolution. The use of the categories cannot be justified on the assumption that the mind must conform to objects. But if objects, to be known, must conform to the mind, and if this means that they must be subjected to the categories of the understanding in order to be objects in the full sense, no further justification of the use of the categories is required.

The argument of Kant's transcendental deduction is by no means easy to follow. But in the course of it he introduces an important idea; and some effort must be made to give a brief account of it, even at the risk of over-simplifying his line of thought. In making this attempt I shall confine my attention to the deduction as given in the second edition of the *Critique of Pure Reason*, which differs considerably from that given in the first edition.

An object of knowledge is defined by Kant as 'that in the concept of which the manifold of a given intuition is *united*'.[1] Without synthesis there can be no knowledge of objects. A mere stream, so to speak, of unconnected representations could not be called knowledge. Now, synthesis is the work of the understanding. 'The connection (*Verbindung* and *conjunctio* are the words used by Kant) of a manifold can never be given us by the sense . . .; for it is an act of the spontaneity of the power of representation. And as one must call this faculty understanding, to distinguish it from sensibility, all connection, whether conscious or unconscious, whether of the manifold of intuition or of several concepts . . . is an act of the understanding. And to this act we give the general name of synthesis.'[2]

Besides the concepts of the manifold and of its synthesis, the idea of connection or conjunction contains another element. This is the representation of the unity of the manifold. Hence connection can be described as 'the representation of the synthetical unity of the manifold'.[3]

---

[1] B, 137.   [2] B, 129–30.   [3] B, 130.

Kant is not referring here to the *a priori* concept or category of unity which figures in the list of categories. He is not saying that all connection involves the application of this category. For the application of any category, whether it be unity or any other, presupposes the unity of which he is speaking. Of what, then, is Kant speaking? He is speaking of the unity which consists in relation to one perceiving and thinking subject. Objects are thought by means of the categories but without this unity they would not be thinkable. In other words, the understanding's work of synthesizing is not possible except within the unity of consciousness.

This means that the manifold of intuition or perception is incapable of being thought and so becoming an object of knowledge unless perceiving and thinking are so united in one subject that self-consciousness is capable of accompanying all representations. Kant expresses this by saying that the *I think* must be capable of accompanying all one's representations. It is not necessary that I should always think of my perceiving and thinking as *mine*. But without the *possibility* of such awareness no unity can be given to the manifold of intuition: no connection is possible. 'The *I think* must be capable of accompanying all my representations. For otherwise something could be represented in me which could not be thought at all. And this is equivalent to saying that the representation would be impossible or at least would be nothing to me. . . . Therefore every manifold of intuition has a necessary relation to the *I think* in the same subject in which this manifold is found.'[1] It would be absurd to speak of my having any idea unless self-awareness could accompany it. And it would be absurd to speak of the manifold of perception being thought, unless the same consciousness could accompany the perceiving and the thinking.

This relation between the subject and the manifold of intuition (namely the relation expressed by saying that the *I think* must be capable of accompanying them all) is called by Kant 'pure apperception', to distinguish it from empirical apperception, that is, the empirical and contingent awareness of a given psychical state as mine. The empirical consciousness which accompanies different representations is fragmentary. At one moment I exercise an empirical act of self-awareness, accompanying a given representation, at another I do not. The empirical consciousness, like the

[1] *B*, 132.

representations which it accompanies, is disunited. But the possibility of an identical *I think* accompanying all representations is a permanent condition of experience. And it presupposes a transcendental (not empirical) unity of self-consciousness which is not given to me as an object but which is the fundamental necessary condition for there being any objects at all for me. Unless the manifold of intuition could be brought, as it were, to the unity of apperception, there could be no experience, no knowledge. Or, to express it less subjectively, there could be no objects.

Kant does not mean, of course, that I have first to be aware of myself as a subject or ego before I can do any synthesizing. I have no prior consciousness of a permanent self-identical ego. It is only with acts directed towards the given that I become conscious of them as mine. Consciousness of self and consciousness of that which is cognitively related to the self are so bound up together in the self that consciousness of self is not a temporally prior experience. At the same time the unity of apperception (in the sense that the *I think* must be capable of accompanying all my representations) and the transcendental unity of consciousness are *a priori* conditions of experience. Without connection there is no experience. And connection entails the unity of apperception.

In speaking of the unity of consciousness, of the unity of perceiving and thinking in one subject, as a condition of experience, Kant may seem to be saying something obvious. But, if so, it is an obvious fact which seems to be passed over by those who forget, as it were, the subject as subject and so concentrate on the empirical ego as object that they feel justified in dissolving the self into a series of psychical events or in describing it as being simply a logical construction, that is, the class of such events. If we bear these phenomenalists in mind, Kant seems to be drawing attention to a point of great importance.

The question arises, however, what has all this to do with justifying the application of the categories? The answer is, in brief, as follows. No objective experience, no knowledge of objects, is possible unless the manifold of intuition is connected in one self-consciousness. But all synthesis is effected by the understanding, and it is thus by the understanding that the manifold of representations is brought into the unity of apperception. Now, the understanding synthesizes by means of its *a priori* categories. Hence no objective experience, no knowledge of objects, is possible except through the application of the categories. The world of experience is formed through the co-operation of perception and thinking in the application of the *a priori* forms of sensibility and of the categories of the understanding. Hence the categories refer to objects, that is, have objective reference, because all objects, to be objects, must conform to them.

Kant's own words are worth quoting. 'The manifold which is given in a sensuous intuition comes necessarily under the original synthetic unity of apperception. For thereby alone is the *unity* of intuition possible. But that operation of the understanding, through which the manifold of given representations (whether intuitions or concepts) is brought under one apperception, is the logical function of judgments. Thus all the manifold, so far as it is given in one empirical intuition, is *determined* in relation to one of the logical functions of judgment, through which, that is to say, it is brought under one consciousness. Now, the *categories* are nothing else but these functions of judgment, so far as the manifold in a given intuition is determined in relation to them. Consequently the manifold in a given intuition is necessarily subject to the categories.'[1] Again, 'a manifold which is contained in an intuition that I call mine is represented by means of the synthesis of the understanding as belonging to the *necessary* unity of self-consciousness. And this takes place by means of the category.'[2]

5. A further question, however, arises. We have on the one hand the manifold data of intuition and on the other a plurality of categories. What determines which category or categories are applied? We need some indication of a connecting link. There must be some proportion or homogeneity between the data of sense intuition and the categories if the former are to be subsumed under the latter. But 'the pure concepts of the understanding are quite heterogeneous when compared with empirical intuitions (or even with sensuous intuitions in general), and they can never be discovered in any intuition. How, then, is the *subsumption* of the latter under the former, and with it the application of the categories to appearances possible?'[3] This is the problem.

To solve this problem Kant has recourse to the imagination (*Einbildungskraft*) conceived as a mediating power or faculty between understanding and sensibility. The imagination is said to produce and to be the bearer, as it were, of *schemata*. A schema is, in general, a rule or procedure for the production of images which schematize or delimit, so to speak, a category so as to permit its

---

[1] *B*, 143.   [2] *B*, 144.   [3] *B*, 176; *A*, 137–8.

application to appearances. The schema is not itself an image but represents a general procedure for the constitution of images. 'This representation of a general procedure of the imagination for providing a concept with its image I call the schema for this concept.'[1] The schema, being general, has an affinity with the concept: the image, being particular, has an affinity with the manifold of intuition. Thus the imagination is able to mediate between the concepts of the understanding and the manifold of intuition.

Kant was not, of course, the first philosopher to emphasize the mediating function of the image. This function had been attributed to the image in, for example, mediaeval Aristotelianism. But the approach to this subject in the philosophy of Kant obviously is, and must be, different from that of the mediaeval Aristotelian. For the latter the image is the result of processes on the level of sense and serves in turn as a basis for intellectual abstraction. With Kant, however, the image is a spontaneous product of the power of imagination working according to a schema which it itself produces. We must never forget that for Kant the object must conform to the mind rather than the other way about.

To show the sort of thing he means Kant gives one or two examples from mathematics. I can produce, for instance, an image of the number five by placing five points one after the other in this way . . . . . But the schema of the number five is not itself this image or any other image: it is the representation of a method whereby a multiplicity can be represented in an image in accordance with a certain concept. The schema permits the bringing together, as it were, of the concept and the manifold of phenomena. That is to say, it permits the application of the concept to phenomena. Kant also cites the non-mathematical example of the concept of a dog. The schema of this concept is a rule for producing a representation which is required for applying the concept to a particular animal.

Such illustrations can be extremely misleading. For we are primarily concerned here, not with mathematical concepts, and still less with empirical *a posteriori* ideas such as that of a dog, but with the pure categories of the understanding. And we are concerned, not with schemata or rules for the production of images which (schemata) we can choose or alter, but with transcendental schemata which determine *a priori* the conditions under which a category can be applied to any manifold. However, Kant's

[1] *B*, 179–80; *A*, 140.

examples, taken from the application of mathematical concepts and of *a posteriori* ideas to the data of perception, are intended to serve only as an introduction to the general notion of a schema.

The transcendental schemata of the categories determine the conditions under which the categories can be applied to appearances. And for Kant this means determining the temporal conditions under which a category is applicable to appearances. For situation in time is the only feature which is common to all appearances whatsoever, including the states of the empirical self. Hence Kant can say that 'the schemata are nothing but temporal determinations *a priori* in accordance with rules'.[1] Time is the formal condition of the connection or conjunction of all representations. And a transcendental determination of time, which is a product of the imagination, has, as it were, a footing in both camps. It is homogeneous with the category of which it is the schema in that it is universal and rests on a *a priori* rule. It is homogeneous with appearances, in that time is contained in every empirical representation of the manifold. 'Thus an application of the category to appearances becomes possible by means of the transcendental determination of time which, as the schema of the concepts of the understanding, permits the subsumption of the latter (appearances) under the former.'[2]

Kant does not discuss at much length the particular schemata of particular categories. And what he does say is in some instances extremely difficult to understand. As, therefore, I do not wish to involve myself in lengthy problems of exegesis, I shall mention only a few examples.

Turning to the categories of relation, we are told that the schema of the category of substance is 'the permanence of the real[3] in time, that is, the representation of it as a substratum of the empirical determination of time; as a substratum, therefore, which remains, while all else changes'.[4] That is to say, in order that the concept of substance should be applicable to the data of perception, it must be schematized or determined by the schema of the imagination; and this involves representing substance as a permanent substratum of change in time. Only in this schematized form is the category applicable to appearances.

The schema of the category of cause is 'the real which, when

[1] *B*, 184; *A*, 145.   [2] *B*, 178; *A*, 139.
[3] Reality, as we learn in the section on the categories of quality, is that whose concept indicates a being in time.   [4] *B*, 183; *A*, 144.

posited, is always followed by something else. It consists, therefore, in the succession of the manifold, in so far as this succession
is subject to a rule.'[1] Kant does not wish to say that the concept
of causality is nothing but the concept of regular succession. What
he means is that the category of cause is not applicable to appearances unless it is so schematized by the imagination that it involves
the representation of regular succession in time.

The schema of the third category of relation, that of community
or reciprocity between agent and patient, is 'the coexistence of the
determinations (accidents) of the one with those of the other
according to a general rule'.[2] Here again Kant does not mean that
the coexistence of substances with their accidents is all that there
is in the concept of interaction. But this concept cannot be applied
to phenomena unless it is given a form which involves this
representation of coexistence in time.

Finally, to take the last two categories of modality, the schema
of the category of existence is being at a certain time, while the
schema of the category of necessity is the being of an object in all
time. Necessity, as a category, does not mean simply being in all
time. It means, as we saw earlier, existence which is given through
the very possibility of existence. But the category could not be
applied, according to Kant, unless the imagination so determined
it in respect of time as to involve the representation of being or
existence in all time. This is a necessary condition of its applicability. We cannot represent to ourselves anything as necessary
except by representing it as existing in all time. This idea belongs
to the schematized category. And it is always the schematized
category which is applied.

A problem arises which can be briefly indicated here. Kant, as
we have seen, uses the terms category and pure or *a priori* concept
to refer to the same thing. Now, the categories are described as
logical functions. They are pure forms of the understanding which
make synthesis possible but which, taken in themselves apart from
their application to appearances, do not represent any objects.
And in this case it can be asked whether the word 'concept' is not
a misnomer. And in his commentary on the *Critique of Pure
Reason*[3] we find Professor Kemp Smith maintaining that when
Kant speaks about the categories he usually means the schemata.
Hence the chapter on the schematism of the categories simply
contains their delayed definitions. The categories proper, as pure

forms of the understanding, are simply logical functions and have
no determinate content or meaning. The concept of substance, for
instance, would be what Kant calls the schema of the category
of substance. There is no room, as it were, for a pure concept of
substance other than the notion of substance defined in the schema.

There is certainly a good deal to be said for this point of view.
And if we turn to mathematical concepts, it might be maintained
that the representation of a general rule or procedure for the
construction of triangles *is* the concept of triangle. At the same
time, while Kant certainly says that the unschematized categories have no sufficient meaning to give us the concept of an
object and that they are 'only functions of the understanding for
the production of concepts',[1] he also attributes to them some
content, even if this content is not sufficient to represent an object.
'Substance, for example, if we leave out the temporal determination of permanence, would mean nothing more than a something,
which can be thought as subject, without being a predicate of
anything else.'[2] It may be that I can 'make nothing' of this idea,
as Kant puts it. But this means that I cannot apply it to represent
an object, an object being a possible object of experience, and
experience being sense-experience. The fact remains, however, that
some meaning or content is attributed by Kant to the unschematized category. This meaning is not sufficiently determinate
to give knowledge; but it is thinkable, as a logical possibility.
According to Kant, metaphysicians have attempted to use the
pure categories as a source of knowledge of things-in-themselves.
And to use the pure categories in this way is to misuse them. But
the very possibility of misuse presupposes that they have *some*
meaning.

6. Now, the understanding produces *a priori* certain principles
which state the conditions of the possibility of objective experience,
that is to say, of experience of objects. Or, to put the same thing
in another way, the understanding produces *a priori* certain
principles which are rules for the objective use of the categories.
To ascertain, therefore, what these principles are, we need only
consider the table of schematized categories. 'The table of categories gives us the natural guide to the table of principles (*Grundsätze*), because the latter are nothing else than rules for the
objective use of the former.'[3]

The principles corresponding to the categories of quantity are

[1] *B*, 187; *A*, 147.   [2] *B*, 186; *A*, 147.   [3] *B*, 200; *A*, 161.

called by Kant 'axioms of intuition'. He does not mention specific axioms; but he tells us that their general principle is, 'All intuitions are extensive magnitudes'.[1] This is a principle of the pure understanding, and so it cannot be (not that one would be tempted to think that it is) a mathematical principle. For mathematical principles are said to be derived from pure intuitions by the mediation of the understanding, not from the pure understanding itself. At the same time this principle of the axioms of intuition explains, according to Kant, why the synthetic *a priori* propositions of mathematics are applicable to experience. For instance, what geometry affirms of the pure intuition of space must be valid for empirical intuitions if all intuitions are extensive magnitudes. In fact, as the principle is itself a condition of objective experience, the applicability of mathematics is also a condition of objective experience. And we may add that if the principle of the axioms of intuition explains why the synthetic *a priori* propositions of mathematics are applicable to phenomenal reality, it also explains the possibility of mathematical physics.

The principles corresponding to the schematized categories of quality are called by Kant 'anticipations of experience'. The general principle of these anticipations is 'in all appearances the real which is an object of sensation has intensive magnitude, that is, a degree'.[2] In discussing the schema of the categories of quality Kant maintained that it involves the representation of degree of intensity, a notion which implies the possibility of increase in intensity and of decrease down to zero (negation). We are now told, in the general principle of the anticipations of experience, that all empirical perceptions, as involving sensation, must have degrees of intensity. This principle, therefore, affords an *a priori* basis for the mathematical measurement of sensation.

If we take these two principles together, namely the principle of the axioms of intuition and the principle of the anticipations of experience, we can see that they enable us to make predictions about future intuitions or perceptions. We cannot, indeed, predict *a priori* what our future perceptions will be; nor can we predict the quality of empirical perceptions (perceptions involving sensation). We cannot predict that the next object of perception will be red, for instance. But we can predict that all intuitions or perceptions will be extensive magnitudes and that all empirical perceptions involving sensation will have intensive magnitude.

[1] *B*, 202; *A*, 162.   [2] *B*, 207; *A*, 166.

These two principles are grouped together by Kant as mathematical principles. Or, rather, they are principles of the mathematical use of the categories. By saying this Kant does not mean that the two principles are mathematical propositions. He means that they bear on intuition, and that they justify the applicability of mathematics.

The principles corresponding to the schematized categories of relation are named 'analogies of experience'. And their general underlying principle runs, 'Experience is possible only through the representation of a necessary connection of perceptions'.[1] Objective experience, that is, knowledge of objects of sense, is not possible without a synthesis of perceptions, implying the presence to consciousness of a synthetic unity of the manifold. But this synthetic unity, which comprehends connections, is contributed by the subject, that is, *a priori*. And *a priori* connections are necessary. Hence experience is not possible except through the representation of necessary connections between objects of perception.

The three analogies are regarded by Kant as rules or guides for the empirical use of the understanding in discovering concrete connections. And they correspond respectively to what Kant calls the three *modi* of time, namely permanence, succession and coexistence. What is meant by this can best be understood by considering the analogies themselves. They are stated as follows. First, 'In every change of appearances the substance remains, and its quantum in Nature neither increases nor diminishes'.[2] Secondly, 'All changes take place according to the law of connection of cause and effect'.[3] Thirdly, 'All substances, so far as they can be perceived as coexistent in space, are in thorough-going interaction'.[4]

These principles obviously correspond respectively to the schematized categories of relation, namely substance and accident, cause and effect, and community or interaction between agent and patient. They are *a priori* principles and thus antecedent to experience. But though they tell us about relations or proportions, they do not predict or enable us to predict the unknown term. They differ, therefore, as Kant notes, from mathematical analogies. The first analogy, for instance, does not tell us what the permanent substance in Nature is: it tells us rather that change involves substance, and that, whatever substance is, it conserves its total

---

[1] *B*, 218; this differs from the version in *A*, 176–7.
[2] *B*, 224; *A*, 182. [3] *B*, 232; *A*, 189. [4] *B*, 256; *A*, 211.

quantum. This will be true whether we decide on empirical grounds that the substance or substratum of change in Nature is to be called matter (as Kant thought) or energy or whatever it may be. To put the matter crudely, the analogy tells us that the total quantum of the basic stuff or substance in Nature is conserved unchanged; but it does not tell us what it is. We cannot discover this *a priori*. Again, the second analogy tells us that all changes are causal, and that any given effect must have a determining cause. But though we may know the effect, we cannot discover what the cause is by the mere use of the second analogy. We must have recourse to experience, to empirical investigation. The analogy or principle is regulative in character: it guides us in the use of the category of causality. As for the third analogy, it is quite obvious that it does not tell us either what things are coexistent in space or what are their interactions. But it tells us *a priori*, and in a general sense, what we should look for.

The principles corresponding to the categories of modality are called 'the postulates of empirical thought in general'. They are as follows.[1] First, 'That which agrees with the formal conditions of experience (intuition and concepts) is *possible*'. Secondly, 'That which is connected with the material conditions of experience (that is of sensation) is *real*'. Thirdly, 'That the connection of which with the real is determined according to general conditions of experience is (exists as) *necessary*'.

It is important to understand that, according to Kant, these postulates concern only the relation of the world, of the objects of experience, to our cognitive faculties. The first postulate, for instance, states that only that which can be subjected, as it were, to the formal conditions of experience is a possible existent, that is, an existent within empirical reality. It does not state that there can be no being or beings which transcend empirical reality by transcending the formal conditions of objective experience. God, for example, is not a possible existent in the physical world; but to say this is not to say that there is not, and cannot be, a God. An infinite spiritual being transcends the application of the formal conditions of experience, and it is, therefore, not possible as a physical or experienced object. But the divine being is logically possible, at least in the sense that no logical contradiction is discernible in the idea of it. And there may be grounds for belief in such a being.

[1] *B*, 265–6; *A*, 218.

The postulates are, as already stated, postulates of empirical thinking. The second postulate, therefore, gives us a definition or explanation of reality in the empirical use of the term. It amounts to saying that in the sciences nothing can be accepted as real which is not connected with an empirical perception, and so with sensation, according to the analysis of experience. As for the third postulate, it concerns inference from what is perceived to what is not perceived according to the analogies of experience and empirical laws. If we take, for instance, the second analogy of experience by itself, we can say only that, given a certain change or event, it must have a cause: we cannot determine *a priori* what the cause is. But, if we take into account the empirical laws of Nature, we can say that a certain definite causal relation is necessary, and that a certain cause must exist, not, of course, with absolute necessity, but with hypothetical necessity, on the hypothesis, that is to say, that a certain change or event occurs.

7. Not only, therefore, is mathematics applicable to Nature, but there are also a number of principles which are derived from the categories of the understanding and which are thus *a priori*. A pure science of Nature is therefore possible. Physics in the narrow sense is an empirical science. Kant never imagined that we could deduce the whole of physics *a priori*. But there is a universal science of Nature, a propaedeutic to physics, as Kant calls it in the *Prolegomena*[1] though he also speaks of it as a universal or general physics.[2] It is true that not all the concepts which are found in this philosophical part of physics, or propaedeutic to physics, are pure in the Kantian sense; for some are dependent on experience. Kant gives as examples the concepts of motion, impenetrability and inertia.[3] And not all the principles of this universal science of Nature are universal in a strict sense. For there are some which apply only to objects of the external sense, and not to objects of the internal sense (namely the psychical states of the empirical ego). But there are at the same time some principles which apply to all objects of experience, whether external or internal; for example, the principle that events are causally determined according to constant laws. In any case there is a pure science of Nature in the sense that it consists of propositions which are not empirical hypotheses but which enable us to predict the course of Nature, and which are synthetic *a priori* propositions.

[1] 15.   [2] *Ibid.*   [3] *Ibid.*

It will be remembered that one of Kant's main problems in the *Critique of Pure Reason* was to explain the possibility of this pure science of Nature. And the question how it is possible has now been answered, namely in the preceding sections of this chapter. A pure science of Nature is possible because objects of experience, to be objects of experience, must of necessity conform to certain *a priori* conditions. Given this necessary conformity, we know that the complex of synthetic *a priori* propositions derived immediately or mediately from the *a priori* categories of the understanding will be always verified. In brief, 'the principles of possible experience are then at the same time universal laws of Nature, which can be known *a priori*. And thus the problem contained in our second question, *How is the pure science of Nature possible?* has been solved'.[1]

We can put the matter in another way. Objects, to be objects, must be related to the unity of apperception, to the unity of consciousness. And they are related by being subsumed under certain *a priori* forms and categories. The complex of possible objects of experience thus forms one Nature in relation to the unity of consciousness in general. And the necessary conditions for thus relating them are themselves the ground of the necessary laws of Nature. Without synthesis there is for us no Nature; and the *a priori* synthesis gives laws to Nature. These necessary laws are in a real sense imposed by the human subject; but they are at the same time objective laws, because they are valid, and necessarily valid, for the whole range of possible experience; that is, for Nature as the complex of possible objects of experience.

Kant has, therefore, settled to his own satisfaction the problems raised by Hume. Newtonian physics postulates the uniformity of Nature. But experience is incapable of proving the uniformity of Nature. It cannot show that the future will resemble the past, in the sense of showing that there are universal and necessary laws of Nature. But while Hume contented himself with observing that we have a natural belief in the uniformity of Nature and with attempting to give a psychological explanation of this belief, Kant attempted to prove this uniformity. As he agreed with Hume that it cannot be proved by empirical induction, he argued that it follows from the fact that Nature, as the complex of objects of possible experience, must conform to the *a priori* conditions of objective experience. It is this fact which enables us to know

[1] *Prol.*, 23.

a priori certain truths which lie at the foundation of Newtonian physics.[1]

We can say, if we like, that Kant undertook to justify the Newtonian physics. But the term 'justify' can, of course, be misleading. For in one sense the only justification needed by a scientific system is its fruitfulness. That is to say, it can be maintained that an *a posteriori* justification is the only kind which is really relevant. But Kant believed that the Newtonian physics involved presuppositions which cannot be theoretically justified *a posteriori*. The question arose, therefore, whether an *a priori* theoretical justification is possible. And Kant was convinced that it was possible on one condition, namely on the condition of accepting the standpoint of his Copernican revolution. Much that Kant says is doubtless either dated or highly disputable. But the questions whether natural science does or does not involve presuppositions and, if so, what is the logical status of these presuppositions are by no means dead questions. For instance, in *Human Knowledge, Its Scope and Limits* Bertrand Russell argues that there are a number of 'postulates' of scientific inference, which are not derived from experience and cannot be proved empirically. To be sure, he goes on to give an account, partly psychological and partly biological, of the genesis of these natural beliefs. And he thus treads in the footsteps of Hume rather than in those of Kant, who tried to show that the presuppositions of physics have objective reference and why they have objective reference and yield knowledge. At the same time Bertrand Russell agrees with both Hume and Kant that pure empiricism is inadequate as a theory of knowledge. In spite, therefore, of his hostility towards Kant he recognizes the reality of the *problem* with which Kant found himself faced. And this is the point which I wish to make.

8. The reader will have noticed that the categories of the understanding, taken by themselves, give us no knowledge of objects. And the schematized categories apply only to the data of sense intuition, that is to say, appearances. The categories can give us no knowledge of things 'except in so far as they can be applied to *empirical intuition*. That is to say, they serve only to

---

[1] For Kant physics very naturally meant the Newtonian physics: given the historical context, it could hardly mean anything else. And it is evident that there is a connection between Kant's principles, as listed in the *Analytic of Principles*, with the Newtonian conception of the physical world. For instance, a principle asserting that all changes take place according to necessary causal relations, would not fit in with a physics which admitted the concept of indeterminacy.

make *empirical knowledge* possible. But this is called experience.'[1] Hence the only legitimate use of the categories, with respect to the knowledge of things, lies in their application to possible objects of experience. This, says Kant, is a conclusion of great importance, because it determines the limits of the use of the categories and shows that they are valid only for objects of sense. They cannot give us theoretical or scientific knowledge of realities which transcend the sphere of sense.

The same must be said, of course, of the *a priori* principles of the understanding. They apply only to possible objects of experience, that is, to phenomena, to objects as given in empirical or sense intuition. 'The final conclusion of this whole section is, therefore, that all principles of the pure understanding are nothing more than *a priori* principles of the possibility of experience; and to this alone do all synthetic *a priori* propositions relate. Indeed, their possibility itself rests entirely on this relation.'[2] Hence the principles, for example, which have reference to substance and to determined causality hold good only for phenomena.

Our knowledge of objects is thus restricted to phenomenal reality. But though we cannot cross the bounds of phenomenal or empirical reality and know what lies beyond these bounds, we have no right to assert that there are only phenomena. And Kant introduces the idea of noumena, an idea which we must now examine.

Literally the word *noumenon* means object of thought. And Kant sometimes speaks of noumena as objects of the understanding (*Verstandeswesen*).[3] But to say that noumenon means object of thought does not carry us far towards a comprehension of Kant's doctrine. Indeed, it can be definitely misleading. For it may suggest that Kant divides up reality into *sensibilia* or objects of sense and *intelligibilia* or noumena considered as objects apprehended by pure thought. The word *noumenon* can, of course, be used in this way. 'Appearances, in so far as they are thought as objects according to the unity of the categories, are called *phenomena*. But if I assume (the existence of) things which are simply objects of the understanding and which at the same time can be given as objects to intuition, although not to sense but to intellectual intuition, things of this kind would be called *noumena* or *intelligibilia*.'[4] But though the word *noumenon can* be used in this way, the notion that human beings enjoy or can enjoy an intellectual intuition of noumena is precisely one of the positions which

[1] *B*, 147.   [2] *B*, 294.   [3] Cf. *Prol.*, 32; *B*, 309.   [4] *A*, 248–9.

Kant is most concerned to exclude. For him at least all intuition is sense intuition. So it is best to drop all etymological considerations and to concentrate on Kant's actual use of the term, which he takes pains to elucidate.

In the first edition of the *Critique of Pure Reason* Kant distinguishes between 'transcendental object' and noumenon. The idea of appearance involves the idea of something which appears. Correlative to the idea of a thing as appearing is the idea of a thing as not appearing; that is, of a thing as it is in itself, apart from its appearing. But if I try to abstract from all that in the object which has reference to the *a priori* conditions of knowledge, that is, of the possibility of objects of knowledge, I arrive at the idea of an unknown 'something', an unknown and, indeed, unknowable *X*. This unknowable *X* is completely indeterminate: it is merely something in general. For example, the idea of the *X* correlative to a cow is no different from the idea of the *X* correlative to a dog. Thus we have here the idea of the transcendental object; that is, 'the completely undetermined idea of something in general'.[1] But this is not yet the idea of a *noumenon*. To transform, as it were, the transcendental object into a noumenon, I must assume an intellectual intuition in which the object can be given. In other words, while the concept of the transcendental object is a mere limiting concept, the noumenon is conceived as an *intelligibile*, a positive reality which could be the object of an intellectual intuition.

Having made this distinction, Kant goes on to say that we possess no faculty of intellectual intuition, and that we cannot conceive even its possibility, not, that is, in a positive concept. Further, though the idea of a noumenon as a thing-in-itself (*ein Ding an sich*) does not contain a logical contradiction, we cannot see the positive possibility of noumena considered as possible objects of intuition. Hence the division of objects into phenomena and noumena is not to be admitted. At the same time the concept of the noumenon is indispensable as a limiting concept; and we can call things-in-themselves, that is, things considered in so far as they do not appear, *noumena*. But our concept is then problematical. We do not assert that there are noumena, which could be intuited if we possessed a faculty of intellectual intuition. At the same time we have no right to assert that appearances exhaust reality; and the idea of the limits of sensibility carries with it as a

[1] *A*, 253.

correlative concept the indeterminate, negative concept of the noumenon.

The trouble with this account is that Kant first says that the word *noumenon* means something more than what is meant by transcendental object and then he proceeds to exclude this something more and to give an interpretation of the noumenon which seems to differ not at all from his interpretation of the transcendental object. However, in the second edition he clears up this at least apparent confusion by carefully distinguishing two senses of the word *noumenon*, though his doctrine concerning the extent of our knowledge remains unaltered.

First there is the negative sense of the word *noumenon*. 'If by noumenon we understand a thing *in so far as it is not the object of our sensuous intuition*, thus abstracting from our mode of intuiting it, this is a noumenon in the negative sense of the term.'[1] The remark about abstracting from our mode of intuiting the noumenon must not be taken to imply that according to Kant we intuit, or can intuit, it in a non-sensuous manner. He means that if we understand by noumenon a thing in so far as it is not the object of sensuous intuition, and if at the same time we make no assumptions about the possibility of any other kind of intuition, we have the idea of a noumenon in the negative sense of the term.

This negative sense of the term is contrasted with a possible positive sense. 'If we understand by it (the noumenon) an object of a non-sensuous intuition, we then assume a particular kind of intuition, namely intellectual intuition, which, however, is not ours and of which we cannot see even the possibility; and this would be a noumenon in the *positive* sense of the term.'[2] Thus a noumenon in the positive sense of the term would be an *intelligibile*, the object of an intellectual intuition. But as, according to Kant, we do not enjoy any such intuition, we can disregard for the moment the positive sense of the term and return to the use of the term in its negative sense.

The concept of the noumenon, Kant insists, is indispensable; for it is bound up with his whole theory of experience. 'The doctrine of sensibility is also the doctrine of noumena in the negative sense.'[3] If we were prepared to say that the human subject is creative in the full sense of the word, we could drop the distinction between phenomena and noumena. But if the subject contributes, as it were, only the formal elements of experience, we

[1] *B*, 307.   [2] *Ibid.*   [3] *Ibid.*

cannot abandon the distinction. For the idea of things conforming to the *a priori* conditions of experience involves the idea of the thing-in-itself.

At the same time, given the restriction of the cognitive use of the categories to phenomenal reality, it follows not only that we cannot know noumena in the sense of knowing their characteristics, but also that we are not entitled to assert dogmatically that they exist. Unity, plurality and existence are categories of the understanding. And though we can think of noumena as existing, the application of the categories in this way beyond their proper range of application does not yield knowledge. The existence of noumena thus remains problematical; and the idea of the noumenon or thing-in-itself becomes a limiting concept (*Grenzbegriff*).[1] The understanding limits sensibility 'by giving the name *noumena* to things considered in themselves and not as phenomena. But it at the same time sets limits to itself, that is, of not knowing them by means of any categories and of thinking them simply as an unknown something.'[2]

Now, in the first section of this chapter we saw how Kant speaks about our being affected by objects. In other words, he started from the common-sense position that things produce an effect on the subject which give rise to sensation, sensation being defined as 'the effect of an object upon the faculty of representation, so far as we are affected by the object'.[3] But this common-sense point of view seems to involve the assertion that there are things-in-themselves. For it appears to involve inference from sensation as an effect to the thing-in-itself as cause. Thus in the *Prolegomena* we read that things-in-themselves are unknowable as they are in themselves but that 'we know them through the representations which their influence on our sensibility procures for us'.[4] But by talking in this way Kant obviously lays himself open to the charge of applying the principle of causality beyond the limits which he himself lays down. It has therefore been a common objection against the doctrine of noumena considered as things-in-themselves that their existence is asserted as a result of causal inference whereas, on Kant's principles, the category of cause is only applicable to phenomena. In asserting the existence of the noumenon as a cause of sensation, it has therefore been said, Kant contradicts himself; that is to say, he is inconsistent with his own principles. It is, indeed, understandable that Kant talks in this

[1] *B*, 311.   [2] *B*, 312.   [3] *A*, 19; *B*, 34.   [4] *Prol.*, 13, remark 2.

way. For he never believed that things can be reduced simply to our representations. And it was natural, for him, therefore, to postulate an external cause or external causes of our representations. But this does not alter the fact that he is guilty of a flagrant inconsistency. And if we wish to maintain the Kantian view of the function of the category of cause, we must abandon the notion of the noumenon as thing-in-itself.

However, though this line of objection is clearly relevant if we regard simply Kant's remarks about the cause of our representations, we have seen that when he discusses explicitly the distinction between phenomena and noumena he adopts a different approach. For the idea of the noumenon is represented as arising, not through inference to a cause of sensation, but as an inseparable correlate of the idea of the phenomenon. We are not presented with subjective representations on the one hand and their external causes on the other. Rather are we presented with the idea of an object which appears and corresponding to the idea we have, as a purely limiting concept, the idea of the object apart from its appearance. It is as though the noumenon were the other side of the picture, a side which we do not and cannot see but the indeterminate notion of which necessarily accompanies the idea of the side which we do see. Further, though Kant clearly believes that there are noumena, he abstains, in theory at least, from asserting their existence. And this line of approach does not seem to lay him open to the line of objection mentioned in the last paragraph. For, even if we use the category of cause to think the noumenon, the use is problematical, not assertorical. And no special difficulty is created by the application of this special category which is not also created by the use of any other category.

A final remark. In this section we have been considering the noumenon as the thing which appears, apart from its appearing. That is to say, we have been considering it as the so-called thing-in-itself (*Ding an sich*). But Kant also speaks about the free, non-empirical ego and about God as being noumena and as possessing noumenal reality. He also speaks occasionally of God as a thing-in-itself. This way of talking is, indeed, justified on his premisses. For God is not a phenomenon and cannot possess phenomenal or empirical reality. He must be conceived, therefore, as a noumenon, as a thing-in-itself, and not as something appearing to us. Further, all that has been said about the non-applicability of the categories to noumena holds good in regard to God. At the same time, if God is thought of at all, He is not thought of as being simply a correlate of spatio-temporal appearances. The concept of God is not the concept of a thing which appears, considered as not appearing. For God cannot be said to appear. Hence the terms *noumenon* and *thing-in-itself*, as applied to God, do not bear precisely the same sense which they bear when applied in the manner described above. It is best, therefore, to reserve any further discussion of the idea of God until we come, in the next chapter, to a consideration of the *Transcendental Dialectic*. For it is in this part of the first *Critique* that Kant discusses the idea of God, when he is dealing with the transcendental Ideas of pure reason.

9. Kant's use of the word *idealism* differs at different stages of the development of his thought. There is no one invariable and consistent use of the term. However, his dislike of the label evidently diminished, and we find him calling his philosophy transcendental or critical or problematical idealism. But when he speaks in this way, he is thinking of the doctrine of the unknowability of things-in-themselves. He does not intend to assert that in his view there are only the human ego and its ideas. Indeed, this is a doctrine which he attacks, as will be seen shortly. And if we can speak of Kant's philosophy as critical idealism, we could also speak of it as critical realism. For he resolutely refused to abandon the idea of things-in-themselves. However, I have no wish to embark on a profitless discussion of the proper nomenclature for Kant's philosophy. And I turn instead to his refutation of idealism; that is, of what he called empirical or material idealism in contrast with transcendental or formal idealism. In his view the acceptance of the latter involves the denial of the former.

Both editions of the *Critique of Pure Reason* contain a refutation of idealism; but I shall confine my remarks to the version given in the second edition. In it Kant distinguishes two kinds of idealism, problematic and dogmatic. According to the first kind, attributed to Descartes, the existence of external things in space is doubtful and indemonstrable, there being only one certain empirical proposition, *I am*. According to dogmatic idealism, attributed to Berkeley, space, together with all the objects of which it is the inseparable condition, is impossible, so that objects in space are mere products of the imagination.

These summaries, if considered as summaries of the actual positions of Descartes and Berkeley, are inadequate, to put it mildly. Berkeley did not hold that all external objects are mere products of the imagination in the sense which would naturally be given to this description. As for Descartes, he certainly maintains that we can apply 'hyperbolical' doubt to the existence of external finite things; but he also maintained that reason can overcome this doubt. Kant may have held that Descartes' demonstration of the existence of finite things other than the self was invalid. But this conviction would not justify his saying that according to problematic idealism the existence of external things in space is indemonstrable, and then ascribing this view to Descartes. However, the accuracy of Kant's historical remarks is of minor importance in comparison with his treatment of the two positions.

Of dogmatic idealism Kant says very little. He just remarks that it is unavoidable if we hold that space is a property of things-in-themselves; for in this case space, together with all the objects of which it is an inseparable condition, is a nonentity (*ein Unding*). But this position has been excluded in the *Transcendental Aesthetic*. In other words, if space is alleged to be a property of things-in-themselves, the concept of space can be shown to be a concept of something unreal and impossible. And it involves in its ruin the things of which it is supposed to be a property, and which must therefore be accounted mere products of the imagination. But it has been shown in the *Critique* that space is an *a priori* form of sensibility which applies only to phenomena and not to things-in-themselves. The latter are left intact, so to speak, while space is shown to possess empirical reality.

The treatment of problematic idealism, ascribed to Descartes, is rather more careful. The main point is that Descartes' approach is all wrong. For he assumes that we possess consciousness of ourselves independently of and prior to experience of external things, and then asks how the ego, certain of its own existence, can know that there are external things. Against this position Kant argues that internal experience is possible only through external experience.

Kant's argument is, indeed, somewhat involved. I am conscious of my own existence as determined in time.[1] But all determination in time, in respect, that is, of succession, presupposes the existence of something permanent in perception. But this something permanent cannot be something within myself. For

---

[1] Kant is speaking, of course, of the empirical ego, which I perceive introspectively only in its successive states. The transcendental ego is not determined in time, but it is not given as an object of self-consciousness. It is thought as the condition of the transcendental unity of apperception.

it is the condition of my existence in time. It follows, therefore, that the perception of my own existence in time is possible only through the existence of something real outside me. Consciousness in time is thus necessarily connected with the *existence* of external things; that is, not merely with the *representation* of things external to me.

The point made by Kant is thus that I cannot be conscious of myself except mediately, that is to say, through the immediate consciousness of external things. 'The consciousness of my own existence is at the same time an immediate consciousness of the existence of other things outside me.'[1] In other words, self-consciousness is not a prior datum: I become conscious of myself in perceiving external things. The question of inferring the existence of external things does not, therefore, arise.

Kant obviously makes a good point here, namely that I become aware of myself concomitantly with acts of attention directed to what is other than myself. But to use this point against Descartes he has to show that this becoming aware of myself is impossible unless external things *exist* and are not merely my representations or ideas. And to show this is, indeed, the burden of his argument. But he then finds himself compelled to admit that 'it does not follow that every intuitive representation of external things involves at the same time the existence of these things; for it may be the mere effect of the power of imagination in dreams as well as in madness.'[2] He argues, however, that these imaginative products are reproductions of previous external perceptions, which would be impossible unless external objects existed. 'Our task here has been to prove only that internal experience in general is possible only through external experience in general.'[3] Whether a particular perception is purely imaginative or not must be decided on the merits of the case.

This treatment of idealism may leave a good deal to be desired; but it at least throws into relief Kant's insistence on the empirical reality of the world of experience as a whole. Within the sphere of empirical reality we cannot justifiably accord a privileged status to the empirical self, reducing external objects, either dogmatically or problematically, to ideas or representations of the empirical self. For the empirical reality of the subject is inseparable from the empirical reality of the external world. That is to say, awareness of the two factors, subject and object, cannot be so divided that

[1] *B*, 276.   [2] *B*, 278.   [3] *Ibid.*

the alleged problem of inferring the existence of objects other than the self becomes a real problem.

10. There are many detailed criticisms of Kant's theory of experience which can be made from within the general framework of the Kantian philosophy, that is, by those who accept the philosopher's general point of view and who would call themselves Kantians or Neo-Kantians. For instance, dissatisfaction may be felt with Kant's idea that he had provided a complete table of categories, based on the table of judgments which he took over, with some changes, from the formal logic with which he was familiar. But such dissatisfaction would not by itself necessitate an abandonment of the general standpoint represented by the theory of categories. Again, it is possible to criticize the ambiguity involved in Kant's habit of referring sometimes to 'categories' and sometimes to *a priori* concepts. But it might be possible to clear up the ambiguity without being compelled at the same time to throw overboard the whole theory. However, the detailed criticisms which can be brought from within the general framework of the system need not concern us here. Something will be said about the Neo-Kantians in a later volume.

If we look on Kant's theory of experience as an attempt to explain the possibility of synthetic *a priori* knowledge, our judgment about it will obviously depend very largely on whether we admit or reject the existence of synthetic *a priori* propositions. If we think that there are no such propositions, we must obviously draw the conclusions that the problem of explaining synthetic *a priori* knowledge does not arise. We shall say, for example, that Kant was mistaken in thinking that the geometrician reads off the properties of space from an *a priori* intuition. In Kantian terminology all propositions are either analytic or synthetic *a posteriori*. If, however, we think that there are synthetic *a priori* propositions, we shall recognize at least that the Kantian problem was a real problem. For *mere* sense-experience does not present us with necessary connections and with true universality.

It does not follow, however, that if we accept the existence of synthetic *a priori* knowledge, we are bound to accept also the hypothesis of Kant's Copernican revolution. For it is possible to allow that there are synthetic *a priori* propositions and at the same time to hold that there is an intellectual intuition which grounds such propositions. I certainly do not wish to commit myself to the view that the geometrician enjoys an intuition of space and that he reads off, as it were, its properties. I am prescinding altogether from the problem of mathematics. That is to say, when I speak about synthetic *a priori* propositions I am thinking, not of the propositions of pure mathematics, but of metaphysical principles, such as the principle that everything which comes into being has a cause. And by intuition I do not mean a direct apprehension of spiritual realities, such as God, but an intuitive apprehension of being, implied by the existential judgment concerning the concrete object of sense-perception. In other words, if the mind can discern, in dependence on sense-perception, the objective, intelligible structure of being, it can enunciate synthetic *a priori* propositions which have objective validity for things in themselves. I do not wish to develop this point of view any further. My intention in mentioning it is simply to indicate that we are not confined to choosing between empiricism on the one hand and the critical philosophy of Kant on the other.

CHAPTER XIII

KANT (4): METAPHYSICS UNDER FIRE

*Introductory remarks—The transcendental Ideas of pure reason
—The paralogisms of rational psychology—The antinomies of
speculative cosmology—The impossibility of proving the existence
of God—The regulative use of the transcendental Ideas of pure
reason—Metaphysics and meaning.*

1. IF we presuppose the analysis of objective experience[1] described
in the last chapter, it may appear that there is really nothing
further to be said about metaphysics. For certain general conclusions about the subject follow directly from the *Transcendental
Aesthetic* and *Transcendental Analytic* taken together. First, to the
extent that transcendental criticism can itself be called metaphysics, the metaphysics, that is to say, of objective experience,
metaphysics is possible, and possible as a science. Secondly, if the
entire system of synthetic *a priori* propositions relating to pure
natural science were worked out, we should have a developed
metaphysics of Nature or of natural science. Thirdly, in so far as
the unschematized categories can be used by the mind to think
things-in-themselves and to form ideas which contain no logical
contradiction, metaphysics of the traditional type is a psychological possibility. It is psychologically possible, for example, to
think of things-in-themselves as substances. But fourthly, inasmuch as this procedure involves applying the categories beyond
their legitimate field of application, it cannot yield knowledge.
The cognitive function of the categories lies in their application to
objects as given in sense intuition, that is, to phenomena. Things-
in-themselves are not, and cannot be, phenomena. And we possess
no faculty of intellectual intuition which could supply objects for
a meta-phenomenal application of the categories. Hence metaphysics of the classical type is excluded, when it is considered as a
possible source of objective knowledge. To take the same example,
application of the category of substance to things-in-themselves
yields no knowledge whatsoever about the latter. Fifthly, we

---

[1] Objective experience, that is to say, in the sense of experience or knowledge
of objects. The analysis of moral experience has not yet been considered. And
moral experience is not an experience of objects in the sense in which we have been
using the term.

cannot use the principles of the understanding to infer the existence of supersensible beings such as God. For the principles of the understanding, like the categories on which they are founded, are of limited application. That is to say, their objective reference is to phenomena alone. Hence they cannot be used to transcend experience (in the Kantian sense).

But Kant's attitude towards metaphysics, as manifested in the *Critique of Pure Reason*, is more complex than this series of conclusions might lead one to expect. As we have already seen, he believed that the impulse to metaphysics is an ineradicable impulse in the human mind. Metaphysics considered as a natural disposition is possible. Moreover, it possesses value. In the *Transcendental Dialectic* Kant tends at least to make of the pure reason (*Vernunft*) a faculty distinct, or distinguishable, from understanding (*Verstand*). It produces transcendental Ideas which cannot, indeed, be used to increase our scientific knowledge of objects, but which at the same time have a positive 'regulative' function to perform. It remains for him, therefore, to investigate the origin and system of these Ideas and to determine their precise function.

Further, Kant is not content with saying simply that the knowledge which traditional speculative metaphysics claims to provide is illusory. He wishes to illustrate and confirm the truth of his contention by a detailed criticism of speculative psychology, speculative cosmology and natural or philosophical theology. This is done in the second book of the *Transcendental Dialectic*.

What did Kant mean by 'transcendental dialectic'? He thought that the Greeks understood by dialectic the art of sophistical disputation. This idea of the historical use of the word is extremely inadequate. But this does not matter for our purposes. The point is that Kant thought of dialectic as a 'logic of semblance' (*eine Logik des Scheins*)[1] or illusion. But he obviously did not wish to produce sophistical illusions. So dialectic came to mean for him a critical treatment of false or sophistical reasoning. And transcendental dialectic meant a critique or criticism of understanding and reason in regard to their claims to provide us with knowledge of things-in-themselves and supersensible realities. 'The second part of the transcendental logic must be, therefore, a critique of this dialectical semblance (or illusion). And it is called transcendental dialectic, not as an art of producing dogmatically such

[1] *B*, 349; *A*, 293.

illusion (an art which is unfortunately too current among the practitioners of manifold metaphysical jugglery), but as a critique of the understanding and reason in regard to their metaphysical use. Its purpose is to expose the false illusion involved in the groundless pretensions of these faculties, and to substitute for their claims to discover new truths and enlarge our knowledge, which they imagine they can do simply by the use of transcendental principles, their proper function of protecting the pure understanding from sophistical delusion.'[1]

Here we have a purely negative conception of the function of transcendental dialectic. But inasmuch as the abuse of transcendental ideas and principles presupposes their rise and presence, and inasmuch as they possess a certain value, transcendental dialectic has also the positive function of determining in a systematic manner what are the transcendental Ideas of pure reason and what is their legitimate and proper function. 'The Ideas of the pure reason can never be, in themselves, dialectical; it is their misuse only which brings it about that we are involved in a deceptive illusion by means of them. For they arise in us through the very nature of our reason; and this supreme tribunal for judging the rights and claims of our speculation cannot possibly contain in itself original deceptions and illusions. We can presume, therefore, that these Ideas will have their sound and proper function, determined by the constitution of our reason.'[2]

2. One characteristic which Kant had in common with Wolff was a respect, not to say passion, for systematic arrangement and deduction. We have seen how he deduced the categories of the understanding from the forms of judgment. In the *Transcendental Dialectic* we find him deducing[3] the Ideas of pure reason from the forms of mediate inference, mediate inference meaning for him syllogistic inference.[4] The deduction seems to me highly artificial and not very convincing. But the general idea can be conveyed by means of the following steps.

[1] B, 88; A, 63–4.   [2] B, 697.

[3] This deduction of the Ideas of pure reason corresponds to the metaphysical deduction of the categories of the understanding, that is, to the systematic derivation of the categories from the forms of judgment. In the *Dialectic* there cannot be anything exactly corresponding to the transcendental deduction or justification of the application of the categories to objects. For the Ideas cannot be applied to objects. However, as the Ideas have a 'regulative' function, the exhibition of this fact is in some way remotely analogous to the transcendental deduction of the categories.

[4] Mediate inference because the conclusion in a syllogism is derived from the major premiss only by means of the minor premiss, which is a condition of the deduction.

The understanding (*Verstand*) is concerned directly with phenomena, unifying them in its judgments. The reason (*Vernunft*) is not directly concerned with phenomena in this way, but only indirectly or mediately. That is to say, it accepts the concepts and judgments of the understanding and seeks to unify them in the light of a higher principle. As an example let us take a syllogism suggested by Kant himself: 'All men are mortal; All scholars are men; Therefore all scholars are mortal.' The conclusion is seen as following from the major premiss by means of, or on the condition of, the minor premiss. But we can obviously go on to seek the condition for the truth of the major premiss. That is to say, we can try to exhibit the major premiss, namely 'All men are mortal', as being itself the conclusion of a prosyllogism. This is achieved, for instance, in the following syllogism: 'All animals are mortal; All men are animals: Therefore all men are mortal.' Our new major premiss can then be seen as unifying a whole series of judgments, such as 'All men are mortal', 'All cats are mortal', 'All elephants are mortal'. And we can then go on to subject the major premiss 'All animals are mortal' to a similar process, exhibiting it as the conclusion of a prosyllogism and thus unifying a wider range of different judgments.

Now, in the examples given it is obvious that reason did not produce the concepts and judgments from itself. It was concerned with the deductive relationship between judgments contributed by the understanding in its empirical use. But it is a peculiar feature of reason that it is not content with stopping this process of unification at any particular premiss which is itself conditioned; that is, which can itself be exhibited as the conclusion of a prosyllogism. It seeks the unconditioned. And the unconditioned is not given in experience.

At this point we must mention a distinction made by Kant, which is important for the line of thought expressed in the *Transcendental Dialectic*. To proceed ever upwards, so to speak, in the chain of prosyllogisms is a logical maxim of pure reason. That is to say, the logical maxim of reason bids us seek an ever greater unification of knowledge, tending more and more towards the unconditioned, towards an ultimate condition which is not itself conditioned. But the logical maxim, taken by itself, does not assert that the chain of reasoning ever does reach an unconditioned. It does not assert that there is an unconditioned: it merely tells us to act as though there were, by telling us to endeavour constantly to complete, as Kant puts it, our conditioned knowledge. When, however, it is assumed that the sequence of conditions reaches the unconditioned, and that there is an unconditioned, the logical maxim becomes a principle of pure reason. And it is one of the main tasks of the *Transcendental Dialectic* to show whether this principle is objectively valid or not. The purely logical maxim is not called in question. But are we justified in assuming that the sequence of conditioned judgments actually is unified in the unconditioned? Or is this assumption the source of deception and fallacy in metaphysics?

Now, there are, according to Kant, three possible types of syllogistic inference, namely categorical, hypothetical and disjunctive. These three types of mediate inference correspond to the three categories of relation, namely substance, cause and community or reciprocity. And corresponding to the three types of inference there are three kinds of unconditioned unity, postulated or assumed by the principles of pure reason. In the ascending series of categorical syllogisms reason tends towards a concept which stands for something which is always subject and never predicate. If we ascend by a chain of hypothetical syllogisms, reason demands an unconditioned unity in the form of a presupposition which itself presupposes nothing else; which is, that is to say, an ultimate presupposition. Finally, if we ascend by a chain of disjunctive syllogisms, reason demands an unconditioned unity in the form of an aggregate of the members of the disjunctive division of such a kind that it makes the division complete.

The reason why Kant endeavours to derive the three kinds of unconditioned unity from the three types of syllogistic inference is, I think, evident. When deducing the categories of the understanding he wished to avoid the haphazard kind of deduction of which he accuses Aristotle of being guilty, and to substitute a systematic and complete deduction. In other words, he wished to show at the same time what the categories are and why there are just these categories and no others. Hence he tried to deduce them from the logical types of judgment, presupposing that his classification of these types was complete. Similarly, in deducing the Ideas of the pure reason he wishes to show at the same time what these Ideas are and why there must be just these Ideas (or, as he puts it, classes of Ideas) and no others. Hence he tries to derive them from the three types of mediate inference which, in accordance with the formal logic which he accepts, are the only possible types. In the whole process we see Kant's passion for systematic arrangement and architectonic at work.

In the course of deducing the Ideas of pure reason, however, Kant introduces a supplementary line of thought which makes the whole matter considerably easier to understand. He introduces, that is to say, the idea of the most general relations in which our representations can stand. These are three. First, there is the relation to the subject. Secondly, there is the relation of our representations to objects as phenomena. Thirdly, there is the relation of our representations to objects as objects of thought in general, whether phenomena or not. We can consider these relations separately.

In the first place it is required for the possibility of experience, as we saw in the last chapter, that all representations should be related to the unity of apperception, in the sense that the *I think* must be capable of accompanying them all. Now, reason tends to complete this synthesis by assuming an unconditioned, namely a permanent ego or thinking subject, conceived as a substance. That is to say, reason tends to complete the synthesis of the inner life by passing beyond the empirical, conditioned ego to the unconditioned thinking self, the substantial subject which is never predicate.

In the second place, turning to the relation of our representations to objects as phenomena, we recall that the understanding synthesizes the manifold of sense intuition according to the second category of relation; namely the causal relation. Now, reason seeks to complete the synthesis by reaching an unconditioned unity conceived as the totality of causal sequences. Understanding provides us, as it were, with causal relations, each of which presupposes other causal relations. Reason postulates an ultimate presupposition which does not presuppose anything else (in the same order), namely the totality of the causal sequences of phenomena. There thus arises the idea of the world, conceived as the totality of causal sequences.

In the third place, that is, in regard to the relation of our representations to objects of thought in general, reason seeks an unconditioned unity in the form of the supreme condition of the possibility of all that is thinkable. Thus arises the conception of God as the union in one Being of all perfections.[1]

[1] Kant admits that the theory according to which the mere form of the disjunctive syllogism necessarily involves the supreme Idea of pure reason, namely the Idea of a Being of all beings (*Wesen aller Wesen*), 'seems at first sight to be

We have, therefore, three principal Ideas of pure reason, namely the soul as permanent substantial subject, the world as the totality of causally related phenomena, and God as absolute perfection, as the unity of the conditions of objects of thought in general. These three Ideas are not innate. At the same time they are not derived empirically. They arise as a result of the pure reason's natural drive towards completing the synthesis achieved by the understanding. This does not mean, as has already been mentioned, that the pure reason carries further the synthesizing activity of the understanding considered as constituting objects by imposing the *a priori* conditions of experience known as the categories. The Ideas of pure reason are not 'constitutive'. But the reason has a natural drive towards unifying the conditions of experience, and this it does by proceeding to the unconditioned, in the three forms already mentioned. In doing this it obviously passes beyond experience. Hence the Ideas of the pure reason are called by Kant 'transcendental Ideas', though he later goes on to speak of the third Idea, that of God, as the 'transcendental Ideal'. For God is conceived as supreme and absolute perfection.

These three Ideas form the principal unifying themes of the three branches of speculative metaphysics according to the Wolffian classification. 'The thinking subject is the object-matter of *psychology*, the totality of all phenomena (the world), the object-matter of *cosmology*, and the entity which contains the supreme condition of the possibility of all that can be thought (the Being of all beings) is the object-matter of *theology*. Thus the pure reason provides its Idea for a transcendental doctrine of the soul (*psychologia rationalis*), for a transcendental science of the world (*cosmologia rationalis*), and finally for a transcendental doctrine of God (*theologia transcendentalis*).'[1]

Now, inasmuch as we do not possess, according to Kant, any faculty of intellectual intuition, objects corresponding to these Ideas cannot be given to us in this way. Nor can they be given through experience in the sense described in the last chapter. The substantial soul, the world as the totality of all appearances, the supreme Being, God: none of these can be given in experience. They are not, and cannot be, phenomena. And the Ideas of them arise, not through the subjection of the material of experience to

extremely paradoxical' (*B*, 393). But he promises a further treatment later (cf. the sections on the Transcendental Ideal; *B*, 599 ff.). We cannot, however, discuss the matter further here.

[1] *B*, 391–2; *A*, 334–5.

the *a priori* conditions of experience, but through unifying the conditions of experience as far as the unconditioned. It is only to be expected, therefore, that if reason makes what Kant calls a 'transcendent' use of them, claiming to prove the existence and nature of corresponding objects and so to enlarge our theoretical knowledge of objects, it will be involved in sophistical arguments and in antinomies. To show that this is in fact the case, and must be the case, is the aim of Kant's critical examination of rational psychology, speculative cosmology and philosophical theology. And we must now consider each of these in turn.

3. Kant conceives rational psychology as proceeding on Cartesian lines and as arguing from the *I think* to the soul as a simple substance which is permanent in the sense that it remains self-identical in time; that is, throughout all accidental changes. In his view rational psychology must proceed *a priori*; for it is not an empirical science. Hence it starts from the *a priori* condition of experience, the unity of apperception. '*I think* is thus the only text of rational psychology, from which it must develop its whole system.'[1]

If we bear in mind the contents of the last chapter, it is easy to see what line Kant's criticism will take. It is a necessary condition for the possibility of experience that *I think* should be capable of accompanying all one's representations. But the ego as a necessary condition for experience is not given in experience: it is a transcendental ego, not the empirical ego. Hence while it is psychologically possible to think of it as a unitary substance, the application of categories such as substance and unity cannot yield knowledge in this context. For this cognitive function lies in their application to phenomena, not to noumena. We can argue to the conclusion that the transcendental ego, as a logical subject, is a necessary condition of experience, in the sense that experience is unintelligible unless objects, to be objects, must be related to the unity of apperception; but we cannot argue to the existence of the transcendental ego as a substance. For this involves a misuse of categories such as existence, substance and unity. Scientific knowledge is bounded by the world of phenomena; but the transcendental ego does not belong to the world; it is a limiting concept. Thus Kant might say with Ludwig Wittgenstein that 'the subject does not belong to the world but it is a limit of the world'.[2]

According to Kant, rational psychology contains a fundamental

---

[1] *B*, 401; *A*, 343.   [2] *Tractatus logico-philosophicus*, 5.632.

paralogism; that is, a logically fallacious syllogism. This syllogism can be expressed as follows:

> 'That which cannot be thought otherwise than as subject, does not exist otherwise than as subject and is therefore substance:
> Now, a thinking being, considered simply as such, cannot be thought otherwise than as subject:
> Therefore it exists only as such, that is, as substance.'[1]

That this syllogism is a paralogism follows from the fact that it contains four terms. That is to say, the middle term, 'that which cannot be thought otherwise than as subject', is understood in one sense in the major and in another sense in the minor premiss. In the major premiss the reference is to objects of thought in general, including objects of intuition. And it is true that the category of substance applies to an object which is given, or can be given, in intuition, and which can be thought only as subject, in the sense of that which cannot be thought as a predicate. But in the minor premiss that which cannot be thought otherwise than as subject is understood in relation to self-consciousness as the form of thought, not in relation to an object of intuition. And it by no means follows that the category of substance can be applied to a subject in this sense. For the ego of pure self-consciousness is not given in intuition, and so it is not a candidate, so to speak, for the application of the category.

It is to be noted that Kant does not question the truth of either premiss when taken by itself. In fact each premiss is, according to him, an analytical proposition. For instance, if the thinking being, considered purely as such, of the minor premiss is understood as the ego of pure apperception, it is analytically true that it cannot be thought otherwise than as subject. But then the word 'subject' is not being used in the same sense in which it is used in the major premiss. And we are not entitled to draw the *synthetic* conclusion that the ego of pure apperception exists as substance.

It is not necessary to enter further into Kant's discussion of rational psychology in order to see the important place in his criticism which is occupied by the concept of intuition. The permanent ego is not given in intuition; on this point Kant agrees with Hume. Hence we cannot apply to it the category of substance. But obviously someone might wish to call in question the view

[1] *B*, 410–11; cf. *A*, 348.

that the permanent ego is not given in intuition. And even if it is not given in intuition as interpreted by Kant, we might well consider that his idea of intuition is too narrow. In any case it might be argued that the presupposition and necessary condition of all experience is precisely a permanent ego; and that if experience is real, its necessary condition must be real. If to say this involves using the categories beyond their allotted sphere, this restriction of their use becomes questionable. If, however, we once admit all Kant's premisses, we can hardly avoid drawing his conclusions. The validity of the *Transcendental Dialectic* obviously depends to a great extent on the validity of the *Transcendental Aesthetic*, and *Analytic*.

It is worth noting that inasmuch as Kant believes that all phenomenal events are causally determined, it is in a sense in his interest to keep the permanent ego in the sphere of noumenal reality beyond experience. For this will enable him later to postulate freedom. At the same time, by placing the permanent self in the noumenal sphere and beyond the range of intuition, he makes it impossible to argue to the existence of the self in this sense. We can assert, of course, the existence of the empirical ego; for this is given in internal intuition. But the empirical ego is the self as studied in psychology. It is an object in time and is reducible to successive states. The ego which is not reducible to successive states and which cannot be thought except as subject is not given in intuition, is not an object and cannot therefore be dogmatically asserted to exist as a simple substance.

4. We have seen that speculative cosmology, according to Kant, centres round the idea of the world as the totality of the causal sequence of phenomena. The speculative cosmologist seeks to extend our knowledge of the world, as a totality of phenomena, through synthetic *a priori* propositions. But this procedure, Kant maintains, leads to antinomies. An antinomy arises when each of two contradictory propositions can be proved. And if speculative cosmology inevitably leads to antinomies in this sense, the conclusion must be drawn that its whole aim is mistaken, namely the aim of building up a science of the world considered as the totality of phenomena. This branch of speculative metaphysics is not, and cannot be, a science. In other words, the fact that speculative cosmology is productive of antinomies shows that we cannot make scientific use of the transcendental Idea of the world as the totality of phenomena.

Kant discusses four antinomies. Each of them is supposed to correspond to one of the four classes of categories. But there is no necessity to dwell upon this typical piece of systematic correlation. I propose to pass it over and to come at once to a brief discussion of each of the four antinomies.

(i) The conflicting propositions of the first antinomy are as follows. '*Thesis:* The world has a beginning in time and is also limited in regard to space. *Antithesis:* The world has no beginning and no limits in space, but is infinite in respect both of time and space.'[1]

The *thesis* is proved as follows. If the world has no beginning in time, an infinite series of events must have occurred. That is to say, before the present moment an infinite series must have been completed. But an infinite series can never be completed. Therefore the world must have had a beginning in time. As for the second part of the thesis, if the world is not limited in regard to space, it must be an infinite given total of coexistent things. But we cannot think an infinite given total of coexistent things filling all possible spaces except by successively adding part to part or unit to unit until the addition is complete. But we cannot regard this addition or synthesis as completed except by regarding it as completed in infinite time. And this involves looking on an infinite time as having elapsed, which is impossible. Hence we cannot regard the world as an infinite given total of coexistent things filling all possible spaces. We must look on it as spatially limited or finite.

The *antithesis* is proved as follows. If the world began in time, there must have been empty time before the world began. But in empty time no becoming or beginning is possible. It makes no sense to speak of something coming into being in empty time. Hence the world has no beginning. As for the world being spatially infinite, let us suppose, for the sake of argument, that it is finite and limited in space. It must then exist in a void or empty space. And in this case it must have a relation to empty space. But empty space is nothing; and a relation to nothing is itself nothing. Hence the world cannot be finite and spatially limited: it must be spatially infinite.

At first sight Kant seems to adopt a position diametrically opposed to that of St. Thomas Aquinas.[2] For while the latter

---

[1] *B*, 454-5.
[2] My references here to mediaeval philosophy must not be understood as involving the suggestion that Kant had the mediaevals in mind. As far as I know, there is no evidence that he knew enough about them for this to have been even possible. But the references are, I think, of general interest.

maintained[1] that it had never been philosophically demonstrated either that the world had a beginning in time or that it had no beginning in time, Kant appears to be saying that both theses can be demonstrated. And we may note in passing that his proof of the thesis that the world had a beginning in time is the same as that advanced by St. Bonaventure[2] in support of this thesis, a proof the validity of which was denied by Aquinas. But both proofs rest, for Kant, on false assumptions. The proof of the thesis rests on the assumption that we can apply to phenomena the principle of pure reason that if the conditioned is given, the totality of conditions, and consequently the unconditioned, is also given. The proof of the antithesis rests on the assumption that the world of phenomena is the world of things-in-themselves. It is assumed, for instance, that space is an objective reality. Given the required assumptions, the proofs are valid.[3] But the fact that each of two contradictory propositions can be proved shows that the assumptions are unwarranted. We can avoid the antinomy only by adopting the standpoint of the critical philosophy and by abandoning the standpoints both of dogmatic rationalism and of uncritical common sense. This is the point which Kant really intends to bring out, though it can hardly be claimed that he does so very clearly. And it would, therefore, be misleading, even if true in a sense, to say that in the long run Kant comes to the position of St. Thomas Aquinas. For, according to Kant's point of view, the inherent futility of trying to prove philosophically either that the world had a beginning in time or that it had no beginning in time can be seen only by adopting a philosophy which was certainly not that of Aquinas.

(ii) The second antinomy is as follows. '*Thesis:* Every composite substance in the world consists of simple parts, and there does not exist anything which is not either itself simple or composed of simple parts. *Antithesis:* No composite thing in the world consists of simple parts, and there does not anywhere exist any simple thing.'[4]

The proof of the *thesis* takes this form. If composite substances

---

[1] For a statement of Aquinas's position, see Vol. II of this *History*, pp. 366–7.

[2] See Vol. II of this *History*, pp. 262–4.

[3] It does not follow, of course, that we have to follow Kant in saying that they are valid. We might wish to say that neither is valid, or that while one is invalid, the other is valid. For a discussion of Kant's proofs of the theses and antitheses in the four antinomies the reader can consult, for instance, Professor N. Kemp Smith's *Commentary to Kant's Critique of Pure Reason*, pp. 483–506.

[4] *B*, 462–3.

did not consist of simple parts, then, if we thought away all composition, nothing at all would remain. But this can be excluded.
For composition is merely a contingent relation. The composite
must, therefore, consist of simple parts. And it follows from this
that everything which exists must be either itself simple or composed of simple parts.

As for the *antithesis*, it can be proved in this way. A composite
substance occupies space. And this space must consist of as many
parts as there are parts in the composite substance. Therefore
every part of the latter occupies a space. But everything which
occupies a space must consist of a manifold of parts. And each of
these will occupy a space, and will thus itself contain parts. And
so on indefinitely. There cannot, therefore, be any composite
thing which consists of simple parts. Nor can there be any simple
thing.   .

As in the first antinomy, the thesis represents the position of
dogmatic rationalism. All composite substances consist of simple
substances, such as the Leibnizian monads. And, again as in the
first antinomy, the antithesis represents an empiricist attack on
dogmatic rationalism. But the thesis treats noumena as though
they were phenomena, objects given in experience; and the antithesis treats phenomena, extended bodies, as though they were
noumena. Again, the only way out of the antinomy is to adopt the
position of the critical philosophy, and to recognize that what is
true of phenomena as phenomena cannot be asserted of noumena,
while of the latter we possess no objective knowledge.[1]

(iii) The third antinomy relates to free causation. '*Thesis:*
Causality according to the laws of Nature is not the only causality
from which the phenomena of the world can be derived. To explain
them, it is necessary to assume another causality, causality through
freedom. *Antithesis:* There is no freedom, but everything in the
world happens solely according to the laws of Nature.'[2]

The *thesis* is proved thus. Let us suppose that there is only one
kind of causality, namely causality according to the laws of
Nature. In this case a given event is determined by a previous
event, and so on indefinitely. There can then be no first beginning;
and consequently the series of causes cannot be completed. But
the law of Nature is that nothing happens without a cause

---

[1] It is arguable that there is in fact no antinomy, on the ground that the thesis
must be interpreted as referring to Leibnizian monads, whereas the antithesis
refers to extended bodies in space.
[2] *B*, 472–3.

sufficiently determined *a priori*. And this law is not fulfilled if the causality of every cause is itself an effect of an antecedent cause. There must therefore be an absolutely spontaneous causality which originates a series of phenomena proceeding according to natural causes.

The proof of the *antithesis* is, in brief, this. Spontaneous, free causation presupposes a state of the cause which stands in no causal relation (that is, as effect) to the preceding state. But this presupposition is contrary to the natural causal law, and it would render impossible the unity of experience. Consequently freedom is not to be found in experience and is a mere fiction of thought.

In this antinomy it is not at all clear in the first place what Kant is talking about. The proof of the thesis naturally suggests that he is thinking about the origination of the natural causal series by a first cause, the causal activity of which is entirely spontaneous in the sense that it does not itself depend on a previous cause. And in his observations on the thesis he explicitly states that he had in mind the origin of the world. But he then goes on to say that if there is a free cause of the total series of phenomenal causal sequences, we are justified in admitting, within the world, free causes of different series of phenomena.

As for the antithesis, it is natural to understand it as referring to human freedom. *Prima facie* at least it makes sense to speak of one state of the human subject being causally determined by another state; but it makes no sense at all to raise the question of the causal relation between states in regard to God. In his observations on the antithesis, however, Kant introduces the idea of a free cause existing outside the world. Even if we admit the existence of such a cause, we cannot, he remarks, admit free causes within the world.

In view of this ambiguity, that is, of the indefinite range of application of thesis and antithesis, it is difficult to maintain that the antinomy is resolved by observing that the thesis and antithesis refer to different things. However, there can be no antinomy at all, in the proper sense, unless thesis and antithesis refer to the same things. If the thesis asserts that a free cause of the total series of phenomenal causal sequences can be proved, while the antithesis states that it can be proved that there is no such cause, we have an antinomy. And if the thesis states that it can be proved that there is free causality within the world, while the antithesis states that it can be proved that there is no free causality within the world, we have again an antinomy. But if the thesis states that it can be proved that there is a free cause of the total series of phenomenal causal sequences, this free cause being outside the series, while the antithesis states that there is no free causality within the phenomenal series, there is, properly speaking, no antinomy at all.

It is not my intention to deny that the third antinomy falls to a great extent into the general pattern of Kant's antinomies. The proof of the thesis, if the latter is understood as referring to a first cause of the total series of phenomenal causal sequences, is valid only on the assumption that we can, as it were, complete the series, using the transcendental Idea of the world as a totality to extend our theoretical knowledge. The thesis, therefore, represents the standpoint of dogmatic rationalism. And the antithesis, whether it is taken as stating that no proof of the existence of a first cause of the total series is possible or as stating that there can be no free causes within the series, represents the empiricist standpoint. But if the antinomy can be resolved only by adopting the standpoint of the critical philosophy, the latter point of view should not be introduced into the proof of either thesis or antithesis. Yet it is at least arguable that this is precisely what Kant does in proving the antithesis. For he states that the admission of free causality destroys the possibility of the unity of experience. And though it may not be necessary to understand this statement in terms of his own peculiar point of view, it is difficult to avoid the impression that this is in fact how it should be understood.

What happens, however, to the antinomy when we explicitly adopt the critical point of view? The proof of the thesis, if the latter is taken as referring to a spontaneous cause of the total series of phenomena, is seen to rest on a misuse of the transcendental Idea of the world. As for the antithesis, the denial of freedom, this is seen to be valid only for the sphere of phenomena. The way is therefore left open for Kant to say later that man is noumenally free and phenomenally determined. If we adopt this point of view we can say that for Kant both thesis and antithesis, when rightly understood, are true. The thesis, that causality 'according to the laws of Nature' is not the only kind of causality, is true, though it is not true that we can prove that this is the case. The antithesis, that there is no freedom, is true if it is taken as referring solely to the phenomenal world, though it is not true if it is taken as referring to all reality whatsoever. For Kant it is only when we adopt the standpoint of the critical philosophy that we can sift out what is true from what is false in thesis and antithesis and rise above the flat contradictions in which reason, in its dogmatic use, has involved itself.

(iv) The fourth antinomy concerns the existence of a necessary being. '*Thesis:* There belongs to the world, either as part of it or as its cause, something which exists as an absolutely necessary being. *Antithesis:* There nowhere exists any necessary being as the cause of the world, either in the world or out of it.'[1]

The *thesis* is proved, as far as the existence of a necessary being is concerned, by the supposed fact that the series of conditions presupposes a complete series of conditions up to the unconditioned, which exists necessarily. Kant then argues that this necessary being cannot be thought of as transcending the world of sense, and that it must therefore be either identical with the whole cosmic series or a part of it.

The *antithesis* is proved by showing that there can be no absolutely necessary being either in or outside the world. There cannot be a first member of the series of changes, which is itself necessary and uncaused. For all phenomena are determined in time. Nor can the whole cosmic series be necessary if no single member is necessary. Therefore there can be no necessary being in the world, either as identical with the latter or as a part of it. But there cannot be a necessary being existing outside the world, as cause of the latter. For if it causes the series of cosmic changes, it must begin to act. And if it begins to act, it is in time. And if it is in time, it is within the world, not outside it.

There is obviously considerable overlapping between the third and fourth antinomies. For though in the fourth antinomy Kant introduces a new term, 'absolutely necessary being', he uses the same line of argument to prove the thesis which he has already used in the third antinomy to prove that there must be a purely spontaneous cause of the series of phenomena. There is thus something to be said in favour of the view that Kant supplies the fourth antinomy precisely in order to make up the number four, each antinomy being supposed to correspond with one of the four classes of categories. It is true, indeed, that the categories of necessity and contingency belong to the fourth class of categories, those of modality, whereas causality belongs to the third class, the

[1] *B*, 480-1.

categories of relation. But Kant, in proving the thesis of the fourth antinomy, makes use precisely of a causal argument.

It is a remarkable fact, according to Kant in his observations on the antithesis of the fourth antinomy, that the same grounds which serve to prove the thesis serve also to prove the antithesis. But he then goes on to say that reason often falls into discord with itself by considering the same object from different points of view. And if thesis and antithesis represent different points of view, it seems to follow that both may be true. That is to say, the antithesis may be correct in so far as it represents the contentions that there is no necessary being in the world, whether as identical with the latter or as part of it, and that no proof can be forthcoming of the existence of such a being outside the world. But the thesis may be true in stating that there is such a being, existing outside the world, though we can never be said to *know* that this is the case.

In regard to the antinomies as a whole, the theses are supposed to represent the point of view of dogmatic rationalist metaphysics, while the antitheses are supposed to represent the empiricist point of view. And Kant sides, of course, with the latter to the extent that he regards as thoroughly sound the empiricist criticism of the pretensions of metaphysics to increase our knowledge. At the same time it is important to understand that he does not commit himself to the empiricist philosophy as such. In his view empiricism, though sound in its negative criticism of speculative metaphysics, is itself a dogmatic system which dogmatically limits reality to phenomena and thus treats them as though they were things-in-themselves. It is not the pretensions of speculative metaphysics alone which have to be exposed. While accepting the empiricist criticism of metaphysical arguments, we have to rise above the narrow limits of dogmatic empiricism (equated pretty well with materialism) and leave room, as it were, for noumenal reality. Further, metaphysics is itself sustained by moral and religious interests. And though this fact easily leads metaphysicians into advancing arguments which are unsound, we must acknowledge that metaphysics represents levels of human life which are not catered for, so to speak, by sheer empiricism. In the critical philosophy, however, Kant maintains, we can avoid both the fallacies of metaphysics and the dogmatic materialism and mechanism of sheer empiricism. We rise above the antinomies by limiting knowledge to its proper sphere while at the same time we leave room for practical faith based on moral experience. Human freedom, for example, cannot be admitted within the phenomenal sphere; but it may be a reality, and later on it turns out to be a necessary postulate of the moral consciousness.

5. The third transcendental Idea of pure reason is called by Kant the transcendental Ideal. Originally, so to speak, it is the idea of the sum total of all possible predicates, containing *a priori* the data for all particular possibilities. That is to say, the mind, ascending the series of disjunctive syllogisms, finds the unconditioned condition of all particular predicates, each of which excludes contradictory or incompatible predicates, in the idea of an aggregate of all predicates. This is the idea of the aggregate or sum total of all possible perfections. But inasmuch as this sum total is thought of as the unconditioned condition of all particular perfections, it is thought of as the prototype of the latter, as that from which the latter are derived and to which they approximate, and not as a mere abstract concept of the conflation, so to speak, of all particular, empirical perfections. It is thought of, therefore, as a real being, indeed as the supreme reality. The idea of the most perfect Being, the *Ens perfectissimum*, is also the idea of the most real Being the *Ens realissimum*. This Being cannot be thought of as a conflation or juxtaposition, so to speak, of empirical, limited and often mutually exclusive perfections. It must be thought of as the union of unlimited, pure perfections in one simple Being. Further, the unconditioned condition of all possible limited perfection and reality is thought of as existing necessarily. We thus reach the idea of God as an individual, necessarily existing, eternal, simple and all-perfect supreme Being, which is not the aggregate of finite realities but their unconditioned condition and ultimate cause. And this idea forms the subject-matter of natural or philosophical theology.[1]

Kant's conception of the procedure of pure reason is clear. The reason seeks the unconditioned unity of all possible predicates. It cannot find this in the aggregate, in a literal sense, of empirical perfections, but has to pass beyond the conditioned. It thus objectifies the indeterminate goal of its search as the *Ens perfectissimum*. This is then 'hypostatized' as the *Ens realissimum*, an individual being. And finally it is personified as the God of theism. But by this procedure of objectification the reason passes beyond all possible experience. We have no right to assert that there *is* a

---

[1] Kant's approach was suggested by the Wolffian philosophy. Baumgarten, for example, approached the idea of God through the idea of the *Ens perfectissimum*, which is then identified with the *Ens realissimum*.

Being which is *Ens perfectissimum* and *Ens realissimum*; that is, that there is an object corresponding to the representation of a sum total of all possible perfections. And even though reason goes on to say that we can possess only an analogical (or symbolic) knowledge of the supreme Being, the very fact of objectifying the idea of a totality of perfection means that we extend the categories beyond their proper field of application.

It is obvious that on Kant's premisses no proof of God's existence is possible. But he wishes to make this impossibility clear by showing that every line of proof is fallacious. The task is not so great as one might suppose. For according to Kant there are only three ways of proving God's existence in speculative metaphysics. The reason can start with what we might call the *how* of the sensible world; that is, with its character as apparently manifesting finality, and proceed to God as cause of this finality. We then have the 'physico-theological' argument. Or reason can start from empirical existence and proceed to God as ultimate cause of this existence. And we then have the 'cosmological' argument. Or reason may proceed from the idea of God to the divine existence. And we then have the 'ontological' argument.

In treating these three lines of proof Kant starts with the third. For the movement of the mind towards God in metaphysics is always guided by the transcendental Ideal of pure reason, which is the goal of its striving. And it is thus only proper to start with the *a priori* argument from the idea of God to the divine existence. Further, it is Kant's conviction that in order to reach God by the other lines of argument reason is forced in the end to make use of the ontological argument. The latter is thus the fundamental argument and the one which must be considered first.

(i) The general form of the ontological argument which Kant has in mind can be stated as follows.[1] In the concept of a most perfect being existence is included. For if it were not, the concept would not be the concept of a most perfect being. Therefore if such a being is possible, it necessarily exists. For existence is included in the full complement of its possibility. But the concept of a most perfect being is the concept of a possible being. Therefore such a being necessarily exists.

Or the argument can be expressed thus. The idea of the *Ens realissimum* is the idea of an absolutely necessary being. And if

[1] For the ontological argument as given by St. Anselm, see Vol. II of this *History*, pp/ 161–4. For the variants given by Descartes and Leibniz, see Vol. IV, pp. 110–15 and 320–3.

such a being is possible, it exists. For the idea of a merely possible (and not actually existent) necessary being is a contradictory idea. But the idea of an absolutely necessary being is the idea of a possible being. Therefore an *Ens realissimum*, namely God, exists.

Kant objects that it is nonsense to talk about the idea of a merely possible necessary being being a contradictory idea. To think of such a being as merely possible I have to think away its existence. But then there is nothing left which could give rise to a contradiction. 'If you think away its existence, you think away the thing with all its predicates. How, then, can there be room for any contradiction?'[1] If someone says that God does not exist, he is not suppressing existence and leaving predicates such as omnipotence: he is suppressing all predicates, and the subject with them. The judgment that God does not exist is not, therefore, self-contradictory, even if it is false.

It may be said that the case of the *Ens realissimum* is unique. I can deny the existence of any other being without involving myself in self-contradiction: for existence does not belong to the concept or idea of any other being. But it does belong to the concept of the *Ens realissimum*. Hence I cannot without self-contradiction admit the possibility of the *Ens realissimum* and at the same time deny its existence.

Kant's answer is on these lines. In the first place, our inability to see any logical contradiction in the idea of God does not constitute a proof that the *Ens realissimum* is positively possible. In the second place, any argument from the idea of the *Ens realissimum* to its existence is worthless; for it is reducible to a mere tautology. If I introduce existence into the idea of a being, then, of course, I can conclude that it exists. But all I am saying is that an existent being exists. And this is true but tautological. I can draw the conclusion that the being exists from its concept or idea only because I have already put existence into the idea, thus begging the whole question. To say that I am arguing from possibility to actuality is self-deception if possibility is made to include actuality.

It is Kant's contention, therefore, that every existential proposition is synthetic and that none is analytic. Hence any existential proposition can be denied without contradiction. The defenders of the ontological argument would reply, indeed, that Kant is missing the whole point of the argument. In all other cases

[1] *B*, 623.

existential propositions are synthetic; but the case of the most perfect being is unique. For in this case, and in this case alone, existence is contained in the idea of the subject. Hence it can be got out of it, so to speak, by analysis. Kant may say that this is possible only because we have already put it there, thus begging the question; but the point is that existence is a predicate which belongs necessarily to this subject.

For Kant, however, existence is not really a predicate at all. If it were, then it would follow that when I affirm existence of anything, I am adding to the idea of this thing. And in this case I do not affirm exactly the same thing which is represented in my idea. The truth of the matter is that when I say that something exists I simply affirm or posit the subject with all its predicates. Hence if I deny God's existence I am not denying a predicate of a subject: I am simply annihilating in thought the total subject, together with all its predicates. And no logical contradiction arises.

We can conclude, therefore, that 'all the trouble and labour bestowed on the famous ontological or Cartesian proof of the existence of a supreme Being from concepts alone is trouble and labour wasted. A man might as well expect to become richer in knowledge by the aid of mere ideas as a merchant to increase his wealth by adding some noughts to his cash-account.'[1]

(ii) Kant's formulation of the cosmological argument for God's existence is based on Leibniz. 'If anything exists, an absolutely necessary being must also exist. Now, I at least exist. Therefore there also exists an absolutely necessary being. The minor premiss contains an experience; the major premiss reasons from an experience in general to the existence of a necessary being.'[2]

It is obvious enough what Kant's line of criticism of the argument as thus presented will be. In his view the major premiss rests on a 'transcendent' use, and therefore on a misuse, of the principle of causality. Everything contingent has a cause. This principle is valid within the realm of sense-experience and it is only there that it possesses significance. We cannot use it to transcend the world as given in sense-experience. Further, the cosmological argument, according to Kant, involves completing the series of phenomena in the unconditioned unity of a necessary being. And though reason has a natural impulse to do this, surrender to the impulse cannot increase our knowledge.

To enter further into this line of criticism is unnecessary. For it

[1] B, 630.   [2] B, 632–3.

follows immediately from Kant's view of the limits of human knowledge. But there is one point in his treatment of the cosmological argument to which attention must be drawn here. It is Kant's contention that in order to pass from the idea of a necessary being to the affirmation of God's existence recourse must be had, at least covertly, to the ontological argument.

The concept of a necessary being is indeterminate. Even if we grant that reflection on experience leads us to a necessary being, we cannot discover its properties by experience. We are forced, therefore, to seek for the concept which is adequate to the idea of a necessary being. And reason believes that it has found what is required in the concept of an *Ens realissimum*. It asserts, therefore, that the necessary being is the *Ens realissimum*, the most real or perfect being. But to do this is to work with concepts alone, which is the characteristic of the ontological argument. Further, if a necessary being is an *Ens realissimum*, an *Ens realissimum* is a necessary being. And here we are saying that the concept of a supremely real or perfect being comprises absolute necessity of existence; which is precisely the ontological argument.

A good many philosophers and historians of philosophy seem to have assumed without more ado that Kant's attempt to show that the cosmological argument necessarily relapses into the ontological argument was successful. But to me it seems singularly unconvincing. Or, rather, it is convincing only on one assumption, namely that the argument based on experience brings us, not to an affirmation of the existence of a necessary being, but only to the vague *idea* of a necessary being. For in this case we should have to look about, as Kant puts it, for a determining concept which would include existence in its content, so that existence could be deduced from the determined idea of a necessary being. And then we should be involved in the ontological argument. If, however, the argument based on experience brings us to the affirmation of the *existence* of a necessary being, the attempt to determine *a priori* the necessary attributes of this being has nothing to do with the ontological argument, which is primarily concerned with deducing existence from the idea of a being as possible, and not with deducing attributes from the idea of a being the existence of which has already been affirmed on other grounds than possibility. It may be said that it was precisely Kant's assumption that the argument based on experience brings us only to the vague idea of a necessary being. But this is no adequate reason for saying that the cosmological argument necessarily relapses into the ontological argument. The question whether the argument based on experience is valid or invalid is not really relevant to the precise point at issue. For if someone is convinced, even unjustifiably, that he has already proved the existence of a necessary being on grounds other than the *a priori* possibility of such a being, his subsequent attempt to determine the attributes of this being is not the same procedure as that adopted in the ontological argument.

(iii) Kant opens his discussion of the physico-theological proof by once more repeating general points of view which exclude from the start any *a posteriori* demonstration of God's existence. For example, 'all laws regarding the transition from effects to causes, yes, all synthetic extension of our knowledge, relate solely to possible experience, and thus to the objects of the sensible world; and it is only in relation to the latter that they have significance.'[1] This being the case, no argument from design in Nature to a transcendent cause can possibly be a valid proof.

The chief steps in the physico-theological argument are these. First, we observe in the world manifest signs of purposeful arrangement; that is, of adaptation of means to ends. Secondly, this adaptation of means to ends is contingent, in the sense that it does not belong to the nature of things. Thirdly, there must exist, therefore, at least one cause of this adaptation, and this cause or these causes must be intelligent and free. Fourthly, the reciprocal relations existing between the different parts of the world, relations which produce an harmonious system analogous to a work of art, justify our inferring that there is one, and only one, such cause.

Kant thus interprets the proof of God's existence from finality as based on an analogy from human constructive adaptation of means to ends. And the proof had indeed been presented in this way in the eighteenth century.[2] But, quite apart from any objections which can be raised on this score, Kant remarks that 'the proof could at most establish the existence of an *architect of the world*, whose activity would be limited by the capacity of the material on which he works, and not of a *creator of the world. . . .*'[3] This contention is obviously true. The idea of design brings us, by itself, to the idea of a designer, and not immediately to the conclusion that this designer is also creator of finite sensible things

---

[1] B, 649–50.
[2] Kant did not, of course, have in mind Paley's *Evidences*; for this work was not published until 1802.
[3] B, 655.

according to their substance. Kant argues, therefore, that to prove the existence of God in the proper sense the physico-theological proof must summon the aid of the cosmological proof. And this, on Kant's view, relapses into the ontological argument. Thus even the physico-theological proof is dependent, even though indirectly, on the *a priori* or ontological argument. In other words, apart from any other considerations God's existence cannot be proved without the use of the ontological argument, and this is fallacious. All three proofs, therefore, have some fallacies in common; and each has also its own fallacies.

Natural theology or, as Kant often calls it, 'transcendental theology' is, therefore, worthless when it is regarded from one particular point of view, namely as an attempt to demonstrate God's existence by means of transcendental ideas or of theoretical principles which have no application outside the field of experience. But to say simply that Kant rejected natural theology would be apt to give a misleading impression of his position. It is, indeed, a true statement. For he describes natural theology as inferring 'the attributes and existence of an author of the world from the constitution of the world and from the order and unity observable in it'.[1] And the attempt to do this is 'completely fruitless'.[2] At the same time the purely negative statement that Kant rejected natural theology may give the misleading impression that he rejected all philosophical theology altogether. In point of fact, however, he admitted what he sometimes called 'moral theology'.[3] 'We shall show later that the laws of morality do not merely presuppose the existence of a supreme Being, but postulate it with right (though only, of course, from the practical point of view), as these laws are themselves absolutely necessary in another relation.'[4] And when we have arrived at practical (moral) faith in God, we can use the concepts of the reason to think the object of our faith in a consistent manner. True, we remain always in the sphere of practical faith; but, if we remember this fact, we are entitled to use the concepts of reason to construct a rational theology.

These last remarks put the statement that Kant rejected natural theology in a rather different light. That is to say, they

---

[1] B, 660.   [2] B, 664.

[3] The term does not, of course, refer to moral theology in the sense of a study of the practical application of Christian moral principles. It refers to a philosophical theology, or doctrine of God, based on the demands or postulates of the moral law.

[4] B, 662.

help to delimit its meaning. The criticism of natural theology has a twofold function. It exposes the fallacies in the theoretical proofs of God's existence, and shows that God's existence cannot be demonstrated. At the same time the very nature of the criticism shows also that the non-existence of God can never be demonstrated. By reason we cannot either prove or disprove God's existence. The criticism of natural theology thus leaves the way open for practical or moral faith. And, when faith is presupposed, the reason can correct and purify our conception of God. Although reason in its speculative use cannot prove God's existence, 'it is, however, of the greatest use in correcting our knowledge of the supreme Being, supposing that this knowledge can be derived from some other source, in making it consistent with itself and with all other concepts of intelligible objects, and in purifying it from all that is incompatible with the concept of a supreme Being and from all admixture of empirical limitations.'[1]

Further, the alleged proofs of God's existence, even though they are fallacious arguments, can be of positive use. Thus the physico-theological argument, for which Kant always retained a real respect, can prepare the mind for theological (practical) knowledge and give it 'a right and natural direction',[2] even though it cannot provide a sure foundation for a natural theology.

6. We have already seen that the transcendental Ideas of pure reason have no 'constitutive' use. That is to say, they do not give us knowledge of corresponding objects. The schematized categories of the understanding, applied to the data of sense intuition, 'constitute' objects and thus enable us to know them. But the transcendental Ideas of pure reason are not applicable to the data of sense intuition. Nor are any corresponding objects supplied by a purely intellectual intuition. For we enjoy no such power of intellectual intuition. Hence the transcendental Ideas have no constitutive use and do not increase our knowledge. If we make use of them to transcend the sphere of experience and to assert the existence of realities not given in experience, we inevitably involve ourselves in those fallacies which it is the aim of the *Transcendental Dialectic* to expose.

At the same time, so Kant tells us, the human reason has a natural inclination to overstep the limits of experience, and he even speaks of the transcendental Ideas as being the parents of 'irresistible illusion'.[3] He does not mean, of course, that it is

---

[1] B, 667-8.   [2] B, 665.   [3] B, 670; cf. A, 297-8.

impossible to correct these illusions. But the impulse which produces them is a natural impulse, and the correction follows, as it were, a natural surrender to them. Historically speaking, speculative metaphysics preceded the *Dialectic*. And the latter, though enabling us in principle to avoid metaphysical illusions, cannot destroy the impulse to produce them and surrender to them. The reason for this is that 'transcendental Ideas are just as natural (to reason) as are the categories to the understanding'.[1]

Now, if the transcendental Ideas are natural to the reason, this suggests that they have a proper use. 'Thus the transcendental Ideas will, in all probability, have their proper and consequently *immanent* use.'[2] That is to say, they will have a use in relation to experience, though this use will not consist in enabling us to know objects corresponding to the Ideas. For there are no such objects *immanent* in experience. And if we give the Ideas a transcendent use, we are, as we have seen, inevitably involved in illusion and fallacy. What, then, is the proper employment of the Ideas? It is what Kant calls their 'regulative' use.

The special task of reason is to give systematic arrangement to our cognitions. We can say, therefore, that 'the understanding is an object for reason, as sensibility is for the understanding. To produce a systematic unity in all possible empirical operations of the understanding is the business of reason, just as the understanding unites the manifold of phenomena by means of concepts and brings them under empirical laws.'[3] In this process of systematization the Idea acts as a regulative principle of unity.

In psychology, for example, the Idea of the ego as a simple, permanent subject stimulates and leads us on to an ever greater unification of psychical phenomena, such as desires, emotions, acts of imagination, and so on; and empirical psychology endeavours to bring them together under laws and to form a unified scheme. In this task it is greatly assisted by the transcendental Idea of the ego as a simple, permanent subject. True, this transcendental ego is not given in experience. And if we are misled by the presence of the Idea into asserting dogmatically the existence of a corresponding object, we go beyond what is legitimate. But this does not alter the fact that the Idea is of great value as a kind of heuristic principle.

As for the cosmological Idea of the world, this would be a hindrance to science if it were taken to involve the assertion that

[1] *B*, 670.   [2] *B*, 671.   [3] *B*, 692: cf. *A*, 302.

the world is a closed totality, so to speak, a completed series. But, when taken without this assertion, the Idea of the world as an indefinite series of events stimulates the mind to proceed ever further along the causal chain. Kant explains that he does not mean to say that in following up a given natural series we are forbidden to find any relatively first term. For instance, we are not forbidden to find the primal members of a given organic species if the empirical evidence so warrants. The cosmological Idea does not tell us what to find or what not to find by scientific investigation. It is a stimulus, a heuristic principle, making us discontented, as it were, with present perceptions and urging us indefinitely to further scientific unification of natural phenomena according to causal laws.

Finally, the transcendental Idea of God as a supreme intelligence and the cause of the universe leads us to think of Nature as a systematic teleological unity. And this presupposition aids the mind in its investigation of Nature. Kant does not mean, of course, that investigation of the eye, for instance, should stop short with saying that God gave eyes to certain creatures for a certain purpose. To assert this would in any case involve asserting something which we do not and cannot know. But if we think of Nature *as if* it were the work of an intelligent work of an intelligent author, we shall be prompted, in Kant's opinion, to carry on the work of scientific investigation by subsumption under causal laws. Perhaps one can interpret Kant's meaning in this way. The idea of Nature as the work of an intelligent creator involves the idea of Nature as an intelligible system. And this presupposition is a spur to scientific investigation. In this way the transcendental Idea of a supreme Being can have a regulative and immanent use.

The transcendental Ideas thus form the basis for a philosophy of *As-if*, to borrow the title of Vaihinger's famous work. It is of practical use in psychology to act *as if* psychical phenomena were related to a permanent subject. It is of use in scientific investigation in general to act *as if* the world were a totality stretching back indefinitely in causal series, and *as if* Nature were the work of an intelligent creator. This utility does not show that the Ideas are true, in the sense of having corresponding objects. Nor is Kant saying that the truth of the statement that there is a God consists in the 'immanent' usefulness of the Idea of God. He is not offering a pragmatist interpretation of truth. At the same time it is easy to see how pragmatists have been able to look on Kant as a forerunner of their philosophy.

7. It will be remembered that Kant's two questions about metaphysics were these. How is metaphysics possible as a natural disposition? Is metaphysics possible as a science? The answers to these questions have, indeed, already been given. But it may be worth while to connect the answers with the foregoing section on the regulative use of the transcendental Ideas of pure reason.

Metaphysics as a natural disposition (that is, the natural disposition to metaphysics) is possible because of the very nature of the human reason. The latter, as we have seen, seeks by its very nature to unify the empirical cognitions of the understanding. And this natural impulse to systematic unification gives rise to the Ideas of an unconditioned unity in different forms. The only proper cognitive use of these Ideas is regulative, in the sense explained above, and therefore 'immanent'. At the same time there is a natural tendency to objectify the Ideas. And then reason seeks to justify this objectification in the various branches of metaphysics. In doing so it oversteps the limits of human knowledge. But this transgression does not alter the fact that the Ideas are natural to reason. They are not abstracted from experience; nor are they innate, in the proper sense of innate. But they arise out of reason's very nature. Hence there is nothing to take exception to in the Ideas considered simply as such. Further, they make possible the development of the necessary postulates of moral experience. The transcendental Ideal (the idea of God), for example, makes possible 'moral theology'; that is, a rational theology based on consideration of the moral consciousness. There is no question, therefore, of dismissing the natural impulse to metaphysics as something perverse in itself.

Metaphysics as a science is, however, impossible. That is to say, speculative metaphysics is supposed to be a science concerning objects corresponding to the transcendental Ideas of pure reason; but there are no such objects. Hence there can be no science of them. The function of the Ideas is not 'constitutive'. Of course, if we mean by 'objects' simply realities, including unknown and, indeed, unknowable realities, we are not entitled to say that there are no 'objects' corresponding to the Ideas of the permanent, simple ego and of God.[1] But the word 'object' should be used as a

---

[1] Kant believed, of course, that there are noumenal realities which we call the soul and God, though he would say that he did not and could not know that this is the case. The arguments to show that there are a soul and God are fallacious;

term correlative to our knowledge. Those things are possible objects which can be given to us in experience. But realities, if there are any, corresponding to the transcendental Ideas cannot be given in experience in the absence of any faculty of intellectual intuition. Hence it is perfectly correct to say that there are no objects corresponding to the Ideas. And in this case there obviously cannot be any science of them.

Now, though there are, strictly speaking, no objects corresponding to the transcendental Ideas, we can *think* realities to which the Ideas of the soul and of God refer. And even if we do not project the Ideas, so to speak, into corresponding realities, the Ideas have content. Hence metaphysics is not meaningless. We cannot know by means of the speculative reason that there is a permanent, simple soul or that God exists; but the Ideas of the soul and of God are free from logical contradiction. They are not mere meaningless terms. Alleged metaphysical knowledge is pseudo-knowledge, illusion, not knowledge at all; and all attempts to show that it is knowledge are fallacious. But metaphysical propositions are not meaningless simply because they are metaphysical.

This seems to me to be Kant's representative position, so to speak, and it differentiates him from the modern positivists who have declared metaphysics to be so much meaningless nonsense. At the same time it must be admitted that the interpretation of Kant's position is by no means such plain sailing as this account would suggest. For sometimes he appears to say, or at least to imply, that speculative metaphysics is meaningless. For instance, he tells us that 'the concepts of reality, substance, causality, and even of necessity in existence lose all meaning and become empty signs of concepts, without any content, if I venture to employ them outside the field of the senses'.[1] And this is not a unique example of this line of thought.

It may well be, as some commentators have suggested, that the apparent diversity in Kant's ways of speaking about the meaning of terms employed in traditional metaphysics is connected with a diversity implicit in his account of the categories. The latter are called *a priori* concepts of the understanding. And in so far as they are concepts, even the unschematized categories must have some content. Hence even in their application outside the field of experience they possess at least some meaning. But the pure

but the ideas, by themselves, do not produce antinomies. The cosmological Idea, however, does produce antinomies. And to this extent it stands in a class by itself.

[1] *B*, 707.

categories are also said to be logical functions of judgments. In this case it seems to follow that they become concepts, as it were, or give rise to concepts only when they are schematized. The unschematized categories would have no content in themselves. They would therefore be meaningless if applied outside the field of experience. Terms such as *Ens realissimum* and *necessary being* would be void of content.

It might be argued, therefore, that Kant's thought points in the direction of the conclusion that the propositions of speculative metaphysics are meaningless. But even if this conclusion appears to follow from one strand in his thought, it certainly does not represent his general position. It seems to me perfectly obvious that a man who insisted on the abiding importance of the fundamental problems of metaphysics, and who tried to show the rational legitimacy of practical faith in freedom, immortality and God did not really believe that metaphysics is simply meaningless nonsense. What he did hold, however, was that if the categories are applied to God, they are not only unable to give knowledge of God but are also of such indeterminate and vague content that they are simply symbols of the unknown. We can, indeed, think God; but we think Him simply by means of symbols. We produce a symbolical conception of the unknown. To think of God in terms of the schematized categories would be equivalent to bringing Him into the sensible world. We therefore try to think away the schematization, as it were, and to apply the term substance, for instance, in an analogical sense. But the attempt to eliminate the concept's reference to the world of sense leaves us with a mere symbol, void of determinate content. Our idea of God is thus symbolical only.

As far as the regulative and so-called immanent use of the transcendental Ideal is concerned, the vagueness of our idea does not matter to Kant. For in making a regulative use of the idea of God we are not asserting that there exists a Being corresponding to this idea. What God may be in Himself, if He exists, can be left indeterminate. We use the idea as 'a point of view' which enables reason to perform its function of unification. 'In a word, this transcendental thing is simply the schema of that regulative principle by means of which reason extends, so far as it can, systematic unity to all experience.'[1]

We may add in conclusion that the Kantian philosophy of

---

[1] *B*, 710.

religion is grounded in reflection on the practical reason; on reason in its moral use. And it is primarily to Kant's moral theory that we have to look for light on the way in which he thought about God. In the *Critique of Pure Reason* he is concerned with delimiting the range of our theoretical knowledge; and his remarks about the regulative use of the idea of God must not be taken as an account of the meaning of the idea for the religious consciousness.

CHAPTER XIV

KANT (5): MORALITY AND RELIGION[1]

Kant's aim—The good will—Duty and inclination—Duty and law—The categorical imperative—The rational being as an end in itself—The autonomy of the will—The kingdom of ends—Freedom as the condition of the possibility of a categorical imperative —The postulates of practical reason; freedom, Kant's idea of the perfect good, immortality, God, the general theory of the postulates —Kant on religion—Concluding remarks.

1. WE have seen that Kant took for granted our ordinary knowledge of objects and our scientific knowledge. Physical science meant for him the Newtonian physics. And it is obvious that he did not consider it the philosopher's business to substitute for the classical physics some other system or to tell us that all our ordinary knowledge of things is no knowledge at all. But, given our ordinary experience and our scientific knowledge, the philosopher can distinguish by a process of analysis between the formal and material, the *a priori* and *a posteriori* elements in our theoretical knowledge of objects. It is the business of the critical philosopher to isolate and exhibit these *a priori* elements in a systematic way.

Now, besides our knowledge of objects which are originally given in sense intuition there is also moral knowledge. We can be said to know, for example, that we ought to tell the truth. But such knowledge is not knowledge of what is, that is to say, of how men actually behave, but of what ought to be, that is to say, of how men ought to behave. And this knowledge is *a priori*, in the sense that it does not depend on men's actual behaviour. Even if they all told lies, it would still be true that they ought not to do so. We cannot verify the statement that men ought to tell the

---

[1] In references in this chapter *G.* denotes the *Groundwork of the Metaphysics of Morals*, *Pr.R.* the *Critique of Practical Reason*, and *Rel.* the *Religion within the bounds of Reason Alone*. These three works are contained respectively in Volumes IV, V and VI of the critical edition. Numbers after the abbreviated titles indicate sections or (if preceded by p.) pages in this edition. In the case of *G.* and *Pr.R.* corresponding references (by page) will be given to the translations contained in T. K. Abbott's *Kant's Theory of Ethics* (see Bibliography) which will be referred to as *Abb.* In the case of *Rel.* corresponding references will be given to the translation by T. M. Greene and H. H. Hudson, abbreviated as *G.-H.*

truth by examining whether they in fact do so or not. The statement is true independently of their conduct, and in this sense is
true *a priori*. For necessity and universality are marks of apriority.
Of course, if we say 'men ought to tell the truth', our knowledge
that there are men depends on experience. But there must be at
least an *a priori* element in the judgment. And for Kant the
primary task of the moral philosopher should be that of isolating
the *a priori* elements in our moral knowledge and showing their
origin. In this sense we can depict the moral philosopher as asking
how the synthetic *a priori* propositions of morals are possible.

The performance of this task obviously does not involve dismissing all our ordinary moral judgments and producing a brand
new system of morality. It means discovering the *a priori* principles according to which we judge when we make moral judgments. In the last chapter we saw that there are, according to
Kant, certain *a priori* categories and principles of judgment. But
Kant did not imagine that he was supplying for the first time a
brand new set of categories. What he wished to do was to show
how the categories which ground the synthetic *a priori* principles
of our theoretical knowledge have their origin in the structure of
the understanding. He wanted to connect them with the pure
reason (the word 'reason' being here used in its wider sense). So
now he wishes to discover the origin in the practical reason of the
fundamental principles according to which we all judge when we
judge morally.

Kant does not mean to imply, of course, that we are all explicitly
aware of the *a priori* principles of morality. If we were, the task
of isolating them would be superfluous. As it is, our moral knowledge taken as a whole contains a variety of elements; and it is
the primary task, though not the only possible task, of the moral
philosopher to lay bare the *a priori* element, freeing it from all
empirically derived elements, and to show its origin in the
practical reason.

What is the practical reason? It is reason[1] in its practical
(moral) use or function. In other words, 'ultimately (there is) only
one and the same reason which has to be distinguished simply in
its application'.[2] Though ultimately one, reason can be concerned,
we are told, with its objects in two ways. It can determine the

---

[1] The word 'reason' must be understood here in the wide sense indicated by the
titles of the first two *Critiques*, not in the narrow sense of the power of mediate
inference.

[2] *G.*, p. 391; *Abb.*, p. 7.

object, the latter being originally given from some other source than reason itself. Or it can make the object real. 'The first is *theoretical*, the second *practical* rational knowledge.'[1] In its theoretical function reason determines or constitutes the object given in intuition, in the sense explained in the last chapter. It applies itself, as it were, to a datum given from another source than reason itself. In its practical function, however, reason is the source of its objects; it is concerned with moral choice, not with applying categories to the data of sense intuition. We can say that it is concerned with the production of moral choices or decisions in accordance with the law which proceeds from itself. We are told, therefore, that whereas reason in its theoretical function is concerned with objects of the cognitive power, in its practical use it is concerned 'with the grounds of the determination of the will; which is a power either of producing objects corresponding to ideas or of determining itself to produce them (whether the physical power to do so is sufficient or not), that is, of determining its causality'.[2] In plain language, theoretical reason is directed towards knowledge, while practical reason is directed towards choice in accordance with moral law and, when physically possible, to the implementation of choice in action. It should be added that while Kant sometimes speaks of practical reason as though it were distinct from will and influenced the latter, he also sometimes identifies it with will. The former way of speaking suggests the picture of practical reason moving the will by means of the moral imperative. The latter way of speaking shows that for Kant the will is a rational power, not a blind drive. Both ways of speaking seem to be required; for practical reason takes the form of willing in accordance with a principle or a maxim,[3] and we can distinguish the cognitive and voluntary aspects involved. But we must not so emphasize the cognitive aspect, knowledge of a moral principle, as to identify it with practical reason to the exclusion of will. For practical reason is said to produce its objects or to make them real. And it is will which produces choice and action in accordance with moral concepts and principles.

Now, we have said that for Kant the moral philosopher must find in the practical reason the source of the *a priori* element in the moral judgment. We cannot say, therefore, that Kant expects the philosopher to derive the whole moral law, form and content,

---

[1] *Critique of Pure Reason*, B, x.   [2] *Pr.R.*, 29–30; *Abb.*, p. 101.
[3] The difference in meaning between these two words will be mentioned later.

from the concept of the practical reason. This follows, indeed, from the statement that the philosopher is concerned with finding the source in practical reason of the *a priori* element in the moral judgment. For the statement implies that there is an *a posteriori* element, which is given empirically. This is perfectly obvious, of course, in the case of a singular moral judgment such as the judgment that I am morally obliged here and now to reply to a certain letter from a particular person. We can distinguish between the concept of moral obligation as such and the empirically given conditions of this particular duty. Further, when Kant speaks of the practical reason or rational will as the fount of the moral law, he is thinking of practical reason *as such*, not of the practical reason as found in a specific class of finite beings, that is, in human beings. True, he does not intend to state that there *are* finite rational beings other than men. But he is concerned with the moral imperative as bearing on all beings which are capable of being subject to obligation, whether they are men or not. Hence he is concerned with the moral imperative regarded as antecedent to consideration of human nature and its empirical conditions. And if practical reason is looked on in this extremely abstract way, it follows that moral laws, in so far as they make sense only on the supposition that there are human beings, cannot be deduced from the concept of practical reason. For instance, it would be absurd to think of the commandment 'Thou shalt not commit adultery' applying to pure spirits, for it presupposes bodies and the institution of marriage. We have to distinguish between pure ethics or the metaphysics of morals, which deals with the supreme principle or principles of morality and with the nature of moral obligation as such, and applied ethics, which applies the supreme principle or principles to the conditions of human nature, calling in the aid of what Kant calls 'anthropology', knowledge of human nature.

The general notion of the division between the metaphysics of morals and applied ethics is reasonably clear. Physics, as we saw, can be divided into pure physics or the metaphysics of Nature and empirical physics. Analogously, ethics or moral philosophy can be divided into the metaphysics of morals and applied ethics or practical anthropology. But when we come down to the details of the division, certain difficulties arise. We would expect the metaphysics of morals to prescind altogether from human nature and to be concerned exclusively with certain fundamental principles which are afterwards applied to human nature in so-called practical anthropology. But in the introduction to the *Metaphysics of Morals* (1797) Kant admits that even in the metaphysics of morals we often have to take account of human nature as such in order to exhibit the consequences of universal moral principles. True, this does not mean that the metaphysics of morals can be founded on anthropology. 'A metaphysics of morals cannot be founded on anthropology, but may be applied to it.'[1] But if the application of moral principles to human nature is admissible in the metaphysical part of ethics, the second part of ethics, namely moral or practical anthropology, tends to become a study of the subjective conditions, favourable and unfavourable, for carrying out moral precepts. It will be concerned, for example, with moral education. And it is, indeed, with such themes that practical anthropology is said to be concerned when Kant describes its function in the introduction to the *Metaphysics of Morals*.

The difficulty, therefore, is this. According to Kant, there is need for a metaphysic of morals which will prescind from all empirical factors. And he blames Wolff for having mixed up *a priori* and empirical factors in his ethical writing. At the same time there seems to be a tendency on Kant's part to push into the metaphysical part of ethics moral laws which seem to include empirical elements. Thus we are told that 'the commandment, *Thou shalt not lie*, is not valid only for human beings as though other rational beings had no need to bother with it; and so with all other moral laws in the proper sense'.[2] But though this precept is *a priori* in the sense that it holds good independently of the way in which human beings actually behave, it is questionable whether it is *a priori* in the sense that it does not depend in any way on 'anthropology'.[3]

However, the main point which Kant wishes to make is that 'the basis of obligation must not be sought in human nature or in the circumstances of the world in which he (man) is placed, but *a priori* simply in the concepts of pure reason'.[4] We must work out a pure ethics which, 'when applied to man, does not borrow the least thing from the knowledge of man himself, but gives laws *a priori* to him as a rational being'.[5] We are really concerned with finding in reason itself the basis of the *a priori* element in the moral

---

[1] *W.*, VI, p. 217; *Abb.*, p. 272.　　[2] *G.*, Preface, p. 389; *Abb.*, pp. 3–4.

[3] It is conceivable that Kant had at the back of his mind the picture of Satan deceiving men. The precept would apply also to 'the father of lies'.

[4] *G.*, Preface, p. 389; *Abb.*, p. 4.　　[5] *Ibid.*

judgment, the element which makes possible the synthetic *a priori* propositions of morals. We are certainly not concerned with deducing all moral laws and precepts by mere analysis from the concept of the pure practical reason. Kant did not think that this can be done.

But though we cannot deduce all moral laws and precepts from the concept of pure practical reason alone, the moral law must ultimately be grounded in this reason. And as this means finding the ultimate source of the principles of the moral law in reason considered in itself, without reference to specifically human conditions, Kant obviously parts company with all moral philosophers who try to find the ultimate basis of the moral law in human nature as such or in any feature of human nature or in any factor in human life or society. In the *Critique of Practical Reason* he refers to Montaigne as founding morality on education, to Epicurus as founding it on man's physical feeling, to Mandeville as founding it on political constitution, and to Hutcheson as founding it on man's moral feelings. He then remarks that all these alleged foundations are 'evidently incapable of furnishing the general principle of morality'.[1] We can also note that Kant's moral theory, by grounding the moral law on reason, is incompatible with modern emotive theories of ethics. In a word, he rejects empiricism and must be classed as a rationalist in ethics, provided that this word is not taken to mean someone who thinks that the whole moral law is deducible by mere analysis from some fundamental concept.

In the following outline of Kant's moral theory we shall be concerned primarily with the metaphysical part of morals. That is to say, we shall be concerned primarily with what Kant calls the metaphysics of morals, not with speculative metaphysics. For Kant did not believe that morality should be founded on natural theology. For him belief in God is grounded in the moral consciousness rather than the moral law on belief in God. And our treatment will be based on the *Groundwork* and the second *Critique*. The work entitled *Metaphysics of Morals* does not seem to add much, if anything, which is required for a brief outline of the Kantian moral theory.

In the *Groundwork of the Metaphysics of Morals* (called by Abbott *Fundamental Principles of the Metaphysics of Morals*) we are told that the metaphysics of morals is concerned to investigate

---

[1] *Pr.R.*, 70; *Abb.*, p. 129.

'the source of the practical principles which are to be found *a priori* in our reason'.[1] The *Groundwork* itself is said to be 'nothing more than the investigation and establishment of *the supreme principle of morality*',[2] and thus to constitute a complete treatise in itself. At the same time it does not profess to be a complete critique of the practical reason. Hence it leads on to the second *Critique*. This fact is indicated, indeed, by the titles of the main divisions of the *Groundwork*. For the first part deals with the transition from common or ordinary moral knowledge to philosophical moral knowledge; the second part with the transition from popular moral philosophy to the metaphysics of morals; and the third with the final step from the metaphysics of morals to the critique of the pure practical reason.

The structure of the *Critique of Practical Reason* recalls the structure of the first *Critique*. There is, of course, nothing corresponding to the *Transcendental Aesthetic*. But the work is divided into an *Analytic* (proceeding from principles to concepts rather than, as in the first *Critique*, from concepts to principles) and a *Dialectic*, dealing with the illusions of reason in its practical use, but also putting forward a positive standpoint. And Kant adds a *Methodology of Pure Practical Reason*, treating of the method of making the objectively practical reason also subjectively practical. That is to say, it considers the way in which the laws of the pure practical reason can be given access to and influence on the human mind. But this section is brief, and it is perhaps inserted more to supply something corresponding to the *Transcendental Doctrine of Method* in the first *Critique* than for any more cogent reason.

2. The fact that the opening words of the *Groundwork of the Metaphysics of Morals* have been quoted time and time again is no reason for not quoting them once more. 'It is impossible to conceive of anything in the world, or indeed out of it, which can be called good without qualification save only a good will.'[3] But though Kant begins his treatise in this dramatic way, he does not consider that he is giving a startling new piece of information. For in his opinion he is making explicit a truth which is present at least implicitly in ordinary moral knowledge. However, it is incumbent on him to explain what he means by saying that a good will is the only good without qualification.

The concept of an unqualified good can be explained without

---

[1] *G.*, Preface, pp. 389–90; *Abb.*, p. 4.
[2] *G.*, Preface, p. 392; *Abb.*, p. 7.
[3] *G.*, p. 393; *Abb.*, p. 9.

much difficulty. External possessions, such as wealth, can be misused, as everybody knows. Hence they are not good without qualification. And the same can be said about mental talents, such as quickness of understanding. A criminal can possess and misuse mental talents of a high order. We can also say the same of natural traits of character, such as courage. They can be employed or manifested in pursuing an evil end. But a good will cannot be bad or evil in any circumstances. It is good without qualification.

This statement, taken by itself, seems to be a mere tautology. For a good will is good by definition; and it is analytically true to say that a good will is always good. Kant must therefore explain what he means by a good will. He refers, indeed, in the first place to a will which is good in itself and not merely in relation to something else. We may say, for example, of a painful surgical treatment that it is good, not in itself, but in relation to the beneficial effect which it is designed to bring about. But the Kantian concept of a good will is the concept of a will which is always good in itself, by virtue of its intrinsic value, and not simply in relation to the production of some end, for example, happiness. We wish to know, however, when a will is good in itself, that is, when it has intrinsic value. According to Kant, a will cannot be said to be good in itself simply because it causes, for instance, good actions. For I may will, for instance, a good action which physical circumstances prevent me from performing. Yet my will can be none the less good. What makes it good? If we are to escape from mere tautology, we must give some content to the term 'good' when applied to the will and not content ourselves with saying that a good will is a good will or that a will is good when it is good.

To elucidate the meaning of the term 'good' when applied to the will, Kant turns his attention to the concept of duty which is for him the salient feature of the moral consciousness. A will which acts for the sake of duty is a good will. The matter has to be stated in this form if it is to be stated with accuracy. For the will of God is a good will, but it would be absurd to speak of God performing His duty. For the concept of duty or obligation involves the concept of at least the possibility of self-conquest, of having to overcome obstacles. And the divine will is not conceived as subject to any possible hindrance in willing what is good. Hence to be quite accurate we cannot say that a good will is a will which acts for the sake of duty; we have to say that a will which acts for the sake of duty is a good will. However, Kant calls a will such as the divine will, which is conceived as always and necessarily good, a 'holy will', thus giving it a special name. And if we prescind from the concept of a holy will and confine our attention to a finite will subject to obligation, we can permit ourselves to say that a good will is one which acts for the sake of duty. But the notion of acting for the sake of duty needs, of course, further elucidation.

3. Kant makes a distinction between actions which are in accordance with duty and acts which are done for the sake of duty. His own example serves to make clear the nature of this distinction. Let us suppose that a tradesman is always careful not to overcharge his customers. His behaviour is certainly in accordance with duty; but it does not necessarily follow that he behaves in this way for the sake of duty, that is, because it is his duty so to behave. For he may refrain from overcharging his customers simply from motives of prudence; for example, on the ground that honesty is the best policy. Thus the class of actions performed in accordance with duty is much wider than the class of actions performed for the sake of duty.

According to Kant, only those actions which are performed for the sake of duty have moral worth. He takes the example of preserving one's life. 'To preserve one's life is a duty, and further, everyone has an immediate inclination to do so.'[1] These are the two presuppositions. Now, if I preserve my life simply because I have an inclination to do so, my action does not, in Kant's view, possess moral worth. To possess such worth my action must be performed because it is my duty to preserve my life; that is, out of a sense of moral obligation. Kant does not explicitly say that it is morally wrong to preserve my life because I desire to do so. For my action would be at least in accordance with duty and not incompatible with it, as suicide would be. But it has no moral value. On the one hand it is not a moral action; but on the other hand it can hardly be called an immoral action in the sense in which suicide is immoral.

This view may be incorrect; but Kant at any rate thinks that it represents the view which everyone who possesses moral convictions implicitly holds and which he will recognize as true if he reflects. Kant tends to complicate matters, however, by giving the impression that in his opinion the moral value of an action performed for the sake of duty is increased in proportion to a decrease in inclination to perform the action. In other words, he

[1] *G.*, p. 397; *Abb.*, p. 13.

gives some ground for the interpretation that, in his view, the less inclination we have to do our duty, the greater is the moral value of our action if we actually perform what it is our duty to do. And this point of view leads to the strange conclusion that the more we hate doing our duty the better, provided that we do it. Or, to put the matter another way, the more we have to overcome ourselves to do our duty, the more moral we are. And, if this is admitted, it seems to follow that the baser a man's inclinations are, the higher is his moral value, provided that he overcomes his evil tendencies. But this point of view is contrary to the common conviction that the integrated personality, in whom inclination and duty coincide, has achieved a higher level of moral development than the man in whom inclination and desire are at war with his sense of duty.

However, though Kant sometimes speaks in a way which appears at first sight at least to support this interpretation, his main point is simply that when a man performs his duty contrary to his inclinations, the fact that he acts for the sake of duty and not simply out of inclination is clearer than it would be if he had a natural attraction to the action. And to say this is not necessarily to say that it is better to have no inclination for doing one's duty than to have such an inclination. Speaking of the beneficent man or philanthropist, he asserts, indeed, that the action of doing good to others has no moral worth if it is simply the effect of a natural inclination, springing from a naturally sympathetic temperament. But he does not say that there is anything wrong or undesirable in possessing such a temperament. On the contrary, actions arising from a natural satisfaction in increasing the happiness of others are 'proper and lovable'.[1] Kant may have been a rigorist in ethics; but his concern to bring out the difference between acting for the sake of duty and acting to satisfy one's natural desires and inclinations should not be taken to imply that he had no use for the ideal of a completely virtuous man who has overcome and transformed all desires which conflict with duty. Nor should it be taken to mean that in his opinion the truly virtuous man would be without any inclinations at all. Speaking of the commandment in the Gospels to love all men, he remarks that love as an affection ('pathological' love, as he puts it) cannot be commanded, but that beneficence for duty's sake ('practical' love) can be commanded, even if a man has an aversion towards beneficent action. But he

<hr>

[1] *G.*, p. 398; *Abb.*, p. 14.

certainly does not say that it is better to have an aversion towards beneficent action, provided that one performs such actions when it is one's duty to do so, than to have an inclination towards it. On the contrary, he explicitly asserts that it is better to do one's duty cheerfully than otherwise. And his moral ideal, as will be seen later, was the greatest possible approximation to complete virtue, to the holy will of God.

4. So far we have learned that a good will is manifested in acting for the sake of duty, and that acting for the sake of duty must be distinguished from acting out of mere inclination or desire. But we require some more positive indication of what is meant by acting for the sake of duty. And Kant tells us that it means acting out of reverence for law, that is, the moral law. 'Duty is the necessity of acting out of reverence for the law.'[1]

Now, by law Kant means law as such. To act for the sake of duty is to act out of reverence for law as such. And the essential characteristic (the form, we may say) of law as such is universality; that is to say, strict universality which does not admit of exceptions. Physical laws are universal; and so is the moral law. But whereas all physical things, including man as a purely physical thing, conform unconsciously and necessarily to physical law, rational beings, and they alone, are capable of acting in accordance with the idea of law. A man's actions, therefore, if they are to have moral worth, must be performed out of reverence for the law. Their moral worth is derived, according to Kant, not from their results, whether actual or intended, but from the maxim of the agent. And this maxim, to confer moral worth on actions, must be that of abiding by law, of obeying it, out of reverence for the law.

We are told, therefore, that the good will, the only good without qualification, is manifested in acting for the sake of duty; that duty means acting out of reverence for law; and that law is essentially universal. But this leaves us with a highly abstract, not to say empty, concept of acting for the sake of duty. And the question arises how it can be translated into terms of the concrete moral life.

Before we can answer this question, we must make a distinction between maxims and principles. A principle, in Kant's technical terminology, is a fundamental objective moral law, grounded in the pure practical reason. It is a principle on which all men would act if they were purely rational moral agents. A maxim is a sub-

[1] *G.*, p. 400; *Abb.*, p. 16.

jective principle of volition. That is to say, it is a principle on which an agent acts as a matter of fact and which determines his decisions. Such maxims can be, of course, of diverse kinds; and they may or may not accord with the objective principle or principles of the moral law.

This account of the nature of maxims may seem to be incompatible with what has been said above about Kant's view that the moral worth of actions is determined by the agent's maxim. For if a maxim can be out of accord with the moral law, how can it confer moral worth on the actions prompted by it? To meet this difficulty we have to make a further distinction between empirical or material maxims and *a priori* or formal maxims. The first refer to desired ends or results while the second do not. The maxim which confers moral value on actions must be of the second type. That is to say, it must not refer to any objects of sensuous desire or to any results to be obtained by action; but it must be the maxim of obeying universal law as such. That is to say, if the subjective principle of volition is obedience to the universal moral law, out of reverence for the law, the actions governed by this maxim will have moral worth. For they will have been performed for the sake of duty.

Having made these distinctions, we can return to the question how Kant's abstract concept of acting for the sake of duty can be translated into terms of the concrete moral life. 'As I have robbed the will of all impulses (or inducements) which could arise for it from following any particular law, there remains nothing but the universal conformity of actions to law in general, which should serve the will as a principle. That is to say, *I am never to act otherwise than so that I can also will that my maxim should become a universal law.*'[1] The word 'maxim' must be taken here to refer to what we have called empirical or material maxims. Reverence for law, which gives rise to the formal maxim of acting in obedience to law as such, demands that we should bring all our material maxims under the form of law as such, this form being universality. We have to ask whether we could will that a given maxim should become a universal law. That is to say, could it assume the form of universality?

Kant gives an example. Let us imagine a man in distress, who can extricate himself from his plight only by making a promise which he has no intention of fulfilling. That is to say, he can

[1] *G.*, p. 402; *Abb.*, p. 18.

obtain relief only by lying. May he do so? If he does act in this way, his maxim will be that he is entitled to make a promise with no intention of fulfilling it (that is, that he is entitled to lie) if only by this means can he extricate himself from a distressful situation. We may put the question in this form, therefore. Can he will that this maxim should become a universal law? The maxim, when universalized, would state that everyone may make a promise with no intention of keeping it (that is, that anyone may lie) when he finds himself in a difficulty from which he can extricate himself by no other means. According to Kant, this universalization cannot be willed. For it would mean willing that lying should become a universal law. And then no promises would be believed. But the man's maxim postulates belief in promises. Therefore he cannot adopt this maxim and at the same time will that it should become a universal law. Thus the maxim cannot assume the form of universality. And if a maxim cannot enter as a principle into a possible scheme of universal law, it must be rejected.

Far be it from me to suggest that this example is immune from criticism. But I do not wish, by discussing possible objections, to distract attention from the main point which Kant is trying to make. It seems to be this. In practice we all act according to what Kant calls maxims. That is to say, we all have subjective principles of volition. Now, a finite will cannot be good unless it is motivated by respect or reverence for universal law. In order, therefore, that our wills may be morally good, we must ask ourselves whether we can will that our maxims, our subjective principles of volition, should become universal laws. If we cannot do so, we must reject these maxims. If we can do so, that is if our maxims can enter as principles into a possible scheme of universal moral legislation, reason demands that we should admit and respect them in virtue of our reverence for law as such.[1]

It is to be noted that up to this point Kant has been concerned with clarifying the idea of acting for the sake of duty. Further, in his opinion we have been moving in the sphere of what he calls the moral knowledge of common human reason. 'The necessity of acting from pure reverence for the practical law is that which constitutes duty, to which every other motive must give place, because it is the condition of a will being good *in itself*; and the

---

[1] There is obviously no question here of *deducing* concrete rules of conduct from the concept of universal law as such. The concept is used as a test of the admissibility or inadmissibility of maxims, but not as a premiss from which they can be deduced.

worth of such a will is above everything. Thus, then, without leaving the moral knowledge of common human reason, we have arrived at its principle.'[1] Although men do not ordinarily conceive this principle in such an abstract form, yet it is known by them implicitly, and it is the principle on which their moral judgments rest.

The principle of duty, that I ought never to act otherwise than so that I can also will that my maxim should become a universal law, is a way of formulating what Kant calls the categorical imperative. And we can now turn our attention to this subject.

5. As we have seen, a distinction must be made between principles and maxims. The objective principles of morality may be also subjective principles of volition, functioning as maxims. But there may also be a discrepancy between the objective principles of morality on the one hand and a man's maxims or subjective principles of volition on the other. If we were all purely rational moral agents, the objective principles of morality would always govern our actions; that is to say, they would also be subjective principles of volition. In point of fact, however, we are capable of acting on maxims or subjective principles of volition which are incompatible with the objective principles of morality. And this means that the latter present themselves to us as commands or imperatives. We thus experience obligation. If our wills were holy wills, there would be no question of command and no question of obligation. But inasmuch as our wills are not holy wills (though the holy will remains the ideal), the moral law necessarily takes for us the form of an imperative. The pure practical reason commands; and it is our duty to overcome the desires which conflict with these commands.

When defining an imperative, Kant makes a distinction between command and imperative.[2] 'The conception of an objective principle, in so far as it is necessitating for a will, is called a command (of reason), and the formula of the command is called an *imperative*. All imperatives are expressed by an *ought* and exhibit thereby the relation of an objective law of reason to a will which, by reason of its subjective constitution, is not necessarily determined by it.'[3] By speaking of the objective principle as being 'necessitating' (*nötigend*) for a will Kant does not mean, of course,

---

[1] *G.*, p. 403; *Abb.*, p. 20.
[2] He does not make much use of it, however. So there is no real need to bother about it
[3] *G.*, p. 413; *Abb.*, p. 30.

that the human will cannot help obeying the law. The point is rather that the will does not necessarily follow the dictate of reason, with the consequence that the law appears to the agent as something external which exercises constraint or pressure on the will. In this sense the law is said to be 'necessitating' for the will. But the latter is not 'necessarily determined' by the law. Kant's terminology may be confusing; but he is not guilty of self-contradiction.

Now, there are three kinds of imperatives, corresponding to three different kinds or senses of good action. And as only one of these imperatives is the moral imperative, it is important to understand the Kantian distinction between the different types.

Let us first consider the sentence, 'If you wish to learn French, you ought to take these means'. Here we have an imperative. But there are two things to notice. First, the actions commanded are conceived as being good with a view to attaining a certain end. They are not commanded as actions which ought to be performed for their own sake, but only as a means. The imperative is thus said to be *hypothetical*. Secondly, the end in question is not one which everyone seeks by nature. A man may wish or not wish to learn French. The imperative simply states that *if* you wish to learn French, you ought to take certain means, that is, perform certain actions. This type of imperative is called by Kant a *problematic* hypothetical imperative or an imperative of skill.

There is no difficulty in seeing that this type of imperative is not the moral imperative. We have taken the example of learning French. But we might equally well have taken the example of becoming a successful burglar. 'If you wish to become a successful burglar, that is, if you wish to burgle and not to be found out, these are the means which you ought to take.' The imperative of skill, or the technical imperative as we might call it, has, in itself, nothing to do with morality. The actions commanded are commanded simply as useful for the attainment of an end which one may or may not desire to attain; and the pursuit may or may not be compatible with the moral law.

In the second place let us consider the sentence, 'You desire happiness by a necessity of nature; therefore you ought to perform these actions'. Here again we have a *hypothetical* imperative, in the sense that certain actions are commanded as means to an end. But it is not a problematic hypothetical imperative. For the desire of happiness is not an end which we set before ourselves or leave aside as we like, in the way that we can choose or not choose to learn French, to become successful burglars, to acquire the carpenter's art, and so on. The imperative does not say, '*if* you desire happiness': it *asserts* that you desire happiness. It is thus an *assertoric* hypothetical imperative.

Now, this imperative has been regarded in some ethical systems as a moral imperative. But Kant will not allow that any hypothetical imperative, whether problematic or assertoric, is the moral imperative. It seems to me that he is somewhat cavalier in his treatment of teleological ethical theories. I mean that he does not seem to give sufficient consideration to a distinction which has to be made between different types of teleological ethics. 'Happiness' may be regarded as a subjective state which is acquired by certain actions but which is distinct from these actions. In this case the actions are judged good simply as means to an end to which they are external. But 'happiness', if we follow, for instance, the customary way of translating Aristotle's[1] *eudaimonia*, may be regarded as an objective actualization of the potentialities of man as man (that is, as an activity); and in this case the actions which are judged good are not purely external to the end. However, Kant would probably say that we then have an ethic based on the idea of the perfection of human nature, and that, though this idea is morally relevant, it cannot supply the supreme principle of morality which he is seeking.

In any case Kant rejects all hypothetical imperatives, whether problemetic or assertoric, as qualifying for the title of moral imperative. It remains, therefore, that the moral imperative must be *categorical*. That is to say, it must command actions, not as means to any end, but as good in themselves. It is what Kant calls an apodictic imperative. 'The categorical imperative, which declares an action to be objectively necessary in itself without reference to any purpose, that is, without any other end, is valid as an *apodictic* practical principle.'[2]

What is this categorical imperative? All that we can say about it purely *a priori*, that is, by considering the mere concept of a categorical imperative, is that it commands conformity to law in general. It commands, that is to say, that the maxims which serve as our principles of volition should conform to universal law. 'There is, therefore, only one categorical imperative, and it is this:

[1] For an outline of Aristotle's ethical theory, see Vol. I of this *History*, Chapter XXXI.
[2] *G.*, p. 415; *Abb.*, p. 32.

*Act only on that maxim through which you can at the same time will
that it should become a universal law.'*[1] But Kant immediately gives
us another formulation of the imperative, namely to *'Act as if the
maxim of your action were to become through your will a Universal
Law of Nature'.*[2]

In the last section we met the categorical imperative expressed
in a negative form. And earlier, in the footnote on page 320, I
remarked that there is no question of deducing concrete rules of
conduct from the concept of universal law as such. So here also we
must remember that Kant does not intend to imply that concrete
rules of conduct can be deduced from the categorical imperative
in the sense in which the conclusion of a syllogism can be deduced
from the premises. The imperative serves, not as a premiss for
deduction by mere analysis, but as a criterion for judging the
morality of concrete principles of conduct. We might speak, however, of moral laws being derived in some sense from the categorical imperative. Suppose that I give money to a poor person in
great distress when there is nobody else who has a greater claim
on me. The maxim of my action, that is, the subjective principle
of my volition, is, let us assume, that I will give alms to an individual who really needs such assistance when there is nobody else
who has a prior claim on me. I ask myself whether I can will this
maxim as a universal law valid for all, namely that one should give
assistance to those who really need it when there is nobody else
who has a prior claim on one. And I decide that I can so will.
My maxim is thus morally justified. As for the moral law which I
will, this is obviously not deducible by mere analysis from the
categorical imperative. For it introduces ideas which are not contained in the latter. At the same time the law can be said to be
derived from the categorical imperative, in the sense that it is
derived through applying the imperative.

Kant's general notion, therefore, is that the practical or moral
law as such is strictly universal; universality being, as it were, its
form. Hence all concrete principles of conduct must partake in this
universality if they are to qualify for being called moral. But he
does not make it at all clear what precisely he means by 'being
able' or 'not being able' to will that one's maxim should become a
universal law. One would perhaps be naturally inclined to understand him as referring to the absence or presence of logical contradiction when one tries to universalize one's maxim. But Kant

[1] *G.*, p. 421; *Abb.*, p. 38.   [2] *Ibid.*; *Abb.*, p. 39.

makes a distinction. 'Some actions are of such a nature that their maxims cannot, without contradiction, be even conceived as a universal law.'[1] Here Kant seems to refer to a logical contradiction between the maxim and its formulation as a universal law. In other cases, however, this 'intrinsic impossibility' is absent; 'but it is still impossible to *will* that the maxim should be raised to the universality of a law of nature, because such a will would contradict itself'.[2] Here Kant seems to refer to cases in which a maxim could be given the formulation of a universal law without logical contradiction, though we could not *will* this law because the will, as expressed in the law, would be in antagonism or, as Kant puts it, contradiction with itself as adhering steadfastly to some purpose or desire the attainment of which would be incompatible with the observance of the law.

A series of examples is, indeed, supplied. The fourth of these appears to be intended as an example of the second type of inability to will that one's maxim should become a universal law. A man enjoys great prosperity but sees that others are in misery and that he could help them. He adopts, however, the maxim of not concerning himself with the distress of others. Can this maxim be turned into a universal law? It can be done without logical contradiction. For there is no logical contradiction in a law that those in prosperity ought not to render any assistance to those in distress. But, according to Kant, the prosperous man cannot *will* this law without a contradiction or antagonism within his will. For his original maxim was the expression of a selfish disregard for others, and it was accompanied by the firm desire of himself obtaining help from others if he should ever be in a state of misery, a desire which would be negated by willing the universal law in question.

Kant's second example appears to be intended as an example of a logical contradiction being involved in turning one's maxim into a universal law. A man needs money, and he can obtain it only by promising to repay it, though he knows very well that he will be unable to do so. Reflection shows him that he cannot turn the maxim (when I am in need of money, I will borrow it and promise to repay it, though I know that I shall not be able to do so) into a universal law without contradiction. For the universal law would destroy all faith in promises, whereas the maxim presupposes faith in promises. From what he says Kant appears to have thought

[1] *G.*, p. 424; *Abb.*, p. 41.   [2] *Ibid.*; *Abb.*, p. 42.

that the law itself would be self-contradictory, the law being that anyone who is in need and can obtain relief only by making a promise which he cannot fulfil may make such a promise. But it is difficult to see that this proposition is self-contradictory in a purely logical sense, though it may be that the law could not be *willed* without the inconsistencies to which Kant draws attention.

It may be said, of course, that we ought not to make heavy weather of concrete examples. The examples may be open to objection; but even if Kant has not given sufficient attention to their formulation, the theory which they are supposed to illustrate is the important thing. This would be an apt observation if the theory, in its abstract expression, were clear. But this does not seem to me to be the case. It seems to me that Kant has not properly clarified the meaning of 'being able' and 'not being able' to will that one's maxim should become a universal law. However, behind his examples we can see the conviction that the moral law is essentially universal, and that the making of exceptions for oneself from selfish motives is immoral. The practical reason commands us to rise above selfish desires and maxims which clash with the universality of law.

6. We have seen that according to Kant there is 'only one' categorical imperative, namely 'Act only on that maxim through which you can at the same time will that it should become a universal law'. But we have also seen that he gives another formulation of the categorical imperative, namely 'Act as if the maxim of your action were to become through your will a Universal Law of Nature'. And he gives further formulations. There seem to be five in all; but Kant tells us that there are three. Thus he asserts that 'the three above-mentioned ways of presenting the principle of morality are at bottom so many formulas of the very same law, each of which involves the other two'.[1] By giving several formulations of the categorical imperative Kant does not, therefore, intend to recant what he has said about there being 'only one' such imperative. The different formulations are intended, he tells us, to bring an idea of the reason nearer to intuition, by means of a certain analogy, and thereby nearer to feeling. Thus the formulation 'Act as if the maxim of your action were to become through your will a Universal Law of Nature' makes use of an analogy between moral law and natural law. And elsewhere Kant expresses the formula in this way: 'Ask yourself whether you could

[1] *G.*, p. 436; *Abb.*, p. 54.

regard the action which you propose to do as a possible object of your will if it were to take place according to a law of nature in a system of nature of which you were yourself a part.'[1] This formula[2] may be the same as the categorical imperative in its original form in the sense that the latter is its principle, as it were; but it is obvious that the idea of a system of Nature is an addition to the categorical imperative as first expressed.

Assuming, however, that the two formulations of the categorical imperative which have already been mentioned can be reckoned as one, we come to what Kant calls the second formulation or way of presenting the principle of morality. His approach to it is involved.

We have, Kant tells us, exhibited the content of the categorical imperative. 'But we have not yet advanced so far as to prove that there really is such an imperative, that there is a practical law which commands absolutely of itself and without any other impulses, and that the following of this law is duty.'[3] The question arises, therefore, whether it is a practically necessary law (that is, a law imposing obligation) for all rational beings that they should always judge their actions by maxims which they can will to be universal laws. If this is actually the case, there must be a synthetic *a priori* connection between the concept of the will of a rational being as such and the categorical imperative.

Kant's treatment of the matter is not easy to follow and gives the impression of being very roundabout. He argues that that which serves the will as the objective ground of its self-determination is the *end*. And if there is an end which is assigned by reason alone (and not by subjective desire), it will be valid for all rational beings and will thus serve as the ground for a categorical imperative binding the wills of all rational beings. This end cannot be a relative end, fixed by desire; for such ends give rise only to hypothetical imperatives. It must be, therefore, an end in itself, possessing absolute, and not merely relative, value. 'Assuming that there is something *the existence of which* has *in itself* absolute value, something which, *as an end in itself*, could be the ground of determinate laws, then in it and in it alone would lie the ground of a possible categorical imperative, that is, of a practical law.'[4]

[1] *Pr.R.*, 122; *Abb.*, p. 161.
[2] This formula is clearly presupposed by Kant's first example of the application of the categorical imperative, namely of the man who is reduced to hopeless misery and who asks himself whether he may commit suicide (*G.*, pp. 421–2; *Abb.*, pp. 39–40).
[3] *G.*, p. 425; *Abb.*, p. 43.   [4] *G.*, p. 428; *Abb.*, p. 46.

Again, if there is a supreme practical principle which is for the human will a categorical imperative, 'it must be one which, being derived from the conception of that which is necessarily an end for everyone because it is *an end in itself*, constitutes an *objective* principle of will, and can thus serve as a universal practical law'.[1]

Is there such an end? Kant postulates that man, and indeed any rational being, is an end in itself. The concept of a rational being as an end in itself can therefore serve as the ground for a supreme practical principle or law. 'The ground of this principle is: *rational nature exists as an end in itself*. ... The practical imperative will thus be as follows: *So act as to treat humanity, whether in your own person or in that of any other, always at the same time as an end, and never merely as a means.*'[2] The words 'at the same time' and 'merely' are of importance. We cannot help making use of other human beings as means. When I go to the hairdresser's, for example, I use him as a means to an end other than himself. But the law states that, even in such cases, I must never use a rational being as a *mere* means; that is, as though he had no value in himself except as a means to my subjective end.

Kant applies this formulation of the categorical imperative to the same cases which he used to illustrate the application of the imperative as originally formulated. The suicide, who destroys himself to escape from painful circumstances, uses himself, a person, as a mere means to a relative end, namely the maintenance of tolerable conditions up to the end of life. The man who makes a promise to obtain a benefit when he has no intention of fulfilling it or when he knows very well that he will not be in a position to keep it, uses the man to whom he makes the promise as a mere means to a relative end.

We may note in passing that Kant makes use of this principle in his treatise *On Perpetual Peace*. A monarch who employs soldiers in aggressive wars undertaken for his own aggrandizement or for that of his country is using rational beings as mere means to a desired end. Indeed, in Kant's view, standing armies should be abolished in the course of time because hiring men to kill or to be killed involves a use of them as mere instruments in the hands of the State and cannot easily be reconciled with the rights of humanity, founded on the absolute value of the rational being as such.

7. The idea of respecting every rational will as an end in itself

[1] *G.*, pp. 428–9; *Abb.*, p. 47.   [2] *G.*, p. 429; *Abb.*, p. 47.

and not treating it as a mere means to the attainment of the object of one's desires leads us on to the 'idea of the will of every rational being as making universal law'.[1] In Kant's view, the will of man considered as a rational being must be regarded as the source of the law which he recognizes as universally binding. This is the principle of the autonomy, as contrasted with the heteronomy, of the will.

One of Kant's approaches to the autonomy of the will is more or less this. All imperatives which are conditioned by desire or inclination or, as Kant puts it, by 'interest' are hypothetical imperatives. A categorical imperative, therefore, must be unconditioned. And the moral will, which obeys the categorical imperative, must not be determined by interest. That is to say, it must not be heteronomous, at the mercy, as it were, of desires and inclinations which form part of a causally determined series. It must, therefore, be autonomous. And to say that a moral will is autonomous is to say that it gives itself the law which it obeys.

Now, the idea of a categorical imperative contains implicitly the idea of the autonomy of the will. But this autonomy can be expressed explicitly in a formulation of the imperative. And then we have the principle 'never to act on any other maxim than one which could, without contradiction, be also a universal law and accordingly always so to act that *the will could regard itself at the same time as making universal law through its maxim*'.[2] In the *Critique of Practical Reason*, the principle is expressed thus: 'So act that the maxim of your will could always at the same time be valid as a principle making universal law.'[3]

Kant speaks of the autonomy of the will as 'the supreme principle of morality'[4] and as 'the sole principle of all moral laws and of the corresponding duties'.[5] Heteronomy of the will, on the other hand, is 'the source of all spurious principles of morality';[6] and, far from being able to furnish the basis of obligation, 'is much rather opposed to the principle of obligation and to the morality of the will'.[7]

If we accept the heteronomy of the will, we accept the assumption that the will is subject to moral laws which are not the result of its own legislation as a rational will. And though reference has already been made to some of the ethical theories which, according

---

[1] *G.*, p. 431; *Abb.*, p. 50.
[2] *G.*, p. 434; *Abb.*, p. 52.
[3] *Pr.R.*, 54; *Abb.*, p. 119.
[4] *G.*, p. 440; *Abb.*, p. 59.
[5] *Pr.R.*, 58; *Abb.*, p. 122.
[6] *G.*, p. 441; *Abb.*, p. 59.
[7] *Pr.R.*, 58; *Abb.*, p. 122

to Kant, accept this assumption, it will clarify Kant's meaning if
we refer to them briefly once again. In the *Critique of Practical
Reason*[1] he mentions Montaigne as grounding the principles of
morality on education, Mandeville as grounding them on the civil
constitution (that is, on the legal system), Epicurus as grounding
them on physical feeling (that is, pleasure), and Hutcheson as
grounding them on moral feeling. All these theories are what Kant
calls subjective or empirical, the first two referring to external
empirical factors, the second two to internal empirical factors. In
addition there are 'objective' or rationalistic theories; that is to
say, theories which ground the moral law on ideas of reason. Kant
mentions two types. The first, attributed to the Stoics and Wolff,
grounds the moral law and obligation on the idea of inner perfection, while the second, attributed to Crusius, grounds the moral
law and obligation on the will of God. All these theories are
rejected by Kant. He does not say that they are all morally
irrelevant; that is, that none of them has any contribution to make
in the field of ethics. What he maintains is that none of them is
capable of furnishing the supreme principles of morality and
obligation. For instance, if we say that the will of God is the norm
of morality, we can still ask why we ought to obey the divine will.
Kant does not say that we ought not to obey the divine will, if it
is manifested. But we must in any case first recognize obedience
to God as a duty. Thus before obeying God we must in any case
legislate as rational beings. The autonomy of the moral will is thus
the supreme principle of morality.

Obviously, the concept of the autonomy of the morally legislating will makes no sense unless we make a distinction in man
between man considered purely as a rational being, a moral will,
and man as a creature who is also subject to desires and inclinations which may conflict with the dictates of reason. And this is,
of course, what Kant presupposes. The will or practical reason,
considered as such, legislates, and man, considered as being subject
to a diversity of desires, impulses and inclinations, ought to obey.

In conceiving this theory of the autonomy of the will Kant was
doubtless influenced to some extent by Rousseau. The latter, as
we have seen, distinguished between the 'general will', which is
always right and which is the real fount of moral laws, and the
merely private will, whether taken separately or together with
other private wills as 'the will of all'. And Kant utilized these

[1] *Pr.R.*, 69; *Abb.*, p. 129.

ideas within the context of his own philosophy. Indeed, it is not unreasonable to suppose that the central position accorded by Kant in his ethical theory to the concept of the good will reflects, to some extent that is to say, the influence of his study of Rousseau.

8. The idea of rational beings as ends in themselves, coupled with that of the rational will or practical reason as morally legislating, brings us to the concept of a kingdom of ends (*ein Reich der Zwecke*). 'I understand by a *kingdom* the systematic union of rational beings through common laws.'[1] And because these laws have in view the relation of these beings to one another as ends and means, as Kant puts it, it can be called a kingdom of ends. A rational being can belong to this kingdom in either of two ways. He belongs to it as a *member* when, although giving laws, he is also subject to them. He belongs to it as a sovereign or supreme head (*Oberhaupt*) when, while legislating, he is not subject to the will of any other. Perhaps Kant can be interpreted as meaning that every rational being is both member and sovereign; for no rational being is, when legislating and as legislating, subject to the will of another. But it is also possible, and perhaps more likely, that *Oberhaupt* is to be taken as referring to God. For Kant goes on to say that a rational being can occupy the place of supreme head only if he is 'a completely independent being without want and without limitation of power adequate to his will'.[2]

This kingdom of ends is to be thought according to an analogy with the kingdom of Nature, the self-imposed rules of the former being analogous to the causal laws of the latter. It is, as Kant remarks, 'only an ideal'.[3] At the same time it is a possibility. It 'would be actually realized through maxims conforming to the rule prescribed by the categorical imperative for all rational beings, *if they were universally followed*'.[4] And rational beings ought to act as though they were through their maxims law-making members of a kingdom of ends. (Hence we have another variation of the categorical imperative.) The ideal of historical development is, we may say, the establishment of the kingdom of ends as an actuality.

9. Now, the categorical imperative states that all rational beings (that is, all rational beings who can be subject to an imperative at all) ought to act in a certain way. They ought to act

---

[1] *G.*, p. 433; *Abb.*, p. 51. [2] *G.*, p. 434; *Abb.*, p. 52.
[3] *G.*, p. 433; *Abb.*, p. 52. [4] *G.*, p. 438; *Abb.*, p. 57.

only on those maxims which they can at the same time will, without contradiction, to be universal laws. The imperative thus states an obligation. But it is, according to Kant, a synthetic *a priori* proposition. On the one hand, the obligation cannot be obtained by mere analysis of the concept of a rational will. And the categorical imperative is thus not an analytic proposition. On the other hand, the predicate must be connected necessarily with the subject. For the categorical imperative, unlike a hypothetical imperative, is unconditioned and necessarily binds or obliges the will to act in a certain way. It is, indeed, a *practical* synthetic *a priori* proposition. That is to say, it does not extend our theoretical knowledge of objects, as is done by the synthetic *a priori* propositions which we considered when discussing the first *Critique*. It is directed towards action, towards the performance of actions good in themselves, not towards our knowledge of empirical reality. But it is none the less a proposition which is both *a priori*, independent of all desires and inclinations, and synthetic. The question arises, therefore, how is this practical synthetic *a priori* proposition possible?

We have here a question similar to that propounded in the first *Critique* and in the *Prolegomena to Any Future Metaphysics*. But there is a difference. As we saw, there is no need to ask *whether* the synthetic *a priori* propositions of mathematics and physics are possible, if we once assume that these sciences do contain such propositions. For the development of the sciences shows their possibility. The only pertinent question is *how* they are possible. In the case of a practical or moral synthetic *a priori* proposition, however, we have, according to Kant, to establish its possibility.

Kant's statement of the problem seems to me to be somewhat confusing. It is not always easy to see precisely what question he is asking. For he formulates it in different ways, and it is not always immediately evident that their meanings are equivalent. However, let us take it that he is asking for a justification of the possibility of a practical synthetic *a priori* proposition. In his terminology this means asking what is the 'third term' which unites the predicate to the subject or, perhaps more precisely, which makes possible a necessary connection between predicate and subject. For if the predicate cannot be got out of the subject by mere analysis, there must be a third term which unites them.

This 'third term' cannot be anything in the sensible world. We cannot establish the possibility of a categorical imperative by referring to anything in the causal series of phenomena. Physical necessity would give us heteronomy, whereas we are looking for that which makes possible the principle of autonomy. And Kant finds it in the idea of freedom. Obviously, what he does is to look for the necessary condition of the possibility of obligation and of acting for the sake of duty alone, in accordance with a categorical imperative; and he finds this necessary condition in the idea of freedom.

We might say simply that Kant finds 'in freedom' the condition of the possibility of a categorical imperative. But, according to him, freedom cannot be *proved*. Hence it is perhaps more accurate to say that the condition of the possibility of a categorical imperative is to be found 'in the idea of freedom'. To say this is not, indeed, to say that the idea of freedom is a mere fiction in any ordinary sense. In the first place the *Critique of Pure Reason* has shown that freedom is a negative possibility, in the sense that the idea of freedom does not involve a logical contradiction. And in the second place we cannot act morally, for the sake of duty, except under the idea of freedom. Obligation, 'ought', implies freedom, freedom to obey or disobey the law. Nor can we regard ourselves as making universal laws, as morally autonomous, save under the idea of freedom. Practical reason or the will of a rational being 'must regard itself as free; that is, the will of such a being cannot be a will of its own except under the idea of freedom'.[1] The idea of freedom is thus *practically* necessary; it is a necessary condition of morality. At the same time the *Critique of Pure Reason* showed that freedom is not logically contradictory by showing that it must belong to the sphere of noumenal reality, and that the existence of such a sphere is not logically contradictory. And as our theoretical knowledge does not extend into this sphere, freedom is not susceptible of theoretical proof. But the assumption of freedom is a practical necessity for the moral agent; and it is thus no mere arbitrary fiction.

The practical necessity of the idea of freedom involves, therefore, our regarding ourselves as belonging, not only to the world of sense, the world which is ruled by determined causality, but also to the intelligible or noumenal world. Man can regard himself from two points of view. As belonging to the world of sense, he finds himself subject to natural laws (heteronomy). As belonging to the intelligible world, he finds himself under laws which have

[1] *G.*, p. 448; *Abb.*, p. 67.

their foundation in reason alone. 'And thus categorical imperatives are possible because the idea of freedom makes me a member of an intelligible world, in consequence of which, supposing that I were nothing else, all my actions *would* always conform to the autonomy of the will; but as I at the same time intuit myself as a member of the world of sense, my actions *ought* so to conform. And this *categorical* 'ought' implies a synthetic *a priori* proposition. . . .'[1]

The matter can be summed up thus in Kant's words. 'The question, therefore, how a categorical imperative is possible, can be answered to this extent, that one can assign the only presupposition on which it is possible, namely the idea of freedom; and one can also discern the necessity of this presupposition, which is sufficient for the *practical use* of reason, that is, for the conviction of the *validity of this imperative,* and hence of the moral law. But no human reason can ever discern how this presupposition itself is possible. However, on the presupposition that the will of an intelligence is free its *autonomy,* as the essential formal condition of its determination, is a necessary consequence.'[2] In saying here that no human reason can discern the possibility of freedom Kant is referring, of course, to positive possibility. We enjoy no intuitive insight into the sphere of noumenal reality. We cannot *prove* freedom, and hence we cannot *prove* the possibility of a categorical imperative. But we can indicate the condition under which alone a categorical imperative is possible. And the idea of this condition is a practical necessity for the moral agent. This, in Kant's view, is quite sufficient for morality, though the impossibility of proving freedom indicates, of course, the limitations of human theoretical knowledge.

10. What we have been saying about the practical necessity of the idea of freedom brings us naturally to the Kantian theory of the postulates of the practical reason. For freedom is one of them. The other two are immortality and God. The ideas, therefore, which Kant declared to be the main themes of metaphysics but which he also judged to transcend the limitations of reason in its theoretical use are here reintroduced as postulates of reason in its practical or moral use. And before we consider the Kantian theory of postulates in general, it may be as well if we consider briefly each of the three particular postulates.

(i) There is no need to say much more about freedom. As we have seen, a theoretical proof that a rational being is free is,

---

[1] *G.,* p. 454; *Abb.,* pp. 73-4.   [2] *G.,* p. 461; *Abb.,* p. 81.

according to Kant, impossible for the human reason. None the less it cannot be shown that freedom is not possible. And the moral law compels us to assume it and therefore authorizes us to assume it. The moral law compels us to assume it inasmuch as the concept of freedom and the concept of the supreme principle of morality 'are so inseparably united that one might define practical freedom as independence of the will on anything but the moral law alone'.[1] Because of this inseparable connection the moral law is said to postulate freedom.

We must note, however, the difficult position in which Kant involves himself. As there is no faculty of intellectual intuition, we cannot observe actions which belong to the noumenal sphere: all the actions which we can observe, either internally or externally, must be objects of the internal or external senses. This means that they are all given in time and subject to the laws of causality. We cannot, therefore, make a distinction between two types of experienced actions, saying that these are free while those are determined. If, then, we assume that man, as a rational being, is free, we are compelled to hold that the same actions can be both determined and free.

Kant is, of course, well aware of this difficulty. If we wish to save freedom, he remarks, 'no other way remains than to ascribe the existence of a thing, so far as it is determinable in time, and therefore also its causality according to the law of *natural necessity*, to *appearance alone*, and to ascribe *freedom* to precisely *the same being as a thing in itself*'.[2] And he then asks, 'How can a man be called completely free at the same moment and in regard to the same action in which he is subject to an inevitable natural necessity?'[3] His answer is given in terms of time-conditions. In so far as a man's existence is subject to time-conditions, his actions form part of the mechanical system of Nature and are determined by antecedent causes. 'But the very same subject, being on the other hand also conscious of himself as a thing in itself, considers his existence also *in so far as it is not subject to time-conditions*, and he regards himself as determinable only through laws which he gives himself through reason.'[4] And to be determinable only through self-imposed laws is to be free.

In Kant's view this position is supported by the testimony of conscience. When I look on my acts which were contrary to the

[1] *Pr.R.*, 167–8; *Abb.*, p. 187.   [2] *Pr.R.*, 170; *Abb.*, p. 189.
[3] *Pr.R.*, 171; *Abb.*, p. 189.   [4] *Pr.R.*, 175; *Abb.*, p. 191.

moral law precisely as past, I tend to attribute them to excusing causal factors. But the feeling of guilt remains; and the reason of this is that when the moral law, the law of my supersensible and supertemporal existence, is in question, reason recognizes no distinctions of time. It simply recognizes the action as mine, without reference to the time of its performance.

The statement, however, that man is noumenally free and empirically determined in regard to the very same actions is a hard saying. But it is one which, given his premises, Kant cannot avoid.

(ii) Before we come directly to the second postulate of the practical reason, namely immortality, it is necessary to say something about Kant's conception of the *summum bonum*, a term which, literally translated, means the highest or supreme good. Indeed, without some understanding of what Kant has to say on this subject we cannot follow his doctrine either of the second postulate or of the third, namely that of God.

Reason, even in its practical function, seeks an unconditioned totality. And this means that it seeks the unconditioned totality of the *object* of practical reason or the will, to which object the name of *summum bonum* is given. This term is, however, ambiguous. It may mean the supreme or highest good in the sense of that good which is not itself conditioned. Or it may mean the perfect good in the sense of a whole which is not itself a part of a greater whole. Now, virtue is the supreme and unconditioned good. But it does not follow that it is the perfect good in the sense that it is the total object of the desires of a rational being. And in point of fact happiness must also be included in the concept of a perfect good. If, therefore, we understand by *summum bonum* the perfect good, it includes both virtue and happiness.

It is very important to understand Kant's view of the relation between these two elements of the perfect good. The connection between them is not logical. If the connection between them were logical or analytic, as Kant puts it, the endeavour to be virtuous, that is, to make one's will accord perfectly with the moral law, would be the same as the rational pursuit of happiness. And if this were what Kant meant to affirm, he would be contradicting his constantly repeated conviction that happiness is not and cannot be the ground of the moral law. The connection, therefore, between the two elements of the perfect good is synthetic, in the sense that virtue produces happiness, as a cause produces its effect.

The *summum bonum* 'means the whole, the perfect good, in which, however, virtue as the condition is always the supreme good, because it has no condition above it; whereas happiness, while it is certainly pleasant to him who possesses it, is not of itself absolutely and in every respect good, but always presupposes morally right behaviour as its condition'.[1]

The truth of the proposition that virtue and happiness constitute the two elements of the perfect good cannot, therefore, be discovered by analysis. A man who is seeking his happiness cannot discover by analysis of this idea that he is virtuous. Nor can a virtuous man, whatever the Stoics may have said, discover that he is happy by analysing the idea of being virtuous. The two ideas are distinct. At the same time the proposition, though synthetic, is *a priori*. The connection between virtue and happiness is practically necessary, in the sense that we recognize that virtue ought to produce happiness. We cannot say, of course, that the desire of happiness must be the motive for pursuing virtue. For to say this would be to contradict the whole idea of acting for the sake of duty and would substitute heteronomy for autonomy of the will. But we must recognize virtue as the efficient cause of happiness. For the moral law, according to Kant, commands us to promote the *summum bonum*, in which virtue and happiness are related as conditions to conditioned, as cause to effect.

But how can we possibly hold that virtue necessarily produces happiness? The empirical evidence does not appear to warrant our making any such assertion. Even if it sometimes happens that virtue and happiness are actually found together, this is a purely contingent fact. We thus seem to arrive at an antinomy. On the one hand the practical reason demands a necessary connection between virtue and happiness. On the other hand the empirical evidence shows that there is no such necessary connection.

Kant's solution to this difficulty consists in showing that the assertion that virtue necessarily produces happiness is only conditionally false. That is to say, it is false only on condition that we take existence in this world to be the only sort of existence that a rational being can have, and if we take the assertion as meaning that virtue exercises in this sensible world a causality productive of happiness. The statement that the search for happiness produces virtue would be *absolutely* false; but the statement that virtue produces happiness is false, not absolutely, but only

[1] *Pr.R.*, 199; *Abb.*, pp. 206–7.

conditionally. It can, therefore, be true if I am justified in thinking that I exist, not only as a physical object in this sensible world, but also as a noumenon in an intelligible and supersensible world. And the moral law, being inseparably connected with the idea of freedom, demands that I should believe this. We must take it, therefore, that the realization of the *summum bonum* is possible, the first element, namely virtue (the supreme or highest good), producing the second element, happiness, if not immediately, yet at least mediately (through the agency of God).

(iii) The conception of existence in another world has already been referred to in what has just been said. But Kant actually approaches the postulate of immortality through a consideration of the first element of the perfect good, namely virtue.

The moral law commands us to promote the *summum bonum*, which is the necessary object of the rational will. This does not mean that the moral law commands us to pursue virtue because it causes happiness. But we are commanded by the practical reason to pursue virtue which causes happiness. Now, the virtue which we are commanded to strive after is, according to Kant, the complete accordance of will and feeling with the moral law. But this complete accordance with the moral law is holiness, and this is 'a perfection of which no rational being of the sensible world is capable at any moment of its existence'.[1] If, therefore, perfect virtue is commanded by reason in its practical use, and if at the same time it is not attainable by a human being at any given moment, the first element of the perfect good must be realized in the form of an indefinite, unending progress towards the ideal. 'But this endless progress is possible only on the supposition of the unending duration of the existence and personality of the same rational being, which is called the immortality of the soul.'[2] As, therefore, the attainment of the first element of the *summum bonum*, the pursuit of which is commanded by the moral law, is possible only on the supposition that the soul is immortal, immortality of the soul is a postulate of the pure practical reason. It is not demonstrable by reason in its theoretical use, which can show only that immortality is not logically impossible. But as the idea of immortality is inseparably connected with the moral law, immortality must be postulated. To deny it is, in the long run, to deny the moral law itself.

A variety of objections have been brought against Kant's

[1] *Pr.R.*, 220; *Abb.*, p. 218.   [2] *Ibid.*

doctrine about the second postulate. It has been objected, for instance, that he contradicts himself. On the one hand, the attainment of virtue must be possible; for it is commanded by the practical reason. If, therefore, it is not attainable in this life, there must be another life in which it is attainable. On the other hand, it is never attainable, either in this life or in any other. There is only unending progress towards an unattainable ideal. It seems, therefore, that the moral law commands the impossible. It has also been objected that we cannot regard the attainment of holiness as a command of the moral law. But, whatever may be the cogency of these objections, Kant himself laid considerable stress on the idea of the moral law commanding holiness as an ideal goal. In his opinion, denial of this command involves a degradation of the moral law, a lowering of standards to fit the weakness of human nature.

(iv) The same moral law which leads us to postulate immortality as the condition of obeying the command to attain holiness leads us also to postulate the existence of God as the condition for a necessary synthetic connection between virtue and happiness.

Happiness is described by Kant as 'the state of a rational being in the world with whom in the totality of his existence *everything goes according to his wish and will*'.[1] It depends, therefore, on the harmony of physical Nature with man's wish and will. But the rational being who is in the world is not the author of the world, nor is he in a position to govern Nature in such a way that a necessary connection is established in fact between virtue and happiness, the latter being proportioned to the former. If, therefore, there is an *a priori* synthetic connection between virtue and happiness, in the sense that happiness ought to follow and be proportioned to virtue as its condition, we must postulate 'the existence of a cause of the whole of Nature which is distinct from Nature and which contains the ground of this connection, namely of the exact harmony of happiness with morality'.[2]

Further, this being must be conceived as apportioning happiness to morality according to the conception of law. For happiness is to be apportioned to morality in the sense that it is to be apportioned according to the degree in which finite rational beings make the moral law the determining principle of their volition. But a being which is capable of acting according to the conception of

[1] *Pr.R.*, 224; *Abb.*, p. 221.   [2] *Pr.R.*, 225; *Abb.*, p. 221.

law is intelligent or rational; and his causality will be his will. Hence the being which is postulated as the cause of Nature must be conceived as acting by intelligence and will. It must, in other words, be conceived as God. Further, we must conceive God as omniscient, as He is conceived as knowing all our inner states; as omnipotent, because He is conceived as capable of bringing into existence a world in which happiness is exactly proportioned to virtue; and so on with other attributes.

Kant reminds us that he is not now affirming what he denied in the first *Critique*, namely that the speculative reason can demonstrate the existence and attributes of God. The admission of God's existence is, of course, an admission by the reason; but this admission is an act of faith. We may speak of it as practical faith as it is connected with duty. We have a duty to promote the *summum bonum*. We can therefore postulate its possibility. But we cannot really conceive the possibility of the perfect good being realized except on the supposition that there exists a God. Hence, though the moral law does not directly enjoin faith in God, it lies at the basis of such faith.

(v) As Kant notes, the three postulates have this in common, that 'they all proceed from the principle of morality, which is not a postulate but a law'.[1] The question arises, however, whether they can be said to extend our knowledge. Kant answers, 'Certainly, but *only from a practical point of view*'.[2] And the customary statement of his view is that the postulates increase our knowledge, not from the theoretical, but only from the practical point of view. But it is by no means immediately clear what is meant by this. If Kant meant merely that it is pragmatically useful, in the sense of morally beneficial, to act as if we were free, as if we had immortal souls, and as if there were a God, his view, whether we agreed with it or not, would present no great difficulty, so far as understanding it was concerned. But in point of fact he appears to mean much more than this.

We are told, indeed, that inasmuch as neither free, immortal soul nor God are given as objects of intuition, 'there is, therefore, no extension of the knowledge *of given supersensible objects*'.[3] This seems to be pretty well a tautology. For if God and the soul are not given as objects, we obviously cannot know them as given objects. But we are also told that though God and the free,

---

[1] *Pr.R.*, 238; *Abb.*, p. 229.   [2] *Pr.R.*, 240; *Abb.*, p. 231.
[3] *Pr.R.*, 243; *Abb.*, p. 233

immortal soul are not given as objects of any intellectual intuition, the theoretical reason's knowledge of the supersensible is increased to this extent that it is compelled to admit 'that there are such objects'.[1] Further, given the practical reason's assurance of the existence of God and the soul, the theoretical reason can think these supersensible realities by means of the categories; and the latter, when so applied, are 'not empty but possess meaning'.[2] To be sure, Kant insists that the categories can be employed to conceive the supersensible in a definite manner 'only in so far as it is defined by such predicates as are necessarily connected with the pure practical purpose given *a priori* and with its possibility'.[3] But the fact remains that through the aid provided by the practical reason Ideas which for the speculative reason were simply regulative take on definite form and shape as ways of thinking supersensible realities, even if these realities are not given as objects of intuition but are affirmed because of their connection with the moral law.

It seems to me, therefore, to be arguable that what Kant is doing is to substitute a new type of metaphysics for the metaphysics which he rejected in the *Critique of Pure Reason*. In the case of the Ideas of a transcendental ego and of God the speculative reason is able to give body to them, as it were, thanks to the practical reason. And this is possible because the latter enjoys a position of primacy when the two co-operate.[4] 'If practical reason could not assume and think as given anything other than that which *speculative* reason can offer it from its own insight, then the latter would have the primacy. But if we suppose that practical reason has of itself original *a priori* principles with which certain theoretical positions are inseparably united, though they are at the same time withdrawn from any possible insight of the speculative reason (which they, however, must not contradict), then the question is, which interest is the superior (not which must give way, for they do not necessarily conflict). . . .'[5] That is to say, the question is whether the interest of speculative reason is to prevail, so that it obstinately rejects all that is offered from any other source than itself, or whether the interest of practical reason is to prevail, so that speculative reason takes over, as it were, the

---

[1] *Pr.R.*, 244; *Abb.*, p. 233.   [2] *Pr.R.*, 246; *Abb.*, p. 234.
[3] *Pr.R.*, 255; *Abb.*, p. 239.
[4] This way of speaking can, of course, be misleading. For ultimately, as we saw earlier, there is only one reason, though it has distinguishable functions or modes of employment.
[5] *Pr.R.*, 216–17; *Abb.*, p. 216.

propositions offered it by the practical reason and tries 'to unite them with its own concepts'.[1] In Kant's opinion, the interest of practical reason should prevail. To be sure, this cannot be maintained if practical reason is taken as dependent on sensible inclinations and desires. For in this case speculative reason would have to adopt all sorts of arbitrary fancies. (Kant mentions Mohammed's idea of Paradise.) In other words, Kant does not wish to encourage mere wishful thinking. But if practical reason is taken as being the pure reason in its practical capacity, that is, as judging according to *a priori* principles; and if certain theoretical positions are inseparably connected with the exercise of pure reason in its practical function; then the pure reason in its theoretical capacity must accept these positions and attempt to think them consistently. If we do not accept this primacy of the practical reason, we admit a conflict within reason itself; for pure practical and pure speculative reason are fundamentally one reason.

That Kant is really engaged in creating a metaphysics based on the moral consciousness seems to me to be clear also from the fact that he appears to admit differences of degree in practical knowledge. The idea of freedom is so united with the concepts of moral law and duty that we cannot admit obligation and deny freedom. 'I ought' implies 'I can' (that is, I can obey or disobey). But we cannot say that the conception of the *summum bonum* or perfect good implies the existence of God in precisely the same way that obligation implies freedom. Reason cannot decide with absolute certainty whether the apportioning of happiness to virtue implies the existence of God. That is to say, it cannot exclude absolutely the possibility that a state of affairs which would render possible this apportioning might come about by the operation of natural laws without the supposition of a wise and good Creator. There is room, therefore, for choice; that is, for practical faith resting on an act of the will. True, we cannot 'demonstrate' freedom, and so it is in a sense an object of belief. But the fact remains that we cannot accept the existence of the moral law and deny freedom whereas it is possible to accept the existence of the moral law and doubt the existence of God, even if faith in God's existence is more in accordance with the demands of reason.

It would be misleading, therefore, to say simply that Kant rejects metaphysics. True, he rejects dogmatic metaphysics when

[1] *P.R.*, 216–17; *Abb.*, p. 216

it is considered either as an *a priori* construction based on *a priori* theoretical principles or as a kind of prolongation or extension of scientific explanation of phenomena. But even if he does not call the general theory of the postulates 'metaphysics', this is what it really amounts to. It is a metaphysics based on the moral consciousness of law and obligation. It does not provide us with an intuition of supersensible reality, and its arguments are conditional on the validity of the moral consciousness and on the Kantian analysis of moral experience. But there are, none the less, reasoned positions in regard to supersensible reality. And we can quite properly speak about a Kantian 'metaphysics'.

11. We have seen that morality, according to Kant, does not presuppose religion. That is to say, man does not need the idea of God to be able to recognize his duty; and the ultimate motive of moral action is duty for duty's sake, not obedience to the commands of God. At the same time morality leads to religion. 'Through the idea of the supreme good as object and final end of the pure practical reason the moral law leads to religion, that is, to the recognition of all duties as divine commands, *not as sanctions, that is, as arbitrary commands of an alien will which are contingent in themselves*, but as essential *laws* of every free will in itself, which, however, must be looked on as commands of the supreme Being, because it is only from a morally perfect (holy and good) and at the same time all-powerful will, and consequently only through harmony with this will, that we can hope to attain the highest good, which the moral law makes it our duty to take as the object of our endeavour.'[1] The moral law commands us to make ourselves worthy of happiness rather than to be happy or make ourselves happy. But because virtue should produce happiness, and because this completion of the *summum bonum* can be achieved only through divine agency, we are entitled to hope for happiness through the agency of a God whose will, as a holy will, desires that His creatures should be worthy of happiness, while, as an omnipotent will, it can confer this happiness on them. '*The hope* of happiness first begins with religion only.'[2]

This point of view reappears in *Religion within the Bounds of Pure Reason* (1793). Thus the preface to the first edition opens in this way. 'Morality, in so far as it is grounded in the concept of man as a being who is free but at the same time subjects himself through his reason to unconditional laws, needs neither the idea

[1] *Pr.R.*, 233; *Abb.*, p. 226.   [2] *Pr.R.*, 235; *Abb.*, p. 227.

of another being above man for the latter to recognize his duty, nor any other motive than the law itself for man to fulfil his duty.'[1] At the same time, however, the question of the final result of moral action and of a possible harmonization between the moral and the natural orders cannot be a matter of indifference to the human reason. And in the long run 'morality leads inevitably to religion'.[2] For we cannot see any other way in which this harmonization could take place than through divine agency.

True religion, for Kant, consists in this, 'that in all our duties we regard God as the universal legislator who is to be reverenced'.[3] But what does it mean to reverence God? It means obeying the moral law, acting for the sake of duty. In other words, Kant attached little value to religious practices in the sense of expressions of adoration and prayer, whether public or private. And this attitude is summed up in the often-quoted words: 'Everything which, apart from a moral way of life, man believes himself capable of doing to please God is mere religious delusion and spurious worship of God.'[4]

This indifference to religious practices in the ordinary sense is coupled, of course, with an indifference to credal varieties as such. The words 'as such' are, I think, required. For some beliefs would be ruled out as incompatible with true morality, while others would be inacceptable to pure reason. But any idea of a unique revelation of religious truths, and still more of an authoritarian Church as custodian and accredited interpreter of revelation, is rejected by Kant. I do not mean that he rejected altogether the idea of a visible Christian Church, with a faith based on the Scriptures; for he did not. But the visible Church is for him only an approximation to the ideal of the universal invisible Church, which is, or would be, the spiritual union of all men in virtue and the moral service of God.

It is not my intention to discuss Kant's treatment of individual dogmas of Christianity.[5] But it is perhaps worth noting that he shows a strong tendency to strip away, as it were, the historical associations of certain dogmas and to find a meaning which fits in with his own philosophy. Thus he does not deny original sin: on the contrary, he affirms it against those who imagine that man is naturally perfect. But the ideas of an historical Fall and of

---

[1] *Rel.*, p. 3; *G.-H.*, p. 3   [2] *Rel.*, p. 6; *G.-H.*, p. 5.
[3] *Rel.*, p. 103; *G.-H.*, p. 95.   [4] *Rel.*, p. 170; *G.-H.*, p. 158.
[5] The reader can consult, for example, *Kant's Philosophy of Religion* by C. C. J. Webb (see Bibliography).

inherited sin give place to the conception of a fundamental propensity to act out of mere self-love and without regard to the universal moral laws, a propensity which is an empirical fact and of which we cannot provide an ultimate explanation, though the Bible does so in picture-language. In this way Kant affirms the dogma in the sense that he verbally admits it, while at the same time he interprets it rationalistically in such a way that he is able to deny on the one hand the extreme Protestant doctrine of the total depravity of human nature and on the other the optimistic theories of the natural perfection of man. This tendency to retain Christian dogmas while giving a rationalistic account of their content becomes much more evident with Hegel. But the latter, with his reasoned distinction between the ways of thinking characteristic of religion and of philosophy, produced a much more profound philosophy of religion than that of Kant.

We can say, therefore, that Kant's interpretation of religion was moralistic and rationalistic in character. At the same time this statement can be misleading. For it may suggest that in the content of true religion as Kant understands it every element of what we may call piety towards God is missing. But this is not the case. He does, indeed, show scant sympathy with mystics; but we have already seen that for him religion means looking on our duties as divine commands (in the sense at least that the fulfilment of them fits into the end which is willed by the holy will of God as the final end of creation). And in the *Opus Postumum* the conception of consciousness of duty as a consciousness of the divine presence comes to the fore. To be sure, it is impossible to know how Kant would have systematized and developed the various ideas contained in the notes which form this volume, if he had had the opportunity to do so. But it appears that though the idea of the moral law as the one valid path to faith in God was retained intact, Kant was inclined to lay greater stress on the immanence of God and on an awareness of our moral freedom and of moral obligation as an awareness of the divine presence.

12. It cannot be denied, I think, that there is a certain grandeur in Kant's ethical theory. His uncompromising exaltation of duty and his insistence on the value of the human personality certainly merit respect. Moreover, a great deal of what he says finds a genuine echo in the moral consciousness. Thus, however much particular moral convictions may differ in different people, the conviction that cases arise when in some sense at least consequences

are irrelevant and the moral law must be obeyed, whatever the consequences may be, is a common feature of the moral consciousness. If we have any moral convictions at all, we all feel, to use popular language, that the line must be drawn somewhere, even if we do not all draw it in the same place. The maxim *Fiat iustitia, ruat coelum* can easily be understood in terms of the ordinary man's moral outlook. Again, Kant rightly drew attention to the universal character of the moral law. The fact that different societies and different individuals have had somewhat different moral ideas does not alter the fact that the moral judgment makes, as such, a universal claim. When I say that I ought to do this or that, I imply at least that anyone else in precisely the same situation ought to act likewise; for I am saying that it is the right thing to do. Even if one adopts an 'emotive' theory of ethics, one must allow for this universal claim of the moral judgment. The statement that I ought to perform action X is obviously, in this as in other respects, of a different type from the statement that I like olives, even if the former is held to be the expression of an emotion or of an attitude rather than of the application of a supreme principle of reason.[1]

At the same time, even if Kant's ethical theory reflects to some extent the moral consciousness, it is open to serious objections. It is easy to understand how Hegel among others criticized Kant's account of the supreme principle of morality on the ground of formalism and abstractness. Of course, from one point of view objections against Kant's ethical theory on the ground of formalism and 'emptiness' are beside the mark. For in pure, as distinct from applied, ethics he was engaged precisely in ascertaining the 'formal' element in the moral judgment, prescinding from the empirically given 'matter'. And what else, it may be pertinently asked, could the formal element possibly be but formalistic? Again, what is the value of the charge of emptiness when the categorical imperative, though applicable to empirically given material, was never intended to be a premiss for the deduction of concrete rules of conduct by sheer analysis? The categorical imperative is meant to serve as a test or criterion of the morality of our subjective principles of volition, not as a premiss for analytic deduction of a concrete moral code. True; but then the question arises whether the Kantian principle of morality is really

---

[1] I do not mean to imply that the defenders of the emotive theory of ethics in its various developed forms do not allow for this feature of the moral judgment.

capable of serving as a test or criterion. We have already noted the difficulty that there is in understanding precisely what is meant by speaking of a rational agent as 'being able' or 'not being able' to will that his maxims should become universal laws. And it may well be that this difficulty is connected with the abstractness and emptiness of the categorical imperative.

Some philosophers would object to Kant's rationalism, to the idea, that is to say, that the moral law rests ultimately on reason and that its supreme principles are promulgated by the reason. But let us assume that Kant was right in his view that the moral law is promulgated by reason. The question then arises whether, as he thought, the concept of duty possesses an absolute primacy or whether the concept of the good is primary, the concept of duty being subordinate to it. And, apart from any other consideration, it is arguable that the second of these theories is better able to serve as a framework for interpreting the moral consciousness. True, any teleological theory of ethics which takes the form of the utilitarianism of, for example, Bentham, lays itself open to the charge of changing the specifically moral judgment into a non-moral empirical judgment, and so of explaining morals by explaining it away. But it does not follow that this must be true of every teleological interpretation of morals. And the question whether it does or does not follow can hardly be regarded as having been finally settled by Kant.

As for Kant's philosophy of religion, it stands in certain obvious ways under the influence of the Enlightenment. Thus in interpreting the religious consciousness Kant attaches too little importance to the historical religions; that is, to religion as it has actually existed. Hegel afterwards attempted to remedy this defect. But, generally considered, the Kantian philosophy of religion is clearly a feature of his attempt to reconcile the world of Newtonian physics, the world of empirical reality governed by causal laws which exclude freedom, with the world of the moral consciousness, the world of freedom. The theoretical reason, of itself, can tell us only that it sees no impossibility in the concept of freedom and in the idea of supra-empirical, noumenal reality. The concept of the moral law, through its inseparable connection with the idea of freedom, gives us a practical assurance of the existence of such a reality and of our belonging to it as rational beings. And theoretical reason, on the basis of this assurance, can attempt to think noumenal reality so far as the practical reason warrants our assuming it. But, so far as we can see, it is God alone who is capable of achieving the ultimate harmonization of the two realms. If, therefore, the 'interest' of practical reason should prevail, and if the moral law demands, at least by implication, this ultimate harmonization, we are justified in making an act of faith in God, even if reason in its theoretical function is incapable of demonstrating that God exists.

But though we are entitled to turn to religion and to hope from God the creation of a state of affairs in which happiness will be apportioned to virtue, it is obvious that we are left here and now with a juxtaposition of the realm of natural necessity and that of freedom. Inasmuch as reason tells us that there is no logical impossibility in the latter, we can say that the two are logically compatible. But this is hardly enough to satisfy the demands of philosophical reflection. For one thing, freedom finds expression in actions which belong to the empirical, natural order. And the mind seeks to find some connection between the two orders or realms. It may not, indeed, be able to find an objective connection in the sense that it can prove theoretically the existence of noumenal reality and show precisely how empirical and noumenal reality are objectively related. But it seeks at least a subjective connection in the sense of a justification, on the side of the mind itself, of the transition from the way of thinking which is in accordance with the principles of Nature to the way of thinking which is in accordance with the principles of freedom.

To find, however, Kant's treatment of this subject we have to turn to the third *Critique*, namely the *Critique of Judgment*.

CHAPTER XV

KANT (6): AESTHETICS AND TELEOLOGY

*The mediating function of judgment—The analytic of the beauti-
ful—The analytic of the sublime—The deduction of pure aesthetic
judgments—Fine art and genius—The dialectic of the aesthetic
judgment—The beautiful as a symbol of the morally good—The
teleological judgment—Teleology and mechanism—Physico-
theology and ethico-theology.*

1. AT the end of the last chapter mention was made of the need
for some principle of connection, at least on the side of the mind,
between the world of natural necessity and the world of freedom.
Kant refers to this need in his introduction to the *Critique of
Judgment*.[1] Between the domain of the concept of Nature or
sensible reality and the domain of the concept of freedom or
supersensible reality there is a gulf of such a kind that no transition from the first to the second is possible by means of the
theoretical use of reason. It appears, therefore, that there are two
sundered worlds, of which the one can have no influence on the
other. Yet the world of freedom must have an influence on the
world of Nature, if the principles of practical reason are to be
realized in action. And it must, therefore, be possible to think
Nature in such a way that it is compatible at least with the
possibility of the attainment in it of ends in accordance with the
laws of freedom. Accordingly, there must be some ground or
principle of unity which 'makes possible the transition from the
way of thinking which is in accordance with the principles of the
one (world) to the way of thinking which is in accordance with
the principles of the other'.[2] In other words, we are looking for a
connecting link between theoretical philosophy, which Kant calls
the philosophy of Nature, and practical or moral philosophy which
is grounded on the concept of freedom. And Kant finds this
connecting link in a critique of judgment which is 'a means to
unite in one whole the two parts of philosophy'.[3]

---

[1] *The Critique of Judgment* (*Kritik der Urteilskraft*), contained in Volume V of
the critical edition of Kant's works, will be referred to in footnotes as *J*.; and references will be given according to sections. Corresponding references will also be given,
by page, to the translation by J. H. Bernard (see Bibliography), which will be
referred to as *Bd*.   [2] *J*., xx; *Bd*., p. 13.   [3] *Ibid*.

To explain why Kant turns to a study of judgment in order to find this connecting link, reference must be made to his theory of the powers or faculties of the mind. In a table given at the end of the introduction to the *Critique of Judgment*[1] he distinguishes three powers or faculties of the mind.[2] These are the cognitive faculty in general, the power of feeling pleasure and displeasure, and the faculty of desire. This suggests at once that feeling mediates in some sense between cognition and desire. He then distinguishes three particular cognitive powers, namely understanding (*Verstand*), judgment (*Urteilskraft*), and reason (*Vernunft*). And this suggests that judgment mediates in some sense between understanding and reason, and that it bears some relation to feeling.

Now, in the *Critique of Pure Reason* we have considered the *a priori* categories and principles of the understanding, which exercise a 'constitutive' function and make possible a knowledge of objects, of Nature. We also considered the Ideas of pure reason in its speculative capacity, which exercise a 'regulative' and not a constitutive function. In the *Critique of Practical Reason* it has been shown that there is an *a priori* principle of pure reason in its practical employment, which legislates for desire (*in Ansehung des Begehrungsvermögens*).[3] It remains, therefore, to inquire whether the power of judgment, which is said by Kant to be a mediating power between the understanding and the reason, possesses its own *a priori* principles. If so, we must also inquire whether these principles exercise a constitutive or a regulative function. In particular, do they give rules *a priori* to feeling; that is, to the power of feeling pleasure and displeasure? If so, we shall have a nice, tidy scheme. The understanding gives laws *a priori* to phenomenal reality, making possible a theoretical knowledge of Nature. The pure reason, in its practical employment, legislates with regard to desire. And judgment legislates for feeling, which is, as it were, a middle term between cognition and desire, just as judgment itself mediates between understanding and reason.

In the technical terms of the critical philosophy, therefore, the problem can be stated in such a way as to throw into relief the similarity of purpose in the three *Critiques*. Has the power of judgment its own *a priori* principle or principles? And, if so, what

---

[1] *J.*, LVIII; *Bd.*, p. 41.
[2] The term used for mind in general is *das Gemüt*. As already noted, Kant uses his term in a very wide sense to cover all psychical powers and activities.
[3] *J.*, V; *Bd.*, p. 2.

are their functions and field of application? Further, if the power or faculty of judgment is related, in regard to its *a priori* principles, to feeling in a manner analogous to the ways in which understanding is related to cognition and reason (in its practical employment) to desire, we can see that the *Critique of Judgment* forms a necessary part of the critical philosophy, and not simply an appendage which might or might not be there.

But what does Kant mean by judgment in this context? 'The faculty of judgment in general', he tells us, 'is the power of thinking the particular as being contained in the universal.'[1] But we must distinguish between determinant and reflective judgment. 'If the universal (the rule, the principle, the law) is given, then the faculty of judgment which subsumes the particular under it is *determinant*, this being true also when the faculty as a transcendental faculty of judgment gives *a priori* the conditions under which alone the particular can be subsumed under the universal. But if only the particular is given, for which the faculty of judgment is to find the universal, then judgment is merely *reflective*.'[2] In considering the *Critique of Pure Reason* we saw that there are, according to Kant, *a priori* categories and principles of the understanding which are ultimately given in the structure of this faculty. And judgment simply subsumes particulars under these 'universals' as under something given *a priori*. This is an example of *determinant* judgment. But there are obviously many general laws which are not given but have to be discovered. Thus the empirical laws of physics are not given *a priori*. Nor are they given *a posteriori* in the sense in which particulars are given. We know *a priori*, for instance, that all phenomena are members of causal series; but we do not know particular causal laws *a priori*. Nor are they given to us *a posteriori* as objects of experience. We have to discover the general empirical laws under which we subsume particulars. This is the work of *reflective* judgment, the function of which, therefore, is not merely subsumptive; for it has to find the universal, as Kant puts it, under which the particulars can be subsumed. And it is with this reflective judgment that we are concerned here.

Now, from our point of view at least empirical laws are contingent. But the scientist is always trying to subsume more particular under more general empirical laws. He does not leave his laws alongside one another, so to speak, without endeavouring

[1] *J.*, xxv; *Bd.*, p. 16.   [2] *J.*, xxvi; *Bd.*, pp. 16–17.

to establish relations between them. He aims at constructing a system of interrelated laws. And this means that he is guided in his inquiry by the concept of Nature as an intelligible unity. The *a priori* principles of science are grounded in our understanding. But 'the special empirical laws . . . must be considered . . . as if (*als ob*) an understanding which is not ours had given them for our powers of cognition, to make possible a system of experience according to special laws of Nature'.[1] Kant adds that he does not intend to imply that the scientist must presuppose the existence of God. What he means is that the scientist presupposes a unity of Nature of such a kind as would obtain if Nature were the work of a divine mind; if, that is to say, it were an intelligible system adapted to our cognitive faculties. The idea of God is here employed simply in its regulative function. And Kant's point is really simply this, that all scientific inquiry is guided by the at least tacit assumption that Nature is an intelligible unity, 'intelligible' being understood in relation to our cognitive faculties. It is on this principle that reflective judgment proceeds. It is an *a priori* principle in the sense that it is not derived from experience but is a presupposition of all scientific inquiry. But it is not an *a priori* principle in precisely the same sense that the principles considered in the *Transcendental Analytic* are *a priori*. That is to say, it is not a necessary condition for there being objects of experience at all. Rather is it a necessary *heuristic* principle which guides us in our study of the objects of experience.

The concept of Nature as unified through the common ground of its laws in a superhuman intelligence or mind which adapts the system to our cognitive faculties is the concept of the purposiveness or finality of Nature. 'Through this concept Nature is represented as though an intelligence contained the ground of the unity of the manifold of Nature's empirical laws. The purposiveness of Nature is thus a special *a priori* concept which has its ultimate source in the faculty of reflective judgment.'[2] And the principle of the purposiveness or finality of Nature is, Kant maintains, a transcendental principle of the faculty or power of judgment. It is transcendental because it concerns possible objects of empirical knowledge in general and does not itself rest on empirical observation. Its transcendental character becomes evident, according to Kant, if we consider the maxims of judgment to which it gives rise. Among the examples given[3] are 'Nature takes the shortest

[1] *J.*, xxvii; *Bd.*, p. 18.   [2] *J.*, xxviii; *Bd.*, pp. 18–19.   [3] *J.*, xxxi; *Bd.*, p. 20.

way' (*lex parsimoniae*) and 'Nature makes no leaps' (*lex continui in natura*). Such maxims are not empirical generalizations; rather are they *a priori* rules or maxims which guide us in our empirical investigation of Nature. And they rest on the general *a priori* principle of the purposiveness or finality of Nature; that is, of the latter's being adapted to our cognitive faculties in respect of the ultimate unity of its empirical laws.

The validity of this *a priori* principle of judgment is subjective rather than objective. In Kantian terminology it does not prescribe to or legislate for Nature considered in itself. It is not a constitutive principle in the sense of a necessary condition for there being any objects at all. And it does not entail the proposition that there is, in an ontological sense, finality in Nature. We cannot deduce from it *a priori* that there actually are final causes operating in Nature. It legislates for the reflective judgment, telling it to regard Nature as though it were a purposive whole, adapted to our cognitive faculties. And if we say that the principle makes Nature possible, we mean that it makes possible an empirical knowledge of Nature in regard to its empirical laws, not that it makes Nature possible in the same sense in which the categories and principles of the understanding make it possible. Of course, the principle is, in a real sense, empirically verified. But in itself it is *a priori*, not the result of observation; and, as an *a priori* principle, it is a necessary condition, not of objects themselves, which are considered as already given, but of the employment of reflective judgment in investigating these objects. Kant is not, therefore, enunciating a metaphysical dogma, namely that there are final causes operating in Nature. He is saying that, because reflective judgment is what it is, all empirical inquiry into Nature involves from the start regarding Nature *as though* it embodied a system of empirical laws which are unified through their common ground in an intelligence other than ours and which are adapted to our cognitive faculties.

Of course, we cannot regard Nature as purposive without attributing purposiveness or finality to Nature. Kant is quite well aware of this fact. 'But that the order of Nature in its particular laws, in this at least possible variety and heterogeneity which transcend our power of comprehension, is yet really adapted to our power of cognition, is, as far as we can discern, a contingent fact. And the discovery of this order is a task of the understanding, a task which is carried out with a view to a necessary end of the understanding, namely the unification of the principles of Nature. And the power of judgment must, then, attribute this end to Nature, because the understanding cannot prescribe any law to Nature in this respect.'[1] But the *a priori* attribution to Nature of finality or purposiveness does not constitute an *a priori* dogma about Nature in itself; it is an attribution with a view to our knowledge. In other words, the *a priori* principle of judgment is, as has already been said, a heuristic principle. If we then find in our empirical investigation that Nature fits in with this principle, this is, as far as we can see, a purely contingent fact. That it *must* fit, is an *a priori* assumption, a heuristic principle of judgment.

Now, the finality or purposiveness of Nature can be represented in two ways. In the first place the finality of a given object of experience can be represented as an accordance of the form of the object with the cognitive faculty, without, however, any reference of the form to a concept with a view to determinate knowledge of the object. The form of the object is considered as the ground of a pleasure which comes from the representation of the object. And when we judge that the representation is necessarily accompanied by this pleasure and that, as a consequence, the representation should be pleasurable for all (and not merely for the particular subject who happens here and now to perceive the form of the object), we have an aesthetic judgment. The object is called beautiful, and the faculty of judging universally on the basis of the pleasure which accompanies the representation is called taste.

In the second place the finality of a given object of experience can be represented as an 'accordance of its form with the possibility of the thing itself, according to a concept of the thing which precedes and contains the ground of its form'.[2] In other words, the thing is represented, in respect of its form, as fulfilling an end or purpose of Nature. And when we judge that this is the case, we have a teleological judgment.

A *Critique of Judgment*, therefore, must pay attention to both the aesthetic and the teleological judgment, distinguishing them carefully. The former is purely subjective, not in the sense that there is no universal claim in the judgment (for there is), but in the sense that it is a judgment about the accordance of the form of an object, whether a natural object or a work of art, with the cognitive faculties on the basis of the feeling caused by the representation of the object and not with reference to any concept.

---

[1] *J.*, xxxix; *Bd.*, p. 27.   [2] *J.*, xlviii–xlix; *Bd.*, p. 34.

Kant can say, therefore, that the faculty of judging aesthetically is 'a special power of judging things according to a rule, but not according to concepts'.[1] The teleological judgment, however, is objective in the sense that it judges that a given object fulfils a conceived purpose or end of Nature, and not that it is the ground of certain feelings in the subject. And Kant tells us that the power of making such judgments is 'not a special power but simply reflective judgment in general. . . .'[2]

Finally, reflective judgment's *a priori*, regulative concept of the purposiveness of Nature serves as a connecting link between the domain of the concept of Nature on the one hand and the domain of the concept of freedom on the other. For although it neither constitutes Nature, in the sense that the categories and principles of the understanding constitute Nature, nor legislates with a view to action, as does the *a priori* principle of pure practical reason, it enables us to think Nature as not being entirely alien, as it were, to the realization of ends. Works of art are phenomenal expressions of the noumenal realm of value; and the beauty which aesthetic appreciation of such works enables us to see in natural objects enables us to regard Nature itself as a phenomenal manifestation of the same noumenal reality, which Kant sometimes calls the 'supersensible substrate'.[3] And the concept of the purposiveness of Nature, which finds expression in the teleological judgment, enables us to conceive the possibility of an actualization of ends in Nature in harmony with the latter's laws.

Kant also puts the matter in this way. A study of the *a priori* principles of the understanding shows that we know Nature only as phenomenon. But at the same time it implies that there is a noumenal reality or 'supersensible reality'. Understanding, however, leaves the latter completely undetermined. As we saw when we considered the concepts of phenomenon and noumenon in connection with the first *Critique*, the term *noumenon* must be taken in its negative sense. Judgment, in virtue of its *a priori* principle for judging Nature, leads us to consider noumenal reality on the 'supersensible substrate', as well within as outside us, as determinable by means of the intellectual faculty. For it represents Nature as being a phenomenal expression of noumenal reality. And reason, by its *a priori* practical law, determines noumenal reality, showing us how we should conceive it. 'And thus the faculty of judgment makes possible the transition from the

[1] *J.*, LII; *Bd.*, p. 37.   [2] *J.*, LII; *Bd.*, p. 37.   [3] Cf. *J.*, LVI; *Bd.*, p. 40.

domain of the concept of Nature to that of the concept of freedom.'[1]

This section has been devoted to lines of thought which are outlined by Kant in his introduction to the *Critique of Judgment*. The main body of the work falls into two parts, the first dealing with aesthetic, the second with teleological judgment. And it is, of course, in these two parts that the main interest of the work lies. But once one turns to the detailed treatment of, for instance, the aesthetic judgment, one is tempted to consider it simply as Kant's aesthetic theory, that is, purely for its own sake, as though it were an isolated part of his philosophy. For this reason it seemed to me appropriate to dwell at some length on the lines of thought which, however involved they may be, at any rate serve to show that the third *Critique* was for Kant an integral part of his system and not a combination of two monographs dealing with subjects interesting in themselves but without intrinsic relation to the first two *Critiques*.

2. Following the usage of English writers on aesthetic, Kant called the judgment which pronounces a thing to be beautiful the judgment of taste (*das Geschmacksurteil*). The word 'taste' immediately suggests subjectivity; and we have already seen that in Kant's view the ground of this judgment is subjective. That is to say, a representation is referred by the imagination to the subject itself, to the feeling of pleasure or displeasure. The ground of our judgment that a thing is beautiful or ugly is the way in which our power of feeling is affected by the representation of the object. In modern language we might say that for Kant the judgment of taste is an emotive proposition, expressing feeling and not conceptual knowledge. As Kant observes, conceptual knowledge about a building is one thing; appreciation of its beauty is another.

But though the ground of the judgment of taste is subjective, what we actually say is obviously something about the thing, namely that it is beautiful. The ground for the statement consists in feeling; but when I say that an object is beautiful I am not simply making a statement about my private feelings. For such a statement would be an empirically verifiable (in principle at least) psychological judgment. It would not be a judgment of taste as such. The latter arises only when I pronounce a thing to be beautiful. There is room, therefore, for an analytic of the beautiful (*Analytik des Schönen*), even though beauty cannot be regarded

[1] *J.*, LVI; *Bd.*, p. 40.

as an objective quality of an object without relation to the subjective ground of the judgment that the object is beautiful.

Kant's analytic of the beautiful takes the form of a study of what he calls four 'moments' of the judgment of taste. Rather oddly perhaps these four moments are correlated with the four logical forms of judgment, namely quality, quantity, relation and modality. I say 'rather oddly perhaps', because the judgment of taste is not itself a logical judgment, even though, according to Kant, it involves a reference or relation to the understanding. However, the study of each moment of the judgment of taste results in a partial definition of the beautiful. We are given, as it were, four complementary elucidations of the meaning of the term 'beautiful'. And Kant's discussion of the theme is of some interest for its own sake, quite apart from the correlation of the four moments with the four logical forms of judgment.

Consideration of the judgment of taste from the standpoint of quality leads us to the following definition of the beautiful. 'Taste is the power of judging of an object or of a way of representing it through an *entirely disinterested* satisfaction or dissatisfaction. The object of such a satisfaction is called *beautiful*.'[1] By saying that aesthetic appreciation is 'entirely disinterested' (*ohne alles Interesse*) Kant does not mean, of course, that it is boring: he means that it is contemplative. In terms of the theory of taste the aesthetic judgment implies that the object which is called beautiful causes satisfaction without reference to desire, to the appetitive faculty. A simple example is sufficient to convey an idea of what Kant means. Suppose that I look at a painting of fruit and say that it is beautiful. If I mean that I should like to eat the fruit, were it real, thus relating it to appetite, my judgment would not be a judgment of taste in the technical sense, that is, an aesthetic judgment; and I should be misusing the word 'beautiful'. The aesthetic judgment implies that the form of the thing is pleasing precisely as an object of contemplation, without any reference to appetite or desire.

Kant distinguishes between the pleasant (*das Angenehme*), the beautiful (*das Schöne*) and the good (*das Gute*) as designating three relations in which representations can stand to the feelings of pleasure and displeasure or pain. The pleasant is that which gratifies inclination or desire, and it is experienced by animals as well as by men. The good is the object of esteem: it is that to which

---

[1] *J.*, 16; *Bd.*, p. 55.

objective worth is attributed. And it concerns all rational beings, including rational beings, if there are any, which are not human beings; that is, which have no bodies. The beautiful is that which simply pleases, without any intrinsic reference to inclination or desire. It is experienced only by rational beings, but not by all. That is to say, it involves sense-perception and so concerns only those rational beings which possess bodies.

Further, the aesthetic judgment, according to Kant, is indifferent to existence. If to take the simple example given above, I relate the painted fruit to my appetite or desire, I am interested in its existence, in the sense that I wish that the fruit were real, so that I could eat it. But if I contemplate it aesthetically, the fact that the fruit is represented fruit and not existent, eatable fruit is entirely irrelevant.

Finally, Kant points out that when he speaks of the aesthetic judgment as entirely disinterested, he does not mean to say that it cannot or that it ought not to be accompanied by any interest. In society men certainly have an interest in communicating the pleasure which they feel in aesthetic experience. And Kant calls this an empirical interest in the beautiful. But interest, though it may accompany or be combined with the judgment of taste, is not its determining ground. Considered in itself, the judgment is disinterested.

Turning to the study of the judgment of taste according to quantity, we find Kant defining the beautiful as 'that which pleases universally, without a concept'.[1] And we can consider these two characteristics separately.

The fact, already established, that the beautiful is the object of an entirely disinterested satisfaction implies that it is the object, or ought to be the object, of a universal satisfaction. Suppose that I am conscious that my judgment that a given statue is beautiful is entirely disinterested. This means that I am conscious that my judgment is not dependent on any private conditions peculiar to myself. In pronouncing my judgment I am 'free', as Kant puts it, neither impelled by desire on the one hand nor dictated to by the moral imperative on the other.[2] And I therefore believe that I have reason for attributing to others a satisfaction similar to that

[1] *J.*, 32; *Bd.*, p. 67.
[2] In introducing the idea of the moral imperative, I do not mean to imply, of course, that it is a private condition, as inclination is. I introduce it simply to complete the notion of being 'free' as Kant uses this term in connection with the aesthetic judgment.

which I experience in myself; for the satisfaction is not grounded in the gratification of my private inclinations. Accordingly, I speak of the statue as if beauty were an objective characteristic of it.

Kant distinguishes, therefore, in respect to universality, between a judgment concerning the pleasant and a judgment concerning the beautiful. If I say that the taste of olives is pleasant, I am quite prepared for someone to say, 'Well, you may find it pleasant, but I find it unpleasant'. For I recognize that my statement was based on private feeling or taste, and that *de gustibus non est disputandum*. But if I say that a certain work of art is beautiful, I tacitly claim, according to Kant, that it is beautiful for all. I claim, that is to say, that the judgment is based, not upon purely private feelings, so that it has validity only for myself, but upon feelings which I either attribute to others or demand of them. We must distinguish, therefore, between the judgment of taste in Kant's technical use of the term and judgments which we might normally be inclined to call judgments of taste. In making the former judgment we claim universal validity, but in the second class of judgments we do not. And it is only the first type of judgment which is concerned with the beautiful.

Naturally, Kant does not mean to imply that when someone calls a statue beautiful, he necessarily believes that all, as a matter of fact, judge it to be beautiful. He means that by making the judgment a man claims that others should recognize the statue's beauty. For, being conscious that his judgment is 'free' in the sense mentioned above, he either attributes to others a satisfaction similar to his own or claims that they should experience it.

What sort of claim or demand is this? We cannot prove logically to others that an object is beautiful. For the claim of universal validity which we make on behalf of an aesthetic judgment does not have any reference to the cognitive faculty, but only to the feeling of pleasure and pain in every subject. In Kant's terminology, the judgment does not rest upon any concept: it rests upon feeling. We cannot, therefore, make good our claim to the universal validity of the judgment by any process of logical argument. We can only persuade others to look again, and to look with more attention, at the object, confident that in the end their feelings will speak for themselves and that they will concur with our judgment. When we make the judgment, we believe that we speak, as it were, with a universal voice, and we claim the assent of others;

but they will give this assent only on the basis of their own feelings, not in virtue of any concepts which we adduce. 'We may now see that in the judgment of taste nothing is postulated but such a *universal* voice in respect of the satisfaction without the intervention of concepts.'[1] We can draw attention as much as we like to different features of the object to persuade others that it is beautiful. But the assent, if it comes, is the result of a certain satisfaction which is at last felt and does not rest on concepts.

But what is this satisfaction or pleasure of which Kant is speaking? He tells us that it is not emotion (*Rührung*), which is 'a sensation in which pleasantness is produced only by means of a momentary checking and a consequent more powerful outflow of the vital force'.[2] Emotion in this sense is relevant to the experience of sublimity, but not to that of beauty. But to say that the satisfaction or state of pleasure which is the determining ground of the judgment of taste is not emotion is not to explain what it is. And we can ask the question in this form. What is the object of the satisfaction or pleasure of which Kant is speaking? For if we know what arouses it, what it is satisfaction at or in, we shall know of what kind of satisfaction or pleasure he is speaking.

To answer this question, we can turn to Kant's study of the third moment of the judgment of taste, corresponding to the category of relation. His discussion of this third moment results in the following definition. '*Beauty* is the form of the *purposiveness* of an object, so far as this is perceived *without any representation of a purpose*.'[3] But as the meaning of this definition is not perhaps immediately evident, some explanation is required.

The fundamental idea is not difficult to grasp. If we look at a flower, say a rose, we may have the feeling that it is, as we say, just right; we may have the feeling that its form embodies or fulfils a purpose. At the same time we do not represent to ourselves any purpose which is achieved in the rose. It is not merely that if someone asked us what purpose was embodied in the rose we should be unable to give any clear account of it: we do not conceive or represent to ourselves any purpose at all. And yet in some sense we *feel*, without concepts, that a purpose is embodied in the flower. The matter might perhaps be expressed in this way. There is a sense of meaning; but there is no conceptual representation of what is meant. There is an awareness or consciousness of finality; but there is no concept of an end which is achieved.

[1] *J.*, 25; *Bd.*, p. 62.   [2] *J.*, 43; *Bd.*, p. 76.   [3] *J.*, 61; *Bd.*, p. 90.

There can, of course, be a concept of purpose, which accompanies the experience of beauty. But Kant will not allow that a judgment of taste is 'pure' if it presupposes a concept of a purpose. He distinguishes between what he calls 'free' and 'adherent' beauty. If we judge that a flower is beautiful, we have, most probably, no concept of a purpose which is achieved in the flower. The beauty of the latter is then said to be free; and our judgment of taste is said to be pure. But when we judge that a building, say a church, is beautiful, we may have a concept of a purpose which is achieved and perfectly embodied in the building. The beauty of the latter is then said to be adherent, and our judgment is said to be impure, in the technical sense that it is not simply an expression of a feeling of satisfaction or pleasure but involves a conceptual element. An aesthetic judgment is pure only if the person who makes it has no concept of a purpose or if he abstracts from the concept, supposing that he has one, when he makes the judgment.

Kant insists upon this point because he wishes to maintain the special and unique character of the aesthetic judgment. If the latter involved a concept of objective purposiveness, of perfection, it would be 'just as much a cognitive judgment as the judgment by which something is pronounced good'.[1] But in point of fact the determining ground of the aesthetic judgment is not a concept at all, and consequently it cannot be a concept of a definite purpose. 'A judgment is called aesthetic precisely because its determining ground is not a concept but the feeling (of the inner sense) of that harmony in the play of the mental powers, so far as it can be experienced in feeling.'[2] Kant admits that we can and do form standards of beauty and that, in the case of man, we form an ideal of beauty which is at the same time a visible expression of moral ideas. But he insists that 'judgment according to such a standard can never be purely aesthetic, and that judgment according to an ideal of beauty is not a mere judgment of taste'.[3]

The fourth partial definition of beauty, derived from a consideration of the judgment of taste according to the modality of the subject's satisfaction in the object, is this. 'The *beautiful* is that which without any concept is recognized as the object of a *necessary* satisfaction.'[4]

This necessity is not a theoretical objective necessity. For if it were, I should know *a priori* that everyone will assent to my

[1] *J.*, 47; *Bd.*, p. 79.   [2] *J.*, 47; *Bd.*, p. 80.
[3] *J.*, 60–1; *Bd.*, p. 90.   [4] *J.*, 68 ;*Bd.*, p. 96.

judgment of taste. And this is certainly not the case. I claim
universal validity for my judgment; but I do not know that it will
be admitted in fact. Nor is this necessity a practical necessity;
that is, the result of an objective law telling us how we ought to
act. It is what Kant calls *exemplary*; 'that is, necessity of the assent
of *all* to a judgment which is regarded as an example of a universal
rule which one cannot state'.[1] When I say that something is
beautiful, I claim that all ought to describe it as beautiful; and
this claim presupposes a universal principle, of which the judgment is an example. But the principle cannot be a logical principle.
It must be regarded, therefore, as a common sense (*ein Gemein-
sinn*). But this is not common sense (*sensus communis*) according
to the ordinary usage of the term. For the latter judges by concepts and principles, however indistinctly represented. Common
sense in the aesthetic understanding of the term refers to 'the
effect resulting from the free play of our cognitive powers'.[2] In
passing an aesthetic judgment we presuppose that a certain
similar satisfaction will arise or should arise from their interplay
in all who perceive the object in question.

What right have we got to presuppose this common sense? We
cannot prove its existence; but it is presupposed or assumed as the
necessary condition of the communicability of aesthetic judgments. According to Kant, judgments, along with the conviction
which accompanies them, must admit of universal communicability. But aesthetic judgments cannot be communicated by
concepts and by appeal to a universal logical rule. Hence 'common
sense' is the necessary condition of their communicability. And
this is our ground for presupposing such a common sense.

In general, it must be understood that in his 'analytic of the
beautiful' Kant is not concerned with giving rules or hints for
educating and cultivating aesthetic taste. He expressly disclaims
any such intention in his preface to the *Critique of Judgment*. He
is concerned first and foremost with the nature of the aesthetic
judgment, with what we can say about it *a priori*; that is, with its
universal and necessary features. In the course of his discussion
he obviously draws attention to ideas which, whether we accept
them or not, are worthy of consideration. The 'disinterestedness'
of the aesthetic judgment and the notion of purposiveness without
any concept of a purpose are cases in point. But the fundamental
question is probably whether the aesthetic judgment expresses

[1] *J.*, 62–3; *Bd.*, p. 91. [2] *J.*, 64–5; *Bd.*, p. 93.

feeling, in the sense that the latter is the only determining ground
of the pure judgment of taste, or whether it is in some sense a
cognitive judgment. If we think that Kant's account of the matter
is too subjectivist and that the aesthetic judgment does in fact
express objective knowledge of a kind for which he does not allow,
we must, of course, be prepared to state what this knowledge is.
If we cannot do so, this is at least a prima facie ground for thinking
that Kant's account was on the right lines. But on this matter the
reader must form his own opinion.

3. Edmund Burke's *Philosophical Inquiry into the Origin of Our
Ideas of the Sublime and the Beautiful* (1756) was regarded by Kant
as the most important work in this line of research which had
appeared. But though he followed Burke in distinguishing between
the beautiful and the sublime,[1] he looked on the English writer's
treatment as being 'purely empirical' and 'physiological'[2] and
considered that what was needed was a 'transcendental exposition'
of aesthetic judgments. Having already considered Kant's study
of the judgment of taste in the sense of a judgment about the
beautiful, we can now turn to the analytic of the sublime. But I
propose to deal with this theme in a more cursory way.

The beautiful and the sublime (*das Erhabene*) have some
common features. For instance, both cause pleasure; and the
judgment that something is sublime no more presupposes a
determinate concept than does the judgment that an object is
beautiful. But there are at the same time considerable differences
between the beautiful and the sublime. For example, the former
is associated with quality rather than with quantity, the latter
with quantity rather than with quality. Natural beauty, as we
have seen, has to do with the form of an object; and form implies
limitation. The experience of the sublime, however, is associated
with formlessness, in the sense of absence of limitation, provided
that this absence of limits is represented together with totality.
(Thus the overpowering grandeur of the tempestuous ocean is felt
as limitless, but the absence of limits is also represented as a
totality.) Kant is thus enabled to associate beauty with the
understanding, the sublime with the reason. Aesthetic experience
of the beautiful does not, as we have seen, depend on any determinate concept. Nevertheless, it involves a free interplay of the
faculties; in this case imagination and understanding. The

---

[1] I do not intend to imply by this remark that Burke was the first to make this
distinction.

[2] *J.*, 128; *Bd.*, p. 147.

beautiful as definite is felt as adequate to the imagination, and the imagination is considered as being in accord, in regard to a given intuition, with the understanding, which is a faculty of concepts. The sublime, however, does violence to the imagination; it overwhelms it, as it were. And it is then represented as being in accord with the reason, considered as the faculty of indeterminate ideas of totality. The sublime, in proportion as it involves absence of limits, is inadequate to our power of imaginative representation; that is to say, it exceeds and overwhelms it. And in so far as this absence of limits is associated with totality, the sublime can be regarded as the 'exhibition', as Kant puts it, of an indefinite idea of the reason. Another difference is that whereas the pleasure produced by the beautiful can be described as a positive joy, prolonged in quiet contemplation, the sublime must be said to cause wonder and awe rather than positive joy. And the experience of it is associated with emotion in the sense alluded to in the last section, namely a momentary checking and a consequent more powerful outflow of the vital force. Finally, the beautiful, though distinct from the charming, can be linked with it. But charm (*Reiz*) and the sublime are incompatible.

From the fact, or supposed fact, that the sublime is experienced as doing violence to the imagination and as being out of accord with our power of representation Kant draws the conclusion that it is only improperly that natural objects are called sublime. For the term indicates approval. And how can we be said to approve what is experienced as in some sense hostile to ourselves? 'Thus the wide tempestuous ocean cannot be called sublime. The sight of it is terrible; and one must have one's mind already filled with many sorts of Ideas, if through such a sight it is to be attuned to a sentiment which is itself sublime because by it the mind is incited to abandon the realm of sense and to occupy itself with Ideas which involve a higher purposiveness.'[1] There are many natural objects which can properly be called beautiful. But, properly speaking, sublimity belongs to our feelings or sentiments rather than to the objects which occasion them.

Kant distinguishes between the mathematical and the dynamical sublime, according as to whether the imagination refers the mental movement involved in the experience of the sublime to the faculty of cognition or to that of desire. The mathematical sublime is said to be 'that which is absolutely great'[2] or '*that in comparison*

---

[1] *J.*, 77; *Bd.*, p. 103.   [2] *J.*, 80; *Bd.*, p. 106.

with which all else is small'.[1] Among examples Kant gives that of St. Peter's at Rome. The dynamical sublime is experienced, for example, when we are confronted with the spectacle of the terrible physical power of Nature but when at the same time we find in our mind and reason a superiority to this physical might.[2]

4. According to Kant, pure judgments of taste (that is, judgments about the beauty of natural objects) stand in need of a deduction, in the sense of justification. The aesthetic judgment demands *a priori* that in representing a given object all should feel the peculiar kind of pleasure (arising from the interplay of imagination and understanding) which is the determining ground of the judgment. As the latter is a particular judgment made by a particular subject, and as its determining ground is subjective (not an objective cognition of a thing), what is the justification of the claim to universal validity? We cannot justify it by logical proof. For the judgment is not a logical judgment. Nor can we justify it by appealing to a factual universal consent. For, quite apart from the fact that people by no means always agree in their aesthetic judgments, the claim on or demand for universal consent is made *a priori*. It is an essential feature of the judgment as such, and it is thus independent of the empirical facts concerning common assent, or the lack of it, to the judgment. The justification, therefore, can take the form neither of a logical deduction nor of an empirical induction, aiming to establish the truth of the judgment when viewed as claiming universal validity.

Kant's way of dealing with the matter amounts to assigning the conditions under which the claim to universal assent can be justified. If the aesthetic judgment rests on purely subjective grounds, on, that is to say, the pleasure or displeasure arising from the interplay of the powers of imagination and understanding in regard to a given representation, and if we have a right to presuppose in all men a similar structure of the cognitive powers and of the relations between them, then the claim to universal validity on the part of the aesthetic judgment is justified. But the judgment does rest on purely subjective grounds. And communicability of representations and of knowledge in general warrants our presupposing in all men similar subjective

---

[1] *J.*, 84; *Bd.*, p. 109.
[2] Kant's remark that the spectacle of, say, the might of the storm-tossed ocean or of a volcano in eruption becomes pleasing when beheld from a safe vantage-point incited Schopenhauer to some sarcastic remarks.

conditions for judgment. Therefore the claim to universal consent is justified.

It does not seem to me that this deduction[1] carries us much further. No deduction is required, Kant tells us, in the case of judgments about the sublime in Nature. For it is only improperly that the latter is called sublime. The term refers to our sentiments rather than to the natural phenomena which occasion them. In the case of the pure judgment of taste, however, a deduction is required; for an assertion is made about an object in respect of its form, and this assertion involves an *a priori* claim to universal validity. And fidelity to the general programme of the critical philosophy demands a deduction or justification of such a judgment. But what we are actually told in the course of the deduction amounts to little more than the statements that the claim to universal validity is warranted if we are justified in presupposing in all men a similarity of the subjective conditions of judgment, and that communicability justifies this presupposition. It is perhaps true that this fits into the general pattern of the critical philosophy, inasmuch as the possibility of the aesthetic judgment, considered as a synthetic *a priori* proposition, is referred to conditions on the part of the subject. But one might have expected to have heard some more about conditions on the part of the object. True, the determining grounds of the judgment of taste are, according to Kant, subjective. But, as we have seen, he allows that natural objects can properly be called beautiful, whereas sublimity is only improperly predicated of Nature.

5. So far we have been concerned with the beauty of natural objects.[2] We must now turn to the subject of art. Art in general 'is distinguished from Nature as making (*facere*), from acting or operating (*agere*), and the product or result of the former from the product or result of the latter as work (*opus*) from effect (*effectus*)'.[3] Fine art (*die schöne Kunst*), as distinguished from merely pleasing art (*die angenehme Kunst*), is 'a kind of representation which has its end in itself, but which none the less, although it has no purpose external to itself, promotes the culture of the mental powers with a view to social communication'.[4]

According to Kant, it pertains to a product of fine art that we

---

[1] For the details of the deduction the reader is referred to the *Critique of Judgment* itself (*J.*, 131 ff.; *Bd.*, pp. 150 ff.).
[2] To judge by the way in which Kant cites the tulip as an example, he appears to have had a predilection for this flower.
[3] *J.*, 173; *Bd.*, p. 183. [4] *J.*, 179; *Bd.*, p. 187.

should be conscious that it is art and not Nature. But at the same time the purposiveness of its form must seem to be as free from the constraint of arbitrary rules as though it were a product of Nature. Kant does not mean, of course, that no rules should be observed in the production of a work of art. He means that their observance should not be painfully apparent. The work of art, to be a work of art, should appear to possess the 'freedom' of Nature. However, whether it is a question of natural beauty or of a work of art, we can say: *'That is beautiful which pleases in the mere act of judging it* (not in sensation, nor by means of a concept).'[1]

Fine art is the work of genius, genius being the talent or natural gift which gives the rule to art. The latter presupposes rules by means of which a product is represented as possible. But these rules cannot have concepts as their determining grounds. Hence the artist, if he is a true artist or genius, cannot devise his rules by means of concepts. And it follows that Nature itself, as operating in the artist (by the harmony of his faculties), must give the rule to art. Genius, therefore, can be defined as 'the inborn mental disposition (*ingenium*) *through which* Nature gives the rule to art'.[2]

It would be out of place to deal here at length with Kant's ideas about art and genius. It is sufficient to mention two points. First, among the faculties which Kant attributes to genius is spirit (*Geist*), which he describes as the animating principle of the mind. It is 'the faculty of presenting aesthetical Ideas',[3] an aesthetical Idea being a representation of the imagination which occasions much thought although no concept is adequate to it, with the consequence that it cannot be made fully intelligible by language. An aesthetical Idea is thus a counterpart of a rational Idea, which, conversely, is a concept to which no intuition or representation of the imagination can be adequate.

The second point which we can note is Kant's insistence on the originality of genius. 'Everyone is agreed that Genius is entirely opposed to the spirit of imitation.'[4] It follows that genius cannot be taught. But it does not follow that genius can dispense with all rules and technical training. Originality is not the only essential condition for genius considered as productive of works of art.

6. We have had occasion to notice Kant's passion for architectonic. This is apparent in the *Critique of Judgment* as well as in

---

[1] *J.*, 180; *Bd.*, p. 187.   [2] *J.*, 181; *Bd.*, p. 188.
[3] *J.*, 192; *Bd.*, p. 197.   [4] *J.*, 183; *Bd.*, p. 190.

the first two *Critiques*. And just as he supplies a deduction of the pure judgment of taste, so also does he supply a short *Dialectic of the Aesthetic Judgment*.[1] This contains the statement of an antinomy and its solution.

The antinomy is as follows. '*Thesis:* The judgment of taste is not based upon concepts; for otherwise it would admit of dispute (would be determinable by proofs). *Antithesis:* The judgment of taste is based upon concepts; for otherwise, in spite of its diversity, we could not quarrel about it (we could not claim for our judgment the necessary assent of others).'[2]

The solution of the antinomy consists in showing that the thesis and antithesis are not contradictory, because the word 'concept' is not to be understood in the same sense in the two propositions. The thesis means that the judgment of taste is not based upon *determinate* concepts. And this is quite true. In the antithesis we mean that the judgment of taste is based upon an *indeterminate* concept, namely that of the supersensible substrate of phenomena. And this also is true. For, according to Kant, this indeterminate concept is the concept of the general ground of the subjective purposiveness of Nature for the judgment; and this is required as a basis for the claim to universal validity on behalf of the judgment. But the concept does not give us any knowledge of the object; nor can it supply any proof of the judgment. Hence thesis and antithesis can both be true, and so compatible; and then the apparent antinomy disappears.

7. The fact that the judgment of taste rests in some sense on the indeterminate concept of the supersensible substrate of phenomena suggests that there is some link between aesthetics and morals. For the aesthetic judgment presupposes, indirectly, this indeterminate concept; and reflection on the moral law gives to the idea of the supersensible or intelligible a determinate content. It is not surprising, therefore, to find Kant saying that 'the beautiful is the symbol of the morally good',[3] and that 'taste is at bottom a power of judging of the sensible illustration of moral ideas (by means of a certain analogy involved in our reflection upon both of these)'.[4]

What does Kant understand by a symbol? His own example is an apt illustration of his meaning. A monarchical State can be represented by a living body if it is governed by laws which spring

---

[1] He also adds to the first part of the *Critique of Judgment* an appendix on the 'Doctrine of Method of Taste'. But this is extremely brief.

[2] *J.*, 234; *Bd.*, p. 231.   [3] *J.*, 258; *Bd.*, p. 250.   [4] *J.*, 263; *Bd.*, p. 255.

from the people,[1] and by a machine (such as a hand-mill) if it is governed according to the individual, absolute will of an autocrat. But the representation is in both cases only *symbolic*. The former type of State is not in actual fact like a body; nor does the latter type bear any literal resemblance to a hand-mill. At the same time there is an analogy between the rules according to which we reflect upon the type of State and its causality on the one hand and the representative symbol and its causality on the other. Thus Kant bases his idea of symbolism on analogy. And the question arises, what are the points of analogy between the aesthetic and the moral judgments, or between the beautiful and the morally good, which justify our looking on the former as a symbol of the latter?

There is an analogy between the beautiful and the morally good in the fact that both please *immediately*. That is to say, there is a similarity between them in the fact that they both please immediately; but there is at the same time a difference. For the beautiful pleases in reflective intuition, the morally good in the concept. Again, the beautiful pleases apart from any interest; and though the morally good is indeed bound up with an interest, it does not precede the moral judgment but follows it. So here too there is an analogy rather than a strict similarity. Further, in the aesthetic judgment the imagination is in harmony with the understanding; and this harmony is analogous to the moral harmony of the will with itself according to the universal law of the practical reason. Lastly, there is an analogy between the claim to universality on the part of the subjective principle in the judgment of taste and the claim to universality on the part of the objective principle of morality.

Kant's way of talking may sometimes suggest a moralizing of aesthetic experience. Thus we are told that 'the true propaedeutic for the foundation of taste is the development of moral ideas and the culture of the moral feeling; for it is only when sensibility is brought into agreement with this that genuine taste can take a definite invariable form'.[2] But Kant does not wish to reduce the aesthetic to the moral judgment. As we have seen, he insists on the special characteristics of the former. The point which he wishes to make is that aesthetic experience forms a connecting link between the sensible world as presented in scientific knowledge and

---

[1] *Nach inneren Volksgesetzen* (*J.*, 256; *Bd.*, p. 249) is Kant's phrase. Perhaps he has at the back of his mind Rousseau's idea of law as the expression of the general will.   [2] *J.*, 264; *Bd.*, p. 255.

the supersensible world as apprehended in moral experience. And it is primarily with this point in mind that he draws attention to analogies between the beautiful and the morally good.

8. We have seen that the judgment of taste is concerned with the form of the purposiveness of an object, so far as this purposiveness is perceived without any representation of a purpose. It is thus in some sense a teleological judgment. In Kant's terminology it is a formal and subjective teleological judgment. It is formal in the sense that it is not concerned with explaining the existence of anything. Indeed, it is not, of itself, concerned with existing things. It is concerned primarily with representations. And it is subjective in the sense that it refers to the feeling of the person who makes the judgment. That is to say, it asserts a necessary connection between the representation of an object as purposive and the pleasure which accompanies this representation.

Besides the subjective formal teleological judgment there is also the objective formal teleological judgment. This is to be found, according to Kant, in mathematics. One of his examples is the following. In so simple a figure as the circle, he remarks, there is contained the ground for the solution of a number of geometrical problems. For instance, if one wishes to construct a triangle, given the base and the opposite angle, the circle is 'the geometrical place for all triangles which conform to this condition'.[1] And the judgment about the suitability of the circle for this purpose is a teleological judgment; for it states 'purposiveness'. It is a formal teleological judgment, because it is not concerned with existing things and with the causal relationship. In pure mathematics nothing is said 'of the existence, but only of the possibility of things'.[2] But it is an objective, and not a subjective, judgment because there is no reference to the feelings or desires of the person making the judgment.

In addition to formal teleological judgments there are also material teleological judgments, which refer to existing things. And these judgments too can be either subjective or objective. They are subjective if they state human purposes; objective if they are concerned with purposes in Nature. The second part of the *Critique of Judgment* deals with the fourth class; that is, with objective, material teleological judgments. And when Kant speaks simply about the 'teleological judgment', it is this sort of judgment which he has in mind.

[1] *J.*, 272; *Bd.*, pp. 262–3. [2] *J.*, 279, note; *Bd.*, p. 268, note.

But there is a further distinction to be made. When we assert that there is purposiveness or finality in Nature, we may be referring either to relative (also called outer or external) or to inner finality. If, for example, we were to say that reindeer exist in the north in order that Eskimos should have meat to eat, we should be asserting a case of relative or outer finality or purposiveness. We should be saying that the natural purpose of the reindeer is to serve something external to itself. If, however, we were to say that the reindeer is a natural purpose in itself, meaning that it is an organic whole in which the parts are mutually interdependent, existing for the whole of which they are parts, we should be asserting a case of inner finality. That is, the natural purpose or end of the reindeer is stated to lie in itself, considered as an organic whole, and not in a relation to something external and other than itself.

Now, let us consider the first judgment, namely that reindeer exist for the sake of human beings. This purports to be an explanation of the existence of reindeer. It is different, however, from a causal explanation. For a causal explanation (in accordance with the schematized category of causality) would merely tell us *how* reindeer come to exist. It would not tell us *why* they exist. The relative teleological judgment purports to supply an answer to the question *why*. But the answer could, at best, be only *hypothetical*. That is to say, it assumes that there must be human beings in the far north. But no amount of study of Nature will show us that there must be human beings in the far north. It is, indeed, psychologically understandable that we should be inclined to think that reindeer should exist for the Eskimos and grass for the sheep and the cows; but, as far as our knowledge is concerned, we might just as well say that human beings are capable of existing in the far north because there happen to be reindeer there, and that sheep and cows are able to live in certain places and not in others because there happens to be appropriate food in the first place and not in the second. In other words, apart from any other possible objections against the assertion of outer finality in Nature, our judgments could never be absolute. We could never be justified in saying absolutely that reindeer exist for men and grass for sheep and cows. The judgments may possibly be true; but we cannot know that they are true. For we cannot see any necessary con-nections which would establish their truth.

Judgments about inner finality, however, are absolute teleological judgments. That is to say, they assert of some product of Nature that it is in itself a purpose or end of Nature (*Naturzweck*). In the case of relative finality we say, equivalently, that one thing exists with a view to some other thing if this other thing embodies a purpose of Nature. But in the case of inner finality we say that a thing embodies a purpose of Nature because the thing is what it is, and not because of its relation to something else. The question arises, therefore, what are the requisite conditions for making this judgment?

'I should say in a preliminary fashion that a thing exists as a purpose of Nature *when it is cause and effect of itself*, although in a twofold sense.'[1] Kant takes the example of a tree. It is not merely that the tree produces another member of the same species: it produces itself as an individual. For in the process which we call growth it receives and organizes matter in such a way that we can regard the whole process as one of self-production. Further, there is a relation of mutual interdependence between a part and the whole. The leaves, for instance, are produced by the tree; but at the same time they conserve it, in the sense that repeated defoliation would eventually kill the tree.

Trying to define more accurately a thing considered as a purpose of Nature, Kant observes that the parts must be so related to one another that they produce a whole by their causality. At the same time the whole can be regarded as a final cause of the organization of the parts. 'In such a product of Nature each part not only exists *by means of* all the other parts but is also regarded as existing *for the sake* of the others and of the whole, that is, as an instrument (organ).'[2] This is not, however, a sufficient description. For a part of a watch can be regarded as existing for the sake of the others and of the whole. And a watch is not a product of Nature. We must add, therefore, that the parts must be regarded as reciprocally producing each other. It is only a product of this kind which can be called a purpose of Nature; for it is not only organized but also a self-organizing being. We regard it as possessing in itself a formative power (*eine bildende Kraft*), which is not present in an artificial production or machine such as a watch. A watch possesses a moving power (*eine bewegende Kraft*), but not a formative power.

We have, therefore, a principle for judging of internal purposiveness in organized beings. 'This principle, which is at the same

---

[1] *J.*, 286; *Bd.*, pp. 273–4.   [2] *J.*, 291; *Bd.*, p. 277.

time a definition, is as follows: *An organized product of Nature is one in which everything is reciprocally end and means.* In it nothing is in vain, without purpose, or to be ascribed to a blind mechanism of Nature.'[1] This principle is derived from experience in the sense that its formulation is occasioned by observation of organic beings. But at the same time 'on account of the universality and necessity which it predicates of such purposiveness'[2] it cannot rest merely on empirical grounds. It must be grounded on an *a priori* principle, the Idea of a purpose of Nature, which is a regulative (and not constitutive) Idea. And the principle quoted above can be called, Kant tells us, a maxim for the employment of this regulative Idea in judging the inner purposiveness of organized beings.

The question arises, however, whether we can be content with a dichotomy in Nature. Internal finality or purposiveness can be said to be verified for us only in self-organizing beings. For, whatever may be the case absolutely speaking, we at least are not in a position to give an adequate explanation of such beings in terms of merely mechanical causality, by working, that is to say, with the schematized category of causality. But this is not the case with inorganic beings, where we do not seem to require the concept of finality. Are we, therefore, to be content with making a split, as it were, in Nature, using the concept of final causality in the case of certain types of beings and not using it in other cases?

According to Kant, we cannot remain content with such a dichotomy. For the Idea of finality, of a purpose of Nature, is a regulative Idea for judgment's interpretation of Nature. And we are thus led to the view of Nature as a system of ends, a view which in turn leads us to refer Nature, as empirically given in sense-perception, to a supersensible substrate. Indeed, the very Idea of a natural purpose takes us beyond the sphere of sense-experience. For the Idea is not given in mere sense-perception; it is a regulative principle for judging what is perceived. And we naturally tend to unify the whole of Nature in the light of this Idea. 'If we have once discovered in Nature a power of bringing forth products which can be thought by us only according to the concept of final causes, we go further and are entitled to judge that those things too belong to a system of ends which do not . . . necessitate our seeking for any principle of their possibility beyond the mechanism of causes working blindly. For the first Idea, as

[1] *J.*, 295–6; *Bd.*, pp. 280–1.   [2] *J.*, 296; *Bd.*, p. 281.

regards its ground, already brings us beyond the world of sense; because the unity of the supersensible principle must be regarded as valid in this way not merely for certain species of natural beings, but for the whole of Nature as a system.'[1]

It is important to understand, of course, that the principle of finality in Nature is for Kant a regulative Idea of reflective judgment, and that the maxims to which it gives rise are heuristic principles. We must not confuse natural science and theology. Thus we should not introduce the concept of God into natural science in order to explain finality. 'Now, to keep itself strictly within its limits, physics abstracts from the question whether ends in Nature (*Naturzwecke*) are *intentional or unintentional*; for this would mean intruding itself into alien territory (namely that of metaphysics). It is enough that there are objects which are *explicable* as regards their internal form, or even intimately *knowable* solely by means of natural laws which we cannot think except by taking the Idea of ends as a principle.'[2] The Idea of a purpose of Nature, so far as natural science is concerned, is a useful, indeed inevitable, heuristic principle. But though teleology leads naturally to theology, in the sense that a teleological view of Nature leads naturally to the assumption that Nature is the work of an intelligent Being acting for a purpose, this does not mean that the existence of God can be regarded as a conclusion which is demonstrable on the basis of natural science. For the regulative Idea of reflective judgment and the maxims which govern its employment are subjective principles. On the side of the mind, the teleological judgment helps us to bridge the gulf between the phenomenal and noumenal spheres; but it cannot form the basis for a dogmatic metaphysics.

9. As we have seen, Kant concentrates on what he calls inner purposiveness or finality; that is, on the finality manifested within an organic being through the relations of the parts to one another and to the whole. A purely mechanistic explanation is insufficient in the case of such beings.

But the situation is not, of course, as simple as this statement of Kant's position might suggest. On the one hand the categories are constitutive in regard to experience. And though this does not tell us anything about noumenal or supersensible reality, it appears to tell us that all phenomena must be explicable in terms of mechanical causality, or at least that they must be considered

---

[1] *J.*, 304; *Bd.*, p. 287.   [2] *J.*, 307–8; *Bd.*, pp. 289–90.

to be explicable in this way. On the other hand consideration of organic beings leads us to use the idea of finality in interpreting them. As Kant puts it, the understanding suggests one maxim for judging corporeal things, while reason suggests another. And these two maxims of judgment appear to be mutually incompatible. There thus arises an antinomy, or at least an apparent antinomy, which Kant discusses under the general heading of *Dialectic of Teleological Judgment*.

The antinomy is first stated as follows. '*The first maxim* of judgment is the *proposition*: All production of material things and their forms can be judged to be possible only according to merely mechanical laws. *The second maxim* is the *counter-proposition*: Some products of material Nature cannot be judged to be possible according to merely mechanical laws. (To judge them requires a quite different law of causality, namely that of final causes.)'[1]

Kant remarks that if we turn these maxims into constitutive principles of the possibility of objects, we are, indeed, faced with a contradiction. For we shall have the following statements. '*Proposition:* All production of material things is possible according to merely mechanical laws. *Counter-proposition:* Some production of material things is not possible according to merely mechanical laws.'[2] And these two statements are clearly incompatible. But judgment does not provide us with constitutive principles of the possibility of objects. And no *a priori* proof of either statement can be given. We must return, therefore, to the antinomy as first stated, where we have two maxims for judging of material objects according to the empirical laws of Nature. And it is Kant's contention that the two maxims do not in fact contradict one another.

The reason why they do not contradict one another is this. If I say that I must judge the production of material things to be possible according to merely mechanical laws (that is, without introducing the idea of purpose or finality), I do not say that the production of material things is only possible in this way. I say that I ought to consider them as being possible only in this way. In other words, I lay down the principle that in the scientific investigation of Nature I must push, as it were, mechanistic explanation as far as it will go. And this does not prevent me from judging that in regard to certain material things I cannot provide an adequate explanation in terms of mechanical causality, and

[1] *J.*, 314; *Bd.*, p. 294.   [2] *J.*, 314–15; *Bd.*, pp. 294–5.

that I have to introduce the idea of final causality. I do not thereby assert dogmatically that organic beings cannot possibly be produced by the operation of mechanical causal laws. I say rather that I do not see how the general principle of explaining the production of material things in terms of mechanical causality can be applied in this case, and that I find myself driven to consider such beings as ends, as embodying purposes of Nature, even if the Idea of a purpose of Nature is not altogether clear to me.

Kant notes that in the history of philosophy there have appeared different ways of explaining purposiveness in Nature. He groups them under two general headings, idealism and realism. The former maintains that such purposiveness is undesigned, while the latter holds that it is designed. Under the heading of idealism Kant includes both the system of the Greek atomists, according to which everything is due to the working of the laws of motion, and the system of Spinoza, according to which purposiveness in Nature arises fatalistically, as it were, from the character of infinite substance. Under realism he includes both hylozoism (the theory, for example, of a world-soul) and theism.

The names are oddly chosen. I mean, it is odd to call the philosophies of Democritus and Epicurus 'idealism'. But the main point to be noticed is that according to Kant theism is by far the most acceptable system of explanation. Epicurus tries to explain purposiveness in Nature through blind chance; but in this way 'nothing is explained, not even the illusion in our teleological judgment'.[1] Spinoza's system leads to the conclusion that all is purposive; for all follows necessarily from Substance, and this is what purposiveness is made to mean. But to say that a thing is purposive simply because it is a thing is tantamount to saying that nothing is purposive. It is true, Kant remarks, that Spinoza's doctrine of the original Being is not easy to refute; but this is because it is not understandable in the first place. As for hylozoism, 'the possibility of a living matter cannot even be thought; for its concept involves a contradiction, because lifelessness, *inertia*, constitutes the essential character of matter'.[2] We are left, therefore, with theism which is superior to all other grounds of explanation in that it refers purposiveness in Nature to an original Being acting intelligently.

But though theism is superior to all other explanations of finality in Nature, it cannot be proved. 'What now in the end does

[1] *J.*, 325; *Bd.*, p. 302.   [2] *J.*, 327; *Bd.*, pp. 304–5.

even the most complete teleology prove? Does it prove that there is such an intelligent Being? No; it proves nothing more than that according to the constitution of our cognitive powers, and in the consequent combination of experience with the highest principles of reason, we can form for ourselves absolutely no concept of the possibility of such a world except by thinking a supreme cause of it *working by design*. Objectively, therefore, we cannot assert the proposition that there is an intelligent original Being; but only subjectively for the use of our faculty of judgment in its reflection upon the purposes in Nature, which cannot be thought according to any other principle than that of the designing (intentional) causality of a highest cause.'[1]

Once more, therefore, the Idea of purpose in Nature (*Natur-zweck*) is a regulative principle, giving rise to heuristic maxims of judgment. These are found useful, even inevitable, in judging of organic beings. And we are led naturally, first to the concept of the whole of Nature as a system of ends, secondly to the concept of an intelligent cause of Nature. But we are dealing here with the implications of a subjective regulative Idea, not with objective proof. At the same time it cannot be shown that final causality is impossible in Nature. True, we cannot understand in a positive way how mechanical and final causality can be ultimately reconciled; how things can be subject, as it were, to two kinds of causal law at the same time. But the possibility remains that they are reconciled in the 'supersensible substrate' of Nature, to which we have no access. And theism provides us with the best frame-work for thinking the universe, though the objective truth of theism, is not capable of being theoretically demonstrated.

10. Towards the close of the *Critique of Judgment* Kant dis-cusses once more the deficiencies of a theology based on the idea of purposiveness or finality in Nature (physico-theology, as he calls it). As we saw when considering his criticism of speculative metaphysics, an argument for the existence of God which is based on empirical evidence of design or purpose in Nature can bring us, at best, only to the concept of a designer, an architect of Nature. It could not bring us to the concept of a supreme cause of the existence of the universe. Nor could it serve to determine any attribute of the suprahuman designer save intelligence. In particular, it could not serve to determine the moral attributes of this Being. Kant now adds that the physico-theological argument

[1] *J.*, 335–6; *Bd.*, p. 311.

could, at best, bring us to the concept of 'an artistic understanding (*Kunstverstand*) for scattered purposes'.[1] That is to say, reflection on certain types of material beings (organisms) would bring us to the concept of a suprahuman intelligence which manifests itself in these beings. But it would not bring us to the concept of a divine wisdom (*Weisheit*)[2] which created the whole universe for one supreme final end. For one thing, the physico-theological argument is based on empirical data; and the universe as a whole is not an empirical datum. We could not refer the 'scattered' purposes which we find in Nature to the unity of a common final end.

If, however, we approach the matter from a different point of view, namely from the point of view of the moral consciousness, the situation is different. As we saw in Chapter XIV, the moral law demands that we should postulate the existence, not simply of a suprahuman intelligence, but of God, the supreme, infinite cause of all finite things. And we must conceive God as creating and sustaining the universe for a final end. What can this end be? According to Kant, it must be man. 'Without man the whole creation would be a mere desert, in vain and without final purpose.'[3] But 'it is only as a moral being that we recognize man as the purpose of creation'.[4] We must look on the end or purpose of creation as a moral purpose, as the full development of man as a moral being in a realized kingdom of ends and as consequently involving human happiness in the final harmonization of the physical and moral orders.

We might, therefore, be inclined to say that in Kant's view 'moral theology' (or ethico-theology) complements and supplies for the deficiencies of physico-theology. And he does sometimes speak in this way. But he also insists that moral theology is quite independent of physico-theology, in the sense that it does not presuppose the latter. Indeed, physical theology is said to be 'a misunderstood physical teleology, only serviceable as a preparation (propaedeutic) for theology'.[5] It can be called theology only when it invokes the aid of the principles of moral theology. In itself, it does not merit the name of theology. For it could just as well, or better, lead to a 'demonology', the indefinite conception of a suprahuman power or powers. In other words, Kant, while retaining his respect for the physico-theological argument for the existence of God once again lays all the emphasis on the moral argument.

[1] *J.*, 408; *Bd.*, p. 368.   [3] *Ibid.*   [3] *J.*, 410; *Bd.*, p. 370.
[4] *J.*, 413; *Bd.*, p. 372.   [5] *J.*, 410; *Bd.*, p. 369.

The moral argument, however, 'does not supply any *objectively-*valid proof of the existence of God; it does not prove to the sceptic that there is a God, but that, if he wishes to think in a way consonant with morality, he must admit the *assumption* of this proposition under the maxims of his practical reason'.[1] We cannot demonstrate the existence or attributes of God. It is a matter of practical faith, not of theoretical cognition.

This faith is free: the mind cannot be compelled to assent by any theoretical proof. But it is worth noting that Kant does not intend to say that this moral faith is irrational. On the contrary, 'faith (as *habitus*, not as *actus*) is the moral way of thinking (*Denkungsart*) of Reason as to belief in that which is unattainable by theoretical knowledge'.[2] To have theoretical knowledge of God we should have to employ the categories of the understanding. But though these can be used to think God analogically or symbolically, their employment cannot give us knowledge of Him. For they give knowledge of objects only by means of their function as constitutive principles of experience. And God is not a possible object of experience for Kant. At the same time belief in God is grounded in reason in its practical or moral employment. It cannot, therefore, be called irrational.

It may seem that Kant's return to the subject of philosophical theology at the close of the *Critique of Judgment* is a case of superfluous repetition. But though it certainly involves repetition, it is not really superfluous. For it re-emphasizes his view that while the aesthetic and teleological judgments enable us to conceive Nature as a possible field for final causality, it is only the practical reason which enables us to give determinate shape, as it were, to the noumenal reality which is vaguely implied by aesthetic experience and by experience of 'objective' finality in certain products of Nature.

[1] *J.*, 424, note; *Bd.*, p. 381, note.   [2] *J.*, 462; *Bd.*, p. 409.

CHAPTER XVI

KANT (7): REMARKS ON THE *OPUS POSTUMUM*

The transition from the metaphysics of Nature to physics—
Transcendental philosophy and the construction of experience—
The objectivity of the Idea of God—Man as person and as
microcosm.

1. *The Critique of Judgment* appeared in 1790. From 1796 until 1803, the year before his death, Kant was engaged in preparing material for a work dealing with the transition from the metaphysics of Nature to physics. For in his opinion this was required to fill a gap in his philosophy. The manuscripts which he left behind him were at length published by Adickes as the *Opus Postumum*[1] or *Posthumous Work* of Kant. As might be expected in what amounts to a collection of notes comprising material for a systematic work, there is a great deal of repetition. Further, while some points are comparatively developed, others remain undeveloped. Again, it is by no means always easy either to elucidate the meaning of Kant's statements or to harmonize apparently divergent points of view. In other words, the commentator is not infrequently unable to decide with any certainty how Kant would have developed his thought if he had had the opportunity to do so, which ideas he would have discarded and which he would have retained, or how precisely he would have reconciled points of view which for us at least it is difficult to reconcile. And study of the chronology of the notes has not done away with these difficulties of interpretation. Hence any account of the movement of Kant's mind as revealed in the *Opus Postumum* is bound by the nature of the case to be largely problematic and conjectural. But this does not mean, of course, that the work is of no interest, or that it can simply be dismissed as an old man's jottings.

The metaphysics of Nature presents us with the concept of matter as that which is subject to motion in space (*das Bewegliche im Raum*)[2] and with its laws so far as these are determinable *a priori*. Physics, however, is concerned with 'the laws of the moving forces of matter in so far as they are given in experience'.[3]

---

[1] The *Opus Postumum* is contained in Vols. XXI–XXII of the Berlin critical edition, and references will be given according to volume and page.
[2] XXI, p. 526.   [3] XXII, p. 497.

At first sight it might appear that no special bridge or transition from the one to the other is required. But Kant is not of this opinion. For experience[1] is not something which is simply given; it is constructed. And physics, considered as concerned with the laws of the moving forces of matter as given in experience, pre-supposes something corresponding to a schematism of the *a priori* concepts of the metaphysics of Nature, a schematism which will form a bridge between the latter and empirical representations. 'The transition from the one science to the other must have (involve) certain mediating concepts (*Zwischenbegriffe*) which are given in the former and applied to the latter, and which belong both to the territory of the one and to that of the other. Otherwise this progress would be, not a regular transition (*ein gesetzmäsziger Uebergang*), but a leap (*Sprung*), in which one does not know where one is going to arrive, and after which, when one looks back, one does not really see the point of departure.'[2]

What Kant appears to be looking for is a schema of physics, in the sense of anticipations of the empirical investigation of Nature. Mere empirical observation of the moving forces of matter cannot be called physics, if physics is a science. As a science physics involves system, not a mere aggregation of observations. And systematization takes place according to *a priori* principles which give us, as it were, guiding lines in empirical investigation. 'From empirical intuition we can take nothing but what we ourselves have put there for physics.'[3] Thus 'there must be *a priori* principles according to which the moving forces are co-ordinated in relation to one another (that is, according to the formal element), while the moving forces in themselves (according to the material element, the object) are considered empirically'.[4] Some definite truths are, indeed, deducible *a priori*; but we also have problematical antici-pations of the empirical investigation of Nature, in the sense that we know that this or that must be the case, though empirical verification alone can tell us which is the case.

Kant aims, therefore, at elaborating a 'schematism of the faculty of judgment for the moving forces of matter'.[5] The meta-physics of Nature, providing us with the concept of matter as that which is subject to motion in space, has a natural tendency towards physics, that is, towards grounding a systematic empirical doctrine of Nature. But for this to be possible we require a

---

[1] Experience is described as the 'absolute unity of the knowledge of the objects of the senses'; XXII, p. 497.

[2] XXI, pp. 525–6.   [3] XXII, p. 323.   [4] XXI, p. 291.   [5] *Ibid.*

mediating concept. And this is provided by the concept of matter in so far as it has moving forces. This concept is partly empirical, inasmuch as it is on the basis of experience that the subject conceives moving forces of matter. But it is also partly *a priori*; for the relations of the moving forces to one another imply *a priori* laws, such as those of attraction and repulsion. The concept of matter in so far as it has moving forces is thus adapted to act as a mediating concept (*Zwischenbegriff*) between the purely *a priori* and the purely *a posteriori* or empirical. And Kant proposes to consider the moving forces of matter in a characteristic manner: 'The moving forces of matter are best divided according to the arrangement of the categories; according to their quantity, quality, relation and modality.'[1]

From one point of view, therefore, the *Opus Postumum* is a programme for working out the transition from the metaphysics of Nature to physics. But this transition falls under the general heading, so to speak, of the subject's construction of experience. Indeed, in his manuscripts Kant gives so much emphasis to this idea that he has appeared to some readers to be adumbrating a purely idealist system. And I wish now to say something about this topic.

2. In the *Opus Postumum* the Ideas of pure reason occupy a prominent place. According to Kant, the system of Ideas is the foundation of the possibility of the whole of experience. 'Transcendental philosophy is the system of synthetic knowledge by *a priori* concepts.'[2] If we took this proposition by itself, we might be inclined to interpret it as referring simply to the system of the categories and of the *a priori* principles of the understanding. But this is not precisely what Kant has in mind. The word 'system', which signifies a 'complete system of the possibility of the absolute whole of experience',[3] is the system of the Ideas of pure reason. 'Transcendental philosophy is pure philosophy (mixed neither with empirical nor with mathematical elements) in a system of the Ideas of the speculative and moral-practical reason, in so far as this constitutes an unconditioned whole.'[4] And this system is made possible 'through the positing of three objects, God, the World and the Idea of Duty':[5] or, we can say, through the positing of God, the World 'and Man in the world, as subject to the principles of duty'.[6] Or, inasmuch as man is in the world,

[1] XXI, p. 291.   [2] XXI, p. 81.   [3] XXI, p. 104.
[4] XXI, p. 77.   [5] XXI, p. 81.   [6] XXI, p. 82.

we can say that 'the totality of beings is God and the World'.[1]
Transcendental philosophy is thus said to be 'the doctrine of God
and the World'.[2] Again, 'highest point of view of the transcendental
philosophy in the two mutually related Ideas, *God and the World*'.[3]
In the Idea of God we think the totality of supersensible or
noumenal reality, and in the Idea of the World we think the
totality of sensible reality. Each Idea contains a 'maximum', and
we can say that 'there is one God and one World'.[4]

These two Ideas together form the Idea of the Universe. 'The
totality of things, *universum*, comprising God and the World.'[5]
Apart from God and the World there can be nothing. But while
these two Ideas are mutually related, the relation is not one of
simple coordination. The World is thought as subordinate to God,
the sensible to the supersensible, the phenomenal to the noumenal.
God and the World as '*entia non coordinata, sed subordinata*'.[6]
Further, the relation between them is synthetic, not analytic.
That is to say, it is man, as thinking subject, who thinks and relates these Ideas. 'God, the World, and the subject which links
together both objects, the thinking being in the World. God, the
World, and that which unites both in one system, the thinking
immanent principle of man (*mens*) in the World.'[7] Again, 'God,
the World and I, the thinking being in the World, which links
them together. God and the World are the two objects of transcendental philosophy, and (subject, predicate and copula) there is
the thinking Man; the subject which binds them together in one
proposition'.[8]

Kant does not mean that the Ideas of God and the World are
conceptual apprehensions of objects given in experience. In a
certain sense, of course, God and the World are thought as objects,
that is, as objects of thought; but they are not given as objects.
The Ideas are the thinking of pure reason as it constitutes itself
as thinking subject. They are 'not mere concepts but laws of
thinking which the subject prescribes to itself. Autonomy.'[9] By
thinking these Ideas the subject gives itself an object and constitutes itself as conscious. 'The first act of reason is consciousness.'[10] But 'I must have objects of my thought and apprehend
them; for otherwise I am not conscious of myself (*cogito, sum:* it
should not run, *ergo*). It is *autonomia rationis purae*. For without
this I should be without ideas . . . like a beast, without knowing

[1] XXI, p. 150.   [2] XXI, p. 6.   [3] XXI, p. 35.   [4] XXI, p. 20.
[5] XXI, p. 22.   [6] XXII, p. 62.   [7] XXI, p. 34.   [8] XXI, pp. 36–7.
[9] XXI, p. 93.   [10] XXI, p. 105.

that I am.'[1] The Ideas supply the material, as it were, for the subject's construction of experience. 'These representations are not mere concepts but also Ideas which provide the material (*den Stoff*) for synthetic *a priori* laws by means of concepts.'[2] God and the World are not 'substances outside my ideas but the thinking whereby we make for ourselves objects through synthetic *a priori* cognitions and are, subjectively, self-creators (*Selbstschöpfer*) of the objects we think'.[3]

The construction of experience can thus be represented as a process of what Kant calls self-positing, self-making, self-constituting, and so on. From the Idea of the World downwards, so to speak, there is a continuous process of schematization which is at the same time a process of objectification. And this process is the work of the self-positing noumenal subject. The categories are said to be acts by which the subject posits itself and constitutes itself as object for the sake of possible experience. And space and time, repeatedly affirmed to be pure subjective intuitions and not things or objects of perception, are said to be primitive products of imagination, self-made intuitions. The subject constitutes or posits itself as object, that is to say, both as the empirical ego and as the object which affects the empirical ego. We can thus speak of the subject as affecting itself.

The transition, therefore, from the metaphysics of Nature to physics, with which the *Opus Postumum* professedly deals, can be seen in the light of this general scheme. For it has to be shown that the possible types of moving forces in Nature and the possible types of quality experienced by the subject in its reaction to these forces are derivable, by a process of schematization, from the self-positing of the subject. At least this has to be shown if it is held that it is the subject itself which constructs experience.

Kant does not attempt to conceal the fact that this theory of the construction of experience through the self-positing of the subject is in some sense an idealist view. 'The transcendental philosophy is an idealism; inasmuch as the subject constitutes itself.'[4] Moreover, this philosophy bears a marked resemblance, at least at first sight, to that of Fichte, who published his *Basis of the Entire Theory of Science* in 1794. And the resemblance becomes all the more striking when we find Kant interpreting the thing in itself as a way in which the subject posits itself or makes itself its

[1] XXI, p. 82.   [2] XXI, p. 20.   [3] XXI, p. 21.   [4] XXI, p. 85.

own object. 'The object in itself (*Noumenon*) is a mere *Gedank-ending* (*ens rationis*), in the representation of which the subject posits itself.'[1] It is 'the mere representation of its own (the subject's) activity'.[2] The subject projects, as it were, its own unity, or its own activity of unification, in the negative idea of the thing in itself. The concept of the thing-in-itself becomes an act of the self-positing subject. The thing-in-itself is 'not a real thing';[3] it is 'not an existing reality but merely a principle',[4] 'the principle of the synthetic *a priori* knowledge of the manifold of sense-intuition in general and of the law of its co-ordination'.[5] And this principle is due to the subject in its construction of experience. The distinction between appearance and thing-in-itself is not a distinction between objects but holds good only for the subject.

At the same time the resemblances between Kant's theory of the construction of experience, as outlined or at least hinted at in the *Opus Postumum*, and Fichte's subjective transcendental idealism[6] do not justify a dogmatic assertion that in his old age Kant abandoned the doctrine of the thing-in-itself and derived the whole of reality from the self-positing of the noumenal subject. For to make such an assertion would be to over-emphasize the use of certain terms and to press certain statements at the expense of others. For example, passages occur in the *Opus Postumum* which appear simply to reaffirm the doctrine about the thing-in-itself which is to be found in the *Critique of Pure Reason*. Thus we are told that though the thing-in-itself is not given as an existing object, and indeed cannot be so given, it is none the less 'a *cogitabile* (and, indeed, as *necessarily thinkable*) which cannot be given but must be thought. . . .'[7] The idea of the thing-in-itself is correlative to that of appearance. Indeed, on one or two occasions Kant seems to go further in a realistic direction than one would expect. 'If we take the world as appearance, it proves precisely the existence (*Dasein*) of something which is not appearance.'[8] He also seems to imply on occasion that the thing-in-itself is simply the thing which appears when considered apart from its appearing. And as for the use of the word 'idealism' for transcendental philosophy, this does not seem to involve any new or revolutionary

---

[1] XXII, p. 36. [2] XXII, p. 37. [3] XXII, p. 24. [4] XXII, p. 34. [5] XXII, p. 33.
[6] 'Subjective' in the sense that the ultimate principle of being and knowledge is the subject; 'transcendental' in the sense that the subject is the pure or transcendental subject, not the empirical ego; 'idealism' in the sense that there is no factor which is not ultimately reducible to the self-positing of the transcendental subject or ego.
[7] XXXII, p. 23. [8] XXI, p. 440.

point of view. For transcendental philosophy is, as we have seen, the system of the Ideas of pure reason. And when Kant emphasizes in the *Opus Postumum* the problematic (not assertoric) character of these Ideas, he is not departing from the doctrine of the *Critiques*.

The fact of the matter seems to be that in the *Opus Postumum* Kant attempts to show that within the framework of the critical philosophy he can answer the objections of those who consider the theory of the thing-in-itself to be inconsistent and superfluous. It is indeed arguable that in the effort to reformulate his views in such a way as to answer his critics and to show that his philosophy contained within itself all that was valid in the development of Fichte and others Kant went a considerable way towards transforming his system into one of pure transcendental idealism. But to admit this is not the same thing as to admit that he ever definitely repudiated or abandoned the general point of view which is characteristic of the *Critiques*. And I do not believe that he did so.

3. Turning to the Idea of God, we can note in the first place that Kant distinguishes carefully between the question what is meant by the term 'God', that is, what is the content of the Idea of God, and the question whether God exists, that is, whether there is a being which possesses the attributes comprised in the Idea of God. 'God is not the world-soul. . . . The concept of God is that of a Being as supreme cause of the things in the world and as a person.'[1] God is conceived as the supreme Being, the supreme intelligence, the supreme good, who possesses rights and is a person. Again, 'a Being for which all human duties are at the same time his commands is God'.[2] Man thinks God according to the attributes which make him (man) a being in the noumenal sphere; but in the Idea of God these attributes are raised, as it were, to the maximum or absolute degree. Man, for instance, is free; but his being involves receptivity, and his freedom is not absolute. God, however, is conceived as supreme spontaneity and freedom, without receptivity and without limitation. For while man is finite and a mixed being, in the sense that he belongs both to the noumenal and to the phenomenal spheres, God is conceived as infinite noumenal reality. The World is conceived as the totality of sensible reality; but it is conceived as subordinate to the creative power of God and to his purposeful and holy will. As we have seen, the relation

[1] XXI, p. 19.   [2] XXI, p. 17.

between the Ideas of God and the World is not one of co-ordination: it is a relation of subordination, in the sense that the World is conceived as dependent on God.

Now, some statements in the *Opus Postumum*, if they are taken in isolation, that is to say, naturally tend to suggest that Kant has abandoned any notion of there being a God independently of the Idea of God. Thus while the Idea of God is said to be necessary, in the sense that it is inevitably thought by pure reason as an ideal, it is said to represent 'a thought thing[1] (*ens rationis*)'.[2] Indeed, 'the concept of such a Being is not the concept of a substance, that is, of a thing which exists independently of any thought, but the Idea (auto-creation, *Selbstgeschöpf*), thought-thing, *ens rationis*, of a reason which constitutes itself as an object of thought, and which produces, according to the principles of transcendental philosophy, *a priori* propositions and an Ideal, in regard to which there is no question of asking whether such an object exists; for the concept is transcendent'.[3]

At first sight at least this last quotation states clearly and explicitly that the Idea of God is a man-made ideal, a creation of thought, and that there is no extramental divine Being which corresponds to the Idea. Elsewhere, indeed, in the *Opus Postumum* Kant appears to be looking for a simpler and more immediate moral argument for God's existence than the argument already advanced in the second *Critique*. And this fact obviously militates against the view that in his old age Kant abandoned any belief in God as an objective reality, especially when there is other evidence to show that he retained this belief up to his death. It is true, indeed, that the *Opus Postumum* consists very largely of jottings, of ideas which occurred to Kant and which were noted for further consideration; and it is not really surprising if in a series of such notes there appear divergent lines of thought which we are not in a position to harmonize or reconcile. At the same time, however, it must be remembered that the ideas expressed in the passages mentioned in the last paragraph can be paralleled, to a great extent at least, in the *Critiques*, and that in the *Critiques* Kant also puts forward a justification of belief in God. Hence even if the divergence of views is sharper in the *Opus Postumum* than in the *Critiques*, it is not a novel phenomenon.

In the *Critique of Pure Reason* Kant had already made it clear that in his opinion the Idea of God, considered as the creation of

---

[1] *Ein Gedankending.* [2] XXI, pp. 32–3. [3] XXI, p. 27.

pure reason, is that of a 'transcendental Ideal'. It does not express any intuition of God; nor can we deduce God's existence from the Idea. And these views reappear in the *Opus Postumum*. We enjoy no intuition of God. 'We see Him as in a mirror; never face to face.'[1] Hence it is impossible to deduce God's existence from the Idea of God:[2] this Idea is a creation of pure reason, a transcendental Ideal. Further, though we think of God as infinite substance, He is not and cannot be a substance; for He transcends the categories of the human understanding. Hence, if we once presuppose this point of view, we cannot sensibly ask whether there is a divine Being corresponding to the Idea of God, at least in so far as the Idea involves thinking of God in terms of the categories. This conclusion substantially repeats the doctrine of the first *Critique*. But, as we have seen, Kant went on in the second *Critique* to offer a moral or practical justification for belief in God. And in the *Opus Postumum* he offers some suggestions for following out or developing this line of thought.

In the second *Critique* Kant justified belief in God as a postulate of the practical reason. We arrive, or can arrive, at belief in God through reflection on the demands of the moral law in regard to the synthesis of virtue with happiness. In the *Opus Postumum* he appears to be concerned with finding a more immediate transition from consciousness of the moral law to belief in God. And the categorical imperative is represented as containing within itself the precept of looking on all human duties as divine commands. 'In the moral-practical reason lies the categorical imperative to regard all human duties as divine commands.'[3] Again, 'To see all in God. The categorical imperative. The knowledge of my duties as divine commands, enunciated through the categorical imperative.'[4] Thus 'the concept of God is the concept of an obligation-imposing subject outside myself'.[5] The categorical imperative is for us the voice of God; and God is manifested in the consciousness of moral obligation, through the moral law.

To be sure, Kant insists that this is not a proof of God's existence as a substance existing outside the human mind. He also insists that nothing is added to the force of the moral law by regarding it as a divine command, and that if a man does not believe in God the obliging force of the categorical imperative is not thereby

---

[1] xxi, p. 33.
[2] Some passages of the *Opus Postumum* seem at first sight to contradict this statement. They will be referred to presently.
[3] xxi, p. 12. [4] xxi, p. 15. [5] *Ibid.*

taken away.'[1] And it is easy to understand that those who concentrate their attention on such statements are inclined to draw
the conclusion that the word 'God' became for Kant simply a
name for the categorical imperative itself or a name for a purely
subjective projection of a voice speaking through the moral law.
But, as we have seen, on Kant's premisses there could not possibly
be a proof of God's existence as a particular substance. And
unless Kant is prepared to reject the doctrine of the second
Critique about the autonomy of the will, he is bound to say that
the moral force of the categorical imperative does not depend on
our regarding it as the expression of a divine command. But it does
not necessarily follow that God is for him no more than a name
for the categorical imperative. What follows is that the only access
we have to God is through the moral consciousness. No theoretical
demonstration of God's existence is possible. This is, indeed, the
doctrine of the *Critique*; but in the *Opus Postumum* Kant seems
to be seeking a more immediate connection between consciousness
of obligation and belief in God. 'Freedom under laws: duties as
divine commands. There is a God.'[2]

It is perhaps in the light of this desire to find a more immediate
justification of belief in God that we should interpret the passages
in the *Opus Postumum* which at first sight appear to amount to a
statement of the *a priori* or ontological argument for God's
existence. Kant tells us, for example, that 'the idea (*Gedanke*) of
Him is at the same time belief in Him and in His personality'.[3]
Again, 'the mere Idea (*Idee*) of God at the same time a postulate
of His existence. To think Him and to believe in Him is an identical
proposition.'[4] And if we were to connect these statements with the
statement that 'a necessary being is one the concept of which is
at the same time a sufficient proof of its existence',[5] we might be
inclined to suppose that Kant, after having rejected the ontological argument in the *Critique of Pure Reason*, came to accept
it in the *Opus Postumum*. But it is most unlikely that he did anything of the kind. He seems to be speaking, not of a theoretical
demonstration, such as the ontological argument purported to be,
but of a 'sufficient proof' for the moral consciousness, that is, from
the purely practical or moral point of view. 'The principle of fulfilling all duties as divine commands in religion, proves the
freedom of the human will . . . and is at the same time, in relation

---

[1] Cf. XXII, p. 64.   [2] XXII, p. 104.   [3] XXII, p. 62.
[4] XXII, p. 109.   [5] XXII, p. 113.

to practical pure principles of reason, a proof of the existence of God as the one God.'[1] It is not that I first have an idea of the divine essence, from which I deduce God's existence. It is rather that through consciousness of the categorical imperative I rise to the idea of God as speaking to me through and in the moral law. And to have this idea of God and to believe in Him are one and the same thing. That is to say, to conceive God as immanent to me, as morally commanding subject, is to conceive Him as existing. But this awareness of God as immanent in the moral consciousness is a 'sufficient proof' of His existence only for this consciousness.

If this interpretation is on the right lines (and one is scarcely in a position to dogmatize on this matter), we can say perhaps that Kant is giving or suggesting a moral equivalent of or analogue to the ontological argument. The latter was thought by its defenders to be a theoretical demonstration of God's existence of such a kind that, once properly understood, it compels assent. Kant does not admit that there is any such argument. But there is something analogous to it. To conceive God as morally commanding subject, immanent in the moral consciousness, and to have a religious belief in Him are one and the same thing. But this does not mean that from a purely abstract idea of a supreme moral legislator one can deduce theoretically the existence of this divine legislator in such a way as to compel the mind's assent. It means rather that within and for the moral consciousness itself the idea of the law as the voice of a divine legislator is equivalent to belief in God's existence. For to have this idea of God is, for the moral consciousness, to postulate His existence. This may not be a very convincing line of argument. For it is arguable that in the long run it amounts to the tautology that to believe in God is to believe in Him. But it is evident at least that Kant is seeking a more immediate approach to belief in God based on the moral consciousness than the one already developed in the second *Critique*. How he would have developed his new approach, if he had had the opportunity of doing so, we cannot, of course, say.

4. We have seen that the synthesis between the Ideas of God and the World is effected by man, the thinking subject. This is possible because man is himself a mediating being; and the concept of man is a mediating concept or idea. For man has a foot, so to speak, in both camps. He belongs to both the supersensible and the sensible, the noumenal and the phenomenal spheres; and

[1] XXII, p. III.

through the moral consciousness the sensible is subordinated to the supersensible. The human reason can thus think the totality of supersensible being in the Idea of God and the totality of sensible being in the Idea of the World; and it synthesizes these Ideas by positing a relation between them whereby the Idea of the World is subordinated to the Idea of God.

That man belongs to the sensible order or sphere is evident. That is to say, it is evident that he belongs to the class of physical organic beings. And, as such, he is subject to the laws of determined causality. But his moral life manifests his freedom; and, as free, he belongs to the noumenal order or sphere. 'Man (a being in the world, *ein Weltwesen*) is at the same time a being which possesses freedom, a property which is outside the causal principles of the world but which nevertheless belongs to man.'[1] And to possess freedom is to possess spirit. 'There is thus a being above the world, namely the *spirit* of man.'[2] And to be free in virtue of a spiritual principle is to be a person. 'The living corporeal being is besouled (*animal*). If it is a person, it is a human being.'[3] Man is a person in that he is a free, self-conscious, moral being.

Does this mean that man is split, as it were, into two elements? It obviously means that we can distinguish between man as noumenon and man as phenomenon. 'Man in the world belongs to the knowledge of the world; but man as conscious of his duty in the world is not phenomenon but noumenon; and he is not a thing but a person.'[4] But though man possesses this dual nature, there is a unity of consciousness. 'I (the subject) am a person, not merely conscious of myself, but also as object of intuition in space and time, and so as belonging to the world.'[5] I possess 'the consciousness of my existence in the world in space and time'.[6] This unity, which is at the same time a unity of two principles, is manifested in the moral consciousness. 'There is in me a reality which, different from me in the causal relation of efficacity (*nexus effectivus*), acts on me (*agit, facit, operatur*). This reality, which is free, that is, independent of the natural law in space and time, directs me interiorly (justifies or condemns me); and I, man, am myself this reality....'[7] Moreover, my freedom can translate itself into action within the world. 'There is in man an active but supersensible principle which, independent of Nature and of natural causality, determines phenomena and is called freedom.'[8]

---

[1] XXI, p. 42. [2] *Ibid.* [3] XXI, p. 18. [4] XXI, p. 61.
[5] XXI, p. 42. [6] XXI, p. 24. [7] XXI, p. 25. [8] XXI, p. 50.

If Kant had developed his theory of the construction of experience, he might, indeed, have derived the empirical ego and man as a phenomenal being from the self-positing of the noumenal ego with a view to moral self-realization. But to say this is to say that there are grounds in the Kantian philosophy for the development of the position adopted by Fichte. And the latter, indeed, always maintained that his own system was a consistent development of the inner tendencies of Kantianism. As it is, however, we are presented rather with the metaphysical concept of man as the microcosm which thinks the macrocosm, namely the Universe. The Universe, as thought by man in the regulative Ideas of God and the World, is a projection of man's dual nature. Neither Idea represents a given object. And from the regulative Idea of God as the transcendental Ideal we cannot deduce God's existence as a substance. So far as His existence can be spoken of as given or manifested, it is manifested only to the moral consciousness in its awareness of obligation. But, as we have seen, this leaves the problem of God's objective existence in suspense. Is the reality corresponding to the term 'God' simply the supersensible principle in man himself, the noumenal ego? Or it is a Being distinct from man, which is known only in and through the awareness of obligation? For my part I think that the second view represents Kant's conviction. But it cannot be said that the jottings which form the *Opus Postumum* make the answer very clear. Rather does the work illustrate the tendency of Kantianism to transform itself into a system of transcendental idealism, subordinating being to thought or, rather, ultimately identifying them. I do not think that Kant himself ever took this decisive step. But the tendency to do so is implicit in his writings, even if Kant did not take kindly to Fichte's suggestions that he should eliminate the element of realism in his system or, as Fichte put it, the element of 'dogmatism'. It is, however, inappropriate to interpret the Kantian philosophy simply in terms of its relation to the speculative idealism which succeeded it. And, if we take it by itself, we can see in it an original attempt to solve the problem of reconciling the two realms of necessity and freedom, not by reducing the one to the other, but by finding the meeting-point in the moral consciousness of man.

CHAPTER XVII

CONCLUDING REVIEW

Introductory remarks — Continental rationalism — British empiricism—The Enlightenment and the science of man—The philosophy of history—Immanuel Kant—Final remarks.

1. In the preface to the present volume I remarked that the fourth, fifth and sixth volumes of this *History*, which together cover the philosophy of the seventeenth and eighteenth centuries, form a trilogy. That is to say, they can be regarded as one whole. At the beginning of Volume IV there was an introductory chapter relating to the matter covered in all three volumes. And I promised to supply a common concluding review at the end of Volume VI.

The purpose of this concluding review is not to give a synopsis of the different philosophies discussed in the trilogy, but to attempt some discussion of the nature, importance and value of the chief styles of philosophizing or philosophical movements in the seventeenth and eighteenth centuries. It will be necessary to confine the discussions to certain selected themes. Further, though reference will, of course, be made to individual philosophers, it will sometimes be necessary to treat complex movements of thought, comprising philosophies which differ from one another in important respects, as though they represented homogeneous styles of philosophizing or even homogeneous systems. In other words, I propose to indulge in discussion of ideal types, as it were, and in generalizations which stand in need of considerable qualification. This procedure may not, indeed, be desirable in itself, but it seems to me to be a legitimate way of drawing attention to certain features of philosophical thought in the period in question, provided, of course, that the different philosophies are treated separately elsewhere.

2. In the introduction to the fourth volume attention was drawn to Descartes' desire to overcome the revived scepticism of the Renaissance which included scepticism about the possibility of solving metaphysical problems and attaining truth in metaphysics. And we saw that he looked to mathematics as a model of clear and certain reasoning. He wished to give to philosophy a clarity and certainty analogous to the clarity and certainty of

mathematics and to distil, as it were, from mathematical method a method which would enable the mind to proceed in an orderly way from step to step without confusion or error.

It is easily understandable that Descartes looked to mathematics as a model of reasoning when one remembers his own mathematical studies and talents and the contemporary advances in this subject. And there is nothing exceptional in this instance of philosophical thought being influenced by extra-philosophical factors. For although philosophy has a continuity of its own, in the sense that we can give an intelligible account of its historical development, this continuity is not absolute, as though philosophy pursued a completely isolated path, without connection with other cultural factors. It can be influenced by other factors in various ways. It can be influenced, for instance, in respect of the concept of the proper method to be employed. Descartes' tendency to look to mathematics as providing a model of method is a case in point. Another example would be modern attempts to interpret metaphysics as hypotheses of wider generality than those of the particular sciences, an interpretation which reflects the influence of an extra-philosophical model, namely the hypothetico-deductive method of modern physics. Again, philosophy can be influenced by extra-philosophical factors in respect of its subject-matter or of the emphasis placed on a certain theme or themes. In the Middle Ages philosophy was powerfully influenced by theology, 'the queen of the sciences'. In the first decades of the nineteenth century we can see the consciousness of historical development, which found expression in the growth of historical science, reflected in the system of Hegel. Marxism obviously showed the influence of the increasing consciousness of the part played by economic factors in the history of civilization and culture. The philosophy of Bergson owed much not only to the scientific hypothesis of evolution but also to the studies of psychologists and sociologists. The thought of Whitehead was influenced by the transition from classical to modern physics. Again, philosophy can be influenced by extra-philosophical factors in regard to the formulation of its problems. For instance, the problem of the relation between soul and body is a classical and a recurrent problem; but the rise of the particular sciences has affected the ways in which the problem has presented itself to different philosophers. The advance of mechanics led to the problem presenting itself to seventeenth-century philosophers in one light, while modern developments in psychology have given a rather different colouring, so to speak, to the problem in the eyes of later thinkers. In one sense we can speak of the same problem, of a 'perennial' problem; but in another sense we can speak of different problems, namely in the sense that different relevant factors which affect our conception and formulation of the basic problem have to be taken into consideration.

To speak in this way is simply to recognize empirical facts: it is not to proclaim the theory that truth is relative. It is, indeed, foolish to deny the historical data to which adherents of the theory of relativism appeal in support of their thesis. But it does not necessarily follow that acknowledgment of the historical data entails acceptance of the thesis that systems of philosophy must be judged simply and solely in terms of their historical contexts and situations, and that no absolute judgments about the truth or falsity of the propositions comprised in them are possible. We can hardly deny that in the course of its development philosophy (that is, the minds of philosophers) has been influenced by extra-philosophical factors. But it is still open to us to discuss, without reference to these factors, whether the propositions enunciated by philosophers are true or false.

Returning to Descartes' admiration for the mathematical model of method, we can recall that other leading rationalist philosophers of the pre-Kantian modern period were also influenced by this model, Spinoza, for example. But what is called 'rationalism'[1] in the history of seventeenth-century philosophy does not consist simply in a preoccupation with method. It is natural to think of philosophy as capable of increasing our knowledge of reality.[2] This is a spontaneous expectation; and any doubt about philosophy's capacity in this respect follows, rather than precedes, the expectation. It is understandable, therefore, that the signal success of the application of mathematics in physical science from the time of the Renaissance onwards should incline some philosophers to think that the application in philosophy of a method analogous to that of mathematics would enable them not only to systematize what was already known or to give the form of knowledge, so to

[1] As was pointed out in the Introduction to Vol. IV rationalism in the present context does not signify simply an attempt to base philosophy on reason rather than on mystical insights. Nor must the term be understood in the sense which has been given it in later times, namely as involving a denial of revealed religion, and perhaps of all religion. There were, indeed, rationalists in this sense in the seventeenth and eighteenth centuries; but the term is not used in this way when we speak of Descartes, for example, as a rationalist.

[2] I use the term 'reality' in preference to 'the world', because the knowledge in question might concern a Being, God, which transcends the world.

speak, to propositions which were true but which had not been logically demonstrated, but also to increase our knowledge through the deduction of unknown or unrecognized truths. The idea of using mathematics for the advance of physical science was not, of course, new. Roger Bacon, for instance, had already insisted on the need for this use in the thirteenth century. But at the same time it is not until the Renaissance that we can really speak of the signal or striking success of the application in physics. It was natural, therefore, that some post-Renaissance thinkers should look to the application in philosophy of a method analogous to that of mathematics to increase the scope of our knowledge of reality. In other words, the rationalists were concerned not only with methodology but also with using the appropriate method to discover new truths, to increase our positive knowledge of reality.

Now, if we put together the idea of giving to philosophy a method analogous to that of mathematics and the idea of deducing from fundamental propositions or from already demonstrated propositions other propositions which give us new factual information about reality, we obtain the idea of a deductive system of philosophy which will be akin to mathematics in its deductive form but different from it in the sense that the system of philosophy will give us truths about existent reality. I do not intend to imply that this distinction would have been universally admitted by Renaissance and post-Renaissance thinkers. Galileo, for example, thought of mathematics, not as a purely formal science exhibiting the implications of freely-chosen definitions and axioms, but as opening to us the very heart of Nature, as enabling us to read the book of Nature. However, it is clear that a proposition about, say, the properties of a triangle, does not tell us that there are triangular objects, whereas the great rationalist philosophers of the pre-Kantian modern period thought of themselves as concerned with existent reality.

Now, the successful application of mathematics in physical science naturally suggested that the world is intelligible or 'rational'. Thus for Galileo God had written the book of Nature in mathematical characters, as it were. And, indeed, if philosophy is to be a deductive system and at the same time to give us certain factual information about the world, it is obviously necessary to assume that the world is of such a kind that it is possible for philosophy to do this. In practice this means that the causal relation will be assimilated to the relation of logical implication. And we find among the rationalist philosophers the tendency to make this assimilation.

Now, let us assume that the world is a rational system in the sense that it has an intelligible structure which can be reconstructed by the philosopher through a process of deduction. Philosophy can then be represented as the unfolding of reason itself, in such a way that the systematic development of philosophical knowledge discloses to us the objective structure of reality. But if the system of reality can be reconstructed by a deductive process which represents the self-unfolding of reason, it is not unnatural to postulate a theory of ideas which are at least virtually innate. For the self-unfolding of reason will mean the development of a philosophical system by the mind from its own resources, so to speak. And the system will be prefigured in the mind in the form of ideas which are virtually present from the start, even though experience may be the occasion of them becoming actual. I do not mean to imply that a deductive system of philosophy necessarily entails a theory of innate ideas. But if it is represented as an unfolding of the mind itself, and if this description signifies anything more than the development of the logical implications of certain definitions and axioms which are either freely chosen or derived in some way from experience, some version of the theory of innate ideas seems to be required. And the theory of virtually innate ideas obviously fits in very much better with the concept of the self-unfolding of mind or reason than would a theory of actual innate ideas.

If philosophy is to rest on virtually innate ideas, and if its conclusions are to be certainly true to reality, it is clear that these ideas must represent real insights into objective essences. Further, we shall require some assurance that in the process of philosophical deduction we are treating of existent reality, and not simply with the realm of possibility. We can understand, therefore, the fondness of the rationalist metaphysicians for the ontological argument for the existence of God. For, if it is valid, it permits an immediate inference from the idea to the existence of the ultimate reality, God or the absolutely perfect and necessary being.

How is this argument of use in a deductive reconstruction of the structure of reality? In this way. If we press the analogy between the development of a deductive system of mathematics and the construction of a philosophical system, we are driven to start in philosophy with a proposition expressing the existence of the ultimate being (a proposition taken as analogous to the fundamental axioms in mathematics) and to deduce finite being by assimilating the causal relation to that of logical implication. We require, therefore, to be assured of the existence of the primary metaphysical principle or ultimate being. And the ontological argument, passing directly from the idea of this being to its existence, fits in much better with the demands of a purely deductive system than does an *a posteriori* argument which explicitly infers the existence of God from the existence of finite being. For we wish to pass, in logical language, from principle to conclusion rather than from conclusion to principle.

The foregoing account of rationalism is, of course, a description of an ideal type, of what might be called pure or ideal rationalism. And it cannot be applied without qualification to the great systems of pre-Kantian continental philosophy. Of the three leading rationalist systems which were discussed in Volume IV it is that of Spinoza which approximates most closely to the description. Descartes, as we saw, did not start with the ultimate reality but with the existence of the finite ego as thinking subject. And he did not think that the existence of the world can be deduced from the existence of God. As for Leibniz, he distinguished between necessary truths or truths of reason and contingent truths or truths of fact. He tended, indeed, to present this distinction as being relative to our finite knowledge; but he made it none the less. And he did not maintain that the creation of the monads which actually exist is logically deducible from the divine essence by a process of reasoning based on the principle of non-contradiction. To explain the transition from the order of necessary essences to that of contingent existences he invoked the principle of perfection or of the best rather than the principle of non-contradiction.

But though the description of rationalism which I have given above cannot be applied without qualification to all those systems which are generally labelled systems of rationalist metaphysics, it represents a tendency which is present in them all. And in my introductory remarks to this chapter I gave notice that for the purpose of discussing different styles of philosophizing I should make use of ideal types and indulge in generalizations which, in their application to particular instances, would stand in need of qualification.

It is scarcely necessary, I think, to discuss at length the theory of innate ideas. For it seems to me that in its main lines at least Locke's criticism of the theory as a superfluous hypothesis is clearly justified. If the theory of virtually innate ideas meant merely that the mind possesses the capacity of forming certain ideas, all ideas could be called innate. But in this case there would be no point in so describing them. The theory can have point only if certain ideas cannot be derived from experience, while other ideas can be so derived. But what is meant by the derivation of ideas from experience? If, of course, experience is reduced to the reception of impressions (in Hume's sense), and if ideas are thought of as automatic effects or as photographic representations of impressions, it becomes very difficult, if not impossible, to explain certain ideas as derived from experience. We have no impression, for instance, of absolute perfection or of absolute infinity. But if we once allow for the constructive activity of the mind, it does not seem to be any longer necessary to suppose that an idea of absolute perfection, for instance, is either imprinted by God or innate. If, indeed, the idea were equivalent to an intuition of absolute perfection, we could not explain its origin in terms of the mind's synthesizing activity based on experience of finite and limited perfection. But there does not appear to be any adequate reason for saying that we possess intuitions of absolute perfection and absolute infinity. And we can give an empirical explanation of the origin of such ideas, provided that we do not understand derivation from experience as meaning photographic representation of the immediate data of sense-perception and introspection. It is not that the theory of innate ideas states a logical impossibility. It is rather that it appears to constitute a superfluous hypothesis to which the principle of economy or Ockham's razor can be profitably applied. The theory can, of course, be transformed in the way that Kant subsequently transformed it in his theory of *a priori* categories, which were moulds of concepts, as it were, rather than concepts or ideas in the ordinary sense. But once it has been transformed in this way it can no longer perform its original function of forming a basis for a metaphysical system in the sense in which the pre-Kantian rationalists understood metaphysics.

Rejection of the theory of innate ideas must, of course, entail rejection of the rationalist ideal if this is taken to be the ideal of deducing a system of reality simply from the resources of the mind itself without recourse to experience. For this ideal would involve the theory of virtually innate ideas. But rejection of this theory does not necessarily entail the rejection of the ideal of a deductive metaphysics as such. For we might be able to arrive at the fundamental principles of such a metaphysics on the basis of experience. That is to say, experience might be the occasion of our seeing the truth of certain fundamental metaphysical propositions. Take the proposition, 'everything which comes into being does so through the agency of an extrinsic cause'. The ideas of coming into being and of causality are obtained through experience: they are not innate ideas.[1] Further, the ideas are distinct. The idea, that is to say, of being caused is not obtained by mere analysis of the idea of coming into being, in a sense which would make it true to say that the proposition in question is a tautology. Hence the proposition is synthetic. But if, as I believe to be the case, the proposition expresses an insight into an objective necessary connection, it is not a synthetic *a posteriori* proposition, in the sense of an empirical generalization which might prove to admit of exceptions. On the contrary, it is a synthetic *a priori* proposition, not in the sense that it is innate but in the sense that its truth is logically independent of empirical verification.[2] And if there are a number of propositions of this type, it may very well be possible to give to general metaphysics or ontology the form of a deductive science.

It certainly does not follow, however, that from propositions of the type mentioned we can deduce existential propositions. The proposition, 'everything which comes into being does so through the agency of an extrinsic cause', states that if anything comes into being it does so through the agency of an extrinsic cause. It does not state that there is anything which comes into being, has done so or will do so. Nor can we deduce from the proposition the conclusion that there is, has been or will be anything of this kind. More accurately, from two propositions, neither of which is an existential proposition, we cannot logically deduce an existential

---

[1] The statement can, of course, be expressed in more 'linguistic' fashion, without the use of the word 'idea'. One might say, for instance, that we learn the meanings of the terms through experience, or through ostensive definition.

[2] I have used the Kantian term 'synthetic *a priori* proposition'. And the use of this particular term can be misleading: for though I agree with Kant that there are propositions which are neither tautologies nor merely probable empirical generalizations, I do not accept Kant's interpretation of their status. In my opinion they express insight into the objective intelligible structure of being. But the term is a convenient one; and it is frequently used today without its use involving, or being thought to involve, the interpretation peculiar to Kant.

conclusion. We may, for instance, be able to deduce a proposition or propositions which will be true of any finite being, if there is any finite being; but we cannot deduce that there is in fact a finite being. In other words, if we once grant that there can be synthetic *a priori* propositions, it follows that we can deduce a scheme of reality in the sense of a body of propositions which will be true of existent things if there are any existent things. But we cannot deduce that this condition is in fact fulfilled. We remain within the sphere of possibility.

Further, from propositions which state what must be true of every existent thing we can deduce only similar propositions. That is to say, from necessary propositions we cannot deduce contingent propositions, the opposite of which is possible. And this holds good whether we confine necessary propositions to those of formal logic and pure mathematics or whether we admit metaphysical principles which are necessarily true. In other words, if we start with premises belonging to general metaphysics or ontology and proceed deductively, we remain within the sphere of general metaphysics or ontology. From such premises we cannot deduce the true propositions which belong to the body of a particular science. We can, of course, apply metaphysical principles which are necessarily true of, say, every finite thing to particular classes of finite things. But this is not the same as deducing the propositions of chemistry or botany or medicine from metaphysical premises. If we assume that the proposition that everything which comes into being does so through the agency of an extrinsic cause is a necessarily true metaphysical proposition, it follows that if there is such a thing as cancer of the lung it will have a cause or causes. But it certainly does not follow that we can deduce from metaphysics what the causes are.

I do not intend to imply that Descartes, for instance, believed that we can in fact start with general metaphysical truths and then deduce logically all the truths of natural science, dispensing with experiment or observation, hypothesis and empirical verification. But the tendency of rationalism was to assimilate the whole body of true propositions to a mathematical system in which all conclusions are logically implied by the fundamental premises. And in so far as the rationalists entertained the ideal of such an assimilation, they were indulging in a vain dream.

Now, it has been said above that from two premises neither of which is an existential proposition we cannot deduce an existential conclusion. But the question arises whether we can start with an existential proposition and deduce other existential propositions in such a way that from the existence of the ultimate ontological principle we can deduce the existence of dependent, finite being. In other words, can we start with the affirmation of the existence of the absolutely perfect and infinite being and deduce the existence of finite being?

To do this, we should have to be able to demonstrate one of two things. We should have to be able to show either that the meaning of the term 'infinite being' contains as part of itself the meaning of the term 'finite being' or that the nature of infinite being is such that it must necessarily cause (that is, create) finite being. In the first case we should have a monistic philosophy. To assert the existence of infinite being would be to assert the existence of finite being, the latter being comprised in some way within the former. If we had already demonstrated the existence of infinite being, by the ontological argument for example, we should only have to analyse the term 'infinite being' to show that finite being exists. In the second case we should not necessarily have a monistic philosophy; but finite being, even if distinct from God, would proceed from Him by a necessity of the divine nature.

As for the first alternative, the term 'infinite being' is used in contradistinction to the term 'finite being', and it comprises the latter within its meaning only in the sense that it involves the negation of finitude. Affirmation of the existence of infinite being involves the negation that this being is finite, not that finite being exists as its modification. Some might perhaps wish to claim that the term 'infinite being', taken in contradistinction to 'finite being', is vacuous; and that to give it content we must understand it as meaning the infinite complex of finite beings. But in this case the assertion that infinite being exists would be equivalent to the assertion that the number of finite beings is infinite. And it would be as idle to talk about deducing the existence of finite being from that of infinite being as it would be to talk about deducing the existence of tea-cups from the statement that the number of tea-cups is infinite. In the present context we are concerned with the deduction of finite being from that of infinite being when the existence of the latter is already known. But if to assert the existence of infinite being were to assert that the number of finite beings is infinite, how could we possibly be said to know that there is infinite being unless we knew that there was an infinite number of finite beings? And in this case the question of deducing their existence would not arise.

As for the second alternative, namely that of showing that God creates by a necessity of His nature, what basis could we possibly have for such an assertion? If we understand by God, an absolutely perfect and infinite being, to affirm God's existence is to affirm the existence of a being which is by nature self-sufficient. That is to say, the creation of finite being cannot add anything to God which would otherwise be lacking. And in this case it does not appear that there could be any conceivable grounds for asserting the necessity of creation. It is significant that Leibniz, when trying to explain divine creation, had recourse to the idea of moral rather than of metaphysical necessity. But if we once understand by God the absolutely perfect being, there does not seem to be any ground for speaking of creation as 'necessary' in any sense of the word.

Of course, if we were discussing theism and pantheism as such, we should have to consider the whole theme of the relation of the finite to the infinite. But we have been discussing a specific point, namely the deduction of finite from infinite being when the existence of the latter is taken as known. And this question implies a distinction between finite and infinite, for it is a question of deducing the existence of the finite from that of the infinite. If, therefore, the term 'infinite being' is analysed in such a way that it means simply an infinite number of finite beings, the problem of deduction, as originally understood, simply disappears. All that is required is an analysis of 'infinite being', and the analysis dissolves the problem. The original question no longer possesses any significance. If, however, we maintain the distinction which is essential for the significance of the problem (that is, the distinction between the infinite and the finite), there seems to be no conceivable ground for a deduction of the existence of finite being from that of infinite being. And it is with this deduction alone that we have been concerned, not with the problems which arise when we proceed the other way round and infer the existence of the infinite from the existence of the finite.

To sum up these critical reflections in dogmatic form. In the first place, from premises which state what must be true of anything if there is anything, we cannot deduce the conclusion that there is something. In the second place, from premises which state what must necessarily be true of anything we cannot deduce conclusions which are in fact true but which could conceivably be false. In the third place, we cannot begin with the affirmation of infinite being and deduce the existence of finite being. We cannot, therefore, construct a purely deductive metaphysics according to the model of a mathematical system, if we mean by a purely deductive metaphysics one in which the affirmation of the being that is first in the ontological order corresponds to the fundamental premisses of a mathematical system and in which the deduction of the existence of the world of finite beings corresponds to the deduction of conclusions in the mathematical system.

Obviously, these critical comments affect the systems of Descartes, Spinoza and Leibniz only in so far as they approximate to what I have called the ideal type of rationalism. And they do this in varying degrees. It is not my intention to deny that these philosophers said anything which was true or interesting. At the very least these philosophers present us with interesting outlooks on the world. And they raise important philosophical problems. Further, they offer programmes, as it were, for subsequent research. Thus Spinoza's description of the awareness or feeling of freedom as ignorance of determining causes can be interpreted, when we look back, as an invitation to the development of depth psychology. And Leibniz' dream of an ideal symbolic language has an obvious importance in the fields of logic and linguistic analysis. But all this does not alter the fact that the history of pre-Kantian continental rationalism has helped to show that metaphysical philosophy cannot take a form suggested by a close analogy with the deductive form of pure mathematics.

3. When we turn our attention to British empiricism, we are turning to a movement of thought which has a much greater significance for contemporary philosophy than pre-Kantian continental rationalism can be said to have. Hume is a living thinker in a sense in which Spinoza is not. The empiricism of the seventeenth and eighteenth centuries has, indeed, been developed; and the language in which it is now expressed is somewhat different from that employed by the classical empiricists. In particular, emphasis is now placed on logical rather than on psychological considerations. But the fact remains that empiricism exercises a powerful influence in modern thought, especially, of course, in England, whereas the influence excercised by pre-Kantian rationalist philosophers on the more metaphysically-minded thinkers of today does not proceed from their approximation to

what I have called rationalism as an ideal type but from other aspects of their thought.

In discussing classical British empiricism one is faced with a difficulty analogous to that with which one is faced in attempting to discuss rationalism as such. For those philosophers of the seventeenth and eighteenth centuries who are traditionally classed as empiricist differed very considerably in their views. If one interprets empiricism in the light of its point of departure, namely Locke's theory that all ideas are derived from experience, then we must obviously include Locke as an empiricist. But if one interprets the movement in the light of its point of arrival in the philosophy of Hume, we shall have to admit that the philosophies of Locke and Berkeley, while containing empiricist elements, are not purely empiricist systems. But this difficulty is, of course, unavoidable if we propose to discuss empiricism as a set of doctrines and as an ideal type rather than as an historical movement. And as in this section I intend to concern myself with empiricism as represented principally by Hume, I remark in advance that I am perfectly well aware that my comments are relevant much more to Hume's thought than to that of either Locke or Berkeley.

Hume's empiricism can, of course, be regarded under different aspects. It can be regarded as a psychological doctrine about the origin and formation of ideas, or as an epistemological doctrine concerning the nature, scope and limits of human knowledge. We can consider it as a logical theory of the different types of propositions or as an essay in conceptual analysis, that is, in the analysis of concepts such as mind, body, cause and so on. But all these different aspects are unified by Hume himself in his idea of the science of human nature, the study of man in his cognitive and reasoning activities and in his moral, aesthetic and social life. As we saw when considering Hume's thought in Volume V, he envisaged an extension of 'experimental philosophy' to what he called, using the term in a wide sense, 'moral subjects'. A study of man is not, as such, a mark of empiricism. Man was studied by the rationalists as well, not to speak of Greek, mediaeval and Renaissance philosophers. But, as has just been mentioned, it was Hume's aim to apply to his subject-matter the method of 'experimental philosophy'. And this meant for him restricting oneself to the evidence offered by observation. True, we ought to endeavour to find the simplest and fewest causes which will explain phenomena. But in doing this we must not go beyond phenomena in the sense of appealing to occult entities, to unobserved substances. There may be occult causes; but even if there are, we cannot have anything to do with them in the experimental science of man. We must try to find general laws (the principle of the association of ideas, for example) which will correlate phenomena and permit verifiable prediction. But we ought not to expect or pretend to discover ultimate causes which transcend the phenomenal level. And any hypothesis which purports to do so should be rejected.

In other words, Hume's plan is to extend to philosophy in general the methodological limitations of Newtonian physics. It is therefore not unreasonable to say that just as continental rationalism was influenced by the model of mathematical deduction, so was the empiricism of Hume influenced by the model of Newtonian physics. This is, indeed, made quite clear by Hume himself in his introduction to the *Treatise of Human Nature*. It is thus possible to look on both rationalism and empiricism as experiments, on rationalism as an experiment to see how far the mathematical model was applicable in philosophy, and on empiricism as an experiment in applying in philosophy the methodological limitations of classical physics.[1]

The feature of Hume's actual procedure which immediately strikes the reader is probably reductive analysis. By this term I understand analysis of the complex into the simple or relatively simple and of wholes into constituent parts. There was, indeed, nothing novel in the use of reductive analysis as such. Without going further back we can recall Locke's reduction of complex to simple ideas and Berkeley's analysis of material things as clusters of phenomena or, as he put it, 'ideas'. But Hume applied this method of investigation in a much more radical way than his predecessors had done. We have only to think of his analysis of causality and of the self.

We cannot say, of course, that Hume's philosophy was all analysis and no synthesis. For one thing he tried to reconstruct the complex out of its elements. Thus he tried to show, for example, how our complex idea of the causal relation arises. For

[1] What Hume called 'experimental philosophy', namely physics, is now, of course, no longer accounted part of philosophy. And one may be tempted to comment that part at any rate of what he regarded as pertaining to the science of man has also tended to separate itself from philosophy, especially if one bears in mind the methodological limitations which he imposed. I am thinking principally of empirical psychology.

another thing he performed an activity of synthesis in the sense of giving a general picture of, say, the extent of human knowledge and of the nature of moral experience. But metaphysical synthesis of the traditional type was excluded. It was excluded by his methodological limitations, and it was excluded by the results of his analysis. Given his analysis of causality, for example, he could not synthesize the multiplicity of phenomenal objects by relating them, as effects to cause, to a One which transcended the objects to be synthesized. Locke and Berkley were able to proceed on these lines; but not Hume. Hence while it would be incorrect to say that there is no synthesis at all in the developed empiricism of Hume, we can legitimately say that in comparison with the rationalist systems it is an analytic philosophy. That is to say, its obvious feature is reductive analysis rather than synthesis as this would be understood by the rationalist metaphysicians.

We can put the matter in this way. Hume was concerned with analysing the meanings of terms such as 'cause', 'self', 'justice', and so on. He was not concerned with deducing the existence of one thing from that of another. In fact, his empiricism did not permit any such deduction. Hence any metaphysical synthesis of the rationalist type was excluded. The emphasis was necessarily placed on analysis. And we can say that a fully empiricist philosophy must be a predominantly analytic philosophy. In the philosophies of Locke and Berkeley analysis, though obviously present, is less predominant than in the philosophy of Hume. And the reason is that their philosophies are only partly empiricist.

There is, of course, no fault to be found with analysis as such. Nor can we reasonably object to a philosopher devoting himself primarily to analysis if he chooses to do so. Quite apart from the fact that metaphysical syntheses constructed without careful analysis of terms and propositions are likely to be houses of cards, it is quite natural that different philosophers should have different bents of mind. Further, the fact that the results of Hume's analysis exclude metaphysical syntheses of the traditional type can hardly be taken to prove without more ado that there must be flaws in his analysis. For the empiricist at least would comment that it is a case of so much the worse for metaphysics.

But though there can be no valid objection to analysis as such, it may be possible to object to the assumption or assumptions which are implicit in a given philosopher's practice of analysis. And it seems to me that Hume's practice of reductive analysis is guided by a mistaken assumption, namely that the real constituents of human experience are atomic, discrete 'perceptions'. Once Hume has assumed or, as he believes, shown that all ideas are derived from impressions[1] and that these impressions are 'distinct existences', it remains only to apply this assumption to the analysis of those ideas which seem to be of importance or interest. And if in the process of application we come upon cases where the general principle fails to work, inasmuch as it leads to insuperable inconsistencies, doubt is inevitably cast upon the validity of the general principle.

Hume's analysis of the self seems to be a case in point. The self is resolved into distinct 'perceptions'. But Hume himself admits that we have a propensity to substitute the notion of identity for that of related objects (that is, distinct perceptions), and that this propensity is so great that we are apt to imagine something substantial connecting the perceptions. And it appears to follow that that which has to be reconstructed out of distinct perceptions must be something to which we can reasonably attribute such a propensity. Yet this is precisely what cannot be done. If the self consists, as Hume says it does, of a series or bundle of perceptions, there is nothing of which it can reasonably be said that it has a propensity to imagine something substantial connecting the perceptions. Hume, indeed, sees the difficulty. He admits his perplexity and openly confesses that he does not know how to correct his opinions or to render them consistent. But this admission really shows that his phenomenalistic analysis of the self will not do. And this conclusion casts doubt upon the general assumption that the ultimate constituents of human experience are atomic, discrete impressions.

It may be objected that it is incorrect to speak of an 'assumption'. Reductive analysis is a method, not an assumption, and Hume shows, to his own satisfaction at least, that it can be successfully applied to ideas such as those of causality and the self. One may think perhaps that the application in the case of the self, for instance, is not successful. But this is no reason for speaking of an assumption.

It is true, of course, that Hume attempts to show in concrete

[1] As we saw in Volume V, Hume admits the possibility of exceptions to this rule. When presented with a graded series of shades of blue in which one shade was missing, we might be able to supply the missing member in the sense of producing the 'idea' though there has been no preceding impression. But, apart from such possible exceptions, Hume presses his general rule throughout.

cases that we can analyse the meanings of words such as 'self' in terms of distinct 'perceptions'. And in this sense it is true to say that he does not simply assume that it can be done. But he certainly assumes as a working hypothesis that our ideas can be explained in terms of discrete impressions. And he does this because he tacitly assumes, again as a working hypothesis, that the ultimate constituents of human experience are atomic, discrete impressions which are the empirical data from which our interpretation of the world is constructed. He takes it that we can reduce our interpretation of the world to the empirical data which are the direct objects of consciousness, and that these data are 'impressions'. But in carrying out this empiricist reduction he forgets the self which enters experience as subject, in order to concentrate on the immediate objects of introspection. This procedure can perhaps be associated with the endeavour to apply the method of 'experimental philosophy' to 'moral subjects'. But its results, in the case of analysis of the self, show the limitations of the method.

In general, we have to be careful not to confuse the results of abstraction with the ultimate data of experience. Perceiving is a form of experiencing. And it may be that within perception we can distinguish by abstraction something corresponding to what Hume calls impressions. But it does not follow that impressions are the actual constituents, as it were, of perception, so that we can reconstruct the total experience simply in terms of impressions. Still less does it follow that what we perceive consists of impressions. It may sound naïve to say that in perceiving we must distinguish between subject, object and act of perceiving. It may seem to some to be no more than a reflection of language, that is, of the subject-verb-object type of proposition. But if one eliminates the subject, it is the subject which performs the elimination. And if we eliminated the object as distinct from the perceiving, we should end in solipsism.

It seems to me that the lines of criticism which I have suggested are applicable not only to Hume's philosophy but also to certain modern versions of his empiricism. Some empiricists have tried to avoid giving the impression that their phenomenalistic analysis is a piece of metaphysics, an ontological theory. Thus according to the theory of 'logical constructions' it is possible, in principle at least, to translate sentences about the mind into other sentences which do not contain the word 'mind' but mention psychical phenomena or events instead, in such a way that if the original sentence is true (or false) the equivalent sentences are true (or false), and *vice versa*. Similarly, a sentence about a table could, in principle at least, be translated into sentences in which the word 'table' would not occur but in which sense-data would be mentioned instead, there being a relation of truth-equivalence between the original sentence and its translation. A table is then said to be a 'logical construction' out of sense-data, and a mind a 'logical construction' out of psychical phenomena or events. Phenomenalism is thus put forward as a logical or linguistic and not as an ontological theory. But it seems to be doubtful whether this ingenious attempt to avoid having to admit that phenomenalism is a rival metaphysical theory to a non-phenomenalistic theory is successful. And in any case it can be asked how, given this analysis of mind, the construction of the 'logical construction' is possible. Further, if the analysis of physical objects such as tables implies that we perceive sense-data (and it is difficult to see how this implication can be successfully avoided), it is arguable that solipsism is the necessary consequence, unless one is willing to hold the strange theory of unattached sense-data, so to speak.

The objection may be raised that, whether my criticism of Hume is valid or not, it does not really touch the most important feature of his empiricism, namely its logical theory. The older empiricists certainly approached philosophy from a psychological angle. Thus Locke began by inquiring into the origin of our ideas. And this was a psychological question. Hume followed him in this path by tracing the origin of almost all ideas to impressions. But though such psychological questions are of importance if we are considering the history of empiricism, the permanent value of classical empiricism consists primarily in its contribution to logical theory. And it is this aspect of Hume's thought which should be stressed. It is the aspect which links him most closely with modern empiricism.

As regards Hume's link with modern empiricism, this is, I think, quite true. As we saw when considering Hume's philosophy in Volume V, he made a distinction between demonstrative reasoning, which concerns the 'relations between ideas' and which is found, for example, in pure mathematics, and moral reasoning, which concerns 'matters of fact' and in which logical demonstration has no place. When we argue, for instance, from an effect to its cause, our conclusions may be more or less probable; but its truth is not, and cannot be, demonstrated. For the contrary of a matter of fact is always conceivable and possible: it never involves a logical contradiction. In pure mathematics, however, where we are concerned with the relations between ideas and not with matters of fact, affirmation of the contrary of the conclusion of a demonstration involves a contradiction.

Hume is here concerned with two kinds of reasoning; and his conclusion is that reasoning about matters of fact cannot amount to demonstration. We cannot, for example, demonstrate the existence of one thing from the existence of another. We may, indeed, feel certain about the truth of our conclusion; but if we prescind from states of feeling and attend to the logical aspect of the matter, we must admit that conclusions attained by reasoning about matters of fact cannot be certain.

In modern empiricism this point of view is retained; but the emphasis is placed on a distinction between two types of proposition. A proposition which, in Hume's language, states a relation between ideas, is said to be analytic and to be true *a priori*. That is to say, its truth is logically independent of empirical verification. A proposition which, in Hume's language, concerns a matter of fact, is said to be synthetic. Its truth cannot be known from the proposition alone but only by empirical verification. It is empirical verification which shows whether the proposition is true or false. The contrary of the proposition is always logically possible; hence no amount of empirical verification can give it more than a very high degree of probability.

This classification of propositions excludes, of course, the possibility of any necessarily true existential propositions. But, as interpreted by the empiricists, it excludes also all propositions which, while not affirming the existence of any thing, purport to be both informative about reality and true *a priori* in the sense that their truth cannot be empirically refuted, even in principle. Take, for example, the statement that everything that comes into being or begins to exist does so through the agency of a cause. In Hume's opinion the truth of this statement is not seen by intuition. For the contrary is conceivable. Nor is its truth demonstrable. It is, therefore, an empirical generalization, an hypothesis which may be generally verified but which, in principle at least, admits of empirical refutation. And I suppose that if Hume were alive today, he would look on what is called 'infra-atomic indeterminacy' as constituting empirical confirmation of his assessment of the logical status of the principle of causality.

In the language of modern empiricism, therefore, there are analytic propositions, which are in some sense 'tautologies', and synthetic *a posteriori* propositions or empirical hypotheses; but there are no synthetic *a priori* propositions. All candidates for this class turn out in the end to be either tautologies, open or concealed, or empirical generalizations, which may enjoy a very high degree of probability but the truth of which cannot be known by analysis of the proposition itself.

The problem of synthetic *a priori* propositions is too complicated to be discussed there. But it may be as well to draw attention to the following points. Let us assume that the phenomena which are grouped under the title of infra-atomic indeterminacy can be so interpreted that the principle of causality can still be offered as a candidate for the rank of synthetic *a priori* proposition. And let us take it that the principle of causality states that anything which comes into being or begins to exist does so through the agency of a cause.[1] In one sense the empiricist is quite right when he says that denial of this proposition involves no logical contradiction. That is to say, there is no verbal contradiction between the propositions 'X comes into being' and 'X has no cause'. If there were a verbal contradiction, the principle of causality, as stated above, would be an analytic proposition in the sense in which the empiricist understands the term. It is thus possible to understand the meanings of the English (or French or German, etc.) words used in stating the principle of causality and yet not to see any necessary connection between coming into being and being caused. We can hardly claim that nobody who denies this necessary connection understands the English words employed in the statement of the principle. We should have, I think, to be able to show that there is a deeper level of understanding than what is ordinarily meant by understanding the meanings of certain words.[2] It might then be claimed that though the empiricist's position cannot be assailed at the level of reflection

---

[1] The principle, be it noted, says nothing about the mode of operation of the cause. That is to say, its application is not confined to mechanical or determined causality.

[2] Obviously, we should have to avoid defining 'understanding the meanings of the terms' as 'seeing a necessary connection between the meanings of the terms'. For in this case the statement that whoever understands the meanings of the terms sees the necessary connection would be equivalent to the tautological statement that whoever sees the necessary connection sees it.

on which he stands, its inadequacy can be seen when one passes to the level of metaphysical insight.

These remarks obviously do not answer the question whether there are or are not synthetic *a priori* propositions. They are designed rather to indicate what must be shown if we claim that there are. It may, indeed, occur to the reader that there is another way of tackling the empiricist position, namely by denying that the propositions of pure mathematics, for example, are purely formal in the sense of being 'tautological'. In other words, it might be claimed that the propositions of pure mathematics are in some sense about reality, even though they are not existential propositions. But if we wish to claim that they are synthetic *a priori* propositions and not analytic propositions in the sense in which the empiricist uses the term, we must be prepared to explain in what sense they are informative about reality.

To return to Hume. Given his classification of propositions, it is clearly impossible to construct an *a priori* deductive system of metaphysics, the propositions of which will be infallibly true of reality. Nor, given his analysis of causality, can we start with the data of experience and infer the existence of God by a causal argument in the way that both Locke and Berkeley thought that we could. But it may appear at first sight that it is still possible to regard metaphysical theories as hypotheses which may enjoy varying degress of probability.

It is true, of course, that Hume discussed some metaphysical problems. And he seems to have been willing to say that it is more probable that there is some cause of order in the universe which bears a remote analogy to human intelligence than that there is no such cause. At the same time it seems to me to follow from his general premises that terms which are used to denote metaphysical entities are void of meaning when used in this context. For ideas are derived from impressions. And if we think that we have an idea because we use a certain word, and if at the same time we cannot indicate, even in principle, the impression or impressions from which this idea is derived, we are forced to conclude that we have no such idea. And in this case the term or word is vacuous. True, Hume allowed for possible exceptions from the general rule that ideas follow impressions. But he certainly did not make this concession in favour of metaphysics. And though it is only in a rhetorical passage that he dismisses metaphysics as meaningless nonsense, I am inclined to think that this passage represents the conclusion to which Hume's premisses logically lead, at least if we press the assertion that ideas are faint images of impressions. And in this case metaphysical theories can hardly be genuine hypotheses.

It seems arguable, therefore, that the empiricism of Hume, if it is developed to the conclusions which are implicitly contained in it, leads to the rejection of metaphysics as so much verbiage. And this development has taken place in the present century at the hands of the neopositivists or logical positivists or radical empiricists, according to whom metaphysical statements can possess no more than 'emotive' significance.[1] So once more we have a link between Hume's philosophy and modern radical empiricism.

It may be objected that this line of interpretation amounts to treating Hume's thought as a kind of preparation for neopositivism, and that this treatment is defective on several counts. In the first place his contemporary relevance lies rather in the emphasis he gave to philosophical analysis in general than in his anticipations of neopositivism in particular, which, in its original dogmatic form at least, has proved to be a passing phase. In the second place a treatment of Hume as a preparation for later thinkers, whether positivists or not, necessarily fails to do justice to his own interpretation of human experience. Whether one agrees or not with what he says, his account of the scope and limitations of human knowledge, his examination of man's affective, moral and aesthetic life and his political theory, which together constitute his attempt to develop a science of man, are only obscured if one persists in treating his thought in function of later philosophical developments.

These objections are, I think, well-founded. At the same time a treatment of Hume's philosophy in the light of later empiricism does help to bring into relief his contemporary relevance. And it is important to do this, even if one confines oneself to a particular aspect of his contemporary relevance. Hume's empiricism suffers from several grave defects. For instance, his atomization of experience is, in my opinion, a fundamental mistake; his theory of ideas is not, I think, tenable; and it might well be claimed that Kant, in

---

[1] This idea of 'emotive' significance also has a basis in Hume's philosophy. For though he complicated his ethical theory by introducing utilitarian elements, his root-idea of the moral judgment was that it expressed 'feeling', specific feelings, that is to say, of approbation or disapprobation. Moral predicates are 'emotive' rather than descriptive terms.

his insistence on the transcendental unity of apperception as a basic condition of human experience, was in a sense more 'empirical' than Hume. But the defects of Hume's philosophy do not diminish its historical importance. And though in some respects his thought falls into older patterns,[1] his concentration on analysis is certainly not the least of his titles to be considered a living thinker.

4. In the introduction to Volume IV we noted that Hume's idea of a science of man represents very well the spirit of the eighteenth-century Enlightenment. And in considering the French Enlightenment in the present volume we saw how philosophers such as Condillac endeavoured to develop Locke's psychological and epistemological theories and to give an empirical account of the genesis and growth of man's mental life; how writers such as Helvetius developed theories of man's moral life; how Montesquieu studied the structure and growth of societies; how Rousseau and others produced their political theories; how the physiocrats began the study of economics; and how thinkers such as Voltaire, Turgot and Condorcet sketched theories of historical development in the light of the ideals of the Age of Reason. All such studies, psychological, ethical, social, political, historical and economic, can be grouped together under the general title of the scientific study of man.

In pursuing this study the philosophers whom we are accustomed to consider as typical representatives of the Enlightenment were concerned to free it from theological and metaphysical presuppositions. This is, I think, one of the salient features of the thought of the period. The aim is not so much to deduce a comprehensive system from self-evident principles as to understand the empirical data by correlating them under empirically verified laws. Thus Condillac was concerned with giving an empirical account of the development of man's mental life, and Montesquieu endeavoured to group the diverse data in the development of different societies under universal laws. In general, Locke's empirical approach exercised a widespread influence. And there is thus a very considerable difference between the atmosphere, so to speak, of the great systems of continental rationalism and the thought of the eighteenth-century Enlightenment. The

---

[1] For example, though professedly concerned with the limits of our knowledge rather than with the nature of reality in itself, he now and again makes incursions into ontology. And his tendency to speak as though the objects of perception are subjective modifications is an unfortunate legacy from his predecessors.

atmosphere of the former is that of deduction, of the latter that of induction. It is true that this statement, like other such rash generalizations, stands in need of qualification. For instance, one would hardly think immediately of empirical induction on hearing the name of Wolff, the hero of the German *Aufklärung*. At the same time the generalization does at any rate draw attention, even if in an over-simplified manner, to a real difference in spirit and atmosphere.

This difference can be illustrated by a reference to moral theory. The moral theory of Spinoza formed an integral part of a deductively-expounded grandiose system; and it was closely associated with metaphysical doctrines. But when we turn to the moral theories of Hume in England or of Helvetius and the Encyclopaedists in France, we find their authors insisting on the autonomy of the moral consciousness and on the separation of ethics from theology.

Similarly, while the idea of the social compact or contract in political theory is not derived from study of the empirical data but constitutes an attempt to give a rational justification of political authority and of the restriction of individual liberty in organized society, we do not find that the political theorists of the eighteenth century are much given to deducing society and authority from metaphysical and theological doctrines. They are concerned rather with the observed needs of man. And it is this approach, of course, which enables Hume to substitute for the more rationalist idea of the social contract the empirical idea of felt utility.

This is not to say, indeed, that the men of the Enlightenment had no presuppositions of their own. As we saw, they assumed a theory of progress according to which progress consists in the advancing rationalization of man, this rationalization involving man's emancipation from religious superstition and from irrational forms of government, ecclesiastical or civil. In their opinion the fruits of progress were best represented by themselves, the enlightened free-thinkers of the Parisian *salons*; and further progress would consist in the spread of the ideas for which they stood and in the refashioning of society according to the ideals of the Enlightenment. Once a reform of the social structure had taken place, men would advance in morality and virtue. For the moral state of man is largely dependent on his environment and on education.

It may be objected that the theory of progress as maintained by the men of the Enlightenment was an empirical generalization rather than a presupposition. And though in the nineteenth century it may have tended to take the form of a 'dogma', especially when it was thought to be supported by the theory of evolution, for the eighteenth-century thinkers it had more the nature of a plastic hypothesis. Even when Turgot anticipated Comte's law of the three stages of human thought, he was propounding an hypothesis based on a study of the historical data rather than an *a priori* pattern to which the data were made to conform.

It is, indeed, obviously true that in the judgment of the thinkers of the Enlightenment the theory of progress was based on historical facts. They did not present it as a conclusion derived from metaphysical premisses. But it is also true that it played the part of a presupposition, based on a value-judgment. That is to say, the Encyclopaedists and those who shared their outlook first formed their ideals of man and of society and then interpreted progress as a movement towards the realization of those ideals. There is, of course, nothing very strange in this procedure. But it meant, for instance, that they came to the study of human history with a presupposition which exercised an undue influence on their interpretation of history. For example, they were unable to appreciate the contribution of the Middle Ages to European culture: the Middle Ages inevitably appeared to them as the Dark Ages. For if progress meant advance towards the fulfilment of the ideals represented by *les philosophes* of the eighteenth century, it involved liberation from some of the leading features of mediaeval culture. Light was represented by the advanced thinkers of the eighteenth century, and the advance of 'reason' was incompatible with mediaeval religion or with a philosophy which was closely associated with theology. In this sense the men of the Enlightenment had a 'dogma' of their own.

Their point of view also meant, of course, that they were unable to do justice to important aspects of human nature and life. It is, indeed, an exaggeration to say that *les philosophes* had no understanding of any aspect of man other than the life of the analytic and emancipated reason. Hume, for instance, insisted on the great part played by feeling and asserted that reason is and ought to be the slave of the passions.[1] And Vauvenargues emphasized the

[1] For the meaning of this statement see Vol. V, p. 319 and pp. 326–7.

importance of the affective side of human nature. Even if
Rousseau's attacks on the Encyclopaedists were not without
foundation, we cannot take his strictures as representing the whole
truth. At the same time *les philosophes* showed little appreciation
of, for example, man's religious life. It would be absurd to turn
to Voltaire among the deists or to d'Holbach among the atheists
for a profound understanding of religion. D'Holbach outlined a
naturalistic philosophy of religion; but it will not bear comparison
with the idealist philosophies of religion which we find in the next
century. The rationalist freethinkers of the eighteenth century
were too much preoccupied with the idea of man's emancipation
from what they regarded as the deadening weight of the chains of
superstition and priestcraft to have any profound understanding
of the religious consciousness.

This element of superficiality shows itself, for instance, in the
materialist current of thought in the philosophy of the Enlightenment. As we saw, the word 'materialist' cannot legitimately be
used as a label to be applied indiscriminately to *les philosophes*.
But there were materialists among them, and they present us with
the somewhat comical spectacle of man as subject engaged in
reducing himself, so to speak, to a purely material object. It is
easy to understand the repugnance and disgust which d'Holbach's
System of Nature aroused in the mind of Goethe as a student. And
d'Holbach was not the crudest of the materialists.

But the superficiality of the philosophy of the French Enlightenment in some of its aspects should not blind one to the
historical importance of the movement. Rousseau, indeed, stands
in a class by himself. His ideas have an intrinsic interest and they
exercised a considerable influence on subsequent thinkers such as
Kant and Hegel. But though the Encyclopaedists and kindred
philosophers, from whom Rousseau chose to dissociate himself,
may not occupy a similar position in the development of philosophy, they nevertheless exercised an important influence which
has to be estimated, I think, not so much in terms of definite
'results' to which we can point as in terms of their contribution to
the formation of a mentality or outlook. Perhaps we can say that
the typical philosophers of the French Enlightenment represent
the idea that man's betterment, welfare and happiness rest in his
own hands. Provided that he frees himself from the notion that his
destiny depends on a supernatural power, whose will is expressed
through ecclesiastical authority, and provided that he follows the

path marked out by reason, he will be able to create the social environment in which true human morality can flourish and in which the greater good of the greatest possible number can be successfully promoted. The idea, which later became so widespread, that the growth of scientific knowledge and a more rational organization of society would inevitably bring with them an increase of human happiness and further the attainment of sound moral ideals was a development of the outlook of the Enlightenment. True, other factors, such as the advance of technical science, were required before the idea could assume its developed form. But the fundamental idea that human welfare depends on the exercise of reason emancipated from the trammels of authority, of religious dogmas and of dubious metaphysical doctrines came into prominence in the eighteenth century. It was not, as at the Reformation, a question of substituting Protestant for Catholic dogma but of substituting 'free thought', the autonomy of reason, for authority.

These remarks are not, of course, intended to express agreement with the point of view of men like Voltaire. Their idea of reason was limited and narrow. To exercise reason meant for them pretty well to think as *les philosophes* thought; whereas to anyone who believes that God has revealed Himself it is rational to accept this revelation and irrational to reject it. And in any case the men of the Enlightenment were not as free from presuppositions and prejudices as they fondly imagined. Further, their optimistic rationalism has obviously met with a powerful challenge in the twentieth century. But all this does not alter the fact that an outlook which has exercised a considerable influence in the modern world took clear shape in the eighteenth century. The ideals of freedom of thought and of toleration, which have played such a part in the civilization of western Europe and of North America, found striking expression in the writings of the eighteenth-century philosophers.[1] No doubt we can add that the philosophers of the French Enlightenment gave a powerful stimulus to the promotion of scientific studies, in psychology, for example. And some of them, such as d'Alembert, made real contributions in the advance of extra-philosophical pursuits. But their chief importance lies, I

[1] I do not mean to imply that toleration and a belief in revealed religion are necessarily incompatible. I am speaking of an historical rather than of a logical connection, unless, of course, one interprets 'freedom of thought' in such a way that it becomes tautological to say that the ideals of 'freedom of thought' and toleration are inseparable.

think, in their contribution to the formation of a general mentality or outlook.

To a certain extent the philosophy of the Enlightenment expressed the development of the middle classes. From the economic point of view the middle class had, of course, been in process of development for a long time. But in the seventeenth and eighteenth centuries its rise was reflected in philosophical currents of thought which, in France, were hostile to the *ancien régime* and which helped to prepare the way for a different organization of society. Such remarks, it may be said, have a Marxist flavour; but they are not for this reason necessarily erroneous.

In conclusion I wish to draw attention to one selected problem which arises out of eighteenth-century philosophy. We have seen that the typical representatives of the Enlightenment tended to insist on the separation of ethics from theology and metaphysics. And I think that behind their attitude there was a genuine philosophical question. But some of the writers of the Enlightenment obscured rather than clarified the nature of this question. I refer to those who were concerned to argue that religion, especially dogmatic Christianity, exercises a baneful influence on moral conduct, with the implication that deism or atheism, as the case may be, is more conducive to morality and virtue. This way of talking obscures the nature of the philosophical question about the relation between ethics on the one hand and metaphysics and theology on the other. For one thing, the question whether virtue is more prevalent among Christians or non-Christians is not a philosophical question. For another thing, if we say, for example, that deism is more conducive to morality and virtue than are Catholicism and Protestantism, we imply that there is a connection between metaphysical beliefs and morals. For deism is, of course, a form of metaphysics. And we ought to make it clear precisely what sort of connection we wish to affirm.

The philosophical question at issue is clearly not whether talk about human conduct can be distinguished from talk about the existence and attributes of God or about things considered simply as beings. For it obviously can be distinguished. In other words, it is clear enough that ethics or moral philosophy has its own subject-matter. This was recognized, for example, by Aristotle in the ancient world and by Aquinas in the Middle Ages.

The immediate question is rather whether fundamental moral principles can be derived from metaphysical or theological premisses. But this question can be reformulated in a broader way, without any specific reference to metaphysical or theological premisses. Let us suppose that someone says: 'We are creatures of God; therefore we ought to obey Him.' The first statement is a statement of fact. The second is a moral statement. And the speaker asserts that the first entails the second. We can ask, therefore, putting the question in a general form, whether a statement of what ought to be the case can be derived from a statement of what is the case, a moral statement from a statement of fact. This general formulation of the question would apply not only to the example which I have given but also, for instance, to the deduction of moral statements from statements of fact about the characteristics of human nature, when no reference is made to theological truths.

This question, we may note, was formulated explicitly by David Hume. 'In every system of morality which I have hitherto met with I have always remarked that the author proceeds for some time in the ordinary way of reasoning and establishes the being of a God or makes observations concerning human affairs, when of a sudden I am surprised to find that instead of the usual copulations of propositions, *is* and *is not*, I meet with no proposition that is not connected with an *ought* or an *ought not*. This change is imperceptible, but is, however, of the last consequence. For as this *ought* or *ought not* expresses some new relation or affirmation, it is necessary that it should be observed and explained, and at the same time that a reason should be given for what seems altogether inconceivable, how this new relation can be a deduction from others, which are entirely different from it'.[1] But though Hume explicitly raised this question, the utilitarians tended to pass it over; and it is only in modern ethical theory that it has been given prominence.

The question is obviously important. For it is relevant not only to authoritarian ethics but also to teleological ethics of the type which first asserts that human nature is of such a kind or that man seeks a certain end and then derives ought-statements from this statement of fact. And I have drawn attention to it because of its importance, not with a view to undertaking a discussion of the right answer. For such a discussion would involve, for instance, an analysis of ought-statements, and this is a task for the writer of a treatise on ethical theory rather than an historian of philosophy.

[1] *Treatise*, I, 3, 1 (Selby-Bigge, p. 469).

However, to avoid any possible misunderstanding of my remarks it may be appropriate to state explicitly that I have no intention of suggesting that the idea of a teleological ethics must be abandoned. On the contrary I think that the concept of the good is paramount in morals, and that 'ought' must be interpreted in function of the idea of the good. At the same time any defender of a teleological ethical theory must take account of the question raised by Hume. And it is worth while having pointed out that behind the polemical utterances of French writers about the separation of ethics from metaphysics and theology there lies a genuine philosophical question. That it was Hume who gave a clear explicit formulation to this question is not, I think, surprising.

5. Mention has been made in the last section of the tendency shown by philosophers of the French Enlightenment to look on history as an advance towards the rationalism of the eighteenth century, an advance out of darkness into light, and to expect in the future further advance which would consist in the fuller implementation of the ideals of the Age of Reason. And in the present volume the fourth Part was devoted to the rise of the philosophy of history in the pre-Kantian modern period. It is appropriate, therefore, to make some general remarks in this Concluding Review about the philosophy of history. But the remarks must be brief. For the idea of philosophy of history is best discussed in connection with later thinkers who developed the theme on the grand scale. At present I wish to content myself with merely suggesting some lines of thought for the reader's reflection.

If by philosophy of history one means a critique of historical method, then philosophy of history is obviously a possible and legitimate undertaking. For just as it is possible to examine scientific method, so is it possible to examine the method or methods employed by historians. We can ask questions about the concept of historical fact, about the nature and role of interpretation of the data, about the part played by imaginative reconstruction, and so on. We can discuss the norms of selection which are observed by historians; and we can inquire what presuppositions, if any, are implicit in historical interpretation and reconstruction.

But when we speak of Bossuet or Vico or Montesquieu or Condorcet or Lessing or Herder as a philosopher of history, it is not of these meta-historical inquiries that we are thinking. For such inquiries are concerned with the nature and method of historiography rather than with the course of historical events. And when we speak of the philosophy of history we think of interpretations of the actual course of historical events rather than of an analysis of the historian's method, norms of selection, presuppositions, and so on. We think of the search for patterns or for a pattern in the course of history and of theories of universal laws which are supposed to be operative in history.

Talk about searching for patterns in history is somewhat ambiguous. We can perfectly well say that historians themselves are concerned with patterns. A man who writes a history of England, for instance, is obviously concerned to trace an intelligible pattern of events. He does not leave us with a series of unconnected historical statements such as the statement that William the Conqueror landed in England in 1066. He tries to show how this event came to pass and why the Conqueror acted as he did: he tries to illustrate the effects which the Norman invasion had on English life and culture. And in doing this he inevitably exhibits a pattern of events. But we do not for this reason call him a philosopher of history. Further, the mere fact that a given historian casts his net more widely and concerns himself with a great range of historical data does not of itself qualify him for the label 'philosopher of history'.

But searching for a pattern in history may mean something more than this. It may mean attempting to show that there is a necessary pattern in history, this pattern taking the form either of a movement towards a goal which will be attained whatever the motives of individuals may be or of a series of cycles the course and rhythm of which are determined by certain universal laws. In the case of such theories we should certainly speak of philosophy of history.

Here again, however, there is room for a distinction. On the one hand a man might believe that in his study of history he had discovered certain recurrent patterns, and he might then endeavour to explain this recurrence in terms of the operation of certain laws. Or he might think that the actual course of history manifests a movement towards a condition of affairs which he regards as desirable and which has come about in spite of obstacles. On the other hand a man might come to the study of history with an already-formed belief, derived from theology or from metaphysics, that human history moves inevitably towards the attainment of a certain end or goal. With this belief in mind he then endeavours to see how the actual course of historical events confirms this belief. The distinction is thus between empirically-grounded philosophy of history and one the main tenet of which is an *a priori* theory, in the sense that the theory is brought ready-made to the study of history.

The distinction, when expressed in this abstract way, seems to be clear enough. But it does not follow, of course, that it is always easy to assign a given philosopher of history to one definite class. Perhaps we can assign Montesquieu to the first class. For he seems to have thought that the laws which he regarded as operative in history were derived from a study of the actual course of events. Bossuet belongs definitely to the second class. For his conviction that a providential divine plan is worked out in history was obviously derived from theology. And Hegel, in the nineteenth century, also belongs to this class. For he explicitly asserts that in studying the course of history the philosopher brings to it the truth (believed to have been demonstrated in what we would call metaphysics) that Reason is the sovereign of history, that is, that Absolute Reason manifests itself in the historical process. But it is not so easy to classify writers such as Condorcet. At the very least, however, we can say that they made a value-judgment about the spirit of the Enlightenment, and that this judgment influenced their interpretation of history. That is to say, they made an approving value-judgment about the culture which they diagnosed as emerging out of the past and as beginning to express itself in the spirit of the Enlightenment; and they then interpreted the past in the light of this judgment. As has already been remarked, this affected, for example, their interpretation of the Middle Ages, which constituted in their eyes a retrogressive movement on the upward path. In other words, their interpretation of history and their tracing of a pattern were permeated and influenced by judgments of value. The same sort of remark could be made, of course, about some historians who are not generally thought of as philosophers of history. Gibbon is a case in point. But Condorcet seems to have assumed that a law of progress operates in historical development (and his concept of what constitutes progress obviously involved value-judgments). And for this reason he can be called a philosopher of history. True, he did not make this assumption very clear; and he laid stress on the need for human effort, particularly in the field of education, to perfect man and human society. But his confident optimistic belief in the advance of history from darkness into light involved an implicit assumption about a teleological movement in historical development.

It does not seem to me that one can justifiably dismiss all philosophy of history in a pure *a priori* manner. As far as those philosophies of history are concerned which purport to be generalizations derived from objective study of historical data, the main question is whether the empirical evidence is such as to render probable the truth of a given theory. We can, of course, raise the question whether the concept of historical laws, as found, for instance, in the philosophy of Vico, does not assume that there is repetition in history; and if we think that this assumption is in fact made, it is open to us to challenge it. But the challenge will have to be based on appeal to historical evidence. And if the reply is made that the concept of historical laws does not assume repetition in history but is based on similarities and analogies between different events or different periods, any discussion of these themes must be conducted in the light of the available evidence. We might, indeed, wish to say that the concept of historical laws can be ruled out *a priori* in virtue of an appeal to human freedom. But though human freedom and initiative would be incompatible with the operation of what one might call 'iron laws', it might be possible to elaborate a conception of historical law which would be compatible with human freedom. In other words, it might be possible to develop a theory of loose-texture cultural cycles which would not make nonsense of human choice. The question whether there was any sufficient ground for the development of such a theory would have to be decided in the light of historical data. At the same time, apart from the question whether the division of history into cultural cycles is legitimate and well-grounded, we should have to ask ourselves whether the so-called laws which are supposed to govern the rhythm of these cycles were anything better than truisms on the one hand or, on the other, propositions which the historian himself would be quite capable of enunciating, without the aid of any philosopher.

As for those philosophies of history in which the philosopher openly brings to the study of historical development a belief derived from theology or from metaphysics, there is at least this to be said in their favour, that they are honest, in the sense that the assumption is explicitly stated. In this respect they are preferable to those philosophies of history which do indeed assume that history moves inevitably towards a certain goal but in which this assumption is concealed. Further, the belief which is taken over from theology or from metaphysics may be quite true. It may be quite true, and in my opinion it is true, that divine providence operates in history and that the divine plan will be realized whether human beings like it or not. But it by no means follows that this belief can be of very much practical use for the study of history. Historical events have their phenomenal causes, and without revelation we cannot really tell how the actual course of events is related to divine providence. We can conjecture and speculate, it is true; we can see in the fall of a nation a symbol of divine judgment, or a symbol of the transitoriness of the things of this world. But neither conjecture nor a deciphering of symbols from the standpoint of faith permit prediction. If these activities are what we mean by philosophy of history, then philosophy of history is, of course, possible. But it is then a pursuit, perhaps profitable and in any case harmless, which the man of faith can undertake if he chooses; but it cannot be said to yield scientific knowledge. Moreover, if we rashly assume that we know the providential plan and that we can discern by philosophical reflection its operation in history, we shall probably find ourselves committed to justifying all that happens.

These remarks are not intended to indicate that the present writer entirely rejects the idea of a philosophy of history which goes beyond meta-historical inquiries such as analysis of the historian's method and presuppositions. But they are intended to express a serious doubt concerning the validity of the idea. I believe that a theology of history is possible; but its scope is extremely limited, being determined by the limits of revelation. And I very much doubt whether it is possible to go further than St. Augustine went. But when we turn from Bossuet to the philosophers of history in the eighteenth century, we find them substituting philosophy for theology in the belief that they are thereby giving to their theories of history the character of scientific knowledge. And I doubt whether philosophy of history is capable of assuming this character. No doubt, the philosophers make true statements; but the question is whether these statements are not the sort of truths which can perfectly well be made by the historian himself. In other words, the question is whether the philosopher as such can achieve anything more in developing a synthetic interpretation of history than can be achieved by the historian. If not, there is no place for philosophy of history in the sense in which the term is being used. But it is, of course, difficult to draw any clear line of demarcation between history and philosophy of history. If by the latter term we mean broad generalizations, the historian himself can make them.

6. The three volumes of this *History* which are devoted to the philosophy of the seventeenth and eighteenth centuries end with a discussion of the Kantian system. And it will obviously be expected of any Concluding Review that it should contain some reflections on Kant's thought. I do not propose, of course, to give a summary of his philosophy. A preliminary summary was provided in the introduction to Volume IV, and after the extended treatment of Kant in the present volume a second summary would be superfluous. Nor do I propose to undertake a direct refutation of Kantianism. I propose instead to make some general reflections about its relations to preceding philosophy and to the German speculative idealism which followed it. And I also wish to draw attention to some of the questions which arise out of Kant's philosophy.

There is, I suppose, a natural temptation to represent the philosophy of Kant as the confluence of the two streams of continental rationalism and British empiricism. It is a natural temptation because there are some obvious grounds for representing his thought in this way. For instance, he was brought up, philosophically speaking, in the scholasticized version of Leibniz' philosophy as presented by Wolff and his successors, and he then underwent the shock, as it were, of Hume's empiricist criticism which awoke him from his dogmatic slumbers. Further, in the construction of Kant's own philosophy we can discern the influence of both movements. For example, his discovery of Leibniz himself, as distinct from Wolff and his successors, had a very considerable influence on Kant's mind; and we may recall that Leibniz had asserted the phenomenal character of space and time. Indeed, the Kantian theory of the *a priori* can be represented as in some sense a development of Leibniz' theory of virtually innate ideas, with the difference that the ideas became innate categorical functions. At the same time we can recall that Hume himself had maintained a subjective contribution to the formation of certain complex ideas, such as that of the causal relation. And thus we might represent Kant's theory of the *a priori* as being also influenced by Hume's position in the light of the former's conviction that Newtonian physics presents us with synthetic *a priori* propositions. In other words, Kant not only offered an answer to Hume's empiricism and phenomenalism but also, in formulating this answer, utilized suggestions made by the British philosopher himself, though the latter did not see their full significance and possibilities.

It would, however, be absurd, were one to represent the Kantian philosophy as a synthesis of continental rationalism and British empiricism in the sense of a conflation of elements borrowed from two mutually opposed currents of thought. Like any other philosopher, Kant was subject to influence by his contemporaries and by his predecessors. And though opinions may differ about the degree of influence which should be ascribed to Leibniz and Hume respectively, we cannot call in question the fact that each man exercised some influence on the development of Kant's thought. So, for the matter of that, did Wolff and his disciples. At the same time any elements which may have been derived from or suggested by other philosophies were taken up and welded together by Kant in a system which was very much more than a conflation. It was intended to supersede both rationalist metaphysics and empiricism, not to combine the incompatible.

The inappropriateness of describing Kant's system as a synthesis of rationalism and empiricism becomes clear if we recall his fundamental problem, the pervasive problem, so to speak, of his philosophy. As we saw, he was faced with the problem of effecting a harmonization between the world of Newtonian physics, the world of mechanistic causality and determinism, and the world of freedom. True, Descartes also had been faced with an analogous problem: it was not a problem peculiar to Kant but one which arose out of the historical situation when natural science had once begun its remarkable development. But the point is that in grappling with this problem Kant submitted to critical examination both rationalism and empiricism and worked out his own philosophy, not as a synthesis of these two movements, but as a triumph over them. Empiricism, he thought, is inadequate because it is unable to account for the possibility of synthetic *a priori* knowledge. If we take scientific knowledge seriously, we cannot embrace sheer empiricism, even if we agree that all knowledge begins with experience. We must have recourse to a theory of the *a priori* formal element in knowledge. That is to say, we cannot explain the possibility of scientific knowledge if we assume that experience is simply given: we have to allow for the subject's construction of experience if we are going to account for the possibility of *a priori* knowledge. But this does not mean that we should accept rationalist metaphysics. If anyone takes moral experience, freedom and religion seriously, it may seem to him that the dogmatic metaphysics of the rationalist philosophers, at least of those who allowed for freedom, offers a sure rational basis for the moral law and for belief in freedom, immortality and God. But this is not the case. Rationalist metaphysics cannot stand up to criticism; and the hollowness of its pretensions to knowledge is shown empirically by the conflict of systems and by the evident incapacity of metaphysics to reach assured results. And the theory of the *a priori*, the transcendental critique of knowledge, shows why this must be the case. But at the same time that this new science shows the hollowness of dogmatic metaphysics it also shows the limitations of scientific knowledge. And for anyone who takes seriously the moral consciousness and the beliefs and hopes which are intimately associated with it the way is left open for a rationally legitimate, though scientifically indemonstrable, belief in freedom, immortality and God. The great truths of metaphysics are then placed beyond the reach of destructive criticism by the very act of removing them from the position of conclusions to worthless metaphysical arguments and linking them with the moral consciousness which is as much a fundamental feature of man as his capacity of scientific knowledge.

In working out his philosophy Kant obviously made use of suggestions and ideas derived from other philosophers. And specialists can trace the origins and development of this or that idea. But this fact does not justify our saying that the Kantian system is a conflation of rationalism and empiricism. He agreed with empiricist criticism of rationalist metaphysics, and at the same time he agreed with the metaphysicians about the importance of the leading metaphysical problems and about the existence of a sphere of noumenal reality to which physical science has no access. But this does not mean that rationalism and empiricism can be combined. It is rather that Kant's measure of agreement, coupled with his measure of disagreement, with each movement drives him forward to the development of an original philosophy. The fact of scientific knowledge rules out sheer empiricism. And a critical analysis of the possibility and conditions of this knowledge rules out dogmatic metaphysics. But man is not simply 'understanding': he is also a moral agent. And his moral consciousness reveals to him his freedom and justifies a practical assurance of spiritual reality, while his aesthetic experience helps him to see the physical world as the manifestation of this reality. To a certain extent, of course, we can see in the Kantian philosophy the culmination of previous lines of thought. Thus it is not unreasonable to regard his theory of the subject's construction of experience as an original development which issued out of a combination of the rationalistic theory of virtually innate ideas with the empiricist tendency to speak as though the immediate objects of experience were phenomena or impressions or sense-data. I have no wish to deny continuity in the development of philosophy or the fact that Kant's philosophy took the form which it did largely because of the character of preceding philosophical thought. But at the same time it remains true that in a certain sense Kant turned his back on both rationalism and empiricism. In other words, if we wished to speak of the Kantian system as a 'synthesis' of rationalism and empiricism, we should have to understand the term in a sense approximating to that given it by Hegel, that is, in the sense that Kant subsumed the elements of positive value (estimated from his own point of view) in the preceding rival traditions or antitheses in an original system, incorporation in which at the same time transformed these elements.

Now, if Kant turned his back on rationalist metaphysics, which he called 'rotten dogmatism', it may appear difficult to explain how it came to pass not only that the critical philosophy was followed in Germany by a series of metaphysical systems but also that the authors of these systems looked on themselves as the true successors of Kant who had developed his thought in the right direction. But if one bears in mind the tension between Kant's theory of the subject's construction of experience and his doctrine of the thing-in-itself, it is an easy matter to understand how German speculative idealism grew out of the critical philosophy.

Kant's doctrine of the thing-in-itself was certainly not unattended by difficulties. Apart from the fact that the nature of the thing-in-itself was declared to be unknowable, not even its existence as cause of the material of sensation could be positively asserted without misuse (on Kant's premisses) of the categories of causality and existence. To be sure, Kant was aware of this fact. And while it seemed to him that the concept of phenomenon demanded as its correlative the concept of thing-in-itself, the former not making any sense without the latter, he maintained that we must refrain from asserting dogmatically the existence of the thing-in-itself, though we cannot help thinking it. It is clear that Kant thought it absurd to reduce reality to a mere construction of the subject, and that he therefore looked on the retention of the concept of the thing-in-itself as a matter of common sense. At the same time he was aware of his difficult position and tried to find formulas which would save him from self-contradiction but which at the same time would enable him to retain a concept which he regarded as indispensable. One can understand Kant's attitude in this matter. But one can also understand Fichte's objections to the theory of the thing-in-itself, which he looked on as a superfluity, indeed as a monstrosity. In his view the thing-in-itself had to be eliminated in the interests of idealism. In his opinion Kant was a man who tried to have things both ways at once, and who therefore involved himself in hopeless inconsistencies. If one had once accepted the Kantian theory of the subject's part in the construction of experience, one was bound, thought Fichte, to go forward to a fully idealist philosophy.

This step involved inevitably a transition from theory of knowledge to metaphysics. If the thing-in-itself is eliminated, it follows that the subject creates the object in its entirety; it does not merely mould, so to speak, a given material. And the theory that the subject creates the object is obviously a metaphysical theory, even if the approach to it is by way of a critique of knowledge.

But what is this creative subject? When Kant spoke about the subject's construction of experience, he was talking about the individual subject. True, he introduced the concept of the transcendental ego as a logical condition of experience; but here again it was of the individual ego that he was thinking, the 'I' which is always subject and never object. But if we transform this logical condition of experience into a metaphysical principle which creates the object, we can hardly identify it with the individual finite ego without being involved in solipsism. For John Smith all other human beings will be objects, and so they will be his own creation. For the matter of fact, John Smith as object, as a phenomenal ego, will be the creation of himself as transcendental ego. If, therefore, we eliminate the thing-in-itself and transform Kant's transcendental ego, a logical condition of experience, into the supreme metaphysical principle, we are driven in the end to interpret it as the universal infinite subject which is productive both of the finite subject and of the finite object. And at once we are involved in a full-blown metaphysical system.

I do not intend, of course, to discuss here the phases of the philosophy of Fichte or the history of German speculative idealism in general. These themes must be reserved for the next volume of this *History*. But I wished to point out that the seeds of speculative idealism were present in the Kantian philosophy itself. Of course, the speculative idealists were concerned to reduce all things to one supreme metaphysical principle from which, in one way or another, they could be philosophically deduced, whereas Kant did not share this concern. And there is an obvious difference in atmosphere and interest between the critical philosophy and the metaphysical systems which succeeded it. At the same time it is not merely a question of 'succeeding'; for the systems of speculative idealism have a more than temporal connection with the philosophy of Kant. And if one admits this and at the same time rejects what grew out of Kant's philosophy, one can hardly accept this philosophy in so far as it formed the point of departure for what one rejects. And this means in practice submitting the idealist and subjectivist aspects of Kant's thought to critical examination. For if one reaffirms these aspects and eliminates instead the thing-in-itself, it is difficult to avoid accompanying Kant's successors along the path which they trod.

It is, indeed, easy to understand that in the middle of the nineteenth century the cry was raised 'Back to Kant!', and that the Neo-Kantians set themselves to develop the critical, epistemological and ethical positions of Kant without falling into what they regarded as the fantastic extravaganzas of the speculative idealists. Kant was for them primarily the patient, methodical, meticulous, analytically-minded author of the first *Critique*; and they thought of the systems of the great idealist metaphysicians from Fichte to Hegel as representing a betrayal of the spirit of Kant. And this point of view is perfectly understandable. At the same time it is, I think, undeniable that the Kantian system lent itself to the very development (or exploitation, if preferred) which it received at the hands of the speculative idealists. In support of the attitude of the Neo-Kantians we can say, of course, that Kant deliberately substituted a new form of metaphysics, a metaphysics of knowledge or of experience, for the older metaphysics which he rejected, and that he regarded this new metaphysics as capable of giving real knowledge, whereas he would certainly not have looked on Hegel's metaphysics of the Absolute, for instance, as constituting knowledge. In other words, he would certainly have disowned those who claimed to be his children, just as he rejected Fichte's preliminary attempts to improve the critical philosophy by eliminating the thing-in-itself. But though one may feel assured that Kant would not have looked with much favour on the metaphysical flights of his successors, this does not alter the fact that he provided them with a promising foundation for their constructions.

It is possible, however, by stressing other aspects of Kant's philosophy than those stressed by his idealist successors, to regard it as pointing in quite a different direction. Kant's rejection of dogmatic metaphysics, it may be said, was more than a rejection of the systems of continental rationalism from Descartes to Leibniz and his disciples. For Kant exposed the fallacious character of all pretended demonstrations in metaphysics and showed that metaphysical knowledge is impossible. True, he offered a new metaphysics of his own; but this was to all intents and purposes analysis of the subjective conditions of experience. It did not pretend to give us a knowledge of so-called noumenal reality. Kant did, indeed, allow for belief in the existence of noumenal reality; but this was inconsistent with his account of the function of the categories. For the categories have content and meaning only in their application to phenomena. Hence it is meaningless, on Kant's premises, to talk of noumenal reality or of a 'supersensuous substrate' as existing. In fact, if reality is itself one of the categories, it is nonsense to talk about noumenal reality at all. We can, it is true, examine the nature of the scientific, moral and aesthetic judgments. But on Kant's premises we are really not entitled to use the moral judgment as the basis for any sort of metaphysics. He would not, of course, have admitted the validity of this interpretation of his thought. But in point of fact, it may be claimed, the valuable service performed by Kant was to show that whatever can be known belongs to the sphere of the sciences, and that metaphysics is not only not science but also meaningless. At best it can have only 'emotive' significance. And this is what Kant's theory of practical faith really amounts to, when it is given its cash-value.

In other words, it can be argued that though the Kantian system gave rise directly to the systems of speculative idealism it is really a half-way house on the road to positivism. And it is in this light, I suppose, that positivists would wish to regard it. They would not follow him, of course, in his theory of synthetic *a priori* propositions and of the conditions of their possibility. But they would regard his partial rejection of metaphysics as a step in the right direction; and they would wish, I think, to emphasize the aspects of his philosophy which seem to point the way to a more radical rejection, even if Kant himself did not understand the full implications of these aspects.

But the fact that both idealist metaphysicians and positivists can offer grounds for claiming that the Kantian system points in the direction of their types of philosophy obviously does not compel us to conclude that we must choose one of the two types. There is another possibility, namely that of rejecting the Kantian theories which lead to this choice. After all, Kant's Copernican revolution was an hypothesis designed to explain the possibility of synthetic *a priori* knowledge on the supposition that it could not be explained on a different hypothesis. And there is plenty of room for questioning here. We can ask whether there is in fact any synthetic *a priori* knowledge. And if we decide that there is, we can still ask whether its possibility cannot be better explained in a different way from that in which Kant explained it. Again, though it is widely taken for granted that Kant showed once and for all that speculative metaphysics cannot lead to knowledge, this assumption is open to question. But it is impossible to deal with these questions in a few words. A thorough discussion of Kant's Copernican revolution would involve discussion not only of Kant's own theories but also of the empiricism of Hume which was partly responsible for his thinking those theories necessary. And the only really satisfactory way of showing that there can be metaphysical knowledge is to produce examples and to show that they are examples. Such tasks cannot be attempted here. But it can be remarked that in any genuine dialogue with Kant a philosopher must endeavour to ascertain his insights and to distinguish between them and what is weak or false. In other words, it would be absurd to suppose that in the case of a thinker of such stature his philosophy can simply be thrown on the rubbish-heap of rejected systems. To take but one example, Kant's insistence on the unity of apperception as a fundamental condition of human experience seems to me to represent a genuine and important insight. Even if he failed to see that the substantial subject affirms its own ontological reality in the judgment, he did not forget the subject.

7. In conclusion we might consider briefly the statement which has sometimes been made that whereas mediaeval philosophy was concerned with the problem of being, modern philosophy has been concerned with the problem of knowledge.[1]

This is a difficult statement to deal with. If it were understood in a sense similar to that of the statement that astronomy is concerned with the heavenly bodies and botany with plants, it would be obviously untrue. On the one hand mediaeval philosophers had a good deal to say about knowledge. On the other hand, if concern with the problem of being is taken to mean concern with problems of existence, with metaphysical explanation of empirical reality and with the problem of the One and the Many, we can hardly say that the problem of being was absent from the minds of men such as Descartes, Spinoza and Leibniz.

Further, statements which involve saying that 'mediaeval philosophy' and 'modern philosophy' are concerned respectively with this or that are obviously open to the criticism that they are, by their very nature, unjustifiable simplifications of complex situations. That is to say, such statements are open to the well-grounded objection that it is thoroughly misleading to speak about mediaeval and post-Renaissance philosophy as though each were a homogeneous unity. The former ranged, for example, from the systematic metaphysical syntheses of Aquinas or Duns Scotus to the critical reflections of Nicholas of Autrecourt, the mediaeval Hume. And the latter, namely post-Renaissance philosophy, was obviously not all of a piece. If we compare Aquinas with Kant, it is certainly true to say that the theory of knowledge occupies a much more prominent position in the latter's thought than it does in that of the former. But if we selected for comparison other mediaeval and modern thinkers, our judgment about the degree to which each was preoccupied with epistemological problems might be somewhat different.

Again, the attempt to give a general interpretation of the world

[1] Some Thomist writers maintain that Aquinas was concerned with the act of existing whereas post-Renaissance rationalist metaphysicians were primarily concerned with the deduction of essences. And there is, I think, some truth in this contention. At the same time we cannot justifiably say that Descartes, for example, bypassed problems of existence. In any case I am concerned in this section with the position occupied by the theory of knowledge in mediaeval and modern philosophy respectively, not with the Thomist contention which I have just mentioned.

and of human experience can be found both in mediaeval philosophy and in the philosophy of the seventeenth and eighteenth centuries. Even Kant was not concerned only with the question: What can I know? He was also concerned, as he put it, with the questions: What ought I to do? and, What may I hope for? Reflection on these questions leads us not only into moral philosophy proper but also to the postulates of the moral law. And though, for Kant, immortality and the existence of God are not demonstrable, a general world-view is opened up to us in which science, morals and religion are harmonized. A critique of the process of reason shows us the limitations of definite knowledge; but it does not destroy the reality or the importance of the chief metaphysical problems.[1] And though the solutions are a matter of practical or moral faith rather than of knowledge, it is both natural and legitimate for reason to attempt to form a general view of reality which goes beyond the field of mathematics and of science, the field, that is, of 'theoretical' knowledge.

True, the extent to which Hume could attempt any such general interpretation of reality was, on his own principles, extremely limited. The nature of reality in itself and the ultimate causes of phenomena were for him shrouded in impenetrable mystery. As far as metaphysical explanation was concerned, the world was for him an enigma. Agnosticism was the only sensible attitude to adopt. His philosophy, therefore, was primarily critical and analytic. But the same can be said of some of the thinkers of the fourteenth century. The difference is that they looked to revelation and theology to supply them with a general view of reality, whereas Hume did not.

But though exception can be taken on several grounds to the statement that mediaeval philosophy is concerned with the problem of being and modern philosophy with the problem of knowledge, the statement may serve to draw attention to certain differences between mediaeval and post-Renaissance thought. If we take mediaeval philosophy as a whole, we can say that the problem of the objectivity of knowledge is not prominent. And one reason for this is, I think, that a philosopher such as Aquinas believed that we perceive directly physical objects such as trees

---

[1] As was remarked in the last section, it is arguable that Kant's doctrine of the categories leads to the conclusion that properly metaphysical problems must be excluded from the rank of meaningful problems. But Kant himself did not think so, of course. On the contrary, he emphasized the importance of what he regarded as the leading problems of metaphysics.

and tables. Our natural knowledge of purely spiritual beings is, indeed, indirect and analogical: there is no natural intuition of God. But we perceive trees and tables and men, not our own subjective modifications or our ideas of trees and tables and men. True, we can make erroneous judgments about the nature of what we perceive. I may judge, for example, that an object in the distance is a man when in point of fact it is a shrub. But the way to correct such error is to do what we are accustomed to do, namely to examine the object more closely. Problems of error arise against the background, so to speak, of a realist theory of perception, the common-sense theory that we enjoy immediate perception of the connatural objects of human cognition. Aquinas was not, of course, so naïve as to suppose that we necessarily know everything that we think that we know. But he believed that we enjoy direct access, as it were, to the world, that the mind is capable of apprehending things in their intelligible being, and that in the act of genuine knowledge it knows that it knows. While, therefore, he was prepared to discuss questions about the origins, conditions and limitations of knowledge and about the nature and causes of erroneous judgments, general questions about the objectivity of knowledge would not have had much meaning for him. For he did not think of ideas as a screen placed between our minds and things.

But if we follow Locke in describing ideas in such a way that they become the immediate objects of perception and thought, it is natural to ask whether our 'knowledge' of the world really is knowledge, that is, whether our representations correspond with reality existing independently of the mind. I do not mean to imply that all philosophers in the seventeenth and eighteenth centuries maintained a representative theory of perception and involved themselves in the problem of the correspondence between our representations and the things which they purport to represent. Locke himself did not maintain the representative theory consistently. And if, with Berkeley, we describe physical objects as clusters of 'ideas', the problem of correspondence between ideas and things simply does not arise. The problem arises only if ideas are said to have a representative function and to be the immediate objects of perception and knowledge. But if the problem does arise, the question whether our *prima facie* knowledge of the world is really objective knowledge pushes itself into the foreground. And it is then natural to treat this question before we embark on any metaphysical synthesis. Epistemology or theory of knowledge becomes basic in philosophy.

Again, while the mediaeval philosopher certainly did not think of the mind as a purely passive recipient of impressions, he regarded its activity as one of penetrating the objective intelligible structure of reality.[1] In other words, he thought of the mind as conforming itself to objects rather than of objects as having to conform themselves to the mind for knowledge to be possible.[2] He did not think of what we call the world as a mental construction. But, given the philosophies of Hume and Kant, it becomes natural to ask whether what we call the world is not a kind of logical construction which lies, as it were, between our minds and reality in itself or things in themselves. And if we think that this is a genuine problem, we shall naturally be inclined to give much more emphasis to the theory of knowledge than we should be if we were convinced that the subject does not construct empirical reality but grasps its intelligible nature.

My point is simply that if we bear in mind the development of post-Renaissance philosophy, especially in British empiricism and in the thought of Kant, it is easy to understand the prominence given in subsequent times to theory of knowledge or epistemology. Kant in particular exercised a most powerful influence in this respect. Of course, different attitudes are possible in regard to the emphasis which came to be laid in large areas of philosophical discussion on problems about the objectivity of knowledge. We may wish to say that it represents an advance from realist naïvety to a more sophisticated and profound understanding of the basic problems of philosophy. Or we may wish to say that the problem of the objectivity arises out of mistaken assumptions. Or we may wish to say that it is silly to talk, for example, about 'the critical problem'. We must try to formulate carefully-defined questions. And in the process of doing so we may find that some alleged problems which appear to be of great moment when they are expressed in vague terms turn out either to be pseudo-problems or to answer themselves. But whatever attitude we may wish to

[1] This is true of the metaphysicians at least.
[2] In a certain sense we can say that for Aquinas things must conform themselves to the subject for knowledge to be possible. For though in his view all being is intelligible in itself, the human subject is of such a kind and possesses such a cognitional structure, so to speak, that the natural scope of its knowledge is limited. For human knowledge as such to be possible conditions are required on the part both of subject and object. But this point of view is different from that represented by Kant's Copernican revolution.

adopt in regard to the emphasis placed on the theory of know-ledge, it is clear, I think, that it arose through the asking of questions which would not come naturally to the mind of the mediaeval philosopher but which were stimulated by develop-ments in the philosophy of the seventeenth and eighteenth centuries.

These remarks are not meant to imply that the prominence given to epistemology or the theory of knowledge in modern philosophy was due exclusively to the British empiricists and to Kant. It is obvious that a theory of knowledge was prominent in the philosophy of Descartes. Indeed, we can describe the difference between rationalism and empiricism in terms of different beliefs about the origins of knowledge and about the ways of increasing knowledge. It is thus true to say that from the very beginning of modern philosophy epistemology occupied a prominent and important position. At the same time it is also true that Kant in particular exercised a powerful influence in pushing epistemology into the foreground of philosophical discussion, if only for the fact that his destructive criticism of metaphysics through a trans-cendental critique of knowledge seemed to imply that the proper subject-matter for the philosopher was precisely the theory of knowledge. And, of course, anyone who wished to refute his criticism of metaphysics had perforce to start with examining his epistemological doctrines.

The fact, discussed briefly in the last section, that the critical philosophy of Kant led, somewhat paradoxically, to a fresh out-burst of metaphysical speculation may appear to count against the assertion that Kant exercised a powerful influence in concen-trating attention on the theory of knowledge. In point of fact, however, the speculative idealism of the first half of the nineteenth century arose, not out of a revulsion against Kant's epistemology, but out of a development of what seemed to Kant's successors to be the proper implications of his point of view. Thus Fichte started with the theory of knowledge, and his idealist metaphysics grew out of it. The Neo-Kantians may have regarded speculative idealism as a betrayal of the true Kantian spirit; but this does not alter the fact that the approach to the new metaphysics was by way of the theory of knowledge. How this transition from the critical philosophy of Kant to idealist metaphysics took place will be recounted in the next volume of this *History*.

APPENDIX

A SHORT BIBLIOGRAPHY[1]

For general remarks and for General Works see the Bibliography at the end of Volume IV, *Descartes to Leibniz.*

For the benefit of the reader who desires some guidance in the selection of a few useful books in English about general movements of thought and the more prominent thinkers an asterisk has been added to some titles. But the absence of this sign must not be taken to indicate a negative judgment about the value of the book in question.

The following works relating to the period of the Enlightenment can be added.

Becker, C. L. *The Heavenly City of the Eighteenth-Century Philosophers.* New Haven, 1932.

Cassirer, E. **The Philosophy of the Enlightenment,* translated by F. Koelln and J. Pettegrove. Princeton and London, 1951.

Hazard, P. *La crise de la conscience européenne (1680–1715).* 3 vols. Paris, 1935.

   *The European Mind, 1680–1715, translated by J. L. May. London, 1953.

   La pensée européenne au XVIIIe siècle, de Montesquieu à Lessing. 3 vols. Paris, 1946.

   *European Thought in the Eighteenth Century, from Montesquieu to Lessing, translated by J. L. May. London, 1954.

Hibben, J. G. *The Philosophy of the Enlightenment.* London and New York, 1910.

Wolff, H. M. *Die Weltanschauung der deutschen Aufklärung.* Berne, 1949.

Wundt, M. *Die deutsche Schulmetaphysik im Zeitalter der Aufklärung.* Tübingen, 1945.

Chapters I–II: The French Enlightenment

1. *Bayle*

Texts

   Dictionnaire historique et critique. 2 vols., Rotterdam, 1695–7; 4 vols., 1730; and subsequent editions.

[1] The abbreviation (*E.L.*) stands, as in previous volumes, for *Everyman's Library.*

Œuvres diverses. 4 vols. The Hague, 1727–31.
Selections from Bayle's 'Dictionary', edited by E. A. Beller and
    M. Du P. Lee. Princeton and London, 1952.
Système de la philosophie. The Hague, 1737.

Studies

André, P. *Le jeunesse de Bayle.* Geneva, 1953.
Bolin, W. *P. Bayle, sein Leben und seine Schriften.* Stuttgart, 1905.
Cazes, A. *P. Bayle, sa vie, ses idées, son influence, son œuvre.* Paris,
    1905.
Courtines, L. P. *Bayle's Relations with England and the English.* New
    York, 1938.
Deschamps, A. *La genèse du scepticisme érudit chez Bayle.* Brussels,
    1878.
Devolve, J. *Essai sur Pierre Bayle, religion, critique et philosophie
    positive.* Paris, 1906.
Raymond, M. *Pierre Bayle.* Paris, 1948.

2. Fontenelle

Texts

Œuvres. 1724 and subsequent editions. 3 vols., Paris, 1818; 5 vols.,
    Paris, 1924–35.
De l'origine des fables, critical edition by J-R. Carré. Paris, 1932.

Studies

Carré, J-R. *La philosophie de Fontenelle ou le sourire de la raison.*
    Paris, 1932.
Edsall, H. Linn. *The Idea of History and Progress in Fontenelle and
    Voltaire* (in Studies by Members of the French Department of
    Yale University, New Haven, 1941, pp. 163–84).
Grégoire, F. *Fontenelle.* Paris, 1947.
Laborde-Milan, A. *Fontenelle.* Paris, 1905.
Maigron, L. *Fontenelle, l'homme, l'œuvre, l'influence.* Paris, 1906.

3. Montesquieu

Texts

Œuvres, edited by E. Laboulaye. 7 vols. Paris, 1875–9.
Œuvres, edited by A. Masson. 3 vols. Paris, 1950–5.
De l'esprit des lois, edited with an introduction by G. Truc. 2 vols.
    Paris, 1945.

Studies

Barrière, P. *Un grand Provincial: Charles-Louis Secondat, baron de La
    Brède et de Montesquieu.* Bordeaux, 1946.

Carcassonne, E. *Montesquieu et le problème de la constitution française au XVIIIᵉ siècle.* Paris, 1927.

Cotta, S. *Montesquieu e la scienza della società.* Turin, 1953.

Dedieu, J. *Montesquieu, l'homme et l'œuvre.* Paris, 1943.

Duconseil, N. *Machiavelli et Montesquieu.* Paris, 1943.

Durkheim, S. *Montesquieu et Rousseau, précurseurs de la sociologie.* Paris, 1953 (reprint of 1892 edition).

Fletcher, F. T. H. *Montesquieu and English Politics, 1750–1800.* London and New York, 1939.

Levin, L. M. *The Political Doctrine of Montesquieu's* Esprit des lois: *Its Classical Background* (dissert.). New York, 1936.

Raymond, M. *Montesquieu,* Fribourg, 1946.

Sorel, A. *Montesquieu.* Paris, 1887.

Struck, W. *Montesquieu als Politiker.* Berlin, 1933.

Trescher, H. *Montesquieus Einfluss auf die Geschichts-und Staatsphilosophie bis zum Anfang. des 19. Jahrhunderts.* Munich, 1918 (*Schmollers Jahrbuch,* vol. 42, pp. 267–304).
Montesquieus Einfluss auf die philosophischen Grundlagen der Staatslehre Hegels. Munich, 1918 (*Schmollers Jahrbuch,* vol. 42, pp. 471–501, 907–44).

Vidal, E. *Saggio sul Montesquieu.* Milan, 1950.

See also:

Cabeen, D. C. *Montesquieu: A Bibliography.* New York, 1947.

Deuxième centenaire de l'Esprit des lois de Montesquieu (lectures). Bordeaux, 1949.

Revue internationale de philosophie, 1955, nos. 3–4.

4. *Maupertuis*

Texts

Œuvres. 4 vols. Lyons, 1768 (2nd edition).

Studies

Brunet, P. *Maupertuis.* 2 vols. Paris, 1929.

5. *Voltaire*

Texts

Œuvres, edited by Beuchot. 72 vols. Paris, 1828–34.

Œuvres, edited by Moland. 52 vols. Paris, 1878–85.

Traité de métaphysique, edited by H. T. Patterson. Manchester, 1937.

Dictionnaire philosophique, edited by J. Benda. Paris, 1954.

Philosophical Dictionary, selected and translated by H. I. Woolf. London, 1923.

Lettres philosophiques, edited by F. A. Taylor. Oxford, 1943.

Bengesco, G. *Voltaire. Bibliographie de ses œuvres*. 4 vols. Paris, 1882–92.

Studies

Aldington, R. *Voltaire*. London, 1926.

Alexander, J. W. *Voltaire and Metaphysics* (in *Philosophy* for 1944).

Bellesort, A. *Essai sur Voltaire*. Paris, 1950.

Bersot, E. *La philosophie de Voltaire*. Paris, 1848.

Brandes, G. *Voltaire*. 2 vols. Berlin, 1923.

Carré, J.-R. *Consistence de Voltaire: le philosophe*. Paris, 1939.

Charpentier, J. *Voltaire*. Paris, 1955.

Craveri, R. *Voltaire, politico dell'illuminismo*. Turin, 1937.

Cresson, A. *Voltaire*. Paris, 1948.

Cuneo, N. *Sociologia di Voltaire*. Genoa, 1938.

Denoisterre, H. *Voltaire et la société au XVIIIe siècle*. 8 vols. Paris, 1867–76.

Fitch, R. E. *Voltaire's Philosophical Procedure*. Forest Grove, U.S.A., 1936.

Girnus, W. *Voltaire*. Berlin, 1947.

Labriola, A. *Voltaire y la filosofia de la liberación*. Buenos Aires, 1944.

Lanson, G. *Voltaire*. Paris, 1906.

Maurois, A. *Voltaire*. Paris, 1947.

Meyer, A. *Voltaire, Man of Justice*. New York, 1945.

Morley, J. *Voltaire*, London, 1923.

Naves, R. *Voltaire et l'Encyclopédie*. Paris, 1938.

    Voltaire, l'homme et l'œuvre. Paris, 1947 (2nd edition).

Noyes, A. *Voltaire*. London, 1938.

O'Flaherty, K. *Voltaire. Myth and Reality*. Cork and Oxford, 1945.

Pellissier, G. *Voltaire philosophe*. Paris, 1908.

Pomeau, R. *La religion de Voltaire*. Paris, 1956.

Rowe, C. *Voltaire and the State*. London, 1956.

Torrey, N. L. *The Spirit of Voltaire*. New York, 1938.

Wade, O. *Studies on Voltaire*. Princeton, 1947.

6. *Vauvenargues*

Texts

Œuvres, edited by P. Varillon. 3 vols. Paris, 1929.

Œuvres choisies, with an introduction by H. Gaillard de Champris. Paris, 1942.

Réflexions et maximes. London, 1936.

Reflections and Maxims, translated by F. G. Stevens. Oxford, 1940.

Studies

Borel, A. *Essai sur Vauvenargues*. Neuchâtel, 1913.
Merlant, J. *De Montaigne à Vauvenargues*. Paris, 1914.
Paléologue, G. M. *Vauvenargues*. Paris, 1890.
Rocheblave, S. *Vauvenargues ou la symphonie inachevée*. Paris, 1934.
Souchon, P. *Vauvenargues, philosophe de la gloire*. Paris, 1947.
   Vauvenargues. Paris, 1954.
Vial, F. *Une philosophie et une morale du sentiment. Duc de Clapiers, Marquis de Vauvenargues*. Paris, 1938.

7. Condillac

Texts

Œuvres. 23 vols. Paris, 1798.
Œuvres philosophiques, edited by G. Le Roy. 3 vols. Paris, 1947–51.
Lettres inédites à Gabriel Cramer, edited by G. Le Roy. Paris, 1952.
Treatise on the Sensations, translated by G. Carr. London, 1930.

Studies

Baguenault de Puchesse G. *Condillac, sa vie, sa philosophie, son influence*. Paris, 1910.
Bianca, G. *La volontà nel pensiero di Condillac*. Catania, 1944.
Bizzarri, R. *Condillac*. Brescia, 1945.
Dal Pra, M. *Condillac*. Milan, 1947.
Dewaule, L. *Condillac et la psychologie anglaise contemporaine*. Paris, 1892.
Didier, J. *Condillac*. Paris, 1911.
Lenoir, R. *Condillac*. Paris, 1924.
Le Roy, G. *La psychologie de Condillac*. Paris, 1937.
Meyer, P. *Condillac*. Zürich, 1944.
Razzoli, L. *Pedagogia di Condillac*. Parma, 1935.
Torneucci, L. *Il problema dell'esperienza dal Locke al Condillac*. Messina, 1937.

8. Helvétius

Texts

Œuvres. 7 vols. Deux-Ports, 1784.
   5 vols. Paris, 1792.
Choix de textes, edited with an introduction by J. B. Séverac, Paris, 1911.
A Treatise on Man, translated by W. Hooper. London, 1777.

Studies

Cumming, I. *Helvetius*. London, 1955.
Grossman, M. *The Philosophy of Helvetius*. New York, 1926.
Horowitz, I. L. C. *Helvetius, Philosopher of Democracy and Enlightenment*. New York, 1954.
Keim, A. *Helvétius, sa vie et son œuvre*. Paris, 1907.
Limentani, L. *Le teorie psichologiche di C. A. Helvétius*. Padua, 1902.
Mazzola, F. *La pedagogia d'Elvetio*. Palermo, 1920.
Mondolfo, R. *Saggi per la storia della morale utilitaria, II: Le teorie morali e politiche di C. A. Helvetius*. Padua, 1904.
Stanganelli, I. *La teoria pedagogica di Helvetius*. Naples, 1939.

9. Encyclopaedia

Texts

Encyclopédie ou Dictionnaire raisonné des sciences, des arts et des métiers. 28 vols. Paris 1751–72.
Supplement in 5 vols.: Amsterdam, 1776–7.
Analytic tables in 2 vols., edited by F. Mouchon, Amsterdam, 1780–1.
The 'Encyclopédie' of Diderot and d'Alembert: selected articles edited with an introduction by J. Lough. Cambridge, 1954.

Studies

Charlier, G., and Mortier, R. *Une suite de l'Encyclopédie, le 'Journal Encyclopédique' (1756–1793)*. Paris, 1952.
Ducros, L. *Les encyclopédistes*. Paris, 1900.
Duprat, P. *Les encyclopédistes, leurs travaux, leur doctrine et leur influence*. Paris, 1865.
Gordon, D. H., and Torrey, N. L. *The Censoring of Diderot's Encyclopaedia*. New York, 1949.
Grosclaude, P. *Un audacieux message, l'Encyclopédie*. Paris, 1951.
Hubert. R. *Les sciences sociales dans l'Encyclopédie*. Paris, 1923.
Mornet, D. *Les origines intellectuelles de la révolution française (1715–87)*. Paris, 1933.
Mousnier, R., and Labrousse, E. *Le XVIIIe siècle. Révolution intellectuelle, technique et politique (1715–1815)*. Paris, 1953.
Roustan, M. *Les philosophes et la société française au XVIIIe siècle*. Lyons, 1906.
The Pioneers of the French Revolution, translated by F. Whyte. Boston, 1926.
Schargo, N. N. *History in the Encyclopaedia*. New York, 1947.
Venturi, F. *Le origini dell'Enciclopedia*. Florence, 1946.

10. *Diderot*

Texts

Œuvres, edited by Assézat and Tournaux. 2 vols. Paris, 1875–9.
Œuvres, edited by A. Billy. Paris, 1952–.
Correspondance, edited by A. Babelon. Paris, 1931.
Diderot: Interpreter of Nature. Selected Writings, translated by J. Stewart and J Kemp. New York, 1943.
Selected Philosophical Writings, edited by J. Lough. Cambridge, 1953.
Early Philosophical Works, translated by M. Jourdain. London and Chicago, 1916.

Studies

Barker, J. E. *Diderot's Treatment of the Christian Religion*. New York, 1931.
Billy, A. *Vie de Diderot*. Paris, 1943.
Cresson, A. *Diderot*. Paris, 1949.
Gerold, K. G. *Herder und Diderot. Ihr Einblick in die Kunst*. Frankfurt, 1941.
Gillot, H. *Denis Diderot. L'homme. Ses idées philosophiques, esthétiques et littéraires*. Paris, 1938.
Hermand, P. *Les idées morales de Diderot*. Paris, 1923.
Johannson, V. *Études sur Diderot*. Paris, 1928.
Le Gras, J. *Diderot et l'Encyclopédie*. Amiens, 1938.
Lefebvre, H. *Diderot*. Paris, 1949.
Löpelmann, M. *Der junge Diderot*. Berlin, 1934.
Loy, J. R. *Diderot's determined Fatalist. A critical Appreciation of 'Jacques le fataliste'*. New York, 1950.
Luc, J. *Diderot. L'artiste et le philosophe. Suivi de textes choisis de Diderot*. Paris, 1938.
Luppol, I. K. *Diderot. Ses idées philosophiques*. Paris, 1936.
Mauveaux, J. *Diderot, l'encyclopédiste et le penseur*. Montbéliard, 1914.
Mesnard, P. *Le cas Diderot, Etude de caractérologie littéraire*. Paris, 1952.
Morley, J. *Diderot and the Encyclopaedists*. 2 vols. London, 1878.
Mornet, D. *Diderot, l'homme et l'œuvre*. Paris, 1941.
Rosenkranz, K. *Diderots Leben und Werke*. 2 vols. Leipzig, 1886.
Thomas, J. *L'humanisme de Diderot*. 2 vols. Paris, 1938 (2nd edition).
Venturi, F. *Jeunesse de Diderot*. Paris, 1939.

11. *D'Alembert*

Texts

Œuvres philosophiques, edited by Bastien. 18 vols. Paris, 1805.
Œuvres et correspondance inédites, edited by C. Henry. Paris, 1887.

Discours sur l'Encyclopédie, edited by F. Picavet. Paris, 1919.
Traité de dynamique. Paris, 1921.

Studies

Bertrand, J. *D'Alembert*. Paris, 1889.
Muller, M. *Essai sur la philosophie de Jean d'Alembert*. Paris, 1926.

12. *La Mettrie*

Œuvres philosophiques. 2 vols. London, 1791; Berlin, 1796.
Man a Machine, annotated by G. C. Bussey. Chicago, 1912.

Studies

Bergmann, E. *Die Satiren des Herrn Machine*. Leipzig, 1913.
Boissier, R. *La Mettrie*. Paris, 1931.
Picavet, F. *La Mettrie et la critique allemande*. Paris, 1889.
Poritzky, Y. E. *J. O. de La Mettrie. Sein Leben und seine Werke*. Berlin, 1900.
Rosenfeld-Cohen, L. D. *From Beast-machine to Man-machine. The Theme of Animal Soul in French Letters from Descartes to La Mettrie*, with a preface by P. Hazard. New York and London, 1940.
Tuloup, G. F. *Un précurseur méconnu. Offray de La Mettrie, médicin-philosophe*. Paris, 1938.

13. *D'Holbach*
Texts

Système de la nature. Amsterdam, 1770.
Système sociale. London, 1773.
La politique naturelle. Amsterdam, 1773.
La morale universelle. Amsterdam, 1776.

Studies

Cushing, M. P. *Baron d'Holbach*. New York, 1914.
Hubert, R. *D'Holbach et ses amis*. Paris, 1928.
Naville, P. *P. T. D'Holbach et la philosophie scientifique au XVIIIe siècle*. Paris, 1943.
Plekhanov, G. V. *Essays in the History of Materialism*, translated by R. Fox. London, 1934.
Wickwaer, W. H. *Baron d'Holbach. A Prelude to the French Revolution*. London, 1935.

14. *Cabanis*

Texts

Œuvres, edited by Thurot. Paris, 1823–5.
Lettre à Fauriel sur les causes premières. Paris, 1828.

Studies

Picavet, F. *Les idéologues*. Paris, 1891.
Tencer, M. *La psycho-physiologie de Cabanis*. Toulouse, 1931.
Vermeil de Conchard, T. P. *Trois études sur Cabanis*. Paris, 1914.

15. *Buffon*

Texts

Histoire naturelle, générale et particulière. 44 vols. Paris, 1749–1804.
Nouveaux extraits, edited by F. Gohin. Paris, 1905.

Studies

Dandin, H. *Les méthodes de classification et l'idée de série en botanique et en zoologie de Linné à Lamarck (1740–1790)*. Paris, 1926.
Dimier, L. *Buffon*. Paris, 1919.
Roule, L. *Buffon et la description de la nature*. Paris, 1924.

16. *Robinet*

Texts

De la nature. 4 vols. Amsterdam, 1761–6.
Considérations sur la gradation naturelle des formes de l'être, ou les essais de la nature qui apprend à faire l'homme. Paris, 1768.
Parallèle de la condition et des facultés de l'homme avec la condition et les facultés des autres animaux. Bouillon, 1769.

Studies

Albert, R. *Die Philosophie Robinets*. Leipzig, 1903.
Mayer, J. *Robinet, philosophe de la nature* (*Revue des sciences humaines*, Lille, 1954, pp. 295–309).

17. *Bonnet*

Texts

Œuvres. 8 vols. Neuchâtel, 1779–83.
Mémoires autobiographiques, edited by R. Savioz. Paris, 1948.

Studies

Bonnet, G. *Ch. Bonnet*. Paris, 1929.
Claparède, E. *La psychologie animale de Ch. Bonnet*. Geneva, 1909.
Lemoine, A. *Ch. Bonnet de Genève, philosophe et naturaliste*. Paris, 1850.
Savioz, R. *La philosophie de Ch. Bonnet*. Paris, 1948.
Trembley, J. *Mémoires pour servir à l'histoire de la vie et des ouvrages de M. Bonnet*. Berne, 1794.

18. *Boscovich*

Texts

Theoria philosophiae naturalis redacta ad unicam legem virium in natura existentium. Vienna, 1758.
(The second edition, Venice, 1763, contains also *De anima et Deo* and *De spatio et tempore*.)
A Theory of Natural Philosophy, Latin (1763)—English edition, translated and edited by J. M. Child. Manchester, 1922.
Opera pertinentia ad opticam et astronomiam. 5 vols. Bassani, 1785.

Studies

Evellin, F. *Quid de rebus vel corporeis vel incorporeis senserit Boscovich*. Paris, 1880.
Gill, H. V., S.J. *Roger Boscovich, S.J. (1711–1787), Forerunner of Modern Physical Theories*. Dublin, 1941.
Nedelkovitch, D. *La philosophie naturelle et relativiste de R. J. Boscovich*. Paris, 1922.
Oster, M. *Roger Joseph Boscovich als Naturphilosoph*. Bonn, 1909.
Whyte, L. L. *R. J. Boscovich, S.J., F.R.S. (1711–1787), and the Mathematics of Atomism*. (Notes and Records of the Royal Society of London, vol. 13, no. 1, June 1958, pp. 38–48.)

19. *Quesnay and Turgot*

Texts

Œuvres économiques et philosophiques de F. Quesnay, edited by A. Oncken. Paris, 1888.
Œuvres de Turgot, edited by Dupont de Nemours. 9 vols. Paris, 1809–11. Supplement edited by Dupont, Daire and Duggard. 2 vols. Paris, 1884.
Œuvres de Turgot, edited by G. Schelle. 5 vols. Paris, 1913–32.

Studies

Bourthoumieux, C. *Essai sur le fondement philosophique des doctrines économiques. Rousseau contre Quesnay*. Paris, 1936.

Fiorot, D. *La filosofia politica dei fisiocrati*. Padua, 1952.
Gignoux, C. J. *Turgot*. Paris, 1946.
Schelle, G. *Turgot*, Paris, 1909.
Stephens, W. W. *Life and Writings of Turgot*. London, 1891.
Vigreux, P. *Turgot*. Paris, 1947.
Weuleresse, G. *Le mouvement physiocratique en France de 1756 à 1770*. Paris, 1910.
La physiocratie sous les ministères de Turgot et de Necker. Paris, 1950.

Chapters III–IV: Rousseau

Texts

Œuvres complètes. 13 vols. Paris, 1910. (There are, of course, other editions of Rousseau's works; but there is as yet no complete critical edition.)
Correspondance générale de J. J. Rousseau, edited by T. Dufour and P. P. Plan. 20 vols. Paris, 1924–34.
Le Contrat social, édition comprenant, avec le texte définitif, les versions primitives de l'ouvrage collationnées sur les manuscrits autographes de Genève et de Neuchâtel. Edition Dreyfus-Brisac. Paris, 1916.
Du contrat social, with an introduction and notes by G. Beaulavon. Paris, 1938 (5th edition).
Discours sur l'origine et les fondements de l'inégalité parmi les hommes, edited with an introduction by F. C. Green. London, 1941.
J-J. Rousseau. Political Writings, selected and translated with an introduction by F. M. Watkins. Edinburgh, 1954.
The Political Writings of Jean Jacques Rousseau, edited by C. E. Vaughan. 2 vols. Cambridge, 1915.
The Social Contract and Discourses, edited with an introduction by G. D. H. Cole. London (*E.L.*).
Emile or Education, translated by B. Foxley. London (*E.L.*).
J-J. Rousseau. Selections, edited with an introduction by R. Rolland. London, 1939.
Citizen of Geneva: Selections from the Letters of J-J. Rousseau, edited by C. W. Hendel. New York and London, 1937.

For a thorough study of Rousseau the student should consult:
Annales de la Société J-J. Rousseau. Geneva, 1905 and onwards.

We can also mention:
Sénelier, J. *Bibliographie générale des œuvres de J-J. Rousseau*. Paris, 1949.

Studies

Attisani, A. *L'utilitarismo di G. G. Rousseau*. Rome, 1930.
Baldanzi, E. R. *Il pensiero religioso di G. G. Rousseau*. Florence, 1934.

Bouvier, B. *J-J. Rousseau*. Geneva, 1912.

Brunello, B. *G. G. Rousseau*. Modena, 1936.

Buck, R. *Rousseau und die deutsche Romantik*. Berlin, 1939.

Burgelin, P. *La philosophie de l'existence de J-J. Rousseau*. Paris, 1952.

Casotti, M. *Rousseau e l'educazione morale*. Brescia, 1952.

Cassirer, E. *Rousseau, Kant, Goethe*, translated by J. Gutman, P. O. Kristeller and J. H. Randall, Jnr. Princeton, 1945.
The Question of J-J. Rousseau, translated and edited with introduction and additional notes by P. Gay. New York, 1954.

Chapman, J. W. *Rousseau, Totalitarian or Liberal?* New York, 1956.

Chaponnière, P. *Rousseau*. Zürich, 1942.

Cobban, A. *Rousseau and the Modern State*. London, 1934.

Cresson, A. *J-J. Rousseau. Sa vie, son œuvre, sa philosophie*. Paris, 1950 (3rd edition).

Derathé, R. *Le rationalisme de J-J. Rousseau*. Paris, 1948.
J-J. Rousseau et la science politique de son temps. Paris, 1950.

Di Napoli, G. *Il pensiero di G. G. Rousseau*. Brescia, 1953.

Ducros, L. *J-J. Rousseau*. 3 vols. Paris, 1908–18.

Erdmann, K. D. *Das Verhältnis von Staat und Religion nach der Sozialphilosophie Rousseaus. Der Begriff der 'religion civile'*. Berlin, 1935.

Faguet, E. *Rousseau penseur*. Paris, 1912.

Fester, R. *Rousseau und die deutsche Geschichtsphilosophie*. Stuttgart, 1890.

Flores d'Arcais, G. *Il problema pedagogico nell'Emilio di G. G. Rousseau*. Brescia, 1954 (2nd edition).

Frässdorf, W. *Die psychologischen Anschauungen J-J. Rousseaus und ihr Zusammenhang mit der französischen Psychologie des 18 Jahrhunderts*. Langensalza, 1929.

Gézin, R. *J-J. Rousseau*. Paris, 1930.

Green, F. C. *Jean-Jacques Rousseau. A Study of His Life and Writings*. Cambridge, 1955.

Groethuysen, B. *J-J. Rousseau*. Paris, 1950.

Guillemin, H. *Les philosophes contre Rousseau*. Paris, 1942.

Hellweg, M. *Der Begriff des Gewissens bei Rousseau*. Marburg-Lahn, 1936.

Hendel, C. W. *Jean-Jacques Rousseau, Moralist*. 2 vols. New York and London, 1934.

Höffding, H. *J-J. Rousseau and His Philosophy*, translated by W. Richards and L. E. Saidla. New Haven, 1930.

Hubert, R. *Rousseau et l'Encyclopédie. Essai sur la formation des idées politiques de Rousseau* (1742–1756). Paris, 1929.

Köhler, F. *Rousseau*. Bielefeld, 1922.

Lama, E. *Rousseau*. Milan, 1952.

Lemaître, J. *J-J. Rousseau.* Paris, 1907.

Léon, P.-L. *L'idée de volonté générale chez J-J. Rousseau et ses antécédents historiques.* Paris, 1936.

Lombardo, S. *Rousseau nel contratto sociale.* Messina, 1951.

Maritain, J. *Three Reformers: Luther, Descartes, Rousseau.* London, 1945 (reprint).

Masson, P. M. *La religion de Rousseau.* 3 vols. Paris, 1916.

Meinhold, P. *Rousseaus Geschichtsphilosophie.* Tübingen, 1936.

Mondolfo, R. *Rousseau e la coscienza moderna.* Florence, 1954.

Moreau, L. *J-J. Rousseau et le siècle philosophique.* Paris, 1870.

Morel, J. *Recherches sur les sources du discours de J-J. Rousseau sur l'origine et les fondements de l'inégalité.* Lausanne, 1910.

Morley, J. **Rousseau.* 2 vols. London, 1883 (2nd edition).

Pahlmann, F. *Mensch und Staat bei Rousseau.* Berlin, 1939.

Petruzzelis, N. *Il pensiero politico e pedagogico di G. G. Rousseau.* Milan, 1946.

Pons, J. *L'éducation en Angleterre entre 1750 et 1800. Aperçu sur l'influence de J-J. Rousseau en Angleterre.* Paris, 1919.

Proal, L. *La psychologie de J-J. Rousseau.* Paris, 1923.

Reiche, E. *Rousseau und das Naturrecht.* Berlin, 1935.

Roddier, H. *J-J. Rousseau en Angleterre au XVIII*e* siècle.* Paris, 1950.

Saloni, A. *Rousseau.* Milan, 1949.

Schiefenbusch, A. *L'influence de J-J. Rousseau sur les beaux arts en France.* Geneva, 1930.

Schinz, A. *La pensée de J-J. Rousseau.* Paris, 1929.
    La pensée religieuse de Rousseau et ses récents interprètes. Paris, 1927.
    État présent des travaux sur J-J. Rousseau. Paris, 1941.

Sutton, C. *Farewell to Rousseau: a Critique of Liberal Democracy,* with an introduction by W. R. Inge. London, 1936.

Thomas, J. F. *Le pélagianisme de Rousseau.* Paris, 1956.

Valitutti, S. *La volontà generale nel pensiero di Rousseau.* Rome, 1939.

Vasalli, M. *La pedagogia di G. G. Rousseau.* Como, 1951.

Voisine, J. *J-J. Rousseau en Angleterre à l'époque romantique.* Paris, 1956.

Wright, E. H. *The Meaning of Rousseau.* London, 1929.

Ziegenfuss, W. *J-J. Rousseau.* Erlangen, 1952.

There are various collections of articles. For example:

F. Baldensperger, etc. *J-J. Rousseau, leçons faites à l'École des hautes études sociales.* Paris, 1912.

E. Boutroux, etc., in *Revue de métaphysique et de morale,* XX, 1912.

Chapters V–VII: The German Enlightenment

1. *Thomasius*

Texts

Institutionum iurisprudentiae divinae libri tres. Frankfurt and
   Leipzig, 1688.
Einleitung zu der Vernunftlehre. Halle, 1691.
Ausübung der Vernunftlehre. Halle, 1691.
Ausübung der Sittenlehre. Halle, 1696.
Versuch vom Wesen des Geistes. Halle, 1699.
Introductio in philosophiam rationalem. Leipzig, 1701.
Kleine deutsche Schriften. Halle, 1701.
*Fundamenta iuris naturae et gentium ex sensu communi deducta in
   quibus secernuntur principia honesti, iusti ac decori.* Halle, 1705.
Dissertationes academicae. 4 vols. Halle, 1733–80.

Studies

Battaglia, F. *Cristiano Thomasio, filosofo e giurista.* Rome, 1935.
Bieber, G. *Staat und Gesellschaft bei C. Thomasius.* Giessen, 1931.
Bienert, W. *Der Anbruch der christlichen deutschen Neuzeit, darge-
   stellt an Wissenschaft und Glauben des Christian Thomasius.*
   Halle, 1934.
   Die Philosophie des Christian Thomasius (dissert.). Halle, 1934.
   Die Glaubenslehre des Christian Thomasius (dissert.). Halle, 1934.
Block, E. *C. Thomasius.* Berlin, 1953.
Lieberwirth, R. *C. Thomasius.* Weimar, 1955.
Neisser, K. *C. Thomasius und seine Beziehung zum Pietismus.*
   Heidelberg, 1928.
Schneider, F. *Thomasius und die deutsche Bildung.* Halle, 1928.

2. *Wolff*

Texts

*Philosophia rationalis, sive logica methodo scientifica pertractata et ad
   usum scientiarum atque vitae aptata.* Frankfurt and Leipzig,
   1728.
Philosophia prima sive Ontologia. Frankfurt, 1729.
Cosmologia generalis. Ibid., 1731.
Psychologia empirica. Ibid., 1732.
Psychologia rationalis. Ibid., 1734.
Theologia naturalis. 2 vols. *Ibid.,* 1736–7.
Philosophia practica universalis. 2 vols., *Ibid.,* 1738–9.
Gesammelte kleinere Schriften. 6 vols. Halle, 1736–40.

Ius naturae methodo scientifica pertractata. 8 vols. Frankfurt and Leipzig, 1740–48.

Ius gentium. Halle, 1750.

Oeconomica. Ibid., 1750.

Philosophia moralis sive Ethica. 5 vols. *Ibid.,* 1750–3.

Studies

Arnsperger, W. *Ch. Wolffs Verhältnis zu Leibniz.* Heidelberg, 1897.

Campo, M. *Ch. Wolff e il razionalismo precritico.* 2 vols. Milan, 1939.

Frank, R. *Die Wolffsche Strafrechtsphilosophie und ihr Verhältnis zur kriminalpolitischen Aufklärung im 18. Jahrhundert.* Göttingen, 1887.

Frauendienst, W. *Ch. Wolff als Staatsdenker.* Berlin, 1927.

Heilemann, P. A. *Die Gotteslehre des Ch. Wolff.* Leipzig, 1907.

Joesten, C. *Ch. Wolffs Grundlegung der praktischen Philosophie.* Leipzig, 1931.

Kohlmeyer, E. *Kosmos und Kosmonomie bei Ch. Wolff.* Göttingen, 1911.

Levy, H. *Die Religionsphilosophie Ch. Wolffs.* Würzburg, 1928.

Ludovici, C. G. *Ausführlicher Entwurf einer vollständigen Historie der Wolffschen Philosophie.* 3 vols. Leipzig, 1736–7.
Sammlung und Auszüge der sämmtlichen Streitschriften wegen der Wolffschen Philosophie. 2 vols. Leipzig, 1737–8.

Utitz, E. *Ch. Wolff.* Halle, 1929.

Wundt, M. *Christian Wolff und die deutsche Aufklärung* (in *Das Deutsche in der deutschen Philosophie,* edited by T. Haering, Stuttgart, 1941, pp. 227–46).

3. *Baumgarten*

Texts

Meditationes philosophicae de nonnullis ad poema pertinentibus. Halle, 1735.

Reflections on Poetry, translated, with the original Latin text, an introduction and notes by K. Aschenbrenner and W. B. Hoelther. Berkeley and London, 1954.

Metaphysica. Halle, 1740.

Aesthetica acroamatica. 2 vols. Frankfurt, 1750–8.

Aesthetica. Iterum edita ad exemplar prioris editionis annorum MDCCL–LVIII spatio impressae.
Praepositae sunt: Meditationes philosophicae de nonnullis ad poema pertinentibus. Bari, 1936.

Ethica philosophica. Halle, 1765.

Philosophia generalis. Halle, 1769.

Studies

Bergmann, E. *Die Begründung der deutschen Aesthetik durch Baumgarten und G. F. Maier.* Leipzig, 1911.

Maier, G. F. *A. G. Baumgartens Leben.* Halle, 1763.

Peters, H. G. *Die Aesthetik A. G. Baumgartens und ihre Beziehungen zum Ethischen.* Berlin, 1934.

Poppe, B. *A. G. Baumgarten, seine Bedeutung und Stellung in der Leibniz-Wolffschen Philosophie.* Berne-Leipzig, 1907.

4. Frederick the Great

Texts

Antimachiavell. The Hague, 1740.

Essai sur l'amour propre envisagé comme principe de la morale. Berlin, 1770.

Œuvres de Frédéric le Grand. 30 vols. Berlin, 1847–57. Vols. 8 and 9 *Œuvres philosophiques.*

Briefwechsel mit Maupertuis, edited by R. Koser. Berlin, 1898.

Briefwechsel mit Voltaire, edited by R. Koser and H. Droysen. Berlin, 1908.

Studies

Berney, A. *Friedrich der Grosse. Entwicklungsgeschichte eines Staatsmannes.* Tübingen, 1934.

Berney, G. *Friedrich der Grosse.* Munich, 1935.

Dilthey, W. *Friedrich der Grosse und die deutsche Aufklärung.* Leipzig, 1927.

Gent, W. *Die geistige Kultur um Friedrich den Grossen.* Berlin, 1936.

Gooch, G. P. *Frederick the Great.* New York, 1947.

Koser, R. *Friedrich der Grosse.* 4 vols. Stockholm, 1912 (4th edition).

Langer, J. *Friedrich der Grosse und die geistige Welt Frankreichs.* Hamburg, 1932.

Muff, W. *Die Philosophie Friedrichs des Grossen* (in *Wissen und Wehr,* Berlin, 1943, pp. 117–33).

Friedrichs des Grossen philosophische Entwicklung (in *Forschungen und Fortschritte,* Berlin, 1943, pp. 156–7).

Pelletan, E. *Un roi philosophe, le grand Frédéric.* Paris, 1878.

Rigollot, G. *Frédéric II, philosophe.* Paris, 1876.

Spranger, E. *Der Philosoph von Sanssouci.* Berlin, 1942.

Zeller, E. *Friedrich der Grosse als Philosoph.* Berlin, 1886.

5. Reimarus

Texts

Abhandlungen von den vornehmsten Wahrheiten der natürlichen Religion. Hamburg, 1754.

Vernunftlehre. Hamburg and Kiel, 1756.
Allgemeine Betrachtungen über die Triebe der Tiere, hauptsächlich über ihren Kunsttrieb. Hamburg, 1760.
Apologie oder Schutzschrift für die vernünftigen Verehrer Gottes. See p. 123.

Studies

Buettner, W. *H. S. Reimarus als Metaphysiker.* Würzburg, 1909.
Koestlin, H. *Das religiöse Erleben bei Reimarus.* Tübingen, 1919.
Loeser, M. *Die Kritik des H. S. Reimarus am alten Testament.* Berlin 1941.
Lundsteen, A. C. *H. S. Reimarus und die Anfänge der Leben-Jesu Forschung.* Copenhagen, 1939.

6. *Mendelssohn*

Texts

Werke, edited by G. B. Mendelssohn. 7 vols. Leipzig, 1843–4.
Gesammelte Schriften, edited by J. Elbogen, J. Guttmann and M. Mittwoch. Berlin, 1929–.

Studies

Bachi, E. D. *Sulla vita e sulle opere di M. Mendelssohn.* Turin, 1872.
Bamberger, F. *Der geistige Gestalt M. Mendelssohns.* Frankfurt, 1929.
Cohen, B. *Ueber die Erkenntnislehre M. Mendelssohns.* Giessen, 1921.
Goldstein, L. *M. Mendelssohn und die deutsche Aesthetik.* Königsberg, 1904.
Hoelters, H. *Der spinozistische Gottesbegriff bei M. Mendelssohn und F. H. Jacobi und der Gottesbegriff Spinozas.* Bonn, 1938.

7. *Lessing*

Texts

Sämtliche Schriften. 30 vols. Berlin, 1771–94.
Sämtliche Werke, critical edition of Lachmann-Muncker (Leipzig, 1886 f.); 4th edition by J. Petersen. 25 vols. Berlin, 1925–35.
Die Erziehung des Menschengeschlechts. Nach dem Urtext von 1780 neu herausgegeben mit Anmerkungen und einem Nachwort von K. R. Riedler. Zürich, 1945.
Lessing's Theological Writings, translated and selected by H. Chadwick. London, 1956.

Studies

Arx, A. von. *Lessing und die geschichtliche Welt.* Frankfurt, 1944.
Bach, A. *Der Aufbruch des deutschen Geistes. Lessing, Klopstock, Herder.* Markkleeberg, 1939.

Fischer, K. *Lessing als Reformator der deutschen Literatur.* 2 vols. Stockholm, 1881.

Fittbogen, G. *Die Religion Lessings.* Halle, 1915.

Flores d'Arcais, G. *L'estetica nel Laocoonte di Lessing.* Padua, 1935.

Garland, H. B. *Lessing, the Founder of Modern German Literature.* London, 1937.

Gonzenbach, H. *Lessings Gottesbegriff in seinem Verhältnis zu Leibniz und Spinoza.* Leipzig, 1940.

Kommerell, M. *Lessing und Aristoteles. Untersuchung über die Theorie der Tragödie.* Frankfurt, 1940.

Leander, F. *Lessing als aesthetischer Denker.* Göteborg, 1942.

Leisegang, H. *Lessings Weltanschauung.* Leipzig, 1931.

Milano, P. *Lessing.* Rome, 1930.

Oehlke, W. *Lessing und seine Zeit.* 2 vols. Munich, 1929 (2nd edition).

Robertson, G. *Lessing's Dramatic Theory.* Cambridge, 1939.

Schmitz, F. J. *Lessings Stellung in der Entfaltung des Individualismus.* Berkeley, U.S.A. and Cambridge, 1941.

Schrempf, C. *Lessing als Philosoph.* Stockholm, 1921 (2nd edition).

Wernle, P. *Lessing und das Christentum.* Leipzig, 1912.

8. *Tetens*

Texts

Gedanken über einige Ursachen, warum in der Metaphysik nur wenige ausgemachte Wahrheiten sind. Bützow, 1760.

Abhandlung von den vorzüglichsten Beweisen des Daseins Gottes. Ibid., 1761.

Commentatio de principio minimi. Ibid., 1769.

Abhandlung über den Ursprung der Sprache und der Schift. Ibid., 1772.

Ueber die allgemeine spekulative Philosophie. Ibid., 1775.

Philosophische Versuche über die menschliche Natur und ihre Entwicklung. 2 vols. Leipzig, 1776. (Reprinted, Berlin, 1913.)

Studies

Schinz, M. *Die Moralphilosophie von Tetens.* Leipzig, 1906.

Schweig, H. *Die Psychologie des Erkennens bei Bonnet und Tetens* (dissert.). Bonn, 1921.

Seidel, A. *Tetens Einfluss auf die kritische Philosophie Kants* (dissert.). Leipzig, 1932.

Uebele, W. *J. N. Tetens nach seiner Gesamtentwicklung betrachtet mit besonderer Berücksichtigung des Verhältnisses zu Kant* (Kantstudien, Berlin, 1911, suppl. vol. 24, viii, 1–238).

Zergiebel, K. *Tetens und sein system der Philosophie (Zeitschrift für Philosophie und Pädagogik,* Langensalza, vol. 19, 1911–12, pp. 273–79, 321–6).

9. *Basedow*

Texts

Philalethie. Lübeck, 1764.
Theoretisches System der gesunden Vernunft. Leipzig, 1765.
Vorstellung an Menschenfreunde und vermögende Männer über Schulen, Studien und ihren Einfluss in die öffentliche Wohlfahrt. Bremen, 1768.
Elementarwerk. 4 vols. Dessau, 1774.

Studies

Diestelmann, R. *Basedow*. Leipzig, 1897.
Pantano-Migneco, G. *G. B. Basedow e il filantropismo*. Catania, 1917.
Piazzi, A. *L'educazione filantropica nella dottrina e nell'opera di G. B. Basedow*. Milan, 1920.
Pinloche, A. *La réforme de l'éducation en Allemagne au XVIIIᵉ siècle. Basedow et le philanthropisme*. Paris, 1889.

10. *Pestalozzi*

Texts

Sämtliche Werke, edited by A. Buchenau, E. Spranger and H. Stettbacker. 19 vols. Berlin, 1927–56.
Sämtliche Werke, edited by P. Baumgartner. 8 vols. Zürich, 1943.
Sämtliche Briefe. 4 vols. Zürich, 1946–51.
Educational Writings. Translated and edited by J. A. Green, with the assistance of F. A. Collie. London, 1912.

Studies

Anderson, L. F. *Pestalozzi*. New York, 1931.
Bachmann, W. *Die anthropologischen Grundlagen zu Pestalozzis Soziallehre*. Berne, 1947.
Banfi, A. *Pestalozzi*. Florence, 1928.
Barth, H. *Pestalozzis Philosophie der Politik*. Zürich and Stockholm, 1954.
Green, J. A. *Life and Work of Pestalozzi*. London, 1913.
Hoffman, H. *Die Religion im Leben und Denken Pestalozzis*. Berne, 1944.
Jónasson, M. *Recht und Sittlichkeit in Pestalozzis Kulturtheorie*. Berlin, 1936.
Mayer, M. *Die positive Moral bei Pestalozzi von 1766–1797* (dissert.). Charlottenburg, 1934.

Otto, H. *Pestalozzi*. Berlin, 1948.
Pinloche, A. *Pestalozzi et l'éducation populaire moderne*. Paris, 1902.
Reinhart, J. *J. H. Pestalozzi*. Basel, 1945.
Schönebaum, H. *J. H. Pestalozzi*. Berlin, 1954.
Sganzini, C. *Pestalozzi*. Palermo, 1928.
Spranger, E. *Pestalozzis Denkformen*. Zürich, 1945.
Wehnes, F. J. *Pestalozzis Elementarmethode*. Bonn, 1955.
Wittig, H. *Studien zur Anthropologie Pestalozzis*. Weinheim, 1952.

11. *Hamann*

Texts

Sämtliche Schriften. Edited by F. Roth. 8 vols. Berlin, 1821–43.
Sämtliche Schriften. Critical edition by J. Nadler. 6 vols. Vienna, 1949–57.
Briefwechsel. Edited by W. Ziesemer and A. Henkel. 2 vols. Wiesbaden, 1955–6.

Studies

Blum, J. *La vie et l'œuvre de J. G. Hamann, le Mage du Nord*. Paris, 1912.
Heinekamp, H. *Das Weltbild J. G. Hamanns*. Düsseldorf, 1934.
Metzger, W. *J. G. Hamann*. Frankfurt, 1944.
Metzke, E. *J. G. Hamanns Stellung in der Philosophie des 18. Jahrhunderts*. Halle, 1934.
Nadler, J. *Die Hamann-Ausgabe*. Halle-Saale, 1930.
    J. G. Hamann. Der Zeuge des Corpus Mysticum. Salzburg, 1949.
O'Flaherty, J. C. *Unity and Language. A Study in the Philosophy of J. G. Hamann*. Chapel Hill, U.S.A., 1952.
Schoonhoven, J. *Natur en genade by Hamann*. Leyden, 1945.
Steege, H. *J. G. Hamann*. Basel, 1954.
Unger, R. *Hamann und die Aufklärung*. 2 vols. Jena, 1911.

12. *Herder*

Texts

Sämtliche Werke. Edited by B. Sulphan and others. 33 vols. Berlin, 1877–1913.
Treatise upon the Origin of Language. Translator anon. London, 1827.
Outlines of a Philosophy of the History of Man. Translated by T. Churchill. London, 1803 (2nd edition).
The Spirit of Hebrew Poetry. Translated by J. Marsh. 2 vols. Burlington, Vt., 1832.

God. Some Conversations. Translated by F. H. Burkhardt. New York, 1949 (2nd edition).

Studies

Andress, J. M. *J. G. Herder as an Educator.* New York, 1916.

Aron, E. *Die deutsche Erweckung des Griechentums durch Winckelmann und Herder* (dissert.). Heidelberg, 1929.

Bach, R. *Der Aufbruch des deutschen Geistes: Lessing, Klopstock, Herder.* Markkleeberg, 1940.

Baumgarten, O. *Herders Lebenzweck und die religiöse Frage der Gegenwart.* Tübingen, 1905.

Bäte, L. *J. G. Herder. Der Weg, das Werk, die Zeit.* Stuttgart, 1948.

Berger, F. *Menschenbild und Menschenbildung. Die philosophisch-pädagogische Anthropologie J. G. Herders.* Stuttgart, 1933.

Bernatzki, A. *Herders Lehre von der aesthetischen Erziehung* (dissert.). Breslau, 1925.

Blumenthal, E. *Herders Auseinandersetzung mit der Philosophie Leibnizens* (dissert.). Hamburg, 1934.

Boor, W. de. *Herders Erkenntnislehre in ihrer Bedeutung für seinen religiösen Idealismus.* Gutersloh, 1929.

Brändle, J. *Das Problem der Innerlichkeit: Hamann, Herder, Goethe.* Berne, 1950.

Clark, R. T., Jnr. **Herder: His Life and Thought.* Berkeley and London, 1955. (Contains full bibliographies.)

Dewey, M. H. *Herder's Relation to the Aesthetic Theory of His Time* (dissert.). Chicago, 1918.

Dobbek, W. *J. G. Herders Humanitätsidee als Ausdruck seines Weltbildes und seiner Persönlichkeit.* Braunschweig, 1949.

Erdmann, H. *Herder als Religionsphilosoph.* Hersfeld, 1868.

Fischer, W. *Herders Erkenntnislehre und Metaphysik* (dissert.). Leipzig, 1878.

Gerold, K. G. *Herder und Diderot, ihr Einblick in die Kunst.* Frankfurt, 1941.

Gillies, A. *Herder.* Oxford, 1945.

Grabowsky, I. *Herders Metakritik und Kants Kritik der reinen Vernunft* (dissert.). Dortmund, 1934.

Hatch, I. C. *Der Einfluss Shaftesburys auf Herder* (dissert.). Berlin, 1901.

Haym, R. *Herder nach seinem Leben und seinen Werken dargestellt.* 2 vols. Berlin, 1954. (Reprint of 1877–85 edition.)

Henry, H. *Herder und Lessing: Umrisse ihrer Beziehung.* Würzburg, 1941.

Joens, D. W. *Begriff und Problem der historischen Zeit bei J. G. Herder.* Göteborg, 1956.

Joret, C. *Herder et la renaissance littéraire en Allemagne au XVIII*° *siècle*. Paris, 1875.

Knorr, F. *Das Problem der menschlichen Philosophie bei Herder* (dissert.). Coburg, 1930.

Kronenberg, M. *Herders Philosophie nach ihrem Entwicklungsgang und ihrer historischen Stellung*. Heidelberg, 1889.

Kuhfuss, H. *Gott und Welt in Herders 'Ideen zur Philosophie der Geschichte der Menschheit'* (dissert.). Emsdetten, 1938.

Kühnemann, E. *Herder*. Munich, 1927 (2nd edition).

Landenberger, A. *J. G. Herder, sein Leben, Wirken und Charakterbild*. Stuttgart, 1903.

Litt, T. *Kant und Herder als Deuter der geistigen Welt*. Heidelberg, 1949 (2nd edition).
Die Befreiung des geschichtlichen Bewusstseins durch Herder. Leipzig, 1942.

McEachran, F. *The Life and Philosophy of J. G. Herder*. Oxford, 1929.

Nevinson, H. *A Sketch of Herder and His Times*. London, 1884.

Ninck, J. *Die Begründung der Religion bei Herder* Leipzig, 1912.

Rasch, W. *Herder, sein Leben und Werk im Umriss*. Halle, 1938.

Rouché, M. *Herder précurseur de Darwin? Histoire d'un mythe*. Paris, 1940.
La philosophie de l'histoire de Herder (dissert.). Paris, 1940.

Salmony, H. A. *Die Philosophie des jungen Herder*. Zürich, 1949.

Siegel, K. *Herder als Philosoph*. Stuttgart, 1907.

Voigt, A. *Umrisse einer Staatslehre bei J. G. Herder*. Stuttgart and Berlin, 1939.

Weber, H. *Herders Sprachphilosophie. Eine Interpretation in Hinblick auf die moderne Sprachphilosophie* (dissert.). Berlin, 1939.

Werner, A. *Herder als Theologe: ein Beitrag zur Geschichte der protestantischen Theologie*. Berlin, 1871.

Wiese, B. von. *Volk und Dichtung von Herder bis zur Romantik*. Erlangen, 1938.
Herder, Grundzüge seines Weltbildes. Leipzig, 1939.

13. *Jacobi*

Texts

Werke. Edited by F. Roth. 6 vols. Leipzig, 1812–25.

Aus F. H. Jacobis Nachlass. Edited by R. Zöpporitz. 2 vols. Leipzig, 1869.

Auserlesener Briefwechsel. Edited by F. Roth. 2 vols. Leipzig, 1825–7.

Briefwechsel zwischen Goethe und F. H. Jacobi. Edited by M. Jacobi. Leipzig, 1846.

Briefe an Bouterwerk aus den Jahren 1800–1819. Edited by W. Meyer. Göttingen, 1868.

Studies

Bollnow, O. F. *Die Lebensphilosophie F. H. Jacobis.* Stockholm, 1933.
Fischer, G. *J. M. Sailer und F. H. Jacobi.* Fribourg, 1955.
Frank, A. *Jacobis Lehre vom Glauben.* Halle, 1910.
Heraens, O. F. *Jacobi und der Sturm und Drang.* Heidelberg, 1928.
Hoelters, H. *Der spinozistische Gottesbegriff bei Mendelssohn und Jacobi und der Gottesbegriff Spinozas* (dissert.). Bonn, 1938.
Lévy-Bruhl, L. *La philosophie de Jacobi.* Paris, 1894.
Schmid, F. A. *F. H. Jacobi.* Heidelberg, 1908.
Thilo, C. A. *Jacobis Religionsphilosophie.* Langensalza, 1905.
Zirngiebl, E. *F. H. Jacobis Leben, Dichten und Denken.* Vienna, 1867.

Chapters VIII–IX: The Rise of the Philosophy of History

1. *Bossuet*

Texts

Œuvres complètes. Edited by P. Guillaume. 10 vols. Bar-le-Duc, 1877.

Studies

Auneau, A. *Bossuet.* Avignon, 1949.
De Courten, C. *Bossuet e il suo 'Discours sur l'histoire universelle'.* Milan, 1927.
Nourisson, A. *Essai sur la philosophie de Bossuet.* Paris, 1852.

2. *Vico*

Texts

Opere. Edited by F. Nicolini. 8 vols. (11 'tomes'). Bari, 1914–41.
La Scienza Nuova seconda, giusta la edizione del 1744, con le varianti del 1730 e di due redazioni intermedie inedite. Edited by F. Nicolini. 2 vols. Bari, 1942 (3rd edition).
There are many other Italian editions of the *Scienza nuova.*
Commento storico alla Scienza seconda. By F. Nicolini. 2 vols. Rome, 1949.
The New Science of Giambattista Vico. Translated from the third edition (1744) by T. G. Bergin and M. H. Fisch. London, 1949.
Il diritto universale. Edited by F. Nicolini. Bari, 1936.
De nostri temporis studiorum ratione. With introduction, translation (Italian) and notes by V. De Ruvo. Padua, 1941.

Giambattista Vico. Autobiography. Translated by M. H. Fisch and T. G. Bergin. New York and London, 1944.
For Bibliography see *Bibliografia vichiana*. Edited by F. Nicolini. 2 vols. Naples, 1947.

Studies

Adams, H. P. *The Life and Writings of Giambattista Vico*. London, 1935.
Amerio, F. *Introduzione allo studio di G. B. Vico*. Turin, 1947.
Auerbach, E. *G. B. Vico*. Barcelona, 1936.
Banchetti, S. *Il significato morale dell'estetica vichiana*. Milan, 1957.
Bellofiore, L. *La dottrina del diritto naturale in G. B. Vico*. Milan, 1954.
Berry, T. *The Historical Theory of G. B. Vico*. Washington, 1949.
Cantone, C. *Il concetto filosofico di diritto in G. B. Vico*. Mazana, 1952.
Caponigri, A. R. *Time and Idea, the Theory of History in Giambattista Vico*. London, 1953.
Cappello, C. *La dottrina della religione in G. B. Vico*. Chieri, 1944.
Chaix-Ruy, J. *Vie de J. B. Vico*. Paris, 1945.
    La formation de la pensée philosophique de J. B. Vico. Paris, 1945.
Chiochetti, E. *La filosofia di Giambattista Vico*. Milan, 1935.
Cochery, M. *Les grandes lignes de la philosophie historique et juridique de Vico*. Paris, 1923.
Corsano, A. *Umanesimo e religione in G. B. Vico*. Bari, 1935.
    G. B. Vico. Bari, 1956.
Croce, B. *La filosofia di G. B. Vico*. Bari, 1911.
Donati, B. *Nuovi studi sulla filosofia civile di G. B. Vico*. Con documenti. Florence, 1936.
Federici, G. C. *Il principio animatore della filosofia vichiana*. Rome, 1947.
Flint, R. *Vico*. Edinburgh, 1884.
Fubini, M. *Stile e umanità in G. B. Vico*. Bari, 1946.
Gentile, G. *Studi vichiani*. Messina, 1915.
    Giambattista Vico. Florence, 1936.
Giusso, L. *G. B. Vico fra l'umanesimo e l'occasionalismo*. Rome, 1940.
    Le filosofia di G. B. Vico e l'età barocca. Rome, 1943.
Luginbühl, J. *Die Axiomatik bei Vico*. Berne, 1946.
    Die Geschichtsphilosophie G. Vicos. Bonn, 1946.
Nicolini, F. *La giovinezza di G. B. Vico*. Bari, 1932.
    Saggi vichiani. Naples, 1955.
Paci, E. *Ingens Sylva, Saggio su G. B. Vico*. Milan, 1949.
Peters, R. *Der Aufbau der Weltgeschichte bei G. Vico*. Stuttgart, 1929.
Sabarini, R. *Il tempo in G. B. Vico*. Milan, 1954.
Severgnini, D. *Nozze, tribunali ed are. Studi vichiani*. Turin, 1956.
Uscatescu, G. *Vico y el mundo histórico*. Madrid, 1956.
Villa, G. *La filosofia del mito secondo G. B. Vico*. Milan, 1949.

Werner, K. *G. B. Vico als Philosoph und gelehrter Forscher*. Vienna, 1881.

There are some collections of articles; for example:

Vico y Herder. Ensayos conmemorativos del secondo centenario de la muerte de Vico y del nacimiento de Herder. Buenos Aires, 1948.

3. *Montesquieu*

See pp. 442–3.

4. *Voltaire*

See pp. 443–4.

5. *Condorcet*

Texts

Œuvres. Edited by Mme Condorcet, Cabanis and Garat. 21 vols. Paris, 1801–4.

Œuvres. Edited by A. Condorcet, O'Connor and M. F. Arago. 12 vols. Paris, 1847–9.

Sketch for a Historical Picture of the Progress of the Human Mind. Translated by J. Barraclough, with an introduction by Stuart Hampshire. London, 1955.

Studies

Alengry, F. *Condorcet, guide de la révolution française*. Paris, 1904.

Brunello, B. *La pedagogia della rivoluzione francese*. Milan, 1951.

Caben, L. *Condorcet et la révolution française*. Paris, 1904.

Frazer, J. G. *Condorcet on the Progress of the Human Mind*. Oxford, 1933.

Jacovello, G. *Introduzione ad uno studio su Condorcet*. Bronte, 1914.

Martin, K. *Rise of French Liberal Thought in the 18th Century*. New York, 1954 (2nd edition).

6. *Lessing*

See pp. 457–8.

7. *Herder*

See pp. 460–2.

Chapters X–XVI: Kant

Texts

Gesammelte Schriften. Critical edition sponsored by the Prussian Academy of Sciences. 22 vols. Berlin, 1902–42.

Immanuel Kants Werke. Edited by E. Cassirer. 11 vols. Berlin, 1912–18.

Kant's Cosmogony. Translated by W. Hastie. Glasgow, 1900. (Contains the *Essay on the Retardation of the Rotation of the Earth* and the *Natural History and Theory of the Heavens*.)

A New Exposition of the First Principles of Metaphysical Knowledge (contained as an Appendix in F. E. England's book, listed below).

An Inquiry into the Distinctions of the Principles of Natural Theology and Morals (contained in L. W. Beck's translation of Kant's moral writings, listed below).

Dreams of a Spirit-Seer Illustrated by the Dreams of Metaphysics. Translated by E. F. Goerwitz, edited by F. Sewall. New York, 1900.

Inaugural Dissertation and Early Writings on Space. Translated by J. Handyside. Chicago, 1929.

Critique of Pure Reason. Translated by N. K. Smith. London, 1933 (2nd edition).

Critique of Pure Reason. Translated by J. M. D. Meiklejohn, with an introduction by A. D. Lindsay. London (*E.L.*).

Prolegomena to Any Future Metaphysic. Translated by J. P. Mahaffy and J. H. Bernard. London, 1889.

Prolegomena to Any Future Metaphysic. Translated by P. Carus, revised by L. W. Beck. New York, 1950.

Prolegomena to Any Future Metaphysics. Translated with introduction and notes by P. G. Lucas. Manchester, 1953.

Immanuel Kant: Critique of Practical Reason and Other Writings in Moral Philosophy. Translated and edited by L. W. Beck. Chicago, 1949. (Contains *An Inquiry*, as mentioned above, *Foundations of the Metaphysics of Morals, Critique of Practical Reason, What is Orientation in Thinking?, Perpetual Peace, On a Supposed Right to Lie from Altruistic Motives*, and selections from the *Metaphysics of Morals*.)

Kant's Critique of Practical Reason and Other Works on the Theory of Ethics. Translated by T. K. Abbott. London, 1909 (6th edition). (Contains a Memoir of Kant, *Fundamental Principles of the Metaphysics of Morals, Critique of Practical Reason*, the Introduction to the *Metaphysics of Morals*, the Preface to the *Metaphysical Elements of Ethics*, the first part of *Religion within the Limits of Reason Alone, On a Supposed Right to Lie from Altruistic Motives*, and *On the Saying 'Necessity has no Law'*.)

The Metaphysics of Ethics. Translated by J. W. Semple. Edinburgh, 1886 (3rd edition).
The Moral Law or Kant's Groundwork of the Metaphysics of Morals. Translated with an introduction by H. J. Paton. London, 1950.
Kant's Lectures on Ethics. Translated by L. Infield. London, 1930.
Critique of Judgment. Translated by J. H. Bernard. London, 1931 (2nd edition).
Religion within the Limits of Reason Alone. Translated by T. M. Greene and H. H. Hudson, with an introduction by T. M. Greene. Glasgow, 1934.
Perpetual Peace, A Philosophical Essay. Translated by M. Campbell Smith. London, 1915 (reprint).
Kant. Selections. Edited with an introduction by T. M. Greene. London and New York, 1929.

Studies

Adickes, E. *Kant als Naturforscher.* 2 vols. Berlin, 1924–5.
    Kant und das Ding an sich. Berlin, 1924.
    Kant und die Als-Ob-Philosophie. Stockholm, 1927.
    Kants Lehre von der doppelten Affektion unseres Ich als Schlüssel zu seine Erkenntnistheorie. Tübingen, 1929.
Aebi, M. *Kants Begründung der 'deutschen Philosophie'.* Basel, 1947.
Aliotta, A. *L'estetica di Kant e degli idealisti romantici.* Rome, 1950
Ardley, G. *Aquinas and Kant.* New York and London, 1950.
Ballauf, T. *Ueber den Vorstellungsbegriff bei Kant.* Eleda, 1938.
Banfi, A. *La filosofia critica di Kant.* Milan, 1955.
Basch, V. *Essai critique sur l'esthétique de Kant.* Paris, 1927 (enlarged edition).
Bauch, B. *Kant.* Leipzig, 1923 (3rd edition).
Bayer, K. *Kants Vorlesungen über Religionslehre.* Halle, 1937.
Bohatec, J. *Die Religionsphilosophie Kants in der 'Religion innerhalb der Granzen der blossen Vernunft'.* Hamburg, 1938.
Borries, K. *Kant als Politiker.* Leipzig, 1928.
Boutroux, E. *La philosophie de Kant.* Paris, 1926.
Caird, E. *The Critical Philosophy of Immanuel Kant.* 2 vols. London, 1909 (2nd edition).
Campo, M. *La genesi del criticismo Kantiano.* 2 vols. Varese, 1953.
Carabellese, P. *La filosofia di Kant.* Florence, 1927.
    Il problema della filosofia da Kant a Fichte. Palermo, 1929.
    Il problema dell'esistenza in Kant. Rome, 1943.
Cassirer, A. W. *A Commentary on Kant's Critique of Judgment.* London, 1938.
    Kant's First Critique: an Appraisal of the Permanent Significance of Kant's Critique of Pure Reason. London, 1955.

Cohen, H. *Kommentar zu Kants Kritik der reinen Vernunft.* Leipzig, 1917 (2nd edition).
Kants Theorie der reinen Erfahrung. Berlin, 1918 (3rd edition).
Kants Begründung der Ethik. Berlin, 1910 (2nd edition).
Vom Kants Einfluss auf die deutsche Kultur. Berlin, 1883.
Kants Begründung der Aesthetik. Berlin, 1889.
Coninck, A. de. *L'analytique de Kant (Part I: La critique kantienne).* Louvain, 1955.
Cornelius, H. *Kommentar zur Kritik der reinen Vernunft.* Erlangen, 1926.
Cousin, V. *Leçons sur la philosophie de Kant.* Paris, 1842.
Cresson, A. *Kant, sa vie, son œuvre. Avec un exposé de sa philosophie.* Paris, 1955 (2nd edition).
Daval, R. *La métaphysique de Kant. Perspectives sur la métaphysique de Kant d'après la théorie du schématisme.* Paris, 1951.
Delbos, V. *La philosophie pratique de Kant.* Paris, 1905.
Denckmann, G. *Kants Philosophie des Aesthetischen.* Heidelberg, 1949.
Döring, W. O. *Das Lebenswerk Immanuel Kants.* Hamburg, 1947.
Duncan, A. R. C. *Practical Rule and Morality. A Study of Immanuel Kant's Foundations for the Metaphysics of Ethics.* London and Edinburgh, 1957.
England, F. E. *Kant's Conception of God.* London, 1929.
Ewing, A. C. *Kant's Treatment of Causality.* London, 1924.
A Short Commentary on Kant's Critique of Pure Reason. London, 1938.
Farinelli, A. *Traumwelt und Jenseitsglaube bei Kant.* Königsberg, 1940.
Fischer, K. *Kants Leben und die Grundlage seiner Lehre.* 2 vols. Heidelberg, 1909 (5th edition).
Friedrich, C. J. *Inevitable Peace.* New Haven, 1948. (Contains *Perpetual Peace* as Appendix.)
Garnett, C. B. Jr. *The Kantian Philosophy of Space.* New York, 1939.
Goldmann, L. *Mensch, Gemeinschaft und Welt in der Philosophie Kants.* Zürich, 1945.
Gottfried, M. *Immanuel Kant.* Cologne, 1951.
Grayeff, P. *Deutung und Darstellung der theoretischen Philosophie Kants.* Hamburg, 1951.
Guzzo, A. *Primi scritti di Kant.* Naples, 1920.
Kant precritico. Turin, 1924.
Heidegger, M. *Kant und das Problem der Metaphysik.* Bonn, 1929.
Heimsoeth, H. *Studien zur Philosophie I. Kants. Metaphysische Ursprünge und ontologische Grundlagen.* Cologne, 1955.
Herring, H. *Das Problem der Affektation bei Kant.* Cologne, 1953.

Heyse, H. *Der Begriff der Ganzheit und die kantische Philosophie.* Munich, 1927.

Jansen, B., S.J. *Die Religionsphilosophie Kants.* Berlin and Bonn, 1929.

Jones, W. T. **Morality and Freedom in the Philosophy of Immanuel Kant.* Oxford, 1940.

Kayser, R. *Kant.* Vienna, 1935.

Klausen, S. *Die Freiheitsidee in ihrem Verhältnis zum Naturrecht und positivem Recht bei Kant.* Oslo, 1950.

Körner, S. **Kant.* Penguin Books, 1955.

Kronenberg, M. *Kant. Sein Leben und seine Werke.* Munich, 1918 (5th edition).

Kroner, R. *Von Kant bis Hegel.* 2 vols. Tübingen, 1921–4.
*Kant's Weltanschauung. Translated by J. E. Smith. Chicago, 1956.

Krüger, G. *Philosophie und Moral in der kantischen Kritik.* Tübingen, 1931.

Kühnemann, E. *Kant.* 2 vols. Munich, 1923–4.

Külpe, O. *Immanuel Kant.* Leipzig, 1921 (5th edition).

Lachièze-Rey, P. *L'idéalisme kantien.* Paris, 1950 (2nd edition).

Lehmann, G. *Kants Nachlasswerk und die Kritik der Urteilskraft.* Berlin, 1939.

Lindsay, A. D. **Kant.* London, 1934.

Litt, T. *Kant und Herder als Deuter der geistigen Welt.* Leipzig, 1930.

Lombardi, F. *La filosofia critica: I, La formazione del problema kantiano.* Rome, 1943.

Lotz, B., S.J. (editor). *Kant und die Scholastik heute.* Munich, 1955.

Lugarini, C. *La logica trascendentale di Kant.* Milan, 1950.

Marc-Wogau, K. *Untersuchungen zur Raumlehre Kants.* Lund, 1932.
Vier Studien zu Kants Kritik der Urteilskraft. Uppsala, 1938.

Maréchal, J., S.J. *Le point de départ de la métaphysique.* 5 vols. Bruges, 1923–46. (Cahiers 3 and 5.)

Martin, G. *Arithmetik und Kombinatorik bei Kant.* Itzehoe, 1938.
*Kant's Metaphysics and Theory of Science. Translated by P. G. Lucas. Manchester, 1955.

Massolo, A. *Introduzione all'analitica kantiana.* Florence, 1946.

Menzer, P. *Kants Aesthetik in ihrer Entwicklung.* Berlin, 1952.

Messer, A. *Kommentar zu Kants ethischen und religionsphilosophischen Hauptschriften.* Leipzig, 1929.

Miller, O. W. *The Kantian Thing-in-itself or Creative Mind.* New York, 1956.

Natorp, P. *Kant über Krieg und Frieden.* Erlangen, 1924.

Nink, C., S.J. *Kommentar zu Kants Kritik der reinen Vernunft.* Frankfurt, 1930.

Noll, B. *Das Gestaltproblem in der Erkenntnistheorie Kants*. Bonn, 1946.

Oggiani, E. *Kant empirista*. Milan, 1948.

Pareyson, L. *L'estetica dell'idealismo tedesco: I, Kant*. Turin, 1950.

Paton, H. J. **Kant's Metaphysic of Experience: A Commentary on the First Half of the Kritik der reinen Vernunft*. 2 vols. London, 1952 (2nd edition).
*The Categorical Imperative: A Study in Kant's Moral Philosophy. London, 1948.

Paulsen, F. *Immanuel Kant: His Life and Doctrine*. Translated by J. E. Creighton and A. Lefèvre. New York, 1902.

Pfleiderer, E. *Kantischer Kritizimus und englische Philosophie*. Tübingen, 1881.

Reich, C. *Die Vollständigkeit der kantischen Urteilstafel*. Berlin, 1932.
Kants Einzigmöglicher Beweisgrund zu einer Demonstration des Daseins Gottes. Berlin, 1932.

Reinhard, W. *Ueber das Verhältnis von Sittlichkeit und Religion bei Kant*. Berne, 1927.

Reininger, R. *Kant, seine Anhänger und Gegner*. Munich, 1923.

Rickert, H. *Kant als Philosoph der modernen Kultur*. Tübingen, 1924.

Riehl, J. *Kant und seine Philosophie*. Berlin, 1907.

Ross, Sir D. *Kant's Ethical Theory. A Commentary on the 'Grundlagen zur Metaphysik der Sitten'*. Oxford, 1954.

Rotta, P. *Kant*. Brescia, 1953.

Ruyssen, T. *Kant*. Paris, 1909.

Scaravelli, L. *Saggio sulla categoria kantiana della realtà*. Florence, 1947.

Scheenberger, G. *Kants Konzept des Moralbegriffs*. Basel, 1952.

Schilling, K. *Kant*. Munich, 1942 (2nd edition).

Schilpp, P. A. *Kant's Pre-Critical Ethics*. Evanston and Chicago, 1938.

Sentroul, C. *La philosophie religieuse de Kant*. Brussels, 1912.
Kant et Aristote. Paris, 1913.

Simmel, G. *Kant*. Munich, 1921 (5th edition).

Smith, A. H. *Kantian Studies*. Oxford, 1947.

Smith, N. K. **A Commentary to Kant's 'Critique of Pure Reason'*. London, 1930 (2nd edition).

Souriau, M. *Le jugement réfléchissant dans la philosophie critique de Kant*. Paris, 1926.

Specht, E. K. *Der Analogiebegriff bei Kant und Hegel*. Cologne, 1952.

Stuckenberg, J. H. W. *The Life of Immanuel Kant*. London, 1882.

Teale, E. *Kantian Ethics*. Oxford, 1951.

Tönnies, I. *Kants Dialektik des Scheins* (dissert.). Würzburg, 1933.

Troilo, E. *Kant*. Milan, 1939.

Vaihinger, H. *Kommentar zur Kritik der reinen Vernunft.* 2 vols. Stuttgart, 1922 (2nd edition).

Vanni-Rovighi, S. *Introduzione allo studio di Kant.* Milan, 1945.

Vleeschauwer, H. J. de. *La déduction transcendentale dans l'œuvre de Kant.* 3 vols. Antwerp, 1934–7.
L'évolution de la pensée kantienne. Histoire d'une doctrine. Paris, 1939.

Vorländer, K. *Immanuel Kant. Der Mann und das Werk.* Leipzig, 1924.

Vuillemin, J. *L'héritage kantien, et la révolution copernicienne.* Paris, 1954.
Physique et métaphysique kantiennes. Paris, 1955.

Wallace, W. *Kant.* Oxford, Edinburgh and London, 1882.

Webb, C. C. J. **Kant's Philosophy of Religion.* Oxford, 1926.

Weldon, T. D. **Introduction to Kant's Critique of Pure Reason.* Oxford, 1945.

Whitney, G. T., and Bowers, D. F. (editors). *The Heritage of Kant* (essays). Princeton, 1939.

Wundt, M. *Kant als Metaphysiker.* Stuttgart, 1924.

Notes

1. R. Eisler's *Kantlexion* (Berlin, 1930) is a useful aid to the study of Kant.
2. *Kantstudien,* the periodical founded in 1896 by H. Vaihinger, contains many important articles on Kant.
3. There are various collections of articles on Kant.
   For example:
   Revue internationale de philosophie, n. 30; Brussels, 1954.
   A Symposium on Kant, by E. G. Ballard and others. Tulane Studies in Philosophy, vol. III. New Orleans, 1954.
4. The more metaphysical aspects of Kant's philosophy are emphasized in the works, listed above, by Daval, Heimsoeth, Martin (second work mentioned) and Wundt. For a discussion of the relations between Kant's thought and Thomism see the works by Audley and Maréchal (Cahier V). Besides the works of Professors Paton and N. K. Smith those of de Vleeschauwer are highly recommended.

INDEX

(The principal references are in heavy type. Asterisked numbers refer to bibliographical information. References in ordinary type to a continuous series of pages, e.g. 33–41, do not necessarily indicate continuous treatment. References to two persons together are usually under the person criticized or influenced. Footnote abbreviations given in italics, e.g. *A.*, are referred to the pages explaining them.)

emotion at the sublime: Kant 360, 364

emotive proposition 356

Empfindung 235

empires, development of 152f

empirical reality *see* reality, empirical

empiricism: British 116, **404-15**, 438f. *See also* Hume, Locke *below*; French 3ff, 8, 16, 28, 46, 58; Hume 186, 207, 266, **405-11**, **413-15**, 434; Kant and 212, 217, 229, 235f, 266, 276, 293, 313, 415, 434; Locke 3ff, 28, 199f, 212, 217, 405, 407, 410, 415; *also* 289, 291, 430

and analysis 407, 414

dogmatic E. 293

and metaphysics 414

modern E. 221, 410ff, 414

and phenomenalism 430

Encyclopaedia, The (1751-65) **39f**, 41-4, 55f, 59f, 169, 446*

Encyclopaedists: Rousseau on 64, 99, 418; *also* 55, 416f

end (as object of a rational will. For purpose in general *see s.v.*): Kant 327f, 331

absolute and relative 327f

kingdom of EE. **331**, 378

E. of creation 378

See also finality in Nature; purpose

energy 16f, 54, 262. *See also* force, physical

England 35, 85, 118, 121, 404

English Constitution 9, 13f

English thought 122f, 140

Enlightenment, The **1-149** (*see* Contents, p. v), **415-20**, 441*

and history 143, 164, 424

opposed: Hamann 135, 137f, 149; Herder 142f, 146, 172f, 175, 177; Rousseau 63, 96; *also* 148f

also 105, 126, 168, 347

See also eighteenth-century

Enlightenment, the French **1-100** (*see* Contents, p. v.), 415, 418f, 422

materialism in 1, 17f, 47, 51, 58

religion opposed 1ff, 58, 100, 103, 417

also 19, 50, 99f, 121

Enlightenment, the German 8, **101-49** (*see* Contents, p. v), 441*

Enquiry into the Distinctness of the Principles of Natural Theology and Morals, Kant's 189-93

ens perfectissimum 294f

ens realissimum 294ff, 298, 306

entelechy 173

Epicurus (B.C. 341-271) 203, 313, 330, 376

epistemology 117, 266, 415, 435, 437ff

epochs of history: Bossuet 152f

equality, human: opposed by Voltaire 23, 25; upheld 95f, 113; *also* 158, 170

Erhabene, das 363

Erläuterungsurteil 219

Erménonville 61

error 174, 274, 437

Erscheinung 236f

Erweiterungsurteil 219

eschatology 151

Esprit des lois, de l', Montesquieu's 9, 163

esse est percipi, Kant on 241

essences, knowledge of: French philosophers 4, 29, 45f, 52; Wolff 107f; *also* 397f, 435n

nominal E. 4, 52

essentialism 109, 435n

Este, history of the House of 154

eternity of the world 287f

ethico-theology *see* theology, moral

ethics: Aristotle 108, 111, 323, 420; French Enlightenment 42f, 46, 49 *and see* Helvetius, Rousseau *below*; Helvetius 36, 38, 415; Hume 405, 409, 414n, 421f; Kant 96f, 181, 189f, 192f, 203f, 208f, 223, 307, **308-48** (*see* Contents, p. vi), 436; Rousseau 63, 67, 96, 99; Thomasius 103ff; Wolff 108, 110f, 312

applied E. 311

emotive theories 313, 346, 414n

empirical theories 312, 330

linked by freedom with philosophy of Nature 349 *and see* free will

metaphysics of morals: Kant 207f, 311-14

pure E: Kant 203, 311f, 346

rationalist E. 313, 330, 347, 416

teleological E. 323, 347, 421f

ethnography 141

eudaimonia 323

Euler, Leonard (1707–83) 195
Europe: Herder
  freedom and slavery in 143
  culture 177, 179
evil 25 ff, 110
evil, problem of 7, 20 f
evolution: Buffon 53; Diderot 43;
  Herder 173 f; Bergson 394
executive power: Rousseau 85,
  93 ff; also 14
existence: Turgot 57; also 189, 398,
  435 and n
  concept of 200, 259 and below
  in idea of the most perfect being
    295 f, 298, 397
  inferability of 156, 398, 400 f,
    403 f, 411
  as predicate 188, 297
existential judgment
  always synthetic: Kant 296 f
  how far deducible 400 f, 403 f
existentialism of St Thomas Aquinas
  109
experience (for Kant see next entry)
  101, 107, 119, 127, 142, 146,
  400
  atomic elements of 408 f, 414
experience: Kant
  aesthetic E. see s.v.
  appearances alone experienced
    198, 240 f
  atomic elements of 408 f, 414
  conditions of 255, 260, 262 f,
    265, 267 382 and see deduction
    of categories
  from sense and intellect 229, 256,
    263
  inner E. 192, 273 f
  moral E. see s.v.
  not merely given 224, 238, 381,
    429 and see under construction,
    mental
  objective E. 260, 277
  occasion of concepts 200 f, 212
  occasion of knowledge 217, 428
  sense E. see s.v.
  source of knowledge see knowledge
  unity of 290 f, 306
  also 182, 193, 237, 240
experiment: Kant 227 f; Vico 156 f
experimental method: Vico 155 f;
  also 42, 47
experimental philosophy: Hume
  405, 406 n, 409

explanation
  causal E. 371
  of phenomena: Kant 224 f, 242,
    also 8, 29, 46, 405 f
extension 17 f, 35, 109, 219, 289
external world: Condillac 32, 35;
  Kant 272 ff and see thing,
  external; also 45, 57, 109, 147

fable see myth
fact, matters of 411. See also truths
  of fact
factions: Rousseau 94. See also
  parties
faculty, faculties: Herder 140 ff,
  144; Kant 350, 354; also 33 ff,
  116 f, 132
faith: Hamann 136, 148 f; Jacobi
  146 f, 148 f; Kant 183, **208** and
  below
  moral F: Kant
    based on moral experience 233,
      293
    in freedom 294, 306, 342
    in future life 195, 306
    in God 233, 300 f, 306, 340,
      342, 379. See also God, belief
      in
    postulates of see postulates of
      practical reason
    in spiritual reality 209, 293 f
    also 208, 379, 433
  practical F. see moral F. above
  religious F: Kant 208, 344
Fall of man: Kant 344 f
fallacies: Kant
  in arguments for existence of God
    295, 301, 304 n
  from misuse of Ideas 231, 301 f,
    304 n
  of metaphysics 305
family
  in history 158, 167, 170, 175
  F. of nations 177
  also 70, 134
fatalism: Kant 233; Spinoza 376
fear 131, 160
federation of small States 95
feeling: Hume 414 n, 416; Kant
  204, 326, 350, 364, 370 and
  below; Rousseau 75 f, 78 f, 100
  and see sentiment